FIND THAT TUNE

AN INDEX
TO ROCK
FOLK-ROCK
DISCO & SOUL
IN COLLECTIONS

Edited by
William Gargan and Sue Sharma

Neal-Schuman Publishers

Published by Neal-Schuman Publishers, Inc.
23 Cornelia Street
New York, NY 10014

Printed and bound in the United States of America.

Library of Congress Cataloging in Publication Data
Main entry under title:

Find that tune.

    1. Rock music—Indexes.   2. Disco music—Indexes.
3. Soul music—Indexes.   I. Gargan, William.
II. Sharma, Sue.
ML128.R6F56   1983   784.5'4'0016   82-22346
ISBN 0-918212-70-7

CONTENTS

PREFACE

FIND THAT TUNE: AN INDEX TO ROCK, FOLK-ROCK, DISCO & SOUL is an index to over 4,000 songs in 203 published collections of sheet music. It concentrates on Rock, Folk-Rock, Disco and Soul music from 1950-1981. This area, hereafter referred to in this preface by the broader term Rock, has been generally neglected by previous song indexes. FIND THAT TUNE is an attempt to fill the gap.

The book is divided in to five parts: Part 1, entitled "Collections Indexed," lists 203 collections of sheet music, each arranged alphabetically and assigned a unique reference number. Part 2, the "Title Index," provides access to over 4,000 songs, supplying information on composers and lyricists, performers, publishers, and copyright dates. The names of the performers are printed in upper case in order to set them off from the composers and lyricists. Each song in the title index contains reference numbers to the collection or collections, listed in Part 1, in which it appears. Part 3 is the "First Line Index." An attempt has been made here to provide enough of the beginning of a song to make a complete thought. When the structure of the lines made it impossible for us to isolate a complete sentence, we truncated the line by use of the traditional four dots. If different collections listed various first lines for the same song, all variants were indexed. (This usually occurred when one collection listed the first line of the verse; another the first line of the chorus.) It was felt that it was best to provide as many access points as possible in order to aid the user in identifying a particular song.

Part 4 is a list of all the composers and lyricists. It provides at a glance a listing of all the songs in the index by any particular composer or lyricist. The letters (m) and (w) after the name of a composer or lyricist indicate that the individual involved is solely responsible for either music(m) or words(w). Part 5, the "Performer Index," lists the performers of the songs indexed. It should be noted that groups such as "Gladys Knight & the Pips," which have individual names as part of their titles, are alphabetized under the name of the group as a whole. Entries for "Gladys Knight & The Pips," therefore, will be found listed under "Gladys." "See" references have been provided from the last names of individuals connected with such groups to insure that material will be accessible.

It is hoped that this format will faciliate the index's use as both a finding list and a ready reference source for general information on the songs included. As such, it should prove a valuable reference tool for musicians, music librarians, and those in the music industry.

The 203 collections indexed were chosen because they represented the broadest possible spectrum of what has generally come to be known as Rock music. The songs included range from Bubble Gum music to Punk Rock, and they encompass a sampling of everything in-between, including Folk-Rock, Disco, and Soul classics. In our desire for completeness, we included a few collections that fit primarily within our scope but contained some songs that were outside it. We decided to retain these songs feeling that it was better to err on the side ot being too inclusive. Although most of the collections indexed are general anthologies, it was necessary to include a number of collections dealing with individual performers as well. This had to be done because a number of important artists such as Elvis Presley, the Grateful Dead, and Buddy Holly are not well-represented in published anthologies; neither are many well-known Folk Rock and Soul performers. To achieve a balanced and representative selection, individual collections of music for performers like Phil Ochs, Arlo Guthrie, James Brown, and Diana Ross had to be added. It is hoped that the presence of these individual song books will enhance the index's value as a ready reference source.

All information regarding composers, lyricists, first lines, performers, and copyright were gleaned, where available, from the collections themselves. Only in cases where anthologies failed to provide such information were additional sources consulted. The three sources we found most useful in verifying information and clearing up discrepancies were: the PHONOLOG REPORTER (Los Angeles: Trade Service Publications), Norm M. Nite's ROCK ON (New York: Thomas Y. Crowell, 2v., 1964, 1978), and Nat Shapiro's POPULAR MUSIC (New York: Adrian Press, 6v., 1969-1973).

In preparing a work of this sort, some problems are bound to arise. By far the most difficult problem encountered throughout the project was verifying copyright information. It is important to realize that this information changes rapidly as publishers sell or assign rights. It should also be noted that the information provided in the collections indexed was not always consistent. The publishers listed, however, should at least provide a starting place for those interested in rights and permissions. Whenever foreign and U.S. rights were listed, we so indicated by use of a slash, for example, Edizioni Curci/Miller Music Corp. For additional information about the complexities of music copyright see Joseph Taubman's IN TUNE WITH THE MUSIC BUSINESS (New York: Law-Arts Publishers, 1980).

Another small problem that presented itself involved identifying whether or not variant forms of a name belonged to one composer or lyricist. Whenever there was some question as to whether J. Jones or James Jones were synonymous, we listed them as distinct individuals. In some instances, we were unable to identify a performer for a song. At times, this was because the song had never been commercially recorded. In these rare instances, we omitted information on aspects of the songs which we were unable to verify. These minor blemishes should not greatly interfere with the index's use.

The arrangement of all sections of the index is alphabetical. Observing general library practice, we have not filed by initial articles such as "a," "an," or "the." In fact, in order to present a clear, straight alphabetical list for the reader, we have dropped the use of initial articles in English completely. We have, however, retained foreign articles and arranged them alphabetically as significant words. "La Bamba," therefore, is filed under "La." We did this because we assumed that many of our users might not be familiar with the meaning of all the foreign articles listed or with the standard library practice for filing them. We thought it wiser to provide "see references" from the first significant word in all such titles which will refer the more experienced user back to the initial foreign articles.

Abbreviations are treated as individual words. "Mr.," therefore, would appear after "Mary." It is important to note that songs beginning with such a word as "Mr." or "Mister" may have to be searched under both forms. Along these same lines, many songs have elisions as part of the title or first line. The user must take care to check a word that sounds like "every" under both "every" and "ev'ry"; a title or first line that begins with a word that sounds like "singing" must check under "singing" and "singin'." Under the index's arrangement, it is incumbent on the user to anticipate any variant possibilities. Nonsense phrases such as "A-Bop-Bop-A-Loom" have been filed as one word both in the title and first line indexes; whenever such a phrase appears as a first line, an additional first line has been entered under the first legitimate sentence in the song. Finally, it is not uncommon to find different songs with the same title. Whenever this occurred, we listed the names of the composers and lyricists in parenthesis next to the title of the song in the first line and performer indexes. This should aid the user in quickly identifying the needed song. We were also generous in providing cross references whenever we saw the need for them.

FIND THAT TUNE: AN INDEX TO ROCK, FOLK-ROCK, DISCO & SOUL is in no way meant as a definitive guide or index to the music in the era covered. It is a beginning to attempt to provide bibliographical access to a rich horde of material that badly needs to be identified, classified, preserved, and made available to the public. It is hoped that this index will be a first step in the right direction, and that it will encourage libraries with popular music collections to continue to develop them for both their entertainment and research value.

ACKNOWLEDGMENTS

Much of the research for this book was completed in the Art & Music Division of the Brooklyn Public Library and at the New York Public Library's Performing Arts Research Center. We are grateful to these libraries and their staffs for their generous assistance. In particular, we would like to thank Charles Eubanks of the Performing Arts Research Center for allowing us access to uncataloged material. We would also like to thank Ken Axthelm and his staff at the Brooklyn Public Library's Audio Visual Division for providing access to the PHONOLOG REPORTER. Moreover, we wish to express our appreciation to all the Brooklyn Public Library staff for their interest and enthusiasm throughout this endeavor.

This project was furthered by a two-week research leave granted Bill Gargan by Brooklyn College (CUNY). We are grateful to the College, and to our colleagues in the Library Department there, for their encouragement and support. We would especially like to thank Ruth Bird, Bernice Clegg, Rita Coleman, and Anne Schreiber who helped type, photocopy, or collate parts of the final manuscript. Thanks also to Anthony Santoro and Michael McLean for sharing their expertise on Rock music.

Finally, we owe our greatest debt to Vir Sharma and Sharon Goodstine Gargan, our respective spouses, for the patience and support they offered throughout the project. Their understanding and encouragement have been important factors in allowing this book to see the light of day.

1

COLLECTIONS INDEXED

COLLECTIONS INDEXED

44. COUNTRY FOLK/ROCK HITS. New York: ARC Music Corp., n.d.

45. CRAZY LITTLE THING CALLED LOVE PLUS 12 POP CHART WINNERS. Hialeah, Florida: Columbia Pictures Publications, 1980.

46. DANCING QUEEN PLUS 12 DYNAMITE HITS. New York: Warner Bros. Publications, 1977.

47. DESIRE; 15 SUPER SONGS OF TODAY. New York: Chappell Music Co., 1980.

48. THE DIANA ROSS SONGBOOK. Hollywood, California: Jobete Music Co., Inc., 1979.

49. DISCO DANCE HITS. New York: Big 3 Music Corp., n.d.

50. DISCO FEVER. New York: Chappell & Co., 1979.

51. DISCO POPS. Hialeah, Florida: Columbia Pictures Publications, 1979.

52. THE DISCOTHEQUE SOUND. New York: Screen Gems-Columbia Pictures, 1975.

53. DON KIRSHNER'S ROCK CONCERT. (Deluxe edition) Miami, Florida: Screen Gems-Columbia Publications, 1975.

54. DOORS-MORRISON HOTEL. New York: Doors Music Co., 1970.

55. DUST IN THE WIND & 50 ROCK CLASSICS. New York: Warner Bros. Publications, 1978.

56. 80 FOR THE 80's. Hialeah, Florida: Columbia Pictures Publications, 1980.

57. ESCAPE (THE PINA COLADA SONG) AND 33 ROCK SMOOTHIES. New York: Warner Bros. Publications, n.d.

58. THE FEMALE SUPERSTAR SONGBOOK. Hialeah, Florida: Columbia Picture Publications, 1980.

59. THE FESTIVAL SONGBOOK. New York: Amsco Music Publishing Co., 1973.

60. THE 5TH DIMENSION: THE AGE OF AQUARIUS. New York: Big 3 Music Corp., n.d.

61. 50 BY JOHN LENNON & PAUL MCCARTNEY. Hollywood, California: Maclen Music, Inc. from the ATV Music Group, n.d.

62. 50 GOLDEN GIANTS. New York: Warner Bros. Publications, 1976.

63. 50 SWINGING SOUNDS. New York: Charles Hansen Educational Music & Books, 1973.

64. 50 TOP TEN HITS. Los Angeles, California: West Coast Publications, Inc., n.d.

65. 1ST BIG HITS OF '79. Hialeah, Florida: Columbia Pictures Publications, 1979.

66. 1ST BIG HITS OF '79. (Soul Edition) Hialeah, Florida: Columbia Pictures Publications, 1979.

67. THE FOLK DECADE: A RETROSPECTIVE. New York: Warner Bros. Publications, 1976.

68. FOLK MUSIC GREATEST HITS. Ojai, California: Creative Concepts, n.d.

69. FOLK ROCK: TOP RECORDED HITS. New York: M. Witmark & Sons, n.d.

70. 40 BEST ALMO SONGS. Hollywood, California: Almo Publications, 1980.

71. 40 BLOCKBUSTERS. Hialeah, Florida: Columbia Pictures Publications, 1979.

72. 48 GREAT HITS OF THE SUPER STARS. New York: Big 3 Music Corp., n.d.

73. 44 NEW SUPERHITS OF THE SUPERSTARS. Hialeah, Florida: Columbia Pictures Publications, 1979.

74. 43 NEW SUPERHITS OF THE SUPERSTARS. Hialeah, Florida: Columbia Pictures Publications, 1978.

75. 40 TOP CHART SONGS. Hialeah, Florida: Columbia Pictures Publications, 1979.

76. 40 TOP OF THE 40. Miami Beach, Florida: Hansen Publications, Inc., n.d.

77. THE GOLDEN BOOK OF ROCK. Hialeah, Florida: Columbia Pictures Publications, 1976.

78. THE GOLDEN ERA OF ROCK & ROLL. New York: The Big 3 Music Corp., n.d.

79. GOOD OLD POP SONGS. VOLUME 1. New York: United Artists Music, n.d.

80. GOOD OLD POP SONGS. VOLUME 2. New York: United Artists Music, n.d.

81. GOLD OLD POP SONGS. VOLUME 3. New York: United Artists Music, n.d.

82. GOOD OLD POP SONGS. VOLUME 4. New York: United Artists Music, n.d.

83. GRATEFUL DEAD. VOLUME 1. New York: Ice Nine Publishing Co., 1975.

84. GRATEFUL DEAD. VOLUME 2. New York: Ice Nine Publishing Co., 1976.

85. GREAT FOLK SONGS OF THE 60s. New York: TRO Ludlow Music, n.d.

86. GREAT MUSIC FESTIVALS FROM MONTEREY TO WOODSTOCK. New York: Charles Hansen Music and Books, n.d.

87. GREAT SUPERSTARS OF TODAY. New York: Warner Bros. Publications, n.d.

88. HANSEN'S HOT FORTY. Miami Beach, Florida: Charles Hansen Publications, n.d.

89. HAPPINESS IS...GREAT SONGS OF THE 70's. New York: Big 3 Music Corp., 1975.

90. HISTORY OF RHYTHM & BLUES--THE GOLDEN YEARS 1953 - 55. VOLUME 2. New York: Progressive Music Publishing Co., Inc., 1969.

91. HISTORY OF RHYTHM & BLUES--ROCK & ROLL 1956 - 57. VOLUME 3. New York: Progressive Music Publishing Co., Inc., 1969.

92. HISTORY OF RHYTHM & BLUES--THE BIG BEAT, 1958 - 60. VOLUME 4. New York: Progressive Music Publishing Co., Inc., 1969.

93. HISTORY OF ROCK MUSIC. Miami Beach, Florida: Charles Hansen, n.d.

94. HITS FOR THE SEVENTIES. New York: MCA Music, a division of MCA Inc., n.d.

95. HITS OF THE DISCO SUPERSTARS. Hollywood, California: Jobete Music Co., Inc. & Black Bull Music, Inc., 1977.

96. THE HOT SHEETS. Hollywood, California: Almo Publications, 1979.

97. HOT 20 SHEET MUSIC POPS. Hialeah, Florida: Florida: Columbia Pictures Publications, 1980.

98. HOT 20 SHEET MUSIC POPS. BOOK 2. Hialeah, Florida: Columbia Pictures Publications, 1980.

99. HOT 20 SHEET MUSIC POPS. BOOK 3. Hialeah, Florida: Columbia Pictures Publications, 1980.

100. I DIG ROCK 'N' ROLL MUSIC. New York: Warner Bros. Publications, n.d.

101. I LOVE THE '50s. New York: Big 3 Music Corp., n.d.

102. I LOVE THE '60s. New York: Big 3 Music Corp., n.d.

103. I WRITE THE SONGS. New York: Charles Hansen Distributor-Educational Sheetmusic & Books, n.d.

104. IN CONCERT ABC. VOLUME 1. Miami, Florida: Screen Gems-Columbia Publications, 1973.

105. IN CONCERT ABC. VOLUME 2. Miami, Florida: Screen Gems-Columbia Publications, 1974.

106. IN CONCERT ABC. VOLUME 3. Miami, Florida: Screen Gems-Columbia Publications, 1974.

107. JAMES BROWN'S SOUL CLASSICS. VOLUME 2. New York: Chappell Music Co., n.d.

108. JEFFERSON AIRPLANE. New York: Music Sales Corp., n.d.

109. JOHN LENNON--ROCK 'N' ROLL. New York: Big Three Music Corp., n.d.

110. JOPLIN IN CONCERT. New York: Warner Bros. Publications, n.d.

111. KILLING ME SOFTLY WITH HIS SONG AND OTHER BIG HITS. New York: Big 3 Music Corp., n.d.

112. LAST DANCE PLUS 12 DISCO CHART WINNERS. Hialeah, Florida: Columbia Pictures Publications, 1979.

113. LATEST HOT FOURTEEN. Miami Beach, Florida: Sheet Music Institute, n.d.

114. LED ZEPPELIN COMPLETE. New York: Superhype Publishing, 1973.

115. LIVE IN CONCERT. New York: Warner Bros. Publications, n.d.

116. LONGER JUST THE WAY YOU ARE & OTHER POP CHART HITS. New York: April-Blackwood Publications, n.d.

117. MACARTHUR PARK & 27 ROCK CLASSICS. New York: Warner Bros. Publications, 1979.

118. MACARTHUR PARK, LE FREAK & MORE GREAT DISCO. New York: Warner Bros. Publications, 1978.

119. THE MAMAS & THE PAPAS--SOUVENIR SONG ALBUM. Miami Beach, Florida: Hansen Publications, Inc., n.d.

120. MEAT LOAF--BAT OUT OF HELL. Melville, New York: Edward B. Marks Music Corp., Neverland Music Co. & Peg Music Co., 1977.

121. MELLOW ROCK. Hialeah, Florida: Columbia Pictures Publications, 1977.

122. THE MEMPHIS SOUND. Hollywood, California: Almo Publications, 1978.

123. THE MOTOWN ERA. Detroit, Michigan: Jobete Music Co., Inc., 1971.

124. MY SHARONA & 25 GREAT ROCK SONGS OF THE '70's. New York: Warner Bros. Publications, n.d.

125. THE NEW BEATLES TOP 40 PLUS POP SONG BOOK. New York: Charles Hansen Distributor/ Educational Music & Books, n.d.

126. THE NEW BIG FOLK-ROCK BOOK, 3rd edition. Hialeah, Florida: Columbia Pictures Publications, 1978.

127. NEW BIG 76. New York: Warner Bros. Publications, 1977.

128. THE NEW BIG TOP 100. Hialeah, Florida: Columbia Pictures Publications, 1979.

129. THE NEW SMASH HITS OF '79. Hollywood, California: Almo Publications, 1979.

130. THE NEW SUPER 79. Hialeah, Florida: Columbia Pictures Publications, 1979.

131. NEW YORK TIMES GREAT SONGS OF THE 70's. New York: Times Books, 1978.

132. THE NOW SOUND OF FOLK MUSIC. New York: Warner Bros.-Seven Arts, Inc., n.d.

133. #1 SONGS OF THE SEVENTIES. New York: Warner Bros. Publications, 1978.

134. 111 HITS OF THE SUPER STARS, 4th Edition. Hialeah, Florida: Columbia Pictures Publications, 1979.

135. 111 HITS OF THE SUPER STARS. VOLUME 3. Hialeah, Florida: Columbia Pictures Publications, 1978.

136. 100 GREAT ROCK SONGS OF THE DECADE. New York: Warner Bros. Publications, n.d.

137. 100 OF THE GREATEST ROCK & ROLL HITS. New York: Big 3 Music Corp., n.d.

138. 110 SUPER SONGS OF THE SUPER STARS. VOLUME 1. New York: Warner Bros. Publications, n.d.

139. 110 SUPER SONGS OF THE SUPER STARS. VOLUME 2. New York: Warner Bros. Publications, 1975.

140. 120 GREATEST HITS OF THE 50's, 60's, 70's. New York: Big 3 Music Corp., 1979.

141. 120 SUPER SONGS OF THE SUPER STARS. New York: Warner Bros. Publications, 1978.

142. 122 SUPERHITS OF THE SUPER STARS. Hialeah, Florida: Columbia Pictures Publications, 1978.

143. PAUL SIMON COMPLETE. New York: Warner Bros. Publications, n.d.

144. PHIL OCHS: THE WAR IS OVER. New York: Barricade Music, Inc., 1968.

145. PLATINUM '78 (SONGBOOK OF THE SUPER-STARS). New York: Warner Bros. Publications, 1979.

146. PLATINUM '79. New York: Warner Bros. Publications, 1979.

147. PLATINUM '80. New York: Warner Bros. Publications, n.d.

148. POP CHART HITS. New York: April-Blackwood Publications, n.d.

149. POPS '70. New York: Warner Bros. Music, n.d.

150. POPULAR RHYTHM & BLUES. Hollywood, California: Jobete Music Co., Inc., 1976.

151. PROGRESSIVE FOLK-ROCK CLASSICS. New York: Warner Bros. Publications, n.d.

152. PROGRESSIVE ROCK CLASSICS. New York: Warner Bros. Publications, n.d.

153. PUNK ROCK 'N' ROLL NEW WAVE. Hollywood, California: Almo Publications, 1978.

154. RHYTHM & BLUES SONG FOLIO. New York: Progressive Music Publishing Co., Inc., 1963.

155. RHYTHM & BLUES: THE ROOTS OF SOUL. New York: Big 3 Music Corp., n.d.

156. ROCK ANTHOLOGY. Miami, Florida: Screen Gems-Columbia Publications, 1975.

157. ROCK ANTHOLOGY: TOP OF THE CHARTS. Hialeah, Florida: Columbia Pictures Publications, 1979.

158. ROCK AROUND THE CLOCK PLUS 12 GOLDEN OLDIES. Hialeah, Florida: Columbia Publications, 1977.

159. ROCK LIVES! Los Angeles, California: ATV Music Publications, 1980.

160. THE ROCK REVIVAL SONG BOOK. Westbury, New York: Cimino Publications Inc., n.d.

161. ROCK: YESTERDAY & TODAY. New York: Big 3 Music Corp., n.d.

162. SAILING & MORE MELLOW GOLD. New York: Warner Bros. Publications, n.d.

163. 77 GIANT HITS OF TODAY. New York: Big 3 Music Corp., 1978.

164. SHEET MUSIC POPS NO. 9. Hialeah, Florida: Columbia Pictures Publications, n.d.

165. SHEET MUSIC SONG BOOK. New York: April-Blackwood Publications, n.d.

166. 16 BIG HITS. VOLUME I. Detroit, Michigan: Jobete Music Co., Inc., 1967.

167. 16 BIG HITS. VOLUME 2. Detroit, Michigan: Jobete Music Co., Inc., 1968.

168. SOLID GOLD ROCK & ROLL. Hialeah, Florida: Screen Gems-Columbia Publications, 1975.

169. SOLID GOLD ROCK & ROLL. New York: Big 3 Music Corp., 1975.

170. THE SONGS OF BOB DYLAN: FROM 1966 THROUGH 1975. New York: Knopf, 1976.

171. SONGS OF LEONARD COHEN. New York: Amsco Music Publishing Co., 1969.

172. SONGS RECORDED BY ELVIS PRESLEY. VOLUME I. New York: Elvis Presley Music, Inc., 1968.

173. SONGS RECORDED BY ELVIS PRESLEY. VOLUME 2. New York: Elvis Presley Music, Inc., 1968.

174. STAIRWAY TO HEAVEN & 51 ROCK CLASSICS. New York: Warner Bros. Publications, n.d.

175. STAIRWAY TO HEAVEN PLUS 24 HEAVY HITS. New York: Warner Bros. Publications, 1977.

176. STAR SONGS. New York: Big 3 Music Corp., n.d.

177. STAR SONGS. VOLUME 2. New York: Big 3 Music Corp., n.d.

178. STAYING ALIVE PLUS 24 SUPER SONGS. New York: Warner Bros. Publications, 1978.

179. STILL & I'LL NEVER LOVE THIS WAY AGAIN PLUS 24 SOLID GOLD SONGS. Hialeah, Florida: Columbia Pictures Publications, 1979.

180. SUPER CHART SONGS OF 1979. Hialeah, Florida: Columbia Pictures Publications, 1980.

181. SUPER HITS OF THE 70's. Hollywood, California: Almo Publications, 1979.

182. SUPERGROUPS! SUPERSTARS! SUPERSONGS! New York: Warner Bros. Publications, n.d.

183. SUPERSTAR SONGBOOK. Trenton, New Jersey: Big Bells Inc., 1975.

184. SUPERSTARS PLAY THE SUPER HITS. New York: Big 3 Music Corp., n.d.

185. 35 ROCK CLASSICS. New York: Warner Bros. Publications, n.d.

186. TODAY'S FANTASTIC HITS. New York: Robbins Music Corp., 1970.

187. TODAY'S SHEET MUSIC POPS. BOOK I. Hialeah, Florida: Columbia Pictures Publications, 1979.

188. TOP HITS OF 1980. VOLUME I. New York: Warner Bros. Publications, n.d.

189. TOP HITS OF 1980. VOLUME 2. New York: Warner Bros. Publications, n.d.

190. TOP HITS OF 1980. VOLUME 3. New York: Warner Bros. Publications, n.d.

191. TOP HITS OF 1970 AND GREAT STANDARDS. New York: Robbins Music Corp., 1971.

192. TOP HITS OF 1971 AND GREAT STANDARDS. New York: Big 3 Music Corp., n.d.

193. TOP HITS OF 1976. New York: Big 3 Music Corp., n.d.

194. TOP HITS OF 1973 AND GREAT STANDARDS. New York: Big 3 Music Corp., n.d.

COLLECTIONS INDEXED

2

TITLE INDEX

TITLE INDEX

Abandoned Love. w&m; Bob Dylan. c1975, 76, Ram's Horn Music. 170

"ABC". w&m; The Corporation. c1970, Jobete Music Co., Inc. JACKSON 5. 20, 123, 150.

ABC's Of Love. w&m; Richard Barrett & George Goldner. c1956, 78, Nom Music Publishing Corp. FRANKIE LYMON & THE TEENAGERS. 2, 101.

Abraham, Martin And John. w&m; Dick Holler. c1968, Roznique Music, Inc. DION. 64, 126, 156.

Absolutely Sweet Marie. w&m; Bob Dylan. c1966, 67, Dwarf Music. BOB DYLAN. 170.

Across 110th Street. w&m; Bobby Womack & J.J. Johnson. c1972, 73, Unart Music Corp. BOBBY WOMACK. 111.

Across the Universe. w&m; John Lennon & Paul McCartney. c1968, Northern Songs, Ltd./Maclen Music, BEATLES. 61.

Act Naturally. w&m; Vonie Morrison & Johnny Russell. c1963, 71, Blue Book Music Co. BEATLES. 125.

Action. w&m; Brian Connolly, Steve Priest, Mick Tucker & Andy Scott. c1975, 76, 77, Sweet Publishing Ltd./WB Music Corp. SWEET. 36, 175.

Action Speaks Louder Than Words. w&m; Lloyd Harris, Jr., Frank Richard, Ernest Dabon, Joseph Smith III, Dwight Richards, Mario G. Tio, Amadee Castenell, Jr., Robert Dabon & Kenneth Williams. c1975, Marsaint Music, Inc. CHOCOLATE MILK. 139.

After Midnight. w&m; John J. Cale. c1966, 70, Warner-Tamerlane Publishing Corp. ERIC CLAPTON. 22, 36, 55, 138, 152, 174, 185.

After The Dance. w&m; Marvin Gaye & Leon Ware. c1976, Jobete Music Co., Inc. MARVIN GAYE. 26.

After The Gold Rush. w&m; Neil Young. c1970, 74, 75, Cotillion Music & Broken Arrow Music. NEIL YOUNG/PRELUDE. 36, 43, 55, 87, 136, 141, 174.

After The Love Has Gone. w&m; David Foster, Jay Graydon & Bill Champlin. c1979, Ninth Music, Bobette Music, Garden Rake Music, Irving Music, Inc. & Foster Frees Music. EARTH, WIND & FIRE. 23, 24, 75, 179, 180.

After The Lovin'. w&m; Alan Bernstein & Ritchie Adams. c1974, 76, Silver Blue Music & Oceans Blue Music. BARBARA MANDRELL/ENGELBERT HUMPERDINCK. 23, 56, 77, 128, 134.

After The Storm. w&m; Dale Noe. c1976, ATV Music Corp. LARRY GATLIN. 37.

After The Thrill Is Gone. w&m; Don Henley & Glenn Frey. c1975, WB Music Corp. EAGLES. 30.

After You. w&m; Doug Frank & Doug James. c1979, 80, Sumac Music Inc. DIONNE WARWICK/MANHATTANS. 23, 24, 45, 58.

Afternoon Delight. w&m; Bill Danoff. c1976, Cherry Lane Music Co. STARLAND VOCAL BAND. 131.

Against The Wind. w&m; Bob Seger. c1980, Gear Publishing Co. BOB SEGER & THE SILVER BULLET BAND. 162, 189.

Ain't Gonna Bump No More. w&m; Bennie Lee McGinty & Buddy Killen. c1976, Tree Publishing Co., Inc. JOE TEX. 196.

Ain't Got No Home. w&m; Clarence Henry. c1956, Arc Music Corp. CLARENCE "FROGMAN" HENRY. 5.

Ain't Love A Bitch. w&m; Rod Stewart & Gary Grainger. c1978, 79, Rod Stewart & Riva Music, Ltd./Riva Music, Inc. ROD STEWART. 27, 147.

Ain't No Mountain High Enough. w&m; Nickolas Ashford & Valerie Simpson. c1967, 69, 70, 71, Jobete Music Co., Inc. DIANA ROSS/MARVIN GAYE & TAMMI TERRELL. 13, 48, 123, 128, 150.

Ain't No Stoppin' Us Now. w&m; J. Whitehead, G. McFadden & J. Cohen. c1978, Mighty Three Music. MC FADDEN & WHITEHEAD. 24, 56, 75, 187.

Ain't No Sunshine. w&m; Bill Withers. c1971, Interior Music Corp. Administered by Irving Music, Inc./U.A. Music International, Inc. BILL WITHERS/EMOTIONS/PROPHETS OF SOUL. 56, 71, 115.

Ain't No Way To Treat A Lady. w&m; Harriet Schock. c1974, 75, Colgems-EMI Music Inc. GONZALEZ/HELEN REDDY. 58, 128, 134.

Ain't No Woman (Like The One I've Got). w&m; Dennis Lambert & Brian Potter. c1972, Trousdale Music Publishers, Inc. & Soldier Music Inc. FOUR TOPS. 32.

Ain't Nothing But A Maybe. w&m; Nickolas Ashford & Valerie Simpson. c1973, 76, Nick-O-Val Music. ASHFORD & SIMPSON/DIANA ROSS/RUFUS. 13.

Ain't Nothing Like The Real Thing. w&m; Nickolas Ashford & Valerie Simpson. c1967, 68, 74, Jobete Music Co., Inc. DONNY & MARIE OSMOND/MARVIN GAYE & TAMMI TERRELL. 13, 123, 150.

Ain't That A Groove (Part 1). w&m; James Brown & Nat Jones. c1966, 68, Dynatone Publishing Co. JAMES BROWN. 18.

Ain't That A Groove (Part 2). w&m; James Brown & Nat Jones. c1966, 68, Dynatone Publishing Co. JAMES BROWN. 18.

Ain't That A Shame. w&m; Antoine Domino & Dave Bartholomew. c1955, Unart Music Corp. CHEAP TRICK/FATS DOMINO/JOHN LENNON. 78, 80, 101, 109, 137, 155, 176, 198.

Ain't That Loving You? (For More Reasons Than One). w&m; Homer Banks & Allen Jones. c1967, East-Memphis Music. BOBBY BLAND. 122.

Ain't That Peculiar. w&m; William Robinson, Warren Moore, Marv Tarplin & Robert Rogers. c1965, 72, Jobete Music Co., Inc. MARVIN GAYE. 123, 150, 166.

Ain't Too Proud To Beg. w&m; Eddie Holland & Norman Whitfield. c1966, Jobete Music Co., Inc. ROLLING STONES/TEMPTATIONS. 52, 53, 123, 150.

Air That I Breathe. w&m; Albert Hammond & Mike Hazelwood. c1972, 73, Landers-Roberts Music, Inc. & April Music Inc. HOLLIES. 106, 165.

Airport Love Theme. SEE Winds Of Chance.

Alabama. w&m; Neil Young. c1971, 1975, Silver Fiddle. NEIL YOUNG. 139.

Alabama Jubilee. w&m; Jack Yellen (w) & George L. Cobb (m). c1915, Jerome H. Remick & Co. ALMANAC SINGERS. 132.

Alfie. w&m; Hal David (w) & Burt F. Bacharach (m.). c1966, 68, Famous Music Corp. CHER/DIAHANN CARROLL/DIONNE WARWICK. 76, 113.

Alice Blue Gown. w&m; Joseph McCarthy (w) & Harry Tierney (m.). c1919, 1947, 1966, Leo Feist Inc. GLENN MILLER/JIMMY WEBB/MANTOVANI. 140.

Alice's Restaurant. w&m; Arlo Guthrie. c1966, 67, 69; Appleseed Music Inc. ARLO GUTHRIE. 7.

Alive Again. w&m; James Pankow. c1978, Make Me Smile Music. CHICAGO. 73.

All Along The Watchtower. w&m; Bob Dylan. c1968, 76, Dwarf Music. BOB DYLAN. 170.

All American Boy. w&m; Bobby Bare. c1958; Mayhew Music Co. BOBBY BARE. 4.

All Around The World. w&m; R. Blackwell & M. Millet. c1956, Venice Music. LITTLE RICHARD. 159.

All By Myself. w&m; Antoine Domino & Dave Bartholomew. c1955, Commodore Music Corp. FATS DOMINO. 137.

All By Myself. w&m; Eric Carmen. c1975, 76, C.A.M.-U.S.A., Inc. ERIC CARMEN. 30, 62, 133, 136, 138, 141, 174.

All God's Children Got Soul. w&m; Booker T. Jones & William Bell. c1969, East-Memphis Music. WILLIAM BELL. 122.

All Good People. w&m; Chris Squire. c1971, 72, Yessongs Ltd. YES. 152.

All I Ever Need Is You. w&m; Jimmy Holiday & Eddie Reeves. c1970, 71, United Artists Music Co. & Racer Music Inc. Administered by United Artists Music Co., Inc. JERRY REED/KENNY ROGERS & DOTTIE WEST/SONNY & CHER. 21, 79, 89, 140, 195.

All I Have To Do Is Dream. w&m; Boudleaux Bryant. c1958, House of Bryant Publications. EVERLY BROTHERS/GLEN CAMPBELL & BOBBIE GENTRY/NITTY GRITTY DIRT BAND. 3, 37, 59, 149.

All I Know. w&m; Jimmy Webb. c1973, Canopy Music Inc. ART GARFUNKEL. 138.

All I Need. w&m; Eddie Holland, Frank Wilson & R. Dean Taylor. c1967, Jobete Music Co., Inc. TEMPTATIONS. 123.

All I Really Want To Do. w&m; Bob Dylan. c1964, M. Witmark & Sons. BOB DYLAN/BYRDS. 35, 69, 138, 151.

All I Want. w&m; Joni Mitchell. c1971, Joni Mitchell Publishing Corp. JONI MITCHELL. 86.

All I Want To Be (Is By Your Side). w&m; Peter Frampton. c1972, Almo Music Corp., Fram-Dee Music Ltd. & United Artists Ltd. PETER FRAMPTON. 12.

All In Love Is Fair. w&m; Stevie Wonder. c1973, 74, Jobete Music Co., Inc. & Black Bull Music, Inc. BARBRA STREISAND/SHIRLEY BASSEY/STEVIE WONDER. 128, 130.

All In My Mind. w&m; Maxine Brown, Fred Johnson & Leroy Kirkland. c1960, 61, Figure Music Inc. Assigned to Frost Music Corp. MAXINE BROWN. 78, 161.

All Is Loneliness. w&m; Louis Hardin. c1969, 72, Prestige Music. JANIS JOPLIN. 110.

All My Loving. w&m; John Lennon & Paul McCartney. c1963, 64, Northern Songs Ltd./Maclen Music, Inc. BEATLES. 61, 127, 145.

All My Trials. w&m; Odetta Gordon (Adapted). c1963, M. Witmark & Sons. JOAN BAEZ/ODETTA. 67.

All My Trials. w&m; Peter Yarrow (Adapted), Paul Stookey (Adapted) & Milton Okun (Adapted). c1963, Pepamar Music Corp. PETER, PAUL & MARY. 41.

All Night Long. w&m; Joe Walsh. c1980, Wow & Flutter Music Publishing. JOE WALSH. 189.

All Revved Up With No Place To Go. w&m; Jim Steinman. c1977, Edward B. Marks Music Corp., Neverland Music Co. & Peg Music Co. MEATLOAF. 120.

All Right Now. w&m; Paul Rodgers & Andy Fraser. c1970, Blue Mountain Music Ltd./Irving Music, Inc. FREE. 191.

All Shook Up. w&m; Otis Blackwell & Elvis Presley. c1957, Unart Music Corp. ELVIS PRESLEY/OTIS BLACKWELL. 78, 81, 101, 137, 155, 161, 163.

All That I Am. w&m; Sid Tepper & Roy C. Bennett. c1966, Gladys Music, Inc. ELVIS PRESLEY. 173.

All That You Dream. w&m; Paul Barrere & Bill Payne. c1976, 78, Naked Snake Music. LINDA RONSTADT. 146.

All The Girls Love Alice. w&m; Elton John & Bernie Taupin. c1973, Dick James Music Ltd./Dick James Music Inc. ELTON JOHN. 138.

All The Tired Horses. w&m; Bob Dylan. c1970, 76, Big Sky Music. BOB DYLAN. 170.

All Things Are Possible. w&m; Dan Peek & Chris Christian. c1978, Home Sweet Home Music & Christian Soldier Music. DAN PEEK. 198.

All Things Must Pass. w&m; George Harrison. c1969, 70, Harrisongs Ltd./Harrisongs Music, Inc. GEORGE HARRISON. 125.

All This And More. w&m; Jimmy Zero. c1978, Bleu Disque Music Co., CBGB Music & Dead Boys Music. DEAD BOYS. 19.

All This And More. w&m; Keith Reid (w) & Gary Brooker (m.). c1969, 72, Essex Music International Ltd./TRO Andover Music, Inc. PROCOL HARUM. 42.

All Together Now. w&m; John Lennon & Paul McCartney. c1968, Northern Songs Ltd./Maclen Music, Inc. BEATLES. 61, 159.

All You Get From Love Is A Love Song. w&m; Steve Eaton. c1973, 77, Hampstead Heath Music Publishers. CARPENTERS. 127.

All You Need Is Love. w&m; John Lennon & Paul McCartney. c1967, Northern Songs Ltd./Maclen Music, Inc. BEATLES. 43, 61, 159.

All Your Love. w&m; Otis Rush. c1965, Arc Music Corp. JOHN MAYALL. 1.

Alley Cat Song. w&m; Jack Harlan (w) & Frank Bjorn (m). c1962, 68, Metorion Music Corp. Controlled by Eureka Anstalt. BENT FABRIC. 113, 163.

Alley-Oop. w&m; Dallas Frazier. c1960, Gary S. Paxton Music, Inc., Kavelin Music & Acoustic Music, Inc. HOLLYWOOD ARGYLES. 6.

Almost Like Being In Love. w&m; Alan J. Lerner (w) & Frederick Loewe (m). c1947, 75, Alan Jay Lerner & Frederick Loewe. Assigned to United Artists Music Co., Inc. FRANK SINATRA/MAGNUM FORCE/MANTOVANI. 140.

Alone Again (Naturally). w&m; Raymond O'Sullivan. c1972, MAM (Music Publishing Ltd.)/Management Agency & Music Publishing, Inc. SARAH VAUGHAN/SHIRLEY BASSEY. 131.

Already Gone. w&m; Jack Tempchin & Robb Strandlund. c1974, WB Music Corp. EAGLES. 117, 185.

Also Sprach Zarathustra (2001). w&m; Richard Strauss (m) & Leonard Moss (Arranged). c1973, Westport Music Corp. 32.

Also Sprach Zarathustra (2001). w&m; Richard Strauss (m) & Eumir Deodato (Arranged). c1973, Three Brothers Music, Inc. DEODATO. 77, 134, 156.

Always And Forever. w&m; Rod Temperton. c1976, 78, Rondor Music Ltd./Almo Music Corp. HEATWAVE. 23, 24, 56, 70, 71, 96, 179.

Always Something There To Remind Me. w&m; Hal David (w) & Burt F. Bacharach (m). c1964, Anne-Rachel Music Corp., Blue Seas Music, Inc. & Jac Music Co., Inc. Administered by Anne-Rachel Music Corp. DIONNE WARWICK. 72, 191, 192.

Alyce Blue Gown SEE Alice Blue Gown.

Am I Blue. w&m; Grant Clarke (w) & Harry Akst (m). c1929, Warner Bros., Inc. CHER/WILLIE NELSON & LEON RUSSELL. 31, 139.

Amarillo. w&m; Neil Sedaka & Howard Greenfield. c1971, 77, Neil Sedaka Music. NEIL SEDAKA. 127.

Amazing Grace. w&m; John A. & Alan Lomax (Collected, adapted & arranged). c1947, 71, Ludlow Music, Inc. JUDY COLLINS. 85.

Amazing Grace (Used To Be Her Favorite Song). w&m; Russell Smith. c1974, 76, Fourth Floor Music, Inc. AMAZING RHYTHM ACES. 122.

Amber Cascades. w&m; Dewey Bunnell. c1976, WB Music Corp. AMERICA. 30, 141.

Amelia. w&m; Joni Mitchell. c1976, 77, Crazy Crow Music. JONI MITCHELL. 141.

America. w&m; Paul Simon. c1968, Paul Simon. SIMON & GARFUNKEL. 143.

American Pie. w&m; Don McLean. c1971, 72, 73, Mayday Music, Inc. & Yahweh Tunes, Inc. Administered by Unart Music Corp. DON MC LEAN. 15, 21, 89, 131, 140, 194, 199.

American Tune. w&m; Paul Simon. c1973, Paul Simon. PAUL SIMON/STARLAND VOCAL BAND. 131, 143.

Among My Souvenirs. w&m; Edgar Leslie & Horatio Nicholls. c1927. Lawrence Wright Music Co., Ltd./Chappell & Co., Inc. CONNIE FRANCIS. 6.

Amoreena. w&m; Elton John & Bernie Taupin. c1970, Dick James Music, Inc. ELTON JOHN. 30, 197.

Amos & Andy Song SEE Like A Sunday In Salem.

Amos Moses. w&m; Jerry Hubbard. c1969, Vector Music Corp. JERRY REED. 64, 88.

Amoureuse SEE Emotion.

Anarchy In The U.K. w&m; Johnny Rotten, Steven Jones, Paul Cook & Glen Matlock. c1978, Glitterbest Ltd. & Glen Matlock. SEX PISTOLS. 19.

And I Love Her. w&m; John Lennon & Paul McCartney. c1964, Northern Songs Ltd./Maclen Music, Inc. BEATLES. 35, 61.

And I Love You So. w&m; Don McLean. c1970, 72, Mayday Music, Inc. & Yahweh Tunes, Inc. Administered by Unart Music Corp. DON MC LEAN/PERRY COMO. 21, 37, 89, 140, 163, 194, 198.

And The Grass Won't Pay No Mind. w&m; Neil Diamond. c1968, 70, Stonebridge Music. NEIL DIAMOND. 88.

And When I Die. w&m; Laura Nyro. c1966, Tuna Fish Music, Inc. Administered by Blackwood Music, Inc. BLOOD, SWEAT & TEARS. 35, 86, 199.

Anderson Tapes, Theme From. w&m; Quincy Jones (m). c1971, 72, Screen Gems-EMI Music Inc. QUINCY JONES. 142.

Angel. w&m; Sid Tepper & Roy C. Bennett. c1962, Gladys Music, Inc. ELVIS PRESLEY. 172.

Angel. w&m; William Sanders & Carolyn Franklin. c1973, Pundit Music, Inc. & Afghan Music Co. ARETHA FRANKLIN. 197.

Angel Eyes. w&m; Earl Brent (w) & Matt Dennis (m). c1946, 75, Matt Dennis. Assigned to Maxey Music Co. & Dorsey Bros. Music, Inc. SHIRLEY BASSEY. 139.

Angel In Your Arms. w&m; Clayton Ivey, Terry Woodford & Tom Brasfield. c1976, 77, Song Tailors Music Co. & I've Got The Music Co. HOT/LYNN ANDERSON/MILLIE JACKSON. 23, 130.

Angel Of The Morning. w&m; Chip Taylor. c1967, Blackwood Music Inc. MERRILEE RUSH/OLIVIA NEWTON-JOHN. 165.

Angie. w&m; Mick Jagger & Keith Richard. c1973, Promopub B.V. ROLLING STONES. 36, 183.

Angie Baby. w&m; Alan O'Day. c1974, WB Music Corp. HELEN REDDY. 133.

Angry Eyes. w&m; Jim Messina & Kenny Loggins. c1972, American Broadcasting Music, Inc., Jasperilla Music Co. & MCA Music. LOGGINS & MESSINA. 28, 36, 142.

Animal. w&m; Ronnie McDowell. c1978, Brim Music. RONNIE MC DOWELL. 74, 135.

Annie's Song. w&m; John Denver. c1974, Cherry Lane Music Co. JOHN DENVER. 131.

Another Brick In The Wall (Part II). w&m; Roger Waters. c1979, Pink Floyd Music Publishers, Ltd./ Unichappell Music, Inc. PINK FLOYD. 47.

Another Day. w&m; Paul & Linda McCartney. c1971, Northern Songs Ltd./Maclen Music, Inc. PAUL MC CARTNEY & WINGS. 141.

Another Saturday Night. w&m; Sam Cooke. c1963, 74, Kags Music Corp. CAT STEVENS/SAM COOKE. 24, 28, 29, 53, 77, 156.

Another Somebody Done Somebody Wrong Song. w&m; Larry Butler & Chips Moman. c1975, Tree Publishing Co., Inc., Press Music Co., Inc. & Screen Gems-EMI Music Inc. B.J. THOMAS/KENNY ROGERS & DOTTIE WEST/LORETTA LYNN. 89, 130.

Another Star. w&m; Stevie Wonder. c1976, Jobete Music Co., Inc. & Black Bull Music Inc. STEVIE WONDER. 142.

Answering Machine. w&m; Rupert Holmes. c1979, 80, WB Music Corp. & The Holmes Line Of Music, Inc. Administered by WB Music Corp. RUPERT HOLMES. 189.

Anthony's Song SEE Movin' Out.

Anticipation. w&m; Carly Simon. c1971, Quackenbush Music, Ltd. CARLY SIMON. 117, 136, 174, 183, 185.

Any Time. w&m; Herbert "Happy Lawson. c1921, 49, Herbert Happy Lawson Music Publishing Co. Renewed & assigned to Hill and Range Songs, Inc. ARLO GUTHRIE. 191.

Any Way You Want It. w&m; Dave Clark. c1964, Sphere Music Co., Ltd./Big Seven Music Corp. DAVE CLARK FIVE. 102.

Any Way You Want It. w&m; S. Erry & N. Schon. c1979, 80, Weed High Nightmare Music. Controlled by Screen Gems-EMI Music Inc. JOURNEY. 99.

Any Way You Want Me (That's How I Will Be). w&m; Aaron Schroeder & Cliff Owens. c1956, Anne-Rachel Music Corp. ELVIS PRESLEY. 173.

Anyday. w&m; Eric Clapton & Bobby Whitlock. c1970, 71, Throat Music Ltd. & Delbon Music/Cotillion. DEREK & THE DOMINOES. 152.

Anyone Who Isn't Me Tonight. w&m; Casey Kelly & Julie Didier. c1978, Bobby Goldsboro Music, Inc. KENNY ROGERS & DOTTIE WEST. 130.

Anyplace Is Paradise. w&m; Joe Thomas. c1956, Elvis Presley Music, Inc. ELVIS PRESLEY. 172.

Anything You Want. w&m; John Valenti & Joe Spinazola. c1975, 76, Minta Music. JOHN VALENTI. 141.

Anytime. w&m; Gregg Rolie, Roger Silver, Robert Fleischman, Neal Schon & Ross Valory. c1978, Weed High Nightmare Music. Controlled by Screen Gems-EMI Music Inc. JOURNEY. 135.

Anytime, Anyplace, Anywhere. w&m; Laurie Tate & Joe Morris. c1950, Progressive Music Publishing Co. Controlled by Unichappell Music, Inc. JOE MORRIS. 155.

Anytime Of The Year. w&m; Robert Brittan (w) & Nurit Hirsch (m). c1970, 71, N. Hirsch, E. Manor & April Music Ltd./Blackwood Music Inc. 192.

Anywhere. w&m; Nickolas Ashford & Valerie Simpson. c1973, 76, Nick-O-Val Music. ASHFORD & SIMPSON. 13.

Apache. w&m; Jerry Lordan & Bert Weedon (Arranged). c1960, 61, Francis, Day & Hunter Ltd./Regent Music Corp. SHADOWS. 168.

Apple Scruffs. w&m; George Harrison. c1970, Harrisongs Ltd./Harrisongs Music, Inc. GEORGE HARRISON. 125.

Apple Sucking Tree. w&m; Bob Dylan. c1970, 75, Dwarf Music. BOB DYLAN/THE BAND. 170.

April Come She Will. w&m; Paul Simon. c1965, Paul Simon. SIMON & GARFUNKEL. 143.

Aquarius. w&m; James Rado (w), Gerome Ragni (w) & Galt MacDermot (m). c1966, 67, 68, 70, James Rado, Gerome Ragni, Galt MacDermot, Nat Shapiro, United Artists Music Co., Inc. Controlled and administered by United Artists Music Co., Inc. CAST OF HAIR/ CHARLES GARLAND. 79, 89, 140, 161, 191.

Aquarius/Let The Sunshine In. w&m; James Rado (w), Gerome Ragni (w) & Galt MacDermot (m). c1966, 67, 68, 70, James Rado, Gerome Ragni, Galt Mac-Dermot, Nat Shapiro, United Artists Music Co., Inc. Controlled and administered by United Artists Music Co., Inc. FIFTH DIMENSION. 21, 60, 72, 102, 192, 194.

Are You From Dixie. w&m; Jack Yellen (w) & George L. Cobb (m). c1915, M. Witmark & Sons. GRANDPA JONES/JERRY REED. 132, 149.

Are You Lonesome Tonight? w&m; Roy Turk & Lou Handman. c1926, 54, Cromwell Music, Inc. & Bourne Inc. ELVIS PRESLEY. 102.

Are You Sure Hank Done It This Way. w&m; Waylon Jennings. c1975, Baron Music Publishing Co. WAYLON JENNINGS. 28.

Ariel. w&m; Dean Friedman. c1976, 77, Blendingwell Music Inc. DEAN FRIEDMAN. 37, 196.

Arkansas Traveler. w&m; Traditional. c1973, Screen Gems-Columbia Publications. SEALS & CROFTS. 104.

Armistice Day. w&m; Paul Simon. c1972, Paul Simon. PAUL SIMON. 143.

Arms Of Mary. w&m; Ian Sutherland. c1975, Smash Brothers & Island Music. SUTHERLAND BROS. & QUIVER. 141.

14

Arrivederci, Roma. w&m; Carl Sigman (w) & R. Rascel (m). c1954, 55, Edizioni Kramer/Anne-Rachel Music Corp. GEORGIA GIBBS. 191.

Art Of Dying. w&m; George Harrison. c1970, Harrisongs Ltd./Harrisongs Music, Inc. GEORGE HARRISON. 125.

As I Went Out One Morning. w&m; Bob Dylan. c1968, 76, Dwarf Music. BOB DYLAN. 170.

As Long As I Have You. w&m; Fred Wise (w) & Ben Weisman (m). c1958, Gladys Music, Inc. ELVIS PRESLEY. 173.

As Tears Go By. w&m; Mick Jagger, Keith Richard & Andrew Long Oldham. c1964, Forward Music Ltd./ TRO-Essex Music, Inc. MARIANNE FAITHFULL/ ROLLING STONES. 5.

As Time Goes By. w&m; Herman Hupfeld. c1931, Harms, Inc. & Warner Bros., Inc. JOHNNY MATHIS/ NILSSON. 31, 139.

Ashes In The Snow. w&m; James Seals. c1969, 74, Dawnbreaker Music Co. & ABC-Dunhill Music, Inc. SEALS & CROFTS. 139.

Ask The Angels. w&m; Patti Smith & Ivan Kral. c1976, 77, Linda Music Corp. PATTI SMITH GROUP. 19.

A' Soalin'. w&m; Paul Stookey, Tracy Batteast & Elena Mezzetti. c1963, Pepamar Music Corp. PETER, PAUL & MARY. 67.

At Last. w&m; Mack Gordon (w) & Harry Warren (m). c1942, 66, 70, Twentieth Century Music Corp. Controlled by Leo Feist, Inc. BOBBY SHORT/RANDY CRAWFORD. 140.

At Seventeen. w&m; Janis Ian. c1974, 75, Mine Music Ltd./April Music Inc. JANIS IAN. 15, 21, 37, 131, 193, 198.

At The Copa SEE Copacabana.

At The Hop. w&m; A. Singer, J. Medora & D. White. c1957, 79, Singular Publishing Co., Inc. DANNY & THE JUNIORS. 4.

At The Zoo. w&m; Paul Simon. c1967, Paul Simon. SIMON & GARFUNKEL. 143.

Attics Of My Life. w&m; Jerry Garcia (m) & Robert Hunter (w). c1971, 73, Ice Nine Publishing Co. GRATEFUL DEAD. 83.

Attitude Dancing. w&m; Carly Simon & Jacob Brackman. c1975, C'est Music & Maya Productions, Ltd. CARLY SIMON. 139.

Autumn Of My Life. w&m; Bobby Goldsboro. c1968, 70, Detail Music, Inc. & Unart Music Corp. BOBBY GOLDSBORO. 79, 140.

Autumn To May. w&m; Paul Stookey & Peter Yarrow. c1962, Pepamar Music Corp. PETER, PAUL & MARY. 67, 132.

Awaiting On You All. w&m; George Harrison. c1970, Harrisongs Ltd./Harrisongs Music, Inc. GEORGE HARRISON. 125.

Babe. w&m; Dennis DeYoung. c1979, Stygian Songs. Administered by Almo Music Corp. STYX. 8, 23, 56, 70, 97, 180.

Babe, I'm Gonna Leave You. w&m; Jimmy Page. c1969, Superhype Publishing. LED ZEPPELIN. 114.

Baby, Baby, Don't Cry. w&m; Alfred Cleveland, Terry Johnson & William Robinson. c1968, 69, Jobete Music Co., Inc. SMOKEY ROBINSON & THE MIRACLES. 123.

Baby Boy (Big Ole Baby Boy). w&m; Mary Kay Place. c1976, Mary Kay Place doing business as Sook Music. MARY KAY PLACE AS LORETTA HAGGERS. 141.

Baby Come Back. w&m; John C. Crowley & Peter Beckett. c1977, Touch of Gold Music, Inc., Crowbeck Music & Stigwood Music, Inc. PLAYER. 128, 134, 157.

Baby Don't Change Your Mind. w&m; Van McCoy. c1976, 77, Warner-Tamerlane Publishing Corp. & Van McCoy Music, Inc. GLADYS KNIGHT & THE PIPS/ STYLISTICS. 127.

Baby Don't Get Hooked On Me. w&m; Mac Davis. c1972, Screen Gems-EMI Music, Inc. & Songpainter Music. MAC DAVIS. 126, 134.

Baby Don't Go. w&m; Karla Bonoff & Kenny Edwards. c1979, Seagrape Music & Valgovind Music. KARLA BONOFF. 99.

Baby, Don't You Do It. w&m; Brian Holland, Lamont Dozier & Eddie Holland. c1964, Jobete Music Co., Inc. BAND/HUMBLE PIE/MARVIN GAYE. 142.

Baby Driver. w&m; Paul Simon. c1969, Paul Simon. SIMON & GARFUNKEL. 143.

Baby Face (Disco Version). w&m; Benny Davis & Harry Akst. c1926, 75, Warner Bros., Inc. WING & A PRAYER FIFE & DRUM CORPS. 30, 46, 62, 118.

Baby, I Don't Care. w&m; Jerry Leiber & Mike Stoller. c1957, Elvis Presley Music, Inc. ELVIS PRESLEY. 172.

Baby, I Love Your Way. w&m; Peter Frampton. c1975, Almo Music Corp. & Fram-Dee Music Ltd. PETER FRAMPTON. 131, 198.

Baby, I Need Your Loving. w&m; Eddie Holland, Lamont Dozier & Brian Holland. c1964, 66, 67, Jobete Music Co., Inc. FOUR TOPS/JOHNNY RIVERS. 123, 150, 167.

Baby I Want You. w&m; Dennis Clifton & John Ingram. c1979, Song Tailors Music Co. & Alan Carter Music. F. C. C. 75.

Baby I'll Give It To You. w&m; Lana Bogan (w) & James Seals (m). c1973, 76, Dawnbreaker Music Co. SEALS & CROFTS. 141.

Baby I'm-A Want You. w&m; David Gates. c1971, Colgems-EMI Music Inc. BREAD. 134, 142, 156.

Baby, I'm Burning. w&m; Dolly Parton. c1978, Velvet Apple Music. DOLLY PARTON. 34, 65, 73, 112, 134, 157.

Baby, I'm Down. w&m; Felix Pappalardi & Gail Collins. c1969, 70, Windfall Music Enterprizes, Inc. FELIX PAPPALARDI. 182.

Baby I'm Yours. w&m; Van McCoy. c1964, 65, Blackwood Music, Inc. BARBARA LEWIS/DEBBY BOONE. 4, 165.

Baby Love. w&m; Brian Holland, Lamont Dozier & Eddie Holland. c1964, 65, Jobete Music Co., Inc. SUPREMES. 123, 150, 166.

Baby Scratch My Back. w&m; James Moore. c1970, Excellorec Music Co. SLIM HARPO. 4.

Baby Sittin' Boogie. w&m; Johnny Parker. c1961, Herb Reis Music Corp. BUZZ CLIFFORD. 4.

Baby (Somethin's Happening). w&m; Peter Frampton. c1974, 76, Almo Music Corp., Fram-Dee Music Ltd. & United Artists Music Ltd. 15

Baby Talk. w&m; Melvin Schwartz. c1958, 79, Admiration Music. JAN & DEAN. 4.

Baby, What A Big Surprise. w&m; Peter Cetera. c1977, Polish Prince Music. CHICAGO. 126, 128, 134.

Baby, What You Want Me To Do. w&m; Jimmy Reed. c1959, 67, 68, Conrad Music, a division of Arc Music Corp. CARL PERKINS. 44, 168.

Baby Workout. w&m; Jackie Wilson & Alonzo Tucker. c1963, Merrimac Music Corp. JACKIE WILSON. 155.

Baby, You're A Rich Man. w&m; John Lennon & Paul McCartney. c1967, Northern Songs Ltd./Maclen Music, Inc. BEATLES. 159.

Baby (You've Got What It Takes). w&m; Clyde Otis & Murray Stein. c1959, 60, 63, Vogue Music, Inc. BROOK BENTON & DINAH WASHINGTON/JOE TEX/MARV JOHNSON. 78, 155, 160.

Back Door Man. w&m; Willie Dixon & C. Burnett. c1961, 70, Arc Music Corp. DEREK/DOORS. 1, 115, 152, 197.

Back In Love Again. w&m; Len Ron Hanks & Zane Grey. c1977, Ice Man Music Corp. & Unichappell Music Inc. L. T. D. 50.

Back In My Arms Again. w&m; Brian Holland, Lamont Dozier & Eddie Holland. c1965, 66, Jobete Music Co., Inc. SUPREMES. 123, 150.

Back In The Saddle. w&m; Steven Tyler & Joe Perry. c1976, Daksel Music Corp., Vindaloo Productions & Song And Dance Music Co. AEROSMITH. 127, 146.

Back In The U.S.A. w&m; Chuck Berry. c1959, Arc Music Corp. CHUCK BERRY/LINDA RONSTADT/MC 5. 155.

Back In The U.S.S.R. w&m; John Lennon & Paul McCartney. c1968, Northern Songs Ltd./Maclen Music, Inc. BEATLES. 36, 145, 175.

Back Off Boogaloo. w&m; Richard Starkey. c1972, Startling Music Ltd. RINGO STARR. 63.

Back On My Feet Again. w&m; Dominic Bugatti, Frank Musker & John Waite. c1979, 80, Dayn Music Ltd. & Pendulum Music Ltd./The Hudson Bay Music Co. BABYS. 99.

Back To The Basics Of Love SEE Luckenbach, Texas.

Bad, Bad Leroy Brown. w&m; Jim Croce. c1972, 73, Blendingwell Music, Inc. & American Broadcasting Music, Inc. JIM CROCE. 15, 21, 31, 89, 111, 131, 140, 161, 163, 193, 194.

Bad Blood. w&m; Neil Sedaka & Phil Cody. c1974, 75, Neil Sedaka Music & Lebasongs. NEIL SEDAKA. 30, 133.

Bad Boy. w&m; Larry Williams. c1959, 65, Venice Music Inc. BEATLES/JIVE BOMBER/SHAUN CASSIDY. 35, 137, 159.

Bad Case Of Loving You. w&m; Moon Martin. c1978, Rockslam Music. ROBERT PALMER. 176, 198.

Bad Girls. w&m; Donna Summer (w), Bruce Sudano (m), Joe Esposito (m) & Eddie Hokenson (m). c1978, Starrin Music Publishing Corp., Earborne Music & Sweet Summer Night Music. DONNA SUMMER. 75, 96, 179.

Bad Moon Rising. w&m; J.C. Fogerty. c1969, Jondora Music. CREEDENCE CLEARWATER REVIVAL. 12, 93, 157.

Bad To Me. w&m; John Lennon & Paul McCartney. c1963, Northern Songs Ltd./Unart Music Corp. BEATLES/BILLY J. KRAMER & THE DAKOTAS/LEIF GARRETT. 81, 102, 137, 161.

Badge. w&m; Eric Clapton & George Harrison. c1969, Dratleaf Ltd. & Apple Publishing Ltd./Casserole. CREAM/ERIC CLAPTON. 152.

Badlands. w&m; Bruce Springsteen. c1978, Bruce Springsteen. BRUCE SPRINGSTEEN. 147.

Baker Street. w&m; Gerry Rafferty. c1978, Rafferty Songs Ltd./Hudson Bay Music Co. GERRY RAFFERTY. 23, 73, 135, 157.

Ball Of Confusion. w&m; Norman Whitfield & Barrett Strong. c1970, Jobete Music Co., Inc. TEMPTATIONS. 123, 150.

Ballad Of Easy Rider. w&m; Roger McGuinn. c1969, 77, Blackwood Music Inc., Last Minute Music & Patian Music. BYRDS. 193.

Ballad Of Frankie Lee And Judas Priest. w&m; Bob Dylan. c1968, 76, Dwarf Music. BOB DYLAN. 170.

Ballad Of Sir Frankie Crisp. w&m; George Harrison. c1970, Harrisongs Ltd./Harrisongs Music, Inc. GEORGE HARRISON. 125.

Ballad Of You & Me Pooneil. w&m; Paul Kantner. c1967, 68, Icebag Corp. JEFFERSON AIRPLANE. 108.

Baltimore Oriole. w&m; Paul Francis Webster (w) & Hoagy Carmichael (m). c1962, M. Witmark & Sons. JUDY RODERICK. 132.

Bama Lama Bama Loo. w&m; Richard Penniman. c1965, Venice Music. LITTLE RICHARD. 159.

Bamba, La SEE La Bamba.

Bamboo. w&m; Dave Van Ronk. c1962, Pepamar Music Corp. DAVE VAN RONK/PETER, PAUL & MARY. 35, 67.

Band On The Run. w&m; Paul & Linda McCartney. c1974, Paul & Linda McCartney/McCartney Music, Inc., by arrangement with ATV Music Corp. PAUL MC CARTNEY & WINGS. 125, 131.

Bang Bang (My Baby Shot Me Down). w&m; Sonny Bono. c1966, Cotillion Music & Five-West Music. SONNY & CHER. 100.

Barbara Ann. w&m; Fred Fassert. c1961, Adam R. Levy, Father Enterprizes, Inc. & Cousins Music, Inc. BEACH BOYS/REGENTS. 5, 93, 102.

Bare Trees. w&m; Danny Kirwan. c1972, Fleetwood Music. FLEETWOOD MAC. 36, 151.

Barefootin'. w&m; Robert Parker. c1965, 67, Bonatemp Music Publishing Co., Inc. ROBERT PARKER. 4.

Barracuda. w&m; Ann & Nancy Wilson, Roger Fisher & Michael Derosier. c1977, Wilsongs, Know Music, Play My Music & Rosebud Music. HEART. 22, 127, 145, 175.

Bartender's Blues. w&m; James Taylor. c1977, 78, Country Road Music, Inc. JAMES TAYLOR. 136, 146.

Bashana Haba' ah--Next Year SEE Anytime Of The Year.

Bat Out Of Hell. w&m; Jim Steinman. c1977, Edward B. Marks Music Corp., Neverland Music Co. & Peg Music Co. MEATLOAF. 120.

Battle Of Evermore. w&m; Jimmy Page & Robert Plant. c1972, 73, Superhype Publishing. LED ZEPPELIN. 114.

Battle Of New Orleans. w&m; Jimmy Driftwood. c1957, 59, Warden Music Co., Inc. JOHNNY HORTON. 3.

Be My Guest. w&m; Antoine Domino, John Marascalco & Tommy Boyce. c1959, Unart Music Corp. FATS DOMINO. 82, 155.

Be My Love. w&m; Sammy Cahn (w) & Nicholas Brodszsky (m). c1949, 50, 65, Metro-Goldwyn-Mayer Inc. Controlled by Miller Music Corp. FERRANTE & TEICHER. 140.

Beach Boy Blues. w&m; Sid Tepper & Roy C. Bennett. c1961, Gladys Music, Inc. ELVIS PRESLEY. 172.

Beat Goes On. w&m; Sonny Bono. c1967, Cotillion Music, Inc. & Chris-Marc Music. SONNY & CHER. 35, 100, 138.

Beaucoups Of Blues. w&m; Buzz Rabin. c1970, Window Music Co., Inc. RINGO STARR. 182.

Beautiful. w&m; Gordon Lightfoot. c1972, Moose Music. GORDON LIGHTFOOT. 115.

Beautiful Girls. w&m; Edward & Alex Van Halen, Michael Anthony & David Lee Roth. c1979, 80, Van Halen Music. VAN HALEN. 147.

Beautiful Loser. w&m; Bob Seger. c1974, 75, Gear Publishing Co. BOB SEGER. 142.

Beautiful Music. w&m; Barry Manilow & Marty Panzer. c1975, 78, Kamakazi Music Corp. BARRY MANILOW. 15.

Beautiful Noise. w&m; Neil Diamond. c1976, Stonebridge Music. NEIL DIAMOND. 145.

Beautiful People. w&m; Melanie Safka. c1967, 71, Avco Embassy Music Publishing Inc., Kama Rippa Music, Inc. & Amelanie Music Publishing Co. MELANIE. 203.

Beautiful Sunday. w&m; Daniel Boone & Rod McQueen. c1972, Stirling-McQueen Music Ltd./Full Of Hits Music, Inc. DANIEL BOONE. 21, 72, 111, 140, 163, 194, 195.

Beauty Is Only Skin Deep. w&m; Eddie Holland &

Norman Whitfield. c1965, 66, Jobete Music Co., Inc. TEMPTATIONS. 123, 167.

Be-Bop-A-Lula. w&m; Gene Vincent & Tex Davis. c1956, 71, Lowery Music Co., Inc. GENE VINCENT. 109.

Because The Night. w&m; Patti Smith & Bruce Springsteen. c1978, Bruce Springsteen. PATTI SMITH GROUP. 22, 124.

Because You Are My Friend. w&m; Leslie West. c1969, 70, Windfall Music Enterprizes, Inc. LESLIE WEST. 182.

Because You're Mine. w&m; Sammy Cahn (w) & Nicholas Brodszsky (m). c1951, 52, 66, Metro-Goldwyn-Mayer Inc. Controlled by Leo Feist, Inc. NAT KING COLE. 140.

Beechwood 4-5789. w&m; William Stevenson, Marvin Gaye & George Gordy. c1962, Jobete Music Co., Inc. MARVELETTES. 150.

Beep Beep. w&m; Donald Claps & Carl Cicchetti. c1958, Big Seven Music Corp. PLAYMATES. 101.

Beethoven's Fifth (Disco Version). w&m; John Lane (Adapted & Arranged). c1976, Robbins Music Corp. 184, 193.

Before The Deluge. w&m; Jackson Browne. c1974, 75, WB Music Corp. JACKSON BROWNE. 117, 136, 139.

Before The Next Teardrop Falls. w&m; Ben Peters & Vivian Keith. c1967, 68, Fingerlake Music Inc. Assigned to Shelby Singleton Music Inc. FREDDY FENDER. 21, 89, 163, 198.

Begin The Beguine. w&m; Cole Porter. c1935, 44, Warner Bros., Inc. JOHNNY MATHIS. 31.

Beginner's Luck. w&m; Sid Tepper & Roy C. Bennett. c1966, Gladys Music, Inc. ELVIS PRESLEY. 173.

Beginnings. w&m; Robert Lamm. c1969, Lamminations Music & Aurelius Music. CHICAGO. 77, 128.

Behind Closed Doors. w&m; Kenny O'Dell. c1973, House of Gold Music, Inc. CHARLIE RICH. 28, 77, 130, 134, 156.

Behind That Locked Door. w&m; George Harrison. c1970, Harrisongs Ltd./Harrisongs Music, Inc. GEORGE HARRISON. 125.

Believe In Me. w&m; Nickolas Ashford & Valerie Simpson. c1975, 76, Nick-O-Val Music. ASHFORD & SIMPSON. 13.

Believe Me. w&m; Conte, Autin & Villa. c1960, 79, Marble Music. ROYAL TEENS. 6.

Bell Bottom Blues. w&m; Eric Clapton. c1970, Throat Music Ltd./Casserole Music, Inc. ERIC CLAPTON. 152.

Belle. w&m; Al Green, Fred Jordan & Reuben Fairfax, Jr. c1977, JEC Publishing & Al Green Music, Inc. AL GREEN. 122.

Bells Of Rhymney. w&m; Idris Davies (w) & Pete Seeger (m). c1959, 64, Ludlow Music, Inc. PETE SEEGER. 85.

Ben. w&m; Don Black (w) & Walter Scharf (m). c1971, 72, Jobete Music Co., Inc. MICHAEL JACKSON. 20, 23, 32, 130, 134, 150.

Bend Me. w&m; Nickolas Ashford & Valerie Simpson. c1973, 76, Nick-O-Val Music. ASHFORD & SIMPSON. 13.

Bend Me, Shape Me. w&m; Scott English & Laurence Weiss. c1967, Helios Music Corp. AMERICAN BREED. 6.

Bennie And The Jets. w&m; Elton John & Bernie Taupin. c1973, Dick James Music Inc. ELTON JOHN. 133, 138.

Bernadette. w&m; Brian Holland, Lamont Dozier & Eddie Holland. c1967, Jobete Music Co., Inc. FOUR TOPS. 123.

Best Disco In Town. w&m; Henri Belolo (w), Phil Hurtt (w), Jacques Morali (m) & Richard Rome (m). c1976, Scorpio Music (Black Scorpio)/Can't Stop Music. RITCHIE FAMILY. 34, 51.

Best Of My Love. w&m; Don Henley, Glenn Frey & John David Souther. c1974, Cass County Music, Red Cloud Music & WB Music Corp. EAGLES. 30, 43, 55, 62, 133, 136, 139, 141, 145, 174, 185.

Best Of My Love. w&m; Maurice White & Al McKay. c1977, Saggifire Music & Steel Chest Music. EARTH, WIND & FIRE/EMOTIONS. 96, 122.

Beth. w&m; Stan Penridge, Peter Criss & Bob Ezrin. c1976, Kiss, Cafe Americana, Inc. & Rock Steady Music, Inc./All By Myself Publishing Co., Ltd. KISS. 71, 179, 181.

Better Love Next Time. w&m; Steve Pippin, Johnny Slate & Larry Keith. c1979, House of Gold Music, Inc. DR. HOOK. 8, 56, 97, 180.

Betty Lou Got A New Pair Of Shoes. w&m; Bobby Freeman. c1958, Clockus Music, Inc. & Benell Music Co. BOBBY FREEMAN. 4.

Beware Of Darkness. w&m; George Harrison. c1970, Harrisongs Ltd./Harrisongs Music, Inc. GEORGE HARRISON. 125.

Bicycle Race. w&m; Freddie Mercury. c1978, Queen Music Ltd./Beechwood Music Corp. QUEEN. 65, 73.

Big Boots. w&m; Sid Wayne (w) & Sherman Edwards (m). c1960, Gladys Music, Inc. ELVIS PRESLEY. 172.

Big Boss Man. w&m; Al Smith & Luther Dixon. c1960, 67, Conrad Music, a division of Arc Music Corp. ELVIS PRESLEY. 44, 168, 169.

Big Bright Green Pleasure Machine. w&m; Paul Simon. c1966, Paul Simon. SIMON & GARFUNKEL. 143.

Big Girls Don't Cry. w&m; Bob Crewe & Bob Gaudio. c1962, BoBob Music Corp. Assigned to Claridge Music Inc. FOUR SEASONS. 37, 78, 102, 137.

Big Hunk Of Love. w&m; Aaron Schroeder & Sid Wyche. c1959, Elvis Presley Music, Inc. ELVIS PRESLEY. 173.

Big Muddy SEE Waist Deep In The Big Muddy.

Big Spender. w&m; Dorothy Fields (w) & Cy Coleman (m). c1965, 69, Notable Music Co., Inc. PEGGY LEE. 21.

Big Yellow Taxi. w&m; Joni Mitchell. c1970, 74, Siquomb Publishing Corp. JONI MITCHELL. 35, 86, 88.

Biggest Part Of Me. w&m; David Pack. c1980, Rubicon Music. AMBROSIA. 189.

Billion Dollar Babies. w&m; Alice Cooper, Michael Bruce & R. Reggie. c1973, Ezra Music. ALICE COOPER. 104.

Billy. w&m; Bob Dylan. c1972, 76, Ram's Horn Music. BOB DYLAN. 170.

Billy, Don't Be A Hero. w&m; Mitch Murray & Pet Callander. c1974, Murray-Callander Music, Inc. BO DONALDSON & THE HEYWOODS. 163.

Bird Dog. w&m; Boudleaux Bryant. c1957, House of Bryant Publications. EVERLY BROTHERS. 3.

Bird On The Wire. w&m; Leonard Cohen. c1968, 69, Stranger Music, Inc. LEONARD COHEN. 59, 171.

Birds And The Bees. w&m; Herb Newman. c1964, 65, Pattern Music. JEWEL AKINS. 3.

Birds Of Fire. w&m; John McLaughlin (m). c1973, 76, Warner-Tamerlane Publishing Corp. & Chinmoy Music Inc. JOHN MC LAUGHLIN MAHAVISHNU ORCHESTRA. 36.

Birthday. w&m; John Lennon & Paul McCartney. c1969, Northern Songs Ltd./Maclen Music, Inc. BEATLES. 159.

Bitch Is Back. w&m; Elton John & Bernie Taupin. c1974, Big Pig Music Ltd./Leeds Music Corp. ELTON JOHN. 183.

Bitter Green. w&m; Gordon Lightfoot. c1968, 69, Warner Bros., Inc. GORDON LIGHTFOOT. 35.

Black And White. w&m; David Arkin (w) & Earl Robinson (m). c1956, 72, 73, Templeton Publishing Co., Inc. THREE DOG NIGHT. 93, 106, 134, 194.

Black Diamond Bay. w&m; Bob Dylan & Jacques Levy (w). c1975, 76, Ram's Horn Music. BOB DYLAN. 170.

Black Dog. w&m; Jimmy Page, Robert Plant & John Paul Jones. c1972, Superhype Publishing. LED ZEPPELIN. 22, 114, 152.

Black Friday. w&m; Walter Becker & Donald Fagen. c1974, MCA Music. STEELY DAN. 142.

Black Mountain Side. w&m; Jimmy Page. c1969, Superhype Publishing. LED ZEPPELIN. 114.

Black Peter. w&m; Jerry Garcia (m) & Robert Hunter (w). c1971, 73, Ice Nine Publishing Co. GRATEFUL DEAD. 83.

Black Slacks. w&m; Joe Bennett & Jimmy Denton. c1957; ABC-Dunhill Music, Inc. SPARKLETONES. 3.

Black Water. w&m; Patrick Simmons. c1974, WB Music Corp. & Lansdowne Music Publishers. DOOBIE BROTHERS. 36, 133, 136, 139.

Black Waters. w&m; Jean Ritchie. c1967, 68, Geordie Music Publishing Inc. JEAN RITCHIE. 132.

Blank Generation. w&m; Richard Hell. c1977, 78, Doraflo Music Co., Automatic Music & Quick Mix Music. RICHARD HELL. 19.

Blazing Saddles. w&m; Mel Brooks (w) & John Morris (m). c1974, 75, Warner-Tamerlane Publishing Corp. & WB Music Corp. FRANKIE LAINE. 139.

Bless The Beasts And Children. w&m; Barry De Vorzon & Perry Botkin, Jr. c1971, Screen Gems-EMI Music Inc. CARPENTERS. 71, 135.

Blessed. w&m; Paul Simon. c1966, Paul Simon. SIMON & GARFUNKEL. 143.

Blind Man. w&m; Deadric Malone & Joseph W. Scott. c1964, Don Music Co., & ABC-Dunhill Music, Inc. BOBBY BLAND. 122.

Blinded By Science. w&m; Mick Jones. c1979, Somerset Songs Publishing Inc./Evansongs Ltd. FOREIGNER. 147.

Blinded By The Light. w&m; Bruce Springsteen. c1972, 77, Laurel Canyon Music Ltd. BRUCE SPRINGSTEEN/MANFRED MANN'S EARTH BAND. 37, 193, 196, 198.

Blitzkrieg Bop. w&m; Joey, Dee Dee, Tommy & Johnny Ramone. c1976, 78, c1976, 78, Bleu Disque Music & Taco Tunes. RAMONES. 19.

Blood Of The Sun. w&m; Leslie West, Felix Pappalardi & Gail Collins. c1969, 70, Windfall Music Enterprises, Inc. MOUNTAIN. 203.

Blowin' In The Wind. w&m; Bob Dylan. c1962, 70, M. Witmark & Sons & Warner Bros., Inc. BOB DYLAN/PETER, PAUL & MARY. 41, 62, 67, 138, 151, 197.

Blue. w&m; Joni Mitchell. c1971, 75, Joni Mitchell Publishing Corp. JONI MITCHELL. 36.

Blue Bonnet Nation. w&m; James Seals & Dash Crofts. c1975, Dawnbreaker Music. SEALS & CROFTS. 41.

Blue Monday. w&m; Dave Bartholomew & Antoine Domino. c1954, 57, Unart Music Corp. BOBBY DARIN/FATS DOMINO. 78, 82, 101, 155.

Blue Money. w&m; Van Morrison. c1971, Caledonia Soul Music & WB Music Corp. VAN MORRISON. 151.

Blue Moon. w&m; Lorenz Hart (w) & Richard Rodgers (m). c1934, 62, 65, Metro-Goldwyn-Mayer Inc. Controlled by Robbins Music Corp. BOB DYLAN/BOSTON POPS/ELVIS PRESLEY/MARCELS/TONY BENNETT. 140.

Blue Moon Of Kentucky. w&m; Bill Monroe. c1947, Peer International Corp. ELVIS PRESLEY. 122.

Blue Morning, Blue Day. w&m; Mick Jones & Lou Gramm (w). c1978, Somerset Songs Publishing, Inc., Evansongs Ltd. & WB Music Corp. FOREIGNER. 87, 146.

Blue Sky. w&m; Forrest Richard Betts. c1972, 74, No Exit Music Co., Inc. JOAN BAEZ. 139.

Blue Suede Shoes. w&m; Carl Lee Perkins. c1956, Hi Lo Music & Hill and Range Songs, Inc. Controlled by Hi Lo Music & Unichappell Music, Inc. CARL LEE PERKINS/ELVIS PRESLEY. 35, 101, 111, 122, 137, 140, 172.

Blue Sunday. w&m; Jim Morrison. c1970, Doors Music Co. DOORS. 54.

Blue Velvet. w&m; Bernie Wayne & Lee Morris. c1951, 63, Meridian Music Corp. Assigned to Vogue Music, Inc. BOBBY VINTON. 160.

Blueberry Hill. w&m; Al Lewis, Larry Stock & Vincent Rose. c1940, Chappell & Co., Inc. FATS DOMINO. 6, 78, 101, 155.

Bluebird Revisited. w&m; Stephen Stills. c1967, 71, 73, Cotillion Music, Inc., Ten East Music & Springalo Toones. BUFFALO SPRINGFIELD. 39.

Bluebirds Over The Mountain. w&m; Ersel Hickey. c1968, Brother Publishing Co. ERSEL HICKEY. 6.

Bluer Than Blue. w&m; Randy Goodrum. c1978, Let There Be Music & Springcreek Music. MICHAEL JOHNSON. 23, 73, 128, 134, 135.

Blues For Allah. w&m; Robert Hunter & Jerry Garcia. c1975, 76, Ice Nine Publishing Co., Inc. GRATEFUL DEAD. 84.

Blues Get Off My Shoulder. w&m; Bobby Parker. c1958, Arc Music Corp. CHAMBERS BROTHERS. 1.

Blues In The Night. w&m; Johnny Mercer (w) & Harold Arlen (m). c1941, Warner Bros., Inc. RAY CHARLES. 31.

Bo Diddley. w&m; Ellas McDaniel. c1955, Arc Music Corp. BO DIDDLEY. 6, 78, 100, 101, 168, 169, 197.

Bo Weevil. w&m; Antoine Domino & Dave Bartholomew. c1956, Unart Music Corp. FATS DOMINO. 78, 82, 137, 155.

Bob Dylan's Blues. w&m; Bob Dylan. c1963, 66, M. Witmark & Sons. BOB DYLAN. 132.

Bobbie's Blues. w&m; Jeffrey M. Comanor. c1968, 70, Mr. Bones Music Inc. FIFTH DIMENSION. 60.

Body And Soul. w&m; Edward Heyman (w), Robert Sour (w), Frank Eyton (w) & John Green (m). c1930, 47, Warner Bros., Inc. & Chappell & Co., Ltd. Assigned to Warner Bros., Inc. MANHATTAN TRANSFER. 31.

Bohemian Rhapsody. w&m; Freddie Mercury. c1975, Feldman & Co., Ltd., Trident Music/Big 3 Music Corp. QUEEN. 15, 21, 193, 198.

Bonfire. w&m; Cat Stevens. c1977, Colgems-EMI Music, Inc. CAT STEVENS. 142.

Bony Moronie. w&m; Larry Williams. c1957, 66, Venice Music, Inc. BILL HALEY & THE COMETS/FLYING BURRITO BROS./JOHN LENNON/JOHNNY WINTER/LARRY WILLIAMS. 29, 35, 100, 109, 159, 197.

Boo, Hoo, Hoo, Hoo (I'll Never Let You Go). w&m; Richard Penniman. c1958, Venice Music. LITTLE RICHARD. 159.

Boogaloo Down Broadway. w&m; Jesse James. c1967, 68, Dandelion Music Co. & James Boy Publishing Co. FANTASTIC JOHNNY C. 4.

Boogie Child. w&m; Barry, Robin & Maurice Gibb. c1976, Brothers Gibb B.V. Controlled by Stigwood Music, Inc. Unichappell Music, Inc., Administrator. BEE GEES. 46, 127.

Boogie Down. w&m; Frank Wilson, Leonard Caston & Anita Poree. c1973, Stone Diamond Music Corp. EDDIE KENDRICKS. 52.

Boogie Fever. w&m; Keni St. Lewis & Freddie Perren. c1975, 76, Perren-Vibes Music Co. & Bull Pen Music Co. SYLVERS. 26, 77.

Boogie Nights. w&m; Rod Temperton. c1976, Rondor Music Ltd./Almo Music Corp. HEATWAVE. 25.

Boogie On Reggae Woman. w&m; Stevie Wonder. c1974, Jobete Music Co., Inc. & Black Bull Music, Inc. STEVIE WONDER. 26, 52, 77, 134, 150.

Boogie Oogie Oogie. w&m; Janice Marie Johnson & Perry Kibble (m). c1978, Conducive Music & On Time Music. G. Q./TASTE OF HONEY. 24, 34, 51, 135.

Boogie Shoes. w&m; H.W. Casey & R. Finch. c1975, 76, Sherlyn Publishing Co., Inc. KC & THE SUN-SHINE BAND. 34.

Boogie Wonderland. w&m; Allee Willis & Jon Lind. c1979, Ninth Music, Irving Music, Inc., Charleville Music & Deertrack Music. EARTH, WIND & FIRE. 75, 96.

Boogie Woogie Dancin' Shoes. w&m; M. Bjoerklund, J. Evers, K. Forsey, J.S. Korduletsch & C. Barry. c1979, Edition Lollipop & Lambda Music. CLAUDIA BARRY. 159.

Book I Read. w&m; David Byrne. c1976, 78, Bleu Disque Music Co. & Index Music. TALKING HEADS. 19.

Book Of Love. w&m; Warren Davis, George Malone & Charles Patrick. c1957, 58, Arc Music Corp. & Nom Music Inc. MONOTONES. 5, 78, 101, 156, 168, 169.

Bookends. w&m; Paul Simon. c1968, Paul Simon. SIMON & GARFUNKEL. 143.

Boom Boom. w&m; John Lee Hooker. c1962, 70, Conrad Music, a division of Arc Music Corp. ANI-MALS/ERIC BURDON. 1, 78, 169.

Border Song. w&m; Elton John & Bernie Taupin. c1969, Dick James Music Ltd./Dick James Music, Inc. ARETHA FRANKLIN/ELTON JOHN. 41, 43, 197.

Border Town. w&m; John David Souther. c1974, Bench-mark Music & Golden Spread Music. SOUTHER-HILLMAN-FURAY BAND. 139.

Born Free. w&m; Don Black (w) & John Barry (m). c1966, Screen Gems-EMI Music Inc. ANDY WILLIAMS. 71.

Born To Be Alive. w&m; Patrick Hernandez. c1979, Radmus Publishing Inc. & Zeldgamous Music Inc. PATRICK HERNANDEZ. 23, 56, 75.

Born To Run. w&m; Bruce Springsteen. c1975, Laurel Canyon Music Ltd. BRUCE SPRINGSTEEN. 15, 21, 37, 131, 193, 198.

Born Under A Bad Sign. w&m; William Bell & Booker T. Jones. c1967, East-Memphis Music. ALBERT KING. 122.

Boss. w&m; Nickolas Ashford & Valerie Simpson. c1979, Nick-O-Val Music, Inc. DIANA ROSS. 27.

Bossa Nova, Baby. w&m; Jerry Leiber & Mike Stoller. c1962, Elvis Presley Music. ELVIS PRESLEY. 172.

Both Sides Now. w&m; Joni Mitchell. c1967, 74, Siquomb Publishing Corp. JONI MITCHELL/JUDY COLLINS. 62, 67, 86, 136, 138, 141, 151.

Bottle. w&m; Brian Jackson (m) & Gil Scott-Heron (w). c1974, Brouhaha Music Inc. GIL SCOTT-HERON. 52.

Bottle Of Red Wine. w&m; Bonnie Bramlett & Eric Clapton. c1970, Casserole Music Corp., Delson Music & Metric Music Co., Inc. ERIC CLAPTON. 199.

Bottle Of Wine. w&m; Tom Paxton. c1963, 68, Deep Fork Music, Inc. & United Artists Music Co., Inc. FIREBALLS/JUDY COLLINS. 79, 140.

Boulevard. w&m; Jackson Browne. c1980, Swallow Turn Music & WB Music Corp. JACKSON BROWNE. 162, 189.

Box Of Rain. w&m; Robert Hunter (w) & Philip Lesh (m). c1970, 73, Ice Nine Publishing Co. GRATEFUL DEAD. 83.

Boxer. w&m; Paul Simon. c1968, Paul Simon. SIMON & GARFUNKEL. 143.

Boy Like Me, A Girl Like You. w&m; Sid Tepper & Roy C. Bennett. c1962, Gladys Music, Inc. ELVIS PRESLEY. 173.

Boys Are Back In Town. w&m; Phil Lynott. c1976, Pippin The Friendly Ranger Music Co., Ltd./Chappell & Co., Inc. THIN LIZZY. 141.

Bracero. w&m; Phil Ochs. c1966, 68, Barricade Music, Inc. PHIL OCHS. 144.

Brand New Key. w&m; Melanie Safka. c1971, April Music Inc. & Neighborhood Music Publishing Corp. Administered by April Music Inc. DANTE'S IN-FERNO/MELANIE. 131.

Brand New Me. w&m; Kenny Gamble, Jerry Butler & Theresa Bell. c1969, Parabut Music Corp. & Associ-ated Music. DUSTY SPRINGFIELD. 6.

Bread And Roses. w&m; James Oppenheim (w) & Mimi Farina (m). c1976, Farina Music. JUDY COLLINS. 141.

Breakdown Dead Ahead. w&m; Boz Scaggs & David Foster. c1980, Boz Scaggs Music & Foster Frees Music-Irving Music. BOZ SCAGGS. 87, 188.

Breaking Up Is Hard To Do. w&m; Neil Sedaka & Howard Greenfield. c1962, 70, Screen Gems-EMI Music Inc. CARPENTERS/NEIL SEDAKA/PART-RIDGE FAMILY. 38, 77, 128, 142, 158.

Breezin'. w&m; Bobby Womack (m). c1971, 76, Unart Music Corp. & Tracebob Music Co. Administered by Unart Music Corp. GEORGE BENSON. 15, 21, 37, 80, 193, 198.

Brian's Song SEE Hands Of Time.

Brick House. w&m; Lionel Richie, Ronald LaPread, Walter Orange, Milan Williams, Thomas McClary & William King. c1977, Jobete Music Co., Inc. & Com-modores Entertainment Publishing Corp. COMMO-DORES. 142.

Bridge Over Troubled Water. w&m; Paul Simon. c1969, Paul Simon. SIMON & GARFUNKEL. 136, 143, 183.

Bright Lights, Big City. w&m; Jimmy Reed. c1961, 68, Conrad Music, a division of Arc Music Corp. ANI-MALS. 169.

Brighton Hill. w&m; Jackie De Shannon, Jimmy Holiday & Randy Myers. c1970, Unart Music Corp. JACKIE DE SHANNON. 186.

Bring It On Home. w&m; Willie Dixon. c1964, 70, Arc Music Corp. LED ZEPPELIN. 1.

Bring It On Home To Me. w&m; Sam Cooke. c1962, Kags Music Corp. ANIMALS/DAVE MASON/SAM COOKE. 29, 53, 109.

Bring It Up. w&m; James Brown. c1967, 68, Dynatone Publishing Co. JAMES BROWN. 18.

Bristol Stomp. w&m; Kal Mann & Dave Appell. c1961, Kalmann Music Inc. DOVELLS. 5.

Brokedown Palace. w&m; Robert Hunter (w) & Jerry Garcia (m). c1971, 73, Ice Nine Publishing Co. GRATEFUL DEAD. 83.

Broken Arrow. w&m; Neil Young. c1967, 74, Cotillion Music, Inc., Ten East Music & Springalo Toones. BUFFALO SPRINGFIELD. 39.

Broken Hearted Me. w&m; Randy Goodrum. c1979, Chappell & Co., Inc. & Sailmaker Music. ANNE MURRAY. 47.

Bron-Y-Aur Stomp. w&m; Jimmy Page, Robert Plant & John Paul Jones. c1970, 73, Superhype Publishing. LED ZEPPELIN. 114.

Brooklyn Roads. w&m; Neil Diamond. c1968, 74, Stonebridge Music. NEIL DIAMOND. 117.

Brother, Can You Spare A Dime? w&m; E.Y. Harburg (w) & Jay Gorney (m). c1932, Harms, Inc. SPANKY & OUR GANG. 132.

Brother Louie. w&m; E. Brown & T. Wilson. c1973, Rak Music Ltd./Buddah Music Inc. STORIES. 106, 156.

Brown Eyed Girl. w&m; Van Morrison. c1957, Web IV Music Inc. VAN MORRISON. 3.

Brown Eyed Handsome Man. w&m; Chuck Berry. c1956, 63, Arc Music Corp. WAYLON JENNINGS. 44, 169.

Brown Sugar. w&m; Mick Jagger & Keith Richard. c1971, Abkco Music, Inc. ROLLING STONES. 29, 52, 53, 77, 134, 142, 156, 157.

Buckets Of Rain. w&m; Bob Dylan. c1974, 76, Ram's Horn Music. BOB DYLAN. 170.

Bunch Of Lonesome Heroes. w&m; Leonard Cohen. c1969, Stranger Music, Inc. LEONARD COHEN. 171.

Burn. w&m; Ritchie Blackmore, Jon Lord, David Coverdale & Ian Paice. c1974, Purple (USA) Music Inc. DEEP PURPLE. 36.

Burn Down The Mission. w&m; Elton John & Bernie Taupin. c1970, Dick James Music Ltd./Dick James Music, Inc. ELTON JOHN. 41.

Burning Bridges. w&m; Mike Curb (w) & Lalo Schifrin (m). c1970, Metro-Goldwyn-Mayer Inc. MIKE CURB CONGREGATION/PAUL MAURIAT/PINK FLOYD. 192.

Bus Stop. w&m; Graham Gouldman. c1966, Man-Ken Music Ltd. HOLLIES. 6.

Bustin' Loose (Part 1). w&m; Chuck Brown. c1978, Ascent Music & Nouvau Music. CHUCK BROWN & THE SOUL SEARCHERS. 25.

But I Do. w&m; Robert Guidry & Paul Gayten. c1960, 61, Arc Music Corp. BOB & MARCIA/CLARENCE "FROGMAN" HENRY. 5, 168, 169.

Butcher. w&m; Leonard Cohen. c1969, Stranger Music, Inc. LEONARD COHEN. 171.

Butterfly For Bucky. w&m; Bobby Goldsboro & Doug Cox (w). c1976, Unart Music Corp. & Pen In Hand Music, Inc. Administered by Unart Music Corp. BOBBY GOLDSBORO. 82.

Buyin' Time. w&m; Stephen Stills & Donnie Dacus. c1976, Gold Hill Music, Inc. & Stephen Stills Music. STEPHEN STILLS. 141.

By The Time I Get To Phoenix. w&m; Jim Webb. c1967, 71, Johnny Rivers Music. Assigned to Dramatis Music Corp. GLEN CAMPBELL. 15, 21, 111, 140, 163, 193, 194, 198.

Bye, Bye Baby. w&m; R.P. St. John, Jr. c1968, 72, Mainspring Watchworks Music. JANIS JOPLIN. 110.

Bye Bye Blackbird. w&m; Mort Dixon (w) & Ray Henderson (m). c1926, 71, H. Remick & Co. & Warner Bros., Inc. JOSE FELICIANO. 132, 182.

Bye, Bye, Johnny. w&m; Chuck Berry. c1960, 64, Arc Music Corp. CHUCK BERRY. 10.

Bye Bye, Love. w&m; Felice & Boudleaux Bryant. c1957, House of Bryant Publications. EVERLY BROTHERS. 93, 158.

Cabaret. w&m; Fred Ebb (w) & John Kander (m). c1966, Times Square Music Publications Co. GORDON LIGHTFOOT/LIZA MINELLI. 23, 56, 58, 130, 179.

Cabin In The Sky. w&m; John Latouche (w) & Vernon Duke (m). c1940, Miller Music Corp. MOSE ALLISON/STANLEY TURRENTINE/TAL FARROW. 140.

Cadillac Walk. w&m; Moon Martin. c1977, Bug Music & Rockslam Music. MINK DE VILLE. 153.

Calendar Girl. w&m; Howard Greenfield (w) & Neil Sedaka (m). c1961, Screen Gems-EMI Music Inc. NEIL SEDAKA. 158.

California. w&m; Joe Brooks. c1976, 78, Big Hill Music Corp. DEBBY BOONE/JOE BROOKS. 23, 58, 131, 134.

California. w&m; Joni Mitchell. c1970, 71, Siquomb Publishing Co. JONI MITCHELL. 86.

California Dreamin'. w&m; John Phillips & Michelle Gilliam Phillips. c1965, 66, American Broadcasting Music, Inc. MAMAS & THE PAPAS. 3, 64, 89, 93, 119, 135.

California My Way. w&m; Willie Hutchison. c1967, 70, Johnny Rivers Music. FIFTH DIMENSION. 60.

California Revisited. w&m; Daniel Peek. c1972, 73, WB Music Corp. AMERICA. 151.

California Soul. w&m; Nickolas Ashford & Valerie Simpson. c1967, Jobete Music Co., Inc. FIFTH DIMENSION. 13.

Call It Stormy Monday. w&m; Aron T. Walker. c1963, Gregmark Music Co. MC COYS. 29.

Call Me. w&m; Deborah Harry & Giorgio Moroder. c1980, Ensign Music Corp., Rare Blue Music, Inc. & Monster Island Music. BLONDIE. 177, 198.

Call Me. w&m; Ellas McDaniel. c1961, Arc Music Corp. BO DIDDLEY. 1.

Call Me (Come Back Home). w&m; Willie Mitchell, Al Jackson & Al Green. c1973, Jec Publishing Co. & Al Green Inc. AL GREEN. 104.

Call On Me. w&m; Lee Loughnane. c1974, Big Elk Music. CHICAGO. 93.

Calling Occupants Of Interplanetary Craft. w&m; Klaatu. c1976, 77, Klaatoons, Inc. Controlled by Welbeck Music Corp. CARPENTERS. 201.

Calypso. w&m; John Denver. c1975, Cherry Lane Music Co. JOHN DENVER. 131.

Can I Carry Your Balloon. w&m; Sandy Linzer & Denny Randell. c1968, Screen Gems-Columbia Music, Inc. SWAMPSEEDS. 76.

Can This Be Real. w&m; J. Hutson, L. Hutson & M. Hawkins. c1973, 74, Silent Giant Publishing Co. & AOPA Publishing Co. NATURAL FOUR. 138.

Can You Read My Mind. w&m; Leslie Bricusse (w) & John Williams (m). c1978, Warner-Tamerlane Publishing Corp. MAUREEN MC GOVERN. 27, 57, 162.

Canadian Railroad Trilogy. w&m; Gordon Lightfoot. c1967, 69, M. Witmark & Sons & Warner Bros. Inc. GORDON LIGHTFOOT. 35, 67.

Candida. w&m; Toni Wine & Irwin Levine. c1969, 70, Pocket Full Of Tunes, Inc. & Big Apple Music Co., a division of 40 West Music Corp. DAWN. 15, 21, 72, 140, 163, 191, 198.

Candle In The Wind. w&m; Elton John & Bernie Taupin. c1973, Dick James Music Ltd./Dick James Music, Inc. ELTON JOHN. 139.

Candles In The Rain. SEE Lay Down (Candles In The Rain).

Candy Man. w&m; Leslie Bricusse & Anthony Newley. c1970, 71, Taradam Music, Inc. SAMMY DAVIS, JR. 64, 89, 134, 195.

Candy Man. w&m; Rev. Gary Davis. c1964, 68, M. Witmark & Sons & Warner Bros.-Seven Arts. REV. GARY DAVIS. 132.

Candyman. w&m; Robert Hunter (w) & Jerry Garcia (m). c1970, 73, Ice Nine Publishing Co. GRATEFUL DEAD. 83.

Candy-O. w&m; Ric Ocasek. c1979, Lido Music Inc. CARS. 147.

Cannons Of Christianity. w&m; Phil Ochs. c1965, 68, Barricade Music, Inc. PHIL OCHS. 144.

Can't Buy Me Love. w&m; John Lennon & Paul McCartney. c1964, Northern Songs Ltd./Maclen Music, Inc. & Unart Music Corp. BEATLES. 35, 61, 138, 159.

Can't Get Enough. w&m; M. Ralphs. c1974, Badco Music Inc. BAD COMPANY. 53.

Can't Give You Anything (But My Love). w&m; Hugo Peretti, Luigi Creatore & George David Weiss. c1975, Avco Embassy Music Publishing, Inc. STYLISTICS. 49.

Can't Help Falling In Love. w&m; George Weiss, Hugo Peretti & Luigi Creatore. c1961, Gladys Music. Controlled by Chappell & Co., Inc. ELVIS PRESLEY. 15, 102, 163, 172.

Can't Hide Love. w&m; Skip Scarborough. c1973, 76, Alexscar Co. Administered by Unichappell Music Inc. EARTH, WIND & FIRE. 16.

Can't Hold On Much Longer. w&m; W. Jacobs. c1970, Arc Music Corp. CANNED HEAT. 1.

Can't Keep A Good Man Down. w&m; Dan Alexander, Eddie Money & Chris Solberg. c1979, Grajonca Music & Davalex Music. EDDIE MONEY. 96.

Can't Smile Without You. w&m; Chris Arnold, David Martin & Geoff Morrow. c1975, 78, Dick James Music Ltd./Dick James Music Inc. BARRY MANILOW. 57, 87, 146.

Can't Stop Loving You. w&m; Wayne Bickerton & Tony Waddington. c1969, 70, Palace Music Co., Ltd. TOM JONES. 63.

Can't We Just Sit Down And Talk It Over. w&m; Tony Macaulay. c1976, 77, Macaulay Music Ltd./Almo Music Corp. DONNA SUMMER. 58.

Can't You Hear My Heart Beat? w&m; Carter-Lewis. c1965, Southern Music Publishing Co., Inc. HERMAN'S HERMITS. 4.

Captain And Me. w&m; Tom Johnston. c1973, Warner-Tamerlane Publishing Corp. DOOBIE BROTHERS. 53.

Cara Mia. w&m; Tulio Trapani & Lee Lange. c1954, 65, Leo Feist, Inc. JAY & THE AMERICANS. 102, 140.

Caretaker. w&m; Nickolas Ashford & Valerie Simpson. c1975, Nick-O-Val Music. ASHFORD & SIMPSON. 13.

Carey. w&m; Joni Mitchell. c1970, 71, Siquomb Publishing Corp. JONI MITCHELL. 86.

Carmelita. w&m; Warren Zevon. c1972, 78, Warner-Tamerlane Publishing Corp. & Darkroom Music. LINDA RONSTADT. 87, 146.

Carol. w&m; Chuck Berry. c1958, 70, Arc Music Corp. CHUCK BERRY/ROLLING STONES/TOMMY ROE. 1, 44, 169, 197.

Carolina In My Mind. w&m; James Taylor. c1969, 70, Blackwood Music Inc. & Country Roads Music, Inc. Administered by Blackwood Music. JAMES TAYLOR. 15.

Carolina In The Pines. w&m; Michael Murphey. c1975, Mystery Music Inc. Administered by Blackwood Music Inc. MICHAEL MURPHEY. 21, 37, 198.

Carpet Man. w&m; Jim Webb. c1967, 70, Johnny Rivers Music. FIFTH DIMENSION. 60.

Carrie. w&m; Terry Britten & Brian Robertson. c1979, 80, Cookaway Music, Inc. & United Artists Music, Inc. CLIFF RICHARD. 31, 188.

Carry It On. w&m; Gil Turner. c1964, Melody Trails Inc. GIL TURNER/JUDY COLLINS. 85.

Carry On. w&m; Stephen Stills. c1970, Gold Hill Music, Inc. CROSBY, STILLS, NASH & YOUNG. 22, 30, 41, 87, 115, 138, 145.

Carry On Wayward Son. w&m; Kerry Livgren. c1976, 77, Don Kirshner Music & Blackwood Music Publications. KANSAS. 117, 127, 145, 148, 175.

Carry That Weight. w&m; John Lennon & Paul McCartney. c1969, Northern Songs Ltd./Maclen Music, Inc. BEATLES. 61.

Casey Jones. w&m; Robert Hunter (w) & Jerry Garcia (m). c1970, 73, Ice Nine Publishing Co. GRATEFUL DEAD. 83.

Cat Scratch Fever. w&m; Ted Nugent. c1977, Magic-land Music Corp. TED NUGENT. 22, 145.

Catch The Wind. w&m; Donovan. c1965, Donovan (Music) Ltd./Southern Music Publishing Co., Inc. DONOVAN. 59, 68.

Catch Us If You Can. w&m; Dave Clark & Lenny Davidson. c1965, Sphere Music Co., Ltd. DAVE CLARK FIVE. 102.

Catchin' Up On Love. w&m; Bobby Harris. c1979, Twentieth Century Music Corp. & All Sunray Publishing Co. KINSMAN DAZZ. 24.

Catfish. w&m; Bob Dylan & Jacques Levy. c1975, 76, Ram's Horn Music. JOE COCKER. 170.

Cat's In The Cradle. w&m; Harry & Sandy Chapin. c1974, Story Songs, Ltd. HARRY CHAPIN. 30, 36, 43, 62, 117, 133, 136, 141.

C. C. Rider. w&m; Chuck Willis. c1957, Progressive Music Publishing Co., Inc. & Rush Music Corp. CHUCK WILLIS. 78, 91, 137, 155, 163.

C. C. Rider. w&m; Huddie Ledbetter. c1936, 1959, 1964, Folkways Music Publishers, Inc. LEADBELLY. 85.

Cecilia. w&m; Paul Simon. c1969. SIMON & GARFUNKEL. 143.

Celebrate. w&m; Alan Gordon & Garry Bonner. c1968, 70, Chardon Music Co., Inc. THREE DOG NIGHT. 186.

Celebration Day. w&m; Jimmy Page, Robert Plant & John Paul Jones. c1970, 73, Superhype Publishing. LED ZEPPELIN. 114.

Certain Girl. w&m; Naomi Neville. c1961, Unart Music Corp. WARREN ZEVON. 177.

Chain. w&m; Lindsey Buckingham, Christine McVie, Stevie Nicks, Mick Fleetwood & John McVie. c1977, 78, Michael Fleetwood, Now Sounds Music & Welsh Witch Music/Warner-Tamerlane Publishing Corp. FLEETWOOD MAC. 22.

Chains Of Love. w&m; A. Nugetre. c1951, 56, Progressive Music Publishing Co., Inc. Assigned to Unichappell Music, Inc. JOE TURNER. 155.

Champagne Jam. w&m; Buddy Buie, Robert Nix & J. R. Cobb. c1978, Low-Sal, Inc. ATLANTA RHYTHM SECTION. 74.

Chances Are. w&m; Al Stillman (w) & Robert Allen (m). c1957, International Korwin Corp. JOHNNY MATHIS. 3.

Change Partners. w&m; Stephen Stills. c1971, 73, Gold Hill Music Inc. STEPHEN STILLS. 36, 43, 138.

Change With The Times. w&m; Van McCoy. c1975, Warner-Tamerlane Publishing Corp. & Van McCoy Music, Inc. GEORGE & GWEN MC CRAE/VAN MC COY. 30, 118.

Changes. w&m; Jim Messina. c1974, 75, Jasperilla Music Co. LOGGINS & MESSINA. 139.

Changes. w&m; Phil Ochs. c1967, 68, Barricade Music, Inc. PHIL OCHS. 37, 144.

Changes In Latitudes, Changes In Attitudes. w&m; Jimmy Buffett. c1977, Coral Reefer Music & Outer Banks Music. Administered by Coral Reefer Music. JIMMY BUFFETT. 146.

Chanson D'Amour. w&m; Wayne Shanklin. c1958, 1965, Thunderbird Music, Inc. Assigned to Bibo Music Publishing Co. ART & DOTTY TODD. 160.

Chantilly Lace. w&m; J.P. Richardson. c1958, Glad Music. BIG BOPPER/JERRY LEE LEWIS. 3, 63.

Charlie Brown. w&m; Jerry Leiber & Mike Stoller. c1959, Tiger Music, Inc. Assigned to Chappell & Co., Inc., Quintet Music, Inc. & Bienstock Publishing Co. Controlled by Chappell & Co. COASTERS. 92, 101, 137, 155.

Charmaine. w&m; Erno Rapee & Lew Pollack. c1926, 54, 66, Miller Music Corp. FRANK SINATRA/HARMONICATS/MANTOVANI. 140.

Chase. w&m; Giorgio Moroder (m). c1978, 79, Gold Horizon Music Corp. Controlled by Screen Gems-EMI Music Corp. THEME FROM THE MOTION PICTURE "MIDNIGHT EXPRESS". 34, 51.

Chattanooga Choo Choo. w&m; Mack Gordon (w) & Harry Warren (m). c1941, 66, Twentieth Century Music Corp. Controlled by Leo Feist, Inc. BILLY STRANGE/BOSTON POPS/GEORGE BENSON/GLENN MILLER/TUXEDO JUNCTION. 140, 199.

Cheater. w&m; John & Mike Krenski. c1965, Son-Kay Publishing. BOB KUBAN & THE IN-MEN. 6.

Checkin' Up On My Baby. w&m; "Sonny Boy" Williamson. c1965, Arc Music Corp. TAJ MAHAL. 1.

Cheeseburger In Paradise. w&m; Jimmy Buffett. c1978, Coral Reefer Music & Outer Banks Music. JIMMY BUFFETT. 178.

Chelsea Morning. w&m; Joni Mitchell. c1967, 74, Siquomb Publishing Corp. DAVE VON RONK/JONI MITCHELL/JUDY COLLINS. 30, 35, 43, 55, 67, 86, 136, 138, 174.

Cherish. w&m; Terry Kirkman. c1966, 71, Beechwood Music Corp. ASSOCIATION/DAVID CASSIDY. 38, 64, 72, 89, 130, 140.

Cherry, Cherry. w&m; Neil Diamond. c1966, 70, Tallyrand Music Inc. NEIL DIAMOND. 93.

Cherry Pie. w&m; Joe Josea & Marvin Phillips. c1954, Modern Music Publishing Co., Inc. SKIP & FLIP. 3.

Chico And The Man. w&m; Jose Feliciano. c1974, 75, J&H Publishing Co. JOSE FELICIANO. 139.

Children Of Darkness. w&m; Richard Farina. c1966, 67, M. Witmark & Sons & Warner Bros. Inc. JOAN BAEZ/MIMI & RICHARD FARINA. 35, 67, 132.

Children Of The Sun. w&m; Billy Thorpe & Spencer Proffer. c1979, Careers Music, Inc., Rock Of Ages Music & Blackwood Music, Inc. BILLY THORPE. 11.

Child's Claim To Fame. w&m; Richie Furay. c1967, Cotillion Music, Inc., Ten East Music & Springalo Toones. BUFFALO SPRINGFIELD. 39.

Chilling Of The Evening. w&m; Arlo Guthrie. c1967, 69, Appleseed Music Inc. ARLO GUTHRIE. 7.

Chimes Of Freedom. w&m; Bob Dylan. c1964, M. Witmark & Sons. BOB DYLAN/BYRDS. 41, 69, 132.

China Doll. w&m; Robert Hunter (w) & Jerry Garcia (m). c1974, 76, Ice Nine Publishing Co., Inc. GRATEFUL DEAD. 84.

China Grove. w&m; Tom Johnston. c1973, Warner-Tamerlane Publishing Corp. DOOBIE BROTHERS. 22, 55, 136, 139, 145, 174, 185.

Chinese Kung Fu. w&m; Subway (m). c1974, 75, Isabelle Music. BANZAII. 49.

Chuck E.'s In Love. w&m; Rickie Lee Jones. c1978, 79, Easy Money Music. RICKIE LEE JONES. 27, 31, 57, 147.

Church Is Burning. w&m; Paul Simon. c1965, Paul Simon. 143.

Chinderella. w&m; Larry Burnett. c1975, 77, Powder Music Inc. Administered by United Artists Music Co., Inc. FIREFALL. 196.

Cinderella Rockefella. w&m; Nancy Ames & Mason Williams. c1966, Irving Music Inc. ESTHER & ABI OFARIM. 76.

Cinnamon Girl. w&m; Neil Young. c1969, 74, Cotillion Music, Inc. & Broken Arrow Music. NEIL YOUNG. 22, 185.

Circle Game. w&m; Joni Mitchell. c1966, 74, Siquomb Publishing Corp. BUFFY SAINT-MARIE/JONI MITCHELL. 35, 43, 88, 141.

Circles. w&m; Harry Chapin. c1971, 74, American Broadcasting Music Inc. HARRY CHAPIN. 37.

Circus, Theme From SEE Computer Game.

Cisco Kid. w&m; Sylvester Allen, Harold R. Brown, Morris Dickerson, Leroy "Lonnie" Jordan, Charles W. Miller, Lee Oskar & Howard Scott. c1972, 73, Far Out Music, Inc. Administered by United Artists Music Co., Inc. WAR. 111, 194.

City Of New Orleans. w&m; Steve Goodman. c1970, 72, Kama Rippa Music Inc. & Turnpike Tom Music. Administered by United Artists Music Co., Inc. ARLO GUTHRIE/STEVE GOODMAN. 21, 37, 156.

Classical Gas. w&m; Mason Williams (m). c1967, 68, Irving Music, Inc. MASON WILLIAMS. 56, 70, 71.

Close Encounters Of The Third Kind, Theme From. w&m; John Williams (m). c1977, Gold Horizon Music Corp. Controlled by Screen Gems-EMI Music Inc. LONDON SYMPHONY ORCHESTRA. 128, 135.

Close To You. w&m; Hal David (w) & Burt Bacharach (m). c1963, 69, U.S. Songs, Inc., Blue Seas Music, Inc. & Jac Music Co., Inc. CARPENTERS/DIONNE WARWICK. 21, 23, 56, 63, 64, 70, 71, 72, 88, 93, 140, 163, 181, 193, 194, 195, 198.

Close To You. w&m; Willie Dixon. c1958, 70, Arc Music Corp. DOORS. 1.

Closer To Home. w&m; Mark Farner. c1970, Storybook Music Co. GRAND FUNK. 93.

Clothes Line Saga. w&m; Bob Dylan. c1970, 75, Dwarf Music. BOB DYLAN & THE BAND. 170.

Cloud Nine. w&m; Barrett Strong & Norman Whitfield. c1968, Jobete Music Co., Inc. TEMPTATIONS. 123.

Cloudy. w&m; Paul Simon. c1966, Paul Simon. SIMON & GARFUNKEL. 143.

C'mon Everybody. w&m; Joy Byers. c1964, Elvis Presley Music, Inc. ELVIS PRESLEY. 173.

Cocaine Blues. w&m; Rev. Gary Davis. c1968, 78, Chandos Music. DAVE VAN RONK. 37.

Cold As Ice. w&m; Mick Jones & Lou Gramm (w). c1977, Somerset Music, Evansongs Ltd. & WB Music Corp. FOREIGNER. 22, 117, 124, 136, 145, 175, 185.

Cold Sweat (Parts 1 & 2). w&m; James Brown & Alfred Ellis. c1967, 68, Dynatone Publishing Co. JAMES BROWN. 18.

Coldblooded. w&m; James Brown. c1974, Dynatone Publishing Co. JAMES BROWN. 107.

Color Him Father. w&m; Richard Spencer. c1969, Holly Bee Music. WINSTONS. 161.

Colorado. w&m; Rick Roberts. c1971, 76, Editions Miriam AG. Controlled by Piccasso Publishing Co. LINDA RONSTADT. 27.

Colour My World. w&m; James Pankow. c1970, Moose Music & Aurelius Music. CHICAGO. 23, 71, 77, 93, 130, 134, 156, 183.

Colours. w&m; Donovan. c1965, Donovan (Music) Ltd./ Southern Music Publishing Co., Inc. DONOVAN. 59.

Come Along. w&m; David Hess. c1966, Gladys Music, Inc. ELVIS PRESLEY. 173.

Come And Get It. w&m; Paul McCartney. c1970, Northern Songs, Ltd./Maclen Music, Inc. BADFINGER. 61, 159.

Come And Go With Me. w&m; Peter Yarrow (Adapted & arranged), Mary Travers (Adapted & arranged), Milton Okun (Adapted & arranged) & Paul Stookey (Adapted & arranged). c1965, Pepamar Music Corp. PETER, PAUL & MARY. 35, 67.

Come Back Baby. w&m; Ray Charles. c1954, 62, Progressive Music Publishing Co., Inc. Controlled by Unichappell Music, Inc. RAY CHARLES. 155.

Come By Here. w&m; Bessie Jones (New words & new music adaptation) & Alan Lomax (Additional lyrics). c1972, Ludlow Music, Inc. B.B. KING/GEORGIA SEA ISLAND SINGERS. 85.

Come Go With Me. w&m; C.E. Quick. c1957, Gil Music Corp. & Fee Bee Music. BEACH BOYS/DEL VIKINGS. 4, 72, 101, 117, 137.

Come In From The Rain. w&m; Melissa Manchester & Carole Bayer Sager. c1975, 76, 77, Rumanian Pickleworks Music Co. & The Times Square Music Publications Co. Administered by Screen Gems-EMI Music Inc. & The Times Square Music Publications Co. CAPTAIN & TENNILLE/DIANA ROSS/MELISSA MANCHESTER/ SHIRLEY BASSEY. 128, 130.

Come Into My Life. w&m; Rick James. c1979, Jobete Music Co., Inc. & Stone City Music Co. RICK JAMES. 24.

Come Live Your Life With Me. w&m; Larry Kusik (w), Billy Meshel (w) & Nino Rota (m). c1972, Famous Music Corp. 63.

Come Monday. w&m; Jimmy Buffett. c1974, ABC-Dunhill Music, Inc. JIMMY BUFFETT. 15, 37.

Come On Over. w&m; Barry & Robin Gibb. c1975, Abigail Music Ltd. & Flam Music Ltd./Casserole Music Corp. Administered by Unichappell Music, Inc. OLIVIA NEWTON-JOHN. 141.

Come 'Round Here SEE I'm The One You Need.

Come Sail Away. w&m; Dennis DeYoung. c1977, Almo Music Corp. & Stygian Songs. Administered by Almo Music Corp. STYX. 23, 56, 70, 71, 96.

Come Saturday Morning. w&m; Dory Previn (w) & Fred Karlin (m). c1969, Famous Music Corp. SAND-PIPERS. 63.

Come See About Me. w&m; Brian Holland, Lamont Dozier & Eddie Holland. c1964, 67, Jobete Music Co., Inc. SUPREMES. 123, 150.

Come Share My Love. w&m; Joe Brooks. c1978, Big Hill Music Corp. DEBBY BOONE. 135.

Come Softly To Me. w&m; Gary Troxel, Gretchen Christopher & Barbara Ellis. c1958, 59, Cornerstone Publishing Co., Inc. & Unart Music Corp. FLEET-WOODS/FRANKIE AVALON. 78, 82.

Come To Me. w&m; Tony Green. c1979, Trumar Music Inc. & Cicada Music Publishing. FRANCE JOLI. 27, 57.

Come Together. w&m; John Lennon & Paul McCartney. c1969, 79, Northern Songs Ltd./Maclen Music, Inc. AEROSMITH/BEATLES. 36, 55, 61, 146, 159, 175.

Come What May. w&m; Frank Tableporter. c1958, Tiger Music, Inc. ELVIS PRESLEY. 172.

Coming In To Los Angeles. w&m; Arlo Guthrie. c1969, Howard Beach Music, Inc. ARLO GUTHRIE. 7, 202.

Communication Breakdown. w&m; Jimmy Page, John Paul Jones & John Bonham. c1969, Superhype Publishing. LED ZEPPELIN. 114.

Computer Game. w&m; Haruomi Hosono (m), Ryuichi Sakamoto (m) & Yukihiro Takahashi (m). c1979, 80, Alfa Music, Ltd./Almo Music Corp. YELLOW MAGIC ORCHESTRA. 24, 99.

Congratulations. w&m; Paul Simon. c1971, Paul Simon. PAUL SIMON. 143.

Conquistador. w&m; Keith Reid (w) & Gary Brooker (m). c1967, 71, Essex Music International Ltd./TRO Essex Music, Inc. PROCOL HARUM. 42, 156.

Cook With Honey. w&m; Valerie Carter. c1972, River Honey Music. JUDY COLLINS. 68.

Cool Change. w&m; Glenn Shorrock. c1979, Fiber-chem International B.V./Screen Gems-EMI Music Inc. LITTLE RIVER BAND. 27, 31, 147, 188.

Copacabana. w&m; Bruce Sussman (w), Jack Feldman (w) & Barry Manilow (m). c1978, Kamakazi Music Corp., Appoggiatura Music, Inc. & Camp Songs Music. BARRY MANILOW. 21, 31, 87, 176.

Copper Kettle (The Pale Moonlight). w&m; Albert F. Beddoe. c1953, 61, 64, Melody Trails, Inc. BOB DYLAN. 85.

Cops Of The World. w&m; Phil Ochs. c1966, 68, Barricade Music, Inc. PHIL OCHS. 144.

Corazon. w&m; Carole King. c1973, Colgems-EMI Music Inc. CAROLE KING. 134.

Corner Of The Sky. w&m; Stephen Schwartz. c1972, Stephen Schwartz, Jobete Music Co., Inc. & Belwin-Mills Publishing Corp. JACKSON 5. 20.

Cotton Fields. w&m; Huddie Ledbetter. c1962, Folkways Music Publishers, Inc. HIGHWAYMEN. 68, 85.

Could I Have This Dance. w&m; Wayland Holyfield & Bob House. c1980, Maplehill Music, Vogue Music & Onhisown Music. ANNE MURRAY. 58, 190.

Could It Be Magic. w&m; Adrienne Anderson & Barry Manilow. c1973, 75, Kamakazi Music Corp. & Angel-dust Music. BARRY MANILOW. 21, 25.

Count Every Star. w&m; Sammy Gallop (w) & Bruno Coquatrix (m). c1950, 68, 78, Pic Corp. Assigned to Gallop Music. HUGO WINTERHALTER/LINDA SCOTT. 4, 113.

Count On Me. w&m; Jesse Barish. c1977, 78, Bright Moments Music & Diamondback Music. JEFFERSON STARSHIP. 134, 135.

Country Girl. w&m; Neil Young. c1970, 71, Cotillion Music, Inc. & Broken Arrow Music. CROSBY, STILLS, NASH & YOUNG. 36.

Country Pie. w&m; Bob Dylan. c1969, 76, Big Sky Music. BOB DYLAN. 170.

Country Road. w&m; James Taylor. c1970, Blackwood Music Inc. & Country Road Music Inc. Administered by Blackwood Music Inc. JAMES TAYLOR. 15, 21, 193, 198.

Country Sunshine. w&m; Billy Davis & Dottie West. c1972, 73, Shada Music Inc. & Tree Publishing Co. DOTTIE WEST. 89.

Cowboy. w&m; Ron Fraser & Harry Shannon. c1976, Welbeck Music Corp. & Sweco Music Corp. EDDIE ARNOLD. 141.

Cowgirl In The Sand. w&m; Neil Young. c1969, 70, 73, Cotillion Music Inc. & Broken Arrow Music. CROSBY, STILLS, NASH & YOUNG/NEIL YOUNG. 127, 151.

Coyote. w&m; Joni Mitchell. c1976, 77, Crazy Crow Music. JONI MITCHELL. 127.

Crackerbox Palace. w&m; George Harrison. c1976, 77, Ganga Publishing B.V. GEORGE HARRISON. 127.

Crackers. w&m; Kye Fleming & Dennis W. Morgan. c1980, Pi-Gem Music, Inc. BARBARA MANDRELL. 58.

Cracklin' Rosie. w&m; Neil Diamond. c1970, 74, Prophet Music, Inc. NEIL DIAMOND. 55, 88, 131, 133, 136, 174, 183.

Crash On The Levee. w&m; Bob Dylan. c1967, 75, Dwarf Music. BOB DYLAN & THE BAND. 170.

Crazy Feelin'. w&m; Jesse Barish. c1978, Diamond-back Music & Bright Moments Music. JEFFERSON STARSHIP. 74.

Crazy Fingers. w&m; Robert Hunter & Jerry Garcia. c1975, 76, Ice Nine Publishing Co., Inc. GRATEFUL DEAD. 84.

Crazy Little Thing Called Love. w&m; Freddie Mercury. c1979, Queen Music Ltd./Beechwood Music Corp. QUEEN. 23, 45, 56, 98.

Crazy Love. w&m; Rusty Young. c1978, 79, Pirooting Publishing. POCO. 27, 31, 57.

Crazy On You. w&m; Ann & Nancy Wilson. c1976, How About Music. HEART. 142.

Crazy Words-Crazy Tune. w&m; Jack Yellen (w) & Milton Ager (m). c1937, Advanced Music Corp. JIM KWESKIN & THE JUG BAND/NITTY GRITTY DIRT BAND. 132.

Creeque Alley. w&m; John Phillips & Michelle Gilliam Phillips. c1967, American Broadcasting Music, Inc. MAMAS & THE PAPAS. 93.

Crimson And Clover. w&m; Tommy James & Peter Lucia. c1968, Big Seven Music Corp. TOMMY JAMES & THE SHONDELLS. 37, 72, 102, 161.

Crocodile Rock. w&m; Elton John & Bernie Taupin. c1972, Dick James Music Ltd./Dick James Music, Inc. ELTON JOHN. 36, 124, 133, 138, 141, 174, 185, 197.

Cross My Heart. w&m; Phil Ochs. c1966, 68, Barricade Music, Inc. PHIL OCHS. 144.

Crossroader. w&m; Felix Pappalardi & Gail Collins. c1971, Upfall Music Corp. MOUNTAIN. 152.

Crucifixion. w&m; Phil Ochs. c1966, 68, Barricade Music. PHIL OCHS. 144.

Cruel To Be Kind. w&m; Nick Lowe & Ian Gomm. c1978, Anglo-Rock, Inc.-Albion Music Ltd. NICK LOWE. 11, 23.

Cruel War. w&m; Paul Stookey & Peter Yarrow. c1962, Pepamar Music Corp. PETER, PAUL & MARY. 67.

Cruisin'. w&m; William "Smokey" Robinson & Marvin Tarplin. c1979, Bertam Music Co. SMOKEY ROBINSON. 24, 98.

Crunge. w&m; John Bonham, John Paul Jones, Jimmy Page & Robert Plant. c1973, Superhype Publishing. LED ZEPPELIN. 114.

Cry Like A Baby. w&m; Dan Penn & Spooner Oldham. c1968, Press Music Co., Inc. BOX TOPS. 76.

Crying In The Chapel. w&m; Artie Glenn. c1953, Hill & Range Songs, Inc. Assigned to Unichappell Music, Inc. DON MC LEAN/ELVIS PRESLEY/ORIOLES. 15, 102, 137, 191.

Crystal Blue Persuasion. w&m; Tommy James, Mike Vale & Ed Gray. c1969, Big Seven Music Corp. TOMMY JAMES & THE SHONDELLS. 102.

Cuckoo. w&m; Dwain Story, Erik Jacobsen, Peter Yarrow, Paul Stookey, Mary Travers & Milton Okun. c1963, 65, M. Witmark & Sons & Pepamar Music Corp. PETER, PAUL & MARY. 67.

Cuddly Toy. w&m; Harry Nilsson. c1967, Screen Gems-Columbia Music Inc. MONKEES. 76.

Cumberland Blues. w&m; Jerry Garcia & Philip Lesh (m) & Robert Hunter (w). c1970, Ice Nine Publishing Co. GRATEFUL DEAD. 83.

Curious Mind. w&m; Curtis Mayfield. c1963, 78, Warner-Tamerlane Publishing Corp. JOHNNY RIVERS. 201.

Da Doo Ron Ron. w&m; Ellie Greenwich, Jeff Barry & Phil Spector. c1963, Trio Music Co., Inc. & Mother Bertha Music, Inc. CARPENTERS/CHIFFONS/MATTHEWS SOUTHERN COMFORT/SHAUN CASSIDY. 128, 135, 142, 164.

Da Ya Think I'm Sexy. w&m; Rod Stewart & Carmine Appice. c1978, Rod Stewart, WB Music Corp. & Nite Stalk Music. ROD STEWART. 22, 27, 31, 136, 146, 185.

Daddy Could Swear, I Declare. w&m; Johnny Bristol, Gladys Knight & Merald Knight. c1972, Jobete Music Co., Inc. GLADYS KNIGHT & THE PIPS. 17.

Daddy, Daddy. w&m; Rudolph Toombs. c1952, Progressive Music Publishing Co., Inc. Controlled by Unichappell Music, Inc. RUTH BROWN. 155.

Daddy Don't Live In That New York City No More. w&m; Walter Becker & Donald Fagen. c1974, MCA Music. STEELY DAN. 142.

Daddy, You Been On My Mind. SEE Mama, You Been On My Mind.

Daddy's Home. w&m; James Sheppard & William Miller. c1961, 73, Nom Music, Inc. SHEP & THE LIMELITES. 102.

Daisy A Day. w&m; Jud Strunk. c1972, Every Little Tune Inc. & Pierre Cossette Music Co. JUD STRUNK. 111, 140, 194.

Daisy Jane. w&m; Gerry Beckley. c1975, WB Music Corp. AMERICA. 139.

Dance SEE Dance (Disco Heat).

Dance Across The Floor. w&m; H.W. Casey & R. Finch. c1978, Sherlyn Publishing Co., Inc. & Harrick Music Inc. Administered by Sherlyn Publishing Co., Inc. JIMMY "BO" HORNE. 135.

Dance, Dance, Dance. w&m; Brian & Carl Wilson. c1964, Sea of Tunes Publishing Co. BEACH BOYS. 9.

Dance Dance Dance. w&m; Neil Young. c1971, 72, Cotillion Music, Inc. & Broken Arrow Music. NEIL YOUNG. 138, 151.

Dance, Dance, Dance. w&m; Steve Miller, Brenda Cooper (w) & Jason Cooper (w). c1976, Sailor Music. STEVE MILLER BAND. 146.

Dance, Dance, Dance. w&m; Windsor King & Morris Levy. c1963, Big Seven Music Corp. 102.

Dance, Dance, Dance (Yowsah, Yowsah, Yowsah). w&m; Kenny Lehman, Bernard Edwards & Nile Rodgers. c1977, Cotillion Music Inc. & Kreimers Music. CHIC. 118, 178.

Dance (Disco Heat). w&m; Eric Robinson & Victor Orsborn. c1978, Jobete Music Co., Inc. SYLVESTER. 34, 51, 74, 112.

Dance Little Dreamer. w&m; Gregg Diamond. c1977, Diamond Touch Publishing, Ltd./Arista Music Inc. BIONIC BOOGIE/GREGG DIAMOND. 34.

Dance The Night Away. w&m; Edward & Alex Van Halen, Michael Anthony & David Lee Roth. c1979, Van Halen Music. VAN HALEN. 22, 27, 147.

Dance To The Music. w&m; Sylvester Stewart. c1968, Daly City Music. SLY & THE FAMILY STONE. 76, 202.

c1968, 75, Northern Songs Ltd./Maclen Music, Inc. BEATLES/FIVE STAIRSTEPS. 30.

December 1963 (Oh, What A Night). w&m; Bob Gaudio & Judy Parker (w). c1975, Jobete Music Co., Inc. & Seasons Music Co. FOUR SEASONS. 95.

Declaration. w&m; Julius Johnsen & Rene De Knight (m). c1969, 70, Mocart-5th Star. FIFTH DIMENSION. 60.

Dedicated To The One I Love. w&m; Lowman Pauling & Ralph Bass. c1957, 67, 71, Trousdale Music Publishers, Inc. & ABC-Dunhill Music, Inc. MAMAS & THE PAPAS/SHIRELLES. 3, 93, 119, 163.

Deep, Theme From. w&m; John Barry. c1977, Gold Horizon Music Corp./Screen Gems-EMI Music Inc. DONNA SUMMER. 142.

Deep Inside My Heart. w&m; Randy Meisner & Eric Kaz. c1980, United Artists Music Co., Inc., Glasco Music & Nebraska Music. RANDY MEISNER. 162, 190.

Deep Purple. w&m; Mitchell Parish (w) & Peter De Rose (m). c1934, 39, 62, 67, Robbins Music Corp. BOOTS RANDOLPH!/DONNY & MARIE OSMOND/ JOHNNY MATHIS/NINO & APRIL. 140.

Deep River Blues. w&m; Doc Watson. c1965, Stormking Music Inc. DOC WATSON. 59.

Deja Vu. w&m; Adrienne Anderson (w) & Isaac Hayes (m). c1979, Ikeco Music Ltd./Angela Music Co. DIONNE WARWICK. 8, 47, 180.

Delilah. w&m; Les Reed & Barry Mason. c1968, Donna Music Ltd./Francis, Day & Hunter, Inc. TOM JONES. 72, 194.

Delta Dawn. w&m; Alex Harvey & Larry Collins. c1972, United Artists Music Co., Inc. & Big Ax Music. Administered by United Artists Music Co., Inc. BETTE MIDLER/HELEN REDDY. 15, 21, 80, 140, 161, 163, 193, 194, 198.

Delta Lady. w&m; Leon Russell. c1969, 71, Cordell-Russell Music Co. & Teddy Jack Music. JOE COCKER/LEON RUSSELL. 12, 29, 134, 152, 156.

Denver. w&m; Dan Penn & Spooner Oldham. c1968, Press Music Co., Inc. STEVE ALAIMO. 76.

Dependin' On You. w&m; Patrick Simmons & Michael McDonald. c1978, 79, Soquel Songs & Snug Music. DOOBIE BROTHERS. 27, 147.

Deportee. w&m; Woody Guthrie (w) & Martin Hoffman (m). c1961, 63, Ludlow Music, Inc. ARLO GUTHRIE/ CISCO HOUSTON/JOAN BAEZ/JUDY COLLINS. 85.

Desire. w&m; Barry, Robin & Maurice Gibb. c1979, 80, Brothers Gibb B.V./Stigwood Music, Inc. Administered by Unichappell Music, Inc. ANDY GIBB. 47.

Desiree. w&m; Neil Diamond. c1977, Stonebridge Music. NEIL DIAMOND. 146.

Desperado. w&m; Don Henley & Glenn Frey. c1973, Cass County Music, Red Cloud Music, WB Music Corp. & Kicking Bear Music. EAGLES/LINDA RONSTADT. 55, 87, 127, 138, 139, 145, 174.

Destiny. w&m; Nickolas Ashford & Valerie Simpson. c1975, 77, Nick-O-Val Music. ASHFORD & SIMPSON. 13.

Devil Or Angel. w&m; Blanche Carter. c1955, Progressive Music Publishing Co., Inc. Controlled by Unichappell Music, Inc. CLOVERS. 91, 154, 155.

Devil Went Down To Georgia. w&m; Charlie Daniels, Tom Crain, James W. Marshall, "Taz" Digregorio, Fred Edwards & Charlie Hayward. c1979, Hat Band Music. CHARLIE DANIELS BAND. 27, 147.

Devil With The Blue Dress On. w&m; William Stevenson & Frederick Long. c1964, 66, Jobete Music Co., Inc. MITCH RYDER/SHORTY LONG. 123, 167.

Devil's Gun. w&m; Barry Blue, Ron Roker & Gerry Shury. c1977, ATV Music Ltd. C. J. & CO. 46, 127.

Devoted To You. Boudleaux Bryant. c1958, House Of Bryant Publications. CARLY SIMON & JAMES TAYLOR/EVERLY BROTHERS. 3, 74, 135.

Diamond Girl. w&m; James Seals & Dash Crofts (m). c1973, Dawnbreaker Music Co. SEALS & CROFTS. 36, 55, 136, 138.

Diamonds And Pearls. w&m; West Tyler. c1960, Lode Publications. PARADONS. 4.

Diamonds And Rust. w&m; Joan Baez. c1975, Chandos Music. JOAN BAEZ. 198.

Diamonds Are Forever. w&m; Don Black (w) & John Barry (m). c1971, United Artists Music Ltd./Unart Music Corp. RONNIE ALDRICH/SHIRLEY BASSEY. 140.

Diana. w&m; Paul Anka. c1957, 63, Spanka Music Corp. PAUL ANKA. 6.

Diane. w&m; Billy Carl, Reid Whitelaw & Richard Bell. c1968, 70, Magic Fleet Music, Inc. & Bates Music Publishing Corp. GOLDEN GATE. 186.

Diane. w&m; Erno Rapee & Lew Pollack. c1927, 55, 66, Miller Music Corp. BACHELORS/MANTOVANI/ MILES DAVIS. 140.

Did She Mention My Name. w&m; Gordon Lightfoot. c1968, 69, Warner Bros. Inc. GORDON LIGHTFOOT. 35, 138.

Dija Ever. w&m; Sid Wayne (w) & Sherman Edwards (m). c1960. Gladys Music, Inc. ELVIS PRESLEY. 172.

Didn't I (Blow Your Mind This Time). w&m; William Hart (w) & Thomas Bell (m). c1969, 70, Mighty Three Music, Nickel Shoe Music Co., Inc. & Bell Boy Music. ARETHA FRANKLIN/DELFONICS/ MILLIE JACKSON. 24, 186.

Didn't Want To Have To Do It. w&m; John B. Sebastian. c1965, 66, Hudson Bay Music Co. JOHN SEBASTIAN. 93.

Different Drum. w&m; Michael Nesmith. c1967, Screen Gems-EMI Music Inc. LINDA RONSTADT. 142.

Dig A Little Deeper. w&m; Benny Latimore. c1978, Sherlyn Publishing Co., Inc. LATIMORE. 66.

Dim All The Lights. w&m; Donna Summer. c1979, Sweet Summer Night Music. DONNA SUMMER. 27, 31, 57, 147.

Dime SEE Feelings.

Dimples. w&m; James Bracken & John Lee Hooker. c1956, 58, Conrad Music, a division of Arc Music Corp. JOHN LEE HOOKER. 169.

Dire Wolf. w&m; Robert Hunter (w) & Jerry Garcia (m). c1970, 73, Ice Nine Publishing Co. GRATEFUL DEAD. 83.

Dirge. w&m; Bob Dylan. c1973, 76, Ram's Horn Music. BOB DYLAN. 170.

Dirty Water. w&m; Ed Cobb. c1965, 66, Equinox Music. STANDELLS. 93.

Dirty White Boy. w&m; Mick Jones & Lou Gramm. c1979, Somerset Songs Publishing Inc./Evansongs Ltd. FOREIGNER. 22, 27, 147.

Disco Baby. w&m; Hugo & Luigi & George David Weiss. c1975, Avco Embassy Music Publishing, Inc. VAN MC COY & THE SOUL CITY SYMPHONY. 49.

Disco Duck (Part I). w&m; Rick Dees. c1976, Stafree Publishing Co. RICK DEES & HIS CAST OF IDIOTS. 46, 133, 141, 145.

Disco Heat   SEE   Dance(Disco Heat).

Disco Inferno. w&m; Leroy Green & Ron Kersey. c1977, Six Strings Music & Golden Fleece Music. TRAMMPS. 34, 51, 135.

Disco Lady. w&m; Harvey Scales, Al Vance & Don Davis. c1976, Groovesville Music & Conquistador Music. Administered by Screen Gems-EMI Music Inc. & Colgems-EMI Music Inc. JOHNNIE TAYLOR. 26, 77.

Disco Nights. w&m; Emmanuel Rahiem Le Blanc, Herb Lane, Keith Crier & Paul Service. c1978, 79, Emmanuel Rahiem Le Blanc, Herb Lave, Keith Crier, Paul Service & Arista Music, Inc. G. Q. 51.

Disco 'Round   SEE   I Love The Nightlife.

Dizzy. w&m; Tommy Roe & F. Weller. c1968, Low-Twi Music, Inc. TOMMY ROE. 64.

Dizzy Miss Lizzie. w&m; Larry Williams. c1958, 65, Venice Music, Inc. BEATLES/LARRY WILLIAMS. 35, 93, 100, 137, 159, 197.

Do Anything You Wanna Do. w&m; Ed Hollis & Graeme Douglas. c1977, 78, Island Music & Anglo-Rock, Inc. EDDIE & THE HOT RODS. 19.

Do I Have To Come Right Out And Say It. w&m; Neil Young. c1966, 74, Cotillion Music, Inc. Ten East Music & Springalo Toones. BUFFALO SPRING-FIELD. 39.

Do It. w&m; Neil Diamond. c1966, 70, Tallyrand Music Inc. NEIL DIAMOND. 63, 88.

Do It Again. w&m; W. Becker & D. Fagen. c1972, 73, MCA Music, a division of MCA Inc., Red Giant Music, Inc. & Wingate Music Corp. STEELY DAN. 105, 134.

Do It Anyway You Wanna. w&m; Leon Huff. c1975, Mighty Three Music. Administered by Blackwood Music Inc. PEOPLES CHOICE. 49.

Do It Baby. w&m; Freddie Perren (w) & Christine Yarian (m). c1974, Jobete Music Co., Inc. MIRACLES. 52.

Do It Or Die. w&m; Buddy Buie, J. R. Cobb & Ronnie Hammond. c1973, 79, Low-Sal, Inc. ATLANTA RHYTHM SECTION. 56, 75, 130, 187.

Do It ('Til You're Satisfied). Billy Nichols. c1974,

Triple "O" Songs, Jeff-Mar Music & Bil-Lee Music. B.T. EXPRESS. 26, 52, 77, 156.

Do Not Disturb. w&m; Bill Giant, Bernie Baum & Florence Kaye. c1965, Elvis Presley Music, Inc. ELVIS PRESLEY. 173.

Do That Stuff. w&m; George Clinton, Garry Shider & Bernie Worrell. c1976, 77, Rick's Music, Inc. & Malbiz Music. PARLIAMENT. 127.

Do That To Me One More Time. w&m; Toni Tennille. c1979, Moonlight and Magnolias Music Publishing Co. CAPTAIN & TENNILLE. 8, 23, 24, 56, 97, 177, 198.

Do The Funky Chicken. w&m; Rufus Thomas. c1969, Birdees Music. RUFUS THOMAS. 122.

Do Wah Diddy Diddy. w&m; Jeff Barry & Ellie Green-wich. c1963, 64, Trio Music Co., Inc. ANDREW GOLD. 142.

Do What You Wanna Do. w&m; J. B. Bingham. c1970, Tiny Tiger Music & Brig Music. FIVE FLIGHTS UP. 88.

Do Ya. w&m; Jeff Lynne. c1972, 77, Roy Wood Music Ltd., Carlin Music Corp. & Sugartown Music Ltd. Administered by United Artists Music Co., Inc. & Chappell & Co., Inc. ELECTRIC LIGHT ORCHES-TRA. 196.

Do You Believe in Magic. w&m; John B. Sebastian. c1965, The Hudson Bay Music Co. LOVIN' SPOON-FUL/SHAUN CASSIDY. 135.

Do You Feel All Right. w&m; Harry Wayne Casey & Richard Finch. c1978, Sherlyn Publishing Co., Inc. & Harrick Music, Inc. Administered by Sherlyn Publishing Co., Inc. K C & THE SUNSHINE BAND. 74.

Do You Know The Way To San Jose. w&m; Hal David (w) & Burt Bacharach (m). c1967, 68, Blue Seas Music, Inc. & Jac Music Co., Inc. DIONNE WAR-WICK/RENAISSANCE. 70, 86.

Do You Know Where You're Going To. w&m; Gerry Goffin (w) & Michael Masser (m). c1973, 75, Screen Gems-EMI Music Inc. & Jobete Music Co., Inc. Controlled by Screen Gems-EMI Music Inc. DIANA ROSS. 23, 24, 48, 56, 58, 71, 77, 128, 150.

Do You Love Me. w&m; Berry Gordy, Jr. c1962, 71, Jobete Music Co, Inc. CONTOURS. 123.

Do You Love What You Feel. w&m; David Wolinski. c1979, 80, Overdue Music. RUFUS FEATURING CHAKA KHAN. 58.

Do You Wanna Dance?. w&m; Robert Freeman. c1958, Clockus Music, Inc. BEACH BOYS/BETTE MIDLER/ BOBBY FREEMAN/MAMAS & THE PAPAS/ RAMONES. 4, 9, 32, 109, 119, 137, 153.

Do You Wanna Make Love. w&m; Peter McCann. c1977, MCA Music & American Broadcasting Music, Inc. PETER MC CANN. 142, 164.

Do You Want To Know A Secret. w&m; John Lennon & Paul McCartney. c1963, Northern Songs Ltd./Unart Music Corp. BEATLES. 82, 102, 137, 161.

Do Your Dance (Part I). w&m; Norman Whitefield & D. Turner. c1977, Warner-Tamerlane Publishing Corp. & May 12th Music, Inc. Administered by

Warner-Tamerlane Publishing Corp. ROSE ROYCE. 30, 118, 145.

Do Your Thing. w&m; Isaac Hayes. c1971, 75, East-Memphis Music. ISAAC HAYES. 122.

Dock Of The Bay. w&m; Steve Cropper & Otis Redding. c1968, 69, 75, East-Memphis Music Corp. & Time Music Co., Inc. OTIS REDDING. 29, 59, 77, 96, 122, 181.

Doctor, Doctor. SEE Bad Case Of Loving You.

Doctor Tarr And Professor Fether. w&m; Eric Woolfson & Alan Parsons. c1976, Fox Fanfare Music, Inc. & Woolfsongs, Inc. ALAN PARSONS PROJECT. 142.

Doctor's Orders. w&m; Roger Cook, Roger Greenaway & Geoff Stephens. c1973, Cookaway Music Ltd. CAROL DOUGLAS. 52.

Does Anybody Really Know What Time It Is. w&m; Robert Lamm. c1969, Lamminations Music & Aurelius Music. CHICAGO. 63, 86, 88, 128, 134, 156, 183.

Does Your Mother Know. w&m; Benny Andersson & Bjorn Ulvaeus. c1979, Union Songs AB & Countless Songs Ltd./Ivan Mogull Music Corp. ABBA. 27.

Doesn't Somebody Want To Be Wanted. w&m; Mike Appel, Jim Cretescos & Wes Farrell. c1971, Screen Gems-Columbia Music, Inc. PARTRIDGE FAMILY. 38.

Dob & Butterfly. w&m; Ann & Nancy Wilson & Susan Ennis. c1978, 79, Wilsongs & Know Music. HEART. 27, 147.

Doin' It To Death. w&m; James Brown. c1973, 74, Dynatone Publishing Co. JAMES BROWN. 107.

Doin' The Best I Can. w&m; Doc Pomus & Mort Shuman. c1960, Elvis Presley Music, Inc. ELVIS PRESLEY. 172.

Doing The Best I Can. w&m; James Brown, Charles Bobbit & Fred Wesley. c1973, 74, Dynatone Publishing Co. JAMES BROWN. 107.

Dominique. w&m; Soeur Sourire, O.P. & Noel Regney (w, Eng.). c1962, Editions Primavera s.a./General Music Publishing Co., Inc. SINGING NUN. 135.

Domino. w&m; Van Morrison. c1969, 71, WB Music Corp. & Caledonia Soul Music. VAN MORRISON. 22, 43, 136, 139, 182.

Donna. w&m; Ritchie Valens. c1958, Kemo Music Co. RITCHIE VALENS. 93.

Don't. w&m; Jerry Leiber & Mike Stoller. c1957, Elvis Presley Music, Inc. ELVIS PRESLEY. 173.

Don't Be A Drop-Out. w&m; James Brown & Nat Jones. c1966, 68, Dynatone Publishing Co. JAMES BROWN. 18.

Don't Be Cruel (To A Heart That's True). w&m; Otis Blackwell & Elvis Presley. c1956, 71, Unart Music Corp. & Elvis Presley Music. Rights of Elvis Presley Music controlled by Unichappell Music, Inc. ELVIS PRESLEY. 78, 82 101, 137, 155, 161.

Don't Break The Heart That Loves You. w&m; Benny Davis & Ted Murry. c1961, Planetary Music Publishing Corp. CONNIE FRANCIS. 102.

Don't Bring Me Down. w&m; Jeff Lynne. c1979, Jet Music Inc. & Blackwood Music Inc. Administered by Blackwood Music Inc. ELECTRIC LIGHT ORCHESTRA. 116, 148, 176, 199.

Don't Cha Hear Me Callin' To Ya. w&m; Rudy Stevenson. c1966, 70, 5th Star Music-Rudy Stevenson Music. FIFTH DIMENSION. 60.

Don't Change On Me. w&m; Eddie Reeves & Jimmy Holiday. c1969, 71, United Artists Music Co., Inc. & Racer Music Inc. 80.

Don't Cry Baby. w&m; Dan Peek. c1977, WB Music Corp. 127.

Don't Cry Out Loud. w&m; Peter Allen & Carole Bayer Sager. c1976, 78, Irving Music, Inc., Woolnough Music, Inc., Jemara Music Corp., Begonia Melodies, Inc. & Unichappell Music, Inc. MELISSA MANCHESTER/ PETER ALLEN. 23, 40, 56, 58, 70, 96, 129, 180.

Don't Do Me Like That. w&m; Tom Petty. c1977, 79, Skyhill Publishing Co., Inc. TOM PETTY & THE HEARTBREAKERS. 56, 98.

Don't Ever Be Lonely. w&m; Eddie Cornelius. c1972, Unart Music Corp. & Stage Door Music Publishing, Inc. Administered by Unart Music Corp. CORNELIUS BROTHERS & SISTER ROSE. 81, 195.

Don't Fear The Reaper. SEE Reaper.

Don't Fence Me In. w&m; Cole Porter. c1944, Warner Bros., Inc. WILLIE NELSON & LEON RUSSELL. 31, 87.

Don't Go Breaking My Heart. w&m; Carte Blanche & Ann Orson. c1976, Big Pig Music Ltd./Jodrell Music, Inc. ELTON JOHN & KIKI DEE. 124.

Don't Go Out Into The Rain (You're Gonna Melt). w&m; Kenny Young. c1966, Unart Music Corp. HERMAN'S HERMITS. 81.

Don't Hang Up. w&m; Kal Mann & Dave Appell. c1963, KalMann Music Inc. ORLONS. 5.

Don't It Make My Brown Eyes Blue. w&m; Richard Leigh. c1976, 77, United Artists Music Co., Inc. CRYSTAL GAYLE. 15, 21, 79, 131, 140, 163, 199.

Don't It Make You Wanta Go Home. w&m; Joe South. c1969, Lowery Music Co. JOE SOUTH. 130.

Don't Jump Me Mother. w&m; Mono Mann. c1978, Doraflo Music Co., Inc. & Go Mental Music. DMZ. 19.

Don't Leave Me Now. w&m; Aaron Schroeder & Ben Weisman. c1957, Gladys Music, Inc. ELVIS PRESLEY. 172.

Don't Leave Me This Way. w&m; Kenny Gamble, Leon Huff & Cary Gilbert. c1975, 77, Mighty Three Music. Administered by Blackwood Music, Inc. THELMA HOUSTON. 196.

Don't Let Go. w&m; Jesse Stone. c1957, 58, Screen Gems-EMI Music Inc. COMMANDER CODY & THE LOST PLANET AIRMEN/ISAAC HAYES/ JERRY LEE LEWIS/MANHATTAN TRANSFER/ PATTY LA BELLE. 24, 98.

Don't Let It Bring You Down. w&m; Neil Young. c1970, 75, Cotillion Music, Inc. & Broken Arrow Music. NEIL YOUNG. 175.

Don't Let Me Be Lonely Tonight. w&m; James Taylor, c1972, 73, Blackwood Music Inc. & Country Roads Music, Inc. Administered by Blackwood Music Inc. ISAAC HAYES/ISLEY BROTHERS/JAMES TAYLOR. 15, 131, 165, 183.

Don't Let The Sun Go Down On Me. w&m; Elton John & Bernie Taupin. c1974, Big Pig Music Ltd. Controlled by Jodrell Music, Inc. ELTON JOHN. 131, 136, 183.

Don't Make Me Over. w&m; Hal David (w) & Burt Bacharach (m). c1962, Blue Seas Music, Inc. & Jac Music Co. DIONNE WARWICK/JENNIFER WARNES. 70.

Don't Mess Up A Good Thing. w&m; Oliver Sain. c1965, 74, Chevis Music Inc. GREG ALLMAN. 142.

Don't Mess With Bill. w&m; William Robinson. c1965, 66, Jobete Music Co., Inc. MARVELETTES. 123, 150.

Don't Miss The Message. w&m; Buddy Buie, Robert Nix & J.R. Cobb. c1976, 77, Low-Sal, Inc. ATLANTA RHYTHM SECTION. 142.

Don't Play That Song. w&m; Ahmet M. Ertegun & Barry Nelson. c1962, Hill And Range Songs, Inc. ARETHA FRANKLIN/BEN E. KING. 137, 191.

Don't Pull Your Love. w&m; Dennis Lambert & Brian Potter. c1970, 71, Trousdale Music Publishers, Inc. & Soldier Music, Inc. HAMILTON, JOE FRANK & REYNOLDS. 64.

Don't Start Me Talkin'. w&m; "Sonny Boy" Williamson. c1955, Arc Music Corp. JOHN HAMMOND. 1.

Don't Stop. w&m; Christine McVie. c1976, 77, 78, Michael Fleetwood & Gentoo Music Inc. Administered by Warner-Tamerlane Publishing Co. FLEETWOOD MAC. 133, 136, 145.

Don't Take It So Hard. w&m; Mark Lindsay. c1968, Boom Music, Inc. PAUL REVERE & THE RAIDERS. 113.

Don't Tell My Heart To Stop Loving You. w&m; Claude Carrere, Jacques Plante, Russ Faith & Allen Hotlen. c1967, Editions Claude Carrere. Controlled by White Plains Music. JERRY VALE. 76.

Don't Think Twice, It's All Right. w&m; Bob Dylan. c1963, M. Witmark & Sons & Warner Bros., Inc. BOB DYLAN/JOAN BAEZ/PETER, PAUL & MARY. 35, 67, 132, 138.

Don't Throw It All Away. w&m; Barry Gibb & Blue Weaver. c1977, 78, Brothers Gibb B.V./Stigwood Music, Inc. Administered by Unichappell Music, Inc. ANDY GIBB. 40.

Don't Worry, Baby. w&m; Brian Wilson & Roger Christian. c1964, Sea Of Tunes Publishing Co. BEACH BOYS. 9.

Don't Worry About The Government. w&m; David Byrne. c1977, 78, Bleu Disque Music Co. & Index Music. TALKING HEADS. 19.

Don't Ya Tell Henry. w&m; Bob Dylan. c1971, 75, Dwarf Music. BOB DYLAN & THE BAND. 170.

Don't You Just Know It. w&m; Huey Smith & John Vincent. c1958, Ace Music Publishing Co., Inc. HUEY "PIANO" SMITH. 6.

Don't You Know. w&m; Ray Charles. c1954, 62, Progressive Music Publishing Co., Inc. Controlled by Unichappell Music, Inc. RAY CHARLES. 90, 155.

Don't You Know I Love You. w&m; A. Nugetre. c1951, Progressive Music Co., Inc. Controlled by Unichappell Music, Inc. CLOVERS. 155.

Don't You Worry 'Bout A Thing. w&m; Stevie Wonder. c1973, Jobete Music Co., Inc. STEVIE WONDER. 150.

Double Life. w&m; Ric Ocasek. c1979, Lido Music, Inc. CARS. 147.

Double Vision. w&m; Mick Jones & Lou Gramm (w). c1978, Somerset Songs Publishing Inc., Evansongs Ltd. & WB Music Corp. FOREIGNER. 22, 27, 146.

Down Along The Cove. w&m; Bob Dylan. c1968, 76, Dwarf Music. BOB DYLAN. 170.

Down By The Riverside. w&m; Dazz Jordan. c1953, Larry Spier, Inc. AL HIRT/BROWNIE MC GHEE. 193.

Down In The Alley. w&m; Clovers & Jesse Stone. c1957, Progressive Music Publishing Co., Inc. CLOVERS. 91.

Down In The Boondocks. w&m; Joe South. c1965, Lowery Music Co. BILLY JOE ROYAL. 93.

Down In The Flood SEE Crash On The Levee.

Down On Me. w&m; Janis Joplin. c1967, 68, 72, Brent Music Corp. & Slow Dancing Music Inc. JANIS JOPLIN. 6, 110, 140, 163.

Down On The Corner. w&m; J. C. Fogerty. c1969, Jondora Music. CREEDENCE CLEARWATER REVIVAL. 86, 93, 157.

Down The Hall. w&m; Bob Gaudio & Judy Parker. c1977. All Seasons Music. FOUR SEASONS. 142.

Down To Love Town. w&m; Don Daniels, Kathy Wakefield & Michael B. Sutton. c1976, Jobete Music Co., Inc. & Stone Diamond Music Corp. ORIGINALS. 95.

Dr. Zhivago, Theme From SEE Somewhere My Love.

Draft Dodger Rag. w&m; Phil Ochs. c1964, Appleseed Music Inc. PHIL OCHS. 59.

Draggin' The Line. w&m; Tommy James & Bob King. c1970, 71, Big Seven Music Corp. TOMMY JAMES. 192.

Draw The Line. w&m; Steven Tyler & Joe Perry. c1977, Daksel Music Corp., Vindaloo Productions & Song And Dance Music Co. AEROSMITH. 145.

Dream Lover. w&m; Bobby Darin. c1959, Screen Gems-EMI Music Inc. & The Hudson Bay Music Co. ANNE MURRAY/BOBBY DARIN. 130, 158.

Dream On. w&m; Steven Tyler. c1973, 76, Daksel Music Corp. AEROSMITH. 22, 36, 55, 117, 124, 136, 141, 147, 174, 175, 185.

Dream Police. w&m; Rick Nielsen. c1978, 79, Screen Gems-EMI Music, Inc. & Adult Music. Controlled by Screen Gems-EMI Music Inc. CHEAP TRICK. 97.

Dream Weaver. w&m; Gary Wright. c1975, 76, High Wave Music Inc. Administered by WB Music Corp. GARY WRIGHT. 30, 55, 62, 133, 136, 141, 174, 185.

Dreamboat Annie. w&m; Ann & Nancy Wilson. c1976, 77, Andorra Music. HEART.

Dreaming. w&m; Deborah Harry & Chris Stein. c1979, Rare Blue Music, Inc. & Monster Island Music. BLONDIE. 177, 198.

Dreams. w&m; Stevie Nicks. c1977, 78, Gentoo Music Inc. & Welsh Witch Music. Controlled by Screen Gems-EMI Music Inc. FLEETWOOD MAC. 133, 142, 145, 164.

Dreams Of The Everyday Housewife. w&m; Chris Gantry. c1968, Combine Music Corp. GLEN CAMP-BELL. 113.

Drift Away. w&m; Mentor Williams. c1972, 73, Almo Music Corp. DOBIE GRAY/HUMBLE PIE/ROD STEWART. 181.

Drifter's Escape. w&m; Bob Dylan. c1968, 76, Dwarf Music. BOB DYLAN. 170.

Driftwood. w&m; Justin Hayward. c1978, Warner Bros. Music Ltd. & Bright Music Ltd. Controlled by WB Music Corp. MOODY BLUES. 147.

Drink The Wind. w&m; Nickolas Ashford & Valerie Simpson. c1972, Jobete Music Co., Inc. VALERIE SIMPSON. 13.

Drive My Car. w&m; John Lennon & Paul McCartney. c1965, 75, Northern Songs Ltd./Maclen Music, Inc. BEATLES. 30, 35.

Driver's Seat. w&m; Paul Roberts. c1978, 79, Complacent Toonz, Inc. SNIFF 'N' THE TEARS. 27.

Duelling Banjos. w&m; Arthur Smith (m). c1955, 73, Combine Music Corp. & Warner-Tamerlane Publishing Corp. ERIC WEISSBERG & DELIVERANCE. 133, 138.

Duke Of Earl. w&m; Earl Edwards, Eugene Dixon & Bernice Williams. c1961, 68, Conrad Music, a division of Arc Music Corp. GENE CHANDLER. 156, 168.

Dum Dum. w&m; Sharon Sheeley & Jackie De Shannon. c1961, Unart Music Corp. & Metric Music Co., Inc. BRENDA LEE. 78, 82.

Duncan. w&m; Paul Simon. c1971, Paul Simon. PAUL SIMON. 143.

Dust In The Wind. w&m; Kerry Livgren. c1977, 78, Don Kirshner Music & Blackwood Music Publishing. KANSAS. 55, 116, 148, 174, 178.

D'yer Mak'er. w&m; John Bonham, John Paul Jones & Robert Plant. c1973, Superhype Publishing. LED ZEPPELIN. 22, 36, 114, 124, 138.

Dynomite (Part I). w&m; Tony Camillo. c1975, Tonob Music. BAZUKA. 49.

Early In The Morning. w&m; Mike Leander & Eddie Seago. c1969, Leeds Music Ltd./Duchess Music Corp. VANITY FARE. 94.

Early In The Morning. w&m; Paul Stookey. c1962, Pepamar Music Corp. PETER, PAUL & MARY. 35, 41, 67.

Early Mornin' Rain. w&m; Gordon Lightfoot. c1964, 66, M. Witmark & Sons & Warner Bros., Inc. BOB

DYLAN/CHAD & JEREMY/GORDON LIGHTFOOT/ JUDY COLLINS/PETER, PAUL & MARY. 35, 67, 138.

Earth Angel. w&m; Dootsi Williams, Gaynell Hodge & Jesse Belvin. c1954, Dootsi Williams Publications, Inc. PENGUINS. 3.

Ease On Down The Road. w&m; Charlie Smalls. c1974, 78, Fox Fanfare Music, Inc. CONSUMER RAPPORT/ DIANA ROSS & MICHAEL JACKSON. 24, 34, 48, 58, 74, 130, 135, 156.

Ease Your Pain. w&m; Hoyt Axton. c1970, 72, Lady Jane Music. ANNE MURRAY/BOBBY WHITLOCK/ HOYT AXTON. 115, 152.

East Is East. w&m; David L'Heureux. c1964, 65, Claridge Music Inc. CASEY PAXTON. 137.

Easy. w&m; Lionel Richie. c1977, Jobete Music Co., Inc. & Commodores Entertainment Publishing Corp. COMMODORES. 24, 138, 142.

Easy Come, Easy Go. w&m; Jack Keller & Diane Hilderbrand. c1969, 70, Screen Gems-Columbia Music, Inc. BOBBY SHERMAN. 38.

Easy Driver. w&m; Jerry Riofelle & David Plehn. c1977, 78, Blue Tampa Music. KENNY LOGGINS. 146.

Easy Evil. w&m; Alan O'Day. c1973, Edwin H. Morris & Co., Inc. & WB Music Corp. TRAVIS WAMMACK. 103.

Easy Living. w&m; Ken Hensley. c1972, Sydney Bron Music Co., Ltd. URIAH HEEP. 138, 152.

Easy Loving. w&m; Freddie Hart. c1970, 71, Blue Book Music. FREDDIE HART. 195.

Easy Question. w&m; Otis Blackwell & Winfield Scott. c1962, Elvis Presley Music, Inc. ELVIS PRESLEY. 172.

Easy Street. w&m; Martin Charnin (w) & Charles Strouse (m). c1977, Charles Strouse & Edwin H. Morris & Co., a division of MPL Communications. CAST OF ANNIE. 21.

Easy To Be Hard. w&m; James Rado (w), Gerome Ragni (w) & Galt MacDermot (m). c1966, 67, 68, 69, James Rado, Gerome Ragni, Galt MacDermot, Nat Shapiro, United Artists Music Co., Inc. Controlled by United Artists Music Co. MELBA MOORE/THREE DOG NIGHT. 79, 161, 163.

Easy Wind. w&m; Robert Hunter. c1970, 73, Ice Nine Publishing Co. GRATEFUL DEAD. 83.

Ebb Tide. w&m; Carl Sigman (w) & Robert Maxwell (m). c1953, 66, Robbins Music Corp. RIGHTEOUS BROTHERS. 140, 163, 192.

Ebony Eyes. w&m; Bob Welch. c1977, Glenwood Music Corp. & Cigar Music. BOB WELCH. 135.

Echoes SEE Everybody's Talkin'.

Echoes Of Love. w&m; Willie Mitchell (w), Earl Randle (w) & Patrick Simmons (m). c1977, Soquel Songs & Jec Publishing. DOOBIE BROTHERS. 145.

Eddie My Love. w&m; Aaron Collins, Maxwell David & Sam Ling. c1955, Modern Music Publishing Co. TEEN QUEENS. 3.

Webb. c1969, 75, Canopy Music, Inc. THELMA HOUSTON. 139.

Everybody Loves A Lover. w&m; Richard Adler & Robert Allen. c1958, International Korwin Corp. SHIRELLES. 4.

Everybody Loves A Rain Song. w&m; Mark James & Chips Moman. c1977, 78, Screen Gems-EMI Music Inc. B.J. THOMAS. 126.

Everybody's Talkin'. w&m; Fred Neil. c1967, 68, Coconut Grove Music, a division of Third Story Music, Inc. NILSSON. 21, 68, 72, 89, 93, 126, 134, 140, 141, 156, 161, 191.

Everyday People. w&m; Sylvester Stewart. c1968, Daly City Music. SLY & THE FAMILY STONE. 4, 203.

Everything I Own. w&m; David Gates. c1972, Colgems-EMI Music Inc. BREAD. 134.

Everything Is Beautiful. w&m; Ray Stevens. c1970, Ahab Music Co., Inc. RAY STEVENS. 23, 28, 64, 133, 135, 156, 181.

Everything Put Together Falls Apart. w&m; Paul Simon. c1971, Paul Simon. PAUL SIMON. 143.

Everything That 'Cha Do (Will Come Back To You). w&m; Ricky Hirsch. c1976, No Exit Music Co., Inc. WET WILLIE. 141.

Everything's Coming Up Love. w&m; Van McCoy. c1973, Warner-Tamerlane Publishing Corp., Van McCoy Music Inc. & Oceans Blue Music. DAVID RUFFIN. 141.

Everything's Gonna Be Alright. w&m; Walter Jacobs. c1959, 71, Arc Music Corp. BUTTERFIELD BLUES BAND. 203.

Everytime Two Fools Collide. w&m; Jeff Tweel & Jan Dyer. c1975, 78, United Artists Music Co., Inc. & Window Music Publishing Co., Inc. KENNY ROGERS & DOTTIE WEST. 21, 199.

Evil. w&m; Maurice White & Phillip Bailey. c1973, Hummit Music, Inc. EARTH, WIND & FIRE. 104.

Evil (Is Going On). w&m; Willie Dixon. c1960, Arc Music Corp. CANNED HEAT. 1.

Evil Ways. w&m; Sonny Henry. c1967, 75, Clarence A. Henry. Assigned to Richcar Music Co. SANTANA. 29, 77, 86, 93, 134, 142, 156.

Evil Woman. w&m; Jeff Lynne. c1975, Unart Music Corp. & Jet Music Inc. Administered by Unart Music Corp. ELECTRIC LIGHT ORCHESTRA. 15, 193, 198.

Ev'ry Day Of My Life. w&m; Jimmie Crane & Al Jacobs. c1953, 54, Miller Music Corp. BOBBY VINTON. 21, 140, 163, 193, 194, 195.

Excitable Boy. w&m; Warren Zevon & LeRoy P. Marinell. c1976, 78, Zevon Music & Polite Music. WARREN ZEVON. 12, 73.

Expecting To Fly. w&m; Neil Young. c1967, 74, Cotillion Music, Inc., Ten East Music & Springalo Toones. BUFFALO SPRINGFIELD. 39.

Express. w&m; B.T. Express. c1973, 75, Triple "O" Songs & Jeff-Mar Music Co. B.T. EXPRESS. 26.

Expressway To Your Heart. w&m; Kenny Gamble & Leon Huff. c1967, Double Diamond Music Co. & Downstairs Music Co. SOUL SURVIVORS. 93.

Eyes Of Silver. w&m; Tom Johnston. c1974, Warner-Tamerlane Publishing Corp. DOOBIE BROTHERS. 139.

Eyes Of The World. w&m; Robert Hunter (w) & Jerry Garcia (m). c1973, 76, Ice Nine Publishing Co., Inc. GRATEFUL DEAD. 84.

Face It, Girl, It's Over. w&m; Frank H. Stanton & Andy Badale. c1967, Richard Irwin Music Publishing Corp. NANCY WILSON. 76.

Fade Away And Radiate. w&m; Chris Stein. c1978, Rare Blue Music, Inc. & Monster Island Music. BLONDIE. 33.

Fair Game. w&m; Stephen Stills. c1977, Gold Hill Music, Inc. CROSBY, STILLS & NASH. 145.

Fairytale. w&m; Anita & Bonnie Pointer. c1974, Polo Grounds Music & Para-Thumb Music Corp. POINTER SISTERS. 93.

Faithless Love. w&m; J.D. Souther. c1974, 75, WB Music Corp. & Golden Spread Music. J.D. SOUTHER/ LINDA RONSTADT. 30, 141.

Fakin' It. w&m; Paul Simon. c1967, Paul Simon. SIMON & GARFUNKEL. 143.

Falling. w&m; Eddie Struzick & Lenny LeBlanc. c1976, 77, Shoals Music Mill Publishing Co., Inc. & Carrhorn Music. LE BLANC & CARR. 128, 135.

Fame. w&m; David Bowie, John Lennon & Carlos Alomar. c1975, Mainman, John Lennon & Ceilidh Prod., Inc. DAVID BOWIE. 49.

Fame. w&m; Dean Pitchford (w) & Michael Gore (m). c1980, Metro-Goldwyn-Mayer Inc. Controlled by MGM Affiliated Music, Inc. IRENE CARA. 189.

Fame And Fortune. w&m; Fred Wise (w) & Ben Weisman (m). c1960, Gladys Music Inc. ELVIS PRESLEY. 172.

Family Affair. w&m; Sylvester Stewart. c1971, Stone Flower Music. SLY & THE FAMILY STONE. 115.

Fancy Dancer. w&m; Ronald La Pread & Lionel Richie. c1976, Jobete Music Co., Inc. & Commodores Entertainment Publishing Corp. COMMODORES. 95.

Fanny Be Tender With My Love. w&m; Barry, Robin & Maurice Gibb. c1975, Abigail Music, Ltd. & Flam Music Ltd./Casserole Music Inc. Administered by Unichappell Music, Inc. BEE GEES. 30.

Fantasy. w&m; Maurice & Verdine White & Eddie Del Barrio. c1977, Saggifire Music. EARTH, WIND & FIRE. 16, 181.

Fat Bottomed Girls. w&m; Brian May. c1978, Queen Music Ltd./Beechwood Music Corp. QUEEN. 65, 73.

Father And Son. w&m; Cat Stevens. c1970, Freshwater Music Ltd./Ackee Music Inc. CAT STEVENS. 127.

Father Of Night. w&m; Bob Dylan. c1970, 76, Big Sky Music. BOB DYLAN. 170.

TITLE INDEX

Fattening Frogs For Snakes. w&m; "Sonny Boy" Williamson. c1964, Arc Music Corp. "SONNY BOY" WILLIAMSON. 1.

Feel Like Makin' Love. w&m; Eugene McDaniels. c1973, Skyforest Music Co., Inc. BAD COMPANY/ ROBERTA FLACK. 93.

Feelin' Alright. w&m; Dave Mason. c1968, 70, Island Music Ltd./Irving Music, Inc. JOE COCKER & THE GREASE BAND. 202.

Feelin' Groovy SEE 59th Street Bridge Song.

Feelin' Stronger Every Day. w&m; Peter Cetera & James Pankow. c1973, Polish Prince Music, Moose Music & Big Elk Music. CHICAGO. 63, 77, 134.

Feelings. w&m; Morris Albert. c1974, 75, Editoria Augusta Ltda./Fermata International Melodies, Inc. MORRIS ALBERT/O'JAYS. 15, 21, 23, 56, 117, 128, 131, 138, 162, 193, 198.

Feelings. w&m; Rick Coonce, Warren Entner & Ken Fukomoto. c1968, Trousdale Music Publishers, Inc. GRASS ROOTS. 76.

Feels Like The First Time. w&m; Mick Jones. c1977, Somerset Music & Evansongs Ltd. FOREIGNER. 22, 127, 145, 175.

Fernando. w&m; Benny Andersson, Stig Anderson & Bjorn Ulvaeus. c1975, Union Songs AB/ Artwork Music Co., Inc. ABBA. 128, 134, 141.

Fess Up To The Boogie. w&m; Gregg Diamond. c1978, 79, Arista Music, Inc. & Diamond Touch Productions Publishing Ltd. GREGG DIAMOND. 51.

Ffun. w&m; Mike Cooper. c1977, Val-le-Joe Music. CON FUNK SHUN. 135.

Fiddle And The Drum. w&m; Joni Mitchell. c1969, Siquomb Publishing Co. JONI MITCHELL. 41.

Fiddler On The Roof. w&m; Jerry Bock (m) & Sheldon Harnick (w). c1964, Times Square Music Publications Co. CAST OF FIDDLER ON THE ROOF. 130.

Fifth Of Beethoven. w&m; Walter Murphy (m). c1976, RFT Music Publishing Corp. WALTER MURPHY BAND. 26, 34, 77, 121, 128, 135, 142.

59th Street Bridge Song. w&m; Paul Simon. c1966, Paul Simon. SIMON & GARFUNKEL. 143.

Fifty Ways To Leave Your Lover. w&m; Paul Simon. c1975, Paul Simon. PAUL SIMON. 131, 143, 147.

Fight SEE Main Event/Fight.

Final Acclaim SEE You're In My Heart.

Fine Old Foxy Self. w&m; James Brown. c1957, 68, Armo Music Corp. JAMES BROWN. 18.

Fingertips (Part 2). w&m; Clarence Paul & Henry Cosby. c1962, 63, Jobete Music Co., Inc. STEVIE WONDER. 123, 150.

Fins. w&m; Jimmy Buffett, Deborah McColl, Barry Chance & Tom Corcoran. c1979, Coral Reefer Music. JIMMY BUFFETT. 27, 147.

Fire. w&m; Bruce Springsteen. c1978, Bruce Springsteen. POINTER SISTERS. 57.

Fire And Rain. w&m; James Taylor. c1969, 70, Blackwood Music Inc. & Country Road Music Inc. Adminis-

tered by Blackwood Music Inc. ANNE MURRAY/ CHER/ISLEY BROTHERS/JAMES TAYLOR/WILLIE NELSON. 21, 59, 68, 116, 148, 165, 183, 198.

Fire In The Morning. w&m; Gary Harju, Larry Herbstritt & Stephen H. Dorff. c1979, 80, Cotton Pickin' Songs & Hobby Horse Music. MELISSA MANCHESTER. 23, 45, 99.

Fire Island. w&m; H. Belolo (w), P. Whitehead (w), P. Hurtt (w) & J. Morali (m). c1977, Scorpio Music (Black Scorpio). Controlled by Can't Stop Music. VILLAGE PEOPLE. 200.

Fire Lake. w&m; Bob Seger. c1979, 80, Gear Publishing Co. BOB SEGER & THE SILVER BULLET BAND. 22, 188.

Fire On The Mountain. w&m; George McCorkle. c1975, No Exit Music Co., Inc. MARSHALL TUCKER BAND. 30, 36.

First Time Ever I Saw Your Face. w&m; Ewan MacColl. c1962, 65, 72, Stormking Music Inc. GORDON LIGHTFOOT/PETER, PAUL & MARY/ROBERTA FLACK/SHIRLEY BASSEY. 21, 58, 64, 68, 72, 89, 111, 131, 134, 140, 163, 194, 195.

Five Hundred Miles. w&m; Hedy West. c1961, 62, Atzal Music, Inc. PETER, PAUL & MARY. 68, 93.

5. 7. 0. 5. w&m; Steve Broughton & Lol Mason. c1978, Chappell & Co., Inc. CITY BOY. 50.

5-10-15 Hours. w&m; Rudolph Toombs. c1952, Progressive Music Publishing Co., Inc. Controlled by Unichappell Music, Inc. RUTH BROWN. 154, 155.

Flip, Flop & Fly. w&m; Charles E. Calhoun & Lou Willie Turner. c1955, Hill & Range Songs, Inc. & Progressive Music Publishing Co., Inc. Controlled by Unichappell Music, Inc. JOE TURNER. 91, 137, 154, 155.

Float On. w&m; Marvin Willis, Arnold Ingram & James Mitchell. c1977, Duchess Music Corp. & Woodsongs Music. FLOATERS. 142.

Floods Of Florence. w&m; Phil Ochs. c1968, Barricade Music, Inc. PHIL OCHS. 144.

Flower In The Sun. w&m; Sam Andrew. c1972, Cheap Thrills Music Co. JANIS JOPLIN. 110.

Flower Lady. w&m; Phil Ochs. c1966, 68, Barricade Music, Inc. PHIL OCHS. 144.

Flowers Never Bend With The Rainfall. w&m; Paul Simon. c1965, Paul Simon. SIMON & GARFUNKEL. 143.

Flowers Of Evil. w&m; Leslie West, David Rea & Felix Pappalardi. c1971, Upfall Music Corp. MOUNTAIN. 152.

Fly Like An Eagle. w&m; Steve Miller. c1976, Sailor Music. STEVE MILLER BAND. 127, 136, 145.

Fly, Robin, Fly. w&m; Sylvester Levay & Stephen Prager. c1975, Edition Meridian-Butterfly. Administered by Midsong Music, Inc. SILVER CONVENTION. 103.

Flying High. w&m; Thomas McClary & Lionel Richie. c1978, Jobete Music Co., Inc. & Commodores Entertainment Publishing Corp. COMMODORES. 74.

35

Flying On The Ground Is Wrong. w&m; Neil Young. c1966, 74, Cotillion Music, Inc., Ten East Music & Springalo Toones. BUFFALO SPRINGFIELD. 39.

FM. w&m; Donald Fagen & Walter Becker. c1978, Feckless Music, Jump Tunes & Duchess Music. STEELY DAN. 57, 87, 146.

Follow. w&m; Jerry Merrick. c1966, 72, Unart Music Corp. RICHIE HAVENS. 37.

Follow That Dream. w&m; Fred Wise (w) & Ben Weisman (m). c1962, Gladys Music Inc. ELVIS PRESLEY. 172.

Fool, Fool, Fool. w&m; A. Nugetre. c1952, Progressive Music Publishing Co., Inc. Controlled by Chappell Music, Inc. CLOVERS. 155.

Fool No. I. w&m; Kathryn R. Fulton. c1961, Sure-Fire Music Co., Inc. BRENDA LEE. 6.

Fool On The Hill. w&m; John Lennon & Paul McCartney. c1967, Northern Songs Ltd./Maclen Music, Inc. BEATLES. 138.

Fooled By A Feeling. w&m; Dennis W. Morgan & Kye Fleming. c1979, Pi-Gem Music, Inc. BARBARA MANDRELL. 56.

Fools Fall In Love. w&m; Jerry Leiber & Mike Stoller. c1957, Tiger Music Inc. DRIFTERS/ELVIS PRESLEY. 91.

Fool's Paradise. w&m; Sonny Le Glaire, Horace Linsley & Norman Petty. c1958, MPL Communications, Inc. BUDDY HOLLY. 14.

Fools Rush In. w&m; Johnny Mercer & Rube Bloom. c1940, 68, Bregman, Vocco & Conn, Inc. Renewed by John H. Mercer. RICKY NELSON. 4.

For A Dancer. w&m; Jackson Browne. c1974, 75, WB Music Corp. JACKSON BROWNE. 141.

For All We Know. w&m; Robb Wilson (w), Arthur James (w) & Fred Karlin (m). c1970, ABC-Dunhill Music, Inc. CARPENTERS/ROBERTA FLACK. 64, 89, 128, 131.

For Crying Out Loud. w&m; Jim Steinman. c1977, Edward B. Marks Music Corp., Neverland Music Co. & Peg Music Co. MEATLOAF. 120.

For Emily, Whenever I May Find Her. w&m; Paul Simon. c1966, Paul Simon. SIMON & GARFUNKEL. 143.

For Everyman. w&m; Jackson Browne. c1973, 75, Benchmark Music. JACKSON BROWNE. 139.

For Lovin' Me. w&m; Gordon Lightfoot. c1964, 65 M. Witmark & Sons & Warner Bros., Inc. GORDON LIGHTFOOT/IAN & SYLVIA/PETER, PAUL & MARY. 35, 43, 67, 139.

For More Reasons Than One SEE Ain't That Loving You?

For Once In My Life. w&m; Ronald Miller (w) & Orlando Murden (m). c1965, 67, 69, 70, 73, Jobete Music Co., Inc. FOUR TOPS/GLADYS KNIGHT & THE PIPS/ JACKIE WILSON/STEVIE WONDER. 17, 24, 53, 71, 123, 130, 134, 154, 183.

For The Good Times. w&m; Kris Kristofferson. c1968, Buckhorn Music Publishers, Inc. KRIS KRISTOFFERSON/RAY PRICE. 63, 86, 88, 93.

For The Love Of Him. w&m; Bobbi Martin & Al Mortimer. c1969, 70, United Artists Music Co., Inc. & Teeger Music Co. Administered by United Artists Music Co., Inc. BOBBI MARTIN. 21, 81, 191.

For The Love Of Money. w&m; Kenny Gamble, Leon Huff & Anthony Jackson. c1974, Mighty Three Music. O'JAYS. 52.

For The Roses. w&m; Joni Mitchell. c1972, 73, Crazy Crow Music. JONI MITCHELL. 139.

For What It's Worth. w&m; Stephen Stills. c1966, 67, Cotillion Music, Inc., Ten East Music & Springalo Toones. BUFFALO SPRINGFIELD. 39, 115, 138, 141, 151.

For You, Blue. w&m; George Harrison. c1970, Harrisongs Ltd./Harrisongs Music, Inc. BEATLES. 125.

For Your Love. w&m; Ed Townsend. c1958, Beechwood Music Corp. GWEN MC CRAE/PEACHES & HERB. 128.

For Your Precious Love. w&m; Arthur Brooks, Richard Brooks & Jerry Butler. c1958, 68, Sunflower Music, Inc. JACKIE WILSON/OSCAR TONEY, JR. 168.

Forever Came Today. w&m; Brian Holland, Lamont Dozier & Eddie Holland. c1968, 74, 75, Jobete Music Co., Inc. SUPREMES. 95.

Forever In Blue Jeans. w&m; Neil Diamond & Richard Bennett. c1978, 79, Stonebridge Music. NEIL DIAMOND. 27, 147.

Forever Mine. w&m; Kenneth Gamble & Leon Huff. c1979, Mighty Three Music. O'JAYS. 24, 98.

Forever Young. w&m; Bob Dylan. c1973, 76, Ram's Horn Music. BOB DYLAN. 170.

Forget To Remember w&m; Teddy Randazzo & Victoria Pike. c1969, 70, Razzle Dazzle Music Inc. FRANK SINATRA. 63.

Fortunate Son. w&m; J.C. Fogerty. c1969, Jondora Music. CREEDENCE CLEARWATER REVIVAL. 157.

Found A Cure. w&m; Nickolas Ashford & Valerie Simpson. c1979, Nick-O-Val Co., Inc. ASHFORD & SIMPSON. 27.

Fountain Of Sorrow. w&m; Jackson Browne. c1974, 76, Warner Bros. Music Corp. JACKSON BROWNE/JOAN BAEZ. 30, 36.

4 + 20. w&m; Stephen Stills. c1969, 71, Gold Hill Music Inc. CROSBY, STILLS, NASH & YOUNG. 203.

Four Sticks. w&m; Jimmy Page & Robert Plant. c1972, 73, Superhype Publishing. LED ZEPPELIN. 114.

Four Strong Winds. w&m; Ian Tyson. c1963, 78, Warner Bros. Inc. BOBBY BARE/IAN & SYLVIA/NEIL YOUNG. 27, 36, 67.

Four Walls. w&m; Marvin Moore & George Campbell. c1957, Unart Music Corp. JIM REEVES/RONNIE MILSAP. 79.

Four Wheel Drive. w&m; Blair Thornton & Randy Bachman. c1975, Ranbach Music & Screen Gems-EMI Music Inc. BACHMAN-TURNER OVERDRIVE. 142.

Fourth Of July (Sandy). w&m; Bruce Springsteen. c1973, Laurel Canyon Music Ltd. BRUCE SPRINGSTEEN/HOLLIES. 37, 199.

Fourth Time Around. w&m; Bob Dylan. c1966, 67, Dwarf Music. BOB DYLAN. 170.

Fox. w&m; Odetta Gordon (Adapted & arranged). c1968, Warner Bros.-Seven Arts Inc. ODETTA. 132.

Fox On The Run. w&m; Brian Connolly, Steve Priest, Mick Tucker & Andy Scott. c1974, 75, 77, Sweet Publishing Ltd./WB Music Corp. SWEET. 77, 141, 142, 175.

Frankenstein. w&m; Edgar Winter. c1972, 74, Hierophant, Inc. EDGAR WINTER GROUP. 53, 105, 156.

Frankfort Special. w&m; Sid Wayne (w) & Sherman Edwards (m). c1960, Gladys Music, Inc. ELVIS PRESLEY. 173.

Frankie And Johnnie. w&m; Fred Karger (New words & arranged), Alex Gottlieb (New words & arranged) & Ben Weisman (New words & arranged). c1966, Gladys Music, Inc. ELVIS PRESLEY. 173.

Frankie's Blues. w&m; Dave Van Ronk. c1968, Warner Bros.-Seven Arts, Inc. DAVE VAN RONK. 132.

Franklin's Tower. w&m; Robert Hunter, Jerry Garcia & William Kreutzmann. c1967, 75 Ice Nine Publishing Co., Inc. GRATEFUL DEAD. 84.

Fraulein. w&m; Lawton Williams. c1956, 57, Unart Music Corp. BOBBY HELMS. 82.

Frederick. w&m; Patti Smith. c1979, Ninja Music. PATTI SMITH GROUP. 11.

Free As The Wind. w&m; Sal Trimachi, Jerry Kasenetz & Jeff Katz. c1969, 70, Kaskat Music, Inc. BROOKLYN BRIDGE. 186.

Free Man. w&m; Bunny Sigler & Ronnie Tyson. c1975, Mighty Three Music. Administered by Blackwood Music, Inc. SOUTH SHORE COMMISSION. 49.

Free Man In Paris. w&m; Joni Mitchell. c1973, 74, Crazy Crow Music. JONI MITCHELL. 36, 139.

Free Me From My Freedom. w&m; Angelo Bond & Truman Thomas. c1977, Stone Diamond Music Corp. BONNIE POINTER. 34, 66.

Free Ride. w&m; Dan Hartman. c1972, 74, Silver Steed Music, Inc. EDGAR WINTER GROUP. 105.

Free The People. w&m; Barbara Keith. c1970, Leo Feist, Inc. OLIVIA NEWTON-JOHN. 82.

Free (Wanna Be Free). w&m; J. Deniece Williams, Hank Redd, Nathan Watts & Susaye Greene. c1975, 77, Kee-Drick. DENIECE WILLIAMS. 127.

Freeways. w&m; Randy Bachman. c1977, Ranbach Music, a division of R.C.B. Ltd. Controlled by Screen Gems-EMI Music Inc. BACHMAN-TURNER OVERDRIVE. 121.

Freight Train. w&m; Paul James & Fred Williams. c1957, Pan-Musik Co./Peter Maurice Music Co., Ltd. PETER, PAUL & MARY. 149.

Friday Night SEE Livin' It Up.

Friday On My Mind. w&m; George Young & Harry Vanda. c1966, 67, J. Albert & Son Pty, Ltd./Unart Music Corp. CHILLY/DAVID BOWIE/EASYBEATS. 81.

Friend Is Dying. w&m; Terry Cashman & T.P. West.

c c1971, 72, Blendingwell Music, Inc. CASHMAN & WEST. 37.

Friend Of The Devil. w&m; Jerry Garcia (m), John Dawson (m) & Robert Hunter (w). c1970, 73, Ice Nine Publishing Co. GRATEFUL DEAD. 83, 136.

Friends. w&m; Jimmy Page & Robert Plant. c1970, 73, Superhype Publishing. LED ZEPPELIN. 114.

From Me To You. w&m; John Lennon & Paul McCartney. c1963, Northern Songs Ltd./Gil Music Corp. BEATLES. 93, 102, 125, 137.

From The Inside. w&m; Alice Cooper, Bernie Taupin, Dick Wagner & David Foster. c1978, 79, Ezra Music, Jodrell Music, Inc., Candlewood Mountain Music Corp. & Foster Frees Music, Inc. ALICE COOPER. 27.

Full Speed Ahead. w&m; Wade Brown, Jr., David H. Jones, Jr. & Robert Bullock. c1975, 76, Jobete Music Co., Inc. TATA VEGA. 95.

Funk #49. w&m; James Kent, Dale Thomas Peters & Joseph Fidler Walsh. c1970, Pamco Music, Inc. & Home Made Music. JAMES GANG. 88.

Funky Street. w&m; Arthur Conley & Earl Simms. c1968, Redwal Music Co., Inc.-Time Music Co., Inc. ARTHUR CONLEY. 76.

Funny Face. w&m; Donna Fargo. c1967, 72, Prima-Donna Music Co. DONNA FARGO. 138.

Gallow Pole. w&m; Jimmy Page & Robert Plant. c1971, 73, Superhype Publishing. LED ZEPPELIN. 114.

Gambler. w&m; Don Schlitz. c1978, Writers Night Music. KENNY ROGERS. 23, 56, 65, 71, 73, 130, 134, 179.

Game Of Love. w&m; Clint Ballard, Jr. c1964, Skidmore Music Co., Inc. WAYNE FONTANA & THE MINDBENDERS. 4

Games People Play. w&m; Joe South. c1968, 70, Lowery Music Co., Inc. JOE SOUTH. 149, 161.

Garden Party. w&m; Rick Nelson. c1972, Matragun Music. RICK NELSON. 37, 131, 156, 194.

Gas Lamps And Clay. w&m; Skip Konte & Dennis Correll (w). c1970, Portofino Music & ATM Music. BLUES IMAGE. 88.

Gates Of Eden. w&m; Bob Dylan. c1965, M. Witmark & Sons. BOB DYLAN. 100.

Gee. w&m; Morris Levy & William E. Davis. c1954, Big Seven Music Corp. CROWS. 155.

Gee Whiz. w&m; Carla Thomas. c1960, 73, East-Memphis Music. CARLA THOMAS. 122.

Genius I. w&m; Nickolas Ashford & Valerie Simpson. c1972, Jobete Music Co., Inc. VALERIE SIMPSON. 13.

Gentle On My Mind. w&m; John Hartford. c1967, 71, Glaser Publications, Inc. GLEN CAMPBELL. 72, 76, 191, 192, 194.

George Jackson. w&m; Bob Dylan. c1971, 76, Ram's Horn Music. BOB DYLAN. 170.

Georgia On My Mind. w&m; Stuart Gorrell (w) & Hoagy Carmichael (m). c1930, Peer International Corp. BAND/BOBBY BLAND. 179.

Georgy Girl. w&m; Jim Dale & Tom Springfield. c1966, Springfield Music Ltd./Chappell & Co., Inc. SEEKERS. 68.

Get A Job. w&m; Silhouettes. c1957, Wildcat Music, Inc. & Dandelion Music Co. SILHOUETTES. 4.

Get Back. w&m; John Lennon & Paul McCartney. c1969, Northern Songs Ltd./Maclen Music, Inc. BEATLES/BILLY PRESTON. 61, 146, 179, 197.

Get Closer. w&m; James Seals & Dash Crofts. c1976, Dawnbreaker Music Co. SEALS & CROFTS FEATURING CAROLYN WILLIS. 62, 141.

Get Dancin'. w&m; Bob Crewe & Kenny Nolan. c1974, Heart's Delight Music Co., Kenny Nolan Publishing Co. & Coral Rock Music Corp. DISCO TEX & HIS SEX-O-LETTES. 49, 89.

Get Down. w&m; Curtis Mayfield. c1971, Curtom Publishing Co. CURTIS MAYFIELD. 104.

Get Down. w&m; James Thompson. c1978, Cachand Music, Inc., Cissi Music & Gaetana Music. GENE CHANDLER. 34, 65, 66, 112.

Get Down Tonight. w&m; H.W. Casey & R. Finch. c1975, Sherlyn PUblishing Co., Inc. KC & THE SUNSHINE BAND. 26, 29, 34, 77.

Get It Right Next Time. w&m; Gerry Rafferty. c1979 Colgems-EMI Music Inc. GERRY RAFFERTY. 11.

Get Off. w&m; C. Driggs & L. Ledesma. c1978, Sherlyn Publishing Co., Inc. & Lindseyanne Music. Administered by Sherlyn Publishing Co., Inc. FOXY. 74, 135.

Get Ready. w&m; William Robinson. c1966, Jobete Music Co., Inc. RARE EARTH. 105, 123.

Get Together. w&m; Chet Powers. c1963, Irving Music Inc. YOUNGBLOODS. 68.

Get Up, Jake. w&m; J. Robbie Robertson. c1969, 70, Canaan Music, Inc. BAND. 151.

Get Used To It. w&m; Michael Omartian & Roger Voudouris. c1979, Spike's Music & See This House Music. ROGER VOUDOURIS. 27.

Get Your Rocks Off. w&m; Bob Dylan. c1968, 76, Dwarf Music. AVIATOR/MANFRED MANN. 170.

Getaway. w&m; Beloyd Taylor & Peter Dor. c1976, Mburu Music. EARTH, WIND & FIRE. 16.

Gettin' Ready For Love. w&m; Tom Snow & Frannie Golde. c1977, Braintree Music, Goldees Gold Publishing Co. & Snow Music. DIANA ROSS. 48.

G.I. Blues. w&m; Sid Tepper & Roy C. Bennett. c1960, Gladys Music, Inc. ELVIS PRESLEY. 172.

Gidget. w&m; Patti Washington & Fred Karger. c1958, Shapiro, Bernstein & Co., Inc. JAMES DARREN. 4.

Gilgarra Mountain. w&m; Peter Yarrow. (Adapted & arranged.) c1965, Pepamar Music Corp. PETER, PAUL & MARY. 67, 132.

Gimme Dat Ding. w&m; Mike Hazelwood & Albert Hammond. c1970, Shaftesbury Music Ltd./Duchess Music Corp. PIPKINS. 94.

Gimme Little Sign. w&m; Alfred Smith, Joseph Hooven & Jerry Winn. c1968, Big Shot Music Inc. BRENTON WOOD. 93.

Gimme Shelter. w&m; Mick Jagger & Keith Richard. c1969, Abkco Music, Inc. ROLLING STONES. 142.

Gimme Some Lovin'. w&m; Steve & Muff Winwood & Spencer Davis. c1966, 80, Island Music Ltd./Island Music. BLUES BROTHERS/SPENCER DAVIS GROUP. 189.

Gimme Something Real. w&m; Nickolas Ashford & Valerie Simpson. c1973, 76, Nick-O-Val Music. ASHFORD & SIMPSON. 13.

Girl Of My Dreams. w&m; Ronald Thomas. c1979, Warner Bros. Music Ltd./WB Music Corp. BRAM TCHAIKOVSKY. 27.

Girl From The North Country. w&m; Bob Dylan. c1963, M. Witmark & Sons. BOB DYLAN. 138.

Girls' Song. w&m; Jim Webb. c1966, 70, Johnny Rivers Music. FIFTH DIMENSION. 60.

Give A Little Bit. w&m; Rick Davies & Roger Hodgson. c1977, Almo Music Corp. & Delicate Music. SUPERTRAMP. 12.

Give A Little More. w&m; Tom & Robert John Pedrick & Mike Piccirillo. c1978, Careers Music, Inc., High Sierra Music & Good Friday Music. ROBERT JOHN. 34.

Give It To Me. w&m; Peter Wolf & Seth Justman. c1973, Walden Music, Inc. & Juke Joint Music. J. GEILS BAND. 197.

Give It What You Got. w&m; Solomon Roberts, Jr. c1975, Triple "O" Songs, Inc. & Jeff-Mar Music Co. B.T. EXPRESS. 49.

Give Me Love. w&m; George Harrison. c1973, Material World Charitable Foundation. GEORGE HARRISON. 93.

Give Peace A Chance. w&m; John Lennon & Paul McCartney. c1969, Northern Songs Ltd./Maclen Music, Inc. JOHN LENNON. 61.

Give The People What They Want. w&m; Kenny Gamble & Leon Huff. c1975, Mighty Three Music, Administered by Blackwood Music Inc. O'JAYS. 49.

Glad All Over. w&m; Dave Clark & Mike Smith. c1958, Ivy Music, Ltd./Campbell-Connelly Inc. DAVE CLARK FIVE. 3.

Glimpses Of Nirvana. w&m; Gary Brooker, Matthew Fisher & Keith Reid. c1968, 72, Essex Music International Ltd./TRO Andover Music, Inc. PROCOL HARUM. 42.

Gloria. w&m; Mike Stokes & Emanuel Johnson. c1976, 77, Desert Moon Songs, Ltd., Willow Girl Music Co. & Desert Rain Music Ltd. ENCHANTMENT. 196.

Go All The Way. w&m; Eric Carmen. c1972, C.A.M.-U.S.A., Inc. RASPBERRIES. 62.

Go And Say Goodbye. w&m; Stephen Stills. c1966, 75, Cotillion Music, Inc., Ten East Music, Springalo Toones & Spinnaker Music Co. BUFFALO SPRINGFIELD. 39.

Go Away Little Girl. w&m; Gerry Goffin & Carole King. c1962, Screen Gems-EMI Music, Inc. DONNY

OSMOND/HAPPENINGS/JANIS IAN/STEVE LAW-RENCE. 38, 130.

Go Down Gamblin'. w&m; David Clayton Thomas (w) & Fred Lipsius (m). c1971, Blackwood Music & Minnesingers Publications, Ltd. BLOOD, SWEAT & TEARS. 104

Go My Way. w&m; Gordon Lightfoot. c1966, 71, Warner Bros., Inc. GORDON LIGHTFOOT. 35, 43.

Go West. w&m; J. Morali, H. Belolo & V. Willis. c1979, Scorpio Music (Black Scorpio). Controlled by Can't Stop Music. VILLAGE PEOPLE. 187.

Go Where You Wanna Go. w&m; John Phillips. c1965, Trousdale Music Publishers, Inc. MAMAS & THE PAPAS. 119.

Go Your Own Way. w&m; Lindsey Buckingham. c1976, 77, 78, Gentoo Music, Michael Fleetwood & Now Sounds Music. Administered by Warner-Tamerlane Publishing Corp. FLEETWOOD MAC. 22, 121, 124, 133, 136, 145.

God Save The Queen. w&m; Johnny Rotten, Steven Jones, Paul Cook & Glen Matlock. c1978, Glitterbest Ltd. & Glen Matlock. SEX PISTOLS. 19.

Goin' Back To Indiana. Corporation. c1970, Jobete Music Co., Inc. JACKSON 5. 20.

Goin' Down Slow. w&m; J. Oden. c1942, 70, Arc Music Corp. BOBBY BLAND/CANNED HEAT. 1, 169.

Goin' Home. w&m; Alan, Wayne & Merrill Osmond. c1973, Kolob Music Co. OSMONDS. 93.

Goin' Out Of My Head. w&m; Teddy Randazzo & Bobby Weinstein. c1964, 1967, South Mountain Music Corp. Assigned to Vogue Music, Inc. LITTLE ANTHONY & THE IMPERIALS. 78, 102, 160.

Goin' To Acapulco. w&m; Bob Dylan. c1975, Dwarf Music. BOB DYLAN & THE BAND. 170.

Goin' Up In Smoke. w&m; Allan Felder & Norman Harris. c1976, Stone Diamond Music Corp. EDDIE KENDRICKS. 95.

Goin' Up The Country. w&m; Alan Wilson. c1968, Metric Music Co. CANNED HEAT. 202.

Going, Going, Gone. w&m; Bob Dylan. c1973, 76, Ram's Horn Music. BOB DYLAN/BOB DYLAN & THE BAND. 170.

Going To A Go Go. William Robinson, Warren Moore, Robert Rogers & Marv Tarplin. c1965, 66, Jobete Music Co., Inc. MIRACLES. 123.

Going To California. w&m; Jimmy Page & Robert Plant. c1972, Superhype Publishing. LED ZEPPE-LIN. 114.

Golden Loom. w&m; Bob Dylan. c1975, 76, Ram's Horn Music. BOB DYLAN. 170.

Goldfinger. w&m; Leslie Bricusse (w), Anthony Newley (w) & John Barry (m). c1964, United Artists Music Ltd. Assigned to Unart Music Corp. SHIRLEY BASSEY. 102.

Gone At Last. w&m; Paul Simon. c1975, Paul Simon. DONNA FARGO/JOHNNY PAYCHECK/PAUL SIMON. 143.

Gone, Gone, Gone. w&m; Boz Burrell. c1978, 79, Badco Music, Inc. BAD COMPANY. 22, 147.

Gone Too Far. w&m; John Ford Coley. c1977, Dawn-breaker Music Co. & Cold Zinc Music. ENGLAND DAN & JOHN FORD COLEY. 127.

Gone With The Wind, Theme From SEE My Own True Love.

Gonna Find Me An Angel SEE Angel (Sander & Franklin).

Gonna Fly Now. w&m; Carol Connors (w), Ayn Robbins (w) & Bill Conti (m). c1976, 77, United Artists Corp. Administered by United Artists Music Co. & Unart Music Corp. BILL CONTI/MAYNARD FERGUSON/RHYTHM HERITAGE. 15, 21, 37, 79, 131, 140, 193, 196, 199.

Gonna Get Along Without Ya Now. w&m; Milton Kellem c1952, 68, Reliance Music Corp. Assigned Bibo Music Publishers. PATIENCE & PRUDENCE. 78, 101, 160.

Gonna Get Back Home Somehow. w&m; Doc Pomus & Mort Shuman. c1962, Elvis Presley Music, Inc. ELVIS PRESLEY. 173.

Gonna Love You More. w&m; Morris Albert. c1974, Editora Augusta Ltda./Fermata International Melodies Inc. & Sunbury Music Inc. GEORGE BENSON. 142.

Gonna Try. w&m; James Brown. c1956, 58, Armo Music Corp. JAMES BROWN. 18.

Good Day Sunshine. w&m; John Lennon & Paul McCart-ney. c1966, Northern Songs Ltd./Maclen Music, Inc. BEATLES. 35, 127.

Good Friend. w&m; Norman Gimbel (w) & Elmer Bernstein (m). c1979, Bernal Music Inc., ASG Music Co., Haliburton Music & Summer Camp Music Publishing. MARY MAC GREGOR. 176.

Good Girls Don't. w&m; Doug Fieger. c1979, Eighties Music. KNACK. 22, 27, 87, 147.

Good Golly Miss Molly. w&m; Robert Blackwell & John Marascalco. c1957, 64, Venice Music, Inc. BEATLES/LARRY WILLIAMS/LITTLE RICHARD. 35, 93, 137, 197.

Good Good Lovin'. w&m; James Brown & Albert Shubert. c1959, 68, Wisto Publishing Co. JAMES BROWN. 18.

Good Hearted Woman. w&m; Waylon Jennings & Willie Nelson. c1971, Baron Music Publishing Co. & Willie Nelson Publishing Co. WAYLON JENNINGS. 142.

Good Lovin'. w&m; Rudy Clark & Art Resnick. c1965, 79, The Hudson Bay Music Co. GRATEFUL DEAD. 73.

Good Luck Charm. w&m; Aaron Schroeder & Wally Gold. c1962, Gladys Music, Inc. ELVIS PRESLEY. 172.

Good Morning Heartache. w&m; Dan Fisher, Irene Higginbotham & Ervin Drake. c1965, 72, Northern Music Co. Renewed Fred Fisher Music Co., Inc. DIANA ROSS. 48.

Good Morning, Little School Girl. w&m; "Sonny Boy" Williamson. c1964, Arc Music Corp. YARDBIRDS. 1.

Good Morning, Little School Girl. w&m; Don Level & Bob Love. c1961, 64, Arc Music Corp. JOHNNY

WINTER/ROD STEWART. 10, 44, 169.

Good Morning Starshine. w&m; James Rado (w), Gerome Ragni (w) & Galt MacDermot (m). c1966, 67, 68, 69, James Rado, Gerome Ragni, Galt MacDermot, Nat Shapiro & United Artists Music Co., Inc. Controlled by United Artists Music Co., Inc. CAST OF HAIR/ LIZA MINELLI/OLIVER. 81, 102, 140.

Good Night Sweetheart. w&m; Ray Noble, Jimmy Campbell & Reg Connelly. c1931, 59, 66, Campbell, Connelly & Co., Ltd./Robbins Music Corp. MANT-OVANI/VAUGHN MONROE/ZOOT SIMS. 140.

Good Sculptures. w&m; John Callis. c1978, Bleu Disque Music Co. REZILLOS. 19.

Good Time Charlie's Got The Blues. w&m; Danny O'Keefe. c1968, 72, Warner-Tamerlane Publishing Corp. & Road Canon Music, Inc. DANNY O'KEEFE/ ELVIS PRESLEY/JERRY LEE LEWIS. 30, 43, 138, 139, 151.

Good Times. w&m; Nile Rodgers & Bernard Edwards. c1979, Chic Music, Inc. Administered by Warner-Tamerlane Publishing Corp. CHIC. 27, 31, 57, 147.

Good Times Bad Times. w&m; Jimmy Page, John Paul Jones & John Bonham. c1969, Superhype Publishing. LED ZEPPELIN. 114.

Good Times Roll. w&m; Ric Ocasek. c1978, 79, Lido Music, Inc. CARS. 27, 147.

Good Timin'. w&m; Brian Wilson & Carl Wilson (w). c1979, Brother Publishing Co., New Executive Music & Murry Gage Music. BEACH BOYS. 96.

Good Timin'. w&m; Clint Ballard, Jr. & Fred Tobias. c1960, United Artists Music Co., Inc. JIMMY JONES. 78, 102, 155.

Goodbye. w&m; John Lennon & Paul McCartney. c1969. Northern Songs Ltd./Maclen Music, Inc. MARY HOPKIN. 61.

Goodbye Girl. w&m; David Gates. c1977, Metro-Goldwyn-Mayer, Inc. & Warner Bros., Inc. DAVID GATES. 87, 201.

Goodbye I Love You. w&m; Rick Roberts. c1977, 79, Stephen Stills Music. FIREFALL. 27, 146.

Goodbye Stranger. w&m; Roger Hodgson & Rick Davies. c1979, Almo Music Corp. & Delicate Music. Ad-ministered by Almo Music Corp. SUPERTRAMP. 11, 56, 75.

Goodbye To Rome SEE Arrivederci, Roma.

Goodbye Yellow Brick Road. w&m; Elton John & Bernie Taupin. c1973, Dick James Music Ltd./Dick James Music Inc. ELTON JOHN. 36, 55, 62, 124, 136, 138, 141, 174, 175, 183.

Goodnight Irene. w&m; Huddie Ledbetter & John A. Lomax. c1936, 50, 64, Ludlow Music, Inc. PETE SEEGER/WEAVERS. 37, 85.

Goodnight, It's Time To Go. w&m; Calvin Carter & James Hudson. c1953, 54, Arc Music Corp. JAY HUDSON/JOHNNY & JACK/SPANIELS. 2, 5, 101, 168, 169.

Goodnight, Sweetheart, Goodnight SEE Goodnight, It's Time To Go.

Goodnight, Well, It's Time To Go SEE Goodnight, It's Time To Go.

Gospel Boogie SEE Wonderful Time Up There.

Got A Feeling. w&m; John Phillips & Dennis Doherty. c1966, Trousdale Music Publishers, Inc. MAMAS & THE PAPAS. 119.

Got A Job. w&m; Berry Gordy, Tyran Carlo & William "Smokey" Robinson. c1958, Jobete Music Co., Inc. SMOKEY ROBINSON & THE MIRACLES. 150.

Got A Lot O' Livin' To Do. w&m; Aaron Schroeder & Ben Wwisman. c1957, Gladys Music, Inc. ELVIS PRESLEY. 173.

Got My Mo-Jo Working. w&m; Preston Foster. c1958, Preston Foster. Assigned to Dare Music Inc. JIMMY SMITH. 4.

Got To Be Real. w&m; David Paich, Cheryl Lynn & David Foster. c1978, 79, Hudmar Publishing Co., Inc., Butterfly-Gong Music & Cotaba Music. CHERYL LYNN. 27.

Got To Be There. w&m; Elliot Willensky. c1971, 72, Jobete Music Co., Inc. & Glenwood Music Corp. JACKSON 5/MICHAEL JACKSON. 20, 138.

Got To Believe In Love. w&m; Neil Goldberg. c1970, Top Floor Music. ROBIN MC NAMARA. 88.

Got To Get You Into My Life. w&m; John Lennon & Paul McCartney. c1966, Northern Songs, Ltd./ Maclen Music, Inc. BEATLES/EARTH, WIND & FIRE. 16, 35, 61, 62, 141, 145.

Got To Give It Up (Part I). w&m; Marvin Gaye. c1977, Jobete Music Co., Inc. MARVIN GAYE. 164.

Got To Have Lovin'. w&m; Cerrone & Don Ray. c1978, Cerrone Music & Don Ray. Controlled by MTB Music, Inc. DON RAY. 25.

Gotta Be The One. w&m; Pierre Tubbs. c1976, Uni-versal Songs Ltd./Unart Music Corp. MAXINE NIGHTINGALE. 184.

Gotta Get Back To You. w&m; Tommy James & Bob King. c1970, Big Seven Music Corp. TOMMY JAMES & THE SHONDELLS. 186.

Gotta Serve Somebody. w&m; Bob Dylan. c1979, Special Rider Music. BOB DYLAN. 27, 147.

Gotta Travel On. w&m; Paul Clayton. c1958, Sanga Music, Inc. BOB DYLAN/LIMELITERS/NITTY GRITTY DIRT BAND. 68, 85.

Graduation Day. w&m; Noel Sherman (w) & Joe Sher-man (m). c1956, Unart Music Corp. ARBOR/BEACH BOYS/FOUR FRESHMEN. 78, 82.

Granada. w&m; Agustin Lara & Dorothy Dodd (w). c1932, 50, 59, Peer International Corp. & Southern Music Publishing Co. AL HIRT/FRANK SINATRA. 194.

Grand Finale. w&m; Gary Brooker, Matthew Fisher & Keith Reid. c1968, 72, Essex Music International Ltd./ TRO Andover Music, Inc. PROCOL HARUM. 42.

Grease. w&m; Barry Gibb. c1978, Brothers Gibb B.V./ Stigwood Music, Inc. Administered by Unichappell Music, Inc. FRANKIE VALLI. 40.

Great Balls Of Fire. w&m; Jack Hammer & Otis Blackwell. c1957, Hill And Range Songs, Inc. Assigned to Unichappell Music, Inc. JERRY LEE LEWIS. 2, 78, 101, 137.

Great Mandella. w&m; Peter Yarrow, Albert Grossman & Mary Travers. c1967, Pepamar Music Corp. PETER, PAUL & MARY. 35, 67, 132.

Great Pretender. w&m; Buck Ram. c1955, Panther Music Corp. PLATTERS. 3.

Greatest Love Of All. w&m; Linda Creed (w) & Michael Masser (m). c1977, Golden Torch Music Corp. & Gold Horizon Corp. Controlled by Colgems-EMI Music & Screen Gems-EMI Music Inc. GEORGE BENSON/ SHIRLEY BASSEY. 24, 71, 134, 142.

Green Eyed Lady. w&m; Jerry Corbetta, J.C. Phillips & David Riordan. c1970, Claridge Music, Inc. SUGARLOAF. 191.

Green Grass Starts To Grow. w&m; Hal David (w) & Burt Bacharach (m). c1970, Blue Seas Music, Inc. & J. C. Music Co. DIONNE WARWICK. 63.

Green, Green. w&m; Randy Sparks & Barry McGuire. c1963, New Christy Music Publishing Co. NEW CHRISTY MINSTRELS. 68.

Green Green Grass Of Home. w&m; Curly Putman. c1965, 70, Tree Publishing Co., Inc. BOBBY BARE/ ELVIS PRESLEY/JOAN BAEZ/TOM JONES. 93, 130, 135, 140, 179.

Green Monkey. w&m; Dewey Bunnell. c1973, WB Music Corp. AMERICA. 138.

Green Onions. w&m; Booker T. Jones, Steve Cropper, Lewis Steinberg & Al Jackson, Jr. c1962, 75, East-Memphis Music. BOOKER T. & THE M.G.'S. 122.

Greenback Dollar. w&m; Hoyt Axton & Ken Ramsey. c1962, 63, Irving Music, Inc. KINGSTON TRIO. 68.

Greenbacks. w&m; Renald Richard. c1954, Progressive Music Publishing Co., Inc. Controlled by Unichappell Music, Inc. RAY CHARLES. 90, 155.

Greenfields. w&m; Terry Gilkyson, Rich Dehr & Frank Miller. c1956, 60, Blackwood Music, Inc. BROTHERS FOUR. 68.

Groove Me. w&m; King Floyd. c1970, Malaco Music Co. KING FLOYD. 64.

Groovin'. w&m; Felix Cavaliere & Edward Brigati, Jr. c1967, 72, Downtown Music Co. & Slacsar Publishing Co., Ltd. Assigned to Coral Rock Music Corp. RASCALS. 21, 37, 72, 102, 140, 161, 163, 199.

Groovy Grubworm. w&m; Harlo Wilcox & B. Warren. c1969, Shelby Singleton Music, Inc. HARLO WILCOX & THE OAKIES. 191.

Growin'. w&m; Kenny Loggins & Ronnie Wilkins. c1974, 75, Gnossos Music, Savona Music & Sugartree Music. BARBARA STREISAND. 139.

G.T.O. w&m; John Wilkin. c1964, 80, Buckhorn Music Publishers. Used by permission of Charles Ryckman Music Publishing. RONNY & THE DAYTONAS. 5.

Guantanamera. w&m; Jose Marti (w), Hector Angulo (m, adapted) & Pete Seeger (m, adapted). c1963, 65, Fall River Music, Inc. JOAN BAEZ/PETE SEEGER/ SANDPIPERS. 85.

Guess Who. w&m; Jesse Belvin. c1959, Michelle Publishing Co. JESSE BELVIN. 3.

Guinnevere. w&m; David Crosby. c1968, 71, Guerilla Music Inc. CROSBY, STILLS, NASH & YOUNG. 203.

Guitar Man. w&m; David Gates. c1972, Kipahulu Music Co. Controlled by Colgems-EMI Music Inc. BREAD. 142.

Gwen (Congratulations). w&m; Ricci Mareno & Jerry Gillespie. c1971, Shenandoah Music. TOMMY OVER-STREET. 191.

Gypsy Good Time. w&m; Nick Gravenites. c1969, 70, Fourth Floor Music, Inc. NICK GRAVENITES. 149.

Gypsy Man. w&m; Sylvester Allen, Harold R. Brown, Morris Dickerson, Leroy "Lonnie" Jordan, Charles W. Miller, Lee Oskar & Howard Scott. c1973, Far Out Music, Inc. Controlled by United Artists Music Co., Inc. WAR. 194.

Gypsy Queen. w&m; Gabor Szabo. c1966, PAB Music Corp. SANTANA. 93.

Gypsy Woman. w&m; Curtis Mayfield. c1961, 69, Curtom Publishing Co., Inc. BRIAN HYLAND/ IMPRESSIONS. 63, 64.

Gypsys, Tramps And Thieves. w&m; Bob Stone. c1971, Peso Music. CHER. 64, 128, 135.

Ha Cha Cha (Funktion). w&m; Randy Muller. c1976, 77, Desert Moon Songs Ltd. & Jeffmar Music Co., Inc. BRASS CONSTRUCTION. 196, 199.

Half A Century High. w&m; Phil Ochs. c1968, Barricade Music, Inc. PHIL OCHS. 144.

Half Breed. w&m; Mary Dean (w) & Al Capps (m). c1973, Blue Monday Music. CHER. 63, 128, 135.

Half Moon. w&m; John & Johanna Hall. c1970, Hall Music & Jojohanna Music, divisions of Open End Music. JANIS JOPLIN. 110.

Half The Way. w&m; Ralph Murphy & Bobby Wood. c1978, Murfezongs Music & Chriswood Music. CRYSTAL GAYLE. 56, 97, 179, 180.

Halfway To Paradise. w&m; Gerry Goffin & Carole King. c1961, 68, Screen Gems-Columbia Music, Inc. BOBBY VINTON. 113.

Hallelujah Day. w&m; Christine Yarian (w) & Freddie Perren (m). c1973, Jobete Music Co., Inc. JACKSON 5. 20.

Hallelujah I Love Her (Him) So. w&m; Ray Charles. c1956, 59, Progressive Music Publishing Co. Controlled by Unichappell Music, Inc. (Belinda Music). RAY CHARLES. 91, 137, 155, 199.

Hammer Song SEE If I Had A Hammer.

Handbags And Gladrags. w&m; Mike D'Abo. c1967, 71, United Artists Music Ltd./United Artists Music Co., Inc. ROD STEWART. 81.

Hands Of Time. w&m; Alan & Marilyn Bergman (w) & Michel Legrand (m). c1972, Colgems-EMI Music Inc. JOHNNY MATHIS/MICHEL LEGRAND/SARAH VAUGHAN & MICHEL LEGRAND. 23, 56, 71, 130.

Handsome Johnny. w&m; Richard Havens & Louis
Goussett. c1967, 70, Unart Music Corp. RICHIE
HAVENS. 37, 202.

Handy Man. w&m; Otis Blackwell & Jimmy Jones.
c1959, 78, Unart Music Corp. DEL SHANNON/
JAMES TAYLOR/JIMMY JONES/OTIS BLACKWELL.
15, 21, 79, 102, 155, 199.

Hang On In There, Baby. w&m; Johnny W. Bristol.
c1974, Bushka Music. JOHNNY BRISTOL. 52.

Hang On Sloopy. w&m; Bert Russell & Wes Farrell.
c1964, Picture Music Publishing Corp., Wren Music
Co., Inc. & Robert Mellin Music Publishing Corp. MC
COYS. 4, 93.

Hangin' Round. w&m; Dan Hartman & Edgar White.
c1972, 74, Hierosphant, Inc. & Silver Steed Music,
Inc. EDGAR WINTER GROUP. 105.

Hanging On The Telephone. w&m; Jack Lee. c1978,
Red Admiral Music, Inc. & Monster Island Music.
BLONDIE. 33.

Hangman. w&m; Peter Yarrow (Adapted & arranged),
Paul Stookey (Adapted & arranged), Mary Travers
(Adapted & arranged), Milton Okun (Adapted &
arranged) & Joel Hendler (Adapted & arranged).
c1965, Pepamar Music Corp. PETER, PAUL & MARY.
67.

Happening. w&m; Eddie Holland (w), Lamont Dozier
(w), Brian Holland (w) & Frank De Vol (m). c1967,
Jobete Music Co., Inc. SUPREMES. 123.

Happier Than The Morning Sun. w&m; Stevie Wonder.
c1972, Jobete Music Co., Inc. & Black Bull Music, Inc.
CAPTAIN & TENNILLE. 142.

Happiest Girl In The Whole U.S.A. w&m; Donna Fargo.
c1971, 72, Prima Donna Music Co. DONNA FARGO.
89, 138, 163.

Happiness. w&m; Allen Toussaint. c1978, 79, Warner-
Tamerlane Publishing Corp. & Marsaint Music, Inc.
POINTER SISTERS. 27.

Happy. w&m; Mick Jagger & Keith Richard. c1972,
Promopub B.V. ROLLING STONES. 183.

Happy. w&m; Smokey Robinson (w) & Michel Legrand
(m). c1972, Jobete Music Co., Inc. BOBBY DARIN/
SMOKEY ROBINSON. 128.

Happy Anniversary. w&m; Beeb Birtles & David
Briggs (m). c1977, 78, Tumbleweed Music PTY.,
Ltd./Australian Tumbleweed Music. LITTLE RIVER
BAND. 201.

Happy Birthday Sweet Sixteen. w&m; Neil Sedaka &
Howard Greenfield. c1961, Screen Gems-EMI Music
Inc. NEIL SEDAKA. 158.

Happy Days Are Here Again. w&m; Jack Yellen (w)
& Milton Ager (m). c1929, Advanced Music Corp.
BARBARA STREISAND. 139.

Happy Ending, Theme From SEE What Are You Doing
The Rest Of Your Life.

Happy, Happy Birthday, Baby. w&m; Margo Sylvia &
Gilbert Lopez. c1956, 57, Arc Music Corp. TUNE
WEAVERS. 5, 78, 100, 101, 168, 169.

Happy Hooker. w&m; Tommy Aldridge. c1973, Pond
Tunes. BLACK OAK ARKANSAS. 105.

H.A.P.P.Y. Radio. w&m; Edwin Starr. c1979, ATV
Music Corp. & Zonal Music, Inc. EDWIN STARR. 159.

Happy Song. w&m; Otis Redding & Steve Cropper.
c1968, East-Memphis Music & Time Music Co., Inc.
OTIS REDDING. 122.

Happy Together. w&m; Garry Bonner & Alan Gordon.
c1966, 67, The Hudson Bay Music Co. CAPTAIN &
TENNILLE/TURTLES. 128, 130.

Harbor Lights. w&m; Boz Scaggs. c1976, Boz Scaggs
Music. BOZ SCAGGS. 146.

Hard Day's Night. w&m; John Lennon & Paul McCartney. c1964, Northern Songs Ltd./Maclen Music, Inc.
& Unart Music Corp. BEATLES. 35, 61, 127, 145,
159.

Hard Headed Woman. w&m; Claude DeMetruis. c1958,
Gladys Music. Controlled by Chappell & Co., Inc.
ELVIS PRESLEY. 155.

Hard Hearted Hannah. w&m; Jack Yellen, Milton Ager,
Bob Bigelow & Charles Bates. c1924, 55, Advanced
Music Corp. NITTY GRITTY DIRT BAND. 132.

Hard Knocks. w&m; Joy Byers. c1964, Elvis Presley
Music, Inc. ELVIS PRESLEY. 172.

Hard Loving Loser. w&m; Richard Farina. c1966, 67,
M. Witmark & Sons. JUDY COLLINS/MIMI &
RICHARD FARINA. 67.

Hard Luck. w&m; Ben Weisman & Sid Wayne. c1966,
Gladys Music, Inc. ELVIS PRESLEY. 173.

Hard Rain's Gonna Fall. w&m; Bob Dylan. c1963,
M. Witmark & Sons & Warner Bros. Inc. BOB DYLAN/
DICK WEISSMAN/JOAN BAEZ. 35, 43, 67, 100, 132,
138, 197.

Hard Rock Cafe. w&m; Carole King. c1977, Colgems-
EMI Music Inc. CAROLE KING. 134, 142.

Hard Times. w&m; Boz Scaggs. c1977, Boz Scaggs
Music. BOZ SCAGGS. 165.

Hard Work. w&m; John Handy. c1976, Hard Work
Music, Inc. JOHN HANDY. 141.

Harder They Fall. w&m; Phil Ochs. c1968, Barricade
Music, Inc. PHIL OCHS. 144.

Harvest. w&m; Neil Young. c1971, 75, Silver Fiddle.
NEIL YOUNG. 117.

Hasten Down The Wind. w&m; Warren Zevon. c1973,
77, Warner-Tamerlane Publishing Corp. & Dark Room
Music. LINDA RONSTADT. 141, 145.

Hats Off To Larry. w&m; Del Shannon. c1961, Mole
Hole Music. Administered by Bug Music Group.
DEL SHANNON. 4.

Hats Off To (Roy) Harper. w&m; Charles Obscure
(Arranged). c1971, 73, Superhype Publishing. LED
ZEPPELIN. 114.

Have A Good Time. w&m; Paul Simon. c1975, Paul
Simon. PAUL SIMON. 143.

Have You Ever Been (To Electric Ladyland). w&m;
Jimi Hendrix. c1968, Bella Godiva Music, Inc. JIMI
HENDRIX. 182, 203.

Have You Ever Seen The Rain? w&m; J. C. Fogerty.
c1970, 71, Jondora Music. CREEDENCE CLEAR-
WATER REVIVAL. 93.

Have You Heard. w&m; Lew Douglas, Frank Lavere & Roy Rodde. c1952, Brandom Music Co. DUPREES. 4.

Have You Never Been Mellow. w&m; John Farrar. c1974, 75, Jumbuck Music Ltd./Irving Music, Inc. BROTHERS FOUR/ISAAC HAYES & DIONNE WARWICK/OLIVIA NEWTON-JOHN. 36, 43, 58, 70, 131, 139.

Haven't Stopped Dancing Yet. w&m; Gloria Jones. c1978, Buckwheat Music & Old Eye Music. GONZALEZ. 25, 96.

Hawaii Five-O. w&m; Mort Stevens (m). c1969, Columbia Broadcasting System, Inc. Publishing rights vested in April Music, Inc. VENTURES. 21, 140, 161, 193.

Hazel. w&m; Bob Dylan. c1973, 76, Ram's Horn Music. BOB DYLAN & THE BAND. 170.

Hazy Shade Of Winter. w&m; Paul Simon. c1966, Paul Simon. SIMON & GARFUNKEL. 143.

He Ain't Heavy...He's My Brother. w&m; Bob Russell (w) & Bobby Scott (m). c1969, Harrison Music Corp. HOLLIES/NEIL DIAMOND/OSMONDS. 63, 93.

He Did With Me. w&m; Gloria Sklerov & Harry Lloyd. c1973, Senor Music. VICKI LAWRENCE. 32.

He Don't Love You (Like I Love You). w&m; Jerry Butler, Curtis Mayfield & Calvin Carter. c1960, 68, Conrad Music, a division of Arc Music Corp. JERRY BUTLER/TONY ORLANDO & DAWN. 78, 102, 128, 133, 139, 156, 168, 169.

He Will Break Your Heart SEE He Don't Love You (Like I Love You).

Head Games. w&m; Lou Gramm (w) & Mick Jones (m). c1979, Somerset Songs Publishing Inc. & Evansongs Ltd. FOREIGNER. 22, 27, 147, 188.

Hear Me Lord. w&m; George Harrison. c1970, Harrisongs Ltd./Harrisongs Music, Inc. GEORGE HARRISON. 125.

Heard It In A Love Song. w&m; Toy Caldwell. c1977, No Exit Music Co., Inc. MARSHALL TUCKER BAND. 127, 146.

Hearsay. w&m; John Colbert & Norman West. c1972, East-Memphis Music. SOUL CHILDREN. 122.

Heart And Soul. w&m; Frank Loesser & Hoagy Carmichael. c1938, Famous Music Corp. JAN & DEAN. 6.

Heart Hotels. w&m; Daniel Fogelberg. c1979, Hickory Grove Music. Administered by April Music Inc. DAN FOGELBERG. 116.

Heart Of Glass. w&m; Deborah Harry & Chris Stein. c1978, Rare Blue Music, Inc. & Monster Island Music. BLONDIE. 25, 33, 96, 129, 181, 198.

Heart Of Gold. w&m; Neil Young. c1971, 72, Silver Fiddle. NEIL YOUNG. 36, 55, 62, 133, 136, 138, 174, 185.

Heart Of Saturday Night. w&m; Tom Waits. c1974, Fifth Floor Music. TOM WAITS. 199.

Heart Of The Night. w&m; Paul Cotton. c1978, 79, Tarantula Music. POCO. 27.

Heartache Tonight. w&m; Don Henley, Glenn Frey, Bob Seger & J. D. Souther. c1979, Cass County Music, Red Cloud Music, Gear Publishing Co. & Ice Age Music. EAGLES. 22, 27, 31, 124, 147.

Heartaches By The Number. w&m; Harlan Howard. c1959, 70, Tree Publishing Co., Inc. JOHNNY TILLOTSON. 89.

Heartbeat. w&m; Bob Montgomery & Norman Petty. c1958, MPL Communications. BUDDY HOLLY. 14.

Heartbeat It's A Lovebeat. w&m; Greg Williams & Mike Kennedy (w). c1972, 73, Schine Music. TONY DE FRANCO. 194.

Heartbreak Hotel. w&m; Mae Boren Axton, Tommy Durden & Elvis Presley. c1956, Tree Publishing Co., Inc. ELVIS PRESLEY. 93, 156.

Heartbreaker. w&m; Cliff Wade & Geoff Gill. c1978, 80, GGA Limited/Dick James Music, Inc. PAT BENATAR. 22.

Heartbreaker. w&m; Jimmy Page, Robert Plant, John Paul Jones & John Bonham. c1969, Superhype Publishing. LED ZEPPELIN. 36, 114, 117, 141, 175.

Heartless. w&m; Ann & Nancy Wilson. c1977, How About Music. HEART. 135.

Heart Of Stone. w&m; Rudolph Jackson (m) & Eddy Ray (w). c1954, Regent Music Corp. BLUE RIDGE RANGERS/CHARMS. 78, 155, 169.

Heat Wave. w&m; Eddie Holland, Lamont Dozier & Brian Holland. c1963, 66, Jobete Music Co., Inc. LINDA RONSTADT/MARTHA & THE VANDELLAS. 29, 58, 77, 123, 142, 150.

Heaven Can Wait. w&m; Jim Steinman. c1977, Edward B. Marks Music Corp., Neverland Music Co., & Peg Music Co. MEATLOAF. 120.

Heaven Help Us All. w&m; Ronald Miller. c1970, Stein & Van Stock, Inc. STEVIE WONDER. 123.

Heaven Knows. w&m; Donna Summer, Giorgio Moroder & Pete Bellotte. c1978, Rick's Music, Inc., O.P. Ed. Intro. & Say Yes Music. DONNA SUMMER. 25, 96, 129, 180, 181.

Heaven Must Have Sent You. w&m; Eddie Holland, Lamont Dozier & Brian Holland. c1966, Jobete Music Co., Inc. BONNIE POINTER/ELGINS. 24, 56, 75, 150, 187.

Heaven On The Seventh Floor. w&m; Dominique Bugatti & Frank Musker. c1977, Chappell & Co., Ltd. & Keyboard Pendulum Ltd. PAUL NICHOLAS. 50.

Heavy Makes You Happy. w&m; Jeff Barry & Bobby Bloom. c1970, 71, Unart Music Corp. STAPLE SINGERS. 81.

Hell. w&m; James Brown. c1974, Dynatone Publishing Co. JAMES BROWN. 107.

Hello/Goodbye. w&m; John Lennon & Paul McCartney. c1967, Northern Songs Ltd./Maclen Music, Inc. BEATLES. 61, 159.

Hello Hello. w&m; T. MacNeil & P. Kraemer. c1967, Great Honesty Music. SOPWITH CAMEL. 6.

Hello It's Me. w&m; Todd Rundgren. c1968, 69, Screen Gems-EMI Music Inc. TODD RUNDGREN. 53, 134.

Hello Old Friend. w&m; Eric Clapton. c1976, Stigwood Music. Administered by Unichappell Music, Inc. ERIC CLAPTON. 141.

Hello Stranger. w&m; Barbara Lewis. c1963, 73, Cotillion Music Inc., Braintree Music & Loveland Music. YVONNE ELLIMAN. 127.

Help. w&m; John Lennon & Paul McCartney. c1965, Northern Songs Ltd./Maclen Music, Inc. BEATLES. 35, 61, 159.

Help Me. w&m; Joni Mitchell. c1973, 74, Crazy Crow Music, JONI MITCHELL. 138.

Help Me Make It. w&m; Bobby Emmons. c1975, Baby Chick Music, Inc. B. J. THOMAS. 28.

Help Me Make It Through The Night. w&m; Kris Kristofferson. c1970, Combine Music Corp. KRIS KRISTOFFERSON. 15, 21, 59, 89, 163, 198.

Help Me Rhonda. w&m; Brian Wilson. c1965, 74, Sea of Tunes Publishing Co. & Irving Music, Inc. BEACH BOYS. 9, 198.

Help On The Way. w&m; Robert Hunter & Jerry Garcia. c1975, 76, Ice Nine Publishing Co., Inc. GRATEFUL DEAD. 84.

Help Yourself. w&m; Jack Fishman (w) & C. Donida (m). c1968, Radio Record Ricordi. TOM JONES. 93.

Helpless. w&m; Neil Young. c1970, 71, Cotillion Music, Inc. & Broken Arrow Music. CROSBY, STILLS, NASH & YOUNG/NEIL YOUNG. 87, 141, 145.

Helplessly Hoping. w&m; Stephen Stills. c1969, 71, Gold Hill Music, Inc. CROSBY, STILLS, NASH & YOUNG. 136.

Helter Skelter. w&m; John Lennon & Paul McCartney. c1968, Northern Songs Ltd./Maclen Music, Inc. BEATLES. 145, 159, 175.

Here At The Western World. w&m; Walter Becker & Donald Fagen. c1978, 79, American Broadcasting Music, Inc. STEELY DAN. 73, 157.

Here Come Those Tears Again. w&m; Jackson Browne & Nancy Farnsworth. c1976, 77, Swallow Turn Music & Open Window Music. Administered by WB Music Corp. & Warner-Tamerlane Publishing Corp. JACKSON BROWNE. 127, 141, 145.

Here Comes Sunshine. w&m; Robert Hunter (w) & Jerry Garcia (m). c1973, 76, Ice Nine Publishing Co., Inc. GRATEFUL DEAD. 84.

Here Comes The Judge. w&m; Billie Jean Brown, Suzanne De Passe & Frederick Long. c1968, Jobete Music, Co., Inc. SHORTY LONG. 123.

Here Come The Sun. w&m; Anthony Middleton, Larry Taylor, Larry James, Len Barry & Art Austin. c1979, Parker Music & Wimot Music. FAT LARRY'S BAND. 24.

Here Comes The Sun. w&m; George Harrison. c1969, Harrisongs Ltd./Harrisongs Music, Inc. BEATLES/GEORGE HARRISON. 125, 183.

Here I Am Again. w&m; Clay McMurray & Patricia Foster. c1971, Jobete Music, Co., Inc. GLADYS KNIGHT & THE PIPS. 17.

Here, There And Everywhere. w&m; John Lennon & Paul McCartney. c1966, Northern Songs Ltd./

Maclen Music, Inc. BEATLES/EMMYLOU HARRIS. 35, 43, 61, 139, 141, 197.

Here 'Tis. w&m; E. McDaniel. c1962, 70, Arc Music Corp. YARDBIRDS. 1.

Here To Love You. w&m; Michael McDonald. c1978, 79, Snug Music. DOOBIE BROTHERS. 147.

Here You Come Again. w&m; Cynthia Weil (w) & Barry Mann (m). c1977, Screen Gems-EMI Music Inc. & Summerhill Songs Inc. Controlled by Screen Gems-EMI Music Inc. B.J. THOMAS/DOLLY PARTON. 128, 134.

He's The Greatest Dancer. w&m; Nile Rodgers & Bernard Edwards. c1979, Chic Music, Inc. Administered by Warner-Tamerlane Publishing Corp. SISTER SLEDGE. 27, 31, 147.

Hey Babe. w&m; Neil Young. c1977, Silver Fiddle. NEIL YOUNG. 127.

Hey! Baby. w&m; Margaret Cobb & Bruce Channel, c1961, Unart Music Corp. & LeBill Music, Inc. BRUCE CHANNEL/RINGO STARR. 4 , 79.

Hey, Deanie. w&m; Eric Carmen. c1977, C.A.M. SHAUN CASSIDY. 124, 145, 178.

Hey Doll Baby. w&m; Titus Turner. c1955, Progressive Music Publishing Co., Inc. Controlled by Unichappell Music, Inc. CLOVERS. 90, 155.

Hey Girl. w&m; Gerry Goffin & Carole King. c1963, Screen Gems-EMI Music Inc. DONNY OSMOND/GEORGE BENSON. 38, 130.

Hey Girl. w&m; John Phillips & Michelle Gilliam. c1966, Trousdale Music Publishers, Inc. MAMAS & THE PAPAS. 119.

Hey Girl, Come And Get It. w&m; Hugo & Luigi & George David Weiss. c1974, Avco Embassy Music Publishing, Inc. STYLISTICS. 49.

Hey, Hey, Hey, Hey (Goin' Back To Birmingham). w&m; Richard Penniman. c1958, Venice Music. LITTLE RICHARD. 159.

Hey Hey, My My. w&m; Neil Young. c1979, Silver Fiddle. NEIL YOUNG & CRAZY HORSE. 22, 27, 57, 147.

Hey Joe. w&m; William M. Roberts. c1962, 65, 66, 70. Third Story Music. JIMI HENDRIX/LEAVES/WILSON PICKETT. 6, 78, 155, 161, 169, 186.

Hey Jude. w&m; John Lennon & Paul McCartney. c1968, Northern Songs Ltd./Maclen Music, Inc. BEATLES. 36, 61, 62, 139, 159.

Hey Little Girl. w&m; Bobby Stevenson & Otis Blackwell. c1959, 73, Screen Gems-EMI Music, Inc. & Odie Music Inc. OTIS BLACKWELL. 2.

Hey, Miss Fannie. w&m; A. Nugetre. c1952, Progressive Music Publishing Co., Inc. Controlled by Unichappell Music, Inc. CLOVERS. 90, 155.

Hey Mister, That's Me Up On The Jukebox. w&m; James Taylor. c1971, 77, Country Road Music, Inc. & Blackwood Music, Inc. Administered by Blackwood Music Inc. LINDA RONSTADT. 199.

Hey Nelly Nelly. w&m; Shel Silverstein & Jim Friedman. c1963, 64, Hollis Music, Inc. SHEL SILVERSTEIN. 85.

Hey Paula. w&m; Ray Hilderbrand. c1962, 63, Le Bill Music & Marbill Music. PAUL & PAULA. 4.

Hey, Schoolgirl. w&m; Paul Simon & Arthur Garfunkel. c1957, Paul Simon. TOM & JERRY. 143.

Hey, That's No Way To Say Goodbye. w&m; Leonard Cohen. c1967, 69, Stranger Music, Inc. LEONARD COHEN. 59, 171.

Hey There Lonely Girl. w&m; Earl Shuman & Leon Carr. c1962, 70, Famous Music Corp. EDDIE HOLMAN/OSMONDS. 6, 93.

Hey What About Me SEE What About Me.

Hey Won't You Play SEE Another Somebody Done Somebody Wrong Song.

Hide And Seek. w&m; Paul Winley & Ethel Byrd. c1955, Progressive Music Publishing Co., Inc. BILL HALEY & THE COMETS. 154.

Hi-De-Ho (That Old Sweet Roll). w&m; Gerry Goffin & Carole King. c1968, 70, Screen Gems-Columbia Music, Inc. BLOOD, SWEAT & TEARS. 86, 88, 104.

High And The Mighty. w&m; Ned Washington (w) & Dimitri Tiomkin (m). c1954, M. Witmark & Sons. DIMITRI TIOMKIN. 138.

High Time. w&m; Robert Hunter (w) & Jerry Garcia (m). c1970, 73, Ice Nine Publishing Co. GRATEFUL DEAD. 83.

Higher. w&m; Sylvester Stewart. c1967, Daly City Music. SLY & THE FAMILY STONE. 202.

Higher And Higher. w&m; Gary Jackson, Carl Smith & Raynard Miner. c1967, 77, Chevis Music, Inc., Warner-Tamerlane Publishing Corp. & BRC Music Corp. RITA COOLIDGE. 87, 117, 127, 133, 136, 145, 185, 201.

Higher Ground. w&m; Stevie Wonder. c1973, Jobete Music Co., Inc. & Black Bull Music. STEVIE WONDER. 52, 77, 106, 134, 150.

Highway In The Wind. w&m; Arlo Guthrie, c1967, 69, Appleseed Music, Inc. ARLO GUTHRIE. 7.

Highway 61 Revisited. w&m; Bob Dylan. c1965, M. Witmark & Sons. & Warner Bros. Inc. BOB DYLAN/JOHNNY WINTER. 35, 149.

Highway Song. w&m; Rick Medlocke & Jackson Spires. c1979, Bobnal Music. BLACKFOOT. 11, 75.

Hi-Heel Sneakers. w&m; Robert Higgenbotham. c1964, 66, Medal Music, Inc. TOMMY TUCKER. 3.

Hi-Lili, Hi-Lo. w&m; Helen Deutsch (w) & Bronislau Kaper (m). c1952, 65, Metro-Goldwyn-Mayer, Inc. Controlled by Robbins Music Corp. RICHARD CHAMBERLAIN. 140.

Him. w&m; Rupert Holmes. c1979, 80, WB Music Corp. & The Holmes Line Of Music, Inc. Adminis-0 tered by WB Music Corp. RUPERT HOLMES. 67, 188.

Himno A La Alegria SEE Song of Joy.

His Latest Flame. w&m; Doc Pomus & Mort Shuman. c1961, Elvis Presley Music, Inc. ELVIS PRESLEY. 1973.

Hit The Road Jack. w&m; Percy Mayfield. c1961, Tangerine Music Corp. RAY CHARLES/ STAMPEDERS. 155, 198.

Hitch A Ride. w&m; Donald T. Scholz. c1970, 77, Pure Songs. Administered by Colgems-EMI Music Inc. BOSTON. 142.

Hitch-Hike. w&m; Marvin Gaye, William Stevenson & Clarence Paul. c1962, 63, 66, Jobete Music Co., Inc. MARVIN GAYE. 150, 166.

Hobo's Blues. w&m; Paul Simon (m) & Stephane Grappelli (m). c1972, Paul Simon. PAUL SIMON. 143.

Hold Me, Thrill Me, Kiss Me. w&m; Harry Noble. c1952, Mills Music Inc. MEL CARTER. 6.

Hold Me Tight. w&m; Johnny Nash. c1968, Dovan Music, Inc. JOHNNY NASH. 6.

Hold On. w&m; Ian Gomm. c1978, 79, Albion Music Ltd. IAN COMM. 27.

Hold On I'm Coming. w&m; Isaac Hayes & David Porter. c1966, East-Memphis Music & Pronto Music, Inc. SAM & DAVE. 122.

Hold On To My Love. w&m; Robin Gibb & Blue Weaver. c1980, Brothers Gibb B.V. & Stigwood Music, Inc. Administered by Unichappell Music, Inc. JIMMY RUFFIN. 47.

Hold The Line. w&m; David Paich. c1977, 78. Hudman Publishing Co., Inc. TOTO. 147.

Hold What You've Got. w&m; Joe Tex. c1964, 65, Tree Publishing Co., Inc. JOE TEX. 93.

Hold Your Head Up. w&m; Rod Argent & Chris White. c1971, Verulam Music Co., Ltd./Mainstay Music, Inc. ARGENT. 106.

Holdin' On For Dear Love. w&m; Johnny Slate, Steve Pippin & Larry Henley. c1978, 79, House of Gold Music, Inc. LOBO. 98.

Holiday. w&m; Barry, Robin & Maurice Gibb. c1967, 75, Abigail Music Ltd. Controlled by Casserole Music Corp. BEE GEES. 35, 43.

Hollywood. w&m; Boz Scaggs & Michael Omartian (m). c1977, 78, Boz Scaggs Music & Meadow Ridge Music. BOZ SCAGGS. 165.

Hollywood. w&m; David Wolinski & Andre Fisher. c1977, American Broadcasting Music, Inc. & Big Elk Music. RUFUS FEATURING CHAKA KHAN. 164.

Hollywood Nights. w&m; Bob Seger. c1978, Gear Publishing Co. BOB SEGER & THE SILVER BULLET BAND. 41, 146.

Hollywood Swinging. w&m; Ricky West & Kool & The Gang. c1973, Delightful Music Publishing & Gang Music Publishing Co. KOOL & THE GANG. 52, 106.

Home And Dry. w&m; Gerry Rafferty. c1979, Rafferty Songs Ltd./The Hudson Bay Music Co. GERRY RAFFERTY. 65, 73.

Home Made Love. w&m; Richard Mainegra. c1974, 76, Unart Music Corp. KENNY ROGERS. 80.

Home To Emily. w&m; Lorenzo Music (m) & Henrietta Music (m). c1974, 76, EJIWA Music Co. 80.

Home To You. w&m; Peter Bowen. c1969, Warner-Tamerlane Publishing Corp. SEATRAIN. 115, 152.

Homecoming. w&m; Hagood Hardy (m). c1975, Hagood Hardy Music. Controlled by ATV Music Corp. HAGOOD HARDY. 30, 62, 141.

Homeward Bound. w&m; Paul Simon. c1966, Paul Simon. SIMON & GARFUNKEL. 143.

Honest I Do. w&m; Damon Stankey, Jim West & Al Candelaria. c1960, 79, Blue Indigo Music. INNOCENTS, 6.

Honest I Do. w&m; Jimmy Reed. c1957, 74, Conrad Music, a division of Arc Music Corp. JIMMY REED. 10, 168, 169.

Honesty. w&m; Billy Joel. c1977, Impulsive Music & April Music Inc. Administered by April Music Inc. BILLY JOEL. 176.

Honey. w&m; Bobby Russell. c1968, Bibo Music Publishers, Inc., a division of T.B. Harms Co. BOBBY GOLDSBORO. 21, 76, 163, 198.

Honey. w&m; Seymour Simons, Haven Gillespie & Richard A. Whiting. c1928, 56, 66. Leo Feist, Inc. ERIC ANDERSEN. 140.

Honey Babe. w&m; Paul Francis Webster (w) & Max Steiner (m). c1955, M. Witmark & Sons. LIGHTNIN' HOPKINS. 132.

Honey Hush. w&m; Lou Willie Turner. c1954, Progressive Music Publishing Co., Inc. Controlled by Unichappell Music, Inc. JOE TURNER. 154, 155.

Honey I'm Rich. w&m; Ray Parker. c1977, 78. Raydiola Music. RAYDIO. 74.

Honey Love. w&m; Clyde McPhatter & J. Gerald. c1954, Progressive Music Publishing Co., Inc. DRIFTERS. 90, 154.

Honeysuckle Rose. w&m; Andy Raxaf (w) & Thomas Waller (m). c1929, 56, Santly Bros., Inc. Assigned to Joy Music, Inc. & Anne-Rachel Music Corp. DUKE ELLINGTON/ELLA FITZGERALD/NAT KING COLE. 191.

Honky Tonk (Parts 1 & 2). w&m; Bill Doggett, Billy Butler, Shep Shephard & Clifford Scott. c1956. W & K Publishing Corp. & Islip Music Publishing Co. BILL DOGGETT. 142.

Honky Tonk Women. w&m; Mick Jagger & Keith Richard. c1969, Abcko Music, Inc. ROLLING STONES. 29, 53, 134, 142.

Hooked On A Feeling. w&m; Mark James. c1968, Screen Gems-EMI Music Inc. B.J. THOMAS. 29, 64, 134.

Hooked On You. w&m; David Gates, c1976, 77, Kipahulu Music Co. Controlled by Colgems-EMI Music, Inc. BREAD. 164.

Hope That We Can Be Together Soon. w&m; Kenny Gamble & Leon Huff. c1969, 75, Blackwood Music Inc. HAROLD MELVIN & THE BLUENOTES/SHARON PAIGE. 49.

Horse With No Name. w&m; Dewey Bunnell. c1971, 72, Warner Bros. Music Ltd./WB Music Corp. AMERICA. 36, 55, 62, 115, 133, 136, 138, 151, 174.

Hot Blooded. w&m; Lou Gramm (w) & Mick Jones (m). c1978, Somerset Songs Publishing Inc., Evansongs Ltd. & WB Music Corp. FOREIGNER. 22, 31, 124, 136, 146.

Hot Butterfly. w&m; Gregg Diamond. c1978, Diamond Touch Publishing Ltd. & Arista Music Inc. BIONIC BOOGIE. 112.

Hot Child In The City. w&m; Nick Gilder & James McCulloch. c1978, Beechwood Music of Canada, a division of Capitol Records (Canada) Ltd. NICK GILDER. 73, 135.

Hot Cop. w&m; J. Morali, H. Belolo & V. Willis. c1978, Scorpio Music (Black Scorpio). Controlled by Can't Stop Music. VILLAGE PEOPLE. 200.

Hot Fun In The Summertime. w&m; Sylvester Stewart. c1969, Stone Flower Music. SLY & THE FAMILY STONE. 203.

Hot Legs. w&m; Rod Stewart. c1977, Rod Stewart. Administered by Riva Music, Inc. ROD STEWART. 22, 87, 146.

Hot Love, Cold World. w&m; Bob Welch & John Henning. c1977, Glenwood Music Corp. & Cigar Music. BOB WELCH. 135.

Hot Rod. w&m; Tommy Aldridge. c1973, Pond Tunes. BLACK OAK ARKANSAS. 105.

Hot Rod Lincoln. w&m; Charles Ryan & W.D. Stevenson. c1960, 72, 4-Star Music Co. COMMANDER CODY & HIS LOST PLANET AIRMEN. 37.

Hot Shot. w&m; Andy Kahn & Kurt Borusiewicz. c1978, Scully Music Co. KAREN YOUNG. 34, 74.

Hot Stuff. w&m; Pete Bellotte, Harold Faltermayer & Keith Forsey. c1979, Rick's Music, Inc. O.P. Revelation Music & Ed. Intro. DONNA SUMMER. 75, 96, 177, 180, 198.

Hot Summer Nights. w&m; Walter Egan. c1977, 78, Swell Sounds Music, Melody Deluxe Music & Seldak Music Corp. NIGHT/WALTER EGAN. 27.

Hot Wax Theme. w&m; Kenny Vance, Ira Newborn & Paul Griffin. c1978, Famous Music Corp., Ensign Music Corp. & Red Giant Music. 2.

Hotel California. w&m; Don Felder, Don Henley & Glenn Frey. c1976, 77, Red Cloud Music, Cass County Music, Fingers Music, Long Run Music & WB Music Corp. EAGLES. 87, 124, 133, 136, 145.

Hound Dog. w&m; Jerry Leiber & Mike Stoller. c1956, Elvis Presley Music, Inc. & American Broadcasting Music, Inc. Assigned to Gladys Music on behalf of Elvis Presley Music. Controlled by Chappell & Co., Inc. BIG MAMA THORNTON/ELVIS PRESLEY. 35, 78, 101, 137, 155, 173, 198.

House At Pooh Corner. w&m; Ken Loggins. c1969, 71, 73, American Broadcasting Music, Inc. LOGGINS & MESSINA. 28, 126, 141.

House Of The Rising Sun. w&m; Traditional. Alan Price (Adapted), Art Summit (Adapted) & Paul Campbell (Adapted). c1951, 64, 76, 78, versions published by Folkways Music Publishers, Inc., Keith Prowse Music Publishing Co., Ltd./Al Gallico Music Corp. & Road Island Co. ALAN PRICE/ANIMALS/FRIJID PINK/JOAN BAEZ/SANTA ESMERALDA/UNIQUES. 3, 29, 68, 78, 85, 93, 102, 128, 129, 135, 156, 157.

How Can I Be Sure. w&m; Felix Cavaliere & Edward Brigati, Jr. c1967, Coral Rock Music Corp. & Downtown Music Co., a division of Purple Records Distributing Corp. DAVID CASSIDY/RASCALS. 21, 72, 140, 195, 199.

How Can I Tell Her (About You). w&m; Lobo. c1973, Famous Music Corp. & Kaiser Music Co., Inc. LOBO. 93.

How Can This Be Love. w&m; Mark Safan & Mark Goldenberg. c1977, 78, Pink Flower Music & Fleedleedle Music. ANDREW GOLD. 74.

How Can You Mend A Broken Heart. w&m; Barry & Robin Gibb. c1971, 75, Abigail Music Ltd. & Robin Gibb Publishing Ltd. Controlled by Frontwheel Music, Inc. on behalf of Robin Gibb Publishing Ltd. BEE GEES. 36, 55, 62, 133, 136, 138, 174.

How Deep Is Your Love. w&m; Barry, Robin & Maurice Gibb. c1977, Brothers Gibb B.V. & Stigwood Music. Administered by Unichappell Music, Inc. BEE GEES. 50, 133.

How Do I Make You. w&m; Billy Steinberg. c1979, 80, Billy Steinberg Music. LINDA RONSTADT. 23, 45, 56, 58, 99.

How Long. w&m; Paul Carrack. c1974, 75, Anchor Music Ltd./American Broadcasting Music Inc. ACE. 37, 49.

How Lucky Can You Get. w&m; John Kander & Fred Ebb. c1975, Screen Gems-EMI Music Inc. BARBRA STREISAND. 58.

How Many More Times. w&m; Jimmy Page, John Paul Jones & John Bonham. c1969, Superhype Publishing. LED ZEPPELIN. 114.

How Much Love. w&m; Barry Mann & Leo Sayer. c1976, 77, Screen Gems-EMI Music Inc., Summerhill Songs, Inc. & Longmanor Ltd. Controlled by Screen Gems-EMI Music Ltd. LEO SAYER. 142.

How Sweet It Is (To Be Loved By You). w&m; Brian Holland, Lamont Dozier & Eddie Holland. c1964, Jobete Music Co., Inc. JAMES TAYLOR/JR. WALKER & THE ALL STARS/MARVIN GAYE. 28, 77, 123, 126, 130, 142, 150, 166.

How Time Flies. w&m; Tommy Jarrett. c1958, Thunderbird Music, Inc. Assigned to Bibo Music. JERRY WALLACE. 160.

How Would You Like To Be. w&m; Ben Raleigh & Mark Barkan. c1963, Elvis Presley Music, Inc. ELVIS PRESLEY. 172.

How You Gonna See Me Now. w&m; Alice Cooper, Dick Wagner & Bernie Taupin. c1978, Ezra Music, Jodrell Music, Inc. & Candlewood Mountain Music Corp. ALICE COOPER. 27.

How You've Changed. w&m; Chuck Berry. c1958, 65, Arc Music Corp. ANIMALS. 10.

Hully Gully. w&m; Fred Smith & Cliff Goldsmith. c1959, Arvee Music Co. OLYMPICS. 6.

Hummingbird. w&m; James Seals & Dash Crofts. c1972, 73, Dawnbreaker Music Co. SEALS & CROFTS. 43, 138, 151.

Hundred Pounds Of Clay. w&m; Bob Elgin, Luther Dixon & Kay Rogers. c1961, Gil Music Corp. GENE MC DANIELS. 4, 35, 78, 102, 137.

Hungry Years. w&m; Neil Sedaka & Howard Greenfield. c1974, 75, Kiddio Music Co. RITA COOLIDGE. 146.

Hurricane. w&m; Bob Dylan & Jacques Levy (w). c1975, Ram's Horn Music. BOB DYLAN. 36, 170.

Hurt. w&m; Cat Stevens. c1973, Freshwater Music Ltd./Ackee Music Inc. CAT STEVENS. 105.

Hurt. w&m; Jimmie Crane & Al Jacobs. c1953, 54, Miller Music Corp. BOBBY VINTON/ELVIS PRESLEY. 163, 198.

Hurt So Bad. w&m; Teddy Randazzo, Bobby Hart & Bobby Wilding. c1965, 67, 72, South Mountain Music Corp. Assigned to Vogue Music, Inc. LINDA RONSTADT/LITTLE ANTHONY & THE IMPERIALS. 78, 102, 160, 177.

Hurting Each Other. w&m; Peter Udell (w) & Gary Geld (m). c1965, 72, Andalusian Music Co., Inc. & Andrew Scott, Inc. CARPENTERS. 64, 115.

Hushabye. w&m; Doc Pomus & Mort Shuman. c1959, Hill & Range Songs, Inc. Assigned to Unichappell Music, Inc. BEACH BOYS/MYSTICS. 2, 78, 101, 137.

Hustle. w&m; Van McCoy. c1975, Warner-Tamerlane Publishing Corp. & Van McCoy Music, Inc. VAN MC COY & THE SOUL CITY SYMPHONY. 30, 36, 46, 62, 118, 133, 139, 141.

I Almost Lost My Mind. w&m; Ivory Joe Hunter. c1950, Hill & Range Songs, Inc. Assigned to Unichappell Music, Inc. HARPTONES/IVORY JOE HUNTER. 137, 163.

I Am A Child. w&m; Neil Young. c1968, 74, Cotillion Music, Inc. & Springalo Toones. BUFFALO SPRINGFIELD. 39.

I Am A Lonesome Hobo. w&m; Bob Dylan. c1968, 76, Dwarf Music. BOB DYLAN. 170.

I Am A Rock. w&m; Paul Simon. c1965, Paul Simon. SIMON & GARFUNKEL. 143.

I Am...I Said. w&m; Neil Diamond. c1971, 74, Prophet Music, Inc. NEIL DIAMOND. 117, 131, 183.

I Am The Walrus. w&m; John Lennon & Paul McCartney. c1967, Northern Songs Ltd./Maclen Music, Inc. BEATLES. 159, 175.

I Am What I Am. w&m; H. Belolo (w), V. Willis (w), P. Whitehead (w) & J. Morali (m). c1978, Scorpio Music (Black Scorpio). Controlled by Can't Stop Music. VILLAGE PEOPLE. 200.

I Am Woman. w&m; Helen Reddy (w) & Ray Burton (m). c1971, Irving Music, Inc. & Buggerlugs Music Co. HELEN REDDY. 58, 70, 93, 131, 181.

I Believe In Miracles. w&m; Barry Mason & Les Reed. c1976, 77, Silver Blue Music, Ltd./Barry Mason Music, Inc. ENGELBERT HUMPERDINCK. 164.

I Believe In Music. w&m; Mac Davis. c1970, 72, Screen Gems-EMI Music Inc. & Songpainter Music. Controlled by Screen Gems-EMI Music Inc. MAC DAVIS. 71, 106, 126, 130, 134, 156.

I Believe (When I Fall In Love It Will Be Forever). w&m; Yvonne Wright & Stevie Wonder. c1972, Jobete

Music Co., Inc. & Black Bull Music Inc. ART GAR-FUNKEL. 142.

I Believe You. w&m; Don & Dick Addrisi. c1977, Musicways, Inc. & Flying Addrisi Music. CARPENTERS. 96.

I Can Help. w&m; Billy Swan. c1974, Combine Music Corp. BILLY SWAN. 21, 89, 163.

I Can See Clearly Now. w&m; Johnny Nash. c1972, Cayman Music Ltd. & Rondor Music Ltd. GLADYS KNIGHT & THE PIPS/JOHNNY NASH. 15, 21, 37, 72, 111, 131, 140, 163, 193, 194, 195, 198.

I Can See For Miles. w&m; Peter Townshend. c1967, Fabulous Music Ltd./TRO-Essex Music, Inc. WHO. 29.

I Can Tell. w&m; Samuel Smith & E. McDaniel. c1962, 64, Arc Music Corp. 10.

I Can Understand It. w&m; Bobby Womack. c1972, 73, Unart Music Corp. & Tracebob Music. NEW BIRTH. 111.

I Can't Be Myself. w&m; Merle Haggard. c1970, Blue Book Music. MERLE HAGGARD. 88.

I Can't Get Next To You. w&m; Barrett Strong & Norman Whitfield. c1969, Jobete Music Co., Inc. TEMPTATIONS. 123, 150.

I Can't Get No Satisfaction SEE Satisfaction.

I Can't Help It. w&m; Barry Gibb. c1980, Brothers Gibb B.V. & Stigwood Music Inc. Administered by Unichappell Music, Inc. ANDY GIBB & OLIVIA NEWTON-JOHN. 47.

I Can't Help Myself. w&m; Brian Holland, Lamont Dozier & Eddie Holland. c1965, 68, 79, Jobete Music Co., Inc. ACE/BONNIE POINTER/FOUR TOPS. 24, 98, 123, 150, 166.

I Can't Hold On. w&m; Karla Bonoff. c1977, Seagrape Music. KARLA BONOFF. 12.

I Can't Make It Anymore. w&m; Gordon Lightfoot. c1966, 68, M. Witmark & Sons & Warner Bros.-Seven Arts, Inc. RICHIE HAVENS/SPYDER TURNER. 132.

I Can't Quit You Baby. w&m; Willie Dixon. c1965, Conrad Music. JOHN MAYALL. 1.

I Can't Stand It "76". w&m; James Brown. c1974, Dynatone Publishing Co. JAMES BROWN. 107.

I Can't Stand My Baby. w&m; John Callis. c1978, Blue Disque Music Co. REZILLOS. 19.

I Can't Stand It No More. w&m; Peter Frampton. c1979, Almo Music Corp., Fram-Dee Music Ltd. & Frampton Music. PETER FRAMPTON. 75, 96.

I Can't Stand The Rain. w&m; Don Bryant, Ann Peebles & Bernard Miller. c1973, JEC Publishing Co. ERUPTION/GRAHAM CENTRAL STATION/HUMBLE PIE. 34, 135, 142.

I Can't Tell You Why. w&m; Timothy B. Schmit, Don Henley & Glenn Frey. c1978, 79, 80, Cass County Music, Red Cloud Music & Jeddrah Music. EAGLES. 162, 188.

I Can't Wait Any Longer. w&m; Bill Anderson & Buddy Killen. c1978, Stallion Music, Inc. BILL ANDERSON. 34.

I Could Never Love Another. w&m; Barrett Strong, Norman Whitfield & Roger Penzabene. c1967, 68, Jobete Music Co., Inc. TEMPTATIONS. 123.

I Count The Tears. w&m; Doc Pomus & Mort Shuman. c1960, Brenner Music, Inc. DRIFTERS. 92.

I Cried A Tear. w&m; Al Julia & Fred Jay. c1958, Progressive Music Publishing Co., Inc. Controlled by Unichappell Music, Inc. LA VERN BAKER. 92, 154, 155.

I Didn't Have The Nerve To Say No. w&m; James Destri & Deborah Harry. c1978, Jiru Music & Monster Island Music. BLONDIE. 19.

I Didn't Know About You. w&m; Bob Russell (w) & Duke Ellington (m). c1944, 72, Robbins Music Corp. JUDY COLLINS. 199.

I Dig Love. w&m; George Harrison. c1970, Harrisongs Ltd./Harrisongs Music, Inc. GEORGE HARRISON. 125.

I Dig Rock And Roll Music. w&m; Paul Stookey, James Mason & Dave Dixon. c1967, Pepamar Music Corp. PETER, PAUL & MARY. 43, 100, 132.

I Do, I Do, I Do, I Do, I Do. w&m; Benny Andersson, Stig Anderson & Bjorn Ulvaeus. c1975, Union Songs, AB. ABBA. 198.

I Do It For Your Love. w&m; Paul Simon. c1975, Paul Simon. PAUL SIMON. 143.

I Don't Hurt Anymore. w&m; Jack Rollins (w) & Don Robertson (m). c1954, Hill & Range Songs, Inc. DINAH WASHINGTON. 137.

I Don't Know How To Love Him. w&m; Tim Rice (w) & Andrew Lloyd Webber (m). c1970, Leeds Music Ltd./Leeds Music Corp. HELEN REDDY/SHIRLEY BASSEY. 131.

I Don't Know Why (I Just Do). w&m; Roy Turk (w) & Fred E. Ahlert (m). c1931, 46, 59, Fred Ahlert Music Corp.-Cromwell Music, Inc. TONY BENNETT. 63.

I Don't Know Why I Love You SEE But I Do.

I Don't Mind. w&m; James Brown. c1961, 68, Wisto Publishing Co. JAMES BROWN. 18.

I Don't Need No Doctor. w&m; Nicholas Ashford, Valerie Simpson & Josie Armstead. c1966, 71, Warner-Tamerlane Publishing Corp., Baby Monica Music, Inc. & Renleigh Music Corp. HUMBLE PIE/NEW RIDERS OF THE PURPLE SAGE. 138, 152, 197.

I Don't Want To Be Right. w&m; Homer Banks, Raymond Jackson & Carl Hampton. c1971, 72, East-Memphis Music & Klondike Ents. Ltd. BARBARA MANDRELL/LUTHER INGRAM/MILLIE JACKSON/ROD STEWART. 56, 75, 96, 122, 129, 181.

I Don't Want To Do Wrong. w&m; John Bristol, William Guest, Catherine Schaffner. Gladys & Merald Knight. c1970, 71, Jobete Music Co., Inc. GLADYS KNIGHT & THE PIPS. 17.

I Don't Want To Hear It Anymore. w&m; Randy Newman. c1964, 69, Unart Music Corp. MELISSA MANCHESTER. 80.

I Don't Want To Talk About It. w&m; Danny Whitten. c1971, 76, Crazy Horse Music. ROD STEWART. 147.

I Dreamed I Saw St. Augustine. w&m; Bob Dylan. c1968, 76, Dwarf Music. BOB DYLAN/JOAN BAEZ. 170.

I Feel Fine. w&m; John Lennon & Paul McCartney. c1964, Northern Songs Ltd./Maclen Music, Inc. BEATLES. 35.

I Feel Like I'm Fixin' To Die Rag. w&m; Joe McDonald. c1968, 70, Tradition Music Co. COUNTRY JOE & THE FISH. 202.

I Feel That I've Known You Forever. w&m; Doc Pomus & Alan Jeffreys. c1962, Elvis Presley Music, Inc. ELVIS PRESLEY. 172.

I Feel The Earth Move. w&m; Carole King. c1971, Colgems-EMI Music Inc. CAROLE KING. 28, 77, 134.

I Forgot To Remember To Forget. w&m; Stanley A. Kesler & Charlie Feathers. c1955, Hi-Lo Music, Inc. ELVIS PRESLEY. 122.

I Get Around. w&m; Brian Wilson. c1964, Sea Of Tunes Publishing Co. BEACH BOYS. 9.

I Get High SEE Every Time You Touch Me.

I Go To Pieces. w&m; Del Shannon. c1964, 80, Mole Hole Music & Rightsong Music. PETER & GORDON. 5.

I Go To Rio. w&m; Peter Allen & Adrienne Anderson. c1976, 77, Irving Music, Inc., Woolnough Music, Inc. & Jemava Music Corp. PABLO CRUISE/PETER ALLEN. 96, 129.

I Got A Bag Of My Own. w&m; James Brown. c1973, Dynatone Publishing Co. JAMES BROWN. 107.

I Got A Name. w&m; Norman Gimbel (w) & Charles Fox (m). c1973, Fox Fanfare Music, Inc. JIM CROCE. 53, 77, 104, 126, 134, 142, 156.

I Got A Woman. w&m; Ray Charles. c1955, 58, Progressive Music Publishing Co., Inc. Controlled by Unichappell Music, Inc. ELVIS PRESLEY/RAY CHARLES. 90, 155.

I Got Ants In My Pants (Part I). w&m; James Brown. c1973, 74, Dynatone Publishing Co. JAMES BROWN. 107.

I Got Lucky. w&m; Ben Weisman, Fred Wise & Dee Fuller. c1962, Gladys Music, Inc. ELVIS PRESLEY. 173.

I Got My Mind Made Up. w&m; Scott Miller, Kim Miller & Raymond Earl. c1979, Lucky Three Music Publishing Co. & Henry Suemay Publishing Co. Administered by Lucky Three Music Publishing Co. INSTANT FUNK. 34, 51, 66.

I Got You Babe. w&m; Sonny Bono. c1965, Cotillion Music, Inc. & Five-West Music. SONNY & CHER. 35, 100, 197.

I Got You (I Feel Good). w&m; James Brown. c1966, 68, Lois Publishing Co. & Try Me Music. JAMES BROWN. 18.

I Hear A Symphony. w&m; Brian Holland, Lamont Dozier & Eddie Holland. c1965, 68, Jobete Music Co., Inc. SUPREMES. 95, 123, 150, 166.

I Hear You Knocking. w&m; Dave Bartholomew & Pearl King. c1955, Unart Music Corp. DAVE EDMUNDS/ FATS DOMINO/GALE STORM/ORION/SMILEY LEWIS. 79, 137, 155.

I Heard It Through The Grapevine. w&m; Norman Whitfield & Barrett Strong. c1966, 67, 69, Jobete Music Co., Inc. CREEDENCE CLEARWATER RE- VIVAL/GLADYS KNIGHT & THE PIPS/MARVIN GAYE. 17, 123, 142, 150.

I Honestly Love You. w&m; Peter Allen & Jeff Barry. c1974, Irving Music Inc., Woolnough Music & Broad- side Music, Inc. OLIVIA NEWTON-JOHN/PETER ALLEN/STAPLES. 58, 70, 71, 131, 181.

I Just Can't Help Believin'. w&m; Cynthia Weil (w) & Barry Mann (m). c1968, 70, Screen Gems-EMI Music Inc. ELVIS PRESLEY. 130.

I Just Can't Say No To You. w&m; Parker McGee (w) & Steve Gibson (m). c1977, Dawnbreaker Music Co. PARKER MC GEE. 37, 196.

I Just Fall In Love Again. w&m; Gloria Sklerov (w), Harry Lloyd (w), Stephen H. Dorff (m) & Larry Herbstritt (m). c1977, Cotton Pickin' Songs, Hobby Horse Music & Peso Music. ANNE MURRAY/ CARPENTERS/DUSTY SPRINGFIELD. 23, 56, 128, 130, 134.

I Just Wanna Stop. w&m; Ross Vannelli. c1978, Ross Vannelli Publishing. GINO VANNELLI/JIMMY CASTOR BUNCH. 70, 181.

I Just Want To Be Your Everything. w&m; Barry Gibb. c1977, Brothers Gibb B.V. Controlled by Stigwood Music, Inc. Administered by Unichappell Music, Inc. ANDY GIBB/FOUR LEAVES. 40, 127, 131, 133, 201.

I Just Want To Celebrate. w&m; Nick Zesses & Dino Fekaris. c1971, Jobete Music Co., Inc. RARE EARTH. 105.

I Knew You When. w&m; Joe South. c1964, 71, Lowery Music. DONNY OSMOND. 38.

I Know. w&m; Barbara George. c1961, At Last Pub- lishing Co. BARBARA GEORGE. 5.

I Know A Heartache When I See One. w&m; Rory Bourke, Kerry Chater & Charlie Black. c1979, Chappell & Co., Inc. & Unichappell Music, Inc. JENNIFER WARNES. 47.

I Know But I Don't Know. w&m; Frank Infante. c1978, Rare Blue Music & Monster Island Music. BLONDIE. 33.

I Know I'm Losing You SEE I'm Losing You.

I Left My Heart In San Francisco. w&m; Douglass Cross (w) & George Cory (m). c1954, General Music Publishing Co., Inc. TONY BENNETT. 113, 130, 135, 140.

I Like Dreamin'. w&m; Kenny Nolan. c1976, Sound of Nolan Music & Chelsea Music Co. KENNY NOLAN. 21, 196.

I Like It Like That. w&m; Chris Kenner & Allen Toussaint. c1961, 65, Thursday Music Corp. CHRIS KENNER/DAVE CLARK FIVE. 5, 93.

I Like It Like That. w&m; William "Smokey" Robinson & Marvin Tarplin. c1964, Jobete Music Co., Inc. SMOKEY ROBINSON & THE MIRACLES. 150.

I Looked Away. w&m; Eric Clapton & Bobby Whitlock. c1970, 71, Throat Music Ltd. & Delbon Music/Cotillion Music Inc. DEREK & THE DOMINOES. 152.

I Love How You Love Me. w&m; Barry Mann & Larry Kolber. c1961, Screen Gems-EMI Music Inc. LYNN ANDERSON/PARIS SISTERS. 130.

I Love Music (Part I). w&m; Kenny Gamble & Leon Huff. c1975, Mighty Three Music. Administered by Blackwood Music, Inc. O'JAYS. 193.

I Love The Life I Live. w&m; Willie Dixon. c1956, Arc Music Corp. MOSE ALLISON. 1.

I Love The Nightlife. w&m; Alicia Bridges & Susan Hutcheson. c1977, 78, Lowery Music Co., Inc. ALICIA BRIDGES. 24, 34, 73, 112, 128, 135, 180.

I Love The Way You Love. w&m; Berry Gordy, Jr. & Mikol Jon. c1959, 60, 71, Jobete Music Co., Inc. MARV JOHNSON. 123.

I Love You. w&m; Chris White. c1965, Verulam Music, Inc. PEOPLE. 76.

I Married An Angel. w&m; Lorenz Hart (w) & Richard Rodgers (m). c1938, 66, Robbins Music Corp. GEORGE WALLINGTON/KENNY CLARKE/NAT ADDERLEY/SHELLY MANNE. 140.

I Need A Man To Love. w&m; Janis Joplin & Sam Andrew. c1968, 70, Cheap Thrills Music. JANIS JOPLIN. 202.

I Need To Know. w&m; Tom Petty. c1977, Skyhill Publishing Co., Inc. TOM PETTY & THE HEART-BREAKERS. 135.

I Need You. w&m; Gerry Beckley. c1971, 72, Kinney Music Ltd. & WB Music Corp. AMERICA. 115, 151.

I Need You So. w&m; Ivory Joe Hunter. c1950, Hill & Range Songs, Inc. Assigned to Unichappell Music, Inc. IVORY JOE HUNTER. 137, 155.

I Need You To Turn To. w&m; Elton John & Bernie Taupin. c1969, Dick James Music, Ltd./Dick James Music, Inc. ELTON JOHN. 197.

I Need Your Help Barry Manilow. w&m; Dale Gonyea. c1979, Ray Stevens Music. RAY STEVENS. 96.

I Need Your Love Tonight. w&m; Sid Wayne & Bix Reichner. c1959, Gladys Music, Inc. ELVIS PRESLEY. 172.

I Never Cry. w&m; Alice Cooper & Dick Wagner. c1976, Ezra Music & Early Frost Music. ALICE COOPER. 141.

I Never Meant To Hurt You. w&m; Laura Nyro. c1966, Tuna Fish Music, Inc. LAURA NYRO. 141.

I Never Promised You A Rose Garden SEE Rose Garden.

I Never Said I Love You. w&m; Hal David (w) & Archie Jordan (m). c1976, 79, Chess Music, Inc. & Casa David Music. BARBARA MANDRELL. 96, 130.

I Never Wanted To Be A Star SEE To Be A Star.

I Only Have Eyes For You. w&m; Al Dubin (w) & Harry Warren (m). c1934, 75, Remick Music Corp. & Warner Bros., Inc. ART GARFUNKEL/FLAMINGOS/SHIRLEY BASSEY. 30, 139.

I Only Want To Be With You. w&m; Ivor Raymonde & Mike Hawker. c1963, Springfield Music Ltd./Chappell & Co., Inc. DUSTY SPRINGFIELD. 6.

I Pity The Poor Immigrant. w&m; Bob Dylan. c1968, 76, Dwarf Music. BOB DYLAN. 170.

I Pledge My Love. w&m; Dino Fekaris & Freddie Perren (m). c1979, 80, Perren-Vibes Music, Inc. PEACHES & HERB. 24, 45, 99.

I Put A Spell On You. w&m; Jay Hawkins. c1956, 78, Unart Music Corp. CREEDENCE CLEARWATER REVIVAL/"SCREAMIN" JAY HAWKINS. 2, 79, 101.

I Put A Spell On You. w&m; Leon Russell. c1970, 71, Skyhill Publishing Co., Inc. LEON RUSSELL. 152, 197.

I Ran All The Way Home SEE Sorry.

I Saw A Man And He Danced With His Wife. w&m; John Durrill. c1974, Señor Music. CHER. 128.

I Saw Her Again Last Night. w&m; John Phillips & Dennis Doherty. c1966, Trousdale Music Publishers, Inc. MAMAS & THE PAPAS. 119.

I Saw Her Standing There. w&m; John Lennon & Paul McCartney. c1963, 64, Northern Songs Ltd./Gil Music Corp. BEATLES/BOB WELCH. 4, 12, 29, 93, 102, 117, 125, 137, 174, 185.

I Saw The Light. w&m; Todd Rundgren. c1971, 72, Earmark Music, Inc. & Screen Gems-Columbia Music, Inc. TODD RUNDGREN. 138, 152, 197.

I Say A Little Prayer. w&m; Hal David (w) & Burt Bacharach (m). c1966, Blue Seas Music, Inc. & Jac Music Co., Inc. ARETHA FRANKLIN/DIONNE WARWICK. 70.

I Second That Emotion. w&m; William Robinson & Alfred Cleveland. c1967, Jobete Music Co., Inc. SMOKEY ROBINSON & THE MIRACLES. 123.

I Shall Be Released. w&m; Bob Dylan. c1967, 70, 76, Dwarf Music. BAND/BOB DYLAN/BOX TOPS/JOAN BAEZ. 30, 170.

I Shall Sing. w&m; Van Morrison. c1970, 73, WB Music Corp. & Caledonia Soul Music. ART GARFUNKEL/TOOTS & THE MAYTALS. 43, 138.

I Shot The Sheriff. w&m; Bob Marley. c1974, Cayman Music Inc. ERIC CLAPTON. 93.

I Should Have Known Better. w&m; John Lennon & Paul McCartney. c1964, Northern Songs Ltd./Maclen Music, Inc. & Unart Music Corp. BEATLES. 159.

I Shoulda Loved Ya. w&m; Narada Michael Walden, T.M. Stevens & Allee Willis. c1979, 80, Irving Music, Inc., Walden Music, Inc. & Gratitude Sky Music, Inc. NARADA MICHAEL WALDEN. 24, 99.

I Slipped, I Stumbled, I Fell. w&m; Fred Wise (w) & Ben Weisman (m). c1961, Gladys Music, Inc. ELVIS PRESLEY. 172.

I Started A Joke. w&m; Barry, Robin & Maurice Gibb. c1968, 75, Abigail Music Ltd. BEE GEES. 35.

I Still Have Dreams. w&m; Billy Batstone. c1979, Batroc Music & Song Mountain Music. RICHIE FURAY. 8.

I Thank You. w&m; David Porter & Isaac Hayes. c1967, 80, Birdees Music Corp. & Walden Music, Inc. Z.Z. TOP. 99.

I Think I Love You. w&m; Tony Romeo. c1970, Screen Gems-Columbia Music, Inc. PARTRIDGE FAMILY. 38, 88.

I Think I'm Gonna Like It Here. w&m; Don Robertson & Hal Blair (w). c1963, Gladys Music, Inc. ELVIS PRESLEY. 173.

I Think We're Alone Now. w&m; Ritchie Cordell. c1967, Patricia Music Publishing Corp. & Big Seven Music Corp. RUBINOOS/TOMMY JAMES & THE SHONDELLS. 102, 137, 161, 196.

I Thought It Took A Little Time. w&m; Michael Masser & Pam Sawyer. c1973, 76, Jobete Music Co., Inc. DIANA ROSS. 48.

I Threw It All Away. w&m; Bob Dylan. c1969, 76, Big Sky Music. BOB DYLAN. 170.

I Walk The Line. w&m; John R. Cash. c1956, Hi-Lo Music, Inc. JOHNNY CASH. 122.

I Wanna Be Free. w&m; Tommy Boyce & Bobby Hart. c1966, 69, Screen Gems-Columbia Music, Inc. MONKEES. 38.

I Wanna Be Selfish. w&m; Nickolas Ashford & Valerie Simpson. c1974, 76, Nick-O-Val Music. ASHFORD & SIMPSON. 13.

I Wanna Be With You. w&m; Eric Carmen. c1972, C.A.M.-U.S.A., Inc. RASPBERRIES. 141.

I Wanna Be Your Boyfriend. w&m; Joey, Dee Dee, Tommy & Johnny Ramone. c1976, 78, Bleu Disque Music Co. & Taco Tunes. RAMONES. 19.

I Wanna Be Your Lover. w&m; Bob Dylan. c1971, 76, Dwarf Music. 170.

I Wanna Be Your Lover. w&m; Prince. c1979, 80, Ecnirp Music. PRINCE. 188.

I Wanna Be Your Man. w&m; John Lennon & Paul McCartney. c1964, Northern Songs, Ltd./Gil Music Corp. BEATLES. 93, 125.

I Want To Learn A Love Song. w&m; Harry Chapin. c1973, 74, Story Songs Ltd. HARRY CHAPIN. 139.

I Want To Take You Higher. w&m; Sylvester Stewart. c1968, Daly City Music. SLY & THE FAMILY STONE. 152, 203.

I Want To Walk You Home. w&m; Antoine Domino. c1959, Unart Music Corp. FATS DOMINO. 81, 101, 137, 155.

I Want You. w&m; Bob Dylan. c1966, 76, Dwarf Music. BOB DYLAN. 170.

I Want You Back. w&m; Corporation. c1969, 72 Jobete Music Co., Inc. JACKSON 5. 20, 123.

I Want You, I Need You, I Love You. w&m; Maurice Mysels (w) & Ira Kosloff (m). c1956, Elvis Presley Music, Inc. ELVIS PRESLEY. 172.

I Want You To Be My Girl. w&m; Morris Levy. c1956, Nom Music Corp. FRANKIE LYMON & THE TEEN-AGERS. 2, 78, 137, 155, 161.

I Want You To Know. w&m; Antoine Domino & David

Bartholomew. c1957, 58, Unart Music Corp. FATS DOMINO. 78, 82.

I Want You To Want Me. w&m; Rick Nielsen. c1977, Screen Gems-EMI Music Inc. & Adult Music. CHEAP TRICK. 11, 56, 75, 187.

I Want Your Love. w&m; Nile Rodgers & Bernard Edwards. c1978, 79, Cotillion Music Inc. & Chic Music, Inc. CHIC. 27, 147.

I Was Born In Love With You. w&m; Alan & Marilyn Bergman (w) & Michel Legrand (m). c1970, Buckminister Music Ltd./Dijon Music Publications. BOB RALSTON. 192.

I Was Made For Dancin'. w&m; Michael Lloyd. c1978, KCM Music, Michael's Music & Scot Tone Music. LEIF GARRETT. 34, 51, 65, 73, 112.

I Was Made For Lovin' You. w&m; Paul Stanley, Vini Poncia & Desmond Child. c1979, Kiss, Mad Vincent Music & Desmobile Music Co. KISS. 75, 96.

I Was Made To Love Her. w&m; Henry Cosby, Lula Hardaway, Stevie Wonder & Sylvia Moy. c1967, Jobete Music Co., Inc. STEVIE WONDER. 123, 150.

I Was Only Joking. w&m; Rod Stewart & Gary Grainger. c1977, 78, Rod Stewart & Riva Music Ltd. ROD STEWART. 145, 147.

I Was The One. w&m; Aaron Schroeder, Claude DeMetruis, Hal Blair & Bill Peppers. c1956, Anne-Rachel Music Corp. ELVIS PRESLEY. 173.

I (Who Have Nothing). w&m; Jerry Leiber (w), Mike Stoller (w) & C. Donida (m). c1961, 63, Radio Record Ricordi, R.R.R./Yellow Dog Music, Inc. BEN E. KING/GLADYS KNIGHT/SHIRLEY BASSEY/ SYLVESTER. 24.

I Will Never Pass This Way Again. w&m; Ronnie Gaylord. c1972, Vegas Music International Publishing Co. GLEN CAMPBELL. 72, 163, 194, 195.

I Will Survive. w&m; Dino Fekaris & Freddie Perren. c1978, Perren-Vibes Music, Inc. BILLIE JO SPEARS/ GLORIA GAYNOR. 24, 25, 56, 70, 75, 96, 129, 179, 180, 181.

I Wish. w&m; Stevie Wonder. c1976, Jobete Music Co., Inc. & Black Bull Music, Inc. PLAYER'S ASSOCIA-TION/STEVIE WONDER. 23, 77, 95, 128, 134.

I Wish I Was Eighteen Again. w&m; Sonny Throck-morton. c1978, 80, Tree Publishing Co., Inc. GEORGE BURNS. 97.

I Wish It Would Rain. w&m; Barrett Strong, Roger Penzabene & Norman Whitfield. c1967, 68, 73, Jobete Music Co., Inc. GLADYS KNIGHT & THE PIPS/TEMPTATIONS. 17, 123, 150.

I Wish You Peace. w&m; Patti Davis & Bernie Leadon. c1975, 76, WB Music Corp. EAGLES. 141.

I Woke Up In Love This Morning. w&m; Irwin Levine & L. Russell Brown. c1971, Screen Gems-Columbia Music, Inc. PARTRIDGE FAMILY. 38.

I Won't Last A Day Without You. w&m; Paul Williams (w) & Roger Nichols (m). c1972, Almo Music Corp. AL WILSON/BARBRA STREISAND/CARPENTERS/ MAUREEN MC GOVERN/SHIRLEY BASSEY. 23, 56, 70, 71, 181.

I Won't Look Back. w&m; Jimmy Zero. c1978, Bleu Disque Music Co., Inc. CBGB Music & Dead Boys Music. DEAD BOYS. 19.

I Write The Songs. w&m; Bruce Johnston. c1974, Artists Music, Inc. Administered by Interworld Music Group, Inc. BARRY MANILOW. 103, 131, 140.

I Wrote This Song For You. w&m; John Valenti & Joey Spinazola. c1976, 77, Mints Music. JOHN VALENTI. 135.

Ice Castles, Theme From. w&m; Carole Bayer Sager (w) & Marvin Hamlisch (m). c1978, 79, Gold Horizon Music Corp. & Golden Torch Music Corp. Administered by Screen Gems-EMI Music Inc. & Colgems-EMI Music Inc. JUDY COLLINS/MELISSA MANCHESTER. 23, 56, 58, 128, 130, 134.

I'd Have You Any Time. w&m; Bob Dylan & George Harrison. c1970, 76, Big Sky Music & Harrisongs Music Ltd. GEORGE HARRISON. 170.

I'd Like To Teach The World To Sing. w&m; B. Backer, B. Davis, R. Cook & R. Greenaway. c1971, 72, The Coca-Cola Co. Assigned to Shada Music, Inc. HILL-SIDE SINGERS/NEW SEEKERS. 21, 72, 111, 140, 163, 193, 194, 195.

I'd Rather Go Blind. w&m; E. Jordan & B. Foster. c1967, 72, Arc Music Corp. CLARENCE GARTER/ROD STEWART. 1, 168.

I'd Rather Leave While I'm In Love. w&m; Peter Allen & Carole Bayer Sager. c1976, 79, Irving Music, Inc., Woolnough Music, Inc., Unichappell Music, Inc. & Begonia Melodies, Inc. MELANIE/PETER ALLEN/RITA COOLIDGE. 8, 47, 56, 58, 98, 180.

I'd Really Love To See You Tonight. w&m; Parker McGee. c1975, 76, Dawnbreaker Music Co. ENGLAND DAN & JOHN FORD COLEY. 15, 62, 68, 77, 128, 135, 141, 142, 198.

Idiot Wind. w&m; Bob Dylan. c1974, 76, Ram's Horn Music. BOB DYLAN. 170.

If. w&m; David Gates. c1971, Colgems-EMI Music, Inc. BREAD/SHIRLEY BASSEY. 23, 56, 71, 130, 142.

If Dogs Run Free. w&m; Bob Dylan. c1970, 76, Big Sky Music. BOB DYLAN. 170.

If Ever I See You Again. w&m; Joe Brooks. c1977, 78, Big Hill Music Corp. DEBBY BOONE/ROBERTA FLACK. 23, 58, 73, 135.

If I Can't Have You. w&m; Barry, Robin & Maurice Gibb. c1977, Brothers Gibb B.V./Stigwood Music, Inc. Administered by Unichappell Music, Inc. BEE GEES. 50.

If I Could SEE El Condor Pasa.

If I Could Build My Whole World Around You. w&m; Johnny Bristol, Vernon Bullock & Harvey Fuqua. c1967, Jobete Music Co., Inc. MARVIN GAYE & TAMMI TERRELL. 123.

If I Could Have Her Tonight. w&m; Neil Young. c1968, 74, Cotillion Music, Inc. & Broken Arrow Music. NEIL YOUNG. 30.

If I Fell. w&m; John Lennon & Paul McCartney. c1964, Northern Songs Ltd./Maclen Music, Inc. BEATLES. 141.

If I Had A Hammer. w&m; Lee Hays & Pete Seeger. c1958, 62, Ludlow Music, Inc. PETE SEEGER/PETER, PAUL & MARY/TRINI LOPEZ/WEAVERS. 68, 85, 126.

If I Had My Way. w&m; Rev. Gary Davis. c1962, Pepamar Music Corp. KINGSTON TRIO/PETER, PAUL & MARY/REV. GARY DAVIS. 35, 41, 67.

If I Sing You A Love Song. w&m; Ronnie Scott & Steve Wolfe. c1978, Scott-Wolfe Songs Ltd. BONNIE TYLER. 74.

If I Were A Carpenter. w&m; Tim Hardin. c1966, Faithful Virtue Music Co., Inc. & Hudson Bay Music Co. BOBBY DARIN/FOUR TOPS/TIM HARDIN. 93, 186.

If I Were A Rich Man. w&m; Sheldon Harnick (w) & Jerry Bock (m). c1964, The Times Square Music Publications Co. TIJUANA BRASS/ZERO MOSTEL. 23, 56, 130.

If I Were Your Woman. w&m; Gloria Jones, La Verne Ware, Pam Sawyer & Clay McMurray. c1970, 72, Jobete Music Co., Inc. GLADYS KNIGHT & THE PIPS. 17, 123.

If It Don't Fit, Don't Force It. w&m; Carolyn Johns (w) & Larry Farrow (m). c1978, Funky Caroline Music & Careers Music. KELLEE PATTERSON. 51.

If Loving You Is Wrong I Don't Want To Be Right SEE I Don't Want To Be Right.

If Not For You. w&m; Bob Dylan. c1970, 76, Big Sky Music. BOB DYLAN. 170.

If The World Ran Out Of Love Tonight. w&m; Blake Mevis, Michael Garvin, Kelly & Steve Wilson. c1977, 78, ABC-Dunhill Music, Inc. & American Broadcasting Music, Inc. ENGLAND DAN & JOHN FORD COLEY. 74.

If We Only Have Love. w&m; Mort Shuman (w), Eric Blau (w) & Jacques Brel (m). c1968, Hill and Range Songs, Inc. JOHNNY MATHIS/SHIRLEY BASSEY. 89.

If You Can't Give Me Love. w&m; Nicky Chinn & Mike Chapman. c1979, Chinnichap Publishing Inc. Administered by Careers Music, Inc. SUZI QUATRO. 11, 75, 187.

If You Could Read My Mind. w&m; Gordon Lightfoot. c1969, 70, Early Morning Music, a division of EMP Ltd. BARBRA STREISAND/GORDON LIGHTFOOT/OLIVIA NEWTON-JOHN. 36, 55, 131, 136, 138, 174, 182.

If You Cry True Love, True Love SEE True Love, True Love.

If You Don't Get It The First Time, Back Up And Try It Again, Party. w&m; James Brown. c1973, 74, Dyna-tone Publishing Co. JAMES BROWN. 107.

If You Gotta Go, Go Now. w&m; Bob Dylan. c1965, M. Witmark & Sons. LIVERPOOL FIVE/MANFRED MANN. 69.

If You Know What I Mean. w&m; Neil Diamond. c1976, Stonebridge Music. NEIL DIAMOND. 62, 145.

If You Leave Me Now. w&m; Peter Cetera. c1976, Polish Prince Music & Big Elk Music. CHICAGO. 23, 77, 128, 130, 142.

If You Love Me (Let Me Know). w&m; John Rostill. c1974, Petal Music, Ltd./Al Gallico Music Corp. OLIVIA NEWTON-JOHN. 28, 106, 134, 156, 198.

If You Remember Me. w&m; Carole Bayer Sager (w) & Marvin Hamlisch (m). c1979, Chappell & Co., Inc., Red Bullet Music, Unichappell & Begonia Melodies Inc. CHRIS THOMPSON. 47.

If You See Her, Say Hello. w&m; Bob Dylan. c1974, 76, Ram's Horn Music. BOB DYLAN. 170.

If You Should Sail. w&m; Reed Nielsen & Mark Pearson. c1980, Third Story Music, Inc. & Poorhouse Publishing Co. NIELSEN & PEARSON. 188.

If You Talk In Your Sleep. w&m; Bobby "Red" West & Johnny Christopher. c1974, Elvis Music, Inc. & Easy Nine Music. ELVIS PRESLEY. 93.

If You Wanna Be Happy. w&m; Frank J. & C. Guida & Joseph Royster. c1962, 63, Rockmasters, Inc. JIMMY SOUL. 5.

If You Wanna Get To Heaven. w&m; Steve Cash & John Dillon. c1974, Lost Cabin Music. OZARK MOUNTAIN DAREDEVILS. 28.

If You Would Just Drop By. w&m; Arlo Guthrie. c1969, Howard Beach Music Inc. ARLO GUTHRIE. 7.

If You're Ready (Come Go With Me). w&m; Homer Banks, Raymond Jackson & Carl Hampton. c1972, 73, East-Memphis Music Corp. STAPLE SINGERS. 105, 122.

If You've Got The Time (I've Got The Place). w&m; Bill Backer. c1971, 73, Shada Music, Inc. HENRY MANCINI. 111.

Il Mio Mondo SEE You're My World.

I'll Always Call Your Name. w&m; Beeb Birtles. c1975, 77, Australian Tumblewood Music. LITTLE RIVER BAND. 128, 135.

I'll Be Back. w&m; Sid Wayne (w) & Ben Weisman (m). c1966, Gladys Music, Inc. ELVIS PRESLEY. 173.

I'll Be Doggone. w&m; William Robinson, Warren Moore & Marv Tarplin. c1965, Jobete Music Co., Inc. MARVIN GAYE. 123, 166.

I'll Be Here. w&m; Wade Brown, Jr., David H. Jones, Jr. & John Bristol. c1972, Jobete Music Co., Inc. GLADYS KNIGHT & THE PIPS. 17.

I'll Be On My Way. w&m; John Lennon & Paul McCartney. c1963, Northern Songs Ltd./Unart Music Corp. BEATLES. 80.

I'll Be There. w&m; Bob West, Hal Davis, Willie Hutch & Berry Gordy. c1970, Jobete Music Co., Inc. JACKSON 5. 20, 123, 128, 150.

I'll Be Your Baby Tonight. w&m; Bob Dylan. c1968, 76, Dwarf Music. BOB DYLAN. 170.

I'll Be Your Shelter (In Time Of Storm). w&m; Homer Banks, Raymond Jackson & Carl Hampton. c1971, East-Memphis Music & Klondike Ents., Ltd. LUTHER LUTHER INGRAM. 122.

I'll Come Running Back To You. w&m; Bill Cook. c1957, Big Billy Music Co. & Venice Music Inc. SAM COOKE. 78, 137.

I'll Get By. w&m; Roy Turk (w) & Fred E. Ahlert (m).

c1928, 56, Bourne, Inc. & Fred Ahlert Music Corp. PEGGY LEE. 63.

I'll Go Crazy. w&m; James Brown. c1960, 68, Wisto Publishing Co. JAMES BROWN. 18.

I'll Have To Say I Love You In A Song. w&m; Jim Croce. c1973, 74, Blendingwell Music Inc. & American Broadcasting Music, Inc. JIM CROCE. 21, 87, 163, 199.

I'll Keep You Satisfied. w&m; John Lennon & Paul McCartney. c1963, Northern Songs, Ltd./Unart Music Corp. BILLY J. KRAMER. 81.

I'll Meet You Halfway. w&m; Wes Farrell & Gerry Goffin. c1971, Screen Gems-Columbia Music, Inc. PARTRIDGE FAMILY. 38.

I'll Never Fall In Love Again. w&m; Hal David (w) & Burt Bacharach (m). c1969, Blue Seas Music, Inc. & Jac Music Co., Inc. CARPENTERS/DIONNE WARWICK/SHIRLEY BASSEY. 70, 71.

I'll Never Find Another You. w&m; Tom Springfield. c1964, Springfield Music, Ltd./Chappell & Co., Inc. SEEKERS. 68.

I'll Never Love This Way Again. w&m; Will Jennings (w) & Richard Kerr (m). c1977, 79, Irving Music, Inc. DIONNE WARWICK. 24, 56, 58, 70, 75, 96, 97, 179, 180.

I'll Never, Never Let You Go. w&m; James Brown. c1961, 68, Wisto Publishing Co. JAMES BROWN. 18.

I'll Play For You. w&m; James Seals & Dash Crofts (w). c1975, Dawnbreaker Music Co. SEALS & CROFTS. 139.

I'll Play The Blues For You. w&m; Jerry Beach. c1971, East-Memphis Music & Rogan Publishing. ALBERT KING. 122.

I'll See You In My Dreams. w&m; Gus Kahn (w) & Isham Jones (m). c1924, 52, 66, Leo Feist, Inc. ART TATUM/CHET ATKINS/JIMMIE LUNCEFORD. 140.

I'll Still Love You. w&m; Jim Weatherly. c1970, 74, Keca Music Inc. JIM WEATHERLY. 139.

I'll Take You There. w&m; Alvertis Isbell. c1972, East-Memphis Music Corp. STAPLE SINGERS. 105, 122.

I'm A Believer. w&m; Neil Diamond. c1966, Screen Gems-Columbia Music, Inc. MONKEES. 38.

I'm A Cruiser. w&m; J. Morali, H. Belolo & V. Willis. c1978, Scorpio Music (Black Scorpio). Controlled by Can't Stop Music. VILLAGE PEOPLE. 200.

I'm A Drifter. w&m; Bobby Goldsboro. c1969, Detail Music, Inc. BOBBY GOLDSBORO. 82.

I'm A Fool For You. w&m; Floyd Huddleston & Robert Colby. c1954, Travis Music Co., Inc. FATS DOMINO. 140.

I'm A Loser. w&m; John Lennon & Paul McCartney. c1964, Northern Songs Ltd./Maclen Music, Inc. BEATLES. 35.

I'm A Road Runner SEE Road Runner (B. Holland, L. Dozier, E. Holland.)

I'm Alone Because I Love You. w&m; Joe Young. c1930, M. Witmark & Sons. LEADBELLY. 132.

I'm Alright. w&m; Kenny Loggins. c1980, Milk Money Music. KENNY LOGGINS. 190.

I'm Comin' Home Again. w&m; Bruce Roberts & Carole Bayer Sager. c1974, Times Square Music Publications Co. & The E.M.P. Co. GLADYS KNIGHT. 66.

I'm Coming Out. w&m; Nile Rodgers & Bernard Edwards. c1980, Chic Music, Inc. Administered by Warner-Tamerlane Publishing Corp. DIANA ROSS. 188.

I'm Easy. w&m; Keith Carradine. c1975, MCA Music, a division of MCA Inc., Duchess Music Corp. & Easy Music. Administered by MCA Music. KEITH CARRADINE. 77, 126, 128, 184, 193.

I'm Every Woman. w&m; Nickolas Ashford & Valerie Simpson. c1978, Nick-O-Val Music, Inc. CHAKA KHAN. 24, 34, 63, 73, 112.

I'm Going Home. w&m; Arlo Guthrie. c1967, 69, Appleseed Music Inc. ARLO GUTHRIE. 7.

I'm Gonna Be A Wheel Someday. w&m; Dave Bartholomew, Roy Hayes & Antoine Domino. c1957, 59, Unart Music Corp. FATS DOMINO. 82.

I'm Gonna Be Strong. w&m; Barry Mann & Cynthia Weil. c1963, Screen Gems-EMI Music Inc. GENE PITNEY. 158.

I'm Gonna Get Married. w&m; L. Price & H. Logan. c1959, Lloyd & Logan Music. LLOYD PRICE. 5.

I'm Gonna Let My Heart Do The Walking. w&m; Brian Holland, Harold Beatty & Edward Holland. c1976, Gold Forever Music Inc., Stone Diamond Music Corp. & Holland-Dozier-Holland Music. Administered by Blackwood Music Inc. SUPREMES. 184.

I'm Gonna Love You Too. w&m; Joe Mauldin, Niki Sullivan & Norman Petty. c1957, 58, MPL Communications, Inc. BLONDIE/BUDDY HOLLY. 14, 33.

I'm Gonna Make You Love Me. w&m; Jerry Ross, Ken Gamble & Jerry Williams. c1966, 68, Act Three Music & Downstair Music, Inc. Administered by Unichappell Music Inc. DIANA ROSS & THE SUPREMES/MADELINE BELL. 6, 93.

I'm Gonna Say It Now. w&m; Phil Ochs. c1965, 68, Barricade Music, Inc. PHIL OCHS. 144.

I'm Happy Just To Dance With You. w&m; John Lennon & Paul McCartney. c1964, Northern Songs Ltd./Maclen Music, Inc. BEATLES. 35, 61, 159.

I'm Her Fool. w&m; Billy Swan & Dennis Linde. c1974, 75, Combine Music Corp. BILLY SWAN. 89.

I'm In Love Again. w&m; Antoine Domino & Dave Bartholomew. c1956, Unart Music Corp. FATS DOMINO/FONTAINE SISTERS/RICK NELSON. 78, 79, 101, 137, 155.

I'm In The Mood For Love. w&m; Jimmy McHugh & Dorothy Fields. c1935, 63, 65, Robbins Music Corp. BOOTS RANDOLPH/FATS DOMINO/FERRANTE & TEICHER/SHIRLEY BASSEY. 140.

I'm Just A Country Boy. w&m; Fred Brooks & Marshall Barer. c1954, Folkways Music Publishers, Inc. DON WILLIAMS. 199.

I'm Leaving It (All) Up To You. w&m; Don Harris & Dewey Terry, Jr. c1957, 63, Venice Music. DALE &

GRACE/DONNY & MARIE OSMOND/FREDDY FENDER/LINDA RONSTADT. 3, 35, 93, 100, 159.

I'm Livin' In Shame. w&m; Pam Sawyer, R. Dean Taylor, Frank Wilson, Henry Cosby & Berry Gordy, Jr. c1969, Jobete Music Co., Inc. SUPREMES. 123.

I'm Lookin' For Someone To Love. w&m; Buddy Holly & Norman Petty. c1957, MPL Communications, Inc. BUDDY HOLLY. 14.

I'm Losing You. w&m; Cornelius Grant, Norman Whitfield & Eddie Holland. c1966, Jobete Music Co., Inc. RARE EARTH/TEMPTATIONS. 123, 167.

I'm Mad Again. w&m; John Lee Hooker. c1961, 68, Conrad Music, a division of Arc Music Corp. JOHN LEE HOOKER. 169.

I'm Never Gonna Be Alone Anymore. w&m; Eddie & Carter Cornelius. c1969, 73, Unart Music Corp. & Stage Door Music Publishing, Inc. CORNELIUS BROTHERS & SISTER ROSE. 72.

I'm Not A Juvenile Delinquent. w&m; George Goldner. c1956, 78, Nom Music Publishing Corp. FRANKIE LYMON & THE TEENAGERS. 2.

I'm Not Gonna Let It Bother Me Tonight. w&m; Buddy Buie, Robert Nix & Dean Daughtry. c1978, Low-Sal, Inc. ATLANTA RHYTHM SECTION. 135.

I'm Not Lisa. w&m; Jessi Colter. c1972, 75, Baron Music Publishing Co. JESSI COLTER. 28, 58, 126, 128, 134.

I'm On My Way. w&m; Mark Safan. c1975, 78, Pink Flower Music. CAPTAIN & TENNILLE. 73, 135, 142.

I'm On The Outside (Looking In). w&m; Teddy Randazzo & Bobby Weinstein. c1964, 67, South Mountain Music Corp. Assigned to Vogue Music, Inc. LITTLE ANTHONY & THE IMPERIALS. 78, 160.

I'm Ready For Love. w&m; Eddie Holland, Lamont Dozier & Brian Holland. c1966, Jobete Music Co., Inc. MARTHA & THE VANDELLAS. 123, 150, 167.

I'm Stickin' With You. w&m; James Bowen & Buddy Knox. c1957, Jackie Music Corp. Assigned to Nom Music. JIMMY BOWEN. 137, 161.

I'm Still In Love With You. w&m; Al Green, Willie Mitchell & Al Jackson. c1972, Jec Publishing & Al Green Music, Inc. AL GREEN. 122.

I'm Still In Love With You. w&m; T-Bone Walker. c1943, Aaron Walker. Assigned to St. Louis Music Corp. & Paul Reiner Music Publishing Co., Inc. Controlled by Unichappell Music, Inc. T-BONE WALKER. 155.

I'm Stone In Love With You. w&m; Thomas Bell, Linda Creed & Anthony Bell. c1972, Assorted Music & Bell Boy Music. JOHNNY MATHIS/STYLISTICS. 130.

I'm Stranded SEE Stranded.

I'm The One You Need. w&m; Eddie Holland, Lamont Dozier & Brian Holland. c1966, Jobete Music Co., Inc. MIRACLES. 167.

I'm Walkin'. w&m; Antoine Domino & Dave Bartholomew. c1957, Unart Music Corp. BILL HALEY & THE COMETS/ELLA FITZGERALD/FATS DOMINO/RICK NELSON. 78, 82, 101, 137, 155, 161.

I'm Your Boogie Man. w&m; H.W. Casey & R. Finch. c1976, Sherlyn Publishing Co. & Harrick Music, Inc. KC & THE SUNSHINE BAND. 24, 34, 135.

I'm Your Puppet. w&m; Dan Penn & Linden Oldham. c1965, Fame Publishing Co., Inc. JAMES & BOBBY PURIFY. 3.

Imaginary Lover. w&m; Buddy Buie, Robert Nix & Dean Daughtry. c1978, Low-Sal Inc. ATLANTA RHYTHM SECTION. 23, 135.

Imagination. w&m; Barry Goldberg & Gerry Goffin. c1973, Screen Gems-Columbia Music, Inc. GLADYS KNIGHT & THE PIPS. 17, 52, 54.

Imagine. w&m; John Lennon. c1971, Northern Songs Ltd./Maclen Music, Inc. JOHN LENNON. 30, 141, 197.

Immigrant. w&m; Neil Sedaka & Phil Cody. c1973, 75, Don Kirshner Music, Inc. & Kirshner Songs Inc. NEIL SEDAKA. 41, 139.

Immigrant Song. w&m; Jimmy Page & Robert Plant. c1970, Superhype Publishing. LED ZEPPELIN. 114, 138, 182.

Immigration Man. w&m; Graham Nash. c1972, Thin Ice Music. DAVID CROSBY & GRAHAM NASH. 151, 197.

Impossible Dream. w&m; Joe Darion (w) & Mitch Leigh (m). c1965, Andrew Scott, Inc., Helena Music Corp. & Sam Fox Publishing Co., Inc. HESITATIONS/JACK JONES/ROGER WILLIAMS. 76.

In America. w&m; Charlie Daniels, Tom Crain, "Taz" DiGregorio, Fred Edwards, Charlie Hayward & Jim Marshall. c1980, Hat Ban Music. CHARLIE DANIELS BAND. 189.

In And Out Of Love. w&m; Brian Holland, Lamont Dozier & Eddie Holland. c1967, Jobete Music Co., Inc. SUPREMES. 123.

In Crowd. w&m; Billy Page. c1964, 65, American Music, Inc. MAMAS & THE PAPAS. 119.

In France They Kiss On Main Street. w&m; Joni Mitchell. c1975, 76, Crazy Crow Music. JONI MITCHELL. 30, 36, 136.

In Held 'Twas In I SEE Individual songs: Glimpses Of Nirvana, 'Twas Teatime At The Circus, In The Autumn Of My Madness, Look To Your Soul & Grand Finale.

In Hollywood (Everybody Is A Star). w&m; H. Belolo (w), P. Hurtt (w) & J. Morali (m). c1977, Scorpio Music (Black Scorpio). Controlled by Can't Stop Music. VILLAGE PEOPLE. 200.

In My Life. w&m; John Lennon & Paul McCartney. c1965, Northern Songs Ltd./Maclen Music, Inc. BEATLES/JUDY COLLINS. 30, 61, 182.

In No Time At All. w&m; Richard Leigh & Archie Jordan. c1979, United Artists Music Co., Inc. & Chess Music, Inc. RONNIE MILSAP. 82.

In Our Time. w&m; Ray Fox (w) & Hod David (m). c1969, 70, Notable Music Co., Inc. ANDREA MARCOVICCI. 186.

In Perfect Harmony SEE I'd Like To Teach The World To Sing.

In The Autumn Of My Madness. w&m; Gary Brooker, Matthew Fisher & Keith Reid. c1968, 72, Essex Music International. PROCOL HARUM. 42.

In The Back Of My Mind. w&m; Brian Wilson. c1965, Sea Of Tunes Publishing Co. BEACH BOYS. 9.

In The Bush. w&m; P. Adams & S. Cooper. c1978, PAP Music Division, Leeds Music Corp. & Phylmar Music. MUSIQUE. 34, 65, 112.

In The Flesh. w&m; Deborah Harry & Chris Stein. c1977, 78, Jiru Music & Monster Island Music. BLONDIE. 19.

In The Hour Of Not Quite Rain. w&m; Richie Furay & Mickeala Callen. c1968, Cotillion Music, Inc., Ten East Music & Springalo Toones. BUFFALO SPRING-FIELD. 39.

In The Midnight Hour. w&m; Wilson Pickett & Steve Cropper. c1966, 67, East-Memphis Music Publishing Co. & Cotillion Music, Inc. MIRETTES/RASCALS/WILSON PICKETT. 35, 100, 122, 138, 197.

In The Mood. w&m; Joe Garland. c1939, 60, Shapiro, Bernstein & Co., Inc. BETTE MIDLER. 58.

In The Navy. w&m; J. Morali, H. Belolo & V. Willis. c1979, Scorpio Music (Black Scorpio). Controlled by Can't Stop Music. VILLAGE PEOPLE. 130, 134.

In The Night-Time. w&m; Michael Henderson & Sylvester Rivers. c1978, Electrocord Publishing Co. MICHAEL HENDERSON. 66.

In The Still Of The Night. w&m; Fred Parris. c1956, Cherio Music Publishers, Inc. FIVE SATINS. 4.

In The Summertime. w&m; Ray Dorset. c1970, Our Music Ltd./Don Kirshner Music, Inc. MUNGO JERRY. 88.

In Thee. w&m; Allen Lanier. c1979, B. O' Cult Songs, Inc. BLUE OYSTER CULT. 27.

In 25 Words Or Less. w&m; Bill LaBounty & Roy Freeland. c1977, 78, Captain Crystal Music. BILL LA BOUNTY. 74.

In Your Arms. w&m; Aaron Schroeder & Wally Gold. c1961, Gladys Music, Inc. ELVIS PRESLEY. 172.

In-A-Gadda-Da-Vida. w&m; Doug Ingle. c1968, 69, Cotillion Music, Inc., Ten East Music & Itasca Music. IRON BUTTERFLY. 36, 55, 149, 152, 174, 182.

Indian Lake. w&m; Tony Romeo. c1968, Pocket Full Of Tunes, Inc. FREDDY WELLER. 192.

Indian Summer. w&m; Jim Morrison & Robbie Krieger. c1970, Doors Music Co. DOORS. 54.

Indiana Wants Me. w&m; R. Dean Taylor. c1970, Jobete Music Co., Inc. R. DEAN TAYLOR. 123.

Inner City Blues (Make Me Wanna Holler). w&m; Marvin Gaye & James Nyx, Jr. c1971, Jobete Music Co., Inc. MARVIN GAYE. 150.

Instant Karma. w&m; John Lennon. c1970, Northern Songs Ltd./Maclen Music, Inc. JOHN LENNON. 61.

Instant Replay. w&m; Dan Hartman. c1978, Silver Steed Music, Inc. DAN HARTMAN. 34, 65, 66.

International Velvet, Sarah's Theme From SEE Ride.

Into The Black SEE Hey Hey, My My.

Into The Mystic. w&m; Van Morrison. c1970, 71, WB Music Corp. & Caledonia Soul Music. VAN MORRISON. 127, 174.

Lo Che Non Vivo SEE You Don't Have To Say You Love Me.

Is It Still Good To Ya. w&m; Nickolas Ashford & Valerie Simpson. c1978, Nick-O-Val Music. ASHFORD & SIMPSON. 65.

Is She Really Going Out With Him. w&m; Joe Jackson. c1979, Albion Music, Ltd./Almo Music Corp. JOE JACKSON. 75.

Is There Anybody Here. w&m; Phil Ochs. c1966, 68, Barricade Music, Inc. PHIL OCHS. 144.

Isis. w&m; Bob Dylan & Jacques Levy (w). c1975, 76, Ram's Horn Music. BOB DYLAN. 170.

Island Girl. w&m; Elton John & Bernie Taupin. c1975, Big Pig Music Ltd. ELTON JOHN. 131.

Island Of Love (Kauai). w&m; Sid Tepper & Roy C. Bennett. c1961, Gladys Music, Inc. ELVIS PRESLEY. 173.

Isn't It A Pity. w&m; George Harrison. c1970, Harrisongs Ltd./Harrisongs Music, Inc. GEORGE HARRISON. 63, 125.

Isn't She Lovely. w&m; Stevie Wonder. c1976, Jobete Music Co., Inc. & Black Bull Music, Inc. JERMAINE JACKSON/STEVIE WONDER. 23, 24, 56, 77, 95, 128, 130, 134.

It Ain't Me, Babe. w&m; Bob Dylan. c1964, M. Witmark & Sons & Warner Bros. Inc. BOB DYLAN/GLEN CAMPBELL/JOAN BAEZ/TURTLES. 35, 67, 69, 132, 138.

It Came To Me. w&m; Nickolas Ashford & Valerie Simpson. c1975, 76, Nick-O-Val Music. ASHFORD & SIMPSON. 13.

It Do Me So Good. w&m; Willie Dixon & Billy Emerson. c1961, Arc Music Corp. LITTLE MISS CORNSHOCK. 1.

It Doesn't Matter Anymore. w&m; Paul Anka. c1958, 74, Spanka Music Corp. BUDDY HOLLY. 6.

It Don't Matter To Me. w&m; David Gates. c1969, 70, Screen Gems-Columbia Music, Inc. BREAD. 88.

It Don't Worry Me. w&m; Keith Carradine. c1975, Lion's Gate Music Co. Administered by American Broadcasting Music, Inc. 28.

It Feels So Good To Be Loved So Bad. w&m; Teddy Randazzo, Victoria Pike & Roger Joyce. c1976, 77, Razzle Dazzle Music, Inc. MANHATTANS. 164.

It Hurts So Bad. w&m; Kim Carnes. No copyright information located. KIM CARNES. 129.

It Keeps Right On A-Hurtin'. w&m; Johnny Tillotson. c1961, 62, Tanridge Music, Inc. Assigned to Ridge Music Corp. JOHNNY TILLOTSON. 3.

It Keeps You Runnin'. w&m; Michael McDonald. c1976, Tauripin Tunes. DOOBIE BROTHERS. 141, 146.

It Must Be Him. w&m; Mack David (w) & Gilbert Becaud (m). c1966, 67, Editions Rouge/Asa Music Co., Inc. VIKKI CARR. 140.

It Never Rains In Southern California. w&m; Albert Hammond & Mike Hazelwood. c1972, 73, Landers-Roberts Music. Administered by April Music Inc. ALBERT HAMMOND/LETTERMEN. 72, 131, 165, 194.

It Only Takes A Minute. w&m; Dennis Lambert & Brian Potter. c1975, ABC-Dunhill Music & One Of A Kind Music Co. TAVARES. 26.

It Was A Good Time. w&m; Mack David (w), Mike Curb (w) & Maurice Jarre (m). c1970, Metro-Goldwyn-Mayer Inc. Controlled by Leo Feist, Inc. LIZA MINELLI/MANTOVANI. 140, 192.

It Was A Very Good Year. w&m; Erwin Drake. c1961, 65, Dolfi Music, Inc. FRANK SINATRA. 93.

It Was Almost Like A Song. w&m; Hal David (w) & Archie Jordan (m). c1977, Chess Music, Inc. & Casa David Music. ACE CANNON/FLOYD CRAMER/JOHNNY MATHIS/RONNIE MILSAP. 23, 56, 96, 126, 128, 134, 142, 181.

It Was So Easy. w&m; Carly Simon & Jacob Brackman. c1972, Quackenbush Music, Ltd. CARLY SIMON. 139.

It Won't Be Long. w&m; John Lennon & Paul McCartney. c1963, 64, Northern Songs Ltd./Maclen Music, Inc. BEATLES. 159.

Itchy, Twitchy Feeling. w&m; Jimmy Oliver. c1958, EmKay Music. BOBBY HENDRICKS. 5.

It'll Come, It'll Come, It'll Come. w&m; Nickolas Ashford & Valerie Simpson. c1975, 76, Nick-O-Val Music. ASHFORD & SIMPSON. 13.

It's A Great Life. w&m; Karen O'Hara & Denny McReynolds. c1967, Tapez Music, Inc. TRINI LOPEZ. 76.

It's A Heartache. w&m; Ronnie Scott & Steve Wolfe. c1977, 78, Mighty Music & Pi-Gem Music Inc. BONNIE TYLER/DAVE & SUGAR/FLOYD CRAMER. 73, 130, 134, 135.

It's A Miracle. w&m; Barry Manilow & Marty Panzer (w). c1974, Kamakazi Music Corp. BARRY MANILOW. 199.

It's A Plain Shame. w&m; Peter Frampton. c1972, 76, Almo Music Corp., Fram-Dee Music Ltd. & United Artists Music Ltd. PETER FRAMPTON. 15, 199.

It's A Sin When You Love Somebody. w&m; Jimmy Webb. c1973, 74, Canopy Music, Inc. GLEN CAMPBELL. 139.

It's A Wonderful World. w&m; Sid Tepper & Roy C. Bennett. c1964, Gladys Music, Inc. ELVIS PRESLEY. 172.

It's All I Can Do. w&m; Ric Ocasek. c1979, Lido Music, Inc. CARS. 27, 147.

It's All In The Game. w&m; Carl Sigman (w) & Gen. Charles G. Dawes (m). c1912, 51, 70, 78, Warner Bros. Inc. FOUR TOPS/GEORGE BENSON/SLIM WHITMAN. 35, 87, 138, 146.

It's All Over Now, Baby Blue. w&m; Bob Dylan. c1965, M. Witmark & Sons & Warner Bros. Inc. BOB DYLAN/BYRDS/JOAN BAEZ. 35, 67, 152.

It's Alright Ma (I'm Only Bleeding). w&m; Bob Dylan. c1965, M. Witmark & Sons & Warner Bros. Inc. BOB DYLAN/JOAN BAEZ. 35, 67.

I've Had It. w&m; Ray Ceroni. c1958, 59, 78, Brent Music Corp. Assigned to Slow Dancing Music, Inc. BELL NOTES. 5.

I've Lost You. w&m; Ken Howard & Alan Blaikley. c1970, Carlin Music Corp. Administered by Gladys Music Inc. ELVIS PRESLEY. 191.

I've Never Been In Love. w&m; Melissa A. Connell. c1977, Big Neck Music. SUZI QUATRO. 176.

I've Passed This Way Before. w&m; James Dean & William Weatherspoon. c1966, Jobete Music Co., Inc. JIMMY RUFFIN. 167.

I've Told Ev'ry Little Star. w&m; Oscar Hammerstein II (w) & Jerome Kern (m). c1932, T.B. Harms Co. LINDA SCOTT. 78, 160.

Jack And Jill. w&m; Ray E. Parker, Jr. c1977, Raydiola Music. RAYDIO. 34, 135, 142.

Jackie Blue. w&m; Larry Lee & Steve Cash. c1974, 75, Larry Lee & Steve Cash. Controlled by Lost Cabin Music. OZARK MOUNTAIN DAREDEVILS. 28, 36, 62, 136, 139, 141.

Jailhouse Rock. w&m; Jerry Leiber & Mike Stoller. c1957, Elvis Presley Music. Assigned to Gladys Music. Controlled by Chappell & Co., Inc. ELVIS PRESLEY. 101, 137, 172.

Jam Up And Jelly Tight. w&m; Tommy Roe (w) & Freddy Weller (m). c1969, 70, Low-Twi Music, Inc. TOMMY ROE. 64, 186.

Jam Up Twist. w&m; Tommy Ridgeley. c1954, Progressive Music Publishing Co., Inc. TOMMY RIDGELEY. 90.

Jamie. w&m; Barrett Strong & William Stevenson. c1961, Jobete Music Co., EDDIE HOLLAND. 150.

Jamie's Cryin'. w&m; Edward & Alex Van Halen, Michael Anthony & David Lee Roth. c1978, 80, Van Halen Music. VAN HALEN. 22, 147.

Jane. w&m; David Freiberg, Jim McPherson, Craig Chaquico (m) & Paul Kantner (m). c1979, Pods Publishing, Kosher Dill Music, Little Dragon Music & Lunatunes. JEFFERSON STARSHIP. 22, 87, 147, 188.

Jawbone. w&m; J. Robbie Robertson & Richard Manuel. c1969, 70, Canaan Music, Inc. BAND. 202.

Jazzman. w&m; David Palmer & Carole King. c1974, Colgems-EMI Music Inc. CAROLE KING. 28, 130, 134, 156.

Jennifer Eccles. w&m; Graham Nash & Allen Clarke. c1968, Gralto Music Ltd. HOLLIES. 76.

Jenny, Jenny. w&m; Enotris Johnson & Richard Penniman. c1957, 69, Venice Music Inc. LITTLE RICHARD. 137, 159.

Jesse. w&m; Carly Simon & Mike Mainieri (w). c1980, Quackenbush Music Ltd. & Redeye Music. CARLY SIMON. 162, 190.

Jesse. w&m; Janis Ian. c1972, 73, Frank Music Corp. JANIS IAN/JOAN BAEZ/ROBERTA FLACK. 165.

Jessica. w&m; Forest Richard Betts (m). c1973, 74, No

Exit Music Co., Inc. ALLMAN BROTHERS BAND. 36, 55, 138, 174.

Jesus Is Just Alright. w&m; Art Reynolds. c1969, 72, Alexis-Yolk. DOOBIE BROTHERS. 28, 77, 104, 156.

Jet Airliner. w&m; Paul Pena. c1977, Sailor Music & No Thought Music. STEVE MILLER BAND. 22, 127, 145.

Jim Dandy. w&m; Lincoln Chase. c1957, 69, Raleigh Music, Inc. Assigned to Shelby Singleton Music Inc. BLACK OAK ARKANSAS. 194.

Jimmy Mack. w&m; Brian Holland, Lamont Dozier & Eddie Holland. c1966, 67, Jobete Music Co., Inc. MARTHA & THE VANDELLAS. 123, 167.

Jive Talkin'. w&m; Barry, Robin & Maurice Gibb. c1975, Abigail Music, Ltd. & Flamm Music, Ltd./ Casserole Music Corp. & Flamm Music, Inc. BEE GEES/RUFUS FEATURING CHAKA KHAN. 131, 133, 139.

Jo-Ann. w&m; John & James Cunningham. c1957, Big Seven Music Corp. PLAYMATES. 101.

Jocko Homo. w&m; Devo. c1977, DEVO Music. DEVO. 153.

Jody Girl. w&m; Bob Seger. c1974, 75, Gear Publishing Co. BOB SEGER. 142.

Joe Hill. w&m; Earl Robinson. c1938, 65, MCA Music, a division of MCA, Inc. JOAN BAEZ. 202.

Joe Hill. w&m; Phil Ochs (w) & Traditional (m). c1966, 68, Barricade Music, Inc. PHIL OCHS. 144.

Joey. w&m; Bob Dylan & Jacques Levy (w). c1975, 76, Ram's Horn Music. BOB DYLAN. 170.

John Looked Down. w&m; Arlo Guthrie. c1968, 69, Appleseed Music Inc. ARLO GUTHRIE. 7.

John Wesley Harding. w&m; Bob Dylan. c1968, 76, Dwarf Music. BOB DYLAN. 170.

Johnny Angel. w&m; Lyn Duddy (w) & Lee Pockriss (m). c1960, 62, Post Music, Inc. & United Artists Music Co., Inc. CARPENTERS/SHELLEY FABARES. 78, 82, 102.

Johnny B. Goode. w&m; Chuck Berry. c1958, Arc Music Corp. CHAMBERS BROTHERS/CHUCK BERRY/ELVIS PRESLEY/GRATEFUL DEAD/ JERRY LEE LEWIS/JIMI HENDRIX/JOHNNY WINTER/ROLLING STONES. 5, 10, 44, 78, 100, 152, 155, 168, 169.

Johnny Strikes Up The Band. w&m; Warren Zevon. c1978, Zevon Music. WARREN ZEVON. 12, 74.

Johnny's Garden. w&m; Stephen Stills. c1972, 74, Gold Hill Music, Inc. STEPHEN STILLS. 138.

Jojo. w&m; Boz Scaggs, David Foster & David Lasley. c1980, Boz Scaggs Music, Foster Frees Music, Irving Music & Almo Music Corp. BOZ SCAGGS. 189.

Joker. w&m; Steve Miller. c1973, Haworth Enterprises doing business as Sailor Music. STEVE MILLER BAND. 53, 106.

Josie. w&m; Walter Becker & Donald Fagen. c1977, 78, ABC-Dunhill Music, Inc. STEELY DAN. 74.

Joy. w&m; J.S. Bach (m). c1972, Westport Music Corp. 64.

Joy. w&m; J.S. Bach (m) & Tom Parker (m, adapted & arranged). c1971, Youngblood Music Ltd. Assigned to Campbell, Connelly & Co., Ltd. APOLLO 100. 195.

Joy 'Round My Brain. w&m; Richard Farina. c1964, 67, M. Witmark & Sons & Warner Bros. Inc. RICHARD FARINA. 41.

Joy To The World. w&m; Hoyt Axton. c1970, 71, Lady Jane Music. THREE DOG NIGHT. 29, 64, 72, 89, 93, 106, 115, 131, 134, 140, 192, 194.

Judy In Disguise (With Glasses). w&m; John Fred & Andrew Bernard. c1967, Su-Ma Publishing Co., Inc. JOHN FRED & HIS PLAYBOY BAND. 4.

Judy Is A Punk. w&m; Joey, Dee Dee, Tommy & Johnny Ramone. c1976, 78, Bleu Disque Music Co. & Taco Tunes. RAMONES. 19.

Judy's Turn To Cry. w&m; Beverly Ross & Edna Lewis. c1963, Glamorous Music Inc. LESLEY GORE. 5.

Julie, Do Ya Love Me. w&m; Tom Bahler. c1970, Lucon Music Publishing Co. & Sequel Music. BOBBY SHERMAN. 38, 63, 64, 88.

Jump Shout Boogie. w&m; Barry Manilow & Bruce Sussman (w). c1976, Kamakazi Music Corp. & Appoggiatura Music, Inc. BARRY MANILOW. 15.

Jumpin' Jack Flash. w&m; Mick Jagger & Keith Richard. c1968, Abkco Music, Inc. PETER FRAMPTON/ROLLING STONES. 29, 53, 142, 157.

Jungle Boogie. w&m; Ronald Bell & Kool & The Gang. c1973, Delightful Music Publishers & Gang Music Publishing Co. KOOL & THE GANG. 52, 106.

Jungle Love. w&m; Lonnie Turner & Greg Douglass. c1977, Sailor Music. STEVE MILLER BAND. 145.

Junior's Farm. w&m; Paul & Linda McCartney. c1974, Paul and Linda McCartney/McCartney Music, Inc. By arrangement with ATV Music Corp. PAUL MC CARTNEY & WINGS. 93, 125.

Just A Dream. w&m; Jimmy Clanton & C. Matassa. c1958, Ace Publishers, Inc. JIMMY CLANTON. 5.

Just A Little. w&m; Ron Elliott & R. Durand. c1965, 67, Clears Music. BEAU BRUMMELS. 6.

Just A Little Bit Of Rain. w&m; Fred Neil. c1965, 66, Third Story Music Co. LINDA RONSTADT. 68.

Just Another Love Song. w&m; Forrest Richard Betts. c1975, Richard Betts Music & No Exit Music Co., Inc. ALLMAN BROTHERS BAND. 30.

Just Because. w&m; Lloyd Price. c1957, ABC-Dunhill Music, Inc. LLOYD PRICE. 109.

Just Don't Want To Be Lonely. w&m; Vinnie Barrett, Bobby Eli & John Freeman. c1973, 74, Bellboy Music. MAIN INGREDIENT. 52.

Just Go Away. w&m; Deborah Harry. c1978, Rare Blue Music, Inc. & Monster Island Music. BLONDIE. 33.

Just Like A Woman. w&m; Bob Dylan. c1966, 76, Dwarf Music. BOB DYLAN/JOAN BAEZ/RICHIE HAVENS. 30, 126, 156, 170, 183.

Just Like Romeo And Juliet SEE Romeo And Juliet.

Just Like Tom Thumb's Blues. w&m; Bob Dylan. c1965, M. Witmark & Sons & Warner Bros. Inc. BOB DYLAN/GORDON LIGHTFOOT/JUDY COLLINS. 35, 69, 132.

Just My Imagination. w&m; Norman Whitfield & Barrett Strong. c1970, 71, 73, Jobete Music Co., Inc. TEMPTATIONS. 123, 150.

Just Once In My Life. w&m; Gerry Goffin, Carole King & Phil Spector. c1965, Screen Gems-EMI Music Inc. BEACH BOYS. 142.

Just One Look. w&m; Gregory Carroll & Doris Payne. c1968, Premier Albums Music Publishing, Inc. DORIS TROY. 4.

Just Remember I Love You. w&m; Rick Roberts. c1977, 78, Stephen Stills Music. FIREFALL. 87.

Just Tell Her Jim Said Hello. w&m; Jerry Leiber & Mike Stoller. c1962, Elvis Presley Music, Inc. ELVIS PRESLEY. 172.

Just The Way You Are. w&m; Billy Joel. c1977, Joelsongs, Impulsive Music & April Music, Inc. Controlled by Blackwood Music, Inc. BILLY JOEL/ENGELBERT HUMPERDINCK/KENNY ROGERS & DOTTIE WEST. 21, 116, 131, 148, 165, 176, 199.

Just To Be Close To You. w&m; Lionel Richie. c1976, Jobete Music Co., Inc. & Commodores Entertainment Publishing Corp. COMMODORES. 142.

Just Too Many People. w&m; Melissa Manchester & Vini Poncia. c1975, Braintree Music & Rumanian Pickleworks Music Co. MELISSA MANCHESTER. 134.

Just What I Needed. w&m; Ric Ocasek. c1978, Lido Music. CARS. 22, 27, 147.

Just When I Needed You Most. w&m; Randy Vanwarmer. c1978, Fourth Floor Music, Inc. RANDY VANWARMER. 23, 56, 75, 96, 181.

Just You And I. w&m; Melissa Manchester & Carole Bayer Sager. c1975, 76, Rumanian Pickleworks Music Co. & The New York Times Music Corp. Controlled by Screen Gems-EMI Music Inc. & The New York Times Music Corp. MELISSA MANCHESTER. 128.

Just You 'N' Me. w&m; James Pankow. c1973, Moose Music & Big Elk Music. CHICAGO. 128, 183.

Justine. w&m; Don Harris & Dewey Terry, Jr. c1958, 65, Venice Music Inc. RIGHTEOUS BROTHERS. 35.

Kansas City. w&m; Jerry Leiber & Mike Stoller. c1952, Halnat Publishing Co. BEATLES/WILBERT HARRISON. 3, 93, 125.

Kathy's Song. w&m; Paul Simon. c1965, Paul Simon. SIMON & GARFUNKEL. 143.

Katmandu. w&m; Bob Seger. c1974, 75, Gear Publishing Co. BOB SEGER. 142.

Kauai. SEE Island Of Love.

K.C. Loving SEE Kansas City.

Keep It Comin' Love. w&m; H.W. Casey & R. Finch. c1976, Sherlyn Publishing Co., Inc. & Harrick Music, Inc. KC & THE SUNSHINE BAND. 34, 135, 142.

Keep On Dancin'. w&m; Eric Matthews & Gary Turnier. c1978, Mideb Music, Inc. & Eric Matthew Music. GARY'S GANG. 25, 96, 129.

Keep On Running Away. w&m; Tim Renwick & Chris White. c1979, Rondor Music Ltd./Almo Music Corp. LAZY RACER. 75.

Keep On Singing. w&m; Danny Janssen & Bobby Hart. c1972, 73, Pocket Full Of Tunes, Inc. HELEN REDDY. 140, 163.

Keep On Truckin'. w&m; Frank Wilson, Leonard Caston & Anita Poree. c1973, Stone Diamond Music Corp. EDDIE KENDRICKS. 52.

Keep On Tryin'. w&m; Timothy B. Schmit. c1975, Fool's Gold. POCO. 30.

Keep The Customer Satisfied. w&m; Paul Simon. c1970, Paul Simon. SIMON & GARFUNKEL. 143.

Keep The Fire. w&m; Kenny Loggins & Eva Ein Loggins (w). c1979, 80, Milk Money Music. KENNY LOGGINS. 147.

Key West. w&m; H. Belolo (w), V. Willis (w), P. Whitehead (w) & J. Morai (m). c1978, Scorpio Music (Black Scorpio). Controlled by Can't Stop Music. VILLAGE PEOPLE. 200.

Killer Queen. w&m; Freddie Mercury. c1974, 78, B. Feldman & Co., Ltd., trading as Trident Music/Glenwood Music Corp. QUEEN. 15, 21, 199.

Killing Floor. w&m; C. Burnett. c1965, Arc Music Corp. ALBERT KING. 1.

Killing Me Softly With His Song. w&m; Norman Gimbel (w) & Charles Fox (m). c1972, Charles Fox & Norman Gimbel, Fox-Gimbel Productions, Inc. BROTHERS FOUR/ROBERTA FLACK. 15, 21, 111, 131, 140, 163, 193, 194, 198.

Killing Of Georgie (Parts I & II). w&m; Rod Stewart. c1976, 77, Rod Stewart. Administered by Riva Music, Inc. ROD STEWART. 145.

Kimberly. w&m; Patti Smith, Allen Lanier & Ivan Kral. c1975, 77, Linda Music Corp. PATTI SMITH GROUP. 19.

King Of A Drag. w&m; James Holvay. c1966, 67, Maryon Music, Bag Of Tunes & Dhaphne Music Co. BUCKINGHAMS. 6, 161.

Kind Woman. w&m; Richie Furay. c1968, Cotillion Music, Inc., Ten East Music & Springalo Toones. BUFFALO SPRINGFIELD. 39, 139.

King Creole. w&m; Jerry Leiber & Mike Stoller. c1958, Elvis Presley Music, Inc. ELVIS PRESLEY. 172.

King Of Nothing. w&m; James Seals. c1970, 74, Dawnbreaker Music Co. & ABC-Dunhill Music, Inc. SEALS & CROFTS. 30.

King Of The Road. w&m; Roger Miller. c1964, 65, Tree Publishing Co. ROGER MILLER. 93, 130.

King Tut. w&m; Steve Martin. c1978, Colorado Music, Inc. STEVE MARTIN. 146.

Kiss An Angel Good Mornin'. w&m; Ben Peters. c1971, Ben Peters Music & Playback Music. CHARLEY PRIDE. 21, 89, 140, 156, 194, 195.

Kiss And Say Goodbye. w&m; Winfred Lovett. c1976, Blackwood Music Inc. & Nattahnam Music Co. MANHATTANS. 184, 198.

Kiss In The Dark. w&m; Michael Lloyd. c1979, KCM Music & Michael Music. PINK LADY. 75.

Kiss Me In The Rain. w&m; Sandy Farina & Lisa Ratner. c1979, Cortlandt Music Publishing, Inc., Emanuel Music Corp. & Songs Of Bandier-Koppelman, Inc. BARBRA STREISAND. 177.

Kiss Me Quick. w&m; Doc Pomus & Mort Shuman. c1961, Elvis Presley Music, Inc. ELVIS PRESLEY. 172.

Kiss You All Over. w&m; Mike Chapman & Nicky Chinn. c1978, Chinnichap Publishing, Inc. Administered by Careers Music, Inc. EXILE. 73, 135, 157.

Kisses Sweeter Than Wine. w&m; Paul Campbell (w) & Joel Newman (m). c1951, 79, Folkways Music Publishers, Inc. ARLO GUTHRIE/JIMMY RODGERS/ WEAVERS. 5, 85.

Knock On Wood. w&m; Eddie Floyd & Steve Cropper. c1966, 73, 79, East-Memphis Music. CHER/EDDIE FLOYD/MELANIE/SPITBALLS. 25, 96, 122, 129, 180, 181.

Knock Three Times. w&m; Irwin Levine & L. Russell Brown. c1970, Pocket Full Of Tunes, Inc., Saturday Music, Inc. & Big Apple Music Co., a division of 40 West Music Corp. BILLY "CRASH" CRADDOCK/ DAWN. 15, 21, 72, 89, 140, 163, 191, 192, 198.

Knockin' On Heaven's Door. w&m; Bob Dylan. c1973, Ram's Horn Music. BOB DYLAN. 126, 131, 156, 170, 183.

Knowing Me, Knowing You. w&m; Benny Andersson, Stig Anderson & Bjorn Ulvaeus. c1976, Polar Music AB & Countless Songs Ltd. Sole selling agent; Ivan Mogull Music Corp. ABBA. 15, 21, 128.

Ko Ko Mo (I Love You So). w&m; Forest Wilson, Jake Porter & Eunice Levy. c1955, Meridian Music Corp. Assigned to Vogue Music Inc. CREW CUTS/PERRY COMO. 78, 160.

Kodachrome. w&m; Paul Simon. c1973, Paul Simon. PAUL SIMON. 124, 136, 143, 146.

Kozmic Blues. w&m; Janis Joplin & Gabriel Mekler. c1969, 70, Strong Arm Music & Wingate Music, Inc. JANIS JOPLIN. 110, 149, 182, 202.

Kumbaya. SEE Come By Here.

La Bamba. w&m; Traditional. Jose Martinez (Adapted), Mort Garson (Adapted) & Tommy LiPuma (Adapted). c1966, 67, 77, versions published by Almo Music Corp., Clara Music Publishing Corp. & Road Island Co. RITCHIE VALENS. 6, 93.

La, La, La (If I Had You). w&m; Danny Janssen. c1969, Green Apple Music Co. BOBBY SHERMAN. 149.

Ladies Night. w&m; George M. Brown & Kool & The Gang. c1979, Delightful Music Ltd. & Gang Music. KOOL & THE GANG. 198.

Ladies Of The Canyon. w&m; Joni Mitchell. c1968, 74, Siquomb Publishing Corp. JONI MITCHELL. 35.

Lady. w&m; Dennis DeYoung. c1973, 75, Wooden Nickel Music. STYX. 139.

Lady. w&m; Graham Goble. c1978, Fiberchem International B.V./Screen Gems-EMI Music Inc. LITTLE RIVER BAND. 27, 147.

Lady Blue. w&m; Leon Russell. c1975, Teddy Jack Music. GEORGE BENSON/LEON RUSSELL. 12, 135.

Lady Godiva. w&m; Mike Leander & Charles Mills. c1966, Dean Street Music Ltd./Regent Music Corp. PETER & GORDON. 10.

Lady Love. w&m; Von Gray. c1977, 78, Mighty Three Music. Administered by Blackwood Music Inc. LOU RAWLS. 15, 130, 165, 199.

Lady Madonna. w&m; John Lennon & Paul McCartney. c1968, Northern Songs Ltd./Maclen Music, Inc. BEATLES. 61, 146.

Lady Marmalade. w&m; Bob Crewe & Kenny Nolan. c1974, Stone Diamond Music Corp., Tanny Boy Music Co. & Kenny Nolan Publishing. LABELLE. 150, 156.

Lady Midnight. Leonard Cohen. c1968, 69, Stranger Music, Inc. LEONARD COHEN. 171.

Lady (Put The Light On Me). w&m; John Goodison & Phil Wainman. c1974, 77, Utopia Music Ltd. Controlled by Utopia Music-Dejamus Music Inc. BROWNSVILLE STATION. 127.

Lady Sings The Blues Love Theme SEE Happy.

Lady Willpower. w&m; Jerry Fuller. c1968, Warner-Tamerlane Publishing Corp. GARY PUCKETT & THE UNION GAP. 35, 138.

Land Ho. w&m; Jim Morrison (w) & Doors (m). c1970, Doors Music Co. DOORS. 54.

Land Of A Thousand Dances. w&m; Chris Kenner & Antoine "Fats" Domino. c1963, Thursday Music Corp. & Anatole Music, Inc. CANNIBAL & THE HEADHUNTERS/WILSON PICKETT. 5, 93.

Lara's Theme From Dr. Zhivago SEE Somewhere, My Love.

Last Child. w&m; Steven Tyler & Brad Whitford. c1976, Daksel Music Corp., Vandaloo Productions & Song & Dance Music Co. AEROSMITH. 87, 141, 145.

Last Dance. w&m; Paul Jabara. c1977, 78, Primus Artists Music & Olga Music. DONNA SUMMER/PAUL JABARA. 23, 24, 25, 34, 56, 58, 74, 87, 96, 112, 118, 128, 136, 146, 176, 181, 199.

Last Night. w&m; Joe Mauldin & Norman Petty. c1957, MPL Communications, Inc. BUDDY HOLLY. 14.

Last Night I Had The Strangest Dream. w&m; Ed McCurdy. c1950, 51, 55, Almanac Music, Inc. ARLO GUTHRIE/SIMON & GARFUNKEL/WEAVERS. 85.

Last Night I Made Love To Somebody Else. w&m; Irwin Levine & L. Russell Brown. c1975, Levine & Brown Music, Inc. BILLY JANE. 103.

Last Of The Singing Cowboys. w&m; George McCorkle. c1979, Marshall Tucker Publishing Co. & No Exit Music Co., Inc. MARSHALL TUCKER BAND. 27.

Last Song. w&m; Larry Evoy. c1972, 73, Eeyor Music, a division of Canadian Bear Ltd. EDWARD BEAR. 72, 89, 111, 163, 194.

Last Tango In Paris. w&m; Dory Previn (w) & Gato Barbieri (m). c1973, Unart Music Corp. GATO BARBIERI/HERB ALPERT & THE TIJUANA BRASS. 89, 111, 140, 194.

Last Thing On My Mind. w&m; Tom Paxton. c1964, 68, United Artists Music Co., Inc. JOAN BAEZ/JUDY COLLINS/NEIL DIAMOND/PETER, PAUL & MARY/TOM PAXTON. 80, 199.

Last Time. w&m; Mick Jagger & Keith Richard. c1965, Abkco Music, Inc. ROLLING STONES. 29.

Last Time I Felt Like This. w&m; Alan & Marilyn Bergman (w) & Marvin Hamlisch (m). c1978, Leeds Music Corp. Controlled by Chappell & Co., Inc. JOHNNY MATHIS & JANE OLIVER. 47.

Last Time I Saw Him. w&m; Pamela Sawyer (w) & Michael Masser (m). c1973, Jobete Music Co., Inc. DIANA ROSS. 48.

Last Train To Clarksville. w&m; Tommy Boyce & Bobby Hart. c1966, Screen Gems-Columbia Music, Inc. MONKEES. 38.

Last Train To London. w&m; Jeff Lynne. c1979, Jet Music Inc. & Blackwood Music Inc. Administered by Blackwood Music Inc. ELECTRIC LIGHT ORCHESTRA. 148.

Last Wall Of The Castle. w&m; Jorma Kaukonen. c1967, 68, Icebag Corp. JEFFERSON AIRPLANE. 108.

Late For The Sky. w&m; Jackson Browne. c1974, 75, WB Music Corp. & Benchmark Music. JACKSON BROWNE. 55, 139, 174.

Late In The Evening. w&m; Paul Simon. c1978, 80, Paul Simon. PAUL SIMON. 162.

Laugh, Laugh. w&m; Ronald Elliott. c1964, 67, Clears Music. BEAU BRUMMELS. 6, 59.

Laughter In The Rain. w&m; Neil Sedaka & Phil Cody. c1974, Neil Sedaka Music & Lebasongs. NEIL SEDAKA. 62, 127, 133, 139, 141.

Laura. w&m; David Raksin (m) & Johnny Mercer (w). c1945, 66, Twentieth Century Music Corp. Controlled by Robbins Music Corp. BOOTS RANDOLPH/BOSTON POPS/DAVE BRUBECK/FERRANTE & TEICHER/MANTOVANI. 140.

Lavender Blue. w&m; Larry Morey (w) & Eliot Daniel (m). c1948, Anne-Rachel Music Corp. SAMMY TURNER. 191.

Lawdy, Miss Clawdy. w&m; Lloyd Price. c1952, 67, Venice Music. BILL HALEY & THE COMETS/BUCKINGHAMS/ELVIS PRESLEY/JOE COCKER/LLOYD PRICE. 3, 35, 100, 159, 197.

Lawyers, Guns And Money. w&m; Warren Zevon. c1978, Zevon Music. LINDA RONSTADT. 135.

Lay Down (Candles In The Rain). w&m; Melanie Safka. c1969, Kama-Rippa & Amelanie Music. MELANIE. 59.

Lay Down Sally. w&m; Eric Clapton, Marcy Levy & George Terry. c1977, 78, Throat Music Ltd./Stigwood Music Inc. Administered by Unichappell Music Inc. ERIC CLAPTON. 47, 178.

Lay, Lady, Lay. w&m; Bob Dylan. c1969, 76 Big Sky Music. BOB DYLAN. 126, 170, 183.

Layla. w&m; Eric Clapton & Jim Gordon. c1970, 77, Throat Music Ltd./Casserole Music Inc. Administered by Unichappell Music, Inc. DEREK & THE DOMINOS/ERIC CLAPTON. 36, 55, 115, 127, 131, 138, 152, 175.

Lazing On A Sunday Afternoon. w&m; Freddie Mercury. c1975, B. Feldman & Co., Ltd., trading as Trident Music/Glenwood Music Corp. QUEEN. 199.

Le Freak. w&m; Nile Rodgers & Bernard Edwards. c1978, Cotillion Music, Inc. & Chic Music, Inc. CHIC. 27, 87, 118, 146.

Lead Me On. w&m; David Lasley & Allee Willis. c1978, Almo Music Corp. & Irving Music, Inc. MAXINE NIGHTINGALE. 24, 70, 75, 96, 179.

Lean On Me. w&m; Bill Withers. c1972, Interior Music. Administered by Irving Music Inc. BILL WITHERS/IKE TURNER/NILSSON/VIKKI CARR. 24, 56, 70, 115.

Learn How To Fall. w&m; Paul Simon. c1973, Paul Simon. PAUL SIMON. 143.

Learn How To Fly. w&m; Willie Hutchison. c1967, 70, Johnny Rivers Music. FIFTH DIMENSION. 60.

Leave Me Alone. w&m; Linda Laurie. c1973, Anne-Rachel Music Corp. & The Brooklyn Music Co. Administered by Chappell & Co., Inc. HELEN REDDY. 21, 89, 140, 163, 194, 198.

Leaves That Are Green. w&m; Paul Simon. c1965, Paul Simon. SIMON & GARFUNKEL. 143.

Leaving On A Jet Plane. w&m; John Denver. c1967, 69, Cherry Lane Music, Inc. PETER, PAUL & MARY. 15, 21, 37, 64, 149, 182, 191.

Leftovers. w&m; Phillip Mitchell. c1975, Muscle Shoals Sound Publishing Co., Inc. MILLIE JACKSON. 103.

Legend In Your Own Time. w&m; Carly Simon. c1971, Quackenbush Music, Ltd. CARLY SIMON. 43.

Legend Of Wooley Swamp. w&m; Charlie Daniels, Tom Crain, "Taz" DiGregorio, Fred Edwards, Charlie Haywood & Jim Marshall. c1980, Hat Band Music. CHARLIE DANIELS BAND. 190.

Legend Of Zanadu. w&m; Howard Blaikley. c1968, Lynn Music Ltd. DAVE, DEE, DOZY, BEAKY, MICK & TICH. 76.

Lemon Tree. w&m; Will Holt. c1960, 61, Dolfi Music Inc. & Boulder Music, Inc. PETER, PAUL & MARY. 68.

Leopard-Skin Pill-Box Hat. w&m; Bob Dylan. c1966, 76, Dwarf Music. BOB DYLAN. 170.

Lesson In Leavin'. w&m; Randy Goodrum & Brent Maher. c1979, Chappell & Co., Inc., Sailmaker Music, Blue Quill Music & Welbeck Music Corp. DOTTIE WEST. 47.

Let It Be. w&m; John Lennon & Paul McCartney. c1970, Northern Songs Ltd./Maclen Music, Inc. BEATLES. 36, 61, 62, 133, 139.

Let It Be Me. w&m; Curtis Mann (w) & Gilbert Becaud (m). c1955, 57, 60, France Music Co. Sole selling agent; MCA Music. GLEN CAMPBELL & BOBBIE GENTRY. 94.

Let It Down. w&m; George Harrison. c1970, Harri-

songs Ltd./Harrisongs Music, Inc. GEORGE HARRISON. 125.

Let It Go, Let It Flow. w&m; Dave Mason. c1976, 78, Dave Mason Music. Administered by Blackwood Music Inc. DAVE MASON. 165.

Let It Rain. w&m; Bonnie Bramlett & Eric Clapton. c1970, Delbon Music, Casserole Music & Cotillion Music. ERIC CLAPTON. 152.

Let It Ride. w&m; Randy Bachman & C.F. Turner. c1973, Ranbach Music, Top Soil Music & Eventide Music. BACHMAN-TURNER OVERDRIVE. 106.

Let Me Be Good To You. w&m; Kenneth Gamble & Leon Huff. c1979, Mighty Three Music. LOU RAWLS. 187.

Let Me Be The Clock. w&m; William "Smokey" Robinson. c1980, Bertam Music Co. SMOKEY ROBINSON. 24.

Let Me Be The One. w&m; Paul Williams (w) & Roger Nichols (m). c1970, Almo Music Corp. ANNE MURRAY/CARPENTERS. 70.

Let Me Be There. w&m; John Rostill. c1973, Petal Music Ltd./Al Gallico Music Corp. OLIVIA NEWTON-JOHN. 28, 106, 126, 134, 156.

Let Me Be Your Angel. w&m; Narada Michael Walden & Bunny Hull. c1980, Walden Music, Gratitude Sky Music, Inc., Cotillion Music, Inc. & Brass Heart Music. Administered by Walden Music, Inc. STACY LATTISAW. 162, 190.

Let Me Be Your Car. w&m; Elton John & Bernie Taupin. c1973, Dick James Music Ltd./Dick James Music Inc. ROD STEWART. 139.

Let Me In. w&m; Yvonne Baker. c1962, Arc Music Corp. & Kae Williams Music Corp. SENSATIONS. 5.

Let Me Know (I Have A Right). w&m; Dino Fekaris & Freddie Perren. c1979, Perren-Vibes Music Inc. GLORIA GAYNOR. 179.

Let Me Lay My Funk On You. w&m; Richard E. Gillyard, Charles A. Morris, David G. Chambliss, Peyton F. Johnson, Herbert A. Dabney III, Janet J. Cook, Marshall F. Smith, Melvin L. Watson & Anthony W. Joyner. c1975, Big Seven Music Corp. & Hot Gold Music Publishing Co. POISON. 49.

Let Me Love You Once Before You Go. w&m; Molly-Ann Leikin & Stephen H. Dorff. c1975, Almo Music Corp. & Peso Music. DUSTY SPRINGFIELD. 135.

Let Me Make Love To You. w&m; Bunny Sigler & Allan Felder. c1975, Mighty Three Music & Golden Fleece Music. Administered by Blackwood Music Inc. O'JAYS. 49.

Let Me Sing Your Blues Away. w&m; Robert Hunter (w) & Keith Godchaux (m). c1973, 76, Ice Nine Publishing Co., Inc. GRATEFUL DEAD. 84.

Let The Four Winds Blow. w&m; Dave Bartholomew & Antoine Domino. c1961, Unart Music Corp. FATS DOMINO. 78, 81, 155.

Let The Good Times Roll. w&m; Leonard Lee. c1956, 59, 60, Atlantic Music Corp. & Unart Music Corp. BARBRA STREISAND/COUNT BASIE/JERRY LEE LEWIS/RAY CHARLES. 82.

Let The Little Girl Dance. w&m; Henry Glover, Carl

Spencer & Bert Lawrence. c1960, Maureen Music, Inc. BILLY BLAND. 3.

Let The Sunshine In SEE ALSO Aquarius/Let The Sunshine In.

Let The Sunshine In. w&m; James Rado (w), Gerome Ragni (w) & Galt MacDermot (m). c1966, 67, 68, James Rado, Gerome Ragni, Galt MacDermot, Nat Shapiro & United Artists Music Co., Inc. Controlled & administered by United Artists Music Co., Inc. FREDERICK KNIGHT/SIL AUSTIN. 80.

Let There Be Music. w&m; Larry Hoppen & Johanna Hall (w). c1974, 75, Borch Music, Mojohanna Music, Sorn Music Co., Inc. & Open End Music. ORLEANS. 142.

Let There Be Peace On Earth. w&m; Sy Miller & Jill Jackson. c1955, 56, Sy Miller & Jill Jackson & Jan-Lee Music. 86.

Let Your Love Flow. w&m; Larry E. Williams. c1975, 76, Loaves & Fishes Music Co., Inc. BELLAMY BROTHERS/JOAN BAEZ. 131, 133.

Let's All Chant. w&m; Alvin Fields & Michael Zager. c1977, Sumac Music. MICHAEL ZAGER BAND. 34.

Let's Be Young Tonight. w&m; Michael L. Smith & Don Daniels. c1976, Jobete Music Co., Inc. & Stone Diamond Music Corp. JERMAINE JACKSON. 95.

Let's Do It Again. w&m; Curtis Mayfield. c1975, Warner-Tamerlane Publishing Corp. STAPLE SINGERS. 30, 36, 133.

Let's Get A Little Sentimental. w&m; Mike Leander & Eddie Seago. c1970, Leeds Music Ltd. MONTANAS. 94.

Let's Get It On. w&m; Marvin Gaye & Ed Townsend. c1973, Jobete Music Co., Inc. & Cherritown Music Co., Inc. MARVIN GAYE. 26, 52, 150.

Let's Go. w&m; Ric Ocasek. c1979, Lido Music, Inc. CARS. 22, 27, 147.

Let's Go Down To The Disco. w&m; Norman Whitfield. c1976, Stone Diamond Music Corp. UNDISPUTED TRUTH. 95.

Let's Go Get Stoned. w&m; Valerie Simpson, Nickolas Ashford & Josephine Armsted. c1965, 66, Warner-Tamerlane Publishing Corp. & Renleigh Music, Inc. JOE COCKER/LOWELL FULSOM. 13, 100, 152.

Let's Spend The Night Together. w&m; Mick Jagger & Keith Richard. c1967, Abkco Music, Inc. ROLLING STONES. 157.

Let's Stay Together. w&m; Willie Mitchell, Al Green & Al Jackson. c1971, Jec Publishing & Al Green Music, Inc. AL GREEN. 104, 122.

Let's Straighten It Out. w&m; Benny Latimore. c1974, Sherilyn Publishing Co., Inc. LATIMORE. 52.

Let's Take The Long Way Around The World. w&m; Archie P. Jordan & Naomi Martin. c1978, Chess Music, Inc. & Pi-Gem Music, Inc. KENNY ROGERS & DOTTIE WEST/RONNIE MILSAP. 74, 130.

Let's Twist Again. w&m; Kal Mann & Dave Appell. c1961, Kalmann Music, Inc. Controlled by Unichappell Music, Inc. CHUBBY CHECKER. 3, 78.

Letter. w&m; Don Harris & Dewey Terry, Jr. c1958, 65, Venice Music Inc. MEDALLIONS. 93.

Letter. w&m; Wayne Carson Thompson. c1967, Earl Barton Music Inc. BOX TOPS/JOE COCKER. 21, 72, 89, 102, 140, 161, 191, 192, 198.

Letter Full Of Tears. w&m; Don Covay. c1962, Abkco Music, Inc. GLADYS KNIGHTS & THE PIPS. 17.

Levon. w&m; Elton John & Bernie Taupin. c1971, Dick James Music Ltd./Dick James Music, Inc. ELTON JOHN. 22, 43, 145.

Liar. w&m; Russ Ballard. c1969, 71, Verulam Music Co., Ltd. Assigned to Mainstay Music, Inc. ARGENT/THREE DOG NIGHT. 64, 93, 106.

Lido Shuffle. w&m; Boz Scaggs & David Paich. c1976, Boz Scaggs Music & Hudmar Publishing Co., Inc. BOZ SCAGGS. 87, 127, 145.

Life Could Be A Dream SEE Sh-Boom.

Life In The Fast Lane. w&m; Joe Walsh, Don Henley & Glenn Frey. c1976, 77, Cass County Music, Red Cloud Music, Wow And Flutter Music Publishing, Long Run Music Publishing & WB Music Corp. EAGLES. 22, 124, 146, 178.

Life Is A Rock (But The Radio Rolled Me). w&m; Norman Dolph, Paul Di Franco & Joe Levine. c1972, 73, 74, Crazy Chords Music & Crushing Music. REUNION. 93.

Life Of The Party. w&m; Hal Davis, Clarence Drayton & Tamy Smith. c1974, Jobete Music Co., Inc. JACKSON 5. 20.

Life's Been Good. w&m; Joe Walsh. c1978, Wow And Flutter Music Publishing. JOE WALSH. 57, 146.

Light My Fire. w&m; Doors. c1967, 70, Nipper Mucik Co., Inc. Assigned to Doors Music Co. DOORS/JOSE FELICIANO. 29.

Light Of A Clear Blue Morning. w&m; Dolly Parton. c1977, Velvet Apple Music. DOLLY PARTON. 164.

Light Up The World With Sunshine. w&m; Ben Findon & Geoff Wilkins. c1976, Black Sheep Music Inc. HAMILTON, JOE FRANK & DENNISON. 184.

Lightnin' Strikes. w&m; Lou Christie & Twyla Herbert. c1966, Rambed Music Publishing Co., Inc. LOU CHRISTIE. 3.

Lights. w&m; Steve Perry & Neal Schon. c1978, Weed High Nightmare Music. Administered & controlled by Screen Gems-EMI Music Inc. JOURNEY. 74.

Lights. w&m; Tommy Shaw & Dennis DeYoung. c1979, Stygian Songs. Administered by Almo Music Corp. STYX. 11.

Like A Hurricane. w&m; Neil Young. c1976, 77, Silver Fiddle. NEIL YOUNG. 22.

Like A Rolling Stone. w&m; Bob Dylan. c1965, 70, M. Witmark & Sons & Warner Bros. Inc. BOB DYLAN/JIMI HENDRIX. 35, 69, 132, 139, 182.

Like A Sunday In Salem. w&m; Gene Cotton. c1978, United Artists Music Co., Inc. GENE COTTON. 81.

Like To Get To Know You. w&m; Stuart Scharf. c1968, Takya Music, Inc. SPANKY & OUR GANG. 4.

Lily, Rosemary And The Jack Of Hearts. w&m; Bob Dylan. c1974, 76, Ram's Horn Music. BOB DYLAN. 170.

Linda Lu. w&m; Ray Sharpe. c1959, Gregmark Music, Inc. RAY SHARPE. 6.

Ling Ting Tong. w&m; Mabel Godwin. c1954, St. Louis Music Corp. Assigned to Unichappell Music Inc. CHARMS/FIVE KEYS. 90, 155.

Lion Sleeps Tonight (Wimoweh). w&m; Hugh Peretti (Adapted), Luigi Creatore (Adapted), George Weiss (Adapted) & Albert Stanton (Adapted). c1951, 52, 61, Folkways Music Publishers. TOKENS/WEAVERS. 5, 68, 85.

Listen To A Country Song. w&m; Jim Messina & Al Garth. c1971, Jasperilla Music Co. LOGGINS & MESSINA. 151.

Listen To Her Heart. w&m; Tom Petty. c1977, 78, Skyhill Publishing Co., Inc. TOM PETTY & THE HEARTBREAKERS. 74.

Listen To Me. w&m; Charles Hardin & Norman Petty. c1957, MPL Communications, Inc. BUDDY HOLLY. 14.

Listen To The Music. w&m; Tom Johnston. c1972, Warner-Tamerlane Publishing Corp. DOOBIE BROTHERS. 55, 136, 138, 145, 174, 185.

Listen To What The Man Said. w&m; Paul McCartney. c1975, McCartney Music, Inc. PAUL MC CARTNEY & WINGS. 125.

Little Bit Of Soap. w&m; Bert Russell. c1961, 66, Robert Mellin Inc. Assigned to Robert Mellin Music Publishing Corp. JARMELS. 4.

Little Bitty Pretty One. w&m; Robert Byrd. c1957, 72, Recordo Music Publishers. JACKSON 5/THURSTON HARRIS. 4, 20, 38, 78, 101, 137.

Little Boy Lost. w&m; Marilyn & Alan Bergman (w) & Michel Legrand (m). c1970, United Artists Music Co., Inc. JOHNNY MATHIS. 21, 198.

Little Darlin'. w&m; Maurice Williams. c1957, Excellorec Music Co. DIAMONDS. 3.

Little Darling (I Need You). w&m; Eddie Holland, Lamont Dozier & Brian Holland. c1965, 66, Jobete Music Co., Inc. DOOBIE BROTHERS/MARVIN GAYE. 142.

Little Girl. w&m; Bob Gonzalez & Don Baskin. c1966, Duane Music & Aim Music. DEAD BOYS/SYNDICATE OF SOUND. 153.

Little Girl Of Mine. w&m; Morris Levy & Herbert Cox. c1956, Nom Music, Inc. CLEFTONES. 101, 137, 161.

Little Green Apples. w&m; Bobby Russell. c1968, Bibo Music Publishers. BOBBY RUSSELL/O.C. SMITH. 21, 102, 163, 194.

Little Honda. w&m; Brian Wilson. c1964, Sea Of Tunes Publishing Co. BEACH BOYS. 9.

Little Jeannie. w&m; Elton John & Gary Osborne. c1980, Big Pig Music Ltd./Jodrell Music, Inc. ELTON JOHN. 162, 189.

Little More Love. w&m; John Farrar. c1978, John Farrar Music. Administered by Irving Music, Inc. OLIVIA NEWTON-JOHN. 58, 96, 129, 180, 181.

Little One. w&m; Danny Seraphine & David "Hawk" Wolinski. c1977, Balloon Head Music & Big Elk Music. CHICAGO. 135.

Little Queenie. w&m; Chuck Berry. c1959, 70, Arc Music Corp. ROLLING STONES. 1.

Little Sister. w&m; Doc Pomus & Mort Shuman. c1961, Elvis Presley Music. ELVIS PRESLEY. 172.

Little Things Mean A Lot. w&m; Edith Lindeman & Carl Stutz. c1954, Leo Feist Inc. MC GUIRE SISTERS. 79.

Little Star. w&m; Morris Levy, Bobby Callender & John Peabody. c1958, 63, 78, Big Seven Music Corp. ELEGANTS. 2, 101.

Little Town Flirt. w&m; Del Shannon & M. McKenzie. c1962, Mole Hole Music & Rightsong Music. Administered by Bug Music Group. DEL SHANNON. 5.

Little Woman. w&m; Danny Janssen. c1969, Green Apple Music Co. BOBBY SHERMAN. 38.

Live And Let Die. w&m; Paul & Linda McCartney. c1973, United Artists Music Ltd., ATV Music Ltd. & McCartney Music Ltd./Unart Music Corp. PAUL MC CARTNEY & WINGS. 140, 163, 194, 198.

Livin' Ain't Livin'. w&m; Rick Roberts. c1976, Stephen Stills Music. FIREFALL. 141.

Livin' It Up. w&m; L. Bell & C. James. c1978, 79, Mighty Three Music. BELL & JAMES. 34, 51.

Livin' Thing. w&m; Jeff Lynne. c1976, United Artists Music Ltd. & Jet Music Inc. Administered by Unart Music Corp. ELECTRIC LIGHT ORCHESTRA. 15, 21, 193, 198.

Living For The City. w&m; Stevie Wonder. c1973, Jobete Music Co., Inc. & Black Bull Music Inc. STEVIE WONDER. 106, 150.

Living Loving Maid. w&m; Jimmy Page & Robert Plant. c1969, Superhype Publishing. LED ZEPPELIN. 114, 186.

Living Next Door To Alice. w&m; Nicky Chinn & Mike Chapman. c1972, 76, Chinnichap-Rak Publishing Ltd. Controlled by Chinnichap Publishing, Inc. SMOKIE. 141.

Living The Blues. w&m; Bob Dylan. c1969, 76, Big Sky Music. BOB DYLAN. 170.

Living Together, Growing Together. w&m; Hal David (w) & Burt Bacharach (m). c1972, Colgems-EMI Music Inc., New Hidden Valley Music Co. & J.C. Music Co. Administered by Colgems-EMI Music Inc. BURT BACHARACH. 128.

Livingston Saturday Night. w&m; Jimmy Buffett. c1975, ABC-Dunhill Music, Inc. & Unart Music Corp. JIMMY BUFFETT. 135.

Lo And Behold. w&m; Bob Dylan. c1967, 75, Dwarf Music. BOB DYLAN & THE BAND. 170.

Loco-Motion. w&m; Gerry Goffin & Carole King. c1962, Screen Gems-EMI Music Inc. GRAND FUNK/LITTLE EVA. 29, 52, 106, 134, 156, 158.

Logical Song. w&m; Roger Hodgson & Rick Davies. c1979, Almo Music Corp. & Delicate Music. Administered by Almo Music. SUPERTRAMP. 23, 56, 70, 75, 96, 180, 181.

Lollipop. w&m; Beverly Ross & Julius Dixon. c1958, Edward B. Marks Music Corp. CHORDETTES. 3.

Lonely Boy. w&m; Andrew Gold. c1976, 77, Luckyu Music. ANDREW GOLD. 27, 127, 128, 134, 142.

Lonely Boy. w&m; Paul Anka. c1958, Spanka Music Corp. PAUL ANKA. 6.

Lonely Days. w&m; Barry, Robin & Maurice Gibb. c1970, Abigail Music Ltd. & Robin Gibb Publishing Ltd./Frontwheel Music Inc. BEE GEES. 55, 136, 174, 182.

Lonely Man. w&m; Bennie Benjamin & Sol Marcus. c1961, Gladys Music, Inc. ELVIS PRESLEY. 173.

Lonely Night (Angel Face). w&m; Neil Sedaka. c1974, 75, Neil Sedaka. CAPTAIN & TENNILLE. 30, 133, 141, 145.

Lonely One. w&m; Janis Ian. c1967, Dialogue Music, Inc. JANIS IAN. 76.

Lonely People. w&m; Dan & Catherine L. Peek. c1974, WB Music Corp. AMERICA. 43, 55, 87, 136, 139, 174, 185.

Lonely Teardrops. w&m; Berry Gordy, Jr., Gwendolyn Gordy & Tyran Carlo. c1957, 58, 74, Merrimac Music Corp. JACKIE WILSON. 6, 155, 168.

Lonely Weekends. w&m; Charlie Rich. c1960, Hi-Lo Music, Inc. CHARLIE RICH. 122.

Lonesome Cowboy. w&m; Sid Tepper & Roy C. Bennett. c1957, Gladys Music, Inc. ELVIS PRESLEY. 172.

Lonesome Death Of Hattie Carroll. w&m; Bob Dylan. c1964, 67, M. Witmark & Sons. BOB DYLAN/JUDY COLLINS. 132.

Lonesome Loser. w&m; David Briggs. c1979, Fiberchem International B.V./Screen Gems-EMI Music Inc. LITTLE RIVER BAND. 27, 31, 57, 87, 147, 162.

Lonesome Tears. w&m; Buddy Holly. c1958, MPL Communications, Inc. BUDDY HOLLY. 14.

Lonesome Traveler. w&m; Lee Hays. c1950, 51, Folkways Music Publishers, Inc. WEAVERS. 85.

Long Ago & Far Away. w&m; James Taylor. c1970, Blackwood Music Inc. & Country Road Music. Administered by Blackwood Music, Inc. JAMES TAYLOR. 183.

Long And Winding Road. w&m; John Lennon & Paul McCartney. c1970, Northern Songs Ltd./Maclen Music, Inc. BEATLES. 36, 61, 127, 133, 139, 145.

Long As I Can See The Light. w&m; J.C. Fogerty. c1970, Jondora Music. CREEDENCE CLEARWATER REVIVAL. 63, 88, 93.

Long Distance Operator. w&m; Bob Dylan. c1971, 75, Dwarf Music. BOB DYLAN & THE BAND. 170.

Long Distance Runaround. w&m; Jon Anderson. c1971, 72, Rondor Music Ltd. & Yessongs Ltd. YES. 36.

Long Haired Lover From Liverpool. w&m; Christopher Dowden. c1969, 72, Virgin Ear Music & Budd Universal Music Group, Inc. DONNY OSMOND. 38.

Long Hot Summer Night. w&m; Jimi Hendrix. c1968, Bella Godiva Music, Inc. JIMI HENDRIX. 203.

Long Lonely Nights. w&m; Lee Andrews, Bernice Davis, Douglas Henderson & Mimi Uniman. c1957, 65, Arc Music Corp. CLYDE MC PHATTER/LEE ANDREWS & THE HEARTS. 168.

Long Lonesome Highway. w&m; James Hendricks. c1969, 70, Rivers Music Co., by arrangement with Hastings Music Corp. MICHAEL PARKS. 191.

Long, Long, Long. w&m; George Harrison. c1968, Harrisongs Ltd./Harrisongs Music, Inc. BEATLES. 125.

Long May You Run. w&m; Neil Young. c1976, Silver Fiddle. STILLS-YOUNG BAND. 141.

Long Run. w&m; Don Henley & Glenn Frey. c1979, Cass County Music & Red Cloud Music. EAGLES. 147, 188.

Long Tall Sally. w&m; Enotris Johnson, Richard Penniman & Robert Blackwell. c1956, Venice Music, Inc. BEATLES/DELANEY & BONNIE/ELVIS PRESLEY/ LITTLE RICHARD. 3, 35, 78, 93, 100, 125, 137, 159, 197.

Long Tall Texan. w&m; Henry Strzelecki. c1959, 77, Adams-Ethridge Publishing Co. Assigned to Isle City Music. MURRY KELLUM. 6.

Long Time. w&m; Donald T. Scholz. c1976, 77, Pure Songs. Controlled by Colgems-EMI Music Inc. BOSTON. 121, 142.

Long Time Gone. w&m; David Crosby. c1968, 70, Guerilla Music. CROSBY, STILLS & NASH/CROSBY, STILLS, NASH & YOUNG. 41, 151, 202.

Long Train Runnin'. w&m; Tom Johnston. c1973, Warner-Tamerlane Publishing Corp. DOOBIE BROTHERS. 117, 136, 138, 145, 197.

Longer. w&m; Daniel Fogelberg. c1978, 79, Hickory Grove Music. Administered by April Music Inc. DAN FOGELBERG. 116, 148.

Look At Me. w&m; Norman Petty, Buddy Holly & Jerry Allison. c1958, MPL Communications, Inc. BUDDY HOLLY. 14.

Look Away. w&m; Randle Chowning. c1974, Lost Cabin Music. OZARK MOUNTAIN DAREDEVILS. 139.

Look In My Eyes Pretty Woman. w&m; Dennis Lambert & Brian Potter. c1970, 74, ABC-Dunhill Music, Inc. TONY ORLANDO & DAWN. 89.

Look Of Love. w&m; Hal David (w) & Burt Bacharach (m). c1967, Colgems-EMI Music Inc. LIZA MINELLI/ RENAISSANCE/SHIRLEY BASSEY. 130.

Look Out For My Love. w&m; Neil Young. c1977, 78, Silver Fiddle. LINDA RONSTADT. 147.

Look Through My Window. w&m; John Phillips. c1966, Trousdale Music Publishers, Inc. & American Broadcasting Music, Inc. MAMAS & THE PAPAS. 93, 119.

Look To Your Soul. w&m; Gary Brooker, Matthew Fisher & Keith Reid. c1968, 72, Essex Music International Ltd./TRO Andover Music, Inc. PROCOL HARUM. 42.

Look To Your Soul. w&m; James Hendricks. c1968, Johnny Rivers Music. JOHNNY RIVERS. 76.

Look What You've Done To Me. w&m; Boz Scaggs & David Foster (m). c1980, Boz Scaggs Music, Foster

FIND THAT TUNE

Frees Music, Inc. & Irving Music, Inc. BOZ SCAGGS. 162, 190.

Look What You've Done To My Heart. w&m; Terri McFaddin, John Footman & Frank Wilson. c1977, Screen Gems-EMI Music Inc. Controlled by Colgems-EMI Music Inc. MARILYN MC COO & BILLY DAVIS, JR. 142.

Lookin' Out My Back Door. w&m; J.C. Fogerty. c1970, Jondora Music. CREEDENCE CLEARWATER REVIVAL. 63, 86, 88, 93.

Lookin' Through The Windows. w&m; Clifton Davis. c1971, Jobete Music Co., Inc. JACKSON 5. 20.

Looks Like We Made It. w&m; Will Jennings (w) & Richard Kerr (m). c1976, 77, Irving Music Inc. & Rondor Music Ltd. BARRY MANILOW. 15, 21, 23, 56, 70, 71, 96, 177, 198.

Loose Caboose. w&m; Joe Tex & Gloria Thompson. c1978, Tree Publishing Co., Inc. JOE TEX. 66.

Loose Lucy. w&m; Robert Hunter (w) & Jerry Garcia (m). c1974, 76, Ice Nine Publishing Co., Inc. GRATEFUL DEAD. 84.

Lord's Prayer. w&m; Traditional (w), Arnold Strals (m) & Les Sands (Arranged). c1973, Du Monde Music & Almo Music Corp. SISTER JANET MEAD. 70, 71, 156.

Lose Again. w&m; Karla Bonoff. c1975, 77, Seagrape Music. KARLA BONOFF/LINDA RONSTADT. 73, 127, 146.

Lost In Love. w&m; Graham Russell. c1980, BRM Publishing, Riva Music Ltd. & Arista Music, Inc. AIR SUPPLY. 45, 56, 99.

Lost In Music. w&m; Nile Rodgers & Bernard Edwards. c1979, Chic Music, Inc. Administered by Warner-Tamerlane Publishing Corp. SISTER SLEDGE. 27, 147.

Lost Without Your Love. w&m; David Gates. c1976, Kipahulu Music Co. Administered & controlled by Colgems-EMI Music, Inc. BREAD. 77, 128, 134.

Lotta Love. w&m; Neil Young. c1978, Silver Fiddle. NEIL YOUNG/NICOLETTE LARSON. 27, 57, 162.

Louisiana 1927. w&m; Randy Newman. c1974, 75, Warner-Tamerlane Publishing Corp. & Randy Newman. RANDY NEWMAN. 36.

Louisville. w&m; Charles Rogers. c1967, Moss Rose Publications, Inc. LEROY VAN DYKE. 76.

Love And Happiness. w&m; Al Green & Mabon Hodges. c1972, 73, Jec Publishing Co. AL GREEN. 104.

Love Ballad. w&m; Skip Scarborough. c1975, 76, Unichappell Music, Inc. GEORGE BENSON. 40.

Love Boat, Main Title From. w&m; Paul Williams (w) & Charles Fox (m). c1977, Aaron Spelling Productions, Inc. & Aaron Spelling Music Co. JACK JONES. 56.

Love Child. w&m; Pam Sawyer, R. Dean Taylor, Frank Wilson & Deke Richards. c1968, Jobete Music Co., Inc. SUPREMES. 123.

Love Comes In Spurts. w&m; Richard Hell. c1977, 78, Doraflo Music Co., Automatic Music & Quick Mix Music. RICHARD HELL. 19.

Love Don't Live Here Anymore. w&m; Miles Gregory. c1978, 79, Warner-Tamerlane Publishing Corp. & May 12th Music Inc. Administered by Warner-Tamerlane Publishing Corp. ROSE ROYCE. 27.

Love Finds Its Own Way. w&m; Jim Weatherly. c1974, 75, Keca Music Inc. GLADYS KNIGHT & THE PIPS. 139.

Love Fire. w&m; Clive Scott & Des Dyer. c1975, 77, Belsize Music Ltd. JIGSAW. 193.

Love For Living. w&m; Clare Torry. c1969, 70, Valley Music Ltd./Duchess Music Corp. GLASS BOTTLE. 94.

Love Hangover. w&m; Pamela Sawyer & Marilyn McLeod. c1976, Jobete Music Co., Inc. DIANA ROSS. 26, 48, 77, 95.

Love Has No Pride. w&m; Eric Kaz & Libby Titus (Additional lyrics). c1973, Glasco Music. Administered by United Artists Music Co., Inc. ERIC KAZ. 37.

Love In The Shadows. w&m; Neil Sedaka & Phil Cody. c1976, Neil Sedaka Music & Lebasongs. NEIL SEDAKA. 141.

Love In Vain. w&m; Mick Jagger & Keith Richard. c1970, Abkco Music, Inc. ROLLING STONES. 77, 156.

Love Is A Rose. w&m; Neil Young. c1975, Silver Fiddle. LINDA RONSTADT/NEIL YOUNG. 30, 36, 145.

Love Is Alive. w&m; Gary Wright. c1975, 76, High Wave Music, Inc. Administered by WB Music Corp. GARY WRIGHT. 62, 141.

Love Is All We Need. w&m; Ben Raleigh & Don Wolf. c1958, Unart Music Corp. TOMMY EDWARDS. 77, 81.

Love Is Here And Now You're Gone. w&m; Eddie Holland, Lamont Dozier & Brian Holland. c1966, 67, Jobete Music Co., Inc. SUPREMES. 123, 167.

Love Is Just A Four-Letter Word. w&m; Bob Dylan. c1967, 68, 69, M. Witmark & Sons & Warner Bros. Inc. JOAN BAEZ. 35, 182.

Love Is Like A Heatwave SEE Heatwave.

Love Is Like An Itching In My Heart. w&m; Eddie Holland, Lamont Dozier & Brian Holland. c1965, 66, Jobete Music Co., Inc. SUPREMES. 123.

Love Is Like Oxygen. w&m; Andrew Scott & Trevor Griffin. c1977, 78, Sweet Publishing Ltd. Controlled by WB Music Corp. & Sweet Publishing Ltd. SWEET. 22, 178.

Love Is The Answer. w&m; Hugo & Luigi & George David Weiss. c1974, Avco Embassy Music Publishing Co., Inc. STYLISTICS. 49.

Love Is The Answer. w&m; Todd Rundgren. c1977, Fiction Music, Inc. & Earmark Music Inc. Administered by Fiction Music, Inc. ENGLAND DAN & JOHN FORD COLEY/TODD RUNDGREN & UTOPIA. 56, 75, 96, 181.

Love Is Thicker Than Water SEE Thicker Than Water.

Love Love Love. w&m; Teddy McCrae, Sid Wyche & Sunny David. c1956, Progressive Music Publishing, Inc. Controlled by Unichappell Music, Inc. CLOVERS. 154, 155.

Love Machine. w&m; Pete Moore & Billy Griffin. c1975, Jobete Music Co., Inc. & Grimora Publishing. MIRACLES. 95, 150.

Love March. w&m; Gene Dinwiddie & Philip Wilson. c1969, 70, Plurb-On Music, Inc. BUTTERFIELD BLUES BAND. 202.

Love Me. w&m; Barry & Robin Gibb. c1976, Brothers Gibb B.V. Administered by Unichappell Music, Inc. YVONNE ELLIMAN. 141.

Love Me Again. w&m; Allee Willis & David Lasley. c1978, Irving Music, Inc. & Almo Music Corp. RITA COOLIDGE. 58.

Love Me Do. w&m; John Lennon & Paul McCartney. c1962, 63, 64, Ardmore & Beechwood Ltd./Beechwood Music Corp. BEATLES. 64, 72, 128, 137, 140, 161.

Love Me, I'm A Liberal. w&m; Phil Ochs, c1965, 68, Barricade Music, Inc. PHIL OCHS. 144.

Love Me Tender. w&m; Elvis Presley & Vera Matson. c1956, Elvis Presley Music. Administered by Unichappell Music, Inc. ELVIS PRESLEY. 35, 78, 101, 137, 140, 163, 173.

Love Me Tonight. w&m; Barry Mason (w), L. Pilat (m) & M. Panzer (m). c1969, Mas Edizioni Musicali/ Duchess Music Corp. TOM JONES. 94.

Love Me With All Your Heart. w&m; Sunny Skylar (w), Carlos Rigual (m) & Carlos Alberto Martinoli (m). c1961, Editorial Mexicana de Musica International S.A./Peer International Corp. BOBBY VINTON/ LETTERMEN. 179.

Love Means (You Never Have To Say You're Sorry). w&m; Warner Wilder. c1971, Bonton Music. Controlled by Colgems-EMI Music Inc. LETTERMEN/ SOUND OF SUNSHINE. 23, 130.

Love Music. w&m; Skip Scarborough. c1978, Alexscar Music. Administered by Irving Music, Inc. EARTH, WIND & FIRE. 16.

Love Or Let Me Be Lonely. w&m; C. "Skip" Scarborough, Jerry Peters & Anita Poree. c1970, Porpete Music. FRIENDS OF DISTINCTION. 64.

Love Potion Number Nine. w&m; Jerry Leiber & Mike Stoller. c1959, Quintet Music Inc. & Freddy Bienstock Music Co. CLOVERS/SEARCHERS. 137.

Love So Right. w&m; Barry, Robin & Maurice Gibb. c1976, 77, Brothers Gibb B.V./Stigwood Music, Inc. Administered by Unichappell Music Inc. BEE GEES. 131, 141.

Love Song. w&m; Kenny Loggins & Dona Lyn George. c1973, 74, Gnossos Music. ANNE MURRAY/LOGGINS & MESSINA. 43, 138.

Love Story, Theme From. w&m; Carl Sigman (w) & Francis Lai (m). c1970, 71, Famous Music Corp. ANDY WILLIAMS/SARAH VAUGHAN. 63, 88, 131.

Love Struck. w&m; Ray Roper & Dave Wills. c1978, Combat Music & Deep Cove Music. STONEBOLT. 129.

Love The One You're With. w&m; Stephen Stills. c1970, 71, 73, Gold Hill Music, Inc. ARETHA FRANKLIN/ BOB SEGER/CROSBY, STILLS, NASH & YOUNG/

ISLEY BROTHERS/STEPHEN STILLS. 36, 43, 55, 117, 136, 138, 151, 174, 182, 185.

Love Theme From Kiss. w&m; Paul Stanley, Gene Simmons, Peter Criss & Ace Frehley. c1974, 77, Cafe Americana, Inc. & Kiss Songs, Inc. KISS. 141.

Love Theme From Lady Sings The Blues SEE Happy.

Love Theme From Superman SEE Can You Read My Mind.

Love Theme From The Sandpiper SEE Shadow Of Your Smile.

Love To Burn. w&m; Paul Harrison & Casey Kelly. c1977, 78, Screen Gems-EMI Music Inc. & Bobby Goldsboro Music Inc. O.C. SMITH. 66.

Love To Love You, Baby. w&m; Pete Bellotte, Giorgio Moroder & Donna Summer. c1976, Sunday Music. Controlled & administered by Rick's Music, Inc. DONNA SUMMER. 147.

Love Will Find A Way. w&m; Cory Lerios & David Jenkins. c1978, Irving Music, Inc. & Pablo Cruise Music. PABLO CRUISE. 96.

Love Will Keep Us Together. w&m; Neil Sedaka & Howard Greenfield. c1973, 75, Don Kirshner Music, Inc. & Neil Sedaka Music. CAPTAIN & TENNILLE. 30, 36, 55, 62, 127, 133, 138, 139, 141.

Love, You Funny Thing. w&m; Roy Turk (w) & Fred E. Ahlert (m). c1932, 60, Leo Feist Inc. Renewed by Fred Ahlert Music Corp.-Cromwell Music Inc. GUY LOMBARDO. 63.

Love You Save. w&m; Corporation. c1970, Jobete Music Co., Inc. JACKSON 5. 20, 123, 150.

Love You To. w&m; George Harrison. c1966, Northern Songs Ltd./Maclen Music, Inc. GEORGE HARRISON. 182.

Lovely Day. w&m; Bill Withers (w) & Skip Scarborough (m). c1977, 78, Golden Withers Music & Unichappell Music, Inc. BILL WITHERS. 178.

Lovely Linda. w&m; Paul McCartney. c1970, Northern Songs Ltd./Maclen Music, Inc. PAUL MC CARTNEY. 61.

Lovely One. w&m; Michael & Randy Jackson. c1980, Mijack Music & Ranjack Music. Administered by Warner-Tamerlane Publishing Corp. JACKSONS. 190.

Lover Please. w&m; Billy Swan. c1962, 75, Lyn-Lou Music Co. CLYDE MC PHATTER/KRIS KRISTOFFERSON & RITA COOLIDGE. 6, 89.

Lover's Question. w&m; Brook Benton & Jimmy Williams. c1955, 65, Eden Music, Inc. & Progressive Music Publishing Co., Inc. Assigned to Unichappell Music, Inc. CLYDE MC PHATTER. 5, 78, 92, 137, 155.

Love's Been Good To Me. w&m; Rod McKuen. c1963, Almo Music Corp. ROD MC KUEN. 68.

Love's Grown Deep. w&m; Kenny Nolan. c1975, 76, Sound Of Nolan Music & Chelsea Music Co. KENNY NOLAN. 196.

Love's Made A Fool Of You. w&m; Buddy Holly & Bob Montgomery. c1958, MPL Communications, Inc. BUDDY HOLLY. 14.

Loves Me Like A Rock. w&m; Paul Simon. c1973, Paul Simon. PAUL SIMON. 143, 146.

Love's Only Love. w&m; Paul Ryan. c1979, 80, Silver Blue Music & Ryan Music Inc. ENGELBERT HUMPERDINCK. 45.

Lovey Dovey. w&m; Ahmet Ertegun & Memphis Curtis. c1954, Progressive Music Publishing Co., Inc. Controlled by Unichappell Music, Inc. CLOVERS/CLYDE MC PHATTER. 91, 154, 155.

Lovey Dovey Kinda Lovin'. w&m; Alfred Smith, Joseph Hooven & Jerry Winn. c1967, Big Shot Music, Inc. BRENTON WOOD. 76.

Lovin' Stew. w&m; Jeffrey M. Comanor & Jules Alexander. c1968, 70, Mr. Bones Music Publishing Inc. & Beechwood Music Corp. FIFTH DIMENSION. 60.

Lovin', Touchin', Squeezin'. w&m; Steve Perry. c1979, Weed High Nightmare Music. Controlled by Screen Gems-EMI Music Inc. JOURNEY. 11.

Lovin' You. w&m; Minnie Riperton & Richard Randolph. c1972, 75, Dickiebird Music and Publishing Co. MINNIE RIPERTON. 134.

Lovin' You Lovin' Me. w&m; Bonnie Bramlett & Eric Clapton. c1970, Throat Music, Ltd. & Delbon Publishing Co. ERIC CLAPTON. 182.

Loving Her Was Easier. w&m; Kris Kristofferson. c1970, Combine Music Corp. KRIS KRISTOFFERSON. 59, 89.

Loving You. w&m; Mike Stoller & Jerry Leiber. c1957, Elvis Presley Music, Inc. ELVIS PRESLEY. 172.

Lowdown. w&m; Boz Scaggs & David Paich. c1976, Boz Scaggs Music & Hudmar Publishing Co., Inc. BOZ SCAGGS. 62, 141, 145.

Lucille. w&m; Albert Collins & Richard Penniman. c1957, 60, Venice Music. JERRY LEE LEWIS/ LITTLE RICHARD. 35, 78, 100, 137, 159, 163, 197.

Lucille. w&m; B.B. King. c1968, 71, ABC-Dunhill Music, Inc. & Sounds Of Lucille. B.B. KING. 105, 122.

Lucille. w&m; Roger Bowling & Hal Bynum. c1976, ATV Music Corp. & Andite Invasion Music. KENNY ROGERS. 15, 21, 196, 199.

Luckenbach, Texas. w&m; Bobby Emmons & Chips Moman. c1977, Baby Chick Music, Inc. WAYLON JENNINGS. 126, 134, 142, 164.

Lucky Me. w&m; Charlie Black & Rory Bourke. c1980, Chappell & Co., Inc. ANNE MURRAY. 47.

Lucretia MacEvil. w&m; David Clayton Thomas. c1970, 71, Blackwood Music Inc. & Bay Music, Ltd. BLOOD, SWEAT & TEARS. 15.

Lucy In The Sky With Diamonds. w&m; John Lennon & Paul Mc Cartney. c1967, Northern Songs Ltd./ Maclen Music, Inc. BEATLES/ELTON JOHN. 36, 55, 62, 133, 139, 145, 159, 175.

Lullaby Of Birdland. w&m; B.Y. Forster (w) & George Shearing (m). c1952, 53, 54, Patricia Music Publishing Corp. AL HIRT/ELLA FITZGERALD. 163.

Lyin' Eyes. w&m; Don Henley & Glenn Frey. c1975, Cass County Music, Red Cloud Music & WB Music Corp. EAGLES. 30, 36, 62, 141, 145, 185.

Ma Belle Amie. w&m; Hans van Eijck, Peter Tetteroo & Gus Howard (Arranged). c1969, 70, Dayglow Music N.V. & Veronica Music Editions C.V. Assigned to & controlled by Legacy Music, Inc. TEE SET. 149.

Mabellene. w&m; Chuck Berry, Russ Fratto & Alan Freed. c1955, Arc Music Corp. CHUCK BERRY/ JERRY LEE LEWIS. 44, 78, 100, 155, 168, 169, 197.

MacArthur Park. w&m; Jimmy Webb. c1968, 73, Canopy Music Inc. DONNA SUMMER/RICHARD HARRIS. 35, 55, 62, 117, 118, 136, 146, 174, 185.

MacDonald's Commercial SEE You, You're The One.

Machine Gun. w&m; Milan Williams (m). c1974, Jobete Music Co., Inc. COMMODORES. 52.

Macho Man. w&m; J. Morali, H. Belolo, V. Willis & P. Whitehead. c1978, Scorpio Music. Controlled by Can't Stop Music. VILLAGE PEOPLE. 34, 51, 73, 112, 135, 177, 198, 200.

Mack The Knife. w&m; Marc Blitzstein (w) & Kurt Weill (m). c1928, 55, Universal Edition. Assigned to Weill-Brecht-Harms Co., Inc. BOBBY DARIN. 100, 138.

Maggie Mae. w&m; John Lennon (Arranged), Paul McCartney (Arranged), George Harrison (Arranged) & Richard Starkey (Arranged). c1970, Northern Songs Ltd./Maclen Music, Inc. BEATLES. 159.

Maggie May. w&m; Rod Stewart & Martin Quittenton. c1971, M.R.C. Music Inc. Administered by Unichappel Music, Inc. ROD STEWART. 131.

Maggie M'Gill. w&m; Jim Morrison (w) & Doors (m). c1970, Doors Music Co. DOORS. 54.

Maggie's Farm. w&m; Bob Dylan. c1965, M. Witmark & Sons & Warner Bros., Inc. BOB DYLAN. 35, 67, 132.

Magic. w&m; John Farrar. c1980, John Farrar Music. OLIVIA NEWTON-JOHN. 58.

Magic Bus. w&m; Peter Townshend. c1967, 69, Fabulous Music, Ltd. Controlled by TRO-Essex Music Inc. WHO. 29, 35.

Magic Garden. w&m; Jim Webb. c1967, 70, Johnny Rivers Music. FIFTH DIMENSION. 60.

Magic Man. w&m; Ann & Nancy Wilson. c1976, How About Music. HEART. 142.

Magical Mystery Tour. w&m; John Lennon & Paul McCartney, c1967, Northern Songs Ltd. Controlled by Comet Music Corp. BEATLES. 36, 127, 138.

Mahogany, Theme From SEE Do You Know Where You're Going To?

Maid Of Constant Sorrow. w&m; Judy Collins. c1968, Warner Bros.-Seven Arts, Inc. JUDY COLLINS. 132.

Main Event/Fight. w&m; Paul Jabara & Bruce Roberts. c1979, Primus Artists Music, Diana Music Corp. & Rick's Music Inc. BARBRA STREISAND. 27, 147.

Mainstreet. w&m; Bob Seger. c1976, 77, Gear Publishing Co. BOB SEGER. 164.

Make It Easy On Yourself. w&m; Hal David (w) & Burt Bacharach (m). c1962, Famous Music Corp. DIONNE WARWICK/JERRY BUTLER. 6, 63, 88.

Make It Last. w&m; Bruce Sudano & Joe Esposito. c1978, Starrin Music Publishing Corp. & Rick's Music Inc. BROOKLYN DREAMS. 25.

Make It With You. w&m; David Gates. c1970, Col-gems-EMI Music Inc. BREAD. 88, 134.

Make Me Smile. w&m; James Pankow. c1970, Moose Music & Aurelius Music. CHICAGO. 63, 86, 134.

Make The World Go Away. w&m; Hank Cochran. c1963, 70, Tree Publishing Co., Inc. AL MARTINO/DONNY & MARIE OSMOND/EDDY ARNOLD/ELVIS PRESLEY. 130, 179.

Makin' It. w&m; Dino Fekaris & Freddie Perren. c1978, 79, Perren-Vibes Music Co. DAVID NAUGHTON. 27, 31.

Making A Good Thing Better. w&m; Pete Wingfield. c1976, 77, Island Music Ltd. & Uncle Doris Music Ltd. Controlled by Ackee Music, Inc. & Uncle Doris Music, Inc. OLIVIA NEWTON-JOHN. 87, 127, 145.

Mama Can't Buy You Love. w&m; Leroy Bell & Casey James. c1977, Mighty Three Music. ELTON JOHN. 24, 56, 75, 180, 187.

Mama, You Been On My Mind. w&m; Bob Dylan. c1964, 67, M. Witmark & Sons & Warner Bros., Inc. BOB DYLAN/JOAN BAEZ/JUDY COLLINS/ROD STEWART. 35, 67, 132, 138, 152.

Mama's Pearl. w&m; Corporation. c1970, 71, Jobete Music Co., Inc. JACKSON 5. 20, 123.

Mammas Don't Let Your Babies Grow Up To Be Cowboys. w&m; Ed & Patsy Bruce. c1975, 78, Tree Publishing Co., Inc. & Sugarplum Music Co. WAYLON & WILLIE. 130, 134, 135.

Man In Me. w&m; Bob Dylan. c1970, 76, Big Sky Music. BOB DYLAN. 170.

Man Of Constant Sorrow. w&m; Peter Yarrow & Paul Stookey. c1962, Pepamar Music Corp. PETER, PAUL & MARY. 67.

Man With All The Toys. w&m; Brian Wilson. c1964, Sea Of Tunes Publishing Co. BEACH BOYS. 9.

Manana. w&m; Jimmy Buffett. c1976, Coral Reefer Music & Outer Banks Music. JIMMY BUFFETT. 145.

Manchester England. w&m; James Rado (w), Gerome Ragni (w) & Galt MacDermot (m). c1966, 67, 70, James Rado, Gerome Ragni, Galt MacDermot, Nat Shapiro. Controlled & administered by United Artists Music Co., Inc. CAST OF HAIR. 161, 186.

Mandy. w&m; Richard Kerr & Scott English. c1971, 74, Screen Gems-EMI Music Inc. & Grahple Music Ltd. Controlled by Screen Gems-EMI Music Inc. & Wren Music Co., Inc. BARRY MANILOW/BROTHERS FOUR. 23, 56, 77, 103, 130, 134, 156.

Maple Leaf Rag. w&m; Scott Joplin (m). c1974, Columbia Pictures Publications. EMERSON, LAKE & PALMER/EUBIE BLAKE. 130.

Margaritaville. w&m; Jimmy Buffett. c1977, Coral Reefer Music. JIMMY BUFFETT. 57, 127, 146.

Marrakesh Express. w&m; Graham Nash. c1969, 71,

Giving Room Music & Siquomb Publishing Corp. CROSBY, STILLS, NASH & YOUNG. 86, 138, 203.

Martha. w&m; Paul Kantner. c1967, 68, Icebag Corp. JEFFERSON AIRPLANE. 108.

Martha (Your Lovers Come And Go). w&m; Terry Lauber. c1978, BEMA Music Co., a division of Sweet City Records Inc. & Terry Lauber Music. GABRIEL. 74.

Mary Jane. w&m; Rick James. c1978, Jobete Music Co., Inc. RICK JAMES. 66.

M*A*S*H, Song From. w&m; Mike Altman & Johnny Mandel. c1970, Twentieth Century Music Corp. BARRY MANILOW/PERCY FAITH/ROGER WILLIAMS. 71, 77, 88, 130, 134.

Mashed Potato Time. w&m; Jon Sheldon & Harry Land. c1962, Rice-Mill Publishing Co. DEE DEE SHARP. 5.

Massachusetts. w&m; Barry, Robin & Maurice Gibb. c1967, 75, Abigail Music Ltd. Controlled by Casserole Music, Inc. Unichappell Music Inc., administrator. BEE GEES. 35, 55, 141.

Master Song. w&m; Leonard Cohen. c1967, 69, Stranger Music, Inc. LEONARD COHEN. 171.

Masterpiece. w&m; J.J. Mouret (m) & Paul Parnes (m). c1972, 74, September Music Corp. CHARLES RANDOLPH GREAN/CHET ATKINS. 163.

Masterpiece Theatre, Theme From SEE Masterpiece.

Masters Of War. w&m; Bob Dylan. c1963, M. Witmark & Sons. BOB DYLAN/JUDY COLLINS. 67, 132, 138.

Matchmaker, Matchmaker. w&m; Sheldon Harnick (w) & Jerry Bock (m). c1964, The Times Square Music Publications Co. CAST OF FIDDLER ON THE ROOF/TEEMATES. 56.

Maybe. w&m; Richard Barrett. c1958, 69, 70, Nom Music, Inc. CHANTELS/DELIGHTS/THREE DEGREES. 2, 78, 101, 155, 161, 191.

Maybe Baby. w&m; Norman Petty & Charles Hardin. c1957, MPL Communications, Inc. BUDDY HOLLY/BUDDY HOLLY & THE CRICKETS. 14.

Maybe I'm A Fool. w&m; Lloyd Chiate, Lee Garrett, Eddie Money & Robert Taylor. c1979, Grajonca Music & Island Music. EDDIE MONEY. 129, 181.

Maybe I'm Amazed. w&m; Paul McCartney. c1970, Northern Songs Ltd/Maclen Music, Inc. PAUL MC CARTNEY/WINGS. 61, 141, 145, 182.

Maybe This Time. w&m; Fred Ebb (w) & John Kander (m). c1963, Times Square Music Publications Co. LIZA MINELLI. 58.

Maybe Tomorrow. w&m; Corporation. c1971, Jobete Music Co., Inc. JACKSON 5. 20.

Me And Baby Brother. w&m; Sylvester Allen, Harold R. Brown, Morris Dickerson, Leroy "Lonnie" Jordan, Charles W. Miller, Lee Oskar & Howard Scott. c1971, 73, Far Out Music, Inc. Administered by United Artists Music Co., Inc. WAR. 194.

Me And Baby Jane. w&m; Leon Russell. c1971, Skyhill Publishing Co., Inc. LEON RUSSELL. 115, 152.

Me And Bobby McGee. w&m; Kris Kristofferson & Fred Foster. c1969, Combine Music Corp. JANIS

JOPLIN/KRIS KRISTOFFERSON. 15, 21, 59, 64, 163, 198.

Me And Julio Down By The Schoolyard. w&m; Paul Simon. c1971, Paul Simon. PAUL SIMON. 124, 131, 143, 146.

Me And Mrs. Jones. w&m; Kenneth Gamble, Leon Huff & Cary Gilbert. c1973, Assorted Music. BILLY PAUL. 130.

Me And My Arrow. w&m; Nilsson. c1970, Dunbar Music Inc. NILSSON. 93.

Me And The Gang. w&m; Hamilton Bohannon. c1978, Intersong USA, Inc. & Bohannon Phase II Music Publishing Co. HAMILTON BOHANNON. 50.

Me And You And A Dog Named Boo. w&m; Kent LaVoie. c1971, Famous Music Corp. & Kaiser Music Co., Inc. LOBO. 63.

Me, The Peaceful Heart. w&m; Tony Hazzard. c1968, Sydney Bron Music Ltd. LULU. 76.

Mean Woman Blues. w&m; Claude DeMetruis. c1957, Gladys Music. Controlled by Chappell & Co., Inc. ELVIS PRESLEY/ROY ORBISON. 155, 173.

Meditation. w&m; Arlo Guthrie. c1968, 69, Appleseed Music Inc. ARLO GUTHRIE. 7.

Meet Me In The Morning. w&m; Bob Dylan. c1974, 76, Ram's Horn Music. BOB DYLAN. 170.

Melissa. w&m; Gregg Allman. c1972, 74, No Exit Music Co., Inc. & Sheralyn Music. ALLMAN BROTHERS BAND. 139.

Mellow Down Easy. w&m; Willie Dixon. c1954, Arc Music Corp. PAUL BUTTERFIELD. 1.

Mellow Lovin'. w&m; T. Monn, J. Cheeks & R. Williams. c1977, 78, Rosalba Music Inc. JUDY CHEEKS. 74.

Mellow Yellow. w&m; Donovan Leitch. c1966, Donovan Music Ltd./Peer International Corp. DONOVAN. 3.

Memories Are Made Of This. w&m; Terry Gilkyson, Rich Dehr & Frank Miller. c1955, Blackwood Music Inc. DEAN MARTIN. 193.

Memphis, Tennessee. w&m; Chuck Berry. c1959, 63, Arc Music Corp. BUCK OWENS/CHUCK BERRY/ ELVIS PRESLEY/JOHNNY RIVERS/ROD STEWART. 6, 44, 78, 100, 156, 168, 169, 197.

Mercedes Benz. w&m; Janis Joplin & Michael McClure. c1970, Strong Arm Music. JANIS JOPLIN. 115.

Mercy, Mercy Me. w&m; Marvin Gaye. c1971, Jobete Music Co., Inc. MARVIN GAYE. 150.

Merry Christmas Baby. w&m; Lou Baxter & Johnny Moore. c1948, St. Louis Music Corp. Assigned to Unichappell Music, Inc. & Chappell & Co., Inc. JOHNNY MOORE'S THREE BLAZERS. 155.

Mess Around. w&m; Ahmet Nugetre. c1954, Progressive Music Publishing Co., Inc. RAY CHARLES. 154.

Mess Of Blues. w&m; Doc Pomus & Mort Shuman. c1960, Elvis Presley Music. Controlled by Unichappell Music, Inc. ELVIS PRESLEY. 155, 172.

Mexico. w&m; James Taylor. c1975, Country Road Music, Inc. JAMES TAYLOR. 136, 146.

Michael. w&m; Traditional. Rev. Earl Osborn (Adapted). c1977, Road Island Co. HIGHWAYMEN. 68.

Michael, Row The Boat Ashore. w&m; Traditional. Jessie Cavanaugh (Adapted) & Albert Stanton (Adapted). c1960, 72, Hollis Music, Inc. WEAVERS. 85.

Michael From Mountains. w&m; Joni Mitchell. c1967, 74, Siquomb Publishing Corp. JONI MITCHELL. 35, 67.

Michelle. w&m; John Lennon & Paul McCartney. c1965, Northern Songs Ltd./Maclen Music, Inc. BEATLES. 35, 61, 62.

Michelle's Song. w&m; Elton John & Bernie Taupin. c1970, Dick James Music Corp. ELTON JOHN. 43.

Mickey's Monkey. w&m; Eddie Holland, Lamont Dozier & Brian Holland. c1963, 72, Jobete Music Co., Inc. SMOKEY ROBINSON & THE MIRACLES. 123, 150.

Midnight Blue. w&m; Carole Bayer Sager & Melissa Manchester. c1974, 75, The Times Square Music Publications Co. & Rumanian Pickleworks Music Co. MELISSA MANCHESTER. 23, 56, 58, 128, 130.

Midnight Confessions. w&m; Lou Josie. c1967, Little Fugitive Music. GRASS ROOTS. 4.

Midnight Cowboy, Theme From SEE Everybody's Talkin'.

Midnight Express, Theme From SEE Chase.

Midnight Light. w&m; Eddie Struzick & Lenny LeBlanc. c1976, Music Mill Publishing Co., Inc. LEBLANC & CARR. 135.

Midnight On The Bay. w&m; Neil Young. c1976, Silver Fiddle. STILLS-YOUNG BAND. 141.

Midnight Rambler. w&m; Mick Jagger & Keith Richard. c1969, Abkco Music, Inc. ROLLING STONES. 77, 142, 156.

Midnight Rider. w&m; Gregg Allman & K. Payne. c1970, 73, No Exit Music Co., Inc. ALLMAN BROTHERS BAND. 36, 117, 138.

Midnight Special. w&m; Traditional. Huddie Ledbetter (Adapted) & Sammy Cash (Adapted). c1936, 59, 64, 76, versions published by Country Glory Music & Folkways Music Publishers Inc. ARLO GUTHRIE/ JOHNNY RIVERS/VAN MORRISON. 68, 85.

Midnight Train. w&m; Richard Havens. c1964, 68, Warner Bros.-Seven Arts, Inc. RICHIE HAVENS. 132.

Midnight Train To Georgia. w&m; Jim Weatherly. c1971, 73, Keca Music, Inc. GLADYS KNIGHT & THE PIPS. 17, 53, 104, 131.

Mighty Idy. w&m; Mono Mann. c1978, Doraflo Music Co. & Go Mental Music. DMZ. 19.

Mighty Joe. w&m; Bobby Van Leeuwen. c1970, Dayglow Music & Skinny Zach Music Inc. SHOCKING BLUE. 186.

Mighty Quinn SEE Quinn The Eskimo.

Miles. w&m; Mimi & Richard Farina. c1966, 68, Warner Bros.-Seven Arts, Inc. MIMI & RICHARD FARINA. 132.

Million Dollar Bash. w&m; Bob Dylan. c1967, 75, Dwarf Music. BOB DYLAN & THE BAND. 170.

Million To One. w&m; Phil Medley. c1960, 71, Jobete Music Co., Inc. JIMMY CHARLES. 123, 150.

Minstrel Boy. w&m; Bob Dylan. c1970, 76, Big Sky Music. BOB DYLAN. 170.

Minute By Minute. w&m; Michael McDonald & Lester Abrams (w). c1978, 79, Snug Music & Loresta Music. DOOBIE BROTHERS. 27, 31, 147.

Minute You're Gone. w&m; Jimmy Gateley. c1963, Regent Music Corp. HANK LOCKLIN. 169.

Miracles. w&m; Marty Balin. c1975, Diamondback Music Co. JEFFERSON STARSHIP. 121.

Miranda. w&m; Phil Ochs. c1966, 68, Barricade Music, Inc. PHIL OCHS. 144.

Misery. w&m; John Lennon & Paul McCartney. c1963, Northern Songs Ltd./Gil Music Corp. BEATLES. 125.

Miss Ann. w&m; Richard Penniman & Enotris Johnson. c1957, Venice Music. LITTLE RICHARD. 159.

Mission Bell. w&m; William Michael. c1960, Bamboo Music, inc. DONNIE BROOKS. 4.

Mission Impossible Theme. w&m; Lalo Schifrin (m). c1966, 67, Bruin Music Co. DICK SCHORY. 76.

Mississippi. w&m; Charlie Daniels. c1978, 79, Hat Band Music. CHARLIE DANIELS BAND. 147.

Mississippi Half-Step Uptown Toodleoo. w&m; Robert Hunter (w) & Jerry Garcia (m). c1973, 76, Ice Nine Publishing Co., Inc. GRATEFUL DEAD. 84.

Mississippi Queen. w&m; Leslie West, Corky Laing, Felix Pappalardi & David Rea. c1970, Upfall Music Co. MOUNTAIN. 115, 152, 182, 197.

Mister SEE ALSO Mr.

Mister Lee. w&m; Heather Dixon, Helen Gathers, Emma Ruth & Jannie Pought & Laura Webb. c1957, Progressive Music Publishing Co., Inc. Controlled by Unichappell Music, Inc. BOBBETTES. 2, 91, 101, 154, 155.

Mister Sandman. w&m; Pat Ballard. c1954, Edwin H. Morris & Co. CHORDETTES. 93.

Misty. w&m; Johnny Burke (w) & Erroll Garner (m). c1954, 55, 75, Vernon Music Corp., by arrangement with Octave Music Publishing Corp. DUKE ELLINGTON/ELLA FITZGERALD/JOHNNY MATHIS/RAY STEVENS. 71, 138.

Misty Mountain Hop. w&m; Jimmy Page, Robert Plant & John Paul Jones. c1972, 73, Superhype Publishing. LED ZEPPELIN. 114.

Misty Roses. w&m; Tim Hardin. c1966, 68, Faithful Virtue Music Co., Inc. FIFTH DIMENSION/TIM HARDIN. 60.

Misunderstanding. w&m; Phil Collins. c1980, Hit And Run Music Ltd./Pun Music. GENESIS. 189.

Moby Dick. w&m; John Bonham, John Paul Jones & Jimmy Page. c1969, Superhype Publishing. LED ZEPPELIN. 114.

Mockingbird. w&m; Inez & Charlie Foxx. James Taylor (Additional lyrics). c1963, 74, Unart Music Corp. CARLY SIMON & JAMES TAYLOR. 79, 140, 163, 198.

Modern World. w&m; Paul Weller. c1977, And Son Music Ltd./Frontwheel Music, Inc. JAM. 153.

Mohair Sam. w&m; Dallas Frazier. c1965, Acclaim Music Inc. Used by permission of Rychman Music Publishing. CHARLIE RICH. 5.

Moments To Remember. w&m; Al Stillman (w) & Robert Allen (m). c1955, 67, Beaver Music Publishing Corp. Assigned to Larry Spier, Inc. FOUR LADS. 193.

Mon Homme SEE My Man.

Mona. w&m; E. McDaniel. c1960, 64, Arc Music Corp. QUICKSILVER MESSENGER SERVICE/ROLLING STONES. 10.

Monday, Monday. w&m; John Phillips. c1966, American Broadcasting Music, Inc. MAMAS & THE PAPAS. 89, 93, 119, 126.

Monday Morning. w&m; Peter Yarrow (Adapted), Paul Stookey (Adapted), Mary Travers (Adapted) & Milton Okun (Adapted). c1965, Pepamar Music Corp. PETER, PAUL & MARY. 35, 67.

Money. w&m; Roger Waters. c1973, Hampshire House Publishing Corp. PINK FLOYD. 142, 156.

Money Blues. w&m; Bob Dylan & Jacques Levy (w). c1975, 76, Ram's Horn Music. BOB DYLAN. 170.

Money Money. w&m; John Barlow (w) & Bob Weir (m). c1974, 76, Ice Nine Publishing Co., Inc. GRATEFUL DEAD. 84.

Money, Money, Money. w&m; Benny Andersson & Bjorn Ulvaeus. c1976, Union Songs AB./Artwork Music Co., Inc. ABBA. 15.

Money (That's What I Want). w&m; Berry Gordy, Jr. & Janie Bradford. c1959, Jobete Music Co., Inc. BARRETT STRONG/BEATLES/DIANA ROSS/JERRY LEE LEWIS/JR. WALKER & THE ALL STARS/MIRACLES/ROLLING STONES. 24, 166.

Money Won't Change You. w&m; James Brown & Nat Jones. c1966, 68, Dynatone Publishing Co. JAMES BROWN. 18.

Monkees, Theme From. w&m; Tommy Boyce & Bobby Hart. c1966, Screen Gems-Columbia Music, Inc. MONKEES. 38.

Monkey See-Monkey Do. w&m; Michael Franks. c1975, 76, Warner-Tamerlane Publishing Corp. & Mississippi Mud Music Co. MELISSA MANCHESTER. 141.

Monster Mash. w&m; Bobby Pickett & Leonard Capizzi. c1962, 73, Acoustic Music, Inc., Gary S. Paxton Music, Inc. & Capizzi Music Co. BOBBY "BORIS" PICKETT. 6, 111.

Montego Bay. w&m; Jeff Barry & Bobby Bloom. c1970, Unart Music Corp. SUGAR CANE. 80.

Mony, Mony. w&m; Bobby Bloom, Ritchie Cordell, Bo Gentry & Tommy James. c1968, Big Seven Music Corp. TOMMY JAMES & THE SHONDELLS. 102.

Moody River. w&m; Gary D. Bruce. c1961, Keva Music, Inc. PAT BOONE. 6.

Moon Is A Harsh Mistress. w&m; Jimmy Webb. c1974, 75, White Oak Songs. JOE CROCKER/JUDY COLLINS. 30.

Moondance. w&m; Van Morrison. c1970, 71, WB Music

Corp. & Caledonia Soul Music. VAN MORRISON. 22, 30, 55, 87, 136, 139, 151, 174, 185.

Moondreams. w&m; Norman Petty. c1957, MPL Communications, Inc. BUDDY HOLLY. 14.

Moonlight Lady. w&m; Iain Sutherland. c1976, 77, Skerry Rock Ltd./Island Music. 127.

Moonlight Serenade. w&m; Mitchell Parish (w) & Glenn Miller (m). c1939, 67, Robbins Music Corp. BOBBY VINTON/BOSTON POPS/GLENN MILLER/NASHVILLE BRASS/TUXEDO JUNCTION. 140, 192, 198.

Moonraker. w&m; Hal David (w) & John Barry (m). c1979, Danjaq S.Z. Controlled & administered by United Artists Music Co., Inc. & Unart Music Corp. SHIRLEY BASSEY. 80.

More I See You. w&m; Mack Gordon (w) & Harry Warren (m). c1945, 73, Twentieth Century Music Corp. Controlled by Bregman, Vocco & Conn, Inc. PETER ALLEN. 130.

More, More, More (Part I). w&m; Gregg Diamond. c1976, Buddah Music, Inc., Gee Diamond Music & MRI Music. ANDREA TRUE CONNECTION. 51.

More Than A Feeling. w&m; Donald T. Scholz. c1975, 76, Pure Songs & Donald T. Scholz. Controlled by Colgems-EMI Music Inc. BOSTON. 23, 121, 128, 134, 142.

More Than A Woman. w&m; Barry, Robin & Maurice Gibb. c1977, Brothers Gibb B.V. Controlled by Stigwood Music, Inc. Unichappell Music Inc., administrator. BEE GEES. 40, 50, 178.

More Than I Can Say. w&m; Sonny Curtis & Jerry Allison. c1960, 80, Warner-Tamerlane Publishing Corp. LEO SAYER. 162, 190.

More Today Than Yesterday. w&m; Pat Upton. c1968, Regent Music Corp., Lynwood Music & Miss Muffit Music. SPIRAL STAIRCASE. 78, 93, 102, 169.

Morning After. w&m; Al Kasha & Joel Hirschhorn. c1972, Twentieth Century Music Corp. & Fox Fanfare Music, Inc. MAUREEN MC GOVERN. 23, 28, 32, 77, 126, 134, 156.

Morning Dance. w&m; Jay Beckenstein. c1978, Harlem Music & Crosseyed Bear Music. SPYRO GYRA. 11, 24.

Morning Has Broken. w&m; Eleanor Farjeon (w) & Cat Stevens (m). c1971, 72, 79, Freshwater Music Ltd./Island Music. CAT STEVENS. 55, 70, 96, 127, 174, 178, 183.

Morningside Of The Mountain. w&m; Dick Manning & Larry Stock. c1951, 74, Remick Music Corp. & Warner Bros. Inc. DONNY & MARIE OSMOND. 139.

Most Beautiful Girl. w&m; Norris Wilson, Billy Sherrill & Rory Bourke. c1973, Al Gallico Music Corp. & Algee Music Corp. BROTHERS FOUR/CHARLIE RICH. 77, 89, 130, 134, 156.

Most Likely You Go Your Way. w&m; Bob Dylan. c1966, 76, Dwarf Music. BOB DYLAN. 170.

Most Peculiar Man. w&m; Paul Simon. c1965, Paul Simon. SIMON & GARFUNKEL. 143.

Mother And Child Reunion. w&m; Paul Simon. c1971, Paul Simon. PAUL SIMON. 136, 143, 147.

Mother Earth. w&m; Peter Chatman & Lewis Simpkins. c1950, Arc Music Corp. ERIC BURDON. 1.

Mother-In-Law. w&m; Allen Toussaint. c1961, Minit Music Co., Inc. & Unart Music Corp. ERNIE K. DOE/ HERMAN'S HERMITS. 78, 81, 102, 137, 155, 161.

Motherless Child. w&m; Mary Travers & Milton Okun. c1965, Pepamar Music Corp. PETER, PAUL & MARY. 67.

Motorcycle Song. w&m; Arlo Guthrie. c1967, 68, 69, Appleseed Music Inc. ARLO GUTHRIE. 7.

Motown Review. w&m; Len Barry & Butch Ingram. c1979, Parker Music & Wimot Music. PHILLY CREAM. 75.

Mountain Of Love. w&m; Harold Doman. c1959, 66, Morris Music, Inc. Controlled by Unichappell Music Inc. HAROLD DOMAN/JOHNNY RIVERS. 6.

Move Over. w&m; Janis Joplin. c1971, Strong Arm Music. JANIS JOPLIN. 110.

Movin' Out (Anthony's Song). w&m; Billy Joel. c1977, 78, Joelsongs. Administered by Blackwood Music Inc. BILLY JOEL. 21, 165.

Mozambique. w&m; Bob Dylan & Jacques Levy (w). c1975, 76, Ram's Horn Music. BOB DYLAN. 145, 170.

Mr. SEE ALSO Mister.

Mr. Bass Man. w&m; Johnny Cymbal. c1963, 74, Regent Music Corp. JOHNNY CYMBAL. 44, 168.

Mr. Big Stuff. w&m; Joe Broussard, Ralph Williams & Carrol Washington. c1971, Malaco Music Co. & Caraljo Music Co. JEAN KNIGHT. 64.

Mr. Blue. w&m; DeWayne Blackwell. c1959, Cornerstone Publishing Co. & Unart Music Corp. DAVID BROMBERG/FLEETWOODS/KEITH CARRADINE. 2, 37, 78, 82, 101.

Mr. BoJangles. w&m; Jerry Jeff Walker. c1968, Cotillion Music, Inc. & Danel Music Inc. JERRY JEFF WALKER/NITTY GRITTY DIRT BAND/SAMMY DAVIS, JR. 35, 62, 115, 138.

Mr. Boom Boom SEE Mr. Bass Man.

Mr. Moonlight. w&m; Roy Lee Johnson. c1962, Lowery Music Co., Inc. BEATLES. 125.

Mr. Soul. w&m; Neil Young. c1967, 74, Cotillion Music, Inc., Ten East Music & Springalo Toones. BUFFALO SPRINGFIELD. 39, 139.

Mr. Tambourine Man. w&m; Bob Dylan. c1964, M. Witmark & Sons & Warner Bros. Inc. BOB DYLAN/ BYRDS/JUDY COLLINS. 35, 67, 69, 138, 151.

Mrs. Robinson. w&m; Paul Simon. c1968, Paul Simon. SIMON & GARFUNKEL. 136, 143.

Muddy Mississippi Line. w&m; Bobby Goldsboro. c1969, Detail Music, Inc. BOBBY GOLDSBORO. 81.

Mundo SEE Un Mundo.

Muscle Of Love. w&m; Alice Cooper & Michael Bruce. c1973, 74, Bizarre Music Inc. & Alive Enterprises. ALICE COOPER. 199.

Music. w&m; John Miles. c1976, Velvet Music Ltd. JOHN MILES. 142.

Music In My Life. w&m; Mac Davis. c1978, Songpainter

Music. Controlled by Screen Gems-EMI Music Inc. MAC DAVIS. 135.

Music Never Stopped. w&m; John Barlow (w) & Bob Weir (m). c1975, Ice Nine Publishing Co., Inc. GRATEFUL DEAD. 84.

Music Will Not End. w&m; Gene Pistilli (w) & Walter Murphy (m). c1978, RFT Music Publishing Corp. WALTER MURPHY BAND. 135.

Muskrat Love. w&m; Willis Alan Ramsey. c1971, Wishbone Music. AMERICA/CAPTAIN & TENNILLE. 77, 126, 128, 134, 142.

Must Of Got Lost. w&m; Peter Wolf & Seth Justman. c1974, Walden Music Inc. & Juke Joint Music. J. GEILS BAND. 36, 139.

Mustang Sally. w&m; Bonny Rice. c1965, 67, Fourteenth Hour Music, Inc. WILSON PICKETT. 4.

My Angel Baby. w&m; Danny McKenna & Balde Silva. c1978, Texongs Music, Inc. & BoMASS Music Corp. TOBY BEAU. 96.

My Babe. w&m; Willie Dixon. c1955, Arc Music Corp. ELVIS PRESLEY. 44, 169.

My Baby Does Good Sculptures SEE Good Sculptures.

My Baby Loves Me. w&m; Sylvia Moy, William Stevenson & Ivy Hunter. c1965, 66, Jobete Music Co., Inc. BARRY MANILOW/MARTHA & THE VANDELLAS. 142, 150.

My Baby Must Be A Magician. w&m; William Robinson. c1967, 68, Jobete Music Co., Inc. MARVELETTES. 123.

My Baby's Baby. w&m; Adrian Baker & Eddie Seago. c1979, Cellar Music Ltd. & Eddie Seago. Controlled by ATV Music Corp. LIQUID GOLD. 159.

My Back Pages. w&m; Bob Dylan. c1964, M. Witmark & Sons & Warner Bros. Inc. BOB DYLAN/BYRDS. 35, 43, 67.

My Best Friend's Girl. w&m; Ric Ocasek. c1978, 79, Lido Music, Inc. CARS. 22, 87, 147.

My Boy Lollipop. w&m; Johnny Roberts & Morris Levy. c1956, 64, Nom Music, Inc. MILLIE SMALL. 78, 102, 155, 157, 161.

My Boyfriend's Back. w&m; Robert Feldman, Gerald Goldstein & Richard Gottehrer. c1963, Blackwood Music, Inc. ANGELS. 4.

My Cherie Amour. w&m; Stevie Wonder, Henry Cosby & Sylvia Moy. c1968, 69, 70, 71, 73, 74, 75, Jobete Music Co., Inc. GEORGE BENSON/STEVIE WONDER. 24, 53, 71, 77, 123, 130, 134, 150, 183.

My Elusive Dreams. w&m; Curly Putman & Billy Sherrill. c1967, 70, Tree Publishing Co., Inc. BOBBY VINTON. 149, 186.

My Eyes Adored You. w&m; Bob Crewe & Kenny Nolan. c1974, Stone Diamond Music Corp., TannyBoy Music Co. & Kenny Nolan Publishing. FRANKIE VALLI. 150, 156.

My Feet Keep Dancing. w&m; Nile Rodgers & Bernard Edwards. c1979, Chic Music Inc. CHIC. 147.

My Foolish Heart. w&m; Ned Washington (w) & Victor Young (m). c1949, Anne-Rachel Music Corp. AL MARTINO. 191.

My Forbidden Lover. w&m; Nile Rodgers & Bernard Edwards. c1979, Chic Music, Inc. Administered by Warner-Tamerlane Publishing Corp. CHIC. 27, 147.

My Front Pages. w&m; Arlo Guthrie. c1969, Howard Beach Music, Inc. ARLO GUTHRIE. 7.

My Generation. w&m; Peter Townshend. c1965, Fabulous Music Ltd. WHO. 35.

My Girl. w&m; William "Smokey" Robinson & Ronald White. c1964, 65, Jobete Music Co., Inc. TEMPTATIONS. 123, 150, 166.

My Girl Josephine. w&m; Antoine Domino & Dave Bartholomew. c1960, Unart Music Corp. FATS DOMINO/JERRY JAYE. 82, 102, 137.

My Guy. w&m; William "Smokey" Robinson. c1964, 65, Jobete Music Co., Inc. MARY WELLS. 123, 150, 166.

My Heart Belongs To Me. w&m; Alan Gordon. c1976, 77, Koppelman-Bandier Music & Kiki Music Corp. BARBRA STREISAND. 15, 21, 199.

My Heart Belongs To Only You. w&m; Frank & Dorothy Daniels. c1952, Merrimac Music Corp. BETTY MC LAURIN/BOBBY VINTON. 168.

My Heart Cries For You. w&m; Carl Sigman & Percy Faith. c1950, Anne-Rachel Music Corp., Gladys Music, Inc. & Massey Music Co., Inc. Administered by Anne-Rachel Music Corp. GUY MITCHELL. 191.

My Heart Is An Open Book. w&m; Hal David (w) & Lee Pockriss (m). c1958, Post Music, Inc. & United Artists Music Co., Inc. CARL DOBKINS, JR. 78, 81.

My Heroes Have Always Been Cowboys. w&m; Sharon Vaughn. c1976, 80, Jack & Bill Music Co. WILLIE NELSON. 177, 199.

My Little Red Book. w&m; Hal David (w) & Burt Bacharach (m). c1965, United Artists Music Co., Inc. LOVE. 79.

My Little Town. w&m; Paul Simon. c1975, Paul Simon. PAUL SIMON/RAY CONIFF SINGERS. 143.

My Love. w&m; Paul & Linda McCartney. c1973, Paul & Linda McCartney. Adminstered by MPL Communications. PAUL MCCARTNEY & WINGS. 93, 125, 131.

My Love. w&m; Tony Hatch. c1965, Welbeck Music Ltd./Duchess Music Corp. PETULA CLARK/SONNY JAMES. 94.

My Love Ain't Never Been This Strong. w&m; Jerry Weaver. c1978, Muscle Shoals Sound Publishing Co., Inc. 7th WONDER. 66.

My Love Don't Come Easy. w&m; Eddie Levert, Dennis Williams & Mike Jackson. c1979, Mighty Three Music & Rose Tree Music. JEAN CARN. 24.

My Love, My Love. w&m; Bob Haymes & Nick Acquaviva. c1952, Unart Music Corp. JONI JAMES. 78.

My Mama Done Tol' Me SEE Blues In The Night.

My Man. w&m; Channing Pollock (w) & Maurice Yvain (m). c1920, 49, Francis Salabert/Leo Feist. BARBRA STREISAND/BILLIE HOLIDAY/DIANA ROSS/IKE & TINA TURNER. 140.

My Melody Of Love. w&m; Bobby Vinton (w) & Henry Mayer (m). c1973, 74, Edition Rhythmus Rolf Budde KG & Radio Music International/Pedro Music Corp. BOBBY VINTON. 21, 134, 156, 163, 198.

My Music. w&m; Jim Messina & Ken Loggins. c1973, Gnossos Music & Jasperilla Music Co. LOGGINS & MESSINA. 138.

My Old Man. w&m; Joni Mitchell. c1970, 71, Siquomb Publishing Corp. JONI MITCHELL. 86.

My Old School. Walter Becker & Donald Fagen. c1973, American Broadcasting Music, Inc. STEELY DAN. 105.

My Own True Love. w&m; Mack David (w) & Max Steiner (m). c1941, 54, Remick Music Corp. MANTOVANI. 139.

My Prayer. w&m; Georges Boulanger (m) & Jimmy Kennedy (w, musical adaptation). c1939, World Wide Music Co., Ltd. Assigned to Skidmore Music Co., Inc. PLATTERS. 4.

My Roommate. w&m; J. Morali, H. Belolo & V. Willis. c1978, Scorpio Music (Black Scorpio). Controlled by Can't Stop Music. VILLAGE PEOPLE. 200.

My Sharona. w&m; Doug Fieger & Berton Averre. c1979, Eighties Music & Small Hill Music. KNACK. 22, 27, 31, 87, 124, 147.

My Special Angel. w&m; Jimmy Duncan. c1957, 68, Viva Music Inc. & Warner-Tamerlane Publishing Corp. BOBBY HELMS/VOGUES. 35, 43, 100, 197.

My Sweet Lord. w&m; George Harrison. c1970, Harrisongs Ltd./Harrisongs Music Inc. BILLY PRESTON/GEORGE HARRISON. 63, 93, 125.

My Thang. w&m; James Brown. c1974, Dynatone Publishing Co. JAMES BROWN. 107.

My True Love. w&m; Jack Scott. c1958, Unart Music Corp. JACK SCOTT. 4.

My Wheels Won't Turn. w&m; Randy Bachman. c1977, Ranbach Music. Controlled by Screen Gems-EMI Music Inc. BACHMAN-TURNER OVERDRIVE. 142.

My Whole World Ended (The Moment You Left Me). w&m; Pam Sawyer, Jimmy Roach, Harvey Fuqua & Johnny Bristol. c1969, Jobete Music Co., Inc. DAVID RUFFIN. 123.

My Wish Came True. w&m; Ivory Joe Hunter. c1957, Unart Music Corp. ELVIS PRESLEY. 4.

My World Is Empty Without You. w&m; Brian Holland, Lamont Dozier & Eddie Holland. c1965, 66, Jobete Music Co., Inc. SUPREMES. 123, 150.

Mystic Eyes. w&m; Van Morrison. c1965, Hyde Park Music Co., Ltd./Wemar Music Corp. VAN MORRISON & THEM. 3.

Nadia's Theme. w&m; Barry DeVorzon & Perry Botkin, Jr. c1971, 73, Screen Gems-EMI Music Inc. BARRY DE VORZON & PERRY BOTKIN, JR./FLOYD CRAMER/VENTURES. 23, 56, 134.

Nadine (Is It You). w&m; Chuck Berry. c1964, Arc Music Corp. CHUCK BERRY. 102, 197.

Name Game. w&m; Shirley Elliston & Lincoln Chase. c1964, Al Gallico Music Corp. SHIRLEY ELLIS. 93.

Name Of The Game. w&m; Benny Andersson, Stig Anderson & Bjorn Ulvaeus. c1977, Polar Music AB/Countless Songs, Ltd. ABBA. 15, 87, 146, 199.

Nanu, Nanu (I Wanna Funcky Wich You). w&m; Lu Janis. c1978, Lymnal Music. ROBIN WILLIAMS. 129.

Nashville Skyline Rag. w&m; Bob Dylan (m). c1969, 76, Big Sky Music. BOB DYLAN. 170.

Native New Yorker. w&m; Denny Randell & Sandy Linzer. c1977, Unichappell Music, Inc. & Featherbed Music. ODYSSEY. 50.

Need You Bad. w&m; Ted Nugent. c1978, 79, Magicland Music Corp. TED NUGENT. 146.

Needle And The Damage Done. w&m; Neil Young. c1971, 75, Broken Arrow Music. NEIL YOUNG. 185.

Needles And Pins. w&m; Sonny Bono & Jack Nitzsche. c1963, Unart Music Corp. & Metric Music Co., Inc. JACKIE DE SHANNON/RAMONES/SEARCHERS. 78, 80.

Neither One Of Us. w&m; Jim Weatherly. c1971, 73, Keca Music Inc. GLADYS KNIGHT & THE PIPS. 17, 104.

Never Be The Same. w&m; Christopher Cross. c1979, 80, Pop 'N' Roll Music. CHRISTOPHER CROSS. 190.

Never Been To Spain. w&m; Hoyt Axton. c1970, Lady Jane Music. THREE DOG NIGHT. 64, 72, 93, 134, 140.

Never Can Say Goodbye. w&m; Clifton Davis. c1970, 71, 73. Jobete Music Co., Inc. GLORIA GAYNOR/ISAAC HAYES/JACKSON 5/LITTLE BEAVER. 20, 24, 29, 52, 77, 95, 123, 126, 134, 142, 150.

Never Ending. w&m; Buddy Kaye & Philip Springer. c1962, Gladys Music, Inc. ELVIS PRESLEY. 172.

Never Ending Song Of Love. w&m; Delaney Bramlett. c1971, Metric Music Co., Inc. & Unart Music Corp. DELANEY & BONNIE. 21, 37, 82, 192.

Never Gonna Be The Same. w&m; Jim Webb. c1967, 70, Johnny Rivers Music. FIFTH DIMENSION. 60.

Never Gonna Fall In Love Again. w&m; Eric Carmen. c1975, 76, C.A.M.-U.S.A. Inc. ERIC CARMEN. 62, 139, 141.

Never Let Her Slip Away. w&m; Andrew Gold. c1978, Luckyu Music. ANDREW GOLD. 135.

Never My Love. w&m; Don & Dick Addrisi. c1967, Warner-Tamerlane Publishing Corp. ASSOCIATION/BLUE SWEDE/FIFTH DIMENSION. 30, 62, 139, 149.

Never On Sunday. w&m; Billy Towne (w) & Manos Hadjidakis (m). c1960, 68, Unart Music Corp. & Lee Corp. CHORDETTES/DON COSTA/TIJUANA BRASS. 113, 163.

Never Say Goodbye. w&m; Bob Dylan. c1973, 76, Ram's Horn Music. BOB DYLAN. 170.

Never Say Never. w&m; Tommy Shaw. c1979, Stygian Songs. Administered by Almo Music Corp. STYX. 12.

Never Say Yes. w&m; Doc Pomus & Mort Shuman.

c1966, Elvis Presley Music, Inc. ELVIS PRESLEY. 173.

Nevertheless. w&m; Gregory L. Allman. c1975, Allbro Publications & No Exit Music Co., Inc. ALLMAN BROTHERS BAND. 30.

New "Frankie And Johnnie" Song. w&m; Shel Silverstein & Bob Gibson. c1962, 64, Hollis Music, Inc. GLEN YARBOROUGH. 68.

New Horizons. w&m; Leon F. Sylvers III & Ricky Sylvers. c1977, Rosy Publishing, Inc. SYLVERS. 142.

New Kid In Town. w&m; Don Henley, Glen Frey & John David Souther. c1976, 77, Ice Age Music Publishing & WB Music Corp. EAGLES. 146, 178.

New Morning. w&m; Bob Dylan. c1970, 76, Big Sky Music. BOB DYLAN. 170.

New Orleans. w&m; Frank J. Guida & Joseph F. Royster. c1960, Rockmasters, Inc. GARY "U.S." BONDS. 5.

New Orleans Ladies. w&m; Hoyt Garrick & Leon Medica. c1976, Break Of Dawn Music, Inc. LOUISIANA'S LE ROUX. 135.

New Rose. w&m; Brian James. c1976, Anglo-Rock, Inc. DAMNED. 153.

New Speedway Boogie. w&m; Jerry Garcia (m) & Robert Hunter (w). c1970, 73, Ice Nine Publishing Co. GRATEFUL DEAD. 83.

New World Coming. w&m; Barry Mann & Cynthia Weil. c1970, Screen Gems-EMI Music Inc. MAMA CASS/ NINA SIMONE. 128.

New York City I Love You. w&m; Walter Zwolinski. c1978, Mother Tongue Music. ZWOL. 74.

New York Mining Disaster 1941. w&m; Barry, Robin & Maurice Gibb. c1967, 75, Abigail Music Ltd. BEE GEES. 35.

New York State Of Mind. w&m; Billy Joel. c1975, 78, Homegrown Music Inc. & Tin Pan Tunes. Administered by Blackwood Music Inc. BARBRA STREISAND/ BILLY JOEL. 15, 27, 116, 148, 165, 199.

Next Hundred Years. w&m; Alan Bernstein & Ritchie Adams. c1977, Silver Blue Music. AL MARTINO/ RAGTIMERS. 128.

Next Time. w&m; Daniel Fogelberg. c1975, Hickory Grove Music. DAN FOGELBERG. 30.

Nice, Nice, Very Nice. w&m; Joe Puerta, Kurt Vonnegut, Jr. (w), David Pack (m), Burleigh Drummond (m) & North (m). c1974, Rubicon Music, The Breakfast Publishing Co. & Epic III Ltd. AMBROSIA. 103.

Nice To Be With You. w&m; Jim Gold. c1971, 72, Interior Music. GALLERY. 195.

Night And Day. w&m; Cole Porter. c1932, 44, 47, Harms, Inc. SAMMY DAVIS JR. 139.

Night Chicago Died. w&m; Pete Callander (w) & Mitch Murray (m). c1974, Murray-Callander Music, Inc. PAPER LACE. 21.

Night Fever. w&m; Barry, Robin & Maurice Gibb. c1977, Brothers Gibb B.V./Stigwood Music, Inc. Administered by Unichappell Music, Inc. BEE GEES. 50, 133.

Night Game. w&m; Paul Simon. c1975, Paul Simon. PAUL SIMON. 143.

Night Has A Thousand Eyes. w&m; Ben Weisman, Dottie Wayne & Marilyn Garett. c1962, Blen Music, Inc. & Mabs Music Co. BOBBY VEE. 3.

Night Moves. w&m; Bob Seger. c1976, Gear Publishing Co. BOB SEGER. 121, 142.

Night They Drove Old Dixie Down. w&m; J. Robbie Robertson. c1969, 70, Canaan Music Inc. BAND/ JOAN BAEZ. 138.

Night Train. w&m; Oscar Washington, Lewis C. Simpkins & Jimmy Forrest. c1952, Frederick Music, Inc. VENTURES. 93.

Nights Are Forever Without You. w&m; Parker McGee. c1976, Dawnbreaker Music Co. ENGLAND DAN & JOHN FORD COLEY. 15, 128, 141, 142, 164, 196, 199.

Nights In White Satin. w&m; Justin Hayward. c1967, 68, Tyler Music Ltd. Controlled by TRO-Essex Music, Inc. MOODY BLUES. 29, 131.

Nights On Broadway. w&m; Barry, Robin & Maurice Gibb. c1975, Abigail Music Ltd. & Flam Music, Ltd. Controlled by Casserole Music, Inc. Administered by Unichappell Music, Inc. BEE GEES/CANDI STATON. 30, 36, 46, 62, 131.

1941. w&m; Harry Nilsson. c1967, Rock Music Co. TOM NORTHCOTT. 76.

99 Miles From L.A. w&m; Hal David & Albert Hammond. c1975, Landers-Roberts Music & Casa David. ALBERT HAMMOND/ART GARFUNKEL/JOHNNY MATHIS. 165.

96 Tears. w&m; Rudy Martinez. c1966, Merlin Music, Inc. ? & THE MYSTERIANS. 93.

Nitty Gritty. w&m; Lincoln Chase. c1963, Al Gallico Music Corp. GLADYS KNIGHT & THE PIPS. 17.

No Communication. w&m; Steve Duboff & Gerald Robinson. c1968, Roosevelt Music Co., Inc. FIVE AMERICANS. 76.

No Love At All. w&m; Wayne Carson Thompson & Johnny Christopher. c1970, 71, Rose Bridge Music, Inc. B.J. THOMAS. 191.

No Matter What. w&m; Peter Ham. c1970, Apple Publishing Ltd. BADFINGER. 63.

No More. w&m; Don Robertson & Hal Blair. c1961, Gladys Music, Inc. ELVIS PRESLEY. 173.

No More Mister Nice Guy. w&m; Michael Bruce & Alice Cooper. c1973, Ezra Music, Bizarre Music, Inc. & Alive Enterprises. ALICE COOPER. 104, 111.

No Night So Long. w&m; Richard Kerr & Will Jennings. c1980, Irving Music, Inc. DIONNE WARWICK. 58.

No, No, No, No. w&m; James Brown. c1956, 68, Armo Music Corp. JAMES BROWN. 18.

No Particular Place To Go. w&m; Chuck Berry. c1964, Arc Music Corp. CHUCK BERRY. 100.

No Quarter. w&m; John Paul Jones, Jimmy Page & Robert Plant. c1973, Superhype Publishing. LED ZEPPELIN. 114.

No Regrets. w&m; Harry Tobias (w) & Roy Ingraham

(m). c1936, 64, Miller Music Corp. PHOEBE SNOW. 21, 37, 184, 191.

No Tell Lover. w&m; Lee Loughnane, Danny Seraphine & Peter Cetera. c1978, Com Music, Street Sense Music & Polish Prince Music. CHICAGO. 65, 73, 157.

Nobody But Me. w&m; Rudolph, Ronald & O'Kelly Isley. c1962, Wemar Music Corp. ISLEY BROTHERS. 93.

Nobody But You. w&m; Jim Messina. c1971, 72, Jasperilla Music Co. LOGGINS & MESSINA. 72.

Nobody 'Cept You. w&m; Bob Dylan. c1973, 76, Ram's Horn Music. BOB DYLAN. 170.

Nobody Does It Better. w&m; Carole Bayer Sager (w) & Marvin Hamlisch (m). c1977, Danjaq S.A. Administered by United Artists Music Co., Inc. & Unart Music Corp. CARLY SIMON. 15, 21, 37, 80, 140, 176, 199.

Norwegian Wood. w&m; John Lennon & Paul McCartney. c1965, Northern Songs Ltd./Maclen Music, Inc. BEATLES. 35, 61, 138.

Not Fade Away. w&m; Charles Hardin & Norman Petty. c1957, MPL Communications, Inc. BUDDY HOLLY. 14.

Nothing But Heartaches. w&m; Eddie Holland, Lamont Dozier & Brian Holland. c1965, Jobete Music Co., Inc. SUPREMES. 123, 150.

Nothing Was Delivered. w&m; Bob Dylan. c1968, 75, Dwarf Music. BOB DYLAN & THE BAND. 170.

Nothing's Too Good For My Baby. w&m; Sylvia Moy, Henry Cosby & William Stevenson. c1966, Jobete Music Co., Inc. STEVIE WONDER. 150.

Now And Then. w&m; Arlo Guthrie. c1967, 69, Appleseed Music Inc. ARLO GUTHRIE. 7.

Now That We've Found Love. w&m; Kenny Gamble & Leon Huff. c1974, 79, Mighty Three Music. O'JAYS/ THIRD WORLD. 51.

Nowadays Clancy Can't Even Sing. w&m; Neil Young. c1966, 74, Cotillion Music, Inc., Ten East Music & Springalo Toones. BUFFALO SPRINGFIELD. 39.

Nowhere Man. w&m; John Lennon & Paul McCartney. c1965, Northern Songs Ltd./Maclen Music, Inc. BEATLES. 35, 61, 141.

Nowhere To Run. w&m; Eddie Holland, Lamont Dozier & Brian Holland. c1965, 66, 73, Jobete Music Co., Inc. MARTHA & THE VANDELLAS. 123, 150.

Nuclear Waste. w&m; John DeSalvo & Jeff Salen. c1978, Bleu Disque Music Co. & Black Disc Music. TUFF DARTS. 19.

#1 Dee Jay. w&m; Vincent Montana, Jr., Bud Ross & Len Rocco. c1978, Vincent Montana Jr. Music Inc. & Bud Ross Music Inc. GOODY GOODY. 34.

Nutbush City Limits. w&m; Tina Turner. c1973, Unart Music Corp. & Huh Music Corp. BOB SEGER/IKE & TINA TURNER. 79.

Ob-La-Di, Ob-La-Da. w&m; John Lennon & Paul McCartney. c1965, Northern Songs Ltd./Maclen Music, Inc. BEATLES. 138, 141.

Obviously Five Believers. w&m; Bob Dylan. c1966, 76, Dwarf Music. BOB DYLAN. 170.

Ocean. w&m; John Bonham, John Paul Jones, Jimmy Page & Robert Plant. c1973, Superhype Publishing. LED ZEPPELIN. 114.

Odds And Ends. w&m; Bob Dylan. c1970, 75, Dwarf Music. BOB DYLAN & THE BAND. 170.

Off The Wall. w&m; Rod Temperton. c1979, 80, Rondor Music Ltd./ Almo Music Corp. MICHAEL JACKSON. 24, 99, 148.

Oh, Baby. w&m; Randy Irwin, Shirley Owens & Charles Simmons. c1975, Adam R. Levy & Father Enterprises Inc. & Rush Release Publishing Co. WAYNE MIRAN & RUSH RELEASE. 49.

Oh Boy. w&m; Sunny West, Bill Tilghman & Norman Petty. c1957, MPL Communications, Inc. BUDDY HOLLY & THE CRICKETS. 14.

Oh! Darling. w&m; John Lennon & Paul McCartney. c1969, Northern Songs Ltd./Maclen Music, Inc. BEATLES/ROBIN GIBB. 61, 146.

Oh Happy Day. w&m; Edwin R. Hawkins. c1969, Kama Rippa Music, Inc. & Edwin R. Hawkins Music Co. Administered by United Artists Music Co., Inc. EDWIN HAWKINS SINGERS/GLEN CAMPBELL. 21, 59, 140, 191, 192.

Oh, In The Morning. w&m; Arlo Guthrie. c1969, Howard Beach Music, Inc. ARLO GUTHRIE. 7.

Oh Julie. w&m; Kenneth R. Moffitt & Noel Ball. c1957, Excellorec Music Co. CRESCENDOS. 3.

Oh Oh I Love Her So. w&m; Joey, Dee Dee, Tommy & Johnny Ramone. c1977, 78, Bleu Disque Music & Taco Tunes. RAMONES. 19.

Oh Me Oh My (I'm A Fool For You Baby). w&m; Jim Doris. c1969, Nootrac Music Ltd. LULU. 186.

Oh, Rock My Soul. w&m; Traditional. Peter Yarrow (Adapted & arranged). c1964, Pepamar Music Corp. PETER, PAUL & MARY. 67.

Oh, Sister. w&m; Bob Dylan & Jacques Levy (w). c1975, 76, Ram's Horn Music. BOB DYLAN. 170.

Oh Very Young. w&m; Cat Stevens. c1974, Freshwater Music Ltd./Ackee Music Inc. CAT STEVENS. 30, 36, 53, 117.

Oh, What A Night. w&m; Marvin Junior & John Funches. c1956, Conrad Music, a division of Arc Music Corp. DELLS. 5, 168.

Oh, What A Night For Dancing. w&m; Barry White & Vance Wilson. c1977, Sa-Vette Music Co. Administered by Super Songs Unlimited. BARRY WHITE. 135.

Okie From Muskogee. w&m; Merle Haggard & Roy Edward Burris. c1969, Blue Book Music. MERLE HAGGARD. 88.

Ol' 55. w&m; Tom Waits. c1972, 74, Fifth Floor Music Inc. EAGLES/ERIC ANDERSEN. 139.

Old Brown Shoe. w&m; George Harrison. c1969, Harrisongs Ltd./Harrisongs Music, Inc. BEATLES. 125.

Old Cape Cod. w&m; Claire Rothrock, Milt Yakus & Allan Jeffrey. c1956, 68, George Pincus & Sons Music Corp. ROBERT GOULET. 113.

Only A Pawn In Their Game. w&m; Bob Dylan. c1963, M. Witmark & Sons. BOB DYLAN. 138.

Only Believe. w&m; Paul Rader & Elvis Presley. c1921, 49, 71, Rodeheaver Co. ELVIS PRESLEY. 191.

Only Living Boy In New York. w&m; Paul Simon. c1969, Paul Simon. SIMON & GARFUNKEL. 143.

Only Love Can Break Your Heart. w&m; Neil Young. c1970, Cotillion Music, Inc. & Broken Arrow Music. NEIL YOUNG. 43, 87, 136, 139, 174, 182.

Only Make Believe. w&m; LeRoy Bell & Casey James. c1979, Mighty Three Music. BELL & JAMES. 24.

Only The Strong Survive. w&m; Kenny Gamble, Leon Huff & Jerry Butler. c1968, 69, Parabut Music Corp., Downstairs Music Co. & Double Diamond Music Co. JERRY BUTLER. 6.

Only Women Bleed. w&m; Alice Cooper & Dick Wagner. c1974, 75, Ezra Music-Early Frost Music. ALICE COOPER. 36, 139, 175.

Only Yesterday. w&m; Richard Carpenter & John Bettis. c1975, Almo Music Corp. & Hammer & Nails Music. CARPENTERS. 183.

Only You. w&m; Buck Ram & Ande Rand. c1955, Hollis Music, Inc. PLATTERS. 5, 78, 101, 137.

O-o-h Child. w&m; Stan Vincent. c1970, Duckstun Music, Inc. & Kama Sutra Music, Inc. Administered by Kama Sutra Music. VALERIE CARTER. 37.

Ooh Poo Pah Doo. w&m; Jesse Hill. c1960, 65, 71, Unart Music Corp. & Minit Music Co., Inc. CHUBBY CHECKER/DR. HOOK/IKE & TINA TURNER/JESSE HILL. 82, 137, 155, 161.

Ooo Baby Baby. w&m; William "Smokey" Robinson & Warren Moore. c1965, 66, 72, 78, Jobete Music Co., Inc. LINDA RONSTADT/SMOKEY ROBINSON & THE MIRACLES. 65, 73, 128, 180.

Open The Door, Homer. w&m; Bob Dylan. c1968, 75, Dwarf Music. BOB DYLAN & THE BAND. 170.

Operator. w&m; Ron McKernan. c1970, 73, Ice Nine Publishing Co. GRATEFUL DEAD. 83.

Operator. w&m; William Spivery. c1959, 75, Conrad Music, a division of Arc Music Corp. MANHATTAN TRANSFER. 37.

Operator (That's Not The Way It Feels). w&m; Jim Croce. c1971, 72, Blendingwell Music, Inc. & American Broadcasting Music, Inc. JIM CROCE. 72, 163.

Our Day Will Come. w&m; Mort Garson (w) & Bob Hilliard (m). c1962, Rosewood Music Corp. RUBY & THE ROMANTICS. 93.

Our House. w&m; Graham Nash. c1970, Giving Room Music, Inc. CROSBY, STILLS, NASH & YOUNG. 182, 197.

Our Love Don't Throw It All Away SEE Don't Throw It All Away.

Out Here On My Own. w&m; Lesley Gore (w) & Michael Gore (m). c1979, 80, Metro-Goldwyn-Mayer Inc. Controlled by MGM Affiliated Music Inc. & Variety Music Inc. IRENE CARA. 162, 189.

Out Of My Mind. w&m; Neil Young. c1966, 74, Cotil-

lion Music, Inc., Ten East Music & Springalo Toones. BUFFALO SPRINGFIELD. 39.

Out Of Sight, Out Of Mind. w&m; Ivory Joe Hunter & Clyde Otis. c1956, Nom Music, Inc. FIVE KEYS/ LITTLE ANTHONY & THE IMPERIALS. 78, 101, 137, 161.

Out Of The Darkness. w&m; David Crosby (w), Graham Nash (w) & Craig Degree (m). c1976, Craig Doerge. Controlled by Fair Star Music, Inc. CROSBY & NASH. 141.

Out On The Tiles. w&m; Jimmy Page, Robert Plant & John Bonham. c1970, 73, Superhype Publishing. LED ZEPPELIN. 114.

Outa Space. w&m; Billy Preston & Joe Greene. c1971, 72, Wep Music Co. & Irving Music. BILLY PRESTON. 104.

Outside My Window. w&m; Stevie Wonder. c1979, 80, Jobete Music Co., Inc. & Black Bull Music. STEVIE WONDER. 24, 45, 99.

Outside Of A Small Circle Of Friends. w&m; Phil Ochs. c1966, 68, Barricade Music. PHIL OCHS. 144.

Over & Over. w&m; Christine McVie. c1979, Fleetwood Mac Music. Administered by Warner-Tamerlane Publishing Corp. FLEETWOOD MAC. 147.

Over And Over. w&m; Nickolas Ashford & Valerie Simpson. c1977, Nick-O-Val Music. ASHFORD & SIMPSON/SYLVESTER. 13.

Over And Over. w&m; Robert Byrd. c1958, Recordo Music Publishers. DAVE CLARK FIVE. 4.

Over My Head. w&m; Christine McVie. c1975, Michael Fleetwood & Gentoo Music, Inc. Administered by Warner-Tamerlane Publishing Corp. FLEETWOOD MAC. 174, 178, 185.

Over The Hills And Far Away. w&m; Jimmy Page & Robert Plant. c1973, Superhype Publishing. LED ZEPPELIN. 114, 197.

Over The Mountains, Across The Sea. w&m; Rex Garvin. c1957, Arc Music Corp. JOHNNIE & JOE. 5.

Over The Rainbow. w&m; E.Y. Harburg (w) & Harold Arlen (m). c1938, 39, 66, 67, 77, Metro-Goldwyn-Mayer, Inc. Controlled by Leo Feist, Inc. GARY TANNER/JACKIE WILSON/JERRY LEE LEWIS/ LITTLE ANTHONY & THE IMPERIALS/LIVINGSTON TAYLOR/SHIRLEY BASSEY/VIKKI CARR. 140, 199.

Overs. w&m; Paul Simon. c1967, Paul Simon. SIMON & GARFUNKEL. 143.

Oye Como Va. w&m; Tito Puente. c1963, 70, 71, Planetary Music Publishing Corp. SANTANA. 21, 72, 89, 163, 192.

Padre. w&m; Paul Francis Webster (w) & Alain Romans (m). c1957, 58, Anne-Rachel Music Corp. TONY ARDEN. 191.

Pagan Love Song. w&m; Arthur Freed (w) & Nacio Herb Brown (m). c1929, 57, 66, Metro-Goldwyn-Mayer & Robbins Music Corp. Controlled by Robbins Music

Corp. FIREHOUSE 5 PLUS 2/GENE AMMONS/ GLENN MILLER/JO ANN CASTLE. 140.

Pain In My Heart. w&m; Naomi Neville. c1964, 71, Arc Music Corp. OTIS REDDING. 169.

Painted Ladies. w&m; Ian Thomas. c1973, Corinth Music Ltd./G.R.T. IAN THOMAS. 194.

Palisades Park. w&m; Chuck Barris. c1962, Claridge Music, Inc. FREDDIE CANNON. 78, 102, 137.

Paloma Blanca. w&m; Hans Bouwens. c1975, Witch Music, Veronica Music Inc. & WB Music Corp. EMERALDS. 30.

Papa Don't Take No Mess (Part I). w&m; James Brown, Fred Wesley, John Starks & Charles Bobbit. c1974, Dynatone Publishing Co. JAMES BROWN. 107.

Papa Hobo. w&m; Paul Simon. c1971, Paul Simon. PAUL SIMON. 143.

Papa Was A Rollin' Stone. w&m; Norman Whitfield & Barrett Strong. c1972, Stone Diamond Music Corp. TEMPTATIONS. 150.

Papa's Got A Brand New Bag (Parts 1 & 2). w&m; James Brown. c1965, 68, Lois Publishing Co. Assigned to Dynatone Publishing Co. JAMES BROWN. 18.

Paper Cup. w&m; Jim Webb. c1967, 70, Johnny Rivers Music. FIFTH DIMENSION. 60.

Paper Roses. w&m; Janice Torre (w) & Fred Spielman (m). c1960, 62, Pambill Music, Inc. Assigned to Lewis Music Publishing Co., Inc. MARIE OSMOND. 21, 63, 140, 163, 194.

Paperback Writer. w&m; John Lennon & Paul McCartney. c1966, Northern Songs Ltd./Maclen Music, Inc. BEATLES. 35, 61, 159.

Paradise. w&m; John Prine. c1971, 72, Cotillion Music, Inc. & Sour Grapes Music. JOHN PRINE. 151.

Paradise By The Dashboard Light. w&m; Jim Steinman. c1977, Edward B. Marks Music Corp., Neverland Music Co. & Peg Music Co. MEATLOAF. 120.

Paradise, Hawaiian Style. w&m; Bill Giant, Bernie Baum & Florence Kaye. c1966, Elvis Presley Music, Inc. ELVIS PRESLEY. 172.

Paranoia Blues. w&m; Paul Simon. c1972, Paul Simon. PAUL SIMON. 143.

Parrty (Parts I & II). w&m; James Brown. c1973, 74, Dynatone Publishing Co. JAMES BROWN. 107.

Part Of The Plan. w&m; Daniel Fogelberg. c1975, Hickory Grove Music. DAN FOGELBERG. 30.

Part-Time Love. w&m; Elton John & Gary Osborne. c1978, Big Pig Music Ltd./Jodrell Music Inc. ELTON JOHN. 146.

Party. w&m; Jessie Mae Robinson. c1957, Gladys Music, Inc. ELVIS PRESLEY. 172.

Party. w&m; Phil Ochs. c1966, 68, Barricade Music. PHIL OCHS. 144.

Party. w&m; Van McCoy. c1976, Warner-Tamerlane Publishing Corp. & Van McCoy Music, Inc. VAN MC COY. 141.

Party Doll. w&m; James Bowen & Buddy Knox. c1957, Jackie Music Corp. & Big Seven Music Corp. As-

signed to Patricia Music Publishing Corp. BUDDY KNOX. 78, 101, 137, 161.

Party Lights. w&m; Claudine Clark. c1962, Rambed Publishing Co., Inc. CLAUDINE CLARK. 3.

Party Lights. w&m; Tennyson Stephens. c1976, 77, Utom Publishing Co. NATALIE COLE. 58, 142.

Pastures Green. w&m; Rod McKuen. c1971, Editions Chanson Co. ROD MC KUEN. 63.

Pastures Of Plenty. w&m; Woody Guthrie. c1960, 63, Ludlow Music, Inc. ODETTA/TOM PAXTON/WOODY GUTHRIE. 85.

Paths Of Victory. w&m; Bob Dylan. c1964, M. Witmark & Sons. PETE SEEGER. 41, 132.

Pattern People. w&m; Jim Webb. c1967, 70, Johnny Rivers Music. FIFTH DIMENSION. 60.

Patterns. w&m; Paul Simon. c1965, Paul Simon. SIMON & GARFUNKEL. 143.

Pause Of Mister Clause. w&m; Arlo Guthrie. c1968, 69, 70, Appleseed Music, Inc. ARLO GUTHRIE. 7, 202.

Payback. w&m; James Brown, Fred Wesley & John Starks. c1973, 74, Dynatone Publishing Co. JAMES BROWN. 107.

Peace Frog. w&m; Jim Morrison (w) & Doors (m). c1970, Doors Music Co. DOORS. 54.

Peace Like A River. w&m; Paul Simon. c1971, Paul Simon. PAUL SIMON. 143.

Peace Of Mind. w&m; Donald Scholz. c1974, 77, Pure Songs. Controlled by Colgems-EMI Music Inc. BOSTON. 142, 164.

Peace Train. w&m; Cat Stevens. c1971, Freshwater Music Ltd. Controlled by Ackee Music Inc. CAT STEVENS. 156, 183.

Peaceful Easy Feeling. w&m; Jack Tempchin. c1972, 73, Benchmark Music, WB Music Corp. & Jazz Bird Music. EAGLES. 38, 138, 145, 151.

Peepin' 'N' Hidin' SEE Baby, What You Want Me To Do.

Peg. w&m; Walter Becker & Donald Fagen. c1977, Duchess Music Corp. & ABC-Dunhill Music, Inc. STEELY DAN. 15, 21, 128, 135, 157.

Peg O' My Heart. w&m; Alfred Bryan (w) & Fred Fisher (m). c1913, 21, 41, 47, 49, 66, Leo Feist Inc. DON BLISS/FOUR ACES/HARMONICATS. 140.

Peggy Day. w&m; Bob Dylan. c1969, 76, Big Sky Music. BOB DYLAN. 170.

Peggy Sue. w&m; Jerry Allison, Norman Petty & Buddy Holly. c1957, MPL Communications, Inc. & Nor Va Jak Music, Inc. BUDDY HOLLY. 14, 109.

Pencil-Thin Mustache. w&m; Jimmy Buffett. c1974, ABC-Dunhill Music, Inc. JIMMY BUFFETT. 15.

Penny Lane. w&m; John Lennon & Paul McCartney. c1967, Northern Songs Ltd./Maclen Music, Inc. BEATLES. 43, 61.

People Got To Be Free. w&m; Felix Cavaliere & Edward Brigati, Jr. c1968, Coral Rock Music Corp. & Slacsar Publishing Co., Ltd. FIFTH DIMENSION/ RASCALS. 60, 140, 199.

FIND THAT TUNE

Peppermint Twist. w&m; Joey Dee & Henry Glover. c1961, 62, Big Seven Music Corp., Frost Music Corp. & Jonware Music Corp. JOEY DEE & THE STAR-LITERS. 78, 102, 137, 161.

Personality. w&m; Harold Logan & Lloyd Price. c1959, Lloyd & Logan, Inc. LLOYD PRICE. 3.

Personality Crisis. w&m; David Johansen (w) & John Genzale (m). c1973, Seldak Music Corp. & Haverstraw Publishing Co. NEW YORK DOLLS. 153.

Philadelphia Freedom. w&m; Elton John & Bernie Taupin. c1975, Big Pig Music Ltd./Jodrell Music Inc. ELTON JOHN/MFSB. 124, 131, 136.

Photograph. w&m; George Harrison & Richard Starkey. c1973, Richoroony Ltd. RINGO STARR. 63.

Piano SEE Softly.

Piano Man. w&m; Billy Joel. c1973, 74, Home Grown Music, Inc. & Tinker Street Tunes. Administered by Blackwood Music Inc. BILLY JOEL. 15, 21, 37, 131, 136, 165, 184, 193, 198.

Piano Picker. w&m; Randy Edelman. c1971, 72, Hasting Music Corp. CARPENTERS. 195.

Picasso Summer, Theme From SEE Summer Me, Winter Me.

Pick Up The Pieces. w&m; Roger Ball & Hamish Stuart. c1974, 75, Average Music. Administered by Cotillion Music, Inc. AVERAGE WHITE BAND. 36, 139.

Picture This. w&m; Deborah Harry, Chris Stein & Jimmy Destri. c1978, Rare Blue Music, Inc. & Monster Island Music. BLONDIE. 33.

Piece Of My Heart. w&m; Bert Berns & Jerry Ragavoy. c1967, 70, Web IV Music Inc. & Ragmar Music Corp. JANIS JOPLIN. 3, 202.

Pieces Of Dreams SEE Little Boy Lost.

Piggies. w&m; George Harrison. c1968, Harrisongs Ltd./Harrisongs Music, Inc. BEATLES. 125.

Pilot Of The Airwaves. w&m; Charlie Dore. c1978, 80, Ackee Music, Inc. CHARLIE DORE. 188.

Pina Colada Song SEE Escape.

Pinball Wizard. w&m; Peter Townshend. c1969, Fabulous Music Ltd./Track Music, Inc. ELTON JOHN/WHO. 36, 62, 86, 139.

Pipeline. w&m; Bob Spickard (m) & Brian Carman (m). c1962, 63, Downey Music Publishing Co. CHANTAYS. 93.

Place In The Sun. w&m; Ronald Miller (w) & Bryan Wells (m). c1966, Stein & Van Stock, Inc. & Jobete Music Co., Inc. STEVIE WONDER. 123, 142, 150, 167.

Plane Wreck At Los Gatos SEE Deportee.

Platinum Heroes. w&m; Bruce Foster. c1977, C.A.M.-U.S.A. BRUCE FOSTER. 142.

Play On Love. w&m; Grace Slick (w) & Pete Sears (m). c1975, Ronin Music & Alien Music. JEFFERSON STARSHIP. 30, 36.

Playboy. w&m; Brian Holland, Robert Bateman, William Stevenson & Gladys Morton. c1961, 71, Jobete Music Co., Inc. MARVELETTES. 123.

Playboys And Playgirls. w&m; Bob Dylan. c1964, 68, M. Witmark & Sons & Warner Bros.-Seven Arts, Inc. BOB DYLAN/PETE SEEGER. 132.

Playground In My Mind. w&m; Paul Vance & Lee Pockriss. c1971, 73, Vanlee Music Corp. & Emily Music Corp. CLINT HOLMES. 89, 111, 194.

Pleasant Valley Sunday. w&m; Gerry Goffin & Carole King. c1967, Screen Gems-Columbia Music, Inc. MONKEES. 38.

Please Come Home For Christmas. w&m; Charles Brown & Gene Redd. c1960, 78, Fort Knox Music Co. EAGLES. 73.

Please Don't Drag That String Around. w&m; Otis Blackwell & Winfield Scott. c1963, Elvis Presley Music, Inc. ELVIS PRESLEY. 172.

Please Don't Go. w&m; Harry Wayne Casey & Richard Finch. c1979, Sherlyn Publishing Co., Inc. & Harrick Music, Inc. Administered by Sherlyn Publishing Co., Inc. K C & THE SUNSHINE BAND. 56, 97.

Please Don't Leave. w&m; Lauren Wood. c1978, Creeping, Licking Music. Administered by Evan Paul Music, a division of the Special Music Group. LAUREN WOOD. 23, 97.

Please Don't Stop Loving Me. w&m; Joy Byers. c1966, Elvis Presley Music, Inc. ELVIS PRESLEY. 173.

Please Let Me Wonder. w&m; Brian Wilson & Mike Love. c1965, Sea Of Tunes Publishing Co. BEACH BOYS. 9.

Please Love Me Forever. w&m; Ollie Blanchard & Johnny Malone. c1961, Selma Music Co., Inc. BOBBY VINTON/CATHY JEAN & THE ROOMMATES. 5.

Please Mr. Postman. w&m; Brian Holland, Robert Bateman, Freddie Gorman, Georgia Dobbins & William Garrett. c1961, 62, 64, 68, 74, Jobete Music Co., Inc. BEATLES/CARPENTERS/MARVELETTES. 28, 29, 123, 138, 142, 150, 156.

Please, Mrs. Henry. w&m; Bob Dylan. c1967, Dwarf Music. BOB DYLAN & THE BAND. 170.

Please, Please, Please. w&m; James Brown & Johnny Terry. c1956, 68, Armo Music Corp. JAMES BROWN. 18.

Please Send Me Someone To Love. w&m; Percy Mayfield. c1950, 51, Venice Music, Inc. B.B. KING/PAUL BUTTERFIELD/PERCY MAYFIELD. 35, 100, 159.

Pleasures Of The Harbor. w&m; Phil Ochs. c1966, 68, Barricade Music, Inc. PHIL OCHS. 144.

Pledging My Time. w&m; Bob Dylan. c1966, 76, Dwarf Music. BOB DYLAN. 170.

Poem On The Underground Wall. w&m; Paul Simon. c1966, Paul Simon. SIMON & GARFUNKEL. 143.

Poetry In Motion. w&m; Paul Kaufman & Mike Anthony. c1960, 63, Meridian Music Corp. Assigned to Vogue Music, Inc. JOHNNY TILLOTSON. 78, 102, 160.

Poetry Man. w&m; Phoebe Snow. c1973, 75, Tarka Music Co. PHOEBE SNOW. 28, 77, 156.

Point Of Know Return. w&m; Steve Walsh, Phil Ehart

& Robby Steinhardt. c1977, Don Kirshner Music. KANSAS. 145.

Poison Ivy. w&m; Jerry Leiber & Mike Stoller. c1959, Tiger Music, Inc. Assigned to Chappell & Co., Inc., Quintet Music, Inc. & Freddy Bienstock Music Co. Controlled by Intersong Music, Inc. COASTERS. 92, 155.

Poor Boy. w&m; Elvis Presley & Vera Matson. c1956, Elvis Presley Music, Inc. ELVIS PRESLEY. 173.

Poor Jenny. w&m; Boudleaux & Felice Bryant. c1959, House of Bryant Publications. EVERLY BROTHERS. 4.

Poor Little Fool Like Me SEE Don't Ever Be Lonely.

Poor Me. w&m; Antoine Domino & Dave Bartholomew. c1955, Commodore Music Corp. FATS DOMINO. 137.

Poor Poor Pitiful Me. w&m; Warren Zevon. c1973, 78, Warner-Tamerlane Publishing Corp. & Darkroom Music. LINDA RONSTADT. 146, 201.

Poor Side Of Town. w&m; Johnny Rivers & Lou Adler. c1967, 70, Johnny Rivers Music. FIFTH DIMENSION/ JOHNNY RIVERS. 60, 163, 199.

Pop Muzik. w&m; Robin Scott. c1978, Robin Scott. M. 8, 11, 24, 56, 98, 180.

Popsicle Toes. w&m; Michael Franks. c1975, 76, War-ner-Tamerlane Publishing Corp. & Mississippi Mud Music Co. MICHAEL FRANKS. 141.

Popsicles And Icicles. w&m; David Gates. c1963, Dra-gonwyck Music Co. MURMAIDS. 5.

Portrait Of My Love. w&m; David West (w) & Cyril Ornadel (m). c1960, 61, Edward Kassner Music Co., Ltd. & Piccadilly Music Corp. Administered by Copy-right Service Bureau Ltd. LETTERMEN/TOKENS. 128.

Positively 4th Street. w&m; Bob Dylan. c1965, M. Wit-mark & Sons & Warner Bros., Inc. BOB DYLAN/ BYRDS. 35, 69, 139.

Prayin'. w&m; Gene McFadden & John Whitehead. c1979, Mighty Three Music. HAROLD MELVIN & THE BLUENOTES. 24.

Precious And Few. w&m; Walter D. Nims. c1970, 72, Caesar's Music Library & Emerald City Music. CLIMAX. 133.

Pretender. w&m; Jackson Browne. c1976, 77, Swallow Turn Music. Administered by WB Music Corp. JACK-SON BROWNE. 127, 145.

Pretty Baby. w&m; Deborah Harry & Chris Stein. c1978 Rare Blue Music, Inc. & Monster Island Music. BLONDIE. 33.

Pretty Blue Eyes. w&m; Teddy Randazzo & Bobby Wein-stein. c1959, 67, Almimo Music Inc. Assigned to Vogue Music Inc. STEVE LAWRENCE. 78, 160.

Pretty Girl Why. w&m; Stephen Stills. c1968, 75, Co-tillion Music, Inc. & Springalo Toones. BUFFALO SPRINGFIELD. 39.

Pretty Girls. w&m; Lisa Dal Bello. c1978, 79, Neve-bianca Productions. MELISSA MANCHESTER. 23, 56, 58, 97.

Pretty Girls Everywhere. w&m; Eugene Church &

Thomas Williams. c1959, Recordo Music Publishers. EUGENE CHURCH. 5.

Pretty Little Angel Eyes. w&m; Tommy Boyce & Curtis Lee. c1961, Bri-Deb Music Corp. CURTIS LEE. 5.

Pretty Vacant. w&m; Johnny Rotten, Steven Jones, Paul Cook & Glen Matlock. c1978, Glitterbest Ltd. & Glen Matlock. SEX PISTOLS. 19.

Pretzel Logic. w&m; Walter Becker & Donald Fagen. c1974, MCA Music. STEELY DAN. 142.

Pride And Joy. w&m; Norman Whitfield, Marvin Gaye & William Stevenson. c1963, 69, Jobete Music Co., Inc. MARVIN GAYE. 123.

Pride Of Cucamonga. w&m; Robert Peterson (w) & Philip Lesh (m). c1974, 76, Ice Nine Publishing Co., Inc. GRATEFUL DEAD. 84.

Priests. w&m; Leonard Cohen. c1967, 69, Stranger Music, Inc. LEONARD COHEN. 171.

Prison Song. w&m; Graham Nash. c1973, 74, Thin Ice Music. GRAHAM NASH. 138.

Prisoner In Disguise. w&m; John David Souther. c1975, 77, WB Music Corp & Golden Spread Music. LINDA RONSTADT. 145.

Prisoner Of Your Love. w&m; John C. Crowley & Peter Beckett. c1978, Touch Of Gold Music, Inc., Crowbeck Music & Stigwood Music, Inc. PLAYER. 74.

Problems. w&m; Boudleaux & Felice Bryant. c1958, House Of Bryant Publications. EVERLY BROTHERS. 4.

Promised Land. w&m; Chuck Berry. c1964, 65, Arc Music Corp. ELVIS PRESLEY. 78, 169.

Promises. w&m; Richard Feldman & Roger Linn. c1978, Narwhal Music. Controlled by Skyhill Publishing Co., Inc. ERIC CLAPTON. 65, 73, 130, 157.

Promises, Promises. w&m; Hal David (w) & Burt Bacharach (m). c1968, Blue Seas Music, Inc. & Jac Music Co., Inc. BURT BACHARACH. 23.

Proud Mary. w&m; J.C. Fogerty. c1968, Jondora Music. CREEDENCE CLEARWATER REVIVAL. 86, 93, 140, 161, 192.

Prove It All Night. w&m; Bruce Springsteen. c1978, Bruce Springsteen. BRUCE SPRINGSTEEN. 22, 124, 146.

P.S. I Love You. w&m; John Lennon & Paul McCartney. c1962, 63, Ardmore & Beechwood Ltd./Beechwood Music Corp. BEATLES. 111, 128, 137, 140, 161.

Psychedelic Shack. w&m; Barrett Strong & Norman Whitfield. c1969, 70, Jobete Music Co., Inc. TEMPT-ATIONS. 123.

Psycho Killer. w&m; David Byrne, Christopher Frantz & Martina Weymouth. c1976, 78, Bleu Disque Music Co. & Index Music. TALKING HEADS. 19.

Pucker Up Buttercup. w&m; Johnny Bristol, Harvey Fuqua & Danny Coggins. c1966, 67, Jobete Music Co., Inc. JR. WALKER & THE ALL STARS. 167.

Puff (The Magic Dragon). w&m; Peter Yarrow & Leonard Lipton. c1963, Pepamar Music Corp. PETER, PAUL & MARY. 67.

Punky's Dilemma. w&m; Paul Simon. c1968, Paul Simon. SIMON & GARFUNKEL. 143.

Puppet On A String. w&m; Sid Tepper & Roy C. Bennett. c1965, Gladys Music, Inc. ELVIS PRESLEY. 172.

Purple People Eater. w&m; Sheb Wooley. c1958, Channel Music Co. SHEB WOOLEY. 3.

Pussywillows, Cat-tails. w&m; Gordon Lightfoot. c1968, Warner Bros., Inc. GORDON LIGHTFOOT. 35.

Put A Little Love In Your Heart. w&m; Jimmy Holiday, Randy Myers & Jackie De Shannon. c1969, Unart Music Corp. ISLEY BROTHERS/JACKIE DE SHANNON/LETTERMEN. 21, 81, 89, 140, 191, 192.

Put Your Hand In The Hand. w&m; Gene MacLellan. c1970, 71, Beechwood Music of Canada, Don Mills/Beechwood Music Corp. ANNE MURRAY/OCEAN. 58, 64, 89, 126, 140, 156, 163, 192.

Put Your Head On My Shoulder. w&m; Paul Anka. c1958, Spanka Music Corp. PAUL ANKA. 6.

Quarter To Three. w&m; F. Guida, G. Barge & J. Royster. c1961, Rockmasters, Inc. GARY "U.S." BONDS. 5.

Queen Of The Highway. w&m; Jim Morrison & Robbie Krieger. c1970, Doors Music Co. DOORS. 54.

Question. w&m; Justin Hayward. c1970, Tyler Music Ltd./TRO-Essex Music International, Inc. MOODY BLUES. 142.

Questions. w&m; Stephen Stills. c1968, 75, Cotillion Music, Inc. & Springalo Toones. BUFFALO SPRINGFIELD. 39, 139.

Quicksand. w&m; Eddie Holland, Lamont Dozier & Brian Holland. c1963, 71, Jobete Music Co., Inc. MARTHA & THE VANDELLAS. 123.

Quinn The Eskimo. w&m; Bob Dylan. c1968, 76, Dwarf Music. BOB DYLAN & THE BAND/MANFRED MANN. 170.

Race Among The Ruins. w&m; Gordon Lightfoot. c1976, Moose Music Ltd. GORDON LIGHTFOOT. 127.

Ra-Da-Da-Da-Da Song SEE Chanson D' Amour.

Rag Mama Rag. w&m; J. Robbie Robertson. c1969, 70, Canaan Music, Inc. BAND. 149, 151, 202.

Rag Mop. w&m; Johnnie Lee Wills & Deacon Anderson. c1950, Hill And Range Songs, Inc. DOC SAUSAGE. 137.

Railroader's Lament SEE Five Hundred Miles.

Rain In My Heart. w&m; Teddy Randazzo & Victoria Pike. c1967, Razzle Dazzle Music, Inc. FRANK SINATRA. 63.

Rain Song. w&m; Jimmy Page & Robert Plant. c1973, Superhype Publishing. LED ZEPPELIN. 114.

Rainbow In Your Eyes. w&m; Leon Russell. c1976, Teddy Jack Music. LEON & MARY RUSSELL. 141.

Raindrops. w&m; Dee Clark. c1961, 68, Conrad Music, a division of Arc Music Corp. DEE CLARK. 5, 168.

Raindrops Keep Fallin' On My Head. w&m; Hal David (w) & Burt Bacharach (m). c1969, Blue Seas Music, Inc., Jac Music Co. & Twentieth Century Music Corp. B.J. THOMAS/VENTURES. 70, 71, 181.

Raining In My Heart. w&m; Boudleaux & Felice Bryant. c1959, House Of Bryant Publications. BUDDY HOLLY/LEO SAYER. 3, 74, 177.

Rainy Day People. w&m; Gordon Lightfoot. c1974, 75, Moose Music. GORDON LIGHTFOOT. 139.

Rainy Day Women #12 & 35. w&m; Bob Dylan. c1966, 76, Dwarf Music. BOB DYLAN. 170.

Rainy Days And Mondays. w&m; Paul Williams (w) & Roger Nichols (m). c1970, Almo Music Corp. CARPENTERS/PAUL WILLIAMS. 15, 23, 70, 131, 181.

Rainy Night In Georgia. w&m; Tony Joe White. c1969, Combine Music Corp. BROOK BENTON. 64, 155, 163.

Raise A Little Hell. w&m; Brian Smith & Raymond McGuire. c1968, 78, Survivor Music. Controlled by Screen Gems-EMI Music Inc. TROOPER. 74.

Raised On Robbery. w&m; Joni Mitchell. c1973, 74, Crazy Crow Music. JONI MITCHELL. 136, 138, 139.

Rama Lama Ding Dong. w&m; George Jones, Jr. c1958, 61, Jimbo Publishing Co. EDSELS. 6.

Ramble On. w&m; Jimmy Page & Robert Plant. c1969, Superhype Publishing. LED ZEPPELIN. 114, 138.

Ramblin' Gamblin' Man. w&m; Bob Seger. c1968, 72, Gear Publishing Co. BOB SEGER. 142.

Ramblin' Man. w&m; Forrest Richard Betts. c1973, No Exit Music Co., Inc. ALLMAN BROTHERS BAND. 43, 55, 136, 138, 141, 174, 185.

Ramona. w&m; Joey, Dee Dee, Tommy & Johnny Ramone. c1977, 78, Bleu Disque Music Co. & Taco Tunes. RAMONES. 19.

Rats. w&m; Jeff Salen & Bobby Butani. c1978, Bleu Disque Music Co. & Black Disc Music. TUFF DARTS. 19.

Rave On. w&m; Sunny West, Bill Tilghman & Norman Petty. c1957, MPL Communications Inc. BUDDY HOLLY. 14.

Reach Out. w&m; Don Wood (w) & David Lucas (m). c1979, 80, Titicus Music Co., Inc. & Elliot Music Co., Inc. BASED ON THE TELEPHONE COMMERCIAL. 189.

Reach Out And Touch (Somebody's Hand). w&m; Nickolas Ashford & Valerie Simpson. c1970, Jobete Music Co., Inc. ARETHA FRANKLIN/DIANA ROSS. 13, 48, 123, 128.

Reach Out I'll Be There. w&m; Brian Holland, Lamont Dozier & Eddie Holland. c1966, 71, Jobete Music Co., Inc. FOUR TOPS. 123, 150, 167.

Reach Out In The Darkness. w&m; Jim Post. c1967, 68, Lowery Music Co., Inc. FRIEND & LOVER. 113.

Ready For The Times To Get Better. w&m; Allen Reynolds. c1976, 78, Aunt Polly's Publishing Co. CRYSTAL GAYLE. 21, 199.

Ready Or Not. w&m; Jack Keller & Amber Dilena. c1978, United Artists Music Co., Inc. HELEN REDDY/ JOHNNY MATHIS. 80, 199.

Ready Teddy. w&m; Robert A. Blackwell & John S. Marascalco. c1956, 69, Venice Music, Inc. LITTLE RICHARD. 3, 109.

Real Love. w&m; Michael McDonald & Patrick Henderson. c1980, Tauripin Tunes, Monosteri Music & April Music Inc. DOOBIE BROTHERS. 162, 190.

Real Man. w&m; Todd Rundgren. c1974, 75, Earmark Music, Inc. TODD RUNDGREN. 12, 139.

Real Wild Child. w&m; Johnny O'Keefe, Johnny Greenan & Dave Owens. c1958, MPL Communications, Inc. BUDDY HOLLY. 14.

Reaper. w&m; D. Roeser. c1976, B. O' Cult Songs, Inc. BLUE OYSTER CULT. 142.

Reason To Be. w&m; Kerry Livgren. c1979, Don Kirshner Music & Blackwood Music Publishing. KANSAS. 148.

Reason To Believe. w&m; Tim Hardin. c1966, 68, Hudson Bay Music Co. TIM HARDIN. 93.

Reasons. w&m; Maurice White, Charles Stepney & Philip Bailey. c1975, Saggifire Music & Eibur Music. EARTH, WIND & FIRE. 16.

Reconsider Baby. w&m; Lowell Fulson. c1955, Arc Music Corp. IKE & TINA TURNER. 1.

Red Rubber Ball. w&m; Paul Simon & Bruce Woodley. c1965, Pattern Music Ltd./Charing Cross Music Inc. CYRKLE. 143.

Red Velvet. w&m; Ian Tyson. c1965, M. Witmark & Sons. JOHNNY CASH. 132.

Redemption. w&m; Bill Conti. c1979, United Artists Corp. Administered by Unart Music Corp. BILL CONTI. 176.

Redondo Beach. w&m; Patti Smith, Lenny Kaye & Richard Sohl. c1975, 77, Linda Music Corp. PATTI SMITH GROUP. 19.

Reelin' And Rockin'. w&m; Chuck Berry. c1958, 65, Arc Music Corp. CHUCK BERRY/DAVE CLARK FIVE/GERRY & THE PACEMAKERS. 2, 10, 100, 101, 155, 169, 197.

Reeling In The Years. w&m; Walter Becker & Donald Fagen. c1972, 73, Wingate Music Corp., MCA Music, a division of MCA Inc. & Red Giant Music Inc. STEELY DAN. 32, 105, 134, 142.

Reflections. w&m; Brian Holland, Lamont Dozier & Eddie Holland. c1967, Jobete Music Co., Inc. SUPREMES. 123.

Refugee. w&m; Tom Petty & Michael Campbell. c1979, 80, Skyhill Publishing Co., Inc. TOM PETTY & THE HEARTBREAKERS. 99.

Rejoyce. w&m; Grace Slick. c1967, 68, Icebag Music Corp. JEFFERSON AIRPLANE. 108.

Relax. w&m; Sid Tepper & Roy C. Bennett. c1963, Gladys Music, Inc. ELVIS PRESLEY. 173.

Relay. w&m; Pete Townshend. c1972, 73, Fabulous Music Ltd./Track Music Inc. WHO. 152.

Release Me. w&m; Eddie Miller & W.S. Stevenson.

c1954, 4-Star Music Co., Inc. ENGELBERT HUMPER- DINCK. 21, 72, 89, 140, 186, 191, 195, 199.

Release Me. w&m; Nickolas Ashford & Valerie Simpson. c1974, 76, Nick-O-Val Music. DYNAMIC SUPERIORS. 13.

Release, Release. w&m; Jon Anderson, Alan White & Chris Squire. c1978, 79, Topographic Music Ltd./WB Music Corp. YES. 146.

Remember Me. w&m; Nickolas Ashford & Valerie Simpson. c1970, Jobete Music Co., Inc. DIANA ROSS. 13, 48, 123.

Remember The Days Of The Old Schoolyard SEE Old Schoolyard.

Reminiscing. w&m; Graham Goble. c1978, Fiberchem International B.V./Screen Gems-EMI Music Inc. LITTLE RIVER BAND. 57, 87, 147.

Renegade. w&m; Tommy Shaw. c1978, Almo Music Corp. & Stygian Songs. STYX. 96.

Reno Nevada. w&m; Richard Farina. c1965, M. Witmark & Sons. RICHARD FARINA. 69.

Requiem: 820 Latham. w&m; Jim Webb. c1967, 70, Johnny Rivers Music. FIFTH DIMENSION. 60.

Rescue Me. w&m; Carl Smith & Raynard Miner. c1965, 75, Chevis Music, Inc. CHER/MELISSA MANCHEST- ER. 37, 89, 184.

Respect. w&m; Otis Redding, Jr. c1965, East-Memphis Music & Time Music Co., Inc. ARETHA FRANKLIN. 122.

Respect Yourself. w&m; Mack Rice & Luther Ingram. c1971, East-Memphis Music Corp. & Klondike Enter- prises, Ltd. STAPLE SINGERS. 105, 122.

Reunited. w&m; Dino Fekaris & Freddie Perren. c1978, Perren-Vibes Music, Inc. PEACHES & HERB. 23, 24, 56, 70, 75, 96, 179, 180, 181.

Revolution. w&m; John Lennon & Paul McCartney. c1968, Northern Songs Ltd./Maclen Music, Inc. BEATLES. 36, 61, 159.

Rhapsody In Blue (Disco Version). w&m; George Gersh- win (m). c1924, 77, New World Music Corp. DEODATO/WALTER MURPHY BAND. 46, 128.

Rhiannon. w&m; Stevie Nicks. c1974, 76, Gentoo Music Inc., Rockhopper Music Inc. & Michael Fleetwood. Administered by Warner-Tamerlane Publishing Co. FLEETWOOD MAC. 55, 77, 121, 174, 178, 185.

Rhinestone Cowboy. w&m; Larry Weiss. c1973, 74, Twentieth Century Music Corp. & House Of Weiss Music Co. GLEN CAMPBELL. 23, 28, 77, 126, 134.

Rhumba Girl. w&m; Jesse Winchester. c1977, Fourth Floor Music, Inc. & Hot Kitchen Music. NICOLETTE LARSON. 96, 181.

Rhumba Man SEE Rhumba Girl.

Rhythms Of Revolution. w&m; Phil Ochs. c1965, 68, Barricade Music, Inc. PHIL OCHS. 144.

Ribbon Of Darkness. w&m; Gordon Lightfoot. c1965, M. Witmark & Sons & Warner Bros. Inc. CONNIE SMITH/GORDON LIGHTFOOT/MARTY ROBBINS. 30, 35, 67, 69.

Rich Man Spiritual. w&m; Gordon Lightfoot. c1964, 66, Warner Bros. Inc. GORDON LIGHTFOOT. 35.

Richard Cory. w&m; Paul Simon. c1966, Paul Simon. SIMON & GARFUNKEL. 143.

Rick-O-Shay SEE Ricochet.

Ricochet. w&m; Larry Coleman, Norman Gimbel & Joe Darion. c1953, Unart Music Corp. TERESA BREWER. 81.

Ride (From The Motion Picture International Velvet). w&m; Leslie Bricusse (w) & Francis Lai (m). c1978, Metro-Goldwyn-Mayer Inc., Variety Music Inc. & M.G.M. Affiliated Music Inc. MOTION PICTURE THEME. 135.

Ride Like The Wind. w&m; Christopher Cross. c1979, Pop 'N' Roll Music. CHRISTOPHER CROSS. 162, 188.

Ride My See-Saw. w&m; John Lodge. c1968, 69, Palace Music Co., Ltd./Felsted Music Corp. MOODY BLUES. 3.

Ride-O-Rocket. w&m; Nickolas Ashford & Valerie Simpson. c1978, Nick-O-Val Music Inc. BROTHERS JOHNSON. 74.

Ridin' The Rainbow. w&m; Fred Wise (w) & Ben Weisman (m). c1962, Gladys Music, Inc. ELVIS PRESLEY. 172.

Right Back Where We Started From. w&m; Pierre Tubbs & Vince Edwards. c1975, 76, Universal Songs-ATV Music, Ltd./Unart Music Corp. & ATV/Music Corp. MAXINE NIGHTINGALE. 62, 193.

Right Down The Line. w&m; Gerry Rafferty. c1978, Rafferty Songs Ltd./Hudson Bay Music Co. GERRY RAFFERTY. 74, 135.

Right Feeling At The Wrong Time. w&m; Barbara Wyrick & Kevin Lamb. c1977, I've Got The Music Co. & Song Tailors Music Co. HOT. 142.

Right Place Wrong Time. w&m; Mac Rebennack. c1973, Walden Music, Inc., Oyster Music & Cauldron Music. DR. JOHN. 197.

Right Thing To Do. w&m; Carly Simon. c1972, Quackenbush Music Ltd. CARLY SIMON. 138, 183.

Right Time Of The Night. w&m; Peter McCann. c1976, 77, American Broadcasting Music, Inc. & MCA Music, a division of MCA Inc. JENNIFER WARNES/ JOHN TRAVOLTA/LYNN ANDERSON/PETER MC CANN. 21, 23, 37, 56, 128, 135, 196.

Rikki, Don't Lose That Number. w&m; Walter Becker & Donald Fagen. c1974, American Broadcasting Music, Inc. STEELY DAN. 157, 161.

Ring Around A Rosy Rag. w&m; Arlo Guthrie. c1967, 68, 69, Appleseed Music Inc. ARLO GUTHRIE. 7.

Ring My Bell. w&m; Frederick Knight. c1979, Two Knight Music. Administered by Island Music. ANITA WARD. 27, 31, 57.

Ring Ring Goes The Bell SEE School Day.

Ringo's Theme. w&m; John Lennon & Paul McCartney. c1963, Northern Songs Ltd./Maclen Music, Inc. BEATLES. 61, 127.

Rings. w&m; Alex Harvey & Eddie Reeves. c1971, Unart Music Corp. LOBO. 79.

Rip Her To Shreds. w&m; Deborah Harry & Chris Stein. c1977, Jiru Music, Inc. & Monster Island Music. BLONDIE. 153.

Rip It Up. w&m; Robert A. Blackwell & John S. Marascalco. c1956, Venice Music. BILL HALEY & THE COMETS/COMMANDER CODY & THE LOST PLANET AIRMEN/ELVIS PRESLEY/GERRY & THE PACEMAKERS/LITTLE RICHARD/SHAUN CASSIDY. 3, 35, 100, 109, 159, 197.

Rip This Joint. w&m; Mick Jagger & Keith Richard. c1972, Promopub B.V. ROLLING STONES. 36.

Ripple. w&m; Robert Hunter (w) & Jerry Garcia (m). c1971, 73, Ice Nine Publishing Co. GRATEFUL DEAD. 83.

Rise. w&m; Andy Armer & Randy Badazz. c1979, Almo Music Corp. & Badazz Music. HERB ALPERT. 23, 24, 56, 70, 97, 179, 180.

Risky Changes. w&m; Gregg Diamond. c1977, Diamond Touch Publishing, Ltd./Arista Music, Inc. GREGG DIAMOND. 34.

Rita May. w&m; Bob Dylan & Jacques Levy (w). c1975, 76, Ram's Horn Music. JERRY LEE LEWIS. 170.

River Of Love. w&m; Jackie De Shannon, Jimmy Holiday & Randy Myers. c1969, 70, Unart Music Corp. B.W. STEVENSON. 79.

Rivers Of Babylon. w&m; F. Farian, G. Reyam, B. Dowe & F. McNaughton. c1978, Far-Musikverlag GmbH-Blue Mountain Music Ltd./Al Gallico Music Corp. & Ackee Music Inc. BONEY M/LINDA RONSTADT. 135.

Road Block. w&m; Janis Joplin & Peter Albin. c1970, 72, Cheap Thrills Music Co. JANIS JOPLIN. 110.

Road Runner. w&m; E. McDaniel. c1960, 66, Arc Music Corp. BO DIDDLEY. 169.

Road Runner. w&m; Eddie Holland, Lamont Dozier & Brian Holland. c1965, Jobete Music Co., Inc. JR. WALKER & THE ALL STARS/PETER FRAMPTON. 142, 150.

Roadhouse Blues. w&m; Jim Morrison (w) & Doors (m). c1970, Doors Music Co. DOORS. 54.

Rock And Roll. w&m; Jimmy Page, Robert Plant, John Paul Jones & John Bonham. c1972, Superhype Publishing. LED ZEPPELIN. 22, 114, 138, 152.

Rock And Roll All Nite. w&m; Paul Stanley & Gene Simmons. c1975, 77, Care Americana, Inc. & Kiss Songs Inc. KISS. 175.

Rock And Roll Hoochie Koo. w&m; Rick Derringer. c1970, 74, Derringer Music, Inc. EDGAR WINTER GROUP. 105, 156.

Rock And Roll Is Here To Stay. w&m; David White. c1958, 78, Singular Publishing Co. DANNY & THE JUNIORS/SHA NA NA. 2, 4.

Rock And Roll Music. w&m; Chuck Berry. c1957, Arc Music Corp. BEACH BOYS/BEATLES/CHUCK BERRY. 5, 78, 101, 155, 168, 169, 184.

Rock And Roll Never Forgets. w&m; Bob Seger. c1976, Gear Publishing Co. BOB SEGER. 142.

Rock And Roll Waltz. w&m; Roy Alfred & Shorty Allen. c1955, Unart Music Corp. KAY STARR. 81.

Rock Around The Clock. w&m; Max C. Freedman & Jimmy DeKnight. c1953, Myers Music, Inc. BILL HALEY & THE COMETS/CARL PERKINS. 93, 128, 158.

Rock Island Line. w&m; Traditional. Huddie Ledbetter (Adapted) & Johnny Cash (Adapted). c1957, 59, versions published by Folkways Music Publishers, Inc. & Hi-Lo Music, Inc. ARLO GUTHRIE/JOHNNY CASH/ODETTA/WEAVERS. 85, 122.

Rock Me. w&m; Nick Gilder & James McCulloch. c1979, Beechwood Music of Canada/Beechwood Music Corp. NICK GILDER. 75, 187.

Rock Me Baby. w&m; Peggy Clinger & Johnny Cymbal. c1972, Pocket Full Of Tunes, Inc. & Every Little Tune, Inc. DAVID CASSIDY. 194.

Rock Me My Baby. w&m; Susan Heather & Shorty Long. c1957, MPL Communications Inc. BUDDY HOLLY. 14.

Rock Me On The Water. w&m; Jackson Browne. c1971, 72, WB Music Corp. JACKSON BROWNE/LINDA RONSTADT. 30, 36, 55, 87, 136, 138, 151, 174, 185.

Rock 'N Me. w&m; Steve Miller. c1976, Sailor Music. STEVE MILLER BAND. 133, 136, 145.

Rock 'N' Roll Fantasy. w&m; Paul Rodgers. c1978, 79, Badco Music Inc. BAD COMPANY. 22, 27, 147.

Rock 'N' Roll Woman. w&m; Stephen Stills. c1967, 75, Cotillion Music, Inc., Ten East Music & Springalo Toones. BUFFALO SPRINGFIELD. 39.

Rock The Boat. w&m; Wally Holmes. c1973, 74, Warner-Tamerlane Publishing Corp. & Jimi Lane Music. HUES CORPORATION. 36, 62, 133.

Rock With You. w&m; Rod Temperton. c1979, Rondor Music Ltd./Almo Music Corp. MICHAEL JACKSON. 24, 45, 56, 70, 99.

Rock Your Baby. w&m; H.W. Casey & R. Finch. c1974, Sherlyn Publishing Co. GEORGE MC CRAE. 26, 52, 77, 156.

Rockaway Beach. w&m; Joey, Dee Dee, Tommy & Johnny Ramone. c1977, 78, Bleu Disque Music Co. & Taco Tunes. RAMONES. 19.

Rocket Man. w&m; Elton John & Bernie Taupin. c1972, Dick James Music Ltd./Dick James Music, Inc. ELTON JOHN. 30, 36, 55, 115, 136, 138, 141, 174, 185.

Rockin' Pneumonia And The Boogie Woogie Flu. w&m; John Vincent & Huey P. Smith. c1957, 66, 67, 72, Ace Publishing Co., Cotillion Music, Inc. & Chris-Marc Music. HUEY "PIANO" SMITH/JOHNNY RIVERS. 5, 93, 138.

Rockin' Robin. w&m; J. Thomas. c1958, Recordo Music Publishers. BOBBY DAY/MICHAEL JACKSON. 4, 38, 64, 72, 137, 140, 195.

Rocky, Theme From SEE Gonna Fly Now.

Rocky Mountain High. w&m; John Denver & Mike Taylor. (m). c1972, Cherry Lane Music Co. JOHN DENVER. 131, 135.

Rocky Raccoon. w&m; John Lennon & Paul McCartney. c1968, Northern Songs Ltd./Maclen Music, Inc. BEATLES. 139.

Rocky II, Theme From SEE Redemption.

Rolene. w&m; Moon Martin. c1978, 79, Rockslam Music. Administered by the Bug Music Group. MOON MARTIN. 22, 27.

Roll Away The Stone. w&m; Leon Russell & Greg Dempsey. c1970, 71, Skyhill Publishing Co. LEON RUSSELL. 128.

Roll On Columbia. w&m; Woody Guthrie (w) & Huddie Ledbetter (m) & John Lomax (m). c1959, 64, Ludlow Music, Inc. WOODY GUTHRIE. 59.

Roll Over Beethoven. w&m; Chuck Berry. c1956, Arc Music Corp. BEATLES/CHUCK BERRY/ELECTRIC LIGHT ORCHESTRA/NAT STUCKEY. 2, 5, 15, 44, 78, 100, 101, 152, 155, 169.

Roller. w&m; Myles Goodwyn. c1978, Goody Two-Tunes Inc. APRIL WINE. 11.

Roller Coaster. w&m; Mark James. c1973, Screen Gems-Columbia Music Inc. BLOOD, SWEAT & TEARS. 104.

Romance In Durango. w&m; Bob Dylan & Jacques Levy (w). c1975, 76, Ram's Horn Music. BOB DYLAN. 170.

Romeo And Juliet. w&m; Bob Hamilton & Freddy Gorman. c1964, 71, Jobete Music Co., Inc. REFLECTIONS. 123.

Romeo's Tune. w&m; Steve Forbert. c1976, 79, Rolling Tide Music. Controlled by Colgems-EMI Music Inc. STEVE FORBERT. 8, 56, 98.

Room Full Of Roses. w&m; Tim Spencer. c1949, Hill And Range Songs, Inc. Assigned to Unichappell Music, Inc. MICKEY GILLEY. 163.

Roots, Theme From. w&m; Gerald Fried (m). c1977, Wolper Productions. Controlled by WB Music Corp. QUINCY JONES. 127.

Rose. w&m; Amanda McBroom. c1977, 79, Fox Fanfare Music, Inc. BETTE MIDLER. 58.

Rose Garden. w&m; Joe South. c1967, 70, Lowery Music Co., Inc. LYNN ANDERSON. 63, 64, 88, 128, 192, 195.

Rosecrans Boulevard. w&m; Jim Webb. c1967, 70, Johnny Rivers Music. FIFTH DIMENSION. 60.

Roses And Love Songs. w&m; Jim Weatherly. c1974, Keca Music Inc. RAY PRICE. 139.

Roses Are Red. w&m; Al Byron & Paul Evans. c1961, 62, United Artists Music Co., Inc. BOBBY VINTON. 78, 82, 102, 137.

Rosy's Theme SEE It Was A Good Time.

Rotation. w&m; Andy Armer & Randy Badazz. c1979, 80, Almo Music Corp. & Badazz Music. HERB ALPERT. 24, 98.

Roundabout. w&m; Jon Anderson & Steve Howe. c1971, 72, Rondor Music Ltd., Topographic Music

Ltd. & Yessongs, Ltd./Cotillion Music Inc. & WB Music Corp. YES. 22, 36, 55, 136, 152, 174, 175, 197.

Roustabout. w&m; Bill Giant, Bernie Baum & Florence Kaye. c1964, Elvis Presley Music, Inc. ELVIS PRESLEY. 173.

Row Jimmy. w&m; Robert Hunter (w) &Jerry Garcia (m). c1973, 76, Ice Nine Publishing Co., Inc. GRATE-FUL DEAD. 84.

Roxanne. w&m; Sting. c1978, Virgin Music Inc. POLICE. 11.

Rubberband Man. w&m; Linda Creed & Thom Bell. c1976, Mighty Three Music. Administered by Black-wood Music Inc. SPINNERS. 21, 193, 196.

Ruby Baby. w&m; Jerry Leiber & Mike Stoller. c1955, Tiger Music, Inc. Assigned to Chappell & Co., Inc., Quintet Music, Inc. & Bienstock Publishing Co. Con-trolled by Chappell & Co., Inc. DION/DRIFTERS. 91, 155.

Ruby Red Dress SEE Leave Me Alone.

Ruby Tuesday. w&m; Mick Jagger & Keith Richard. c1967, Abkco Music, Inc. MELANIE/ROLLING STONES. 121, 128, 130, 157.

Rueben James. w&m; Barry Etris & Alex Harvey. c1969, Unart Music Corp. KENNY ROGERS. 79.

Run For Your Life. w&m; John Lennon & Paul McCartney. c1965, Northern Songs Ltd./Maclen Music, Inc. BEATLES. 159.

Run Home Girl. w&m; Paul Young & Ian Wilson. c1978, Man-Ken Music, Ltd. SAD CAFE. 129.

Run Of The Mill. w&m; George Harrison. c1970, Har-risongs Ltd./Harrisongs Music, Inc. GEORGE HAR-RISON. 125.

Run Sally Run. w&m; Paul Vance & Lee Pockriss. c1969, 70, Vanlee Music Corp. & Emily Music Corp. CUFF LINKS. 161, 186.

Run That Body Down. w&m; Paul Simon. c1971, Paul Simon. PAUL SIMON. 143.

Run To Me. w&m; Barry, Robin & Maurice Gibb. c1972, Abigail Music Ltd. & Robin Gibb Publishing Ltd./ R.S.O. Publishing, Inc. & WB Music Corp. BEE GEES. 136, 139, 197.

Run, Woman, Run. w&m; Ann Booth, Duke Goff & Dan Hoffman. c1970, Algee Music Corp. TAMMY WYNETTE. 88.

Runaround. w&m; Cirino Colacrai. c1954, Regent Music Corp. CHUCK BERRY. 78, 169.

Runaway. w&m; Del Shannon & Max Crook. c1961, Mole Hole Music & Noma Music, Inc. Controlled by Bug Music Group. DEL SHANNON. 4.

Runaway. w&m; N.Q. Dewey. c1978, Diamondback Music. JEFFERSON STARSHIP. 73, 135.

Runaway Child, Running Wild. w&m; Barrett Strong & Norman Whitfield. c1969, Jobete Music, Co., Inc. TEMPTATIONS. 123.

Runaway Love. w&m; Gilbert A. Askey. c1978, Gemigo Publishing Co., Inc. & Andrask Music Pub-lishing. LINDA CLIFFORD. 74, 135.

Runnin' With The Devil. w&m; Edward & Alex Van Halen, Michael Anthony & David Lee Roth. c1978, 80, Van Halen Music. VAN HALEN. 147.

Running Down The Road. w&m; Arlo Guthrie. c1969, Howard Beach Music Inc. ARLO GUTHRIE. 7.

Running On Empty. w&m; Jackson Browne. c1977, 78, Swallow Turn Music. Administered by WB Music Corp. JACKSON BROWNE. 22, 136, 146, 178.

Sacred. w&m; Bill Landau & Adam Ross. c1961, Bam-boo Music Co. & Daywin Music, Inc. CASTELLS. 6.

Sad Eyed Lady Of THe Lowlands. w&m; Bob Dylan. c1966, 76, Dwarf Music. BOB DYLAN/JOAN BAEZ. 170.

Sad Eyes. w&m; Robert John. c1979, Careers Music, Inc. ROBERT JOHN. 23, 56, 75, 97, 130, 179, 180, 187.

Sad Song. w&m; Melanie Safka. c1967, 71, H & L Music Corp. & Unart Music Corp. Administered by Unart Music Corp. MELANIE. 37.

Safe In My Garden. w&m; John Phillips. c1968, American Broadcasting Music, Inc. & Honest John Music. MAMAS & THE PAPAS. 93.

Sail Away. w&m; Rafe Vanhoy. c1976, Tree Publishing Co., Inc. OAK RIDGE BOYS. 187.

Sail Away. w&m; Randy Newman. c1972, 73, 75, WB Music Corp. & Randy Newman. LINDA RONSTADT/ RANDY NEWMAN. 36, 43, 55, 87, 136, 139, 151, 174, 185.

Sail On. w&m; Lionel Richie. c1979, Jobete Music Co., Inc. & Commodores Entertainment Publishing Corp. COMMODORES. 23, 24, 56, 97, 179, 180.

Sailboat Song. w&m; Jeffrey M. Comanor. c1968, 70, Mr. Bones Music Publishing Inc. FIFTH DIMENSION. 60.

Sailing. w&m; Christopher Cross. c1979, 80, Pop 'N' Roll Music. CHRISTOPHER CROSS. 162, 189.

Sailing. w&m; Gavin Sutherland. c1972, 75, Island Music Ltd./Ackee Music Inc. ROD STEWART. 30, 147.

Sailor's Life. w&m; Judy Collins. c1968, Warner Bros. Seven Arts, Inc. JUDY COLLINS. 132.

Salty Dog. w&m; Keith Reid (w) & Gary Brooker (m). c1969, 71, Essex Music International Ltd./TRO Andover Music, Inc. PROCOL HARUM. 42.

Sam. w&m; John Farrar, Hank Marvin & Don Black. c1976, 77, Blue Gum Music LTd. & Lords Music Ltd./ Blue Gum Music, Inc. OLIVIA NEWTON-JOHN. 128.

San Diego Serenade. w&m; Tom Waits. c1974, 78, Fifth Floor Music, Inc. TOM WAITS. 37.

San Francisco Bay Blues. w&m; Jesse Fuller. c1958, 63, Hollis Music, Inc. JESSE FULLER/PHOEBE SNOW/ RICHIE HAVENS. 59, 68, 85, 126.

San Francisco (Be Sure To Wear Some Flowers In Your Hair). w&m; John Phillips. c1967, American Broad-casting Music, Inc. & Honest John Music. SCOTT MC KENZIE. 89, 135.

San Francisco (You've Got Me). w&m; H. Belolo (w),
P. Whitehead (w), P. Hurtt(w) & J. Morali (m). c1977,
Scorpio Music (Black Scorpio). Controlled by Can't
Stop Music. VILLAGE PEOPLE. 34, 200.

Sandman. w&m; Dewey Bunnell. c1971, 72, Warner
Bros. Music Ltd./WB Music Corp. AMERICA. 43, 87,
136, 139, 174, 197.

Sandpiper, Love Theme From SEE Shadow Of Your
Smile.

Santo Domingo. w&m; Phil Ochs. c1965, 68, Barricade
Music. Inc. PHIL OCHS. 144.

Sara. w&m; Bob Dylan. c1975, 76, Ram's Horn Music.
BOB DYLAN. 145, 170.

Sara. w&m; Stevie Nicks. c1979, Fleetwood Mac
Music/Warner Bros. Inc. FLEETWOOD MAC.
147.

Sara Smile. w&m; Daryl Hall & John Oates (w). c1975,
Unichappell Music, Inc. HALL & OATES. 37.

Sarah's Theme SEE Ride.

Satisfaction. w&m; Mick Jagger & Keith Richard.
c1965, Abkco Music, Inc. ROLLING STONES. 29,
128, 134, 156, 157.

Satisfaction. w&m; William "Smokey" Robinson.
c1971, Jobete Music Co., Inc. SMOKEY ROBINSON
& THE MIRACLES. 24.

Saturday In The Park. w&m; Robert Lamm. c1972,
Lamminations Music & Big Elk Music. CHICAGO.
77, 121, 134.

Saturday Night. w&m; Brood (w) & Lademacher (w).
c1979, Radmus Publishing Inc. HERMAN BROOD. 11.

Saturday Night. w&m; Randy Sparks. c1963, Cherry-
bell Music Publishing Co. NEW CHRISTY
MINSTRELS. 68.

Saturday Night's Alright. w&m; Elton John & Bernie
Taupin. c1973, Dick James Music, Inc. ELTON
JOHN. 139.

Save The Country. w&m; Laura Nyro. c1968, 70, Tuna
Fish Music, Inc. FIFTH DIMENSION/LAURA NYRO.
35, 41, 86, 199.

Save The Last Dance For Me. w&m; Doc Pomus & Mort
Shuman. c1960, Hill & Range Songs, Inc. Assigned
to Unichappell Music, Inc. DE FRANCO FAMILY/
DRIFTERS. 78, 92, 102, 137, 155, 161, 163.

Save The Life Of My Child. w&m; Paul Simon. c1968,
Paul Simon. SIMON & GARFUNKEL. 143.

Savoy Truffle. w&m; George Harrison. c1968, Harrisongs Ltd./Harrisongs Music, Inc. BEATLES. 125.

Say Goodbye To Hollywood. w&m; Billy Joel. c1976,
78, Blackwood Music, Inc. BETTE MIDLER/BILLY
JOEL. 165.

Say, Has Anybody Seen My Sweet Gypsy Rose. w&m;
Irwin Levine & L. Russell Brown. c1973, Levine &
Brown Music Inc. TONY ORLANDO & DAWN. 63.

Say Maybe. w&m; Neil Diamond. c1978, 79, Stonebridge Music. NEIL DIAMOND. 27, 147.

Say You Love Me. w&m; Christine McVie. c1974, 76,
Rockhopper Music, Inc. FLEETWOOD MAC. 77.

Say You'll Stay Until Tomorrow. w&m; Roger Greenaway & Barry Mason. c1976, 77, Dick James Music
Ltd./Dick James Music, Inc. & WB Music Corp.
Dick James Music Inc., Administrator. TOM JONES.
127, 141.

Scarborough Fair. w&m; Traditional. Woody Hayes
(Adapted). c1965, 72, versions published by Ludlow
Music, Inc. & Road Island Co. SERGIO MENDES &
BRASIL '66/WES MONTGOMERY. 68, 85.

Scarborough Fair/Canticle. w&m; Paul Simon & Art
Garfunkel (Arrangement & Original Counter Melody).
c1966, Paul Simon. SIMON & GARFUNKEL. 126,
143.

Scarlet Begonias. w&m; Robert Hunter (w) & Jerry
Garcia (m). c1974, 76, Ice Nine Publishing Co., Inc.
GRATEFUL DEAD. 84.

School Day. w&m; Chuck Berry. c1957, Arc Music
Corp. CHUCK BERRY. 6, 155.

School Is Out. w&m; Gene Barge & Frank Guida. c1961,
Rockmasters Inc. GARY "U.S." BONDS. 5.

School's Out. w&m; Alice Cooper & Michael Bruce.
c1972, Bizarre Music, Inc. & Alive Enterprises.
ALICE COOPER. 72, 156, 195.

Scorpio. w&m; Dennis Coffey. c1970, 72, Interior
Music Corp. DENNIS COFFEY. 115.

Scotch And Soda. w&m; Traditional. Dave Guard
(Adapted). c1959, 61, Beechwood Music Corp.
KINGSTON TRIO. 93.

Sea Cruise. w&m; Huey Smith & John Vincent. c1959,
66, 78, Ace Publishing Co., Lancer Music & Cotillion
Music, Inc. FRANKIE FORD. 2, 5.

Sealed With A Kiss. w&m; Gary Geld (m) & Peter Udell
(w). c1960, 68, Post Music Inc. & United Artists
Music Co., Inc. BOBBY VINTON/GARY LEWIS/
BRIAN HYLAND. 78, 79, 102, 113, 137, 161, 195.

Search And Destroy. w&m; James Osterberg & James
Williamson. c1972, Mainman Ltd. IGGY POP &
THE STOOGES. 153.

Searchin'. w&m; Jerry Leiber & Mike Stoller. c1957,
Tiger Music, Inc. Assigned to Chappell & Co., Inc.
Quintet Music Inc. & Freddy Bienstock Music Co.
Controlled by Intersong Music, Inc. COASTERS. 91,
155.

Searchin' For A Rainbow. w&m; Toy T. Caldwell. c1975,
No Exit Music Co., Inc. MARSHALL TUCKER BAND.
141.

Searchin' So Long. w&m; James Pankow. c1974, Big
Elk Music. CHICAGO. 93.

Searching For A Thrill. w&m; James Cobb & Bruce
Blackman. c1978, Brother Bill's Music. STARBUCK.
74.

Seasons In The Sun. w&m; Rod McKuen (w) & Jacques
Brel (m). c1961, 64, 74, Societe Nouvelle des Editions
Musicales/Edward B. Marks Music Corp. BOBBY
VINTON/BROTHERS FOUR/ROD MC KUEN. 68, 131.

Secret Love. w&m; Paul Francis Webster (w) & Sammy
Fain (m). c1953, 75, Remick Music Corp. & Warner
Bros. Inc. FREDDY FENDER. 30, 87.

Secretly. w&m; Al Hoffman, Dick Manning & Mark

Markwell. c1958, Planetary Music Publishing Corp. JIMMIE RODGERS. 78, 101, 161.

Security. w&m; Otis Redding & Margaret Wessen. c1964, East Publications. ETTA JAMES. 76.

See Me, Feel Me. w&m; Peter Townshend. c1969, 70, Fabulous Music Ltd. Controlled by Track Music, Inc. WHO. 36, 63, 86, 88.

See Saw. w&m; Don Covay & Steve Cropper. c1965, East-Memphis Music. ARETHA FRANKLIN. 122.

See The Changes. w&m; Stephen Stills. c1977, Gold Hill Music, Inc. CROSBY, STILLS, & NASH. 127, 146.

See The Funny Little Clown. w&m; Bobby Goldsboro. c1963, 64, Unart Music Corp. BOBBY GOLDSBORO. 81.

See You In September. w&m; Sid Wayne (w) & Sherman Edwards (m). c1959, Vibar Music, HAPPENINGS. 198.

See You Later, Alligator. w&m; Robert Guidry. c1955, 56, Arc Music Corp. BILL HALEY & THE COMETS. 5, 78, 101, 155, 168, 169.

Seems So Long Ago, Nancy. w&m; Leonard Cohen. c1969, Stranger Music, Inc. LEONARD COHEN. 171.

Sell The House. w&m; Nickolas Ashford & Valerie Simpson. c1975, 76, Nick-O-Val Music. ASHFORD & SIMPSON. 13.

Send In The Clowns. w&m; Stephen Sondheim. c1973, Rilting Music Inc. & Revelation Music Publishing Corp. JUDY COLLINS/LOU RAWLS. 131.

Send Me Some Lovin'. w&m; Leo Price & John Marascalco. c1957, 75, Venice Music. JOHN LENNON/LITTLE RICHARD/SAM COOKE. 35, 100, 109, 137, 159.

Send One Your Love. w&m; Stevie Wonder. c1979, Jobete Music Co., Inc. & Black Bull Music. STEVIE WONDER. 8, 23, 24, 56, 97, 180.

Sentimental Journey. w&m; Bud Green, Les Brown & Ben Homer. c1944, Morley Music CO., Inc. BEATLES. 125.

Sentimental Lady. w&m; Bob Welch. c1972, Fleetwood Music Ltd./Sonheath Music & WB Music Corp. FLEETWOOD MAC. 30, 138, 146, 178.

September. w&m; Maurice White, Al McKay & Allee Willis. c1978, Saggifire Music, Steelchest Music, Irving Music, Inc. & Ninth Music. EARTH, WIND & FIRE. 16, 96, 181.

September Morn. w&m; Neil Diamond & Gilbert Becaud. c1978, 80, Stonebridge Music & Ema-Suisse. NEIL DIAMOND. 87, 147, 188.

Serpentine Fire. w&m; Maurice & Verdine White & Sonny Burke. c1977, Saggifire Music & Free Delivery Music. EARTH, WIND & FIRE. 24, 34, 51, 128.

Set Me Free. w&m; Todd Rundgren, Roger Powell, Kasim Sulton & John Wilcox. c1979, 80, Unearthly Music Inc. & Fiction Music Inc. UTOPIA. 99.

Seul Sur Son Etoile SEE It Must Be Him.

Seven Days. w&m; Willis Carroll & Carmen Taylor.

c1956, Progressive Music Publishing CO., Inc. Controlled by Unichappell Music Inc. CLYDE MC PHATTER. 154, 155.

Seven Little Girls Sitting In The Back Seat. w&m; Bob Hilliard & Les Pockriss. c1959, Post Music, Inc. & United Artists Music Co., Inc. PAUL EVANS. 78, 82, 101.

7 O'Clock News/Silent Night. w&m; Paul Simon & Arthur Garfunkel (Narration & arrangement). c1966, Paul Simon, SIMON & GARFUNKEL. 143.

7 Rooms Of Gloom. w&m; Brian Holland, Lamont Dozier & Eddie Holland. c1967, Jobete Music, Co., Inc. FOUR TOPS. 123.

7-6-5-4-3-2-1 (Blow Your Whistle). w&m; Roger Cook. c1974, Cookaway Music Inc. GARY TOMS EMPIRE. 46.

Seven Song SEE Half Moon.

Seventh Son. w&m; Willie Dixon. c1955, 65, 70, 74, Arc Music Corp. CLIMAX BLUES BAND/JOHN HAMMOND/JOHNNY RIVERS/MOSE ALLISON. 1, 100, 168.

Sex Machine. w&m; Sylvester Stewart (m). c1970, Daly City Music. SLY & THE FAMILY STONE. 202.

Sexy. w&m; Kenny Gamble & Leon Huff. c1975, Mighty Three Music. Administered by Blackwood Music Inc. MSFB. 49.

Sexy Eyes. w&m; Bob Mather, Keith Stegall & Chris Waters. c1979, April Music, Inc. & Blackwood Music, Inc. DR. HOOK. 116.

Sgt. Pepper's Lonely Hearts Club Band. w&m; John Lennon & Paul McCartney. c1967, Northern Songs Ltd./Maclen Music, Inc. BEATLES/BEE GEES. 36, 61, 138, 146, 159.

Shadow Dancing. w&m; Andy, Barry, Robin & Maurice Gibb. c1978, Stigwood Music Inc. Brothers Gibb, Andy Gibb Music, Joye USA Music Co. & Hugh & Barbara Gibb. Administered by Unichappell Music Inc. ANDY GIBB. 50, 178.

Shadow Of Your Smile. w&m; Paul Francis Webster Johnny Mandel (m). c1965, 67, Metro-Goldwyn-Mayer, Inc. Controlled by Miller Music Corp. TONY BENNETT. 21, 111, 192.

Shaft, Theme From. w&m; Isaac Hayes, c1971, 75, East-Memphis Music. ISAAC HAYES. 122.

Shake. w&m; Sam Cooke. c1964, Kags Music Corp. SAM COOKE. 93

Shake And Dance With Me. w&m; M. Cooper. c1978, Val-Le-Joe Music. CON FUNK SHUN. 51, 74.

Shake It. w&m; Terence Boylan. c1978, 79, Steamed Clam Music. IAN MATTHEWS. 27.

Shake Me, Wake Me (When It's Over). w&m; Eddie Holland, Lamont Dozier & Brian Holland. c1966, 68, Jobete Music CO., Inc. FOUR TOPS. 150.

Shake, Rattle And Roll. w&m; Charles Calhoun. c1954, Hill And Range Songs, Inc. & Progressive Music Publishing Co., Inc. Controlled by Unichappell Music, Inc. ARTHUR CONLEY/BILL HALEY & THE COMETS/ELVIS PRESLEY/JOE TURNER. 78, 90, 101, 137, 154, 155.

Shake, Shake, Shake, Shake Your Booty SEE Shake Your Booty.

Shake Some Action. w&m; Cyril Jordan & Chris Wilson. c1976, 78, Bleu Disque Music Co. & Photon Music. FLAMIN' GROOVIES. 19.

Shake That Tambourine. w&m; Bill Giant, Bernie Baum & Florence Kaye. c1965, Elvis Presley Music, Inc. ELVIS PRESLEY. 173.

Shake Your Booty. w&m; Harry Wayne Crosby & Richard Finch. c1976, Sherlyn Publishing Co. & Harrick Music, Inc. K C & THE SUNSHINE BAND. 26, 34, 77.

Shake Your Groove Thing. w&m; Dino Fekaris & Freddie Perren. c1978, Perren-Vibes Music, Inc. PEACHES & HERB. 25, 96, 129.

Shake Your Rump To The Funk. w&m; Larry Dodson, James Alexander, Michael Beard, Winston Stewart, Lloyd Smith, Charles Allen, Harvey Henderson & Frank Thompson. c1976, Warner-Tamerlane Publishing Corp. & Barkay Music. BAR-KAYS. 46, 118, 141.

Shakedown Cruise. w&m; Jay Ferguson. c1978, Painless Music. JAY FERGUSON. 27.

Shakedown Street. w&m; Robert Hunter (w) & Jerry Garcia (m). c1978, 79, Ice Nine Publishing Co., Inc. GRATEFUL DEAD. 22

Shakin' All Over. w&m; Johnny Kidd. c1960, Mills Music Ltd./Mills Music Inc. GUESS WHO. 6.

Shambala. w&m; Daniel Moore. c1973, ABC-Dunhill Music, Inc. & Speed Music. THREE DOG NIGHT. 32, 93, 106.

Shangri-la. w&m; Carl Sigman (w), Matt Malineck (m) & Robert Maxwell (m). c1946, 56, 66, Robbins Music Corp. BOOTS RANDOLPH/LETTERMAN/ROBERT MAXWELL. 140, 163.

Shannon. w&m; Henry Gross. c1975, 76, Blendingwell Music, Inc. HENRY GROSS. 37, 193.

Sharing The Night Together. w&m; Ava Alridge & Eddie Struzick. c1975, 78, Alan Cartee Music, Inc. & Shoals Music Mill Publishing Co., Inc. DR. HOOK. 73, 74, 128, 157, 180.

Sh-Boom. w&m; James Keyes, Claude & Carl Feaster, Floyd F. McCrae & James Edwards. c1954, Hill And Range Songs, Inc. Controlled by Unichappell Music, Inc. CHORDS/CREWCUTS. 90, 101, 137, 155.

She Belongs To Me. w&m; Bob Dylan. c1965, M. Witmark & Sons & Warner Bros, Inc. BOB DYLAN/RICK NELSON. 35, 138, 149.

She Came In Through The Bathroom Window. w&m; John Lennon & Paul McCartney. c1969, Northern Songs Ltd./Maclen Music, Inc. BEATLES/JOE COCKER. 61.

She Did It. w&m; Eric Carmen. c1976, 77, C.A.M.-U.S.A., Inc. ERIC CARMEN. 127.

She Knows Me Too Well. w&m; Brian Wilson. c1964, Sea of Tunes Publishing Co. BEACH BOYS. 9.

She Loves You. w&m; John Lennon & Paul McCartney. c1963, 64, Northern Songs, Ltd./Gil Music Corp. BEATLES. 4, 93, 102, 117, 125, 137, 145, 163, 174, 185.

She Never Knew Me. w&m; Bob McDill & Wyland Holyfield. c1975, Hall-Clement Publications, Maplehill Music & Vogue Music, Inc. DON WILLIAMS. 199.

She Said "Yeah". w&m; Roddy Jackson & Sonny Bono. c1959, Venice Music. ROLLING STONES. 159.

Sheena Is A Punk Rocker. w&m; Joey, Dee Dee, Tommy & Johnny Ramone. c1977, 78, Bleu Disque Music Co. & Taco Tunes. RAMONES. 19.

Shelter From The Storm. w&m; Bob Dylan. c1974, 75 76, Ram's Horn Music, BOB DYLAN. 36, 131, 170.

Shenandoah. w&m; Traditional. Odetta Gordon (Adapted & Arranged). c1963, M. Witmark & Sons. ODETTA. 67.

Sherry. w&m; Bob Gaudio. c1962, 63, BoBob Music Corp. Assigned to Claridge Music, Inc. FOUR SEASONS. 78, 102, 137.

Sherry Don't Go. w&m; Danny & Myrna Janssen & Wally Keske. c1968, Grey Fox Music Inc. LETTERMEN. 76.

She's A Lady. w&m; Paul Anka. c1970, 71, Spanka Music Corp. TOM JONES. 64.

She's Always A Woman. w&m; Billy Joel. c1977, Impulsive Music and April Music Inc. Administered by April Music Inc. BILLY JOEL. 177.

She's Just A Woman SEE Living/Loving Maid.

She's Not There. w&m; Rod Argent. c1964, Marquis Music Ltd./Al Gallico Music Corp. SANTANA/VANILLA FUDGE/ZOMBIES. 29, 126, 128, 135, 157.

She's Some Kind Of Wonderful SEE Some Kind Of Wonderful.

She's Your Lover Now. w&m; Bob Dylan. c1971, 76 Dwarf Music. 170.

Shine A Little Love. w&m; Jeff Lynn. c1979, United Artists Music Ltd. & Jet Music. Administered by Unart Music Corp. ELECTRIC LIGHT ORCHESTRA. 176.

Shine On. w&m; Peter Frampton. c1971, 76, United Artists Music Ltd./Unart Music Corp. PETER FRAMPTON. 37.

Shinnin' On. w&m M. Franer & D. Brewer. c1974, Cram Renraff Co. & Brew Music Co. GRAND FUNK. 93.

Shinning Star. w&m; Leo Graham & Paul Richmond. c1980, Content Music, Inc. MANHATTANS. 162, 189.

Shining Star. w&m; Maurice White, Philip Bailey & Larry Dunn. c1975, Saggifire Music. EARTH, WIND, & FIRE. 16, 103, 156.

Ship Of Fools. w&m; Jim Morrison (w) & Doors (m). c1970, Doors Music Co. DOORS. 54.

Ship Of Fools. w&m; Robert Hunter (w) & Jerry Garcia (m). c1974, 76, Ice Nine Publishing Co., Inc. GRATEFUL DEAD. 84.

Ships. w&m; Ian Hunter. c1979, April Music Inc. & Ian

Hunter Music, Inc. Administered by April Music. BARRY MANILOW/IAN HUNTER. 116, 148, 198.

Shoe, Shoe Shine. w&m; Nickolas Ashford & Valerie Simpson. c1974, 76, Nick-O-Val Music. DYNAMIC SUPERIORS. 13.

Shoo-Be-Doo-Be-Doo-Da-Day. w&m; Stevie Wonder, Henry Cosby & Sylvia Moy. c1968, Jobete Music Co., Inc. STEVIE WONDER. 123.

Shoop Shoop Shoop Song SEE It's In His Kiss.

Shop Around. w&m; Berry Gordy, Jr. & William "Smokey" Robinson. c1961, Jobete Music Co., Inc CAPTAIN & TENNILLE/MIRACLES/SMOKEY ROBINSON & THE MIRACLES. 77, 123, 142, 150, 166.

Shoppin' Around. w&m; Sid Tepper, Roy C. Bennett & Aaron Schroeder. c1957, Gladys Music, Inc. ELVIS PRESLEY. 173.

Short Fat Fannie. w&m; Larry Williams. c1957, Venice Music. LARRY WILLIAMS. 159.

Short People. w&m; Randy Newman. c1977, Hightree Music. RANDY NEWMAN. 181.

Shotgun. w&m; Autry De Walt. c1965, 69, Jobete Music Co., Inc. JR. WALKER & THE ALL STARS. 123, 150, 166.

Should I. w&m; Arthur Freed (w) & Nacio Herb Brown (m). c1929, 57, 66, Metro-Goldwyn-Mayer Inc. Controlled by Robbins Music Corp. BEN WEBSTER/ JO JONES. 140.

Shouldn't I Know. w&m; Meredith Brothers & Sam Azrael. c1951, Progressive Music Publishing Co., Inc. Controlled by Unichappell Music Inc. CARDINALS. 155.

Should've Never Let You Go. w&m; Neil Sedaka & Phil Cody. c1978, Kirshner Songs & April Music. Publishing. NEIL SEDAKA. 116.

Shout. w&m; O'Kelly, Ronald & Rudolph Isley. c1959, 62, Wemar Music Corp. & Nom Music, Inc. ISLEY BROTHERS. 3, 101, 155, 163.

Shout And Shimmy. w&m; James Brown. c1962, 68, Lois Publishing Co. JAMES BROWN. 18.

Shout It Out. w&m; Bill Giant, Bernie Baum & Florence Kaye. c1966, Elvis Presley Music Inc. ELVIS PRESLEY. 172.

Show And Tell. w&m Jerry Fuller. c1973, Fullness Music Co. AL WILSON. 52.

Show Me How. w&m; Isaac Hayes & David Porter. c1971, East-Memphis Music. EMOTIONS. 122.

Show Me The Way. w&m; Peter Frampton. c1975, Almo Music Corp. & Fram-Dee Music Ltd. PETER FRAMPTON. 12, 131, 181.

Showdown. w&m; Jeff Lynne. c1973, Carlin Music Corp. & Sugartown Music Ltd. Administered by Chappell & Co.,Inc. & United Artists Music Co., Inc. ELECTRIC LIGHT ORCHESTRA. 184.

Shower The People. w&m; James Taylor. c1975, 76, Country Road Music, Inc. JAMES TAYLOR. 136, 146.

Shutters And Boards. w&m; Audie Murphy & Scott

Turner. c1962, 64, Camp & Canyon. Assigned to Vogue Music, Inc. JERRY WALLACE. 160.

Sign On The Window. w&m; Bob Dylan. c1970, 76, Big Sky Music. BOB DYLAN. 170.

Signed, Sealed, Delivered I'm Yours. w&m; Stevie Wonder, Syreeta Wright, Lula Mae Hardaway & Lee Garrett. c1970, Jobete Music Co., Inc. PETER FRAMPTON/STEVIE WONDER. 123, 134, 142, 150.

Signs. w&m; Les Emmerson. c1971, 4-Star Music Co., Inc. FIVE MAN ELECTRICAL BAND. 192.

Silent Eyes. w&m; Paul Simon. c1975, Paul Simon. PAUL SIMON. 143.

Silent Weekend. w&m; Bob Dylan. c1973, 74, Dwarf Music. 170.

Silhouettes. w&m; Frank C. Slay, Jr. & Bob Crewe. c1957, 65, Regent Music Corp. HERMAN'S HERMITS/RAYS. 5, 10, 78, 101, 168, 169.

Silver Dreams. w&m; John Waite & Anthony Brock. c1977, Dayn Music Ltd./The Hudson Bay Music Co. BABYS. 135.

Silver Lining. w&m; Peter Beckett. c1978, Touch Of Gold Music Inc., Crowbeck Music & Stigwood Music, Inc. PLAYER. 73.

Silver Threads And Golden Needles. w&m; Dick Reynolds & Jack Rhodes. c1956, Central Songs, a division of Beechwood Music Corp. CHARLIE MC COY/LINDA RONSTADT. 140, 142.

Simple Desultory Philippic. w&m; Paul Simon. c1965, Paul Simon. SIMON & GARFUNKEL. 143.

Simple Man, Simple Dream. w&m; John David Souther. c1976, 78, WB Music Corp. & Golden Spread Music. LINDA RONSTADT. 146.

Simple Song Of Freedom. w&m; Bobby Darin. c1969, Hudson Bay Music CO. BOBBY DARIN. 93.

Simple Twist Of Fate. w&m; Bob Dylan. c1974, 76, Ram's Horn Music. BOB DYLAN. 170.

Since I Don't Have You. w&m; James Beaumont (w) Janet Vogel (w), Joseph Verscharen (w), Walter Lester (w), John Taylor (w), Joseph Rock (m) & Lennie Martin (m). c1958, Bonnyview Music Corp. ART GARFUNKEL/SKYLINERS. 3, 75, 187.

Since I Fell For You. w&m; Buddy Johnson. c1948, 75, Advanced Music Corp. & Warner Bros., Inc. BOBBY BLAND/CAPTAIN & TENNILLE/DINAH WASHINGTON/JOHNNY MATHIS/LENNY WELCH. 30, 100.

Since I Lost My Baby. w&m; William "Smokey" Robinson & Warren Moore. c1965, Jobete Music Co., Inc. TEMPTATIONS. 150.

Since I Met You Baby. w&m; Ivory Joe Hunter. c1956, Progressive Music Publishing Co., Inc. Controlled by Unichappell Music, Inc. IVORY JOE HUNTER. 91, 137, 154, 155.

Since I've Been Loving You. w&m; Jimmy Page, Robert Plant & John Paul Jones. c1970, 73, Superhype Publishing. LED ZEPPELIN. 114.

Since You've Been Gone. w&m; Aretha Franklin & Ted White. c1968, Fourteenth Hour Music, Inc. & Cotillion Music, Inc. ARETHA FRANKLIN. 4.

Sincerely. w&m; Harvey Fuqua & Allan Freed. c1954, 74, Arc Music Corp. MC GUIRE SISTERS/MOONGLOWS. 2, 101, 168.

Sing. w&m; Joe Raposo. c1971, 72, Jonico Music, Inc. CARPENTERS. 30, 127, 138, 139, 197.

Sing. w&m; Leo Gianangelo. c1976, 77, Churn Music. TONY ORLANDO & DAWN. 23, 128, 142, 164.

Sing A Simple Song. w&m; Sylvester Stewart. c1968, Daly City Music. SLY & THE FAMILY STONE. 202.

Sing For The Day. w&m; Tommy Shaw. c1978, Almo Music Corp. & Stygian Songs. STYX. 129.

Singasong. w&m; Maurice White & Al McKay. c1975, Saggifire Music & Mburu Music. EARTH, WIND & FIRE. 16, 103.

Singin' In The Rain. w&m; Arthur Freed (w) & Nacio Herb Brown (m). c1929, 57, 66, Metro-Goldwyn-Mayer Inc. Controlled by Robbins Music Corp. DEBBIE REYNOLDS/JUDY GARLAND/SHEILA & B. 140.

Single Girl. w&m; Paul Stookey & Mary Travers. c1964, Pepamar Music Corp. PETER, PAUL & MARY. 132.

Sir Duke. w&m; Stevie Wonder. c1976, Jobete Music Co., Inc. & Black Bull Music, Inc. LOU RAWLS/ STEVIE WONDER. 24, 121, 128, 135, 164.

Sister Golden Hair. w&m; Gerry Beckley. c1975, Warner Bros. Inc. Music Corp. AMERICA. 30, 36, 117, 133, 136, 139, 141, 174, 185.

Sisters Of Mercy. w&m; Leonard Cohen. c1967, 69, Stranger Music, Inc. LEONARD COHEN. 171.

Sit Down And Talk To Me. w&m; Kenneth Gamble & Leon Huff. c1977, Mighty Three Music. LOU RAWLS. 24.

Sittin' On The Dock Of The Bay SEE Dock Of The Bay.

Sittin' On Top Of The World. w&m; Doc Watson. c1970, Hellgreen Music. DOC WATSON. 59.

Sitting. w&m; Cat Stevens. c1972, Freshwater Music Ltd./ Ackee Music, Inc. CAT STEVENS. 28, 30, 105.

Sitting On Top Of The World. w&m; Chester Burnett. c1958, Arc Music Corp. CREAM. 1.

Sixteen Candles. w&m; Luther Dixon & Allyson R. Khent. c1958, Coronation Music, Inc./January Corp. CRESTS. 5, 93.

Sixteen Tons. w&m; Merle Travis. c1947, Hill And Range Songs Inc., Elvis Presley Music, Gladys Music Noma Music Inc. TENNESSEE ERNIE FORD. 137.

Sky High w&m; Buddy Buie, Robert Nix, Dean Daughtry & Ronnie Hammond. c1976, 77, Low-Sal, Inc. ATLANTA RHYTHM SECTION. 142.

Skybird. w&m; Carole Bayer Sager & Bruce Roberts. c1974, 76, New York Times Music Corp. (Sunbeam Music Division & Dramatis Music Corp. TONY ORLANDO & DAWN. 103.

Skylark. w&m John Mercer (w) & Hoagy Carmichael (m). c1941, 42, 68, 69, George Simon, Inc. Twentieth Century Music Corp. & Frank Music Corp. BETTE MIDLER. 58.

Sleeping Single In A Double Bed. w&m; Dennis Morgan & Kye Fleming. c1978, Pi-Gem Music, Inc. BARBARA MANDRELL. 58.

Slicin' Sand. w&m; Sid Tepper & Roy C. Bennett. c1961, Gladys Music, Inc. ELVIS PRESLEY. 172.

Slip Slidin' Away. w&m; Paul Simon. c1977, Paul Simon. PAUL SIMON. 143, 146.

Slippin' And Slidin'. w&m; Richard Penniman, Edwin Bocage, Albert Collins & James Smith. c1956, 69, Venice Music & Bess Music, Inc. BILLY PRESTON/ BUDDY HOLLY/JOHN LENNON/JOHNNY WINTER/ LITTLE RICHARD. 35, 100, 109, 137, 159, 197.

Sloop John B.. w&m; Traditional. Brian Wilson (Adapted) & Lee Hays (Adapted). c1951, 66, versions published by Foldways Music Publishers, Inc. &New Executive Music. BEACH BOYS/KINGSTON TRI/WEAVERS. 3, 85.

Slow Dance. w&m; Bruce Sussmer (w), Jack Feldman (w) & Barry Manilow (m). c1979, Kamakazi Music Corp., Appoggiatura Music, Inc. & Camp Songs Music. BARRY MANILOW. 199.

Slow Dancin' SEE Swayin' To The Music.

Slow Dancin' Don't Turn Me On. w&m; Dick & Don Addrisi. c1977, Musicways, Inc. & Flying Addrisi Music. ADDRISI BROTHERS. 164, 196.

Slow Down. w&m; Larry Williams. c1957, 64, Venice Music, Inc. BEATLES/LARRY WILLIAMS/SHAUN CASSIDY. 35, 93, 125, 137, 159.

Slowly. w&m; David Raksin & Kermit Goell. c1945, Foundation Music Corp. Assigned to Planetary Music Publishing Corp. SARAH VAUGHAN. 161.

Slowly But Surely. w&m; Sid Wayne (w) & Ben Weismen (m). c1963, Gladys Music, Inc. ELVIS PRESLEY. 172.

Smilin'. w&m; Sylvester Stewart. c1971, 72, Stone Flower Music Co. SLY & THE FAMILY STONE. 152.

Smiling Faces Sometimes. w&m; Norman Whitfield & Barrett Strong. c1971, Jobete Music Co, Inc. UNDISPUTED TRUTH. 150.

Smoke Gets In Your Eyes. w&m; Otto Harback (w) & Jerome Kern (m). c1933, T. B. Harms Co. PLATTERS. 78, 101, 160.

Smoke On The Water. w&m; Ian Paice, Jon Lord, Ian Gillan, Ritchie Blackmore & Roger Glover. c1973, 73, B. Feldman & Co., Ltd., trading as Hec Music. DEEP PURPLE. 21, 89, 140, 163, 194, 198.

Smokestack Lightning. w&m; C. Burnett. c1956, 64, 70, Arc Music Corp. YARDBIRDS. 1, 10.

Smokey Joe's Cafe. w&m; Jerry Leiber & Mike Stoller. c1955, Quintet Music Inc. Controlled by Chappell & Co. COASTERS/ROBINS. 91, 155.

Smokie (Part I). w&m; Bill Black. c1959, Jec Publishing. BILL BLACK COMBO. 122.

Smokin' In The Boys Room. w&m; Michael Lutz & Cub Koda. c1973, Big Leaf Music. BROWNSVILLE STATION. 138.

Smorgasbord. w&m; Sid Tepper & Roy C. Bennett. c 1966, Gladys Music, Inc. ELVIS PRESLEY. 173.

Snowbird. w&m; Gene MacLellan. c1970, Beechwood Music of Canada/Beechwood Music Corp. ANNE MURRAY. 58, 63, 64, 72, 126, 128, 140, 191, 192, 194.

So Close. w&m; Jake Holmes. c1970, Out Of Business Publishing, Ltd. JAKE HOLMES. 63, 88.

So Close, Yet So Far (From Paradise). w&m; Joy Byers. c1965, Elvis Presley Music, Inc. ELVIS PRESLEY. 173.

So Far Away. w&m; Carole King. c1971, Col-Gems Music Corp. CAROLE KING. 183.

So Into You. w&m; Buddy Buie, Robert Nix & Dean Daughtry. c1976, 77, Low-Sal, Inc. ATLANTA RHYTHM SECTION. 23, 121, 142, 164.

So Long. w&m; Rick Roberts. c1977, 79, Warner-Tamerlane Publishing Corp. & El Sueno Music. Administered by Warner-Tamerlane Publishing Corp. FIREFALL. 201.

So Long, Frank Lloyd Wright. w&m; Paul Simon. c1969, Paul Simon. SIMON & GARFUNKEL. 143.

So Long It's Been Good To Know Yuh. w&m; Woody Guthrie. c1940, 50, 51, 68, 78, 79, Folkways Music Publishers, Inc. WOODY GUTHRIE. 68.

So Long, Marianne. w&m; Leonard Cohen. c1967, 69, Stranger Music, Inc. LEONARD COHEN. 171.

So Many Roads. w&m; Marshall Paul. c1960, Arc Music Corp. JOHN MAYALL. 1.

So, So Satisfied. w&m; Nickolas Ashford & Valerie Simpson. c1976, 77, Nick-O-Val Music. ASHFORD & SIMPSON. 13.

So This Is Love. w&m; Herbert New man. c1962, Pattern Music, Inc. CASTELLS. 3.

So You Win Again. w&m; Russ Ballard. c1976, 77, Island Music Ltd./Island Music. HOT CHOCLATE. 127.

Sodom And Gomorrah. w&m; H. Belolo (w), V. Willis (w), P. Whitehead (w) & J. Morali (m). c1978, Scorpio Music (Black Scorpio). Controlled by Can't Stop Music. VILLAGE PEOPLE. 200.

Soft Summer Breeze. w&m; Tim Hardin. c1971, Hudson Bay Music Co. TIM HARDIN. 93.

Softly, As I Leave You. w&m; Hal Shaper (w) & A. De Vita (m). c1960, 62, Edizioni Curci/Miller Music Corp. ELVIS PRESLEY/EYDIE GORME. 21, 193, 195, 199.

Solitaire. w&m; Neil Sedaka & Phil Cody. c1972, 75, Don Kirshner Music, Inc. & Don Kirshner Songs, Inc. CARPENTERS. 139.

Solitary Man. w&m; Neil Diamond. c1966, 70, Tallyrand Music, Inc. NEIL DIAMOND. 88.

Some Folk's Lives Roll Easy. w&m; Paul Simon. c1975, Paul Simon. PAUL SIMON. 143.

Some Kind Of Wonderful. w&m; John Ellison. c1967, Dandelion Music Co. FANTASTIC JOHNNY C/GRAND FUNK. 5, 52, 77, 156.

Some Things You Never Get Used To. w&m; Nickolas Ashford & Valerie Simpson. c1968, Jobete Music Co., Inc. DIANA ROSS & THE SUPREMES. 13.

Somebody Groovy. w&m; John Phillips. c1965, Trousdale Music Publishers, Inc. MAMAS & THE PAPAS. 119.

Somebody To Love. w&m; Darby Slick. c1966, Irving Music, Inc. & Copper Penny Music Publishing Co., Inc. JEFFERSON AIRPLANE. 59.

Somebody To Love. w&m; Freddie Mercury. c1976, EMI Music Publishing Ltd. & Queen Music Ltd./Beechwood Music Corp. QUEEN. 196.

Somebody Told A Lie. w&m; Nickolas Ashford & Valerie Simpson. c1975, 76, Nick-O-Val Music. ASHFORD & SIMPSON. 13.

Someday Never Comes. w&m; J. C. Fogerty. c1972, Primeval Ltd. CREEDENCE CLEARWATER REVIVAL. 63, 93.

Someday Soon. w&m; Ian Tyson. c1963, 69, M. Witmark & Sons & Warner Bros., Inc. CRYSTAL GAYLE/IAN & SYLVIA/JUDY COLLINS. 67.

Someday We'll Be Together. w&m; Jackey Beavers, Johnny Bristol & Harvey Fuqua. c1961, 69, 73, Jobete Music, Co., Inc. SUPREMES, 123, 150.

Someone Saved My Life Tonight. w&m; Elton John & Bernie Taupin. c1975, Big Pig Music Ltd./Jodrell Music Inc. ELTON JOHN. 136.

Someone That I Used To Love. w&m; Gerry Goffin (w) & Michael Masser (m). c1978, 80, Screen Gems-EMI Music Inc., Princestreet Music & Arista Music, Inc. NATALIE COLE. 58.

Someone To Lay Down Beside Me. w&m; Karla Bonoff. c1976, Sky Harbor Music. KARLA BONOFF/LINDA RONSTADT. 12, 73, 87, 135, 141, 146.

Someone To Watch Over Me. w&m; Ira Gershwin (w) & George Gershwin (m). c1926, New World Music Corp. WILLIE NELSON. 31, 87.

Something. w&m; George Harrison. c1969, Harrisongs Ltd./Harrisongs Music, Inc. BEATLES/GEORGE HARRISON/TONY BENNETT. 63, 86, 88, 93, 125, 183.

Something About You. w&m; Eddie Holland, Lamont Dozier & Brian Holland. c1965, Jobete Music Co., Inc. FOUR TOPS. 150.

Something Better Change. w&m; Hugh Cornwell, Dave Greenfield, Jean Jacques-Burnel & Jet Black. c1978, Albion Music. Adminsitered by Irving Music, Inc. STRANGLERS. 153.

Something He Can Feel. w&m; Curtis Mayfield. c1975, 76, Warner-Tamerlane Publishing Corp. ARETHA FRANKLIN. 141.

Something So Right. w&m; Paul Simon. c1973, Paul Simon. PAUL SIMON. 143.

Something There Is About You. w&m; Bob Dylan. c1973, 76, Ram's Horn Music. BOB DYLAN. 170.

Something You Got. w&m; Chris Kenner. c1961, 65, Thursday Music Corp. CHUCK JACKSON & MAXINE BROWN. 5.

Something's Got A Hold On Me. w&m; Pearl Woods, Leroy Kirkland & Etta James. c1962, Figure Music, Inc. & Big Seven Music Corp. ETTA JAMES. 137, 155, 161.

Somethin's Happening SEE Baby Somethin's Happening.

Spanish Harlem. w&m; Jerry Leiber & Phil Spector. c1960, 61, Progressive Music Publishing Co., Inc., Hill & Range Songs, Inc. & Trio Music Co., Inc. Controlled by Unichappell Music, Inc. ARETHA FRANKLIN/BEN E. KING. 21, 72, 92, 102, 137, 140, 154, 155, 192.

Sparrow. w&m; Paul Simon. c1964, 66, Duchess Music Corp. SIMON & GARFUNKEL. 143.

Speak Softly Love. w&m; Larry Kusik (w) & Nino Rota (m). c1972, Famous Music Corp. JOHNNY MATHIS. 131.

Special Lady. w&m; H. Ray, A. Goodman & L. Walter. c1979, Dark Cloud Music Inc. & H.A.B. Publishing, Inc. RAY, GOODMAN & BROWN. 177, 198.

Speedo. w&m; Esther Navarro. c1955, 78, Adam R. Levy & Father Enterprises Inc. CADILLACS. 2.

Speedy Gonzales. w&m; Buddy Kaye, David Hill & Ethel Lee. c1961, 62, Budd Music Corp. PAT BOONE. 6.

Spicks And Specks. w&m; Barry Gibb. c1967, 78, Belinda Music, Pty., Ltd/Unichappell Music Inc. BEE GEES. 15, 199.

Spiders And Snakes. w&m; Jim Stafford & David Bellamy. c1973, 74, Kaiser Music, Inc. & Boo Music. JIM STAFFORD. 93.

Spill The Wine. w&m; Howard Scott, Morris Dickerson, Harold R. Brown, Charles W. Miller, Leroy "Lonnie" Jordan, Sylvester Allen & Lee Oskar. c1970, Far Out Music. ERIC BURDEN & WAR. 37, 191.

Spinning Wheel. w&m; David C. Thomas. c1968, 69, Blackwood Music Inc. & Minnesingers Publishers Ltd. BLOOD SWEAT & TEARS. 21, 72, 86, 89, 93, 140, 161, 191, 192, 193, 194, 195, 199.

Spinout. w&m; Sid Wayne, Ben Weisman & Darrell Fuller. c1966, Gladys Music Inc. ELVIS PRESLEY. 173.

Spirits (Having Flown). w&m; Barry, Robin & Maurice Gibb. c1968, 79, Brothers Gibb B.V./Stigwood Music, Inc. Administered by Unichappell Music Inc. BEE GEES. 47.

Splish Splash. w&m; Bobby Darin & Jean Murray. c1958, Travis Music Co. & Unart Music Corp. BARBRA STREISAND/BOBBY DARIN/FRANKIE AVALON/LOGGINS & MESSINA. 2, 78, 81, 101, 137, 161, 199.

Spooky. w&m; Harry Middlebrooks, Mike Shapiro, Buddy Buie, & J. R. Cobb. c1965, 67, Lowery Music Co., Inc. ATLANT RHYTHM SECTION/DENNIS YOST & THE CLASSICS IV. 11, 64, 179.

Spoonful. w&m; Willie Dixon. c1960, 70, Arc Music Corp. CREAM/ERIC CLAPTON/SCREAMING MOTHERS. 1, 152, 197.

Spring Affair. w&m; Donna Summer, Giorgio Moroder & Peter Bellotte. c1976, 77, Ricks Music, Inc. & Sunday Music. DONNA SUMMER. 58.

Spring Is Here. w&m; Lorenz Hart (w) & Richard Rodgers (m). c1938, 66, Robbins Music Corp. JOHN COLTRANE/SHIRLEY BASSEY/TONY BENNETT. 140.

Springtime Mama. w&m; Henry Gross. c1975, 76, Blendingwell Music, Inc. HENRY GROSS. 184, 193, 199.

Spy. w&m; Jim Morrison. c1970, Doors Music Co. DOORS. 54.

Squeeze Box. w&m; Pete Townshend. c1975, Eel Pie Publishing Ltd./Towser Tunes Inc. WHO. 30, 36.

St. Judy's Comet. w&m; Paul Simon. c1973, Paul Simon. PAUL SIMON. 143.

Stagger Lee. w&m; Harold Logan & Lloyd Price. c1958, 59, Travis Music Co., Inc. & Unart Music Corp. DION/GRATEFUL DEAD/LLOYD PRICE/NEIL DIAMOND/WILSON PICKETT. 78, 82, 101, 137, 155, 161, 192.

Stairway To Heaven. w&m; Jimmy Page & Robert Plant. c1972, Superhype Publishing. LED ZEPPELIN. 22, 36, 55, 87, 114, 124, 136, 152, 174, 175, 185.

Stairway To The Stars. w&m; Mitchell Parish (w), Matt Malneck (m) & Frank Signorelli (m). c1935, 39, 63, 65, 67, Robbins Music Corp. BOSTON POPS/FERRANTE & TEICHER/JOHN COLTRANE/NATALIE COLE. 140.

Stand. w&m; Sylvester Stewart. c1969, Daly City Music. SLY & THE FAMILY STONE. 115, 202.

Stand By Me. w&m; Ben E. King, Jerry Lieber & Mike Stoller. c1961, Hill And Range Songs, Inc. & Trio Music Co., Inc. Assigned to Unichappell Music Inc. BEN E. KING. 102, 109, 137.

Stand By Your Man. w&m; Tammy Wynette & Billy Sherrill. c1968, Al Gallico Music Corp. TAMMY WYNETTE. 63.

Stand Tall. w&m; Burton Cummings. c1976, Shillelagh Music Co. BURTON CUMMINGS. 121, 128, 142, 164.

Standing At The Threshold. w&m; Arlo Guthrie. c1968, 69, Appleseed Music Inc. ARLO GUTHRIE. 7.

Standing In The Shadows Of Love. w&m; Eddie Holland, Lamont Dozier & Brian Holland. c1966, Jobete Music Co., Inc. DEBORAH WASHINGTON/FOUR TOPS. 112, 123, 150.

Standing Ovation. w&m; Emmanuel Rahiem Le Blanc, Herb Lane, Keith Crier & Paul Service. c1980, Arista Music Inc., Careers Music, Inc. & Emmanuel Rahiem Le Blanc, Herb Lane, Keith Crier & Paul Service. G.Q. 24.

Star. w&m; Maurice White. Eddie Del Barrio & Allee Willis. c1979, Saggifire Music, Ninth Music, Irving Music, Inc. & Criga Music. EARTH, WIND & FIRE. 24.

Star On A T.V. Show. w&m; Hugo & Luigi & George David Weiss. c1974, Avco Embassy Music Publishing, Inc. STYLISTICS. 89.

Star Teck, Theme From. w&m; Gene Roddenberry (w) & Alexander Courage (m). c1966, 70, Bruin Music Co. DEODATO/MAYNARD FERGUSON. 103.

Star Wars. w&m; John Williams (m). c1977, Fox Fanfare Music, Inc. DON ELLIS & SURVIVAL/JOHN WILLIAMS/LONDON SYMPHONY ORHESTRA/MECO. 23, 34, 56, 71, 128, 135, 142.

Starcruiser. w&m; Gregg Diamond. c1978, Diamond

Touch Publishing, Ltd. & Arista Music Inc. GREGG DIAMOND. 34, 66, 112.

Stargazer. w&m; Peter Brown. c1979, 80, Sherlyn Publishing Co., Inc. Decibel Publishing Co. & Penguin Publishing Co. PETER BROWN. 98.

Starry, Starry Night. SEE Vincent.

Starsky & Hutch Theme. w&m; Thomas W. Scott. c1976, 77, Spellgold Music. TOM SCOTT. 128.

Started Out Dancing, Ended Up Making Love. w&m; Alan O'Day. c1977, WB Music Corp. ALAN O'DAY. 30.

Starting Today. w&m; Don Robertson. c1961, Gladys Music, Inc. ELIVS PRESLEY. 172.

Stay. w&m; Chaka Khan & Richard Calhoun. c1978, American Broadcasting Music, Inc. & High Seas Music. RUFUS FEATURING CHAKA KHAN. 135.

Stay. w&m; Maurice Williams. c1960, Cherio Music Publishers, Inc. MAURICE WILLIAMS. 4.

Stay Awhile. w&m; Ken Tobias. c1970, 71, CoBurt Music Publishing Co., Inc. DUSTY SPRINGFIELD. 64.

Stay Close To Me. w&m; Buddy Holly. c1958, MPL Communications, Inc. BUDDY HOLLY. 14.

Stay With Me. w&m; Ronald David Wood & Rod Stewart. c1971, 72, WB Music Corp. ROD STEWART & FACES. 115, 138.

Stayin' Alive. w&m; Barry, Robin & Maurice Gibb. c1977, Brothers Gibb B.V./Stigwood Music, Inc. Administered by Unichappell Music Inc. BEE GEES. 50, 133, 178, 201.

Stealin'. w&m; (Arranged & adapted) Gus Cannon & Arlo Guthrie. c1969, Howard Beach Music Inc. ARLO GUTHRIE. 7.

Steamboat. w&m; Buddy Lucas. c1955, Progressive Music Publishing Co., Inc. DRIFTERS. 90, 154.

Steel Rail Blues. w&m; Gordon Lightfoot. c1966, M. Witmark & Sons. GORDON LIGHTFOOT. 132.

Stella Blue. w&m; Robert Hunter (w) & Jerome Garcia (m). c1973, 76, Ice Nine Publishing Co., Inc. GRATE-FUL DEAD. 84.

Steppin' Out. w&m; James Bracken. c1959, 70, Conrad Music. JOHN MAYALL. I.

Steppin' Out. w&m;Neil Sedaka & Phil Cody. c1976, Neil Sedaka Music & Lebasongs. NEIL SEDAKA. 141.

Steppin' Out, I'm Gonna Boogie Tonight. w&m; Irwin Levine & L. Russel Brown. c1973, Levine And Brown Music Inc. TONY ORLANDO & DAWN. 93.

Steppin' Out Of line. w&m; Ben Weisman, Fred Wise & Dee Fuller. c1962, Gladys Music, Inc. ELVIS PRESLEY. 173.

Still. w&m; Lionel RIchie. c1979, Jobete Music Co., Inc. & Commodores Entertainment Publishing Corp. COMMODORES. 23, 24, 56, 97, 179, 180.

Still Crazy After All These Years. w&m; Paul Simon. c1974, Paul Simon. PAUL SIMON. 143, 146.

Still The Lovin' Is Fun. w&m; Chris Christian. c1977, Home Sweet Home Music. B. J. THOMAS. 128, 142.

Still The Same. w&m; Bob Seger. c1977, 78, Gear Publishing Co. BOB SEGER & THE SILVER BULLET BAND. 22, 57, 146.

Still Waters Run Deep. w&m; Bob Perper, Paul Gasper & Jack Aranda. c1962, Ambassador Music Ltd. BROOK BENTON. 137.

Sting, Theme From SEE Entertainer S. Joplin).

Stir It Up. w&m; Bob Marley. c1972, Cayman Music Ltd. JOHNNY NASH. 72, III.

Stir It Up And Servie it. w&m; T. Roe & F. Weller. c1968, 69, Low-Twi Music, Inc. & Lowery Music Co., Inc. TOMMY ROE. 161.

Stomp. w&m; Louis, George & Valerie Johnson & Rod Temperton. c1980, Bodsong, State Of The Arts Music. JOHNSON BROTHERS. 24.

Stone To The Bone. w&m; James Brown. c1973, 74, Dynatone Publishing Co. JAMES BROWN. 107.

Stoned Love. w&m; Yennik Samoht & Frank Wilson. c1970, Jobete Music Co., Inc. SUPREMES. 123.

Stoned Soul Picnic. w&m; Laura Nyro. c1967, 68, Tuna Fish Music, Inc. FIFTH DIMENSION. 15, 35, 60, 64, 136.

Stoney End. w&m; Laura Nyro. c1966, 68, Tuna Fish Music, Inc. BARBRA STREISAND/LAURA NYRO. 35, 115, 136.

Stop And Smell The Roses. w&m; Mac Davis & Doc Severinsen. c1974, Screen-Gems-Columbia Music, Inc., Colgems Music Corp. & Songpainter Music. Controlled by Screen-Gems-Columbia Music, Inc. & Colgems Music Corp. MAC DAVIS. 28, 106,134, 156.

Stop! In The Name Of Love. w&m; Brian Holland, Lamont Dozier & Eddie Holland. c1965, Jobete Music Inc. SUPREMES. 123.

Stop, Look, Listen. w&m; Joy Byers. c1964, Elvis Presley Music, Inc. ELVIS PRESLEY. 173.

Stories Of The Street. w&m; Leonard Cohen. c1967, 69, Stranger Music, Inc. LEONARD COHEN. 171.

Stormy. w&m; Buddy Buie & J.R. Cobb. c1968, 79, Low-Sal Music, Inc. DENNIS YOST & THE CLASSICS IV/SANTANA. 64, 65, 73, 157.

Story Of Isaac. w&m; Leonard Cohen. c1967, 69, Stranger Music, Inc. LEONARD COHEN. 171.

Straight Shooter. w&m; John Phillips. c1966, Trousdale Music Publishers, Inc. MAMAS & THE PAPAS. 119.

Stranded. w&m; Ed Kuepper & Chris Baily. c1976, Saints Music-Sinners Music Publishers, Inc. MAMAS & THE PAPAS. 119.

Stranded In A Limousine. w&m; Paul Simon. c1977, Paul Simon. PAUL SIMON. 143, 147.

Strange Magic. w&m; Jeff Lynne. c1975, 76, Unart Music Corp. & Jet Music Inc. ELECTRIC LIGHT ORCHESTRA. 193, 198.

Strange Way. w&m; Rick Roberts. c1978, Warner-Tamerlane Publishing Corp., El Sueno Music & Stephen Stills Music. Administered by Warner-Tamerlane Publishing Corp. on behalf of El Sueno Music. FIREFALL. 27, 146.

Stranger Song. w&m; Leonard Cohen. c1966, Project Seven Music. LEONARD COHEN. 171.

Strawberry Fields Forever. w&m; John Lennon & Paul McCartney. c1967, Northern Songs Ltd./Maclen Music, Inc. BEATLES. 43, 55, 61, 146, 197.

Street Fighting Man. w&m; Mick Jagger & Keith Richard. c1968, Abkco Music, Inc. ROLLING STONES. 142.

Street Life. w&m; Will Jennings (w) & Joe Sample (m). c1979, Irving Music, Inc. & Four Knights Music Co. CRUSADERS/HERB ALPERT. 24, 56.

Street Singin'. w&m; Barry Manilow & Adrienne Anderson. c1976, Kamakazi Music Corp. & Angeldust Music Co. LADY FLASH. 184.

Stroll. w&m; Clyde Otis & Nancy Lee. c1957, Meridian Music Corp. Assigned to Vogue Music Inc. DIAMONDS. 160.

Stubborn Kind Of Fellow. w&m; William Stevenson, Marvin Gaye & George Gordy. c1962, 68, Jobete Music Co., Inc. MARVIN GAYE. 167.

Stuck In The Middle With You. w&m; Joe Egan & Gerry Rafferty. c1973, Baby Bun Music Ltd. & Ricochet Music, Ltd./Hudson Bay Music Co. STEALERS WHEEL. 32.

Stuck Inside Of Mobile With The Memphis Blues Again. w&m; Bob Dylan. c1966, 76, Dwarf Music. BOB DYLAN. 170.

Stuff Like That. w&m; Quincy Jones, Valerie Simpson, Nickolas Ashford, Eric Gale, Steve Gadd, Richard Tee & Ralph McDonald. c1978, Yellow Brick Road Music Co., & Nick-O-Val Music. QUINCY JONES. 24, 34, 135.

Stumblin' In. w&m; Nicky Chinn & Mike Chapman. c1979, Chinnichap Publishing, Inc. Administered by Careers Music, Inc. SUZI QUATRO & CHRIS NORMAN. 27, 31, 57, 162.

Substitute. w&m; Willia Harry Wilson. c1978, Touch of Gold Music, Inc. CLOUT. 74.

Subterranean Homesick Blues. w&m; Bob Dylan. c1965, M. Witmark & Sons & Warner Bros., Inc. BOB DYLAN. 35, 132.

Such A Woman. w&m; Mark Krieder & Norman Mershon. c1979, Morning Dew Music. TYCOON. 11.

Such An Easy Question SEE Easy Question.

Sugar Daddy. w&m; Corporation. c1971, 72, Jobete Music Co., Inc. JACKSON 5. 20.

Sugar Magnolia. w&m; Bob Weir & Robert Hunter (w). c1970, 73, Ice Nine Publishing Co. GRATEFUL DEAD. 83.

Sugar On The Floor. w&m; Kiki Dee. c1973, Rocket Music Ltd./Yellow Dog Music, Inc. ELTON JOHN. 103.

Sugar Pie, Honey Bunch SEE I Can't Help Myself.

Sugar Shack. w&m; Keith McCormack & Faye Voss. c1962, Dundee Music. JIMMY GILMER & THE FIREBALLS. 4.

Sugar, Sugar. w&m; Jeff Barry & Andy Kim. c1969, Don Kirshner Music Inc. ARCHIES. 138.

Suicide Is Painless SEE M*A*S*H, Song From.

Suite: Judy Blue Eyes. w&m; Stephen Stills. c1969, 70, Gold Hill Music Inc. CROSBY, STILLS & NASH/ CROSBY, STILLS, NASH & YOUNG. 55, 136, 197, 202.

Sultans Of Swing. w&m; Mark Knopfler. c1978, 79, Straitjacket Songs Ltd. & Rondor Music Ltd./ Almo Music Corp. DIRE STRAITS. 11, 96, 129, 180, 181.

Summer. w&m; Bobby Goldsboro. c1973, Unart Music Corp. & Pen In Hand Music, Inc. Administered by Unart Music Corp. BOBBY GOLDSBORO/MILLIE JACKSON. 80.

Summer Breeze. w&m; James Seals & Dash Crofts (m). c1971, 72, Dawnbreaker Music Co. & ABC-Dunhill Music, Inc. ISLEY BROTHERS/SEALS & CROFTS. 36, 62, 117, 131, 136, 138, 151, 174, 197.

Summer In The City. w&m; John B. Sebastian, Steve Boone & Mark Sebastian. c1966, 67, Hudson Bay Music Co. JOHN SEBASTIAN. 93.

Summer Knows. w&m; Marilyn & Alan Bergman (w) & Michel Legrand (m). c1971, WB Music Corp. ANDY WILLIAMS/PETER NERO. 62, 138.

Summer Love Sensation. w&m; Bill Martin & Phil Coulter Music Ltd. Controlled by Martin-Boulter Music, Inc. & Al Gallico Music Corp. BOBBY VINTON. 135.

Summer Me, Winter Me. w&m; Marilyn & Alan Bergman (w) & Michel Legrand (m). c1969, WB Music Corp. SARAH VAUGHAN. 139.

Summer Of '42 SEE ALSO Summer Knows.

Summer Of '42 (Disco Version). w&m; Michel Legrand (m). c1971, 75, WB Music Corp. BIDDU ORCHESTRA. 30.

Summer Place, Theme From. w&m; Mack Discant (w) & Max Steiner (m). c1959, 60, M. Witmark & Sons. LETTERMEN. 43.

Summer Place '76. w&m; Max Steiner (m). c1959, 75, Warner Bros., Inc. PERCY FAITH. 30.

Summer Side Of Life. w&m; Gordon Lightfoot. c1970, 71, Early Morning Music. GORDON LIGHTFOOT. 151.

Summer Wind. w&m; Johnny Mercer (w) & Henry Mayer (m). c1965, Edition Primus Rolf Budde KG/M. Witmark & Sons. FRANK SINATRA. 43.

Summertime. w&m; Du Bose Heyward (w) & George Gershwin (m). c1935, Gershwin Publishing Corp. & New Dawn Music Corp. JANIS JOPLIN. 110.

Summertime Blues. w&m; Eddie Cochran & Jerry Capehart. c1958, Viva Music, Inc. , Hill & Range Songs, Inc., Elvis Presley Music, Inc. & Gladys Music Inc. Administered by Viva Music, Inc. BLUE CHEER/WHO. 76, 100, 152, 191.

Summertime Dream. w&m; Gordon Lightfoot. c1976, Moose Music Ltd. GORDON LIGHTFOOT. 141.

Summertime, Summertime. w&m; Tom Jameson & Sherm Feller. c1958, Templeton Publishing Co., Inc. JAMIES. 3.

Sun Is Shining. w&m; Elmore James. c1960, Arc Music Corp. ELMOREJAMES. 1.

TITLE INDEX

Sunday Girl. w&m; Chris Stein. c1978, Rare Blue Music Inc. & Monster Island Music. BLONDIE. 33.

Sunday Mornin' Comin' Down. w&m; Kris Kristofferson. c1969, Combine Music Corp. KRIS KRISTOFFERSON. 15, 88, 89, 199.

Sundown. w&m; Gordon Lightfoot. c1973, 74, Moose Music Ltd. BROTHERS FOUR/GORDON LIGHTFOOT. 30, 36, 43, 62, 117, 133, 136, 138.

Sunflower. w&m; Neil Diamond. c1976, 77, Stonebridge Music. GLEN CAMPBELL. 127.

Sunny. w&m; Bobby Hebb. c1965, 66, Portable Music Co., Inc. BOBBY HEBB. 21, 102, 140, 161, 163, 191, 193, 195.

Sunny And Me. w&m; Wes Farrell & Tony Romeo. c1968, Pocket Full Of Tunes Inc. & Pamco Music, Inc. D. GOOD & G. PLENTY. 76.

Sun's Gonna Shine Again. w&m; Sam Sweet. c1953, Progressive Music Publishing Co., Inc. RAY CHARLES. 90.

Sunrise. w&m; Eric Carmen. c1975, 76, C.A.M.-U.S.A., Inc. ERIC CARMEN. 141.

Sunrise, Sunset. w&m; Sheldon Harnick (w) & Jerry Bock (m). c1964, The Times Square Music Publications Co. CAST OF FIDDLER ON THE ROOF/LOUIS ARMSTRONG. 56, 179.

Sunshine (Go Away Today). w&m; Jonathan Edwards. c1971, Castle Hill Publishing Ltd. JONATHAN EDWARDS. 37, 72, 140, 195.

Sunshine Of My World. w&m; Dallas Frazier. c1968, Blue Crest Music Inc. DALLAS FRAZIER. 76.

Sunshine Of Your Love. w&m; Jack Bruce, Peter Brown & Eric Clapton. c1968, Dratleaf Ltd. Controlled by Casserole Music, Inc. Administered by Unichappell Music, Inc. CHALLENGERS/CREAM/ERIC CLAPTON. 141, 152, 175, 182, 197.

Sunshine On My Shoulders. w&m; John Denver, Mike Taylor (m) & Dick Kniss (m). c1971, Cherry Lane Music, Co. BROTHERS FOUR/JOHN DENVER. 131, 135.

Sunshine Superman. w&m; Donovan. c1966, Donovan Ltd./Peer International Corp. DONOVAN. 3.

Super Strut. w&m; Eumir Deodato. c1973, 74, Kenya Musuc. DEODATO. 156.

Superfly. w&m; Curtis Mayfield. c1972, Warner-Tamerlane Publishing CO. CURTIS MAYFIELD. 138.

Superman. w&m; Richie Snyder. c1976, 77, Brial Music Co., Emanuel Music Corp. & Magusta Music. BARBRA STREISAND. 15, 176.

Superman, Love Theme From SEE Can You Read My Mind.

Superstar. w&m; Leon Russell & Bonnie Bramlett. c1970, 71, Skyhill Publishing Co., Inc., Teddy Jack Music & Delbon Music. BETTE MIDLER/CARPENTERS/JOE COCKER/LEON RUSSELL/MAC DAVIS. 28, 115, 131, 134, 138, 142, 156.

Superstar. w&m; Tim Rice (w) & Andrew Lloyd Webber (w). c1969, Leeds Music Ltd./Leeds Music Corp. CAST OF JESUS CHRIST SUPERSTAR. 131.

Superstition. w&m; Stevie Wonder. c1972, Jobete Music Co., Inc. & Black Bull Music, Inc. STEVIE WONDER. 26, 29, 77, 106, 134, 142, 150.

Sure Gonna Miss Her. w&m; Leon Russell. c1965, Viva Music, Inc. & Tennessee Music, Inc. GARY LEWIS & THE PLAYBOYS. 100.

Surf City. w&m; Brian Wilson & Jan Berry. c1963, Screen Gems-Columbia Music Inc. JAN & DEAN. 156.

Surfer Girl. w&m; Brian Wilson. c1962, Guild Music Co. BEACH BOYS. 4, 64.

Surfin. w&m; Brian Wilson & Mike Love. c1961, 62, Guild Music Co. BEACH BOYS. 4

Surfin' Safari. w&m; Brian Wilson & Mike Love. c1962, Guild Music Co. BEACH BOYS. 4.

Surfin' U.S.A.. w&m; Brian Wilson (w) & Chuck Berry (m). c1958, 63, Arc Music Corp. BEACH BOYS. 168.

Surrender. w&m; Doc Pomus (w), Mort Shuman (w) & E. De Curtis (m). c1960, Elvis Presley Music, Inc. ELVIS PRESLEY. 172.

Surrender. w&m; Nickolas Ashford & Valerie Simpson. c1971, Jobete Music CO., Inc. DIANA ROSS. 13.

Surrender. w&m; Rick Nielsen. c1976, Screen Gems-EMI Music Inc. & Adult Music. CHEAP TRICK. 135.

Surrender To Me. w&m; Rick Vito. c1978, Richard F. Vito, doing business as Fat Frog Music. MC GUINN, CLARK & HILLMAN. 11.

Susie Darlin'. w&m; Robin Luke. c1958, Congressional Music Publicaitons. ROBIN LUKE. 3.

Susie-Q. w&m; Dale Hawkins, Stanley J. Lewis & Eleanor Broadwater. c1957, 70, Arc Music Corp. CHET ATKINS/CREEDENCE CLEARWATER REVIVAL/DALE HAWKINS/JOSE FELICIANO/ROLLING STONES. 1, 5, 44, 78, 100, 168, 169, 197.

Suspicion. w&m; Doc Pomus & Mort Shuman. c1962, Elvis Presley Music, Inc. ELVIS PRESLEY/TERRY STAFFORD. 173.

Suspicions. w&m; Eddie Rabbitt, Randy McCormick, David Malloy & Even Stevens. c1979, DebDave Music, Inc. & Briarpatch Music. EDDIE RABBITT. 75, 187.

Suspicious Minds. w&m; Mark James. c1968, 69, 70, 71, Press Music Co. & Screen Gems-EMI Music Inc. ELVIS PRESLEY/THELMA HOUSTON/WAYLON JENNINGS & JESSIE COLTER. 77, 130, 149, 161, 182.

Suzanne. w&m; Leonard Cohen. c1966, Project Seven Music. JUDY COLLINS/LEONARD COHEN. 68, 171.

Swallow My Pride. w&m; Joey, Dee Dee, Tommy & Johnny Ramone. c1977, 78, Bleu Disque Music Co. & Taco Tunes. RAMONES. 19.

S.W.A.T., Theme From. w&m; Barry De Vorzon. c1975, Spelling-Goldberg Productions. RHYTHM HERITAGE. 26, 128.

Swayin' To The Music. w&m; Jack Tempchin. c1975, 76, WB Music Corp. FUNKY KINGS/JOHNNY RIVERS. 30, 127, 141.

Sweet And Innocent. w&m; Billy Sherrill & Rich Hall. c1958, 71, Tree Publishing Co. DONNY OSMOND. 38, 64.

97

Sweet Baby James. w&m; James Taylor. c1970, Blackwood Music Inc. & Country Road Music Inc. Administered by Blackwood Music Inc. JAMES TAYLOR. 131.

Sweet Blindness. w&m; Laura Nyro. c1967, Tuna Fish Music, Inc. Administered by Blackwood Music Inc. FIFTH DIMENSION. 15.

Sweet Caroline. w&m; Neil Diamond. c1969, 74, Stonebridge Music. NEIL DIAMOND. 55, 136, 145, 174.

Sweet City Song. w&m; Terry Cashman & T.P. West. c1972, Blendingwell Music Inc. CASHMAN & WEST. 72.

Sweet Emotion. w&m; Steven Tyler & Tom Hamilton. c1975, Daksel Music Corp. AEROSMITH. 139.

Sweet Georgia Brown. w&m; Ben Bernie, Marco Pinkard & Kenneth Casey. c1962, Jerome H. Remick & Co. DOC WATSON. 132.

Sweet Green Fields. w&m; James Seals. c1967, 4-Star Music Co., Inc. SEALS & CROFTS. 199.

Sweet Hitch-Hiker. w&m; J. C. Fogerty. c1971, Primeval Ltd. CREEDENCE CLEARWATER REVIVAL. 93.

Sweet Inspiration. w&m; Dan Penn & Spooner Oldham. c1967, Press Music Co. SWEET INSPIRATIONS. 76.

Sweet Life. w&m; Paul Davis & Susan Collins. c1977, 78, Chappell & Co., Inc. Tanta Music & Webb IV Music, Inc. PAUL DAVIS. 40.

Sweet Little Sixteen. w&m; Chuck Berry. c1958, Arc Music Corp. CHUCK BERRY/JERRY LEE LEWIS/ JIMMY & JESSE/JOHN LENNON. 2, 10, 44, 78, 101, 109, 155, 169, 197.

Sweet Love. w&m; Lionel Richie. c1975, Jobete Music, Inc. & Commodores Music Corp. COMMODORES. 26.

Sweet Marjorene. w&m; Arnold Capitanelli & Robert O'Connor. c1975, Silver Blue Music & Arnold Jay Music ENGLEBERT HUMPERDINCK. 135.

Sweet Painted Lady. w&m; Elton John & Bernie Taupin. c1973, Dick James Music Ltd./Dick James Music Inc. ELTON JOHN. 127.

Sweet Seasons. w&m; Carole King & Toni Stern. c1971, Screen Gems-Columbia Music, Inc. CAROLE KING. 183.

Sweet Talkin' Guy. w&m; Doug Morris, Elliott Greenberg, Barbara Baer & Robert Schwartz. c1966, Elmwin Music Inc. & Roznique Music, Inc. Rights for Roznique assigned to Robert Mellin Music Publishing Corp. CHIFFONS. 4.

Sweet Talkin' Woman. w&m; Jeff Lynne. c1977, 79, United Artists Music Ltd. & Jet Music. Administered by Unart Music Corp. ELECTRIC LIGHT ORCHESTRA. 21, 199.

Sweetest Pain. w&m; Dexter Wansel & Cynthia Biggs. c1979, Mighty Three Music. DEXTER WANSEL. 24.

Sweetheart. w&m; Barry & Maurice Gibb. c1969, 70, Abigail Music Ltd./Casserole Music, Inc. ENGLEBERT HUMPERDINCK. 182.

Sweets For My Sweet. w&m; Doc Pomus & Mort Shuman. c1961, Brenner Music, Inc., Progressive Music Publishing Co., Inc. & Trio Music, Inc. Controlled by

Unichappell Music, Inc. & Trio Music Co., Inc. DRIFTERS/TONY ORLANDO. 176.

Swing Your Daddy. w&m; Kenny Nolan. c1974, 75, Kenny Nolan Publishing Co. & Hearts Delight Music Co. JIM GILSTRAP. 49.

Swingin' Shepherd Blues. w&m; Rhoda Roberts (w), Kenny Jacobsen (w) & Moe Koffman (m). c1958, 62, Nom Music, Inc. MOE KOFFMAN & HIS ORCHESTRA. 161, 191.

System Of Doctor Tarr & Professor Fether SEE Doctor Tarr & Professor Fether.

Take A Chance On Me. w&m; Benny Andersson & Bjorn Ulvaeus. c1977, 78, Union Songs AB/Artwork Music Co., Inc. ABBA. 135, 147, 199.

Take Care Of Your Homework. w&m; Homer Banks, Don Davis, Raymond Jackson & Tom Kelly. c1969, East-Memphis Music. JOHNNIE TAYLOR. 122.

Take Good Care Of My Baby. w&m; Gerry Goffin & Carole King. c1961, Screen Gems-Columbia Music Inc. BOBBY VEE. 156.

Take It Easy. w&m; Jackson Browne & Glenn Frey. c1972, 76, WB Music Corp. & Red Cloud Music. EAGLES/JACKSON BROWNE. 36, 55, 57, 124, 127, 138, 145, 174, 185.

Take It Like A Woman. w&m; Norman Sallitt. c1978, Al Gallico Music Corp. & Turtle Music. MARY WELCH. 65.

Take It To The Limit. w&m; Randy Meisner, Don Henley & Glenn Frey. c1975, Cass County Music, Red Cloud Music, Nebraska Music & WB Music Corp. EAGLES. 30, 87, 124, 136, 146.

Take Life A Little Easier. w&m; John Annarino (w) & Sid Woloshin (m). c1973, Senor Music & G.&W. Publishing Co. RODNEY ALLEN RIPPY. 63.

Take Me Home. w&m; Michele Aller & Bob Esty. c1978, Rick's Music, Inc. CHER/STANLEY TURRENTINE. 25, 96, 129, 198.

Take Me Home, Country Roads. w&m; Bill Danoff, Taffy Nivert & John Denver. c1971, Cherry Lane Music. JOHN DENVER. 15, 21, 64, 72, 93, 131, 135, 136, 151, 156, 192, 197, 199.

Take Me I'm Yours. w&m; Michael Henderson. c1978, Electrochord Publishing Co. MICHAEL HENDERSON. 74.

Take Me To The Mardi Gras. w&m; Paul Simon. c1973, Paul Simon. PAUL SIMON. 143.

Take Me To The Pilot. w&m; Elton John & Bernie Taupin. c1969, Dick James Music Ltd./Dick James Music, Inc. ELTON JOHN. 197.

Take Me To The River. w&m; Al Green & Mabon Hodges. c1974, 78, Jec Publishing & Al Green Music, Inc. Controlled by Jec Publishing. TALKING HEADS. 65, 73, 157.

Take That To The Bank. w&m; Leon F. Sylvers III & Kevin Spencer. c1978, Rosy Publishing, Inc. SHALIMAR. 25, 129.

Take The Long Way Home. w&m; Roger Hodgson &

Rick Davies. c1979, Almo Music Corp. & Delicate Music. Administered by Alamo Music Corp. SUPER-TRAMP. 56, 97, 180.

Take The Money And Run. w&m; Steve Miller. c1976, Sailor Music. STEVE MILLER BAND. 146.

Take Time To Know Her. w&m; Steve Davis. c1968, Al Gallico Music Corp. PERCY SLEDGE. 76.

Take Your Time. w&m; Norman Petty & Buddy Holly. c1958, MPL Communications, Inc. BUDDY HOLLY. 14.

Takin' Care Of Business. w&m; Randy C. Bachman. c1973, Ranbach Music, a division of R.C.B. Ltd./ Screen Gems-EMI Music, Inc. BACHMAN-TURNER OVERDRIVE. 12, 29, 77, 106, 134, 142, 156.

Takin' It To The Streets. w&m; Michael McDonald. c1978, Tauripin Tunes. DOOBIE BROTHERS. 22, 136, 146.

Taking A Chance On Love. w&m; John Latouche (w), Ted Fetter (w) & Vernon Duke (m). c1940, Miller Music Corp. BARBRA STREISAND/SHIRLEY BAS-SEY. 140.

Talkin' In Your Sleep. w&m; Roger Cook & Bobby Woods. c1977, 78, Roger Cook Music & Chriswood Music. CRYSTAL GAYLE. 73, 130, 135.

Talking Folklore Center. w&m; Bob Dylan. c1969, Folklore Center & Consolidated Music Publishers, Inc. BOB DYLAN. 59.

Tall Oak Tree. Tall Oak Tree. w&m; Dorsey Burnette. c1960, Bamboo Music Inc. DORSEY BURNETTE. 6.

Tallahassee Lassie. w&m; Frank C. Slay, Jr., Bob Crewe & Frederick A. Piscariello. c1958, 59, Conley Music, Inc. FREDDIE CANNON. 78, 137.

Tangerine. w&m; Jimmy Page. c1970, 73, Superhype Publishing. LED ZEPPELIN. 114.

Tangled Up In Blue. w&m; Bob Dylan. c1974, 76, Ram's Horn Music. BOB DYLAN. 170.

Tangles-Up Puppet. w&m; Harry & Sandy Chapin. c1975, Sandy Songs. HARRY CHAPIN. 30.

Tape From California. w&m; Phil Ochs. c1968, Barri-cade Music, Inc. PHIL OCHS. 144.

Tapestry. w&m; Carole King. c1971, Colgems-EMI Music Inc. MARY O'HARA. 130.

Tara Theme SEE My Own True Love.

Taste Of Honey. w&m; Ric Marlow (w) & Bobby Scott (m). c1960, 62, Songfest Music Corp. BEATLES/ HERB ALPERT & THE TIJUANA BRASS. 93, 102, 125, 137, 163.

Taurus. w&m; Dennis Coffey. c1971, 72, Interior Music Corp. DENNIS COFFEY. 115.

Teach Your Children. w&m; Graham Nash. c1970, Giving Room Music, Inc. CROSBY, STILLS, NASH & YOUNG. 41, 139.

Teachers. w&m; Leonard Cohen. c1967, 69, Stranger Music, Inc. LEONARD COHEN. 171.

Tear The Roof Off The Sucker. w&m; George Clinton, Bootsie Collins & Jerome Brailey. c1976, Rick's Music Inc. & Malbiz Music. PARLIAMENT. 46, 141.

Tears Of A Clown. w&m; Henry Cosby, William "Smokey" Robinson & Stevie Wonder. c1967, 70, 71, Jobete Music Co., Inc. SMOKEY ROBINSON & THE MIRACLES. 123, 150.

Tears Of Rage. w&m; Bob Dylan (w) & Richard Manuel (m). c1968, 75, Dwarf Music. BAND/BOB DYLAN & THE BAND/JOAN BAEZ. 170.

Teddy Bear. w&m; Dale Royal, Billy Joe Burnette, Red Sovine & Tommy Hill. c1978, Cedarwood Publishing Co., Inc. RED SOVINE. 184.

Teddy Bears' Picnic. w&m; Jimmy Kennedy (w) & John W. Bratton (m). c1947, M. Witmark & Sons. NITTY GRITTY DIRT BAND. 132.

Teen-Age Crush. w&m; Audrey & Joe Allison. c1956, Central Songs Inc. TOMMY SANDS. 137.

Teenage Idol. w&m; Jack Lewis. c1962, Nelson Music Publishing Co. Controlled by Mills Music, Inc./Mills Music Ltd. RICK NELSON. 6.

Telephone Commercial SEE Reach Out And Touch Someone.

Telephone Line. w&m; Jeff Lynne. c1976, 77, United Artists Music Ltd. & Jet Music Inc./Unart Music Corp. ELECTRIC LIGHT ORCHESTRA. 21, 148, 199.

Telephone Man. w&m; Meri Wilson. c1977, Castle-ridge Music. MERI WILSON. 128.

Tell It All. w&m; Nickolas Ashford & Valerie Simpson. c1975, 76, Nick-O-Val Music. ASHFORD & SIMPSON. 13.

Tell It Like It Is. w&m; George David & Lee Diamond. c1966, 67, Conrad Music, a division of Arc Music Corp. & Olrap Publishing Co., Inc. ARRON NEVILLE/ HEART. 5, 102, 137, 155, 161, 190.

Tell It On The Mountain. w&m; Traditional. Peter Yarrow (Adapted), Paul Stookey (Adapted), Milton Okun (Adapted) & Mary Travers (Adapted). c1963, Pepamar Music Corp. PETER, PAUL & MARY. 67.

Tell Laura I Love Her. w&m; Jeff Barry & Ben Raleigh. c1960, Edward B. Marks Music Corp. RAY PETER-SON. 3.

Tell Me. w&m; Chester Burnett. c1960, Arc Music Corp. HOWLING WOLF. 1.

Tell Me. w&m; J. Will Callahan (w) & Max Kortlander (m). c1919, Jerome H. Remick & Co. BURL IVES. 132.

Tell Me, Momma. w&m; Bob Dylan. c1971, 76, Dwarf Music. 170.

Tell Me Something Good. w&m; Stevie Wonder. c1974, Jobete Music Co., Inc. & Black Bull Music, Inc. RUFUS/STEVIE WONDER. 52, 150.

Tell Me That It Isn't True. w&m; Bob Dylan. c1969, 76, Big Sky Music. BOB DYLAN. 170.

Tell Me To My Face. w&m; Allan Clarke, Tony Hicks & Graham Nash. c1966, 79, Gralto Music Ltd./Maribus Music, Inc. DAN FOGELBERG & TIM WEISBERG/ KEITH. 22, 87, 146.

Tell Me What You're Gonna Do. w&m; James Brown. c1964, 68, Wisto Publishing Co. JAMES BROWN. 18.

Tell Me Why. w&m; John Lennon & Paul McCartney.

c1964, Northern Songs Ltd./Maclen Music, Inc. & Unart Music Corp. BEATLES. 159.

Tell Me You'll Wait For Me. w&m; Charles Brown & Oscar Moore. c1945, Progressive Music Publishing Co., Inc. Controlled by Unichappell Music Inc. CHARLES BROWN. 155.

Temporary Like Achilles. w&m; Bob Dylan. c1966, 76, Dwarf Music. BOB DYLAN. 170.

Temptation Eyes. w&m; Dan Walsh & Harvey Price. c1970, Trousdale Music Publishers. GRASS ROOTS. 105.

Ten Commandments Of Love. w&m; M. Paul. c1958, 74, Arc Music Corp. LITTLE ANTHONY & THE IMPERIALS. 168.

Ten Percent. w&m; Talmadge G. Conway & Allan Felder. c1976, Mighty Three Music, Golden Fleece Music & Lucky Three Publishing Co. Administered by Blackwood Music Inc. DOUBLE EXPOSURE. 184.

Tenderness. w&m; Paul Simon. c1973, Paul Simon. PAUL SIMON. 143.

Tenderness On The Block. w&m; Warren Zevon & Jackson Browne. c1978, Zevon Music & Swallow Turn Music. Administered on behalf of Swallow Turn Music by WB Music Corp. WARREN ZEVON. 74.

Tequila Surprise. w&m; Don Henley & Glenn Frey. c1973, WB Music Corp., Benchmark Music & Kicking Bear Music. EAGLES. 139, 145.

Texas. w&m; Charlie Daniels. c1975, 76, Kama Sutra Music, Inc. & Rada Dara Music. CHARLIE DANIELS BAND. 37.

Thank God I'm A Country Boy. w&m; John Martin Sommers. c1974, Cherry Lane Music Co. JOHN DENVER. 131.

Thank You. w&m; Jimmy Page & Robert Plant, c1969, Superhype Publishing. LED ZEPPELIN. 114.

Thank You For Being A Friend. w&m; Andrew Gold. c1978, Luckyu Music. ANDREW GOLD. 135.

Thank You Girl. w&m; Paul McCartney & John Lennon. c1963, 64, Northern Songs, Ltd./Conrad Music, a division of Arc Music Corp. BEATLES. 10, 125, 168 169.

That Girl Could Sing. w&m; Jackson Browne. c1980, Swallow Turn Music. Administered by WB Music Corp. JACKSON BROWNE. 162, 190.

That Lucky Old Sun. w&m; Haven Gillespie (w) & Beasley Smith (m). c1949, 66, 77, Robbins Music Corp. ARTISTS/GEORGE BENSON/JACKIE WILSON/LOUIS ARMSTRONG/RAY CHARLES/WILLIE NELSON. 140, 163, 199.

That Same Old Obsession. w&m; Gordon Lightfoot. c1972, Moose Music. GORDON LIGHTFOOT. 151.

That Would Be Something. w&m; Paul McCartney. c1970, Northern Songs Ltd./Maclen Music Inc. PAUL MCCARTNEY. 61.

That'll Be The Day. w&m; Norman Petty, Buddy Holly & Jerry Allison. c1957, MPL Communications, Inc. BUDDY HOLLY & THE CRICKETS. 14.

That's All. w&m; Alan Brandt & Bob Haymes. c1952, Unart Music Corp. RICK NELSON. 78.

That's All For Everyone. w&m; Lindsey Buckingham. c1979, Fleetwood Mac Music/Warner-Tamerlane Publishing Corp. FLEETWOOD MAC. 147.

That's All Right. w&m; Jimmy Rogers. c1958, Arc Music Corp. MOSE ALLISON. 1.

That's How Much I Love You. w&m; Eddy Arnold, Wally Fowler & J. Graydon Hall. c1946, Wallace Fowler Publications. Assigned to Vogue Music Inc. PAT BOONE. 160.

That's It, I Quit, I'm Movin' On. w&m; Roy Alfred & Del Serno. c1961, Planetary Music Publishing Corp. SAM COOKE. 102, 137, 140, 163.

That's Rock 'N Roll. w&m; Eric Carmen. c1975, 76, C.A.M.-U.S.A., Inc. ERIC CARMEN/SHAUN CASSIDY. 124, 127, 145.

That's The Way. w&m; Jimmy Page & Robert Plant. c1970, 73, Superhype Publishing. LED ZEPPELIN. 114.

That's The Way I Feel About Cha. w&m; Bobby Womack, Joe Hicks & John Grisby. c1971, 72, Unart Music Corp. & Tracebob Music. Administered by Unart Music Corp. O.V. WRIGHT. 81.

That's The Way I Like It. w&m; H.W. Casey & R. Finch. c1975, Sherlyn Publishing Co. K C & THE SUNSHINE BAND. 26, 34.

That's The Way It's Gonna Be. w&m; Bob Gibson & Phil Ochs. c1964, 68, M. Witmark & Sons & Warner Bros.-Seven Arts, Inc. BACK PORCH MAJORITY/GLENN YARBOROUGH. 132.

That's The Way I've Always Heard It Should Be. w&m; Carly Simon & Jacob Brackman. c1970, 71, Carly Simon & Jacob Brackman/Quackenbush Music Ltd. & Kensho Music. CARLY SIMON. 43.

That's The Way Love Is. w&m; Norman Whitfield & Barrett Strong. c1969, Jobete Music Co., Inc. MARVIN GAYE, 123.

That's The Way Of The World. w&m; Maurice & Verdine White & Charles Stepney. c1975, Saggifire Music & Eibur Music. EARTH, WIND & FIRE. 16.

That's What You Get For Lovin' Me. SEE For Lovin' Me.

That's When The Music Takes Me. w&m; Neil Sedaka. c1972, 75, Don Kirschner Music, Inc. NEIL SEDAKA. 139.

That's Where I Went Wrong. w&m; Terry Jacks. c1969, 70, Gone Fishin' Music Ltd. POPPY FAMILY. 63, 88.

That's Why. w&m; Berry Gordy, Jr. & Tyran Carlo. c1957, 78, Merrimac Music Co. & Pearl Music Co. JACKIE WILSON. 2, 6, 155.

Theme For An Imaginary Western. w&m; Pete Brown (w) & Jack Bruce (m). c1969, Bruce Music Ltd./Casserole Music, Inc. MOUNTAIN. 203.

Theme From.... SEE Name of particular motion picture, play, musical, television series, etc.

Then Came You. w&m; Phil Pugh & Sherman Marshall. c1974, Mighty Three Music. SPINNERS. 52.

There Ain't No Way. w&m; Lobo. c1972, 73, Famous Music Corp. & Kaiser Music Co., Inc. LOBO. 63.

There But For Fortune. w&m; Phil Ochs. c1963, 64, Appleseed Music Inc. JOAN BAEZ. 68.

There Goes Another Love Song. w&m; Hugh Edward Thomasson Jr. & Byron Lamont Yoho. c1975, Hustlers, Inc. OUTLAWS. 28, 128.

There Goes My Baby. w&m; Lover Patterson, George Treadwell & Benjamin Nelson. c1959, Hill & Range Songs, Progressive Music Publishing Co., Inc. & Jot Music. Administered by Unichappell Music, Inc. DRIFTERS. 2, 92, 137, 154, 155.

There It Is (Part I). w&m; James Brown & St. Clair Pickney. c1972, 74, Dynatone Publishing Co., JAMES BROWN. 107.

There Was A Tall Oak Tree SEE Tall Oak Tree.

They'll Never Be. w&m; Bobby Debarge. c1978, Jobete Music Co., Inc. SWITCH. 66.

There's A Kind Of Hush. w&m; Les Reed & Geoff Stephens. c1966, 67, Donna Music Ltd/Francis, Day & Hunter, Inc. HERMAN'S HERMITS. 192.

There's A Lesson To Be Learned. w&m; Pam Sawyer & Gloria Jones. c1970, Jobete Music Co., Inc. GLADYS KNIGHT & THE PIPS. 17.

There's A Meetin' Here Tonight. w&m; Traditional. Bob Gibson (Adapted). c1960, 64, Melody Trails, Inc. LIMELITERS. 68.

There's A Moon Out Tonight. w&m; Alfred Striano, Joseph Luccisano & Alfonso Gentile. c1960, 64, Maureen Music Corp. CAPRIS. 3.

There's A Place. w&m; John Lennon & Paul McCartney. c1963, 64, Northern Songs, Ltd./ Gil Music Corp. BEATLES. 125.

There's Always Something There To Remind Me SEE Always Something There To Remind Me.

These Boots Are Made For Walkin'. w&m; Lee Hazelwood. c1965, 66, Criterion Music Corp. NANCY SINATRA. 35.

These Eyes. w&m; Randall Bachman & Burton Cummings. c1969, Cirrus Music, Inc./Dunbar Music, Inc. GUESS WHO. 64.

They Call The Wind Maria. w&m; Alan Jay Lerner (w) & Frederick Loewe (m). c1951, Chappell & Co. JOE & EDDIE. 68.

They Just Can't Stop It. w&m; Charles Simmons, Bruce Hawes & Joseph B. Jefferson. c1974, Mighty Three Music. Administered by Blackwood Music Inc. SPINNERS. 49.

They Long To Be Close To You SEE Close To You.

Thicker Than Water. w&m; Barry & Andy Gibb. c1977, Stigwood Music, Inc., Brothers Gibb, Andy Gibb Music, Joye Publishing, Hugh & Barbara Gibb. Controlled by Stigwood Music, Inc. Administered by Unichappell Music, Inc. ANDY GIBB. 133.

Things We Do For Love. w&m; Eric Steward & Graham Gouldman. c1977, Man-Ken Music Ltd. 10CC. 127.

Think About Me. w&m; Christine McVie. c1979, Fleetwood Mac Music/Warner-Tamerland Publishing Corp. FLEETWOOD MAC. 188.

Think It Over. w&m; Brian Russell & Brenda Gordon Russell. c1978, Kengorus Music. BRENDA RUSSELL/ CHERYL LADD. 23, 74, 135.

Think It Over. w&m; Cissy Houston, Alvin Fields & Michael Zager. c1978, Sumac Music, Inc. CISSY HOUSTON. 34, 74.

Third Time Lucky. w&m; Dave Peverett. c1979, Riff Bros. Music. FOGHAT. 8, 56, 98.

Thirsty Boots. w&m; Eric Andersen. c1965, United Artists Music Co., Inc. ERIC ANDERSEN/JUDY COLLINS. 37, 80.

This Boy SEE Ringo's Theme.

This Girl. w&m; Peter Yarrow & Mary MacGregor. c1976, 77, Silver Dawn Music. MARY MAC GREGOR. 127.

This Guy's In Love With You. w&m; Hal David (w) & Burt Bacharach (m). c1968, Blue Seas Music, Inc. & Jac Music Co. DIONNE WARWICK/ETTA JONES/ HERB ALPERT. 70, 71.

This I Swear. w&m; James Beaumont (w), Janet Vogel (w), Joseph Verscharen (w), Walter Lester (w), John Taylor (w), Joseph Rock (m) & Lennie Martin (m). c1959, Bonnyview Music Corp. SKYLINERS. 4.

This Is All I Ask. w&m; Gordon Jenkins. c1958, Anne-Rachel Music Corp. & Massey Music Co., Inc. TONY BENNETT. 195.

This Is It. w&m; Kenny Loggins & Michael McDonald. c1979, Milk Money Music, Snug Music & Tauripin Tunes. KENNY LOGGINS. 87, 147, 188.

This Is Love. w&m; Madeline Sunshine (w) & Robert Tepper (m). c1978, Camerica Music Inc. PAUL ANKA. 73, 134.

This Is My Heaven. w&m; Bill Giant, Bernie Baum & Florence Kaye. c1966, Elvis Presley Music, Inc. ELVIS PRESLEY. 173.

This Is The Way I Feel. w&m; George Jackson. c1977, Fame Publishing Co., Inc. MARIE OSMOND. 164.

This Land Is Your Land. w&m; Woody Guthrie. c1956, 58, 72, Ludlow Music, Inc. NEW CHRISTY MINSTRELS/SEEKERS/WEAVERS. 85.

This Magic Moment. w&m; Doc Pomus & Mort Shuman. c1960, Rumbalero Music, Inc. Controlled by Unichappell Music, Inc. DRIFTERS. 92, 155.

This Masquerade. w&m; Leon Russell. c1972, 73, Teddy Jack Music. CARPENTERS/GEORGE BENSON/HELEN REDDY/LEON RUSSELL. 23, 56, 71, 77, 128, 131, 135, 142.

This Moment In Time. w&m; Alan Bernstein & Ritchie Adams. c1978, Silver Blue Music, Ltd. ENGELBERT HUMPERDINCK. 23, 65, 73, 130.

This Night Won't Last Forever. w&m; Bill LaBounty & Roy Freeland. c1976, 79, Captain Crystal Music. MICHAEL JOHNSON. 23, 97, 180.

This Old Heart Of Mine (Is Weak For You). w&m; Brian Holland, Lamont Dozier & Eddie Holland. c1966, Jobete Music Co., Inc. ISLEY BROTHERS. 167.

This One's For You. w&m; Marty Panzer (w) & Barry Manilow (m). c1976, Kamakazi Music Corp. BARRY MANILOW. 21, 162, 193, 198.

This Song. w&m; George Harrison. c1976, Ganga Publishing B.V. GEORGE HARRISON. 141.

This Time I'm In It For Love. w&m; Steve Pippin & Larry Keith. c1976, Windchime Music Inc. & House of Gold Music Inc. PLAYER. 135.

This Train. w&m; Paul Stookey & Peter Yarrow. c1962, Pepamar Music Corp. LIMELITERS/PETER, PAUL & MARY. 41, 67.

This Wheel's On Fire. w&m; Bob Dylan (w) & Rick Danko (m). c1967, 75, Dwarf Music. BAND/BOB DYLAN & THE BAND. 170.

Thomas Crown Affair, Theme From SEE Windmills Of Your Mind.

Those Were The Days. w&m; Gene Raskin. c1962, 68, Essex Music, Inc. LIMELITERS/WING & A PRAYER FIFE & DRUM CORP/MARY HOPKIN. 85.

Thousand Miles Away. w&m; James Sheppard & William H. Miller. c1956, Nom Music, Inc. HEARTBEATS. 2, 78, 101, 155, 161.

Thousand Stars. w&m; Gene Pearson. c1960, Bryden Music. KATHY YOUNG & THE INNOCENTS. 6.

Three Angels. w&m; Bob Dylan. c1970, 76 Bid Sky Music. BOB DYLAN. 170.

Three Coins In The Fountain. w&m; Sammy Cahn (w) & Jule Styne (m). c1954, 67, Robbins Music Corp. FOUR ACES/FRANK SINATRA/MONTOVANI. 140.

Three Times A Lady. w&m; Lionel Richie. c1978, Jobete Music Co., Inc. & Commodores Entertainment Publishing Corp. COMMODORES. 23, 24, 56, 71, 73, 128, 130, 135.

Three Times In Love. w&m; Tommy James & Ronald Serota. c1979, Big Teeth Music Publishing Corp. & Tommy James Music Inc. TOMMY JAMES. 177.

Thrill Is Gone. w&m; Roy Hawkins. c1951, 71, Modern Music Publishing Co., Inc. B.B. KING. 105, 122, 156.

Through The Eyes Of Love SEE Ice Castles, Theme From.

Thunder Island. w&m; Jay Ferguson. c1977, 78, Painless Music. JAY FERGUSON. 22.

Thunder And Light' ning. w&m; Chi Coltrane. c1972, 73, Chinick Music & Trane Music. CHI COLTRANE. 139.

Ticket To Ride. w&m; John Lennon & Paul McCartney. c1965, Northern Songs Ltd./Maclen Music, Inc. BEATLES. 30, 35, 55, 61, 127, 159.

Tie A Yellow Ribbon Round The Ole Oak Tree. w&m; Irvine Levine & L. Russell Brown. c1972, 73, Tridem Music. Assigned to Five Arts Music & Levine & Brown Music, Inc. TONY ORLANDO & DAWN. 30, 62, 93, 133, 138, 141, 197.

Tight Rope. w&m; Leon Russell. c1972, Skyhill Publishing Co., Inc. LEON RUSSELL. 12, 138, 142.

Till The Morning Comes. w&m; Robert Hunter (w) & Jerry Garcia (m). c1971, 73, Ice Nine Publishing Co. GRATEFUL DEAD. 83.

Time. w&m; Michael Merchant. c1965, Edmark Production Co. & Regent Music Corp. GLEN CAMPBELL. 44, 169.

Time And A Word. w&m; Jon Anderson & David Foster. c1970, 75, Yessongs, Ltd. YES. 36.

Time In A Bottle. w&m; Jim Croce. c1971, 72, Blendingwell Music, Inc. & American Broadcasting Music, Inc. JIM CROCE. 21, 31, 87, 89, 131, 140, 162, 163, 193, 194, 199.

Time Is On My Side. w&m; Jerry Ragovoy. c1963, Rittenhouse Music, Inc. & Magyar Music Inc. ROLLING STONES. 4.

Time Of The Seasons. w&m; Rod Argent. c1967, 69, Verulam Music Co., Ltd./Mainstay Music, Inc. ZOMBIES. 64.

Time Passages. w&m; Al Stewart & Peter White. c1978, Dick James Music, Inc., Frabjous Music & Approximate Music. AL STEWART. 27, 31, 57, 146.

Time Passes Slowly. w&m; Bob Dylan. c1970, 76, Big Sky Music. BOB DYLAN. 170.

Time To Kill. w&m; Robbie Robertson. c1970, Canaan Music, Inc. BAND. 182.

Time Won't Let Me. w&m; Chet Kelly (w) & Tom King (m). c1966, Beechwood Music Corp. OUTSIDERS. 128.

Times They Are A-Changin'. w&m; Bob Dylan. c1963, M. Witmark & Sons & Warner Bros., Inc. BOB DYLAN/BYRDS. 35, 41, 67, 138.

Tin Man. w&m; Dewey Bunnell. c1974, WB Music Corp. AMERICA. 136.

Tiny Dancer. w&m; Elton John & Bernie Taupin. c1971, Dick James Music, Inc. ELTON JOHN. 36, 139.

Tiny Montgomery. w&m; Bob Dylan. c1967, 75, Dwarf Music. BOB DYLAN & THE BAND. 170.

Tired Of Toein' The Line. w&m; Rocky Burnette & Ron Coleman. c1979, 80, Cheshire Music, Inc. ROCKY BURNETTE. 189.

To Be A Star. w&m; Cat Stevens. c1977, Colgems-EMI Music Inc. CAT STEVENS. 142.

To Be Alone With You. w&m; Bob Dylan. c1969, 76, Big Sky Music. BOB DYLAN. 170.

To Electric Ladyland SEE Have You Ever Been To Electric Ladyland.

To Know You (Him) Is To Love You (Him). w&m; Phil Spector. c1958, Warman Music Co. Assigned to Vogue Music Inc. DAVID BROMBERG/TEDDYBEARS. 78, 101, 160.

To Love Somebody. w&m; Barry, Robin & Maurice Gibb. c1967, 75, Abigail Music Ltd. BEE GEES. 35.

To Sir, With Love. w&m; Don Black (w) & Marc London (m). c1967, Screen Gems-EMI Music, Inc. AL GREEN/LULU. 66, 130.

To The Aisle. w&m; Billy Dawn Smith & Stuart Weiner. c1957, Wemar Music Corp. FIVE SATINS. 6.

To The Morning. w&m; Daniel Fogelberg. c1975, Hickory Grove Music. DAN FOGELBERG. 36, 141.

Tobacco Road. w&m; John D. Loudermilk. c1960, 64, Cedarwood Publishing Co., Inc. EDGAR WINTER GROUP/NASHVILLE TEENS. 3, 104.

Today. w&m; Randy Sparks. c1964, Metro-Goldwyn-

Mayer Inc. Controlled by Miller Music Corp. BOBBY BLAND/JIMMIE RODGERS/JOHN DENVER/NEW CHRISTY MINSTRELS. 21, 140, 186, 199.

Today, Tomorrow And Forever. w&m; Bill Giant, Bernie Baum & Florence Kaye. c1964, Elvis Presley Music, Inc. ELVIS PRESLEY. 172.

Today's The Day. w&m; Dan Peek. c1976, WB Music Corp. AMERICA. 141.

Tom Cat. w&m; Tom Scott. c1974, 75, Hollenbeck Music. TOM SCOTT & THE L.A. EXPRESS. 36.

Tom Dooley. w&m; Traditional. Frank Warner (Collected, adapted & arranged) & John A. & Alan Lomax (Collected, adapted & arranged). c1947, 58, 75, Ludlow Music, Inc. KINGSTON TRIO. 68, 85.

Tomorrow. w&m; Martin Charnin (w) & Charles Strouse (m). c1977, Charles Strouse & Edwin H. Morris & Co., a division of MPL Communications, Inc. All rights of Charles Strouse administered by AGAC. BARBRA STREISAND/LOU RAWLS/MANHATTANS. 15, 21, 131, 176, 199.

Tomorrow Is A Long Time. w&m; Bob Dylan. c1963, M. Witmark & Sons. BOB DYLAN/BROTHERS FOUR/ IAN & SYLVIA/JUDY COLLINS/KINGSTON TRIO. 67, 132.

Tonight I'll Be Staying Here With You. w&m; Bob Dylan. c1969, 76, Big Sky Music. BOB DYLAN. 170.

Tonight Will Be Fine. w&m; Leonard Cohen. c1967, 69, Stranger Music, Inc. LEONARD COHEN. 171.

Tonight's The Night (Gonna Be Alright). w&m; Rod Stewart. c1967, Rod Stewart. Administered by Riva Music, Inc. ROD STEWART. 57, 117, 124, 127, 133, 136, 145.

Too Busy Thinking About My Baby. w&m; Norman Whitfield, Janie Bradford & Barrett Strong. c1966, 69, Jobete Music Co., Inc. MARVIN GAYE. 123, 150.

Too Far Gone. w&m; Billy Sherrill, c1967, 75, Al Gallico Music Corp. EMMYLOU HARRIS. 134.

Too Hot. w&m; George M. Brown & Kool & The Gang. c1979, Delightful Music Ltd./Gang Music. KOOL & THE GANG. 177, 198.

Too Hot To Stop (Part I). w&m; F. Freeman, H. Nehls III, Larry Dodson, James Alexander, Michael Beard, Winston Stewart, Lloyd Smith, Charles Allen, Harvey Henderson & Frank Thompson. c1977, Warner-Tamerlane Publishing Corp., Barkay Music & Dunbar Music, Inc. Administered by Warner-Tamerlane Publishing Corp. BAR-KAYS. 118.

Too Late. w&m; Steve Perry & Neal Schon. c1979, Weed High Nightmare Music. Controlled by Screen Gems-EMI Music, Inc. JOURNEY. 56, 98.

Too Late To Turn Back Now. w&m; Eddie Cornelius. c1971, 72, Unart Music Corp. & Stage Door Music Publishing Inc. CORNELIUS BROTHERS & SISTER ROSE. 79, 195.

Too Many Fish In The Sea. w&m; Eddie Holland & Norman Whitfield. c1964, Jobete Music Co., Inc. MARVELETTES. 150, 167.

Too Much Of Nothing. w&m; Bob Dylan. c1967, 75, Dwarf Music. BOB DYLAN & THE BAND/PETER, PAUL & MARY. 170.

Too Much, Too Little, Too Late. w&m; Nat Kipner & John Vallins. c1978, Homewood House Music. JOHNNY MATHIS & DENIECE WILLIAMS. 57, 87, 146.

Too Young. w&m; Sylvia Dee & Sid Lippman. c1951, Jefferson Music Co., Inc. DONNY OSMOND. 38.

Took The Last Train. w&m; David Gates & Larry Knechtel (m). c1978, Kipahulu Music Co. Administered & controlled by Colgems-EMI Music Inc. DAVID GATES. 74.

Top Of The World. w&m; John Bettis (w) & Richard Carpenter (m). c1972, Almo Music Corp. & Hammer And Nails Music. CARPENTERS. 70, 71, 183.

Torn Between Two Lovers. w&m; Peter Yarrow & Phillip Jarrell. c1976, Muscle Shoals Sound Publishing Co., Inc. & Silver Dawn Music. MARY MAC GREGOR. 131.

Tossin' And Turnin'. w&m; Malou Rene & Ritchie Adams. c1961, Harvard Music Inc. & Viva Music Inc. BOBBY LEWIS. 78, 102, 137, 163.

Touch A Hand, Make A Friend. w&m; Homer Banks, Raymond Jackson & Carl Hampton. c1973, 75, East-Memphis Music. STAPLE SINGERS. 122.

Touch Me In The Morning. w&m; Ron Miller (w) & Michael Masser (m). c1972, 73, 74, Jobete Music Co., Inc. DIANA ROSS/MFSB. 24, 48, 58, 134, 150.

Touch Of Class. w&m; Sammy Cahn (w) & George Barrie (m). c1972, 73, Brut Music Publishing Co. MOTION PICTURE THEME. 140.

Tough Mama. w&m; Bob Dylan. c1973, 76, Ram's Horn Music. BOB DYLAN. 170.

Towering Inferno, Theme From SEE We May Never Love This Way Again.

Town Without Pity. w&m; Ned Washington (w) & Dimitri Tiomkin (m). c1961, United Artists Music Co., Inc. GENE PITNEY. 102.

Traces. w&m; Buddy Buie, James Cobb & Emory Gordy. c1969, 70, Low-Sal Music, Inc. DENNIS YOST & THE CLASSICS IV. 64, 111, 130, 161.

Tracks Of My Tears. w&m; Marv Tarplin, Warren Moore & William "Smokey" Robinson. c1965, 67, Jobete Music Co., Inc. GLADYS KNIGHT & THE PIPS/JOHNNY RIVERS/LINDA RONSTADT/ SMOKEY ROBINSON & THE MIRACLES. 17, 58, 123, 142, 150.

Tragedy. w&m; Barry, Robin & Maurice Gibb. c1978, 79, Brothers Gibb B.V./Stigwood Music Inc. Administered by Unichappell Music Inc. BEE GEES. 40, 50.

Tranquillo (Melt My Heart). w&m; Carly Simon, James Taylor & Arif Mardin. c1978, C'est Music. CARLY SIMON. 147.

Travelin' Band. w&m; J.C. Fogerty. c1970, Jondora Music. CREEDENCE CLEARWATER REVIVAL. 86, 157.

Treasure Of Love. w&m; J. Shapiro & Lou Stallman. c1956, Progressive Music Publishing Co., Inc. Controlled by Unichappell Music, Inc. CLYDE MCPHATTER. 91, 155.

Treat Her Like A Lady. w&m; Eddie Cornelius. c1969,

71, Unart Music Corp. & Stage Door Music Publishing. Administered by Unart Music Corp. CORNELIUS BROTHERS & SISTER ROSE/DETROIT EMERALDS. 80, 192.

Treat Her Right. w&m; Roy Head. c1965, Don Music Co., a division of ABC-Dunhill Music, Inc. ROY HEAD. 3.

Treat Me Nice. w&m; Jerry Leiber & Mike Stoller. c1957, Elvis Presley Music, Inc. ELVIS PRESLEY. 173.

Trick Of The Light. w&m; John Entwistle. c1978, Whistle Rhymes Ltd./Hot Red Music. WHO. 147.

Tried Tested And Found True. w&m; Nickolas Ashford & Valerie Simpson. c1976, Nick-O-Val Music. ASHFORD & SIMPSON. 13.

Truckin'. w & m; Robert Hunter (w), Jerry Garcia (m), Bob Weir (m) & Phil Lesh (m). c1971, 73, Ice Nine Publishing Co., Inc. GRATEFUL DEAD. 22, 36, 83, 136, 185.

True Love, True Love. w&m; Doc Pomus & Mort Shuman. c1959, Brittany Music Inc. Controlled by Unichappell Music, Inc. DRIFTERS. 92, 155.

True Love Ways. w&m; Norman Petty & Buddy Holly. c1958, MPL Communications, Inc. BUDDY HOLLY. 14.

Trust Me. w&m; Cindy Bullens. c1979, 80, Gooserock Music & Fleur music. CINDY BULLENS. 98.

Try A Little Kindness. w&m; Bobby Austin & Curt Sapaugh. c1969, Airefield Music, a division of Beechwood Music Corp. & Glen Campbell Music. GLEN CAMPBELL. 89.

Try A Little Tenderness. w&m; Harry Woods, Jimmy Campbell & Reg Connelly. c1932, 60, 66, Campbell Connelly, Inc. assigned to Robbins Music Corp. THREE DOG NIGHT. 72, 140, 163.

Try It Baby. w&m; Berry Gordy. c1964, 74, Jobete Music Co., Inc. MARVIN GAYE. 150.

Try (Just A Little Bit Harder). w&m; Jerry Ragovoy & Chip Taylor. c1968, 70, Ragmar Music Corp. JANIS JOPLIN. 110.

Try Me. w&m; James Brown. c1958, 68, Wisto Publishing Co. JAMES BROWN. 18.

Try To Remember. w&m; Tom Jones (w) & Harvey Schmidt (m). c1960, Tom Jones & Harvey Schmidt. Controlled by Chappell & Co., Inc. BROTHERS FOUR/HARRY BELAFONTE. 68.

Tryin' To Get The Feeling. w&m; David Pomeranz. c1974, 76, Warner-Tamerlane Publishing Corp. & Upward Spiral Music. BARRY MANILOW. 30, 57, 62, 133, 141, 145.

Tryin' To Love Two. w&m; William Bell & Paul F. Mitchell. c1976, 77, Bell Kat Publishing Co. WILLIAM BELL. 121, 164.

TSOP (The Sound Of Philadelphia). w&m; Kenny Gamble & Leon Huff. c1973, 74, Mighty Three Music. MFSB. 52.

Tubular Bells. w&m; Mike Oldfield (m). c1974, Virgin Music. MIKE OLDFIELD. 156.

Tuesday Afternoon. w&m; Justin Hayward. c1968, 70,

Tyler Music Ltd. Controlled by TRO-Essex Music International Inc. MOODY BLUES. 142, 156.

Tulsa Time. w&m; Danny Flowers. c1978, Bibo Music Publishers. DON WILLIAMS. 140.

Tumbleweed. w&m; Douglas Van Arsdale. c1971, 72, Denny Music, Inc. JOAN BAEZ. 151.

Tupelo Honey. w&m; Van Morrison. c1971, 72, WB Music Corp. & Caledonia Soul Music. VAN MORRISON. 36, 117, 136, 138, 185.

Turn Around. w&m; Malvina Reynolds, Allen Greene & Harry Belafonte. c1958, Clara Music Publishing Corp. HARRY BELAFONTE. 68.

Turn Around, Look At Me. w&m; Jerry Capehart. c1961, Warner-Tamerlane Publishing Corp., Viva Music, Inc., Hill & Range Songs, Inc., Elvis Presley Music, Inc. & Gladys Music, Inc. LETTERMEN/VOGUES. 35, 43, 197.

Turn Back The Hands Of Time. w&m; Jack Daniels & Bonnie Thompson. c1970, Dakar Productions, Inc. & Jadan Music. TYRONE DAVIS. 64.

Turn Back the Pages. w&m; Stephen Stills & Donnie Dacus. c1975, Gold Hill Music, Inc. & Donnie Dacus Publishing. STEPHEN STILLS. 139.

Turn Off The Lights. w&m; Kenneth Gamble & Leon Huff. c1979, Mighty Three Music. TEDDY PENDERGRASS. 75.

Turn To Stone. w&m; Jeff Lynne. c1977, United Artists Music Ltd. & Jet Music Inc. Administered by Unart Music Corp. ELECTRIC LIGHT ORCHESTRA. 15, 199.

Turn! Turn! Turn!. Traditional. Pete Seeger (Adapted). c1962, Melody Trails, Inc. BYRDS/PETE SEEGER. 85, 126.

Tusk. W&m; Lindsey Buckingham. c1979, Fleetwood Mac Music. Administered by Warner-Tamerlane Publishing Corp. FLEETWOOD MAC. 27, 31, 124, 147.

Tutti Frutti. w&m; Richard Penniman & Dorothy La Bostrie. c1955, 56, Venice Music, Inc. CHUCK BERRY/ELVIS PRESLEY/LITTLE RICHARD. 2, 3, 35, 78, 100, 137, 159.

Tuxedo Junction. w&m; Buddy Feyne (w), Erskine Hawkins (m), William Johnson (m) & Julian Dash (m). c1940, 68, 74, Lewis Music Publishing Co., Inc. GLEN MILLER/MANHATTAN TRANSFER. 193.

'Twas Teatime At The Circus. w&m; Gary Brooker, Matthew Fisher & Keith Reid. c1968, 72, Essex Music International Ltd.-TRO Andover Music, Inc. PROCOL HARUM. 42.

Tweedlee Dee. w&m; Winfield Scott. c1954, Hill & Range Songs, Inc. & Progressive Music Publishing Co., Inc. Assigned to Unichappell Music, Inc. GEORGIA GIBBS/LAVERN BAKER. 78, 90, 101, 137, 154, 155.

Twelfth Of Never. w&m; Paul Francis Webster (w) & Jerry Livingston (m). c1956, 57, Frank Music Corp. CHI-LITES/DONNY OSMOND/TYMES. 165.

Twenty-Five Miles. w&m; Edwin Starr, Johnny Bristol & Harvey Fuqua. c1968, 69, 73, Jobete Music Co., Inc. EDWIN STARR. 123, 150.

25 Or 6 To 4. w&m; Robert Lamm. c1970, Lammina-

tions Music & Aurelius Music. CHICAGO. 29, 63, 77, 86, 88, 93, 134, 142, 156.

Twenty Seventy Five. w&m; Willie Mitchell, c1964, Jec Publishing. WILLIE MITCHELL. 122.

Twilight Time. w&m; Buck Ram (w) & Morty & Al Nevins (m). c1944, 72, TRO & Devon Music, Inc. PLATTERS. 5, 140.

Twist. w&m; Hank Ballard. c1959, Armo Music Corp. & Fort Knox Music Co. CHUBBY CHECKER. 93.

Twist And Shout. w&m; Bert Russell & Phil Medley. c1960, 63, Robert Mellin Inc. & Progressive Music Inc. BEATLES/ISLEY BROTHERS. 4, 72.

Two Doors Down. w&m; Dolly Parton. c1977, Velvet Apple Music. DOLLY PARTON. 135.

Two Faces Have I. w&m; Lou Sacco & Twyla Herbert. c1963, Painted Desert Music Corp. LOU CHRISTIE. 4.

Two Heads. w&m; Grace Slick. c1967, 68, Icebag Corp. JEFFERSON AIRPLANE. 108.

Two Lovers. w&m; William "Smokey" Robinson. c1962, 68, 71, Jobete Music Co., Inc. MARY WELLS. 123, 150, 167.

Two Out Of Three Ain't Bad. w&m; Jim Steinman. c1977, Edward B. Marks Music Corp., Neverland Music Co. & Peg Music Co. MEATLOAF. 120.

Two Places At the Same Time. w&m; Ray Parker, Jr. c1980, Raydiola Music Co. RAY PARKER JR. & RAYDIO. 189.

Two Sides. w&m; Scott Davis. c1975, Sedso Music. CARPENTERS. 135.

2001 SEE Also Sprach Zarathustra.

Two Tickets To Paradise. w&m; Eddie Money. c1977, Grajonca Music. EDDIE MONEY. 96.

Un Mundo. w&m; Stephen Stills. c1968, 75, Cotillion Music, Inc. & Springalo Toones. BUFFALO SPRING-FIELD. 39.

Unbroken Chain. w&m; Robert Peterson (w) & Philip Lesh (m). c1974, 76, Ice Nine Publishing Co., Inc. GRATEFUL DEAD. 84.

Unchained Melody. w&m; Hy Zaret (w) & Alex North (m). c1955, Frank Music Corp. ELVIS PRESLEY/ GEORGE BENSON/RIGHTEOUS BROTHERS/SONNY & CHER/STYLISTICS. 165, 199.

Uncle Albert/Admiral Halsey. w&m; Paul & Linda Mc Cartney. c1971, Northern Songs Ltd,/Maclen Music Inc. PAUL & LINDA MCCARTNEY. 133.

Uncle John's Band. w&m; Robert Hunter (w) & Jerry Garcia (m). c1970, 73, Ice Nine Publishing Co. GRATEFUL DEAD. 83.

Under My Thumb. w&m; Mick Jagger & Keith Richard. c1966, Abkco Music, Inc. ROLLING STONES. 12.

Under The Boardwalk. w&m; Artie Resnick & Kenny Young. c1964, Hudson Bay Music Co. DRIFTERS. 158.

Under The Falling Sky. w&m; Jackson Browne. c1971, 76, WB Music Corp. JACKSON BROWNE. 30.

Undercover Angel. w&m; Alan O'Day. c1977, WB Music Corp. ALAN O'DAY. 127, 133, 141.

Understanding. w&m; Jimmy Holiday & Ray Charles. c1967, Unart Music Corp. RAY CHARLES. 82.

Unicorn. w&m; Shel Silverstein. c1962, 68, Hollis Music, Inc. IRISH ROVERS. 85.

Unmarried Woman, Theme From. w&m; Bill Conti. c1978, Fox Fanfare Music, Inc. BILL CONTI. 135.

Until It's Time For You To Go. w&m; Buffy Saint-Marie. c1965, 67, 73, Gypsy Boy Music, Inc. BUFFY SAINTE-MARIE/NEIL DIAMOND. 35, 67, 86, 88, 134.

Up On Cripple Creek. w&m; J. Robbie Robertson. c1969, Canaan Music Inc. BAND. 115, 149, 202.

Up On The Roof. w&m; Gerry Goffin & Carole King. c1962, Screen Gems-EMI Music Inc. DRIFTERS/ JAMES TAYLOR/LAURA NYRO/STUFF. 75, 88, 130, 156, 187.

Up The Ladder To The Roof. w&m; Vincent Dimirco. c1970, Jobete Music Co., Inc. SUPREMES. 123.

Up To Me. w&m; Bob Dylan. c1974, 76, Ram's Horn Music. ROGER MCGUINN. 170.

Up, Up And Away. w&m; Jim Webb. c1967, 70, 71, Johnny Rivers Music. Assigned to Dramatis Music Corp. FIFTH DIMENSION. 15, 21, 24, 60, 72, 86, 89, 102, 163, 193, 194, 199.

Ups And Downs. w&m; J. Morali, H. Belolo & V. Willis. c1978, Scorpio Music (Black Scorpio). Controlled by Can't Stop Music. VILLAGE PEOPLE. 200.

Upside Down. w&m; Nile Rodgers & Bernard Edwards. c1980, Chic Music, Inc. Administered by Warner-Tamerlane Publishing Corp. DIANA ROSS. 189.

Uptight (Everything's Alright). w&m; Henry Cosby, Sylvia Moy & Stevie Wonder. c1965, 66, Jobete Music Co., Inc. STEVIE WONDER. 123, 166.

Us And Love. w&m; Kenny Nolan. c1979, 80, Sound of Music. KENNY NOLAN. 99.

U.S. Blues. w&m; Robert Hunter (w) & Jerry Garcia (m). c1974, 76, Ice Nine Publishing Co., Inc. GRATEFUL DEAD. 84.

U.S. Male. w&m; Jerry Reed. c1966, Vector Music Corp. ELVIS PRESLEY. 4.

Valhalla. w&m; Elton John & Bernie Taupin. c1968, Dick James Music Inc. ELTON JOHN. 197.

Valley Below SEE One More Cup Of Coffee.

Valley Of Tears. w&m; Antoine Domino & Dave Bartholomew. c1957, Unart Music Corp. FATS DOMINO. 81, 137.

Valley Of The Dolls, Theme From. w&m; Dory Previn (w) & Andre Previn (m). c1967, Twentieth Century Music Ltd./Twentieth Century Music Corp. DIONNE WARWICK. 58.

Vengeance. w&m; Carly Simon. c1979, C'est Music. CARLY SIMON. 27.

Ventura Highway. w&m; Dewey Bunnell. c1972, Warner Bros. Music Ltd./WB Music Corp. AMERICA. 43, 138.

Venus. w&m; Edward H. Marshall. c1959, 76, Kirshner Songs, Inc. & Welbeck Music Corp. FRANKIE AVALON. 30, 35.

Venus And Mars Rock Show. w&m; Paul McCartney. c1975, McCartney Music, Inc. PAUL MC CARTNEY & WINGS. 103.

Very Special Love Song. w&m; Billy Sherrill & Norris Wilson. c1974, Algee Music Corp. BARBARA MANDRELL/CHARLIE RICH. 89, 128, 134, 163.

Video Killed The Radio Star. w&m; Bruce Wooley, Trevor Horn & Geoff Downes. c1979, Carlin Music Corp. & Island Music Ltd. Controlled by Carbert Music, Inc. & Ackee Music, Inc. BUGGLES. 27, 97.

Village People. w&m; H. Belolo (w), P. Whitehead (w), P. Hurtt (w) & J. Morali (m). c1977, Scorpio Music (Black Scorpio). Controlled by Can't Stop Music. VILLAGE PEOPLE. 200.

Vincent. w&m; Don McLean. c1971, 72, Mayday Music Inc. & Yahweh Tunes, Inc. DON MC LEAN. 21, 37, 72, 89, 131, 194, 198.

Visions Of Johanna. w&m; Bob Dylan. c1966, 76, Dwarf Music. BOB DYLAN. 170.

Vo-Do-Do-De-O Blues. w&m; Jack Yellen (w) & Milton Ager (m). c1927, Advanced Music Corp. GOOFUS FIVE. 132.

Voices. w&m; Rick Nielsen. c1978, 79, Screen Gems-EMI Music, Inc. & Adult Music. Controlled by Screen Gems-EMI Music, Inc. CHEAP TRICK. 8, 98.

Volare. w&m; Mitchell Parish (w) & Domenico Modugno (m). c1958, Edizioni Curci/Robbins Music Corp. AL MARTINO/BOBBY RYDELL/DOMENICO MODUGNO. 163, 193.

Volcano. w&m; Jimmy Buffett, Keith Sykes & Harry Dailey. c1979, Coral Reefer Music & Keith Sykes Music. JIMMY BUFFETT. 147.

Voodoo Chile. w&m; Jimi Hendrix. c1968, Bella Godiva Music Inc. JIMI HENDRIX. 203.

Wabash Cannon Ball. w&m; William Kindt. c1943, 66, Robbins Music Corp. BOOTS RANDOLPH/DOC WATSON/NASHVILLE BRASS. 140.

Wah-Watusi. w&m; Kal Mann & Dave Appell. c1962, Kalmann Music Inc. & Lowe Music Publishing Co. ORLONS. 5.

Waist Deep In The Big Muddy. w&m; Pete Seeger. c1967, Melody Trails, Inc. PETE SEEGER. 85.

Waiting For The Sun. w&m; Jim Morrison (w) & Doors (m). c1970, Doors Music. DOORS. 54.

Wake Up Everybody. w&m; G. McFadden, J. Whitehead & V. Carstarphen. c1975, 77, Mighty Three Music. Administered by Blackwood Music Inc. HAROLD MELVIN & The BLUENOTES. 193.

Wake Up, Little Susie. w&m; Boudleaux & Felice Bryant. c1957, House Of Bryant Publications. EVERLY BROTHERS. 3, 86, 93, 158.

Wake Up Susan. w&m; Sherman Marshall & Thom Bell. c1976, 77, 78, Mighty Three Music. Administered by Blackwood Music Inc. SPINNERS. 184, 193.

Walk A Mile In My Shoes. w&m; Joe South. c1969, Lowery Music Co., Inc. JOE SOUTH. 149, 191.

Walk Away From Love. w&m; Charles H. Kipps, Jr. c1974, 75, Charles Kipps Music, Inc. DAVID RUFFIN. 30.

Walk, Don't Run. w&m; Johnny Smith. c1960, Forshay Music, Inc. VENTURES. 93.

Walk Hand In Hand. w&m; Johnny Cowell, c1956, Republic Music Corp. LETTERMAN. 63.

Walk Like A Man. w&m; Bob Crewe & Bob Gaudio. c1963, Saturday Music Inc. FOUR SEASONS. 137.

Walk On. w&m; Neil Young. c1973, 74, Silver Fiddle. NEIL YOUNG. 139.

Walk On By. w&m; Hal David (w) & Burt Bacharach (m). c1964, Blue Seas Music, Inc. & Jac Music Co., Inc. AVERAGE WHITE BAND/DIONNE WARWICK/ RENAISSANCE/WILDARE EXPRESS. 71, 96.

Walk Right By. w&m; Sonny Curtis. c1960, 78, Warner-Tamerlane Publishing Corp. ANNE MURRAY. 146.

Walk Right In. w&m; Gus Cannon, H. Woods, Erik Darling (Arranged) & Willard Svanoe (Arranged). c1930, 63, Peer International Corp. ROOFTOP SINGERS. 68.

Walk This Way. w&m; Steven Tyler & Joe Perry. c1975, Daksel Music Corp. AEROSMITH. 141, 147, 175.

Walkin' Miracle. w&m; George David Weiss & Adam R. Levy. c1963, Planetary Music Publishing Corp. ESSEX. 161.

Walking By Myself. w&m; J.A. Lane. c1957, Arc Music Corp. CANNED HEAT. 1.

Walking Man. w&m; James Taylor. c1974, 78, Country Road Music, Inc. JAMES TAYLOR. 136.

Walking The Dog. w&m; Rufus Thomas. c1963, Birdees Music & East-Memphis Music Corp. RUFUS THOMAS. 59, 122.

Walking Through The Country. w&m; Dennis Provisor. c1972, TCB Music Co., Inc. GRASS ROOTS. 105.

Wallflower. w&m; Bob Dylan. c1971, 76, Ram's Horn Music. DOUG SAHM. 170.

Wallflower. (Otis) SEE Dance With Me Henry.

Walls Have Ears. w&m; Sid Tepper & Roy C. Bennett. c1962, Gladys Music, Inc. ELVIS PRESLEY. 173.

Wanderer. w&m; Donna Summer (w) & Girogio Moroder (m). c1980, Giorgio Moroder Publishing Co. & Sweet Summer Night Music. Administered by WB Music Corp. DONNA SUMMER. 190.

Wanderer. w&m; Ernie Maresca. c1960, 64, Schwartz Music Co., Inc. DION. 198.

Wang-Dang-Doodle. w&m; Willie Dixon. c1962, 74, Arc Music Corp. HOWLING WOLF/POINTER SISTERS. 1, 138.

Wanted Man. w&m; Bob Dylan. c1969, 76, Big Sky Music. BOB DYLAN. 170.

War. w&m; Norman Whitfield & Barrett Strong. c1970, Jobete Music Co., Inc. EDWIN STARR. 123.

War Is Over. w&m; Phil Ochs. c1968, Barricade Music, Inc. PHIL OCHS. 144.

Warmth Of The Sun. w&m; Brian Wilson & Mike Love. c1964, Sea Of Tunes Publishing Co. BEACH BOYS. 9.

Was A Sunny Day. w&m; Paul Simon. c1973, Paul Simon. PAUL SIMON. 143.

Wasn't It Good. w&m; Michele Aller & Bob Esty. c1978, Rick's Music, Inc. CHER. 75.

Wasted Days And Wasted Nights. w&m; Wayne M. Duncan & Freddy Fender. c1960, 75, Travis Music Co., Inc. & Unart Music Corp. FREDDY FENDER. 21, 80, 163, 198.

Watch Closely Now. w&m; Paul Williams & Kenny Ascher. c1976, First Artists Music Co., Emanuel Music Corp. & 20th Century Music Corp. Administered by WB Music Corp. BARBRA STREISAND & KRIS KRISTOFFERSON. 127, 145.

Watch Her Ride. w&m; Paul Kantner. c1967, 68, Icebag Corp. JEFFERSON AIRPLANE. 108.

Watchin' Scotty Grow. w&m; Mac Davis. c1970, 71, 72, Screen Gems-EMI Music Inc. BOBBY GOLDSBORO/MAC DAVIS. 130.

Whatcha See Is Whatcha Get. w&m; Tony Hester. c1971, Groovesville Music, Inc. DRAMATICS. 192.

Watching The River Flow. w&m; Bob Dylan. c1971, 76, Big Sky Music. BOB DYLAN. 170.

Watching The River Run. w&m; Jim Messina & Ken Loggins. c1973, 74, Gnossos Music & Jasperilla Music Co. LOGGINS & MESSINA. 138.

Water Sign. w&m; Gary Wright. c1976, 77, High Wave Music, Inc. Administered by WB Music Corp. GARY WRIGHT. 127.

Waterfall. w&m; Carly Simon. c1975, C'est Music. CARLY SIMON. 30.

Watusi, El. SEE El Watusi.

Way Back When. w&m; Brenda Russell. c1979, Almo Music Corp. & Rutland Road Music. BRENDA RUSSELL. 24.

Way Down. w&m; Layng Martine, Jr. c1977, Ray Stevens Music. ELVIS PRESLEY. 122.

Way Downtown. w&m; Traditional. Doc Watson (Adapted & arranged). c1972, Hillgreen Music. DOC WATSON. 37.

Way I Feel. w&m; Gordon Lightfoot. c1965, 66, Warner Bros., Inc. GORDON LIGHTFOOT. 35.

Way We Were. w&m; Alan & Marilyn Bergman (w) & Marvin Hamlisch (m). c1973, Colgems-EMI Music, Inc. BARBRA STREISAND/ERUPTION/GLADYS KNIGHT & THE PIPS/SHIRLEY BASSEY. 23, 56, 58, 71, 134, 156.

Way You Do The Things You Do. w&m; William "Smokey" Robinson & Robert Rogers. c1964, 66, 68, 72, Jobete Music Co., Inc. RITA COOLIDGE/TEMPTATIONS. 123, 135, 150.

Way You Look To-Night. w&m; Dorothy Fields (w) & Jerome Kern (m). c1936, T.B. Harms Co. LETTERMAN. 160.

Ways. w&m; Buddy Buie & John Adkins. c1968, LowSal Music. CANDYMEN. 76.

We Are Family. w&m; Nile Rodgers & Bernard Edwards. c1979, Chic Music, Inc. Administered by Warner-Tamerland Publishing Corp. SISTER SLEDGE. 27, 31, 57, 87, 147.

We Are Not Helpless. w&m; Stephen Stills. c1970, 73, Gold Hill Music, Inc. STEPHEN STILLS. 41.

We Are The Champions. w&m; Freddie Mercury. c1977, Queen Music Ltd./Beechwood Music Corp. QUEEN. 23, 128, 134, 142, 157.

We Belong Together. w&m; Robert Carr, Johnny Mitchell & Sam Weiss. c1958, Nom Music, Inc. & Maureen Music. ROBERT & JOHNNY/WEBS. 78, 101, 137, 155, 161.

We Can Work It Out. w&m; John Lennon & Paul McCartney. c1965, Northern Songs Ltd./Maclen Music, Inc. BEATLES. 35, 61, 159, 197.

We Don't Talk Anymore. w&m; Alan Tarney. c1979, ATV Music Ltd./ATV Music Corp. CLIFF RICHARD. 159.

We Got To Get You A Woman. w&m; Todd Rundgren. c1970, Earmark Music Inc. & Screen Gems-EMI Music Inc. TODD RUNDGREN. 12.

We Gotta Get Out Of This Place. w&m; Barry Mann & Cynthia Weil. c1965, Screen Gems-Columbia Music, Inc. ANIMALS. 29.

We Just Disagree. w&m; Jim Krueger. c1976, 77, Blackwood Music Inc. & Bruiser Music. DAVE MASON. 165.

We May Never Love Like This Again. w&m; Al Kasha & Joel Hirschhorn. c1974, WB Music Corp., 20th Century Music Corp., Warner-Tamerlane Publishing Corp. & Fox Fanfare Music, Inc. MAUREEN MC GOVERN. 139.

We May Never Pass This Way Again. w&m; James Seals & Dash Crofts (m). c1973, Dawnbreaker Music Co. SEALS & CROFTS. 36, 43.

We Shall Overcome. w&m; Traditional. Zilphia Horton (Adapted), Frank Hamilton (Adapted), Guy Carawan (Adapted) & Pete Seeger (Adapted). c1960, 63, Ludlow Music, Inc. JOAN BAEZ/PETE SEEGER. 59, 85.

We Will Rock You. w&m; Brian May. c1977, 78, Queen Music Ltd./Beechwood Music Corp. QUEEN. 11, 134, 157.

Wear My Ring Around Your Neck. w&m; Bert Carroll & Russell Moody. c1958, Elvis Presley Music, Inc. & Rush Music Corp. Administered by Elvis Presley Music, Inc. ELVIS PRESLEY. 172.

Weather Report I. w&m; Bob Weir & Eric Andersen (w). c1973, 76, Ice Nine Publishing Co., Inc. GRATEFUL DEAD. 84.

Weather Report II: Let It Grow. w&m; John Barlow (w) & Robert Weir (m). c1973, 76, Ice Nine Publishing Co., Inc. GRATEFUL DEAD. 84.

Wedding Bell Blues. w&m; Laura Nyro. c1966, Tuna Fish Music, Inc. Administered by Blackwood Music Inc. FIFTH DIMENSION/LAURA NYRO. 15, 35, 55, 68, 86, 136, 174, 198.

Wedding Song. w&m; Bob Dylan. c1973, 76, Ram's Horn Music. BOB DYLAN/BUFFY SAINTE-MARIE. 170.

Wedding Song (There Is Love). w&m; Traditional. c1971, Public Domain Foundation, Inc. PAUL STOOKEY/ PETULA CLARK. 138, 139.

Wednesday Morning, 3 a.m. w&m; Paul Simon. c1966, Paul Simon. SIMON & GARFUNKEL. 143.

Weekend. w&m; Mick Jackson & Tommy Mayer. c1978, Global Musikverlag-Global Musik GmbH & Co., Kg./Almo Music Corp. MICK JACKSON/WET WILLIE. 75, 96.

Weekend In New England. w&m; Randy Edelman. c1975, 76, Unart Music Corp. & Piano Picker Music. Administered by Unart Music Corp. BARRY MANILOW. 21, 37, 80, 193, 196, 198.

Weekend Lover. w&m; Denny Randell & Sandy Linzer. c1977, 78, Unichappell Music Inc. & Featherbed Music. ODYSSEY. 50.

Weep For Jamie. w&m; Peter Yarrow. c1967, Pepamar Music Corp. PETER, PAUL & MARY. 132.

Welcome. w&m; John Coltrane (m). c1974, Jowcol Music. SANTANA. 142.

Welcome Back. w&m; John Sebastian. c1976. John Sebastian Music. JOHN SEBASTIAN. 62, 133, 141.

Welcome To My Nightmare. w&m; Alice Cooper & Dick Wagner. c1974, 76, Ezra Music-Early Frost Music. ALICE COOPER. 30.

Welfare Cadillac. w&m; Guy Drake. c1969, Birmingham Music, Inc. Assigned to Bull Fighter Music. GUY DRAKE. 186.

Well All Right. w&m; Norman Petty, Buddy Holly, Jerry Allison & Joe Mauldin. c1958, MPL Communications, Inc. BUDDY HOLLY. 14.

We'll Never Have To Say Goodbye Again. w&m; Jeffrey Comanor. c1975, 78, Dawnbreaker Music Co. ENGLAND DAN & JOHN FORD COLEY. 15, 21, 199.

We'll Sing In The Sunshine. w&m; Gale Garnett. c1963, Lupercalia Music Publishing Co. GALE GARNETT. 68.

Wendy. w&m; Brian Wilson. c1964, Sea Of Tunes Publishing Co. BEACH BOYS. 9.

Went To See The Gypsy. w&m; Bob Dylan. c1970, 76, Big Sky Music. BOB DYLAN. 170.

We're All Alone. w&m; Boz Scaggs. c1976, 78, Boz Scaggs Music. FRANKIE VALLI/RITA COOLIDGE. 87, 141, 145, 162, 178, 201.

We're All The Way. w&m; Don Williams. c1974, 78, Jack Music Inc. ERIC CLAPTON. 199.

We're An American Band. w&m; Don Brewer. c1973, Cram Renraff Co. GRAND FUNK. 93.

We're Coming In Loaded. w&m; Otis Blackwell & Winfield Scott. c1962, Elvis Presley Music, Inc. ELVIS PRESLEY. 173.

Werewolves Of London. w&m; LeRoy P. Marinell, Waddy Wachtel & Warren Zevon. c1975, Zevon Music & Polite Music. FLAMIN' GROOVIES/WARREN ZEVON. 11, 23, 135, 157.

Western Movies. w&m; Fred Smith & Cliff Goldsmith. c1958, Elizabeth Music Publishing & Aries Music Co. OLYMPICS. 6.

We've Got A Groovy Thing Goin'. w&m; Paul Simon. c1966, Paul Simon. SIMON & GARFUNKEL. 143.

We've Got Love. w&m; Dino Fekaris & Freddie Perren. c1978, 79, Perren-Vibes Music, Inc. PEACHES & HERB. 31, 147.

We've Got Tonite. w&m; Bob Seger. c1976, 78, Gear Publishing Co. BOB SEGER & THE SILVER BULLET BAND. 27, 57, 146.

We've Only Just Begun. w&m; Paul Williams (w) & Roger Nichols (m). c1970, 72, Irving Music Inc. CARPENTERS. 15, 21, 23, 56, 70, 71, 72, 131, 140, 156, 163, 179, 181, 191, 192, 193, 198.

What A Difference You've Made In My Life. w&m; Archie P. Jordan. c1977, Chess Music, Inc. RONNIE MILSAP. 128, 130.

What A Fool Believes. w&m; Michael McDonald & Kenny Loggins. c1978, 79, Snug Music & Milk Money Music. DOOBIE BROTHERS. 22, 27, 31, 57, 136, 146, 162.

What A Wonderful World SEE Wonderful World.

What About Me. w&m; Scott McKenzie. c1966, Hudson Bay Music Co. ANNE MURRAY. 32.

What Are Heavy. w&m; Cy Coleman. c1972, Notable Music Co., Inc. CY COLEMAN CO-OP. 195.

What Are You Doing The Rest Of Your Life. w&m; Alan & Marilyn Bergman (w) & Michel Legrand (m). c1969, United Artists Music Co., Inc. BARBRA STREISAND/ MICHAEL DEES/SHIRLEY BASSEY. 21, 191.

What Becomes Of The Brokenhearted. w&m; James Dean, Paul Riser & William Witherspoon. c1966, Jobete Music Co., Inc. JIMMY RUFFIN. 123, 150, 166.

What Can I Say After I Say I'm Sorry. w&m; Walter Donaldson & Abe Lyman. c1926, 54, 66, Miller Music Corp. KING PLEASURE. 140.

What Does It Take. w&m; Johnny Bristol, Harvey Fuqua & Vernon Bullock. c1968, 69, Jobete Music Co., Inc. JR. WALKER & THE ALL STARS. 123.

What Every Woman Lives For. w&m; Doc Pomus & Mort Shuman. c1966, Elvis Presley, Inc. ELVIS PRESLEY. 173.

What Gives. w&m; Warwick Gilbert & Deniz Tek. c1978, Bleu Disque Music & McGarrett Music. RADIO BIRDMAN. 19.

What Have They Done To My Song, Ma. w&m; Melanie Safka. c1970, Kama Rippa Music, Inc. & Amelanie Music. MELANIE/NEW SEEKERS/RAGTIMERS. 28, 130.

What I Did For Love. w&m; Marvin Hamlisch (m) & Edward Kleban (w). c1975, Marvin Hamlisch & Edward Kleban. Controlled by Wren Music Co., Inc. & American Compass Music Corp. ENGELBERT HUMPERDINCK/MARVIN HAMLISCH/SHIRLEY BASSEY. 103, 131.

What In The World's Come Over You. w&m; Jack Scott. c1959, Unart Music Corp. JACK SCOTT. 3.

What Is And What Should Never Be. w&m; Jimmy Page & Robert Plant. c1969, Superhype Publishing. LED ZEPPELIN. 114.

What Is Life. w&m; George Harrison. c1970, Harrisongs Ltd./Harrisongs Music, Inc. GEORGE HARRISON. 125.

What Is Love. w&m; Lee Pockriss & Paul Vance. c1959, Planetary Music Publishing Corp. PLAYMATES. 161.

What It Is. w&m; Randy Muller & Jeff Lane. c1977, 79, Big Boro Music Publishing Corp. & Careers Music. GARNET MIMMS. 51.

What Kind Of Love Is This. w&m; Johnny Nash. c1962, Planetary Music Publishing Corp. JOEY DEE & THE STARLITERS. 78, 155, 161.

What Now My Love. w&m; G. Becaud (m) & Carl Sigman (w). c1962, Editions Le Rideau Rouge/Remick Music Corp. HERB ALPERT & THE TIJUANA BRASS. 139.

What The World Needs Now Is Love. w&m; Hal David (w) & Burt Bacharach (m). c1965, Blue Seas Music, Inc. & Jac Music Co., Inc. ARTISTICS/DELANEY & BONNIE/JACKIE DE SHANNON. 70, 71.

What You See Is What You Get SEE Whatcha See Is Whatcha Get.

What You Won't Do For Love. w&m; Bobby Caldwell & Alfons Kettner. c1978, Sherlyn Publishing Co., Inc. & Lindseyanne Music Co., Inc. Administered by Sherlyn Publishing Co., Inc. BOBBY CALDWELL/NATALIE COLE & PEABO BRYSON. 24, 65, 66, 73, 157.

What'd I Say. w&m; Ray Charles. c1959, 71, Progressive Music Publishing Co., Inc. Controlled by Unichappell Music, Inc. RAY CHARLES. 92, 101, 137, 155, 199.

Whatever Gets You Thru The Night. w&m; John Lennon. c1974, Lennon Music-ATV Music Corp. JOHN LENNON. 89.

Whatever You Got, I Want. w&m; Mel Larson & Jerry & Gene Marcellino. c1973, Jobete Music Co., Inc. JACKSON 5. 20.

What's A Matter, Baby. w&m; Clyde Otis & Joy Byers. c1962, Eden Music Corp. TIMI YURO. 5.

What's Going On. w&m; Alfred Cleveland, Marvin Gaye & Renauldo Benson. c1970, 71, Jobete Music Co., Inc. MARVIN GAYE. 123.

What's Happened To Blue Eyes. w&m; Jessi Colter. c1975, Baron Music Publishing Co. JESSI COLTER. 28.

What's New Pussycat. w&m; Hal David (w) & Burt Bacharach (m). c1965, United Artists Music Co., Inc. TOM JONES. 102.

What's So Good About Goodbye. w&m; William "Smokey" Robinson. c1961, Jobete Music Co., Inc. SMOKEY ROBINSON & THE MIRACLES. 150.

What's Your Name, What's Your Number. w&m; Roger Cook & Bobby Woods. c1976, 78, Dick James Music, Inc. ANDREA TRUE CONNECTION. 118.

Wheel In The Sky. w&m; Neal Schon, Robert Fleischman & Diane Valory. c1978, Weed High Nightmare Music. Controlled by Screen Gems-EMI Music Inc. JOURNEY. 135.

Wheel Of Fortune. w&m; Arlo Guthrie. c1969, Howard Beach Music Inc. ARLO GUTHRIE. 7.

Wheel Of Life SEE Great Mandella.

Wheels Of Life. w&m; Gino Vannelli. c1978, 79, Almo Music Corp. & Giva Music. GINO VANNELLI. 129.

When. w&m; Paul Evans & Jack Reardon. c1958, Sounds Music Co. & Bib Hurry Music Inc. KALIN TWINS. 4.

When A Man Loves A Woman. w&m; Calvin Lewis & Andrew Wright. c1966, 80, Pronto Music, Inc. & Quincy Music Pub. Co. BETTE MIDLER/PERCY SLEDGE. 100, 162.

When He Walked Me Home SEE Da Doo Ron Ron.

When I Grow Too Old To Dream. w&m; Oscar Hammerstein II (w) & Sigmund Romberg (m). c1934, 35, 62, 63, 66, Metro-Goldwyn-Mayer. Controlled by Robbins Music Corp. LINDA RONSTADT. 140.

When I Grow Up (To Be A Man). w&m; Brian Wilson. c1964, Sea Of Tunes Publishing Co. BEACH BOYS. 9.

When I Need You. w&m; Albert Hammond (w) & Carole Bayer Sager (m). c1976, 77, Unichappell Music, Inc. & Begonia Melodies. LEO SAYER. 40.

When I Paint My Masterpiece. w&m; Bob Dylan. c1971, 76, Big Sky Music. BAND/BOB DYLAN. 131, 170.

When I Wanted You. w&m; Gino Cunico. c1979, Home Grown Music Inc. Administered by Blackwood Music, Inc. BARRY MANILOW/ENGELBERT HUMPERDINCK. 116, 148.

When I'm Gone. w&m; Phil Ochs. c1966, 68, Barricade Music, Inc. PHIL OCHS. 144.

When In Rome. w&m; Phil Ochs. c1968, Barricade Music, Inc. PHIL OCHS. 144.

When It Comes To Having Love SEE Honey I'm Rich.

When It's Over. w&m; Joe Brooks. c1978, Big Hill Music Corp. DEBBY BOONE/ROBERTA FLACK. 73, 128, 130, 135.

When The Levee Breaks. w&m; Jimmy Page, Robert Plant, John Paul Jones, John Bonham & Memphis Minnie. c1972, 73, Superhype Publishing. LED ZEPPELIN. 114.

When The Love Light Starts Shining Through His Eyes. w&m; Eddie Holland, Lamont Dozier & Brian Holland. c1963, 64, 65, 69, Jobete Music Co., Inc. SUPREMES. 150.

When The Moon Comes Over The Mountain. w&m; Kate Smith, Howard Johnson & Harry Woods. c1931, 59, 66, Metro-Goldwyn-Mayer & Robbins Music Corp. Controlled by Robbins Music Corp. KATE SMITH. 140.

When The Party's Over. w&m; Janis Ian. c1974, 75, Mine Music Ltd./April Music Inc. JANIS IAN. 37, 199.

When The Ship Comes In. w&m; Bob Dylan. c1963, M. Witmark & Sons & Warner Bros., Inc. ARLO GUTHRIE/BOB DYLAN/PETER, PAUL & MARY. 35, 41, 43, 67.

When Will I See You Again. w&m; Kenneth Gamble & Leon Huff. c1974, Mighty Three Music. JOHNNY MATHIS/THREE DEGREES. 52, 130.

When You Dance. w&m; Andrew Jones. c1955, Angel Music Inc. TURBANS. 2, 3.

When You Get Right Down To It. w&m; Barry Mann. c1970, Screen Gems-Columbia Music, Inc. DELFONICS. 88.

When Your Heart's On Fire SEE Smoke Gets In Your Eyes.

When You're Hot You're Hot. w&m; Jerry Hubbard. c1971, Vector Music Corp. JERRY REED. 64.

When You're In Love With A Beautiful Woman. w&m; Even Stevens. c1979, DebDave Music, Inc. DR. HOOK. 23, 56, 75, 187.

When You're Loved. w&m; Richard M. & Robert B. Sherman. c1977, 78, Wrather Music Publishing, Inc. DEBBY BOONE. 58, 74.

When You're Next To Me. w&m; Tom Gunn. c1974, Plain & Simple Music. Administered by Music Of The Times Publishing Corp. LOVEMAKERS. 103.

Whenever I Call You "Friend". w&m; Kenny Loggins & Melissa Manchester (w). c1978, Milk Money Music & Rumanian Pickle Works. KENNY LOGGINS. 57, 146, 162.

Where Angels Go, Trouble Follows. w&m; Lalo Schifrin, Tommy Boyce & Bobby Hart. c1968, Screen Gems-Columbia Music, Inc. TOMMY BOYCE & BOBBY HART. 76.

Where Are They Now. w&m; Richard Kerr (w) & John Bettis (m). c1979, Sweet Harmony Music, Inc. & Irving Music Inc. Administered on behalf of Sweet Harmony Music, Inc. by WB Music Corp. BARRY MANILOW. 27, 147.

Where Did All The Good Times Go. w&m; Buddy Buie & James R. Cobb. c1969, Low-Sal, Inc. DENNIS YOST & THE CLASSICS IV. 63, 88.

Where Did Our Love Go. w&m; Eddie Holland, Lamont Dozier & Brian Holland. c1964, Jobete Music Co., Inc. SUPREMES. 123, 150.

Where Do I Begin SEE Love Story, Theme From.

Where Do You Come From. w&m; Ruth Batchelor & Bob Roberts. c1962, Elvis Presley Music. ELVIS PRESLEY. 172.

Where Does The Lovin' Go. w&m; David Gates. c1979, 80, Kipahulu Music Co. Controlled by Colgems-EMI Music Inc. DAVID GATES. 45, 99.

Where Have All The Flowers Gone. w&m; Pete Seeger & Joe Hickerson (Additional verses). c1961, 62, Fall River Music, Inc. JOAN BAEZ/KINGSTON TRIO/PETE SEEGER. 68, 85.

Where Is The Love. w&m; H.W. Casey, R. Finch, W. Clarke & B. Wright. c1975, Sherlyn Publishing Co. BETTY WRIGHT. 26, 77.

Where Is The Love. w&m; Ralph MacDonald & William Salter. c1971, 72, Antisia Music, Inc. ROBERTA FLACK & DONNY HATHAWAY. 58, 134.

Where Peaceful Waters Flow. w&m; Jim Weatherly. c1972, 73, Keca Music, Inc. GLADYS KNIGHT & THE PIPS. 17.

Where Were You When I Was Falling In Love. w&m; Jeff Silbar, Steve Jobe & Sam Lorber. c1979, Bobby Goldsboro Music, Inc. & House Of Gold Music Inc. LOBO. 23.

Which Way To Nowhere. w&m; Jim Webb. c1967, 70 Johnny Rivers Music. FIFTH DIMENSION. 60.

Whiffenpoof Song. w&m; Meade Minnigerode, George S.

Pomeroy, Todd B. Galloway & Rudy Vallee (Revision). c1936, 64, 66, Miller Music Corp. LOUIS ARMSTRONG/MANTOVANI. 140.

While My Guitar Gently Weeps. w&m; George Harrison. c1968, Harrisongs Ltd./Harrisongs Music, Inc. BEATLES/GEORGE HARRISON. 125, 183.

Whippin' Post. w&m; Gregg Allman. c1970, 74, No Exit Music Co., Inc. ALLMAN BROTHERS BAND. 22, 136.

Whispering. w&m; John Schonberger, Richard Coburn & Vincent Rose. c1920, 48, 66, Miller Music Corp. MANTOVANI/MILES DAVIS/NINO & APRIL. 140.

Whispering Bells. w&m; F. Lowry & C.E. Quick. c1957, Gil Music Corp. & Fee Bee Music. DEL VIKINGS. 5.

White Boots Marchin' In A Yellow Land. w&m; Phil Ochs. c1966, 68, Barricade Music, Inc. PHIL OCHS. 144.

White Light, White Heat. w&m; Lou Reed. c1967, Oakfield Avenue Music. VELVET UNDERGROUND. 153.

White Rabbit. w&m; Grace Slick. c1967, Irving Music, Inc. & Copper Penny Music Publishing Co., Inc. JEFFERSON AIRPLANE. 59.

White Silver Sands. w&m; Charles G. (Red) Matthews & Gladys Hart. c1956, Sharina Music. BILL BLACK COMBO. 6, 122.

Whiter Shade Of Pale. w&m; Keith Reid & Gary Brooker. c1967, Essex Music International Ltd./TRO-Essex Music Inc. PROCOL HARUM. 29, 42.

Who Are You. w&m; Peter Townshend. c1978, Eel Pie Publishing Ltd./Towser Tunes, Inc. WHO. 146.

Who Are You Now? w&m; Bruce Hart (w) & Stephen Lawrence (m). c1973, Cinegroup Co. & Music Of The Times Publishing Corp. OLIVIA NEWTON-JOHN. 103.

Who Do Ya Love. w&m; Harry Wayne Casey & Richard Finch. c1978, Sherlyn Publishing Co., Inc. & Herrick Music Inc. K C & THE SUNSHINE BAND. 24, 34, 65, 66.

Who Do You Love. w&m; Ellas McDaniel. c1956, Arc Music Corp. DOORS. 1.

Who Done It. w&m; Keni St. Lewis & Freddie Perren. c1977, Bull Pen Music Co. & Perren-Vibes Music Co. TAVARES. 164.

Who Listens To The Radio. w&m; Steve Cummings & Andrew Pendlebury. c1979, Emu Music & Australian Tumbleweed Music. SPORTS. 97.

Who Will The Next Fool Be. w&m; Charlie Rich. c1961, Knox Music. CHARLIE RICH. 122.

Whodunit SEE Who Done It.

Whole Lotta Love. w&m; Jimmy Page, Robert Plant, John Paul Jones & John Bonham. c1969, Superhype Publishing. LED ZEPPELIN. 22, 36, 55, 114, 136, 138, 139, 174, 191.

Whole Lotta Loving. w&m; Antoine Domino & Dave Bartholomew. c1958, 59, Unart Music Corp. B.B. KING/FATS DOMINO. 82.

Who'll Stop The Rain. w&m; J.C. Fogerty. c1970, Jondora Music. BILL HALEY & THE COMETS/CREEDENCE CLEARWATER REVIVAL/VENTURES. 12, 130, 157.

Who's Been Sleepin' Here. w&m; Jeff Salen & Mikael

Kirke. c1978, Bleu Disque Music Co. & Black Disc Music. TUFF DARTS. 19.

Who's Been Talking. w&m; C. Burnett. c1960, Arc Music Corp. SMOKESTACK LIGHTNING. 1.

Who's Making Love. w&m; Homer Banks, Bettye Crutcher, Don Davis, Raymond Jackson & Jo Ann Bullard. c1968, East-Memphis Music. JOHNNIE TAYLOR. 122.

Who's Sorry Now. w&m; Bert Kalmar, Harry Ruby & Ted Snyder. c1923, 51, Mills Music Inc. CONNIE FRANCIS. 6.

Whose Garden Was This. w&m; Tom Paxton. c1970, United Artists Music Co., Inc. JOHN DENVER/TOM PAXTON. 37, 81, 198.

Why. w&m; Bill Crompton & Tony Sheridan. c1964, Pan Musik Ltd./Al Gallico Music Corp. BEATLES. 125.

Why. w&m; Bob Marcucci & Peter De Angelis. c1959, Debmar Publishing Co. FRANKIE AVALON. 4.

Why Baby Why. w&m; Luther Dixon & Larry Harrison. c1957, Winneton Music Corp. PAT BOONE. 5.

Why Do Fools Fall In Love. w&m; Frankie Lymon & Morris Levy. c1956, 78, Patricia Music Publishing Corp. & Big Seven Music Corp. BEACH BOYS/ FRANKIE LYMON & THE TEENAGERS/JONI MITCHELL. 2, 78, 101, 111, 137, 155, 161, 163.

Why Don't They Understand. w&m; Joe Henderson & Jack Fishman. c1957, Henderson Music Ltd./TRO-Hollis Music Inc. GEORGE HAMILTON IV. 5.

Why Don't We Try A Slow Dance SEE Slow Dance.

Why Don't You Write Me. w&m; Paul Simon. c1969, Paul Simon. SIMON & GARFUNKEL. 143.

Why Have You Left The One (You Left Me For). w&m; Mark True. c1978, Mother Tongue Music. CRYSTAL GAYLE. 65, 73.

Why Me. w&m; Dennis DeYoung. c1979, Stygian Songs. Administered by Almo Music Corp. STYX. 56, 98.

Why Me. w&m; Kris Kristofferson. c1972, Resaca Music Publishing Co. KRIS KRISTOFFERSON. 21, 138, 193, 198.

Wichita Lineman. w&m; Jimmy Webb. c1968, Canopy Music, Inc. GLEN CAMPBELL. 35, 139.

Wicked Messenger. w&m; Bob Dylan. c1968, 76, Dwarf Music. BOB DYLAN. 170.

Wigwam. w&m; Bob Dylan (m). c1970, 76, Big Sky Music. BOB DYLAN. 170.

Wild About My Lovin'. w&m; John B. Sebastian & Geoffrey Muldaur. c1965, Faithful Virtue Music Co., Inc. LOVIN' SPOONFUL. 132.

Wild Mountain Thyme. w&m; Judy Collins. c1968, Warner Bros.-Seven Arts, Inc. JUDY COLLINS. 132.

Wild Night. w&m; Van Morrison. c1971, WB Music Corp. & Caledonia Soul Music. VAN MORRISON. 141.

Wild One. w&m; Bernie Lowe, Kal Mann & Dave Appell. c1960, 79, Lowe Music Publishing Corp. BOBBY RYDELL. 4.

Wild Side Of Life. w&m; W. Warren & A.A. Carter. c1976, 78, Unart Music Corp. ROD STEWART. 199.

Wild Tyme. w&m; Paul Kantner. c1967, 68, Icebag Corp. JEFFERSON AIRPLANE. 108.

Wild World. w&m; Cat Stevens. c1970, 71, Freshwater Music Ltd./Island Music. CAT STEVENS. 136, 183.

Wildfire. w&m; Michael Murphey (w) & Larry Cansler (m). c1975, Warner-Tamerlane Publishing Corp. MICHAEL MURPHEY. 36, 62, 139.

Wildwood Weed. w&m; Jim Stafford & Don Bowman. c1964, Famous Music Corp., Ensign Music Corp. & Parody Publishing Corp. JIM STAFFORD. 106.

Will Anything Happen. w&m; Jack Lee. c1978, Red Admiral Music, Inc. & Monster Island Music. BLONDIE. 33.

Will It Go 'Round In Circles. w&m; Billy Preston & Bruce Fisher. c1972, Irving Music, Inc. & Wep Music Corp. BILLY PRESTON. 53, 104.

Will You Love Me Tomorrow. w&m; Gerry Goffin & Carole King. c1960, 61, 71, Screen Gems-EMI Music Inc. CAROLE KING/DAVE MASON/FOUR SEASONS/ SHIRELLES/ROBERTA FLACK. 28, 58, 76, 134, 135, 156, 158.

Wimoweh SEE Lion Sleeps Tonight.

Wimp. w&m; Javier Escovedo. c1978, Bug Music-Cruisin' Music. ZEROS. 159.

Windflowers. w&m; James & Danny Seals. c1974, Dawn-breaker Music Co. SEALS & CROFTS. 139.

Windmills Of Your Mind. w&m; Marilyn & Alan Bergman (w) & Michel Legrand (m). c1968, United Artists Music Co., Inc. DUSTY SPRINGFIELD/MICHEL LE-GRAND. 21, 192, 193, 195, 198.

Winds Of Chance. w&m; Paul Francis Webster (w) & Alfred Newman (m). c1969, 70, Shamley Music Corp. VINCENT BELL. 94.

Windy. w&m; Ruthann Friedman. c1967, Irving Music, Inc. ASSOCIATION. 64, 70.

Winter Lady. w&m; Leonard Cohen. c1967, 69, Stranger Music, Inc. LEONARD COHEN. 171.

Winter Melody. w&m; Donna Summer, Giorgia Moroder & Pete Bellotte. c1976, 77, Rick's Music, Inc. & Sunday Music. DONNA SUMMER. 58, 128.

Winter Time. w&m; Steve Miller. c1977, Sailor Music. STEVE MILLER BAND. 146.

Winterlude. w&m; Bob Dylan. c1970, 76, Big Sky Music. BOB DYLAN. 170.

Wipe Out. w&m; Surfaris. c1963, Richard Delvy Enter-prises, Inc. & Robin Hood Music Co. SURFARIS. 93.

Wishin' On A Star. w&m; Billie Calvin. c1977, 78, Warner-Tamerlane Publishing Corp. & May 12th Music, Inc. ROSE ROYCE. 146.

Wishing You Were Here. w&m; Peter Cetera. c1974, Big Elk Music. CHICAGO. 93, 128, 156.

Witchy Woman. w&m; Bernie Leadon & Don Henley. c1972, Benchmark Music, WB Music Corp. & Kicking Bear Music. EAGLES. 138, 146, 151.

With A Child's Heart. w&m; Vicki Basemore, Sylvia

Moy & Henry Cosby. c1966, Jobete Music Co., Inc. MICHAEL JACKSON. 32.

With A Little Help From My Friends. w&m; John Lennon & Paul McCartney. c1967, Northern Songs Ltd./ Maclen Music, Inc. BEATLES/JOE COCKER. 61, 159, 182, 202.

With God On Our Side. w&m; Bob Dylan. c1963, M. Witmark & Sons. BOB DYLAN & JOAN BAEZ. 67, 132.

With Pen In Hand. w&m; Bobby Goldsboro. c1968, Detail Music, Inc. & Unart Music Corp. ACE CANNON/ BILLY VERA/BOBBY GOLDSBORO/EDDY ARNOLD/ JOHNNY DARRELL/VIKKI CARR. 80, 140, 191.

With You I'm Born Again. w&m; Carol Connors (w) & David Shire (m). c1979, 80, Check Out Music. Administered by Stone Diamond Music. BILLY PRESTON & SYREETA. 24, 45, 99.

With Your Love. w&m; Marty Balin, Joey Covington & Victor Smith. c1976, Diamondback Music Co. JEFFERSON STARSHIP. 142.

Without Her. w&m; Nilsson. c1967, 68, Rock Music. NILSSON. 93.

Without You. w&m; Peter Ham & Tom Evans. c1970, 72, Apple Publishing Ltd. NILSSON. 63.

Wizard. w&m; Ken Hensley & Mark Clarke. c1972, 73, Sydney Bron Music Co., Ltd./WB Music Corp. URIAH HEEP. 36, 175.

Woman, A Lover, A Friend. w&m; Sid Wyche. c1959, Merrimac Music Corp. JACKIE WILSON. 5, 155.

Woman Tonight. w&m; Dan Peek. c1975, WB Music Corp. AMERICA. 30.

Woman's Gotta Have It. w&m; Bobby Womack, Linda Cooke & Darryl Carter. c1969, 72, Unart Music Corp. & Tracebob Music. Administered by Unart Music Corp. BOBBY WOMACK/JAMES TAYLOR. 82.

Women. w&m; J. Morali, H. Belolo & V. Willis. c1978, Scorpio Music (Black Scorpio). Controlled by Can't Stop Music. VILLAGE PEOPLE. 200.

Wonder Of You. w&m; Baker Knight. c1958, 59, Duchess Music Corp. ELVIS PRESLEY. 94.

Wonderful Baby. w&m; Don McLean. c1974, The Benny Bird Co. & Unart Music Corp. Administered by Unart Music Corp. DON MC LEAN. 82.

Wonderful One. w&m; Adapted from a theme by Marshall Neilan. Dorothy Terriss (w), Paul Williams (m) & Ferde Grofe (m). c1922, 50, 66, Leo Feist, Inc. BOSTON POPS/GLENN MILLER. 140.

Wonderful Time Up There. w&m; Lee Roy Abernathy. c1947, Lee Roy Abernathy. Assigned to Wallace Fowler Publications. PAT BOONE. 160.

Wonderful! Wonderful. w&m; Ben Raleigh & Sherman Edwards. c1956, Edward B. Marks Music Corp. JOHNNY MATHIS. 3.

Wonderful World. w&m; Sam Cooke, Herb Alpert & Lou Adler. c1959, 78, Kags Music Corp. ART GARFUNKEL. 134.

Wonderland. w&m; Milan Williams. c1979, Jobete Music Co., Inc. & Commodores Entertainment Publishing Corp. COMMODORES. 8, 24, 98.

Wonderous Stories. w&m; Jon Anderson. c1977, 78, Topographic Music. Controlled by WB Music Corp. YES. 145.

Won't Get Fooled Again. w&m; Peter Townshend. c1971, Fabulous Music Ltd./Track Music, Inc. WHO. 86.

Won't You Try/Saturday Afternoon. w&m; Paul Kantner. c1967, 68, Icebag Corp. JEFFERSON AIRPLANE. 108, 203.

Wooden Heart. w&m; Fred Wise, Ben Weisman, Kay Twomey & Berthold Kaempfert. c1960, Gladys Music. Controlled by Chappell & Co., Inc. BOBBY VINTON/ ELVIS PRESLEY. 21, 172.

Wooden Ships. w&m; David Crosby & Stephen Stills. c1969, 70, Gold Hill Music & Guerilla Music. CROSBY, STILLS & NASH/CROSBY, STILLS, NASH & YOUNG. 41, 202.

Woodstock. w&m; Joni Mitchell. c1969, 74, Siquomb Publishing Corp. CROSBY, STILLS, NASH & YOUNG/ JONI MITCHELL. 35, 41, 43, 67, 86, 139, 185.

Woogie-Boogie. w&m; Bob Dylan (m). c1970, 76, Big Sky Music. BOB DYLAN. 170.

Wooly Bully. w&m; Domingo Samudio. c1964, 65, Beckie Publishing Co., Inc. SAM THE SHAM & THE PHARAOHS. 4.

Words. w&m; Barry, Robin & Maurice Gibb. c1968, 75, Abigail Music Ltd. BEE GEES. 35.

Words Of Love. w&m; Buddy Holly. c1957, MPL Communications. BUDDY HOLLY & THE CRICKETS. 14.

Words Of Love. w&m; John Phillips. c1966, Trousdale Music Publishers, Inc. MAMAS & THE PAPAS. 119.

Workin' At The Car Wash Blues. w&m; Jim Croce. c1973, 74, Blendingwell Music Inc. & American Broadcasting Music Inc. JIM CROCE. 21, 87, 163, 199.

Workin' My Way Back To You. w&m; S. Linzer & D. Randell. c1965, 66, 79, Screen Gems-EMI Music Inc. & Seasons Four Music Corp. Controlled by Screen Gems-EMI Music, Inc. FOUR SEASONS/SPINNERS. 24, 45, 98.

World. w&m; Barry, Robin & Maurice Gibb. c1967, 75, Abigail Music Ltd. BEE GEES. 35.

World I Used To Know. w&m; Rod McKuen. c1963, 64, Almo Music Corp. JIMMIE RODGERS. 68.

World Is A Ghetto. w&m; Sylvester Allen, Harold R. Brown, Morris Dickerson, Leroy "Lonnie" Jordan, Charles W. Miller, Lee Oskar & Howard Scott. c1972, Far Out Music, Inc. Administered by United Artists Music Co., Inc. WAR. 72, 89, 194.

World Of Our Own. w&m; Tom Springfield. c1965, Springfield Music, Ltd./Chappell& Co. SEEKERS. 68/

World Without Love. w&m; John Lennon & Paul McCartney. c1964, Northern Songs Ltd./Maclen Music Inc. PETER & GORDON. 61.

Worst That Could Happen. w&m; Jim Webb. c1967, 70, Johnny Rivers Music. Assigned to Dramatis Music Corp. BROOKLYN BIRDGE/FIFTH DIMENSION. 60, 163.

Would You. w&m; Arthur Freed (w) & Nacio Herb Brown (m). c1936, 64, 66, Metro-Goldwyn-Mayer. Controlled trolled by Robbins Music Corp. DEBBIE REYNOLDS. 140.

Wouldn't You Believe It. w&m; Arlo Guthrie. c1968, 69, Appleseed Music Inc. ARLO GUTHRIE. 7.

Wreck Of The Edmund Fitzgerald. w&m; Gordon Lightfoot. c1976, Moose Music Ltd. GORDON LIGHTFOOT. 127, 131, 141.

Wreck Of The "John B" SEE Sloop John B.

Wurlitzer Prize. w&m; Chips Moman & Bobby Emmons. c1977, Baby Chick Music, Inc. WAYLON & WILLIE. 128.

X-Offender. w&m; Deborah Harry & Gary Valentine. c1977, Jiru Music, Inc. BLONDIE. 19, 153.

Ya Ya. w&m; Clarence L. Lewis & Morris Levy. c1961, Big Seven Music Corp., Frost Music Corp. & Jon Ware Music Corp. LEE DORSEY. 102, 109, 137, 155.

Yakety Yak. w&m; Jerry Leiber & Mike Stoller. c1958, Tiger Music, Inc. Assigned to Chappell & Co., Inc., Quintet Music, Inc. & Bienstock Publishing Co. Controlled by Chappell & Co. COASTERS. 92, 101, 137, 155.

Yama-Yama-Man. w&m; Wollin Davis (w) & Karl Hoschna (m). c1908, M. Witmark & Sons. GEORGE SEGAL. 132.

Yank Me, Crank Me. w&m; Ted Nugent. c1978, Magicland Music Corp. TED NUGENT. 145.

Yankee Lady. w&m; Jesse Winchester. c1969, Fourth Floor Music, Inc. JESSE WINCHESTER. 37.

Yea! Heavy And A Bottle Of Bread. w&m; Bob Dylan. c1967, 75, Dwarf Music. BOB DYLAN & THE BAND. 170.

Year Of The Cat. w&m; Al Stewart & Peter Wood. c1976, Gwyneth Music Ltd./Unichappell Music, Inc. Controlled on behalf of Gwyneth Music Ltd. by Dick James Music, Inc. AL STEWART. 55, 57, 127, 136, 141, 145, 174.

Years. w&m; Dennis W. Morgan & Kye Fleming. c1979, 80, Pi-Gem Music, Inc. BARBARA MANDRELL/WAYNE NEWTON. 58, 99.

Yellow Bird. w&m; Marilyn Keith (w), Alan Bergman (w) & Norman Luboff (m). c1957, 58, Walton Music Corp. Controlled by Frank Music Corp. EMERALDS/JOHN GARY. 165.

Yellow Days. w&m; Alan Bernstein (w) & Alvaro Carillo (m). c1965, 66, Edward B. Marks Music Corp. EARL "FATHA" HINES. 68.

Yellow Submarine. w&m; John Lennon & Paul McCartney. c1966, Northern Songs Ltd./Maclen Music, Inc. BEATLES. 35, 61.

Yes I'm Ready. w&m; Barbara Mason. c1965, Stilran Music & Dandelion Music Co. BARBARA MASON/CHI-LITES/MAUREEN MC GOVERN/TERI DE SAIRO & K.C. 5, 24, 97.

Yes It's True. w&m; Cyril Jordan & Chris Wilson. c1976, 78, Bleu Disque Music Co. & Photon Music. FLAMIN' GROOVIES. 19.

Yes, It's You. w&m; Nugetre. c1953, Progressive Music Publishing Co., Inc. CLOVERS. 90.

Yes Sir, That's My Baby. w&m; Gus Kahn (w) & Walter Donaldson (m). c1925, 52, Donaldson Publishing Co. BAJA MARIMBA BAND/ETTA JONES/FRANK SINATRA. 140.

Yes We Can-Can. w&m; Allen Toussaint. c1970, 73, Marsaint Music, Inc. POINTER SISTERS. 138.

Yesterday. w&m; John Lennon & Paul McCartney. c1965, Northern Songs Ltd./Maclen Music, Inc. BEATLES. 30, 35, 61, 62, 138, 141, 145.

Yesterday Once More. w&m; Richard Carpenter & John Bettis. c1973, Almo Music Corp., Sweet Harmony Music & Hammer & Nails Music. BROTHERS FOUR/CARPENTERS. 70, 183.

Yester-Me, Yester-You, Yesterday. w&m; Ron Miller (w) & Bryan Wells (m). c1966, Jobete Music Co., Inc. STEVIE WONDER. 123, 142, 150.

Y.M.C.A. w&m; J. Morali, H. Belolo & V. Willis. c1978, Scorpio Music (Black Scorpio). Controlled by Can't Stop Music. VILLAGE PEOPLE. 24, 34, 51, 65, 66, 73, 112, 128, 130, 134, 198, 200.

Yo Yo. w&m; Joe South. c1966, Lowery Music Co., Inc. OSMONDS. 64.

You. w&m; George Harrison. c1975, Ganga Publishing B.V./Loaves And Fishes Music Co., Inc. GEORGE HARRISON. 103.

You. w&m; Randy Edelman. c1975, 76, Unart Music Corp. & Piano Picker Music. Administered by Unart Music Corp. CARPENTERS. 81.

You. w&m; Tom Snow. c1975, Beechwood Music Corp. & Snow Music. RITA COOLIDGE. 58, 135.

You Ain't Goin' Nowhere. w&m; Bob Dylan. c1967, 75, Dwarf Music. BOB DYLAN & THE BAND/JOAN BAEZ. 170.

You Ain't Never Been Loved. w&m; Jessi Colter. c1975, Baron Music Publishing Co. JESSI COLTER. 28.

You Ain't Seen Nothing Yet. w&m; Randy Bachman. c1974, Ranbach Music, a division of R.C.B. Ltd./Screen Gems-EMI Music. BACHMAN-TURNER OVERDRIVE/BURTON CUMMINGS. 77, 134, 142, 156.

You And I. w&m; Johnny W. Bristol. c1974, Bushka Music. JOHNNY BRISTOL. 139.

You And I. w&m; Michaele (w) & L. & P. Sebastian. c1978, Fire Hole Music Corp. & Boona Music. BARBRA STREISAND/MADLEEN KANE. 24, 58, 179.

You And I. w&m; Rick James. c1978, Jobete Music Co., Inc. RICK JAMES & THE STONE CITY BAND. 34, 74.

You And Me. w&m; Alice Cooper & Dick Wagner. c1977, Ezra Music Corp.-Early Frost Music/Kru Music Ltd. ALICE COOPER. 127.

You And Me Against The World. w&m; Paul Williams & Ken Ascher. c1974, Almo Music Corp. HELEN REDDY/PAUL WILLIAMS. 58, 70, 71.

You Angel You. w&m; Bob Dylan. c1973, 76, Ram's Horn Music. BOB DYLAN. 170.

You Are A Song. w&m; Jim Weatherly. c1973, 74, Keca Music Inc. BATDORF & RODNEY. 139.

You Are My Destiny. w&m; Paul Anka. c1958, Spanka Music Corp. PAUL ANKA. 6.

You Are My Heaven. w&m; Stevie Wonder & Eric Mercury. c1979, Jobete Music Co., Inc., Black Bull Music, Inc. & Stone Diamond Music Corp. ROBERTA FLACK. 24.

You Are On My Mind. w&m; James Pankow. c1976, Make Me Smile Music & Big Elk Music. CHICAGO. 121, 164.

You Are So Beautiful. w&m; Billy Preston & Bruce Fisher. c1973, 74, Irving Music, Inc., Wep Music Corp., Almo Music Corp. & Preston Songs. JOE COCKER/OSMONDS/RAY STEVENS. 15, 23, 56, 70, 71.

You Are The Sunshine Of My Life. w&m; Stevie Wonder. c1972, 73, Jobete Music Co., Inc. & Black Bull Music, Inc. STEVIE WONDER. 23, 24, 32, 53, 71, 77, 121, 134, 150, 156, 183.

You Are The Woman. w&m; Rick Roberts. c1976, Stephen Stills Music. FIREFALL. 141.

You Baby (Nobody But You). w&m; P.F. Sloan & Steve Barri. c1965, 66, Trousdale Music Publishers, Inc. & ABC-Dunhill Music, Inc. MAMAS & THE PAPAS/ TURTLES. 3, 119.

You Beat Me To The Punch. w&m; William "Smokey" Robinson & Ronald White. c1962, Jobete Music Co., Inc. MARY WELLS. 123, 150.

You Belong To Me. w&m; Carly Simon (w) & Michael McDonald (m). c1977, 78, Snug Music & C'est Music. CARLY SIMON. 57, 146, 178.

You Better Move On. w&m; Arthur Alexander. c1962, Keva Music Inc. ARTHUR ALEXANDER. 6.

You Came A Long Way From St. Louis. w&m; Bob Russell (w) & John Benson Brooks (m). c1948, Jewel Music Publishing Co., Inc. CHUCK BERRY. 169.

You Can Get It Girl   SEE   I Got My Mind Made Up.

You Can't Always Get What You Want. w&m; Mick Jagger & Keith Richard. c1969, Abkco Music, Inc. ROLLING STONES. 12, 128.

You Can't Catch Me. w&m; Chuck Berry. c1956, Snapper Music Inc. Assigned to Big Seven Music Corp. CHUCK BERRY. 109, 137, 161.

You Can't Change That. w&m; Ray Parker, Jr. c1979, Raydiola Music. RAYDIO. 27, 57.

You Can't Hurry Love. w&m; Eddie Holland, Lamont Dozier & Brian Holland. c1965, 66, Jobete Music Co., Inc. SUPREMES. 123, 150, 166.

You Can't Sit Down. w&m; Delecta Clark, Cornell Muldrow & Kal Mann. c1963, 68, Conrad Music, a division of Arc Music Corp. DOVELLS. 168.

You Can't Win. w&m; Charlie Smalls. c1974, 78, Fox Fanfare Music, Inc. MICHAEL JACKSON. 51.

You Caught Me Smilin'   SEE   Smilin'.

You Cheated. w&m; Don Burch. c1958, Balcones Publishing Co. SHIELDS. 6.

You Decorated My Life. w&m; Bob Morrison & Debbie Hupp. c1978, Music City Music, Inc. KENNY ROGERS. 176, 198, 199.

You Don't Bring Me Flowers. w&m; Neil Diamond & Marilyn & Alan Bergman (w). c1977, 78, Stonebridge Music & Threesome Music. NEIL DIAMOND & BARBRA STREISAND. 27, 57, 73, 87, 136, 146.

You Don't Have To Be A Baby To Cry. w&m; Bob Merrill & Terry Shand. c1950, R.F.D. Music Publishing Co., Inc. CARAVELLES. 4.

You Don't Have To Be A Star. w&m; J. Dean & J. Glover. c1976, Groovesville Music. Controlled by Screen Gems-EMI Music Inc. MARILYN MC COO & BILLY DAVIS JR. 134.

You Don't Have To Say You Love Me. w&m; Vicki Wickham (w), Simon Napier-Bell (w) & P. Donaggio (m). c1965, 66, Accordo Edizioni Musicali/Miller Music Corp. DUSTY SPRINGFIELD/ELVIS PRESLEY. 21, 72, 102, 137, 192.

You Don't Know Where Your Interest Lies. w&m; Paul Simon. c1967, Paul Simon. 143.

You Don't Love Me Anymore. w&m; Alan Ray & Jeff Raymond. c1977, 78, Debdave Music, Inc. & Briarpatch Music. EDDIE RABBITT. 199.

You Don't Mess Around With Jim. w&m; Jim Croce. c1971, 72, Blendingwell Music, Inc., Wingate Music Corp. & American Broadcasting Music, Inc. JIM CROCE. 89, 104, 195.

You Don't Own Me. w&m; John Madara & Dave White. c1963, Jerjoda Music, Inc. Controlled by Unichappell Music, Inc. LESLEY GORE. 6.

You Gonna Make Me Love Somebody Else. w&m; Kenneth Gamble & Leon Huff. c1978, Mighty Three Music. JONES GIRLS. 75.

You Got It. w&m; Jerry Ragovoy & Linda Laurie. c1978, Society Hill Music, Inc. & Brooklyn Music Co. DIANA ROSS. 48, 73, 135.

You Got Me Hummin'. w&m; Isaac Hayes & David Porter. c1966, 70, Pronto Music, Inc. & East-Memphis Music Corp. COLD BLOOD. 149.

You Gotta Make Your Own Sunshine. w&m; Neil Sedaka & Howard Greenfield. c1976, Neil Sedaka Music. NEIL SEDAKA. 141.

You Haven't Done Nothin'. w&m; Stevie Wonder. c1974, Jobete Music Co., Inc. & Black Bull Music, Inc. STEVIE WONDER. 52, 53, 150.

You Keep Me Dancin'. w&m; Denny Randell & Sandy Linzer. c1977, 78, Unichappell Music, Inc. & Featherbed Music. SAMANTHA SANG. 40.

You Keep Me Hangin' On. w&m; Brian Holland, Lamont Dozier & Eddie Holland. c1966, 67, 68, Jobete Music Co., Inc. SUPREMES. 95, 123.

You Know Who I Am. w&m; Leonard Cohen. c1967, 69, Stranger Music, Inc. LEONARD COHEN. 171.

You Lied   SEE   Don't Play That Song.

You Light Up My Life. w&m; Joe Brooks. c1976, 77,

Big Hill Music Corp. DEBBIE BOONE. 23, 56, 58, 71, 73, 128, 134, 142.

You Little Trustmaker. w&m; Christopher Mark Jackson. c1973, 74, Dramatis Music Corp. TYMES. 52.

You Love The Thunder. w&m; Jackson Browne. c1977, 78, Swallow Turn Music. Administered by WB Music Corp. JACKSON BROWNE. 87, 146.

You Make Loving Fun. w&m; Christine McVie. c1976, 77, Michael Fleetwood/Warner-Tamerlane Publishing Corp. FLEETWOOD MAC. 22, 87, 136, 146.

You Make Me Feel Brand New. w&m; Thom Bell & Linda Creed. c1974, Mighty Three Music. Administered by Blackwood Music, Inc. STYLISTICS. 21, 24, 52, 131, 165.

You Make Me Feel Like Dancing. w&m; Leo Sayer & Vincent Poncia. c1976, Long Manor Music, Ltd. & Braintree Music, Inc. Controlled by Chrysalis Music Corp. LEO SAYER. 46, 96, 118, 121, 124, 127, 128, 131, 133, 141, 145, 177, 181, 198.

You Make Me Feel (Mighty Real). w&m; Sylvester (w) & James "Tip" Wirrick (m). c1978, 79, Bee Keeper Music & Tipsyl Music. SYLVESTER. 24, 34, 51.

You Make Me Real. w&m; Jim Morrison. c1970, Doors Music Co. DOORS. 54.

You May Be Right. w&m; Billy Joel. c1979, 80, Impulsive Music & April Music Inc. BILLY JOEL. 116.

You Need A Woman Tonight. w&m; Dana Merino. c1976, 78, ABC-Dunhill Music, Inc. CAPTAIN & TENNILLE. 65, 73.

You Needed Me. w&m; Randy Goodrum. c1975, 76, 78, Chappell & Co., Inc. & Ironside Music. Administered by Chappell & Co., Inc. ANNE MURRAY. 40, 47.

You Never Have To Say You're Sorry SEE Love Means.

You + Me = Love. w&m; Norman Whitfield. c1976, Stone Diamond Music Corp. UNDISPUTED TRUTH. 95, 164.

You Really Got Me. w&m; Ray Davies. c1964, Edward Kassner Music Ltd./Jay Boy Music Corp. KINKS/VAN HALEN. 135.

You Really Rock Me SEE Rock Me.

You Shook Me. w&m; Willie Dixon & J.B. Lenore. c1962, Arc Music Corp. LED ZEPPELIN. 1.

You Should Be Dancing. w&m; Barry, Robin & Maurice Gibb. c1976, Stigwood Music. By arrangement with Brothers Gibb. Administered by Unichappell Music, Inc. BEE GEES. 46, 62, 131, 133, 141.

You Should Do It. w&m; Peter Brown & Robert Rans (w). c1977, 78, Sherlyn Publishing Co., Inc. & Decibel Publishing Co. Administered by Sherlyn Publishing Co., Inc. PETER BROWN. 74.

You Stepped Into My Life. w&m; Barry, Robin & Maurice Gibb. c1976, Brothers Gibb B.V./Stigwood Music Inc. Administered by Unichappell Music, Inc. MELBA MOORE. 40, 50.

You Take My Breath Away. w&m; Bruce Hart (w) & Stephen Lawrence (m). c1978, 79, The Laughing Willow Music Co. REX SMITH. 140, 176, 198, 199.

You Take My Heart Away. w&m; Carol Connors (w),

Ayn Robbins (w) & Bill Conti (m). c1976, United Artists Corp. Administered by United Artists Music Co., Inc. & Unart Music Corp. SHIRLEY BASSEY/STEVE LAWRENCE. 81.

You Talk Too Much. w&m; Joe Jones & Reginald Hall. c1960, Nom Music, Inc. & Ben-Ghazi Enterprises. JOE JONES. 78, 102, 137, 155, 161.

You Took The Words Right Out Of My Mouth. w&m; Jim Steinman. c1977, Edward B. Marks Music Corp., Neverland Music & Peg Music Co. MEATLOAF. 120.

You Tore Me Down . w&m; Cyril Jordan & Chris Wilson. c1976, 78, Bleu Disque Music Co. & Photon Music. FLAMIN' GROOVIES. 19.

You Turn Me On I'm A Radio. w&m; Joni Mitchell. c1972, Crazy Crow Music. JONI MITCHELL. 127, 151.

You Were On My Mind. w&m; Sylvia Fricker. c1964, 65, M. Witmark & Sons & Warner Bros. Inc. IAN & SYLVIA/LETTERMEN/WE FIVE. 35, 67, 69, 100, 132, 139.

You Won't See Me. w&m; John Lennon & Paul McCartney. c1965, 74, Northern Songs Ltd./Maclen Music, Inc. BEATLES. 139, 159.

You, You're The One. w&m; Keith Reinhard (w), Dan Nichols (w) & Ginny Redington (m). c1975, 77, G. & W. Publishing Corp. MACDONALD'S COMMERCIAL. 193.

You'll Accomp'ny Me. w&m; Bob Seger. c1979, 80, Gear Publishing Co. BOB SEGER & THE SILVER BULLET BAND. 162, 190.

You'll Never Find Another Love Like Mine. w&m; Kenny Gamble & Leon Huff. c1976, Mighty Three Music. Administered by Blackwood Music Inc. LIVING VOICES/LOU RAWLS. 130, 184, 193.

Young And The Restless, Theme From SEE Nadia's Theme.

Young Blood. w&m; Jerry Leiber, Mike Stoller & Doc Pomus. c1957, Tiger Music Inc. Assigned to Unichappell Music, Trio Music Inc, & Freddy Bienstock Music Co. Administered by Unichappell Music, Inc. BAD COMPANY/COASTERS. 91, 155, 198.

Young Blood. w&m; Rickie Lee Jones. c1978, 79, Easy Money Music. RICKIE LEE JONES. 147.

Young Dreams. w&m; Aaron Schroeder & Martin Kalmanoff. c1958, Gladys Music, Inc. ELVIS PRESLEY. 173.

Young Girl. w&m; Jerry Fuller. c1968, Viva Music & Warner-Tamerlane Publishing Corp. GARY PUCKETT & THE UNION GAP. 35, 138, 161.

Young Girl Sunday Blue. w&m; Marty Balin & Paul Kantner. c1967, 68, Icebag Corp. JEFFERSON AIRPLANE. 108.

Young Hearts Run Free. w&m; Dave Crawford. c1976, DaAnn Music. CANDI STATON. 118, 141.

Your Love. w&m; Walter Johnson & H.B. Barnum. c1975, 77, El Patricio Music. MARILYN MC COO & BILLY DAVIS, JR./TASTE OF HONEY. 128, 164.

Your Love Has LIfted Me Higher And Higher. SEE Higher And Higher.

Your Love Is Like Nuclear Waste SEE Nuclear Waste.

Your Mamma Don't Dance. w&m; Jim Messina & Kenny Loggins. c1972, 73, Jasperilla Music Co., Wingate Music Corp. & American Broadcasting Music, Inc. LOGGINS & MESSINA. 36, 55, 72, 136, 174.

Your Mother Should Know. w&m; John Lennon & Paul McCartney. c1967, Northern Songs Ltd./Maclen Music, Inc. BEATLES. 141.

Your Move. w&m; Jon Anderson. c1971, Yessongs, Ltd./Cotillion Music, Inc. YES. 152.

Your Own Special Way. w&m; Michael Rutherford. c1976, 77, Fuse Music Ltd./WB Music Corp. GENESIS. 127, 175.

Your Precious Love. w&m; Valerie Simpson & Nickolas Ashford. c1967, Jobete Music Co., Inc. IKE & TINA TURNER/MARVIN GAYE & TAMMI TERRELL. 13, 123.

Your Smiling Face. w&m; James Taylor. c1977, Country Road Music Inc. JAMES TAYLOR. 136, 146.

Your Song. w&m; Elton John & Bernie Taupin. c1969, Dick James Ltd./Dick James Music, Inc. ELTON JOHN. 62, 115, 117.

Your Time Is Gonna Come. w&m; Jimmy Page & John Paul Jones. c1969, Superhype Publishing. LED ZEPPELIN. 114.

You're A Big Girl Now. w&m; Bob Dylan. c1974, 76, Ram's Horn Music. BOB DYLAN. 170.

You're A Wonderful One. w&m; Eddie Holland, Lamont Dozier & Brian Holland. c1964, 65, 74, Jobete Music Co., Inc. MARVIN GAYE. 150.

You're All I Need To Get By. w&m; Nickolas Ashford & Valerie Simpson. c1968, 70, Jobete Music Co., Inc. ARETHA FRANKLIN/JOHNNY MATHIS & DENIECE WILLIAMS/MARVIN GAYE & TAMMI TERRELL/ TONY ORLANDO & DAWN. 13, 123, 135, 150.

You're Gonna Hear From Me. w&m; Dory Previn (w) & Andre Previn (m). c1965, Remick Music Corp. FRANK SINATRA/SHIRLEY BASSEY. 43.

You're Gonna Make Me Lonesome When You Go. w&m; Bob Dylan, c1974, 79, Ram's Horn Music. BOB DYLAN. 170.

You're In My Heart. w&m; Rod Stewart. c1977, Rod Stewart/Riva Music, Inc. ROD STEWART. 145, 178.

You're Kind. w&m; Paul Simon. c1975, Paul Simon. PAUL SIMON. 143.

You're My Best Friend. w&m; John Deacon. c1975, B. Feldman & Co., Ltd., trading as Trident Music/Big 3 Music Corp. QUEEN. 184, 198.

You're My Everything. w&m; Norman Whitfield, Roger Penzabene & Cornelius Grant. c1967, Jobete Music Co., Inc. TEMPTATIONS. 123, 150.

You're My World. w&m; Carl Sigman (w) & Umberto Bindi (m). c1963, 64, Edizioni Musicali M.E.C./Chappell & Co., Inc. HELEN REDDY. 15, 21, 196.

You're Only Lonely. w&m; J.D. Souther. c1979, Ice Age Music. J.D. SOUTHER. 57, 188.

You're Sixteen. w&m; Bob & Dick Sherman. c1960, Viva Music, Inc. & Warner-Tamerlane Publishing Corp. JOHNNY BURNETTE/RINGO STARR. 35, 100, 133, 138, 197.

You're So Fine. w&m; W. Schofield, L. Finney & R. West. c1958, C & B West Publishing Co. FALCONS. 5.

You're So Square Baby, I Don't Care SEE Baby, I Don't Care.

You're So Vain. w&m; Carly Simon. c1972, 73, Quackenbush Music Ltd. CARLY SIMON. 22, 36, 55, 62, 124, 133, 136, 139, 141, 174, 183, 185.

You're Still A Young Man. w&m; E. Castillo & S. Kupka. c1972, Kuptillo Music. TOWER OF POWER. 105.

You're The Best Thing That Ever Happened To Me. w&m; Jim Weatherly. c1972, Keca Music Inc. GLADYS KNIGHT & THE PIPS. 17.

You're The Devil In Disguise. w&m; Bill Giant, Bernie Baum & Florence Kaye. c1963, Elvis Presley Music, Inc. ELVIS PRESLEY. 172.

You're The Love. w&m; David Batteau & Louis Shelton (m). c1978, Dawnbreaker Music, Blue Harbor Music & David Batteau Music. SEALS & CROFTS. 135, 142.

You're The One That I Want. w&m; John Farrar. c1978, Stigwood Music, Inc., John Farrar Music & Ensign Music Inc. JOHN TRAVOLTA & OLIVIA NEWTON-JOHN. 178.

You're The Reason. w&m; Bobby Edwards, Mildred Imes, Fred Henley & Terry Fell. c1960, 64, American Music Inc. Assigned to Vogue Music Inc. JOHNNY TILLOTSON. 160.

Yours Is No Disgrace. w&m; Jon Anderson, Chris Squire, Steve Howe, Tony Kaye & Bill Bruford. c1971, 72, Yessongs Ltd. YES. 36.

You've Got A Friend. w&m; Carole King. c1971, Colgems-EMI Music Inc. ANNE MURRAY/CAROLE KING/JAMES TAYLOR/LETTERMEN/ROBERTA FLACK & DONNY HATHAWAY. 23, 58, 71, 130, 134, 142, 183.

You've Got Love. w&m; Johnny Wilson, Roy Orbison & Norman Petty. c1957, MPL Communications, Inc. BUDDY HOLLY. 14.

You've Got Personality. SEE Personality.

You've Got To Hide Your Love Away. w&m; John Lennon & Paul McCartney. c1965, Northern Songs Ltd./ Mavlrn Music, Inc. BEATLES/SILKIE. 35, 61, 141, 159.

You've Got What It Takes. w&m; Berry & Gwen Gordy & Tyran Carlo. c1957, 59, 67, 71, Jobete Music Co., Inc. MARV JOHNSON. 123, 150.

You've Got Your Troubles. w&m; Roger Greenaway & Roger Cook. c1965, Mills Music, Ltd./Mills Music, Inc. FORTUNES. 6.

You've Lost That Lovin' Feelin'. w&m; Barry Mann, Cynthia Weil & Phil Spector. c1964, 65, 71, Screen Gems-EMI Music Inc. BILLY PRESTON/ELVIS PRESLEY/MARTHA REEVES/RIGHTEOUS BROTHERS/ROBERTS FLACK & DONNY HATHAWAY. 128, 158.

You've Made Me So Very Happy. w&m; Berry Gordy, Jr., Patrice & Brenda Holloway & Frank Wilson. c1967, 69, 70, Jobete Music Co., Inc. BLOOD, SWEAT & TEARS. 123, 150.

You've Really Got A Hold On Me. w&m; William "Smokey" Robinson. c1962, 63, Jobete Music Co. SMOKEY ROBINSON & THE MIRACLES. 123, 150.

Yowsah, Yowsah, Yowsah. SEE Dance, Dance, Dance (K. Lehman, B. Edwards & N. Rodgers).

Zoom. w&m; Esther Navarro. c1956, 78, Adam R. Levy & Father Enterprises, Inc. CADILLACS. 2.

Zorba The Greek, Theme From. w&m; Mikis Theodorakis (m). c1964, 65, Twentieth Century Music Corp. Controlled by Miller Music Corp. MANTOVANI/ TIJUANA BRASS. 140.

3

FIRST LINE INDEX

"A-bop-bop-a-loom-op a-lap bop boom, tutti frutti au ruti." Tutti Frutti.

"Across the bay a lady waits to hold me tight." Sail Away (R. Vanhoy).

"Action speaks louder than words." Action Speaks Louder Than Words.

"After a while I began wanting to be with you." Still The Lovin' Is Fun.

"After a while we took in the clothes." Clothes Line Saga.

"After long enough of being alone...." Only Yesterday.

"After mignight, we're gonna let it all hang down." After Midnight.

"After six hours of school, I've had enough for the day." Dance, Dance, Dance (B. & C. Wilson)

"After you get rid of me who will the next fool be?" Who Will The Next Fool Be.

"After you go, I can catch up on my readin'." Bluer Than Blue.

"Ah (22x), you're gonna say ya miss me." I'm Gonna Love You Too.

"Ah, ah, ah, ah, I get a little peck and you're off to bed." Let Me Know (I Have A Right).

"Ah, ah, ah, I don't know how many stars there are up in the heavenly sky." Maybe Tomorrow.

"Ah, ah, ah, woo oo, please stay with me now, don't you let me go." Stay (C. Khan & R. Calhoun).

"Ah, ah hah, you've got a cute way of talkin'." You Make Me Feel Like Dancing.

"Ah, ah, oo, if you need me, call me, no matter where you are." Ain't No Mountain High Enough.

"Ah, ah, we come from the land of the ice and snow." Immigrant Song.

"Ah, ah, we may be big or small, or black and white eternally." Desire.

"Ah, caught you smiling at me." Bron-Y-Aur-Stomp.

"Ah, dance with me, come on dance with me baby." After The Dance.

"Ah, do ya, do ya, do ya, do you love what you feel? Do You Love What You Feel.

"Ah ha yeah, yeah, what's an hour of the day." It Only Takes A Minute.

"Ah! I got a feeling inside of me." New Rose.

"Ah, let's do it!" Dance Across The Floor.

"Ah, look at all the lonely people!" Eleanor Rigby.

"Ah, love, soft as an easy chair," Evergreen.

"Ah, oo, in my own way I say too much." Such A Woman.

"Ah, peace like a river ran through the city." Peace Like A River.

"Ah, you can talk about the pit barbecue." Mess Around.

"Ain't it foggy outside, all the planes have been grounded." Sandman.

"Ain't it just like the night to play tricks when you're tryin' to be so quiet?" Visions Of Johanna.

"Ain't no more Motown review, and the Beatles have broken up too." Motown Review.

"Ain't no stoppin' us now, we're on the move." Ain't No Stoppin' Us Now.

"Ain't no sunshine when she's gone." Ain't No Sunshine.

"Ain't no woman like the one I've got." Ain't No Woman Like The One I've Got.

"Ain't nothing like the real thing baby. Ain't Nothing Like The Real Thing.

"All alone at the end of the evening, and the bright lights have faded to blue." Take It To The Limit.

"All around the world, rock and roll is all they play. All Around The World.

"All day long I hear my telephone ring, friends calling giving their advice." Back In My Arms Again.

"All day long you're asking me what I see in you." I Don't Know Why (I Just Do).

"All hands on deck." Salty Dog.

"All I want is a party doll, to come along with me when I'm feelin' wild." Party Doll.

"All I want is a room with a view." Picture This.

"All is fair in love." All In Love Is Fair.

"All is loneliness here for me." All Is Loneliness.

"All it took was a special look, and I felt I knew you before." Think About Me.

"All my bags are packed, I'm ready to go." Leaving On A Jet Plane.

"All my boyhood friends told me I'd fail. I Won't Look Back.

"All my friends had to ask me something they didn't understand." Treat Her Like A Lady.

"All my life was a paper once plain, pure and white." You Decorated My Life.

"All my life's a circle, sunrise and sundown." Circles.

"All my trials, Lord, soon be over." All My Trials (P. Yarrow, P. Stookey & M. Okun).

"All of a sudden she was on my mind." <u>If I Could Have Her Tonight</u>.

"All of my days were long, none of my nights would end." <u>I Never Said I Love You</u>.

"All of my friends come to see me last night." <u>Black Peter</u>.

"All of my love, all of my kissin'." <u>Oh Boy</u>.

"All of the ladies attending the ball are requested to gaze in the faces found on their dance card." <u>Change Partners</u>.

"All our times have come." <u>Reaper</u>.

"All that I am or ever hope to be lies in your hands." <u>All That I Am</u>.

"All the empty words I've spoken...." <u>Livin Ain't Livin'</u>.

"All the leaves are brown, and the sky is grey." <u>California Dreamin'</u>.

"All the lovin' is lovin'." <u>All Your Love</u>.

"All the tired horses in the sun, how'm I s'posed to get any ridin' done." <u>All The Tired Horses</u>.

"All the world loves a lover." <u>Love, You Funny Thing</u>.

"All the world over, it's so easy to see, people ev'rywhere just wanna be free." <u>People Got To Be Free</u>.

"All the years combine, they melt into a dream." <u>Stella Blue</u>.

"All through this long and sleepless night I hear my neighbors talking." <u>Shake Me, Wake Me (When It's Over)</u>.

"All you gotta do is dance, dance, dance." <u>Life Of The Party</u>.

"All your life you've waited for love to come and stay." <u>Goodbye Girl</u>.

"All you fellows gather 'round me and let me give you some good advice." <u>Who's Making Love</u>.

"All you've got is one life, living once can be rough." <u>Once Is Enough</u>.

"Almost heaven, West Virginia, Blue Ridge Mountains, Shenandoah River." <u>Take Me Home, Country Roads</u>.

"Along a mountain pass, there is a patch of grass where the swingin' shepherd plays his tune." <u>Swingin' Shepherd Blues</u>.

"Although I know our love is going strong, little surprises kind of help it along." <u>Making A Good Thing Better</u>.

"Although the things you've done I wouldn't criticize." <u>Shine A Little Love</u>.

"Always and forever, each moment with you is just like a dream to me that somehow came true." <u>Always And Forever</u>.

"Always together, together, forever, always together forever." <u>I Pledge My Love</u>.

"Am I fool number one or am I fool number two?" <u>Fool No. 1</u>.

"Am I really hard to please?" <u>I Thought It Took A Little Time</u>.

"Amazing grace how sweet the sound, that saved a wretch like me." <u>Amazing Grace</u>.

"'Amazing grace' used to be her fav'rite song." <u>Amazing Grace (Used To Be Her Favorite Song)</u>.

"Amber cascades all over today." <u>Amber Cascades</u>.

"And he'll tell her he's been working late again." <u>Daytime Friends</u>.

"And here's to you, Mrs. Robinson, Jesus loves you more than you will know." <u>Mrs. Robinson</u>.

"And I just got to be me, me, me." <u>Free (Wanna Be Free)</u>.

"And I know if I don't go I'll never ever be like a rolling stone." <u>I'll Always Call Your Name</u>.

"And I love you so." <u>And I Love You So</u>.

"And I wake up in the morning with my hair down in my eyes and she says 'Hi.'" <u>Little Green Apples</u>.

"And if I say to you tomorrow take my hand child, come with me." <u>What Is And What Should Never Be</u>.

"And if it's bad, don't let it get you down, you can take it." <u>Hold Your Head Up</u>.

"And it looks like daylight, gonna catch me up, gonna catch me up again." <u>Daylight</u>.

"And so once again, my dear Johnny, my dear friend, and so once again, you are fighting us all." <u>Fiddle And The Drum</u>.

"And the crabs are crazy; they scuttle back and forth." <u>Santa Domingo</u>.

"And the night comes again to the circle studded sky." <u>Crucifixion</u>.

"And the ship sets the sail." <u>Pleasures Of The Harbor</u>.

"And the sign said: 'Long-haired freaky people need not apply.'" <u>Signs</u>.

"And though you try to justify the meaning of the note you sent this evening to my door, you're not deceiving me." <u>Tell Me To My Face</u>.

"And when God gave out rhythm, He sure was good to you." <u>Popsicle Toes</u>.

"And when I die and when I'm dead, dead and gone." <u>And When I Die</u>.

"And when I go away I know my heart can stay with my love." <u>My Love</u> (L. & P. McCartney).

"And who will write love songs for you when I am lord at last." <u>Priests</u>.

"Angel whispered to me, when I woke this morning." <u>You Are My Heaven</u>.

"Angel, with those angel eyes." <u>Angel</u> (S. Tepper & R. Bennett).

"Angie, Angie, when will those clouds all disappear?" <u>Angie</u>.

"Another date has ended at the door." <u>No Communication</u>.

"Another day, another dollar, after I've sang and hollered." <u>Highway Song</u>.

"Another day is at end." <u>Shannon</u>.

"Another night has gone by." It's Not Killing Me.

"Another Saturday night and I ain't got nobody." Another Saturday Night.

"Anthony works in the grocery store savin' his pennies for some day." Movin' Out (Anthony's Song).

"Any time, any day, you can hear the people say that love is blind, well, I don't know but I say love is kind." Listen To What The Man Said.

"Any time that you want me..." Anytime.

"Any time you're feeling lonely, any time you're feeling blue, any time you feel downhearted, that will prove your love for me is true." Any Time.

"Any way you want it, that's the way you need it, any way you want it." Any Way You Want It (S. Erry and N. Schon).

"Any way you want it, you can call me any day." Any Way You Want It. (D. Clark).

"Anything you want, any time at all." Anything You Want.

"April, come she will." April Come She Will.

"Aquarius, Libra, Leo, Cancer." Float On.

"Arabian wind, the needle's eye is thin." Blues For Allah.

"Are we really happy with this lonely game we play?" This Masquerade.

"Are you feelin' happy?" Do You Feel All Right.

"Are you from Dixie?" Are You From Dixie.

"Are you going to Scarborough Fair?" Scarborough Fair.

"Are you going to Scarborough Fair: parsley, sage, rosemary and thyme." Scarborough Fair/Canticle.

"Are you gonna take me home tonight?" Fat Bottomed Girls.

"Are you lonesome tonight?" Are You Lonesome Tonight.

"Arrested on charges of unemployment, he was sittin' in the witness stand." Brown Eyed Handsome Man.

"Arrivederci, Roma." Arrivederci, Roma.

"As I approach the prime of my life, I find I have the time of my life." This Is All I Ask.

"As I got on a city bus and found a vacant seat...." Nadine (Is It You).

"As I stand alone on this moonful night for the first time I feel alone in life." I'm Ready For Love.

"As I walk along I wonder what went wrong with our love." Runaway. (D. Shannon and M. Crook).

"As I walk down the highway all I do is sing this song." Out On The Tiles.

"As I walk this land with broken dreams, I have visions of many things." What Becomes Of The Broken-Hearted.

"As I walk through this world, nothing can stop the Duke of Earl." Duke Of Earl.

"As I was goin' over Gilgarra mountain, I spied Colonel Farrell and his money he was countin'." Gilgarra Mountain.

"As I was out walking on a corner one day, I spied an old hobo, in a doorway he lay." Only A Hobo.

"As I was walkin' 'roun' Grosvenor Square...." Scarlet Begonias.

"As I was walking down the street last night, a pretty little girl came into sight." Greenbacks.

"As I was walking down the street one day...." Does Anybody Really Know What Time It Is.

"As I went out one morning to breathe the air around Tom Paine's...." As I Went Out One Morning.

"As I write this letter, send my love to you." P.S. I Love You.

"As my life goes on I believe somehow something's changed." Searchin' So Long.

"As the bitter tears fall from your eyes...." That's The Way Love Is.

"As the son of a son of a sailor, I went out on the sea for adventure." Son Of A Son Of A Sailor.

"As time goes on I realize just what you mean to me...." Colour My World.

"As we go marching, marching in the beauty of the day...." Bread And Roses.

"As we walk along and I hold your hand...." Still Waters Run Deep.

"As you brush your shoes and stand before the mirror...." Wild Night.

"Ask the angels who they're callin'." Ask The Angels.

"Asked a girl what she wanted to be." Drive My Car.

"At a bar down in Dallas, an old man chimed in." I Wish I Was Eighteen Again.

"At first I was afraid, I was petrified." I Will Survive.

"At last, my love has come along." At Last.

"At seventeen we fell in love high school sweethearts." Too Hot.

"At the first flash of Eden we raced down to the sea." Waiting For The Sun.

"At times I just don't know how you could be anything but beautiful." Beautiful.

"Aw, ev'rybody get on the floor, let's dance." Shake Your Booty.

"Aw, I'm itchin' and I don't know where to scratch." Baby Scratch My Back.

"Away above my head I see the strangest sight." Fiddler On The Roof.

"Away out here they got a name for rain, and wind, and fire." They Call The Wind Maria.

"A-well-a, bless my soul what's wrong with me?" All Shook Up.

" Ba do di o di o di o di o do mm, ba do di o di o di o di do mm, sat in on my shoulder and a smile on my lips, how lucky can you get?" How Lucky Can You Get.

"Babe, Baby, Baby, I'm gonna leave you." Babe, I'm Gonna Leave You.

"Babe, I'm leaving, I must be on my way." Babe.

"Babe, somewhere I know I'm gonna find it, babe." Very Special Love Song.

"Babe, you're gettin' closer, the lights are goin' dim." Way Down.

"Baby, babe let's get together honey, honey me and you." Get Down Tonight.

"Baby, baby, baby don't leave me." Where Did Our Love Go.

"Baby, oh baby, boogaloo down Braodway." Boogaloo Down Broadway.

"Baby, please, please don't take your love from me." Heaven Knows.

"Baby, so they give you anything." Mama Can't Buy You Love.

"Baby, there's a chance you ought to take, a chance of a mistake you gotta make." One Step Closer.

"Baby, we can talk all night." Two Out Of Three Ain't Bad.

"Baby's good to me you know." I Feel Fine.

"Baby's into runnin' 'round hangin' with the crowd." Lowdown.

"Back home you'll see those ruby berries shine." I'm On My Way.

"Back off, boogaloo, I said." Back Off Boogaloo.

"Backstroke lover always hidin' 'neath the covers till I talked to your daddy." Walk This Way.

"Bad girls, talkin' 'bout the sad girls." Bad Girls.

"Bad little kid moved into my neighborhood." Bad Boy.

"Bad news, bad news!" We've Got A Groovy Thing Goin'.

"Baltimore oriole took a look at the mercury, forty below." Baltimore Oriole.

"Bam bam bamba, bam bam." La Bamba. (M. Garson and T. L. Puma)

"Bama lama bama loo, got a gal name Lucinda; we call her the great pretender." Bama Lama Bama Loo.

"Bar-bar Ann, Bar-bar-bar Ann, Bar-bar Ann, Bar-bar-bar Ann, Bar-bar Ann, take my hand." Barbara Ann.

"Bare trees grey light oh yeah it was a cold night." Bare Trees.

"B. B. Bumble and the Stingers..." Life Is A Rock.

"Be careful, girls, for Mighty Joe, be careful." Mighty Joe.

"Be my love, for no one else can end this yearning." Be My Love.

"Beat goes on, the beat goes on." The Beat Goes On.

"Beat is getting stronger, music gettin' longer too." I Want To Take You Higher.

"Beautiful people, you live in the same world as I do." Beautiful People.

"Beautiful soul music chimin' out of the jukebox." Saturday Night.

"Be-bop-a-lu-la, she's my baby." Be-Bop-A-Lula.

"Because you're mine, the brightest star I see looks down, down, my love, and envies me because you're mine." Because You're Mine.

"Because you're sweet and lovely, girl, I love you so." For You, Blue.

"Bee-bah! I love you, baby." I'm Stickin' With You.

"Been a long time since you touched me and made me feel that wonderful glow the way you do." Is It Still Good To Ya.

"Been away, haven't seen you in a while." We Just Disagree.

"Been dazed and confused for so long it's not true." Dazed And Confused.

"Been in pain and I been in shame, but ain't love a bitch." Ain't Love A Bitch.

"Before I knew that I was blessed..." Beautiful Music.

"Before this dance is through I think I'll love you too." I'm Happy Just To Dance With You.

"Being alone at night makes me sad, girl." Julie, Do Ya Love Me.

"Bell bottom blues, you made me cry." Bell Bottom Blues.

"Belle, the Lord and I've been friends for a mighty long time." Belle.

"Bells will be ringing and birds will be singing." Summer Place, Theme From.

"Bells will be ringing the sad sad news, oh what a Christmas to have the blues." Please Come Home For Christmas.

"Ben, the two of us need look no more." Ben.

"Bend me mold me just do what you got to do, yeah." Bend Me.

"Beneath this snowy mantle cold and clean, the unborn grass lies waiting for its coat to turn to green." Snowbird.

"Bernadette, people are searchin' for the kind of love that we possess." Bernadette.

"Best of friends never part." It's Over.

"Best things in life are free." Money (That's What I Want.

"Bet you're wond'ring how I knew." I Heard It Through The Grapevine.

"Beth, I hear you callin' but I can't come home right now." Beth.

"Betty Lou got a new pair of shoes." Betty Lou Got A New Pair Of Shoes.

"Beyond the rim of the starlight..." Star Trek, Theme From.

"Bicycle, bicycle, bicycle, I want to ride my bicycle bicycle, bicycle." Bicycle Race.

"Big boss man, can't you hear me when I call." Big Boss Man.

"Big girls don't cry." Big Girls Don't Cry.

"Big ole Ruby Red Dress wanders 'round the town." Leave Me Alone.

"Bill, I love you so." Wedding Bell Blues.

"Billion dollar baby." Billion Dollar Babies.

"Black slacks." Black Slacks.

"Blackbird, blackbird singing the blues all day." Bye Bye Blackbird.

"Bless the beasts and the children, for in this world they have no voice." Bless The Beasts And Children.

"Blessed are the meek for they shall inherit." Blessed.

"Blind man, standing on the corner, crying out the blues." Blind Man.

"Blinded by science, I'm on the run." Blinded By Science.

"Blow me a kiss from across the room." Little Things Mean A Lot.

"Blue and lonely was I." My Own True Love.

"Blue jean baby, L.A. lady, seamstress for the band." Tiny Dancer.

"Blue light rain, whoa, unbroken chain." Unbroken Chain.

"Blue Monday, how I hate blue Monday." Blue Monday.

"Blue moon, blue moon, blue moon, keep a-shinin' bright." Blue Moon Of Kentucky.

"Blue Moon, you saw me standing alone." Blue Moon.

"Blue songs are like tattoos you know I've been to sea before. Blue.

"Blue Spanish eyes, teardrops are falling from your Spanish eyes." Spanish Eyes.

"Bluebirds over the mountain, sea gulls over the sea." Bluebirds Over The Mountain.

"Bm Bm (32x), you send cold chills up and down my spine." Mama's Pearl.

"Bo Diddley'll buy baby a diamond ring." Bo Diddley.

"Bobby's drivin' through the city tonight through the lights in a hot new rent' a' car." Say Goodbye To Hollywood.

"Body wanna feel my body?" Macho Man.

"Bom bom bom bom bom bom bom, now they up and call me Speedo but my real name is Mister Earl." Speedo.

"Bom dee doo dee doo lee doo lee bom bom bom wa wa wa wa, well zoom went the strings of my heart." Zoom.

"Boo, hoo, hoo, hoo, I'm cryin' over you." Boo, Hoo, Ho Hoo, Hoo (I'll Never Let You Go).

"Boogie, ah, you sexy, boogie child." Boogie Child.

"Boogie, boogie down, baby." Boogie Down.

"Boogie fever, got to boogie down." Boogie Fever.

"Boogie nights oh boogie nights, boogie nights boogie nights ain't no doubt we are here to party." Boogie Nights.

"Boom, boom, boom, boom, gonna shoot you right down." Boom, Boom.

"Boop bop boo dee doo wah doo wap." Swing Your Daddy.

"Born a natural loser, I can't recall just where." Go Down Gamblin'.

"Born free, as free as the wind blows." Born Free.

"Born in February, you were always very shy as a child." Water Sign.

"Born in Red Hook, Brooklyn in the year of who knows when." Joey.

"Bottle of wine, fruit of the vine, when you gonna let me me get sober?" Bottle Of Wine.

"Bows and flows of angel hair, and ice cream castles in the air, and feather canyons ev'rywhere, I've looked at clouds that way." Both Sides Now.

"Boy is born in Hardtime, Mississippi, surrounded by four walls that ain't so pretty." Living For The City.

"Boy, the look of love is in my eyes." You + Me = Love.

"Boy, you're gonna carry that weight." Carry That Weight.

"Brand new boots I bought ya, fine fine blew your mind." Sugar Daddy.

"Bright light almost blinding." Friends.

"Bright lights, big city, gone to my baby's head." Bright Lights, Big City.

"Brighton Hill, where the sky changes its color..." Brighton Hill.

"(Br-r-r) Black slacks." Black Slacks.

"Buck was born on a beautiful mornin' and I felt very proud." Butterfly For Bucky.

"Buckets of rain, buckets of tears, got all them buckets comin' out of my ears." Buckets Of Rain.

"Buddy you're a boy make a big noise playin' in the street ...". We Will Rock You.

"Buh, buh, buh, buh, buh, boo-buh, buh, buh, buh, buh, you went to school to learn girl." ABC.

"Bullet from the back of a bush took Medgar Evers' blood." Only A Pawn In Their Game.

"Bunch of lonesome and very quarrelsome heroes were smoking out along the open road." Bunch Of Lonesome Heroes.

"Burn, baby, burn. (disco inferno)." Disco Inferno.

"Bury the bottle, mama, it's grapefruit wine." FM

"Bus stop wet day she's there I say please share my my um'brella." Bus Stop.

"Busted flat in Baton Rouge, headin' for the trains." Me And Bobby McGee.

"But, all I've got is the photograph." Photograph.

"But I'd like to get to know you." Like To Get To Know You.

"But I'm gonna get married." I'm Gonna Get Married.

"By the rivers of Babylon there we sat down." Rivers Of Babylon.

"By the time I get to Phoenix, she'll be risin'." By The Time I Get To Phoenix.

"Bye, baby, see you around, didn't I tell you I wouldn't hold you down." Remember Me.

"Bye, bye, bye baby, bye, bye." Bye, Bye Baby.

"California my way, any day, oo oo." California My Way. Way.

"Call me, call me, call me; what a beautiful time we had together." Call Me (Come Back Home).

"Calling out around the world are you ready for a brand new beat?" Dancing In The Street.

"Can anybody find me somebody to love?" Somebody To Love. (F. Mercury)

"Can I describe what it's like to have sex with the light on?" All This And More. (J. Zero).

"Can you hear the drums Fernando?" Fernando.

"Can you read my mind?" Can You Read My Mind.

"Can you surry, can you picnic?" Stoned Soul Picnic.

"Candy man, salty dog...." Candy Man (Rev. G. Davis).

"Candy-O, I need you." Candy-O.

"Can't buy me love." Can't Buy Me Love.

"Can't get no rest, don't know how I'll work all day." They Just Can't Stop It.

"Can't let the sun go down on me, oh no more." New Horizons.

"Can't you feel it in your bones, y 'all?" Touch A Hand, Make A Friend.

"Can't you hear that rooster crowin'?" New Morning.

"Can't you see I love you?" Wooden Heart.

"Cara mia why must we say goodbye?" Cara Mia.

"Carry on my wayward son; there'll be peace when you are done." Carry On Wayward Son.

"Cast a pebble on the water, watch the ripples gently spreading." Michelle's Song.

"Cause breaking up is so very hard to do." Make It Easy On Yourself.

"Celia, you're breaking my heart." Cecilia.

"Chains of love have tied my heart to you." Chains Of Love.

"Chances are 'cause I wear a silly grin...." Chances Are.

"Change with the times." Change With The Times.

"Chanson d'amour ra da da da da, play encore." Chanson D'Amour.

"Chantilly lace and a pretty face...." Chantilly Lace.

"Checkin' up on my baby and I'm watching from now." Checkin' Up On My Baby.

"Checkmate, honey; beat you at your own damned game." Draw The Line.

"Chemical change like a laser beam you've shattered the warning amber light." Rejoyce.

"Cherish is the word that I use to describe all the feeling that I have hiding here for you inside." Cherish.

"Cherry cherry pie...." Cherry Pie.

"Chewin' out a rhythm on my bubble gum." Rockaway Beach.

"Chewing on a piece of grass, walking down the road." Ventura Highway.

"Chico, don't be discouraged." Chico And The Man.

"Childhood part of my life, it wasn't very pretty." Cloud Nine.

"Children behave, that's what they say when we're together." I Think We're Alone Now.

"Children play in the park, they don't know." Make Me Smile.

"Christian cannons have fired at my days." Cannons Of Christianity.

"Christopher Robin and I walked along under branches lit up by the moon." House At Pooh Corner.

"Church house, gin house, a school-house, out-house on highway number nineteen." Nutbush City Limits.

"Church is burning." Church Is Burning.

"Cisco Kid was a friend of mine." Cisco Kid.

"City girls just seem to find out early how to open doors with just a smile." Lyin' Eyes.

"City streets are empty now." Turn To Stone.

"Clap your hands now ev'rybody we're gonna have some fun tonight." I Like It Like That (W. Robinson & M. Tarplin).

"Close the door, light the light." World Of Our Own.

"Close the door, put out the light." No Quarter.

"Close your eyes and I'll kiss you." All My Loving.

"Close your eyes, close the door." I'll Be Your Baby Tonight.

"Clouds so swift, rain won't lift." You Ain't Goin' Nowhere.

"Cloudy, the sky is grey and white and cloudy." Cloudy.

"Cold late nights so long ago...." Magic Man.

"Color me, your color, baby, color me, your car." Call Me (D. Harry & G. Moroder).

"Come all you pretty women with your hair a-hanging down." Candyman (J. Garcia & R. Hunter).

"Come along, come along, there's a full moon shinin' bright." Come Along.

"Come and a-walk with me; we can go where peaceful waters flow." Where Peaceful Waters Flow.

"Come and go with me to that land." Come And Go With Me.

"Come and sing a simple song of freedom." Simple Song Of Freedom.

"Come bring me your softness." <u>With You I'm Born Again</u>.

"Come by here, my Lord, come by here." <u>Come By Here</u>.

"Come, come, come into my life." <u>Come Into My Life</u>.

"Come gather 'round people where ever you roam." <u>Times They Are A-Changin'</u>.

"Come, get out of the way, boys, quick, get out of the way." <u>Cops Of The World</u>.

"Come here sister, papa's in there safe." <u>Papa's Got A Brand New Bag (Part I)</u>.

"Come, let's stroll--stroll across the floor." <u>Stroll</u>.

"Come on all you big strong men, Uncle Sam needs your help again." <u>I Feel Like I'm Fixin' To Die Rag</u>.

"Come on and dance, yeah dance." <u>Dance, Dance, Dance</u> (W. King & M. Levy).

"Come and do it, do it, do it 'til you're satisfied." <u>Do It ('Til You're Satisfied)</u>.

"Come on and ease on down, ease on down the road." <u>Ease On Down The Road</u>.

"Come on, baby, and be my guest." <u>Be My Guest</u>.

"Come on, baby, let the good times roll." <u>Let The Good Times Roll</u>.

"Come on baby, let's do the twist." <u>Twist</u>.

"Come on, come on, come on, come on, didn't I make you feel like you were the only man?" <u>Piece Of My Heart</u>.

"Come on, come on, let me show you where it's at!" <u>I Like It Like That</u> (C. Kenner & A. Toussaint).

"Come on down to the glory river." <u>Save The Country</u>.

"Come on ev'rybody and snap your fingers now." <u>C'mon Everybody</u>.

"Come on ev'rybody, I say now let's play a game." <u>Name Game</u>.

"Come on, ev'rybody, take a trip with me." <u>New Orleans</u>.

"Come on feet, start movin', got to get me there, wow!" <u>Twenty Five Miles</u>.

"Come on, little baby, play hide and go seek with me." <u>Hide And Seek</u>.

"Come on mama, give me a break." <u>Champagne Jam</u>.

"Come on, operator, gimme Rolene on my line." <u>Rolene</u>.

"Come on, people, come on, children, come on down to the glory river." <u>Save The Country</u>.

"Come on, take me to the Mardi Gras." <u>Take Me To The Mardi Gras</u>.

"Come on turn on your radio." <u>Don't Miss The Message</u>.

"Come out here on the floor, let's rock some more." <u>Baby Workout</u>.

"Come over to the window, my little darling." <u>So Long, Marianne</u>.

"Come Saturday morning...." <u>Come Saturday Morning</u>.

"Come sing a song of joy for peace shall come, my brother." <u>Song of Joy</u>.

"Come softly, darling." <u>Come Softly To Me</u>.

"Come take my hand, you should know me." <u>Magic</u>.

"Come to me when you're all alone and feelin' down." <u>Come To Me</u>.

"Come with me and we shall run across the sky." <u>Up The Ladder To The Roof</u>.

"Come with me where moonbeams light Tahitian skies." <u>Pagan Love Song</u>.

"Come you masters of war." <u>Masters Of War</u>.

"Comin' to you on a dusty road, good lovin' I got a truckload." <u>Soul Man</u>.

"Coming in from London from over the pole, flying in a big airliner." <u>Coming In To Los Angeles</u>.

"Comouna promesa, eres tu, eres tu." <u>Eres Tu</u>.

"Congratulations!" <u>Congratulations</u>.

"Conquistador, your stallion stands in need of company." <u>Conquistador</u>.

"Cookin' on my feet in the disco heat." <u>Dance (Disco Heat)</u>.

"Corazon, mi corazon, corazon mi corazon, yo te quiero mi corazon." <u>Corazon</u>.

"Could be a spoonful of diamonds, could be a spoonful of gold." <u>Spoonful</u>.

"Could it be she's int'rested or am I just wanting it to be so." <u>Ain't Nothing But A Maybe</u>.

"Could you ever need me?" <u>Over & Over</u> (C. McVie)

"Count ev'ry star in the midnight sky." <u>Count Every Star</u>.

"Couple in the next room bound to win a prize." <u>Duncan</u>.

"Cowboys ain't easy to love and they're harder to hold." <u>Mammas Don't Let Your Babies Grow Up To Be Cowboys</u>.

"Cracklin' Rosie, get on board." <u>Cracklin' Rosie</u>.

"Crash on the levee, mama, water's gonna overflow." <u>Crash On The Levee</u>.

"Crazy words, crazy tune." <u>Crazy Words--Crazy Tune</u>.

"Creme tangerine and montelimat." <u>Savoy Truffle</u>.

"Crimson flames tied through my ears rollin' high and mighty traps." <u>My Back Pages</u>.

"Crops are all in and the peaches are rott'ning." <u>Deportee</u>.

"Crossroads seem to come and go." <u>Melissa</u>.

"Cruel war is raging; Johnny has to fight." <u>Cruel War</u>.

"Cryin' on my pillow, lonely in my bed." <u>Undercover Angel</u>.

"Da doot dot doo dot dot dey." <u>Get Dancin'</u>.

"Daddy, daddy, daddy, love me strong." <u>Daddy, Daddy</u>.

"Daddy don't live in that New York City no more." <u>Daddy Don't Live In That New York City No More</u>.

"Daddy was a cop on the eastside of Chicago back in the U.S.A." <u>Night Chicago Died</u>.

"Dah dah dah dah dah dah dah dah dah dah dah dah dah, rockets and moonshots spent it on the have-nots." <u>Inner City Blues</u>.

"Dance, boogie wonderland, ha, ha, dance." <u>Boogie Wonderland</u>.

"Dance, dance, dance, dance, keep on dancin'." <u>Dance, Dance, Dance (Yowsah, Yowsah, Yowsah)</u>.

"Dance, dance, dance, disco baby." <u>Disco Baby</u>.

"Dance just a little bit longer." <u>Stay</u>.

"Dance little dreamer on a joy ride." <u>Dance Little Dreamer</u>.

"Dance to the music." <u>Dance To The Music</u>.

"Dance wit me, baby, baby, dance wit me." <u>Dance Wit Me</u>.

"Dance with me, hold, hold me closer, closer and closer." <u>Dance With Me</u> (L. Lebish, G. Treadwell, I. Nahan & E. Glick.)

"Dancin', dancin', dancin', she's a dancin' machine." <u>Dancing Machine</u>.

"Dancing, dancing, my feet keep dancing." <u>My Feet Keep Dancing</u>.

"Dancing days are here again." <u>Dancing Days</u>.

"Danger in the shape of something wild." <u>Hot Child In The City</u>.

"Daniel is trav'ling tonight on a 'plane." <u>Daniel</u>.

"Darkness at the break of noon shadows even the silver spoon." <u>It's Alright Ma</u>.

"Darkness of night with the moon shining bright." <u>Superfly</u>.

"Darlin', darlin', darlin', I can't wait to see you." <u>In The Flesh</u>.

"Darlin', I know I'm another head on your pillow." <u>Real Love</u>.

"Darlin' if you want me to be closer to you, get closer to me." <u>Get Closer</u>.

"Darling dumpling, if I could have you to call my very own." <u>Something About You</u>.

"Darling, you can count on me till the sun dries up the sea." <u>Devoted To You</u>.

"Day after day alone on a hill." <u>Fool On The Hill</u>.

"Day after day I must face a world of strangers where I don't belong." <u>I Won't Last A Day Without You</u>.

"Day after day I'm more confused." <u>Drift Away</u>.

"Day by day, day by day, oh, dear Lord three things I pray." <u>Day By Day</u> (S. Schwartz).

"Day by day I'm falling more in love with you." <u>Day By Day</u> (S. Cahn, A. Stordahl, & P. Weston.)

"Day is night in New York City." <u>Hitch A Ride</u>.

"Day oh! Day oh! Day light break an' I wanna go home." <u>Day Light Break</u>.

"Daylight, all right." <u>Head Games</u>.

"Daytime dreaming, getting involved only halfway deed." <u>Sound Asleep</u>.

"Dear darling, surprised to hear from me?" <u>How You Gonna See Me Now</u>.

"Dear Landlord, please don't put a price on my soul." <u>Dear Landlord</u>.

"Dear sir or madam will you read my book?" <u>Paperback Writer</u>.

"Deep as a river, wide as the sea." <u>Captain And Me</u>.

"Deep down in Louisiana, close to New Orleans..." <u>Johnny B. Goode</u>.

"Delta Dawn, what's that flower you got on?" <u>Delta Dawn</u>.

"Desmond had a barrow in the market place." <u>Ob La Di, Ob La Da</u>.

"Desperado, why don't you come to your senses?" <u>Desperado</u>.

"Devil in the blue dress..." <u>Devil With The Blue Dress On</u>.

"Devil or angel, I can't make up my mind." <u>Devil Or Angel</u>.

"Devil went down to Georgia." <u>Devil Went Down To Georgia</u>.

"Diamond girl, you sure do shine." <u>Diamond Girl</u>.

"Diamonds are forever." <u>Diamonds Are Forever</u>.

"Did I see you down in a young girl's town with your mother in so much pain?" <u>Harvest</u>.

"Did ya ever see starlight come rushin' from the skies?" <u>Walkin' Miracle</u>.

"Did you hear about the midnight rambler?" <u>Midnight Rambler</u>.

"Did you know I'd go to sleep and leave the lights on?" <u>Last Song</u>

"Did you write the book of love and do you have faith in God above?" <u>American Pie</u>.

"Didja ever, didja ever get, didja ever get one, didja ever get one of them days?" <u>Didja Ever</u>.

"Didn't I hear you cry this morning?" <u>Strange Way</u>.

"Didn't I make you feel like you were the only man?" <u>Piece Of My Heart</u>.

"Didn't wanna hafta do it." <u>Didn't Want To Have To Do It.</u>"

"Dim all the lights, sweet darlin', cause tonight, it's all the way." <u>Dim All The Lights</u>.

"Dirty rain is falling." <u>There Ain't No Way</u>.

"Dizzy, I'm so dizzy." <u>Dizzy</u>.

"Do be do be do be do...you little trustmaker." <u>You Little Trustmaker</u>.

"Do, do, do, do, do, do, do, do, do, do, do, do, do, do, do, tonight I wanna give it all to you." <u>I Was Made For Lovin' You</u>.

"Do do do do, it came to me in the middle of the night." <u>It Came To Me</u>.

"Do do do do Mary Jane, I'm in love with Mary Jane." <u>Mary Jane</u>.

"Do I have to come right out and say it, tell you that you

look so fine?" <u>Do I Have To Come Right Out And Say It.</u>

"Do it again, do it." <u>Let's Do It Again.</u>

"Do it any way ya wanna do it." <u>Do It Anyway You Wanna.</u>

"Do it while your soul's still burnin'." <u>Do It.</u>

"Do me wrong, do me right." <u>Don't Let Me Be Lonely Tonight.</u>

"Do people have a tendency to dump on you?" <u>Big Bright Green Pleasure Machine.</u>

"Do that to me one more time; once is never enough with a man like you." <u>Do That To Me One More Time.</u>

"Do the Hustle." <u>Hustle.</u>

"Do what you do, don't bring me down." <u>All I Want To Be (Is By Your Side).</u>

"Do ya do ya o tenda, do ya oo tenda...way back when I saw magic." <u>Way Back When.</u>

"Do you believe in magic in a young girl's heart?" <u>Do You Believe In Magic.</u>

"Do you have a problem?" <u>Miranda.</u>

"Do you know the way to San Jose?" <u>Do You Know The Way To San Jose.</u>

"Do you know where you're going to?" <u>Do You Know Where You're Going To.</u>

"Do you love me (yes, I love you)." <u>Ain't That A Groove (Part II).</u>

""Do you love what you feel?" <u>Do You Love What You Feel.</u>

"Do you or don't you love me?" <u>Easy Question.</u>

"Do you recall a year ago tonight?" <u>Blueberry Hill.</u>

"Do you remember the twenty-first night of September." <u>September.</u>

"Do you remember when you loved me before the world took me astray?" <u>Make The World Go Away.</u>

"Do you think I'm such a fool to believe ev'rything you say is true?" <u>Angel In Your Arms.</u>

"Do you wanna dance and hold my hand?" <u>Do You Wanna Dance.</u>

"Doctor my woman is comin' back late today." <u>Tryin' To Get The Feeling Again.</u>

"Doctor said, "Come back again next week ' cause I think that you need me." <u>Heartless.</u>

"Do-do-do-do-do-do-do-do (4x), Jesus is just alright with me." <u>Jesus Is Just Alright.</u>

"Does he love me, I wanna know." <u>It's In His Kiss.</u>

"Does she love me with all her heart?" <u>Lover's Question.</u>

"Doesn't take much to make me happy and make me smile with glee." <u>Best Of My Love</u> (M. White & A. McKay).

"Dominique, nique, nique, over the land he plods along, and sings a little song." <u>Dominique.</u>

"Don't break the heart that loves you, handle it with care." <u>Don't Break The Heart That Loves You.</u>

"Don't, don't that's what you say." <u>Don't.</u>

"Don't ever be lonely, a poor little fool like me." <u>Don't Ever Be Lonely.</u>

"Don't ever stop no." <u>Crazy Feelin'.</u>

"Don't get me mad, don't tell me lies." <u>Straight Shooter.</u>

"Don't go breaking my heart." <u>Don't Go Breaking My Heart.</u>

"Don't go changing to try and please me." <u>Just The Way You Are.</u>

"Don't go out into the rain, you're gonna melt, sugar, oh no." <u>Don't Go Out Into The Rain.</u>

"Don't hang up." <u>Don't Hang Up.</u>

"Don't it make you wanta go home now?" <u>Don't It Make You Wanta Go Home.</u>

"Don't jump me mother, or you'll end up buried under, understand?" <u>Don't Jump Me Mother.</u>

"Don't know what's happened to me since I met you." <u>With Your Love.</u>

"Don't know when I've been so blue." <u>Don't It Make My Brown Eyes Blue.</u>

"Don't know why I'm surviving ev'ry lonely day." <u>If I Can't Have You.</u>

"Don't leave me now, now that I need you." <u>Don't Leave Me Now.</u>

"Don't leave me this way I can't survive, can't stay alive, without your love." <u>Don't Leave Me This Way.</u>

"Don't let your troubles make you cry." <u>Do It Or Die.</u>

"Don't look so sad; I know it's over." <u>For The Good Times.</u>

"Don't look so sad, it's not so bad, ya know." <u>It's Just Another New Year's Eve.</u>

"Don't make me over, now that I'd do anything for you." <u>Don't Make Me Over.</u>

"Don't mess with Bill." <u>Don't Mess With Bill.</u>

"Don't play that song for me." <u>Don't Play That Song.</u>

"Don't pull your love out on me, baby." <u>Don't Pull Your Love.</u>

"Don't stop dancing to the music." <u>Shake Your Rump To The Funk.</u>

"Don't take your love away from me." <u>Breaking Up Is Hard To Do.</u>

"Don't wanna know your name 'cause you don't look the same." <u>Fox On The Run.</u>

"Don't want a four leaf clover." <u>Good Luck Charm.</u>

"Don't want to discuss it, I think it's time for a change." <u>Domino.</u>

"Don't you ever feel sad." <u>Hold On I'm Coming.</u>

"Don't you feel it growin' day by day, people gettin' ready for the news." <u>Listen To The Music.</u>

"Don't you know that I danced, I danced 'till a quarter to three with the help, last night, of Daddy 'G'." <u>Quarter To Three.</u>

"Don't you know that I love you?" <u>Honest I Do.</u> (J. Reed)

"Don't you let nothin', nothin' stand in your way." Ain't No Stoppin' Us Now.

"Don't you like the way I move when you see me?" Something Better Change.

"Don't you wonder sometimes 'bout sound and vision?" Sound And Vision.

"Don't you worry 'bout what's on your mind." Let's Spend The Night Together.

"Don't-cha hear me callin' to ya?" Don't-cha Hear Me Calling' To You.

"Do dit dit dit, doo dit dit, doo dit dit, doo dit dit dit doo, sha la la la la la, my lady, in the sun with your hair undone." Thunder Island.

"Doo doo ba doo doo doo doo doo doo ba doo doo doo doo doo doo ba doo doo doo doo doo doo, ba doo doo doo doo doo doo brand new boots I bought ya, fine fine blew your mind." Sugar Daddy.

"Doo doo bee doo, dom dom dom doo dom doo bee doo dom dom dom doo dom doo bee doo dom, dom doo dom doo bee doo dom dom doo dom doo bee." Come Softly To Me.

"Doo (18x), that's the way (un-huh, un-huh), I like it." That's The Way (I Like It).

"Doo doo doo down doo bee..." Breaking Up Is Hard To Do.

"Doo doo doot, doo doo doot, doo doo doo doo doo doot." Get Dancin'.

"Doo doot doo doo doot doot doo doot doo, you and I we fit together like a glove on hand, that's right." You And I (R. James).,

"Doo doot n doo doot n doo doo doo." My Music.

"Door it opened slowly, my father he came in." Story Of Isaac.

"Down along the cove, I spied my true love comin' my way." Down Along The Cove.

"Down around the corner half a mile from here, see them old trains runnin' and then watch them disappear." Long Train Runnin'.

"Down at the Lido they welcome you with sausage and beer." Here At The Western World.

"Down by the river..." Dirty Water.

"Down in Jamaica they got lots of pretty women." On And On.

"Down in the boondocks." Down In The Boondocks.

"Down on me, down on me, looks like ev'rybody in this whole round world is down on me." Down On Me.

"Down on the boulevard they take it hard." Boulevard.

"Downtown anywhere U.S.A. you can find yourself a hard rock cafe." Hard Rock Cafe.

"Downtown my darlin' dimestore thief..." In France They Kiss On Main Street.

"Dream, dream, dream, dream, dream, dream, dream, dream." All I Have To Do Is Dream.

"Dream police, they live inside of my head." Dream Police.

"Dreamin', I must be dreamin', or am I really lyin' here with you?" I Just Fall In Love Again.

"Drivin' in a beat-up car." Freeways.

"Driving along with my radio on feeling good." Hangin' Round.

"Driving that train, high on cocaine, Casey Jones, you'd better watch your speed." Casey Jones.

"Dry your eyes my little friend." Johnny Strikes Up The Band.

"Du bop shu boom bom bom bom bom bom du bop shu boom bom bom bom bom bom, I'll always want you, because my heart is true." ABC's Of Love.

"Dum deedle lee dum dum little girl where did you come from?" She Said "Yeah".

"Dynomite!" Dynomite (Part I).

"Each day just goes so fast." Love You To.

"Each day through my window I watch her as she passes by." Just My Imagination.

"Each day when I rise and I look at you, I can't believe I'm livin' a dream come true." Your Love.

"Each man must find a pasture green." Pastures Green.

"Each night as I go wandering down the street of tears...." Believe Me.

"Each time I look at you it's like the first time." More I See You.

"Earlier tonight I wished that I could share a dance and some romancin' with someone who really cared." Love Struck

"Early in the evenin' just about supper time...." Down On The Corner.

"Early in the mornin'...." Obviously Five Believers.

"Early one mornin' the sun was shinin." Tangled Up In Blue.

"Early one morning, one morning in spring to hear the birds whistle, the nightingales sing." Monday Morning.

"Earth angel, earth angel, will you be mine?' Earth Angel.

"Easy driver, she's a wicked rider." Easy Driver.

"Easy loving so sexy looking." Easy Loving.

"Eddie my love, I love you so." Eddie My Love

"Eli's comin', Eli's comin!" Eli's Comin'.

"Emptiness and just a memory, love is gone and nothin' left for me." Winter Melody.

"End of the spring and here she comes back." Hot Fun In The Summertime.

"Enjoy yourself, enjoy yourself, enjoy yourself with me." Enjoy Yourself.

"Even now, when there's someone else who cares...." Even Now.

"Even tho' the pain and heartache seem to follow me wherever I go..." Never Can Say Goodbye.

"Ever Forever, ever and ever and ever." Forever Came Today.

"Ever had the feelin' that the world's gone and left you behind? Angel Eyes.

"Ever seen a blind man cross the road tr'n to make the other side." Handbags And Gladrags.

"Ever since I met ya, seems I can't forget ya." Then Came You.

"Ever since I was a kid in school, I messed around with all the rules." I Was Only Joking.

"Ever since I was a young boy, I played the silver ball. Pinball Wizard.

"Ever since we've been together, you've been bugging me about another woman." Hearsay.

"Every night I'm lyin' in bed, holdin' you close in my dreams." Best Of My Love.

"Everybody have you heard, he's gonna buy me a mockingbird." Mockingbird.

"Everybody sing yeah, yeah, say yeah." Fingertips (Part II).

"Evil running through our brain." Evil.

"Ev'ry day ev'ry day I have the blues." Every Day (I Have The Blues).

"Ev'ry day I get in the queue." Magic Bus.

"Ev'ry day it's a-gettin' closer." Every Day.

"Ev'ry day of my life I'll be in love with you." Ev'ry Day Of My Life.

"Ev'ry day she takes a morning bath, she wets her hair." Another Day.

"Ev'ry day there's something new, honey, to keep me loving you." Your Precious Love.

"Ev'ry day's a new day in love with you." More Today Than Yesterday.

"Ev'ry hand in the land shakes along with me." Every Hand In The Land.

"Ev'ry man has a place, in his heart there's a space, and the world can't erase his fantasies." Fantasy.

"Ev'ry morning about this time, she get me out of bed, a-crying get a job." Get A Job.

"Ev'ry night I hope and pray a dream lover will come my way." Dream Lover.

"Ev'ry night I just want to go out, get out of my head." Every Night.

"Ev'ry now and then I cry." Broken Hearted Me.

"Ev'ry rolling stone gets to feel alone when home sweet home is far away." Sentimental Journey.

"Ev'ry time I look at you I don't understand why you let the things you did get so out of hand." Superstar (T. Rice & A.L. Webber).

"Ev'ry time I move I lose, when I look I'm in." Back In Love Again.

"Ev'ry time I see you lookin' my way...." Can't You Hear My Heart Beat.

"Ev'ry time that I look in the mirror, all these lines on my face gettin' clearer." Dream On.

"Ev'ry time you kiss me I'm still not certain that you love me." Suspicion.

"Ev'ry time you look at me, I'm as helpless as can be." Puppet On A String.

"Ev'ry time you see me smile, I'm really blue." Yes, It's True.

"Ev'ry time you touch me, I get high." Every Time You Touch Me.

"Ev'rybody always asks me how I got to play so fine." Piano Picker.

"Ev'rybody come aboard the showboat tonight." Everybody Come Aboard.

"Ev'rybody dance." Everybody Dance.

"Ev'rybody get off your feet." Barefootin'.

"Ev'rybody I talk to is ready to leave with the light of the morning." For Everyman.

"Ev'rybody knows him as 'old folks.'" Old Folks.

"Ev'rybody knows that you've been untrue." You Tore Me Down.

"Ev'rybody likes a celebration." This Night Won't Last Forever.

"Ev'rybody listen to me." Shout It Out.

"Ev'rybody, listen to me and return me my ship." Closer To Home.

"Ev'rybody loves a lover." Everybody Loves A Lover.

"Ev'rybody's building the big ships and the boats." Quinn The Eskimo.

"Ev'rybody's doin' a brand new dance now." Loco'motion.

"Ev'rybody's gone away, said they're movin' to L.A." Good Time Charlie's Got The Blues.

"Ev'rybody's got a thing, but some don't know how to handle it." Don't You Worry 'Bout A Thing.

"Ev'rybody's talkin' at me." Everybody's Talkin'.

"Ev'rybody's talkin' 'bout the seventh son." Seventh Son.

"Ev'rybody's talking about Bagism, Shagism, Dragism, Madism, Ragism, Tagism, Thisism, Thatism, isn't it the most?" Give Peace A Chance.

"Ev'ryday, there's something new." Your Precious Love.

"Ev'ryone has a choice when to and not to raise their voices." Run Of The Mill.

"Ev'ryone tells me to know my place, but that ain't the way I play." You're Gonna Hear From Me.

"Ev'rything has its season, ev'rything has its time." Corner Of The Sky.

"Ev'rything went from bad to worse." Up To Me.

"Ev'rywhere I go I see a pretty girl." Pretty Girls Everywhere.

"Ev'rywhere I hear the sound of marching, charging feet." Street Fighting Man.

"Extra, extra, I'm in love." Main Event Fight.

"Eyes of silver, hungry and aware; eyes of silver, your mystic love I share." Eyes Of Silver.

"Eyes that hypnotize...." <u>My Baby Must Be A Magician</u>.

"Faded photograph, covered now with lines and creases." <u>Traces</u>.

"Faded photographs, the feelin's all come back, even now, sometimes you feel so near." <u>Years</u>.

"Faithless love like a river flows." <u>Faithless Love</u>.

"Fame and fortune, how empty they can be." <u>Fame And Fortune</u>.

"Fame makes a man take things over." <u>Fame</u> (D. Bowie, J. Lennon & C. Alomar).

"Fancy me." <u>Boss</u>.

"Far across the blue waters, lives an old German's daughter, by the banks of the river Rhine." <u>Fraulein</u>.

"Far between sundown's finish and midnight's broken toll, we ducked inside the doorway, thunder went crashing." <u>Chimes Of Freedom</u>.

"Fare thee well, I know you're leaving for the new love that you found." <u>He Don't Love You (Like I Love You)</u>.

"Fare you well, my honey." <u>Brokedown Palace</u>.

"Father of night, father of day, father who taketh the darkness away...." <u>Father Of Night</u>.

"Fee fee fi fi fo fo fum; I smell smoke in the auditorium." <u>Charlie Brown</u>.

"Fee fi fo fum, I'm looking down the barrel of the devil's gun." <u>Devil's Gun</u>.

"Feel I'm going back to Massachusetts." <u>Massachusetts</u>.

"Feelin' down and dirty, feelin' kind of mean." <u>Double Vision</u>.

"Feelin' low, rockin' slow." <u>Tuxedo Junction</u>.

"Feeling is clear." <u>Call On Me</u>.

"Feelings, nothing more than feelings, trying to forget my feelings of love." <u>Feelings</u>.

"Feels so good, words can't explain, it's got to be the sweetest pain." <u>Sweetest Pain</u>.

"Fellas, a brand new funk, a brand new funk." <u>My Thang</u>.

"Fellas, can we still do it?" <u>If You Don't Get It The First Time, Back Up And Try It Again, Party</u>.

"Fellas, I wonder would you mind if I talk to you a minute." <u>Woman's Gotta Have It</u>.

"Festival was over." <u>Lily, Rosemary And The Jack Of Hearts</u>.

"Find it hard to see you in the dark." <u>Shine On</u>.

"Finding a job tomorrow morning." <u>Romeo And Juliet</u>.

"Fine fine foxy lady get down." <u>Get Down</u> (J. Thompson).

"Fire breathing rebels arrive at the party early." <u>Party</u> (P. Ochs).

"Fire Island! It's a funky weekend, a funky, funky weekend." <u>Fire Island</u>.

First a boy and a girl meet each other." <u>To The Aisle</u>.

"First I rise, then I fall." <u>Fanny Be Tender With My Love</u>.

"First I'm here, then I'm there." <u>Ways</u>.

"First of all, I would like to say a word or two." <u>Song Is Love</u>.

"First of all, let's get one thing straight." <u>Shoe, Shoe Shine</u>.

"First the tide rushes in, plants a kiss on the shore." <u>Ebb Tide</u>.

"First thing I remember, I was lying in my bed." <u>Late In The Evening</u>.

"First thing I remember is askin' Papa 'why?'." <u>Someday Never Comes</u>.

"First time ever I saw your face, I thought the sun rose in your eyes." <u>First Time Ever I Saw Your Face</u>.

"First time I fell in love, I fell in love with you." <u>Beginner's Luck</u>.

"First time I met ya', I knew you'd be all I'd dreamed of." <u>New York City I Love You</u>.

"First time I saw you, baby, I knew right away I wanted you for my lady." <u>Two Places At The Same Time</u>.

"Fishing boats go out across the water, smuggling guns and arms across the Spanish border." <u>On The Border</u>.

"Five seven o five but there's no reply." <u>5. 7. 0. 5.</u>

"Flew in from Miami Beach, B.O.A.C., didn't get to bed last night." <u>Back In The U.S.S.R.</u>

"Fly, robin, fly." <u>Fly, Robin, Fly</u>.

"Fly silly sea birds; no dreams can possess you." <u>Song To A Seagull</u>.

"Flyin' high, gonna be there." <u>Flying High</u>.

"Flyin' me back to Memphis, gotta find my Daisy Jane." <u>Daisy Jane</u>.

"Folks say that you found someone new." <u>I'll Come Running Back To You</u>.

"Follow me, baby, show you a gypsy good time." <u>Gypsy Good Time</u>.

"(Folsom) Folsom Street on the way to Polk and Castro." <u>San Francisco (You've Got Me)</u>.

"Fool, fool, fool, that I was to fall for you." <u>Fool, Fool, Fool</u>.

"Fooled by a feelin', I was fooled." <u>Fooled By A Feeling</u>.

"Fools fall in love in a hurry." <u>Fools Fall In Love</u>.

"Fools rush in where angels fear to tread." <u>Fools Rush In</u>.

"For awhile, to love was all we could do." <u>After The Love Has Gone</u>.

"For once in my life I have someone who needs me, someone I've needed so long." <u>For Once In My Life</u>.

"For so long, you and me been finding each other for so long." <u>I Just Want to Be Your Everything</u>.

"For the last year I've been searching." <u>Silver Dreams</u>.

"For you, there might be a brighter star." Another Star.

"For you, there'll be no more cryin'." Songbird (C. McVie).

"For your love...." I Just Wanna Stop.

"For your love, I would do anything." For Your Love.

"Forever mine, all because you're my kind." Forever Mine.

"Forgive me if my fantasies might seem a little shop-worn." Dark Star.

"Forgive me, Lord." Hear Me Lord.

"Fortunata woman, you know I wanted to fly." Gotta Get Back To You.

"Fortune queen of New Orleans was brushing her cat in her black limousine." Dark Lady.

"Found a cure." Found A Cure.

"Four and twenty years ago I come into this life." 4+20.

"Four months ago in April on a day coach she came down." Red Velvet.

"Four strong winds that blow lonely, seven seas that run high." Four Strong Winds.

"Fox went out one chilly night." Fox.

"Freak out!" Le Freak.

"Free as the wind." Free As The Wind.

"Free the people from the fire." Free The People.

"Freight train, freight train goin' so fast." Freight Train.

"Friday night I crashed your party." You May Be Right.

"Friday night, it was late, I was walkin' you home." Reminiscing.

"Friends all tried to warn me, but I held my head up high." Burning Bridges.

"Friends I used to know are coming by." If You Would Just Drop By.

"Friends that I knew and gave up for you...." I'm Alone Because I Love You.

"From nowhere through a caravan around the camp-fire light...." Gypsy Woman.

"From rags to riches, here I stand." One Love In My Lifetime.

"From the time I fall asleep till the mornin' comes I dream about you baby." You Baby (Nobody But You).

"Funny face, I love you." Funny Face.

"Funny, just seems kinda funny that ev'ry time it's sunny, can't get along with my honey." In The Night Time.

"Gather 'round cats and I'll tell ya' a story." All American Boy.

"Gather 'round, clap your hands, come on and dance, hey come on." Bring It Up.

"Gee but it's great to be back home." Keep The Customer Satisfied.

"Gee whiz, look at his eyes." Gee Whiz.

"Get away, let's leave today, let's get away!" Getaway.

"Get dancin'--here come D.J. Disco Tex." Get Dancin'.

"Get down baby to the funky, funky, funky groove." Get Down (C. Mayfield).

"Get down, get down, get down, get down." Jungle Boogie.

"Get on down and party." Party (V. McCoy).

"Get out from that kitchen and rattle those pots and pans." Shake, Rattle And Roll.

"Get up, get your man a bottle of red wine." Bottle Of Red Wine.

"Get up, Jake, it's late in the mornin'." Get Up, Jake.

"Get you a copper kettle." Copper Kettle (The Pale Moonlight).

"Giddy up, giddy up, well I'm a long tall Texan." Long Tall Texan.

"Girl, close your eyes, let that rhythm get into you." Rock With You.

"Girl, I can't believe my ears." I Could Never Love Another.

"Girl, I know I've been neglecting you." Catchin' Up On Love.

"Girl, I love you, I need you by my side." I'll Never, Never Let You Go.

"Girl, I'm a free man." Free Man.

"Girl, I've heard you're gettin' married." Worst That Could Happen.

"Girl, I've known you very well." More Than A Woman.

"Girl, to be with you is my fav'rite thing." Boogie Shoes.

"Girl, we had our romp in the sun." Once In A Lifetime Thing.

"Girl, we made it to the top." Hungry Years.

"Girl, we've come a long way from nowhere." Love Finds Its Own Way.

"Girl, when I'm alone with you...." Heartbeat, It's A Lovebeat.

"Girl, you really got me going." You Really Got Me.

"Girl, you're gettin' that look in your eyes, and it's starting to worry me." Baby Don't Get Hooked On Me.

"Girl, you're my sunshine; you chase away the raindrops, make it all worthwhile." Don't Change On Me.

"Give a little bit, give a little bit of your love to me." Give A Little Bit.

"Give a little more, give a little more, little bit more than you ever had to give me before." Give A Little More.

"Give it what you got!" Give It What You Got.

"Give me a ticket for an airplane, ain't got time to take the fastest train." Letter (W. Thompson).

133

"Give me love, give me love, give me peace on earth." Give Me Love.

"Gloria, my Gloria, things ain't been the same since you went away." Gloria.

"Go away, little girl." Go Away Little Girl.

"Go far enough and you will reach a place where the sea runs underneath." Your Own Special Way.

"Go my way and I'll be good to you." Go My Way.

"Go tell it on the mountain." Go Tell It On The Mountain.

"Go 'way from my window, leave at your own chosen speed." It Ain't Me, Babe.

"God save the Queen the fascist regime." God Save The Queen.

Goin' back to Birmingham, way down in Alabam." Hey, Hey, Hey, Hey (Goin' Back to Birmingham.

"Goin' down that long lonesome highway, bound for the mountains and the plains." Long Lonesome Highway.

"Goin' up?" Heaven On The Seventh Floor.

"Gold coast slave ship bound for cotton fields, sold in a market down in New Orleans." Brown Sugar.

"Goldfinger, he's the man, the man with the Midas touch." Goldfinger.

"Gone, swirling tears come, she went today." Last Wall Of The Castle.

"Gonna break out of this city." Do Anything You Wanna Do.

"Gonna buy me a long white robe." Rich Man Spiritual.

"Gonna find her." Searchin'.

"Gonna find me an angel to fly away with me." Angel (W. Sanders & C. Franklin).

"Gonna find my baby, gonna hold her tight." Afternoon Delight.

"Gonna fly now, flying high now." Gonna Fly Now.

"Gonna love you more than anything you've heard about." Gonna Love You More.

"Gonna tell Aunt Mary 'bout Uncle John." Long Tall Sally.

"Good day sunshine." Good Day Sunshine.

"Good God, don't jump." Save The Life Of My Child.

"Good golly Miss Molly, yeah you sure like a ball." Good Golly Miss Molly.

"Good, good timin', good, good timin', ooo, ah ooo, you need good timin'." Good Timin' (B. & C. Wilson).

"Good morning heartache, you old gloomy sight." Good Morning Heartache.

"Good morning little school girl." Good Morning, Little School Girl (D. Level & B. Love).

"Good morning little school girl, good morning little school girl, can I come home with, can I come home with you." Good Morning Little School Girl (S. Williamson).

"Good morning, Mister Sunshine." Lonely Days.

"Good morning morning, hello sunshine, wake up sleepy head." Happiest Girl In The Whole USA.

"Good morning starshine, the earth says hello." Good Morning Starshine.

"Good night sweetheart, till we meet tomorrow." Good Night Sweetheart.

"Good times, these are the good times." Good Times.

"Goodbye, I lied." Let It Ride.

"Goodbye, my love, happy life my love." I'm Gonna Let My Heart Do The Walking.

"Goodbye Norma Jean though I never knew you at all." Candle In The Wind.

"Goodbye, old friend." For Once In My Life.

"Goodnight sweetheart, well, it's time to go." Goodnight, It's Time To Go.

"Got a feeling that I'm wasting time on you babe." Got A Feeling.

"Got a gal named Lucinda; we call her the great pretender." Bama Lama Bama Loo.

"Got a good reason for loving you." Kind Woman.

"Got a good reason for taking the easy way out." Day Tripper.

"Got a new dance and it goes like this." Peppermint Twist.

"Got a surprise especially for you." Two Tickets To Paradise.

"Got along without ya before I met ya, gonna get along without ya now." Gonna Get Along Without Ya Now.

"Got on board a west bound seven forty seven." It Never Rains In Southern California.

"Got something for you darling, that you never, never had." Good Good Lovin'.

"Got to be there, got to be there in the morning." Got To Be There.

"Gotta get away from you fast as I can." End Of Our Road.

"Gotta get off, gonna get, have to get off from this ride." Valley Of The Dolls, Theme From.

"Granada, I'm falling under your spell." Granada.

"Grandma loved a sailor who sailed the frozen sea." Land Ho.

"Great grandfather met great grandmother when she was a shy young miss." Lavender Blue.

"Green Douglas firs where the waters cut through." Roll On Columbia.

"Green eyed lady, lovely lady, strolling slowly towards the sun." Green-Eyed Lady.

"Green, green, it's green, they say, on the far side of the hill." Green Green.

"Groovin' on a Sunday afternoon." Groovin'.

"Groovy day, a sunny day, walking through the country." Walking Through The Country.

"Ground control to Major Tom." Space Oddity.

"Guantanamera, guajira, Guantanamera." Guantanamera.

"Guess it's over, call it a day." Too Much, Too Little, Too Late.

"Guess who just got back today?" Boys Are Back In Town.

"Guilty undertaker sighs." I Want You.

"Guinnevere had green eyes, like yours, mi'lady like yours." Guinnevere.

"Gwen, congratulations." Gwen.

"Gypsy wind is blowing warm tonight." You'll Accomp'ny Me.

"Ha, ha, ha, ha, ha, oh you sweet thing." Chantilly Lace.

"Half moon in a night-time sky." Half Moon.

"Half of your love is just not what I'm after." Half The Way.

"Hallelujah day sing hallelujah, love is on its way." Hallelujah Day.

"Hand me down my walkin' cane, hand me down my hat." Rubberband Man.

"Hang down your head, Tom Dooley." Tom Dooley.

"Hang in there baby, gonna make love tonight." Hang On In There, Baby.

"Hang on Sloopy, Sloopy hang on." Hang On Sloopy.

"Hangman, hangman, hold it a little while." Gallows Pole.

"Happier tha the morning sun...." Happier Tha The Morning Sun.

"Happy birthday, sweet sixteen." Happy Birthday Sweet Sixteen.

"Happy, happy birthday, baby." Happy, Happy Birthday, Baby.

"Happy radio...an automatic alarm turns my radio on." H.A.P.P.Y. Radio.

"Harbors open their arms to the young searching foreigners." Immigrant.

"Hard work!" Hard Work.

"Has anybody here seen my old friend Abraham." Abraham, Martin And John.

"Have mercy, baby, on a poor girl like me." Say You Love Me.

"Have no use for other sweets of any kind since the day you came around." Honeysuckle Rose.

"Have you ever been, have you ever been to Electric Ladyland." Have You Ever Been (To Electric Ladyland).

"Have you found yourself in love before?" Fancy Dancer.

"Have you heard about the lonesome loser, beaten by the Queen of Hearts ev'ry time?' Lonesome Loser.

"Have you heard about the new dance craze?" Le Freak.

"Have you heard before, hit it out, don't look back, rock is the medium of our generation?" Release, Release.

"Have you heard I married an angel?" I Married An Angel.

"Have you heard, who's kissing her now?" Have You Heard.

"Have you seen her?" Dance The Night Away.

"Have you seen the little piggies crawling in the dirt?" Piggies.

"Haven't you heard about the guy known as the cheater?" Cheater.

"Hawaii, U.S.A." Paradise, Hawaiian Style.

"Hazel, dirty blonde hair, I wouldn't be ashamed to be seen with you anywhere." Hazel.

"He came down through the fields of green on the summer side of life." Summer Side Of Life.

"He came from somewhere back in her long ago." What A Fool Believes.

"He gave me the eye but I just passed him by." When The Love Light Starts Shining Through His Eyes.

"He goes on the prowl each night like an alley cat." Alley Cat Song.

"He holds her in his arms." Would You.

"He is now to be among you at the calling of your hearts." Wedding Song (There Is Love).

"He remembers the first time he met her." Daisy A Day.

"He rocks in the treetop all day long, hoppin' and a-boppin' and a-singin' his song." Rockin' Robin.

"He rode a blazing saddle; he wore a shining star." Blazing Saddles.

"He took a hundred pounds of clay." Hundred Pounds Of Clay.

"He wants to dream like a young man." Beautiful Loser.

"He was a hardheaded man." Life In The Fast Lane.

"He was a mean individual; he had a heart like a bone." Stranded In A Limousine.

"He was a most peculiar man." Most Peculiar Man.

"He was born in the summer of his twenty seventh year." Rocky Mountain High.

"He was born on a summer day, nineteen fifty-one." Lonely Boy (A. Gold).

"He was sittin' in the lounge of the Empire Hotel." Raised On Robbery.

"He was the wizard of a thousand kings and I chanced to meet him one night wandering." Wizard.

"Headin' up to San Francisco for the Labor Day weekend show." Come Monday.

"Heading out this morning into the sun." Dreamboat Annie.

"Hear that old train whistle howlin' in the night." Gonna Get Back Home Somehow.

"Hear that whistle, it's ten o'clock, don't let go, don't let go." Don't Let Go.

"Heard you talking then I thought I heard you say yeah, please leave me alone." Anyday.

"Heart and soul, I fell in love with you." Heart And Soul.

"Heartache number one was when you left me." Heartaches By The Number.

"Heartbeat, why do you miss when my baby kisses me?" Heartbeat.

"Hearts go astray, leaving hurt when they go." Everlasting Love.

"Hearts made of stone will never break." Hearts Of Stone.

"Hearts of fire create love desire, take you higher and higher to the world you belong." That's The Way Of The World.

"Heaven can wait." Heaven Can Wait.

"Heaven help the child who never had a home." Heaven Help Us All.

"Heaven knows we've seen the storm clouds gather." After The Storm.

"Heaven may be an answer if you're looking for Eden in the sky." California Revisited.

"Heaven, please send to all mankind understanding and peace of mind." Please Send Me Someone To Love.

"Heavenly shades of night are falling, it's twilight time." Twilight Time.

"Hello again." Now And Then.

"Hello, baby, I'm sorry I said the things I did." Crackers.

"Hello, cowgirl in the sand." Cowgirl In The Sand.

"Hello darkness, my old friend." Sound Of Silence.

"Hello, hello, I like your smile." Hello Hello.

"Hello honey, this is your lucky day." Wonderland.

"Hello, how are you?" Telephone Line.

"Hello, I don't even know your name, but I'm hopin' all the same this is more than just a simple hello." Last Time I Felt Like This.

"Hello it's me, I've thought about us for a long, long time." Hello It's Me.

"Hello Josephine, how do you do?" My Girl Josephine.

"Hello stranger, it seems so good to see you back again." Hello Stranger.

"Hello, y'all! We've got the long march goin' on here." Love March.

"Hello, yeah, it's been a while." I'd Really Love To See You Tonight.

"Help! I need somebody." Help.

"Help me, I think I'm fallin' in love again." Help Me.

"Helplessly hoping her harlequin hovers nearby, awaiting a word." Helplessly Hoping.

"Her face is cracked from smiling." Celebration Day.

"Her name was Lola, she was a showgirl, with yellow feathers in her hair and a dress cut down to there." Copacabana.

"Here come old flat top, he come grooving up slowly." Come Together.

"Here come the express." Express.

"Here come those tears again." Here Come Those Tears Again.

"Here comes D.J. Disco Tex truckin' with his Sexolettes." Get Dancin'.

"Here comes the judge." Here Comes The Judge.

"Here comes the mailman, walking up the street." Letter Full Of Tears.

"Here comes the sun." Here Comes The Sun (G. Harrison).

"Here I am again: I'm knocking on your front door again." Here I Am Again.

"Here I lie in a lost and lonely part of town." Tragedy.

"Here I stand with head in hand, turn my face to the wall." You've Got To Hide Your Love Away.

"Here in the dark a dusty light is fading." Out Of The Darkness.

"Here inside my paper cup ev'rything is looking up." Paper Cup.

"Here is my song for the asking." Song For The Asking.

"Here, making each day of the year." Here, There And Everywhere.

"Here she comes now, say, Mony, Mony." Mony Mony.

"Here she comes riding, rolling it down the line." Shake It.

"Here she comes, that little town flirt." Little Town Flirt.

"Here they come again, mm." Catch Us If You Can.

"Here we are in a room full of strangers." Nights On Broadway.

"Here we come, walkin' down the street." Monkees, Theme From.

"Here you come again." Here You Come Again.

"He's a one-trick pony." One Trick Pony.

"He's a real nowhere man." Nowhere Man.

"He's doin' the jerk, he's doin' the fly." Papa's Got A Brand New Bag (Part II).

"He's on his way, he's goin' to Hollywood." Hollywood.

"He's the kind of guy puts on a motorcycle jacket and he weighs about a hundred and five." Hard Loving Loser.

"He's the man with all the toys." Man With All The Toys.

"He's triggered by the rise of their suburban eyes." Pretty Girls.

"Hey babe, say you're mine, all mine." Hey Babe.

"Hey, baby! I ain't askin' much of you." Big Hunk O' Love.

"Hey! Baby! I want to know if you'll be my girl." Hey Baby.

"Hey, baby, if you're feelin' down, I know what's good for you all day." <u>Dirty White Boy</u>.

"Hey baby, I'm your telephone man." <u>Telephone Man</u>.

"Hey baby, what do I have to do to make a hit with you?" <u>Dance With Me Henry</u>.

"Hey, baby, why you goin' that-a way." <u>Shake And Dance With Me</u>.

"Hey! Can I carry your balloon." <u>Can I Carry Your Balloon</u>.

"Hey, Chubby Checker!" <u>Loose Caboose</u>.

"Hey, Colorado, it was not so long ago I left your mountains to try life on the road." <u>Colorado</u>.

"Hey, did you happen to see the most beautiful girl in the world?" <u>Most Beautiful Girl</u>.

"Hey, doll baby, can we have a little talk together?" <u>Hey, Doll Baby</u>.

"Hey, don't worry." <u>Minute By Minute</u>.

"Hey fellas, have you heard the news?" <u>Heartbreaker</u> (J. Page, R. Plant, J.P. Jones & J. Bonham).

"Hey girl, come and get it while I still got it." <u>Hey Girl, Come And Get It</u>.

"Hey girl, I know he put you down." <u>Hey Girl</u> (J. Phillips & M. Gilliam).

"Hey girl, I want you to know, I'm gonna miss you so much if you go." <u>Hey Girl</u> (G. Goffin & C. King).

"Hey, girl, stop what you doin'!" <u>Communication Breakdown</u>.

"Hey, girl, watcha doin' down there." <u>Knock Three Times</u>.

"Hey girls, gather round, because of what I'm puttin' down." <u>Handy Man</u>.

"Hey! Gotta, gotta payback, revenge." <u>Payback</u>.

"Hey, have you ever tried, really reaching out for the other side." <u>Make It With You</u>.

"Hey hey baby, I wanna know yeah if you'll be my girl." <u>Hey! Baby</u>.

"Hey, hey, hey a-what you got to say." <u>Hollywood Swinging</u>.

"Hey, hey, hey, hey, beat is getting stronger." <u>I Want To Take You Higher</u>.

"Hey, hey, look at me and tell me, what's gonna happen to you." <u>Look At Me</u>.

"Hey, hey, mama, said the way you move gonna make you sweat, gonna make you groove." <u>Black Dog</u>.

"Hey, hey, my, my, rock and roll can never die." <u>Hey Hey, My My</u>.

"Hey! Hey! Paula I wanna marry you." <u>Hey! Paula</u>.

"Hey, hey, pretty baby, with your fine old foxy self." <u>Fine Old Foxy Self</u>.

"Hey hey, tell me whatcha gonna do about that." <u>I Got Ants In My Pants (Part I)</u>.

"Hey ho, let's go, hey ho, let's go!" <u>Blitzkrieg Bop</u>.

"Hey ho, nobody home, meat nor drink nor money have I none." <u>A'Shoalin'</u>.

"Hey Joe, where ya goin' with that gun in your hand." <u>Hey Joe</u>.

"Hey Johnny, hey Dee Dee; little Tom and Joey." <u>Ramona</u>.

"Hey Jude, don't make it bad, take a sad song and make it better." <u>Hey Jude</u>.

"Hey kids shake it loose together." <u>Bennie And The Jets</u>.

"Hey, lady, you got the love I need, maybe more than enough." <u>Over The Hills And Far Away</u>.

"Hey! Life, look at me." <u>Happening</u>.

"Hey, little girl, I wanna be your boyfriend." <u>I Wanna Be Your Boyfriend</u>.

"Hey, little girl in the high school sweater." <u>Hey Little Girl</u>.

"Hey, little girl, won't you meet me at the school yard gate?" <u>My Music</u>.

"Hey, little girl, you don't have to hide nothin' no more!" <u>Little Girl</u>.

"Hey, little woman, please make up your mind." <u>Little Woman</u>.

"Hey, look what you have done, showing me the sun." <u>It's Nice To Be With You</u>.

"Hey, look yonder, tell me what's that you see marching to the fields of Concord." <u>Handsome Johnny</u>.

"Hey, mama don't you treat me wrong." <u>What'd I Say</u>.

"Hey mister, please, spare me some time." <u>Mellow Lovin'</u>.

"Hey! Mister Tambourine man play a song for me." <u>Mr. Tambourine Man</u>.

"Hey, mister, that's me up on the jukebox." <u>Hey Mister, That's Me Up On The Jukebox</u>.

"Hey, Nelly Nelly, come to the window." <u>Hey Nelly Nelly</u>.

"Hey nonny ding dong alang, alang, alang, boom, ba-deh, ba-doo, ba-doo, life could be a dream, sh-boom." <u>Sh-Boom</u>.

"Hey, pretty baby, you can't sit down." <u>You Can't Sit Down</u>.

"Hey! Psst, psst! Here she comes now." <u>Rip Her To Shreds</u>.

"Hey, say wait a minute." <u>Just Don't Want To Be Lonely</u>.

"Hey, schoolgirl in the second row...." <u>Hey, Schoolgirl</u>.

"Hey, sister, go sister, soul sister, go sister." <u>Lady Marmalade</u>.

"Hey there! Georgy girl...." <u>Georgy Girl</u>.

"Hey there, lonely girl, lonely girl...." <u>Hey There Lonely Girl</u>.

"Hey, Venus, oh, Venus...." <u>Venus</u>.

"Hey, what about me?" <u>Hey, What About Me</u>.

"Hey, where did we go days when the rains came." <u>Brown Eyed Girl</u>.

"Hey, who's that stompin' all over my face?" <u>Nowadays Clancy Can't Even Sing</u>.

FIND THAT TUNE

"Hey, woman, you got the blues." Evil Woman.

"Hey, yeah, here come the jesters, one, two, three." Rock 'N' Roll Fantasy.

"Hey, y' know?" I Know But I Don't Know.

"Hi, hello, awake from thy sleep." Frederick.

"Hi-de-ho, hi-de-hi, gonna get me a piece of the sky." Hi-De-Ho.

"Higher than the highest mountain...." Endlessly.

"Hit it, how you feelin', brother?" Doin' It To Death.

"Hit the road Jack and don't you come back no more." Hit The Road Jack.

"Ho ho ho, just like a yo yo." Yo Yo.

"Hold me close." Today's The Day.

"Hold me close and tell me how you feel." Words Of Love (B. Holly).

"Hold me close, hold me tight." I Want You, I Need You, I Love You.

"Hold me, hold me, never let me go until you've told me, told me what I want to know and then just hold me, hold me." Hold Me, Thrill Me, Kiss Me.

"Hold the boat steady; don't-a let it rock." We're Coming In Loaded.

"Holy Moses I have been removed." Border Song.

"Home made love, just like mama used to make." Home-Made Love.

"Honey, I'll always love you." You Can't Change That.

"Honey, you are my shining star." Shining Star (L. Graham & P. Richmond).

"Honey-e-e, you do me wrong but still I'm crazy 'bout you." Ain't That Peculiar.

"Hoo, ha, ha, hoo, precious moments...when will I see you again." When Will I See You Again.

"Hope they never end this song." Look What You've Done To Me.

"Hot chili peppers in the blistering sun." Romance In Durango.

"Hot summer night fell like a net." Bad Case Of Loving You.

"Hot town, summer in the city." Summer In The City.

"Hoverin' by my suitcase, tryin' to find a warm place to spend the night." Rainy Night In Georgia.

"How can I be sure in a world that's constantly changing?" How Can I Be Sure.

"How can people be so heartless?" Easy To Be Hard.

"How can this be love if it makes us cry?" How Can This Be Love.

"How can you tell me how much you miss me?" Poor Side Of Town.

"How come he don't come and p.l.p. with me down at the meter no more?" Chuck E's In Love.

"How do I say goodbye to what we had?" It's So Hard To Say Goodbye To Yesterday.

"How does it feel to be one of the beautiful people?" Baby, You're A Rich Man.

"How it all started, I hardly remember, a casual walk through the park in winter." Gone Too Far.

"How long has this been going on?" How Long.

"How many more times, treat me the way you wanna do?" How Many More Times.

"How many roads must a man walk down before you call him a man?" Blowin' In The Wind.

"How many times do I see your face?" Count Every Star.

"How many times have I been downhearted?" Everybody Gets To Go To The Moon.

"How much love do you need before you give your love to me?" How Much Love.

"How sweet it is to be loved by you." How Sweet It Is (To Be Loved By You).

"How the time flies, when I'm near you." How Time Flies.

"How would you like to be a little circus clown?" How Would You Like To Be.

"Huh, well, the music is coming to an end." Me And The Gang.

"Huh! You know life is funny when you look at it." That's The Way I Feel About Cha.

"Human race was dying out, no one left to scream and shout." Ship Of Fools (J. Morrison & Doors).

"Hurt to think that you lied to me, hurt way down deep inside of me." Hurt (J. Crane & A. Jacobs).

"Hush little baby don't you cry, though you know your mama was born to die." All My Trials (O. Gordon).

"Hushabye, hushabye; oh, my darling, don't you cry." Hushabye.

"I ain't gonna marry in the fall." I'm Just A Country Boy.

"I ain't gonna work on Maggie's farm no more." Maggie's Farm.

"I ain't got no home, a-no place to roam." Ain't Got No Home.

"I ain't got no money." I Wanna Be Your Lover.

"I ain't got time to think about money." Too Busy Thinking About My Baby.

"I ain't lookin' to compete with you." All I Really Want To Do.

"I ain't never been with a woman long enough for my boots to get old." Heard It In A Love Song.

"I always said you could make it." Will Anything Happen.

"I am a back door man." Back Door Man.

"I am a child." I Am A Child.

"I am a lineman for the county, and I drive the main road." Wichita Lineman.

"I am a lonesome hobo without family or friends." <u>I Am A Lonesome Hobo</u>.

"I am a maid of constant sorrow." <u>Maid Of Constant Sorrow</u>.

"I am a man of constant sorrow." <u>Man Of Constant Sorrow</u>.

"I am down in the sea of confusion 'neath the waves of no recovery." <u>Hard Times</u>.

"I am he as you are he as you are me and we are all together." <u>I Am The Walrus</u>.

"I am just a poor boy, though my story's seldom told." <u>Boxer</u>.

"I am on a lonely road and I am traveling." <u>All I Want</u>.

"I am only five years old and my baby's three." <u>Baby Talk</u>.

"I am sailing, I am sailing home again, 'cross the sea." <u>Sailing</u> (G. Sutherland).

"I am so in love for once in my life." <u>Lovin' You Lovin' Me</u>.

"I am the entertainer and I know just where I stand." <u>Entertainer</u> (B. Joel).

"I am the one who can please you." <u>Even It Up</u>.

"I am what I am, what I am, I'll be." <u>I Am What I Am</u>.

"I am woman, hear me roar." <u>I Am Woman</u>.

"I am yours and you are mine, come what may." <u>Come What May</u>.

"I asked that man what he wanted to be." <u>Drive My Car</u>.

"I awoke this morning, love laid me down by the river." <u>Wonderous Stories</u>.

"I been ballin' a shiny black jack hammer, been chippin' rocks for the great highway." <u>Easy Wind</u>.

"I been had my eyes on you for a while." <u>Too Hot To Stop</u> (Part I).

"I been in the right place, but it must-a been the wrong time." <u>Right Place Wrong Time</u>.

"I been Norman Mailered, Maxwell Taylored." <u>Simple Desultory Phillippic</u>.

"I been standin' here for oh so long tryin' to figure out, girl, where we went wrong." <u>Maybe I'm A Fool</u>.

"I been trying to get to you for a long time." <u>Expressway To Your Heart</u>.

"I beg your pardon, I never promised you a rose garden." <u>Rose Garden</u>.

"I believe in miracles and all because of you." <u>I Believe In Miracles</u>.

"I believe that you heard your master sing when I was sick in bed." <u>Master Song</u>.

"I believe the children are the future." <u>Greatest Love Of All</u>.

"I believe you, when you say that you will reach into the sky and steal a star so you can put it on my finger." <u>I Believe You</u>.

"I bet you're wondrin' how I knew baby..." <u>I Heard It Through The Grapevine</u>.

"I bless the day I found you." <u>Let It Be Me</u>.

"I bought a brand new airmobile." <u>You Can't Catch Me</u>.

"I bruise you, you bruise me." <u>All I Know</u>.

"I call you." <u>Breakdown Dead Ahead</u>.

"I came by myself to a very crowded place." <u>Lady Midnight</u>.

"I came down to New York town." <u>Talking Folklore Center</u>.

"I came upon a butcher, he was slaughtering a lamb." <u>Butcher</u>.

"I came upon a child of God; he was walking along the road." <u>Woodstock</u>.

"I can hear the soft breathing of the girl that I love as she lies here beside me asleep with the night." <u>Somewhere They Can't Find Me</u>.

"I can hear the soft breathing of the girl that I love as she lies here beside me asleep with the night." <u>Wednesday Morning, 3 a.m.</u>

"I can hear the turning of the key." <u>Abandoned Love</u>.

"I can only give you love that lasts forever." <u>That's All</u>.

"I can see clearly now the rain has gone." <u>I Can See Clearly Now</u>.

"I can see her body pushin' at her clothes." <u>Started Out Dancing, Ended Up Making Love</u>.

"I can see her lyin' back in her satin dress in a room where you do what you don't confess." <u>Sundown</u>.

"I can see the dancing, the silhouettes on the shade." <u>Let Me In</u>.

"I can see us in an empty house, not worried about the things going on outside." <u>I Wanna Be Selfish</u>.

"I can see where I'm goin', although the road's not clear." <u>Can't Keep A Good Man Down</u>.

"I can see you're slipping away from me." <u>I'm Gonna Be Strong</u>.

"I can tell because it's plain to see." <u>I Can Tell</u>.

"I can tell by your eyes that you've prob'bly been cryin' forever." <u>I Don't Want To Talk About It</u>.

"I can think of younger days when living for my life was ev'rything a man could want to do." <u>How Can You Mend A Broken Heart</u>.

"I can turn the grey sky bluer, and I can make it rain whenever I want it to." <u>I Can't Get Next To You</u>.

"I cannot follow you, my love, you cannot follow me." <u>You Know Who I Am</u>.

"I can't budge, baby." <u>Bonfire</u>.

"I can't cover up my feelings in the name of love...." <u>It's My Turn</u>.

"I can't get no satisfaction." <u>Satisfaction</u> (M. Jagger & K. Richard).

"I can't light no more of your darkness." <u>Don't Let The Sun Go Down On Me</u>.

"I can't love you, baby, any more." <u>Gotta Be The One</u>.

"I can't quit you baby." <u>I Can't Quit You Baby</u>.

"I can't remember when I've felt this high." You (T. Snow).

"I can't seem to face up to the facts." Psycho Killer.

"I can't seem to find the words, Diane." Diane (B. Carl, R. Whitelaw & R. Bell).

"I can't stand my baby, it's a real drag." I Can't Stand My Baby.

"I can't stand the rain 'gainst my window ho--bringin' back sweet memories." I Can't Stand The Rain.

"I can't stand to wait a minute longer." Wake Up Susan.

"I can't stay much longer, Melinda; the sun is getting high." Cumberland Blues.

"I can't stay, yes I know, you know why I hate to go." Just A Little.

"I can't stop this feeling deep inside of me." Hooked On A Feeling.

"I can't wait any longer." I Can't Wait Any Longer.

"I can't wait forever, even though you want me to." Time Won't Let Me.

"I close my eyes only for a moment, and the moment's gone." Dust In The Wind.

"I come fresh from the street, fast on my feet, kinda lean and lazy." I Want To Learn A Love Song.

"I come from the mountains, Kentucky's my home." Black Waters.

"I come to this garden, I come here to rest." That Same Old Obsession.

"I could keep trying, look the rest of my life to find that special love." We've Got Love.

"I couldn't stop moving when it first took hold." Rock And Roll Hoochie Koo.

"I cried a tear because of you." I Cried A Tear.

"I cried a tear, you wiped it dry." You Needed Me.

"I cried when they shot Medgar Evers." Love Me, I'm A Liberal.

"I cry myself to sleep each night." It Keeps Right On A-hurtin'.

"I did not know what you were about." Get Used To It.

"I did you wrong." Ooo Baby Baby.

"I didn't know what day it was when you walked into the room." You're In My Heart.

"I didn't know you were the one for me." Watch Her Ride.

"I didn't mean to treat you so bad." One Of Us Must Know.

"I dig love." I Dig Love.

"I dig rock 'n' roll music and I love to get the chance to play." I Dig Rock 'N' Roll Music.

"I do believe in you and I know you believe in me." Feelin' Stronger Every Day.

"I don't care about your past, I just want our love to last." Cold Sweat (Parts 1 & 2).

"I don't care if you never come home." Promises.

"I don't even know how to love you just the way you want me to." Yes I'm Ready.

"I don't have plans and schemes and I don't have hopes and dreams." Since I Don't Have You.

"I don't hurt any more." I Don't Hurt Any More.

"I don't know, but it seems that ev'ry single dream is painting pretty pictures in the air." Cross My Heart.

"I don't know how I'm gonna tell you I can't play with you no more." That's The Way.

"I don't know how to love him, what to do, how to move him." I Don't Know How To Love Him.

"I don't know what it is that makes me love you so." I Only Want To Be With You.

"I don't know what you can do, let me lay my funk on you." Let Me Lay My Funk On You.

"I don't know what you got." You Got Me Hummin'.

"I don't know where I'm agonna go when the volcano blow, let me say it now." Volcano.

"I don't know why I love you but I do." But I Do.

"I don't know why I love you like I do, all the changes you put me through." Take Me To The River.

"I don't like you, but I love you." You've Really Got A Hold On Me.

"I don't mind you coming here, wasting all my time." Just What I Needed.

"I don't mind your love." I Don't Mind.

"I don't need a whole lots of money." Some Kind Of Wonderful.

"I don't need anyone." Sonic Reducer.

"I don't need no doctor if 'cause I know what's ailin' me." I Don't Need No Doctor.

"I don't remember mama, she died when I was born." Keep On Singing.

"I don't remember what day it was." More Today Than Yesterday.

"I don't wanna know the reason why." Don't Throw It All Away.

"I don't wanna know your name 'cause you don't look the same, the way you did before." Fox On The Run.

"I don't want a pickle, just want to ride on my motor-sickle." Motorcycle Song.

"I don't want the world to know." Two Faces Have I.

"I don't want to do wrong, but you've been gone, baby, so long." I Don't Want To Do Wrong.

"I don't want to hear it, no more fussin' and a fightin', baby." Hold Me Tight.

"I don't want to lose you, this good thing that I got." Knock On Wood.

"I don't want your lonely mansion, with a tear in ev'ry room." Silver Threads And Golden Needles.

"I dreamed I saw Joe Hill last night alive as you and me." Joe Hill (E. Robinson).

"I dreamed I saw St. Augustine, alive as you or me." I Dreamed I Saw St. Augustine.

"I drive so hard, I drive so far, won't you watch me wheelin' around?" Hot Rod.

"I feel good, I knew that I would now." I Got You (I Feel Good).

"I feel it in my leg; I feel it in my shoe." Party (J. Robinson).

"I feel like a lonesome tumbleweed rolling across an open plain." Tumbleweed.

"I feel the earth move under my feet." I Feel The Earth Move.

"I finally broke into prison." Old Revolution.

"I forgot to remember to forget her." I Forgot To Remember To Forget.

"I found a river I'm so proud of." River Of Love.

"I found a woman, I thought I truly loved." Take Time To Know Her.

"I found my own true love was on a blue Sunday." Blue Sunday.

"I found my thrill on Blueberry Hill." Blueberry Hill.

"I gave my heart and soul to you, boy, didn't I do it, baby?" Didn't I (Blow Your Mind This Time).

"I gave my heart, I gave my love." Doin' The Best I Can (D. Pomus & M. Shuman).

"I get around from town to town." I Get Around.

"I get too low with no reason." I Can't Make It Anymore.

"I give, give you my heart, today, tomorrow and forever." Today, Tomorrow And Forever.

"I give her all my love, that's all I do." And I Love Her.

"I go downtown and roam around." Doesn't Somebody Want To Be Wanted.

"I go out to work on Monday morning." Lazing On A Sunday Afternoon.

"I got a bag of my own." I Got A Bag Of My Own.

"I got a call the other day." Angel (W. Sanders & C. Franklin).

"I got a feeling you're feeling good tonight." Standing Ovation.

"I got a girl, I got a girl, I got a girl named Bony Moronie." Bony Moronie.

"I got a girl named Rama Lama, Rama Lama Ding Dong." Rama Lama Ding Dong.

"I got a good thing." Stone To The Bone.

"I got a woman mean as she can be." Mean Woman Blues.

"I got a woman way over town." I Got A Woman.

"I got chills, they're multiplyin'." You're The One That I Want.

"I got excited when I first heard that you wanted to meet me." Take Me I'm Yours.

"I got lost on the road somewhere." From The Inside.

"I got lumps in my throat when I saw her comin' down the aisle." Little Queenie.

"I got my mo-jo working but it just won't work on you." Got My Mo-Jo Working.

"I got something to tell you that I think you ought to know." I've Got A Thing About You Baby.

"I got the blues when my baby left me by the San Francisco Bay." San Francisco Bay Blues.

"I got the feelin' the feelin's gone, my heart has gone to sleep." My Heart Belongs To Me.

"I got to find my baby, I wonder where she can be." I've Got To Find My Baby.

"I got up this mornin' and while I was havin' my coffee...." I've Found Someone Of My Own.

"I grew up a-dreaming of being a cowboy, and loving the cowboy ways." My Heroes Have Always Been Cowboys.

"I guess I'll learn how to fly." Learn How To Fly.

"I guess it was yourself you were involved with." Ain't No Way To Treat A Lady.

"I guess we used to be the lucky ones." Why Me (D. De Young).

"I guess you wonder where I've been." What You Won't Do For Love.

"I had a dream, oh, my, crazy dream, oh, oh." Song Remains The Same.

"I had a friend, a friend I could trust." Ring Around A Rosy Rag.

"I had a friend one time, at least I thought he was my friend." I'm Mad Again.

"I had a girl, Donna was her name." Donna.

"I had a sweetheart, her name was Jo-Ann." Jo-Ann.

"I hate myself for lovin' you and the weakness that it showed." Dirge.

"I hate to say it but I told you so." Laugh, Laugh.

"I have a mansion but forget the price." Life's Been Good.

"I have been a rover, I have walked alone." Love's Been Good To Me.

"I have counted ev'ry day since you've been away." I Count The Tears.

"I have heard rumors all over town." Tell Me That It Isn't True.

"I have known you all my life." Feelings (R. Coonce, W. Entner & K. Fukomoto).

"I have never been so much in love." Love Ballad.

"I have not come, yeah, to testify about our bad, bad misfortune." It's Not My Cross To Bear.

"I have often heard you say you love me as a friend." Lead Me On.

"I have seen the morning burning golden on the mountain in the skies." Loving Her Was Easier.

"I have these moments all steady and strong." Part Of The Plan.

"I have watched you sitting there." Apple Scruffs.

"I haven't stopped dancing yet, since we met on our first

date." I Haven't Stopped Dancing Yet.

"I hear mariachi static on my radio." Carmelita.

"I hear some people talkin' me down, bring up my name, pass it 'round." Walk On.

"I hear the drizzle of the rain." Kathy's Song.

"I hear your voice everywhere." Echoes Of Love.

"I heard about it raining on a Georgia night, never saw clearly in the mornin' light." Everybody Loves A Rain Song.

"I heard he sang a good song, I heard he had a style." Killing Me Softly With His Song.

"I heard it in the wind last night." For The Roses.

"I heard that you're on your own now." Sam.

"I heard the knock on my door, I heard the ring of the bell." Lights (T. Shaw & D. DeYoung).

"I heard the men saying something." Point Of Know Return.

"I heard the weather man predict a sunny day." This Time I'm In It For Love.

"I heard you on the wireless back in fifty-two, lying awake intently tuning in on you." Video Killed The Radio Star.

"I, I love, love, n' I n' I love you." You (G. Harrison).

"I, I who have nothing." I (Who Have Nothing).

"I just can't help believin'." I Just Can't Help Believin'.

"I just closed my eyes again." Dream Weaver.

"I just got out my little red book the minute that you said goodbye." My Little Red Book.

"I just got your letter, baby; a-too bad you can't come home." Mess Of Blues.

"I just had to get on the Texas plane, yeah, when it was bringin' me down." Ego Rock.

"I just lay here at night." You're The Reason.

"I just wanna see ya dancin' ev'rywhere we go." Dancin'.

"I just want to celebrate another day of living." I Just Want To Celebrate.

"I keep a close watch on this heart of mine." I Walk The Line.

"I knew a man Bojangles and he danced for you in worn out shoes." Mr. Bojangles.

"I knew you when you were lonely." I Knew You When.

"I know a girl from a lonely street." Sunday Girl.

"I know a place, ain't nobody cryin'." I'll Take You There.

"I know each time she smiles at you." Where Angels Go, Trouble Follows.

"I know if I'd been wiser, this would never have occurred." Look To Your Soul (G. Brooker, M. Fisher & K. Reid).

"I know it's late." We've Got Tonite.

"I know it's late to call, I don't blame you if you're angry." Fire In The Morning.

"I know she's waiting in Denver." Denver.

"I know that it's late and I really must leave you alone." Love Me Tonight.

"I know that somewhere there's someone you love more than me." Too Far Gone.

"I know the reason you've been crying oh, yes! What's A Matter, Baby.

"I know we only met just the other day." Next Hundred Years.

"I know you don't know what I'm going through standing here looking at you." Hurt So Bad.

"I know you don't love me no more, no more, no, no more." I Know.

"I know you had a hard time keeping it together." It'll Come, It'll Come, It'll Come.

"I know you wanna leave me but I refuse to let you go." Ain't Too Proud To Beg.

"I know your eyes in the morning sun." How Deep Is Your Love.

"I know your type." Kiss In The Dark.

"I know you're a lonely woman and I love you." If You Talk In Your Sleep.

"I know you've deceived me." I Can See For Miles.

"I laid on a dune." Sara (B. Dylan).

"I learned the truth at seventeen that love was meant for beauty queens." At Seventeen.

"I left Louisian'; I had no big plans." Beaucoups Of Blues.

"I left my heart in San Francisco." I Left My Heart In San Francisco.

"I left my home in Norfolk, Virginia, California on my mind." Promised Land.

"I left Oklahoma drivin' in a Pontiac, just about to lose my mind." Tulsa Time.

"I like dreamin' 'cause dreamin' can make you mine." I Like Dreamin'.

"I like love music, that's my kind of music." Love Music.

"I like springtime flowers that grow along the lane." In 25 Words Or Less.

"I like the way you walk, I like the way you talk." Let The Four Winds Blow.

"I like the way your sparklin' earrings lay, against your skin so brown." Peaceful Easy Feeling.

"I like to see you boogie right across the floor." Boogie On Reggae Woman.

"I like to spend some time in Mozambique." Mozambique.

"I lit a thin green candle to make you jealous of me." One Of Us Can Not Be Wrong.

"I lit out from Reno, I was trailed by twenty hounds." Friend Of The Devil.

"I live my life like there's no tomorrow." Running With The Devil.

"I lived with the decent folks in the hills of old Vermont." Yankee Lady.

"I look at the rain and look at the stars tonight all falling down on me." Moonlight Lady.

"I look at you all see the love there that's sleeping while my guitar gently weeps." While My Guitar Gently Weeps.

"I look at you and, wham, I'm head over heels." I Slipped, I Stumbled, I Fell.

"I look pretty young, but you know that I'm dyin'." Who's Been Sleepin' Here.

"I lost at love before." You've Made Me So Very Happy.

"I love a girl and a-Ruby is her name." Ruby Baby.

"I love how your eyes close whenever you kiss me." I Love How You Love Me.

"I love, I love, I love my calendar girl." Calendar Girl.

"I love music, any kind of music." I Love Music (Part I).

"I love the little wiggle in your walk." Sweet And Innocent.

"I love the way you love to live." Happiness.

"I love the way you walk." Dimples.

"I love to love you, baby." Love To Love You, Baby.

"I love you." Please Don't Go.

"I love you and that's simply all there is to it." Destiny.

"I love you, baby, and I want you to be my girl." I Want You To Be My Girl.

"I love you, I love you." I Love You.

"I love you more than ever, more than time and more than love." Wedding Song.

"I love you more than I can say." More Than I Can Say.

"I love you the best, better than all the rest." Indian Summer.

"I loved you in the morning, our kisses sweet and warm." Hey, That's No Way To Say Goodbye.

"I make up things to say on my way to you." I've Told Ev'ry Little Star.

"I married Isis on the fifth day of May." Isis.

"I may not seem your ideal when you look into my eyes." Let Me Be Your Car.

"I mean come in this house, stop all that yakkity yak." Honey Hush.

"I met a devil woman." You Ain't Seen Nothing Yet.

"I met a gin soaked, barroom queen in Memphis." Honky Tonk Women.

"I met a man who bought up land wherever his foot would tread." My Wheels Won't Turn.

"I met a woman long ago, her hair the black that black can go." Teachers.

"I met him on a Monday and my heart stood still." Da Doo Ron Ron.

"I met my little bright-eyed doll, down by the riverside." Down By The Riverside.

"I met my old lover on the street last night." Still Crazy After All These Years.

"I met you on somebody's island." Jungle Love.

"I miss you." You And I (Michaele & L. & P. Sebastian).

"I must decide how I live." Love For Living.

"I nearly lost myself tryin' to be someone else." Look To Your Soul (J. Hendricks).

"I need a man." I Need A Man To Love.

"I need love, love to ease my mind." You Can't Hurry Love.

"I need somebody groovy." Somebody Groovy.

"I need you, baby, like a dog needs a bone." Yank Me, Crank Me.

"I need you so to keep me happy." I Need You So.

"I need you, when the moon is bright." Honey Love.

"I need your sweet inspiration." Sweet Inspiration.

"I never did so much to make her stay here, and words of love to her, I never say." Sure Gonna Miss Her.

"I never feel, a thing is real, when I'm away from you." It's Only A Paper Moon.

"I never fell in love so easily, where the four winds blow I carry on." Spirits (Having Flown).

"I never knew how complete love could be till she kissed me and said baby please go all the way." Go All The Way.

"I never meant to hurt you." I Never Meant To Hurt You.

"I never met a girl who makes me feel the way that you do." Get Ready.

"I never read it in a book, I never saw it on a show." If You Wanna Get To Heaven.

"I never won for losing, but it ceased to be amusing when you told me...." Everybody Be Dancin'.

"I once had a girl, or should I say she once had me." Norwegian Wood.

"I once held her in my arms." I Threw It All Away.

"I picked up the paper this morning, and read all the daily blues." I'm Not Gonna Let It Bother Me Tonight.

"I pity the poor immigrant who wishes he would've stayed home." I Pity The Poor Immigrant.

"I plan it all and I take my place." Odds And Ends.

"I play the street life, because there's no place I can go." Street Life.

"I prayed to the Lord to send a love." My True Love.

"I pulled out for San Anton', I never felt so good." Lo And Behold.

"I put a spell on you because you're mine." I Put A Spell On You (J. Hawkins).

"I ran all the way home just to say I'm sorry." Sorry.

"I ran around with my own little crowd." I Didn't Know About You.

"I read the news today, oh boy, about a lucky man who made the grade." Day In The Life.

"I realize the best part of love is the thinnest slice." Lost In Love.

"I realize the way your eyes deceived me with tender looks that I mistook for love." Paper Roses.

"I really love you, honest I do." Honest I Do (D. Stankey, J. West & A. Candelaria).

"I really want you, really do." You Make Me Real.

"I recall when I was young, my pappy said, 'Don't cry.'" Roller Coaster.

"I remember a time, rompin' through the woods." It Was So Easy.

"I remember all my life raining down as cold as ice." Mandy.

"I remember every little thing as if it happened only yesterday." Paradise By The Dashboard Light.

"I remember finding out about you." Day After Day.

"I remember my first love affair." Only The Strong Survive.

"I remember nineteen sixty four, there was nothing playing on the radio." Platinum Heroes.

"I remember now the time you left." My Front Pages.

"I remember setting out just to see what I could see." Painted Ladies.

"I remember sitting on the front steps feeling the softness of a warm summer rain." Kiss Me In The Rain.

"I remember standing on the corner at midnight." Mainstreet.

"I remember the thirty five sweet goodbyes when you put me on the Wolverine up in Annandale." My Old School.

"I remember the way our sainted mother would sit and croon us her lullaby." Easy Street.

"I remember times, my love, when we really had it all." Love Me.

"I remember to this day...." Me And You And A Dog Named Boo.

"I remember when Mary Lou said, 'You wanna walk me home from school?'" Spiders And Snakes.

"I remember when rock was young." Crocodile Rock.

"I remember when the sunlight had a special kind of brightness." Yellow Days.

"I rode into town today." Searchin' For A Rainbow.

"I rode my bicycle past your window last night." Brand New Key.

"I said, 'Babe, ya gotta bring it on home to me.'" Bring It On Home.

"I said, 'Shotgun shoot 'em 'fore he run now.'" Shotgun.

"I said, 'Take it easy, baby, I worked all day and my feet feel just like lead.'" Bossa Nova, Baby.

"I said, 'Upside down you're turnin' me.'" Upside Down.

"I saw a werewolf, with a Chinese menu in his hand." Werewolves Of London.

"I saw her again last night." I Saw Her Again Last Night.

"I saw her standing on the corner, a yellow ribbon in her hair." Young Blood (J. Leiber, M. Stoller, & D. Pomus).

"I saw her today at the reception, a glass of wine in her hand." You Can't Always Get What You Want.

"I saw him today." Needles And Pins.

"I saw the light on the night that I passed by her window." Delilah.

"I saw you standing on the corner." X-Offender.

"I see a bad moon arising." Bad Moon Rising.

"I see in the paper nearly ev'ry day, people breakin' up and just walkin' away from love, and that's wrong, that's so wrong." No Love At All.

"I see that worried look upon your face; you've got your troubles, I got mine." You've Got Your Troubles.

"I see the clouds that move across the sky." Don't Worry About The Government.

"I see the party lights shining in the night." Party Lights (T. Stephens).

"I see your teeth flash, Jamaican honey so sweet." Island Girl.

"I set to sea on a ship called emptiness." She Did It.

"I shall sing, sing my song, be it right, be it wrong." I Shall Sing.

"I shot the sheriff, but I did not shoot the deputy." I Shot The Sheriff.

"I should have known better with a girl like you." I Should Have Known Better.

"I should have known you'd bid me farewell." Red Rubber Ball.

"I shoulda loved ya." I Shoulda Loved Ya.

"I shoulda quit you a long time ago." Killing Floor.

"I sing woe, woe, woe." Here 'Tis.

"I sit by the telephone waiting for you to call me." Gettin' Ready For Love.

"I smell smoke in the auditorium." Charlie Brown.

"I solve my problems and I see the light." Grease.

"I spend the night in a chair." Without Her.

"I stand at your gate and the song that I sing is of moonlight." Moonlight Serenade.

"I started a joke which started the whole world crying." I Started A Joke.

"I stayed up all night waiting for you to call." Deep Inside My Heart.

"I stood a-watchin' all night long." Susie Darlin'.

"I talked to my baby on the telephone long distance." Never Let Her Slip Away.

"I tell myself what's done is done." It Must Be Him.

"I think about winter when I was with her and the snow was fallin' down." Falling.

"I think I'm going to Katmandu." Katmandu.

"I think I'm gonna be sad, I think it's today, yeh!" Ticket To Ride.

"I think it's so groovy now, that people are finally getting together." Reach Out In The Darkness.

"I think of her." Friend Is Dying.

"I think that you don't care, and it's more than I can bear." All In My Mind.

"I thought I knew you." Turn Back The Pages.

"I thought love was only true in fairy tales." I'm A Believer.

"I told myself the day you left it's just a matter of time till I regain my peace of mind." Never Gonna Be The Same.

"I took my little Jenny to a party last night." Poor Jenny.

"I took my troubles down to Madam Ruth." Love Potion Number Nine.

"I took off for a weekend last month just to try and recall the whole year." Changes In Latitudes, Changes In Attitudes.

"I try to believe you when you tell me you love me." Baby I Want You.

"I used to be a rolling stone, you know." Philadelphia Freedom.

"I used to be such a sweet, sweet thing till they got a hold of me." No More Mister Nice Guy.

"I used to go out to parties and stand around." Got To Give It Up (Part I).

"I used to hurry a lot." Long Run.

"I used to know you was a heavy lady." Keep On Running Away.

"I used to run around; you never tied me down. Lady (Put The Light On Me).

"I walk along the city streets you used to walk along with me." Always Something There To Remind Me.

"I walk forty seven miles of barb wire." Who Do You Love.

"I wanna be free, like the bluebirds flying by me." I Wanna Be Free.

"I wanna be your lover, babe, I wanna be your man." I Wanna Be Your Man.

"I wanna get close to you, baby, as white on white." Close To You (W. Dixon).

"I wanna live, I wanna give, I've been a miner for a heart of gold." Heart Of Gold.

"I wanna live with a cinnamon girl." Cinnamon Girl.

"I wanna tell you a story ev'ry man ought to know." Treat Her Right.

"I wanna tell you about my good friend." Crunge.

"I want a love that's right but right is only half of what's wrong." Old Brown Shoe.

"I want security, yeah." Security.

"I want me somebody to hold my hand." Woman, A Lover, A Friend.

"I want the love that you deny me that I need so desperately." Surrender (N. Ashford & V. Simpson).

"I want to be your lover, but your friend is all I stay." Halfway To Paradise.

"I want to jump but I'm afraid I'll fall." Rockin' Pneumonia And The Boogie Woogie Flu.

"I want to ride out in the morning air." Ride.

"I want tell you 'bout ooh poo pah doo." Ooh Poo Pah Doo.

"I want to say I love you." Love Me Again.

"I want to walk with you; I'd like to talk to you." I'm Still In Love With You (T-B. Walker).

"I want to walk you home." I Want To Walk You Home.

"I want you in my arms." All I Have To Do Is Dream.

"I want you to call me baby." Call Me (E. McDaniel).

"I want you to know I love her so well and I love her so much I could never, never tell." I Want You To Know.

"I want you to love me even when the leaves turn brown." Soft Summer Breeze.

"I want you to take me where I belong, where hearts have been broken with a kiss and a song." Valley Of Tears.

"I want you to tell me why you walked out on me." Walk Right Back.

"I want you to want me." I Want You To Want Me.

"I want your love." I Want Your Love.

"I was a child who wanted a love so wild." Love Comes In Spurts.

"I was a fool for your love from the moment I saw you." Hey, Deanie.

"I was a fool to ever leave your side." Reunited.

"I was a little too tall, could've used a few pounds." Night Moves.

"I was alone, I took a ride, I didn't know what I would find there." Got To Get You Into My Life.

"I was born from love, and my poor mother worked the mines." Stoney End.

"I was born in a crossfire hurricane." Jumpin' Jack Flash.

"I was born in a dump." Tobacco Road.

"I was born in 'Lil Rock, had a childhood sweetheart." I Was Made To Love Her.

"I was born in love with you." I Was Born In Love With You.

"I was born in the wagon of a travelin' show." Gypsys, Tramps And Thieves.

"I was born lonely down by the riverside." Ramblin' Gamblin' Man.

"I was by myself drinking chilled lonely wine then he walked in with some woman whose place was once mine." I Saw A Man And He Danced With His Wife.

"I was down by the old mill pond a week ago today." Gas Lamps And Clay.

"I was driving across the burning desert when I spotted six jet planes." Amelia.

FIND THAT TUNE

"I was five and she was six...." Bang Bang.

"I was high and mighty." High And The Mighty.

"I was justified when I was five." Bitch Is Back.

"I was lost till you were found." For Crying Out Loud.

"I was making my way through the wasteland the road into town passes through." Song On The Radio.

"I was nothing but a lonely boy, looking for something new." All Revved Up With No Place To Go.

"I was on the outskirts of a little southern town." Teddy Bear.

"I was once out strolling one very hot summer's day...." Spill The Wine.

"I was raised on country sunshine, green grass beneath my feet." Country Sunshine.

"I was sayin' 'Let me outta here'--before I was even born." Blank Generation.

"I was searchin' on a one-way street." Sweet Talkin' Woman.

"I was seventeen." To Be A Star.

"I was sitting all alone, watching people get it on with each other." Sexy Eyes.

"I was so lonely until I met you." Back On My Feet Again.

"I was so young when I was born, my eyes could not yet see." Crackerbox Palace.

"I was standing on the corner when I heard my bulldog bark." Stagger Lee.

"I was strolling down the garden path." Hello Old Friend.

"I was sure I'd lost my chance forever." It's Like We Never Said Goodbye.

"I was talkin' with a friend of mine, said a woman had hurt his pride." Don't Do Me Like That.

"I was the one who taught her to kiss the way that she kisses him now." I Was The One.

"I was the third brother of five." Across 110th Street.

"I was tired of my lady; we'd been together too long." Escape.

"I was twenty-one years when I wrote this song." Leaves That Are Green.

"I was working in the lab late one night, when my eyes beheld an eerie sight." Monster Mash.

"I watch the leaves falling to the ground." Can't Stop Loving You.

"I went dancing at the disco last night." What's Your Name, What's Your Number.

"I went down to the river on a Saturday morn, a-lookin' around just to see who's born." Don't Ya Tell Henry.

"I went home with the waitress the way I always do." Lawyers, Guns And Money.

"I went on, darlin', best I can." Sun's Gonna Shine Again.

"I went to a garden party to reminisce with my old friends." Garden Party.

"I went to Chinatown 'way back in old Hong Kong." Ling Ting Tong.

"I went to see the doctor today 'cos ever since you've been gone...." Doctor's Orders.

"I will find a way to get to you some day." Shake Some Action.

"I will pass this way but once." I Will Never Pass This Way Again.

"I will spend my whole life through loving you." Loving You.

"I wish you peace when the cold winds blow." I Wish You Peace.

"I woke up this mornin', looked around my four walls." On The Road Again.

"I woke up this mornin', there were tears in my bed." George Jackson.

"I woke up this morning and the sun was gone." More Than A Feeling.

"I wonder how you're feeling; there's a ringing in my ears." Show Me The Way.

"I wonder why you keep me waiting, Charmaine cries in vain." Charmaine.

"I won't ever leave while you want me to stay." Liar.

"I work all night, I work all day to pay the bills I have to pay." Money, Money, Money.

"I would climb any mountain, sail across a stormy sea...." Feels Like The First Time.

"I would love to tour the Southland in a trav'ling minstrel show." Pretzel Logic.

"I wrote this song for you." I Wrote This Song For You.

"I'd like to build the world a home and furnish it with love." I'd Like To Teach The World To Sing.

"I'd like to make a long distance call to a number in west L.A." Girls Song.

"I'd rather be a sparrow than a snail." El Condor Pasa.

"I'd rather crawl through poison." Nuclear Waste.

"I'd rather leave while I'm in love, while I still believe the meaning of the word." I'd Rather Leave While I'm In Love.

"If a picture paints a thousand words, then why can't I paint you?' If.

"If dogs run free, then why not me." If Dogs Run Free.

"If ever you've got rain in your heart, someone has hurt you and torn you apart." Run To Me (B., R. & M. Gibb).

"If ev'rybody had an ocean across the U.S.A...." Surfin' U.S.A.

"If he brings you happiness then I wish you both the best." Before The Next Teardrop Falls.

"If I close my eyes...." Brooklyn Roads.

"If I could be you and you could be me for just one hour." Walk A Mile In My Shoes.

"If I could build my whole world around you, darling...." If I Could Build My Whole World Around You, Darling.

"If I could ease your pain, if I could lighten your load...." Ease Your Pain.

"If I could I'd like to be a great big movie star." I'm Stone In Love With You.

"If I could make a wish I think I'd pass." Air That I Breathe.

"If I could save time in a bottle...." Time In A Bottle.

"If I could stick my pen in my heart." It's Only Rock N Roll.

"If I fell in love with you, would you promise to be true?" If I Fell.

"If I had a hammer, I'd hammer in the morning." If I Had A Hammer.

"If I had a nickel I know what I would do." That's How Much I Love You.

"If I had money I'd go wild." Can't Give You Anything (But My Love).

"If I listened long enough to you...." Reason To Believe.

"If I sent a rose to you for ev'ry time you made me blue...." Room Full Of Roses.

"If I should leave you, try to remember the good times." Just A Little Bit Of Rain.

"If I sing you a love song, will you always remember?" If I Sing You A Love Song.

"If I were a carpenter and you were a lady...." If I Were A Carpenter.

"If I were a rich man, daidle, deedle, daidle, digguh, digguh, deedle, daidle, dum." If I Were A Rich Man.

"If I were your woman and you were my man." If I Were Your Woman.

"If it don't fit, don't force it." If It Don't Fit, Don't Force It.

"If it keeps on rainin', levee's goin' to break." When The Levee Breaks.

"If it's kinky they'll try it." Searching For A Thrill.

"If little David hadn't grabbed that stone...." Good Timin' (C. Ballard & F. Tobias).

"If lovin' you is wrong, I don't want to be right." I Don't Want To Be Right.

"If my life gets like a jigsaw with the pieces out of place." Come On Over.

"If my words did glow, with the gold of sunshine...." Ripple.

"If not for you babe, I couldn't find the door." If Not For You.

"If only you believe like I believe baby, we'd get by." Miracles.

"If the hands of time were hands that I could hold, I'd keep them warm and in my hands they'd not turn cold." Hands Of Time.

"If the music makes you move and you feel in the groove, groove on." Do Your Thing.

"If the sun refused to shine, I would still be lovin' you." Thank You.

"If the world ran out of love tonight...." If The World Ran Out Of Love Tonight.

"If there's a cure for this I don't want it." Love Hangover.

"If there's a tear on my face it makes me shiver to the bone." I Never Cry.

"If there's anything that you want...." From Me To You.

"If there's one thing in my life that's missing, it's the time I spend alone, sailing on the cool and bright clear water." Cool Change.

"If today was not an endless highway...." Tomorrow Is A Long Time.

"If we only have love, then tomorrow will dawn." If We Only Have Love.

"If we were older we wouldn't have to be worried tonight." I Wanna Be With You.

"If you change your mind I'm the first in line." Take A Chance On Me.

"If you could read my mind, love, what a tale my thoughts could tell." If You Could Read My Mind.

"If you cry I think my heart would break." True Love, True Love.

"If you disrespect ev'rybody that you run into, how in the world do you think ev'rybody 'sposed to respect you?" Respect Yourself.

"If you do want me, gimme little sugar." Gimme Little Sign.

"If you ever change your mind about leaving...." Bring It On Home To Me.

"If you ever leave me, I'll be sad and blue." Bad To Me.

"If you feel that it's real, I'm on trial." Take Me To The Pilot.

"If you feel that you can't go on...." Reach Out I'll Be There.

"If you go down in the woods today...." Teddy Bears' Picnic.

"If you leave me, I'll go crazy." I'll Go Crazy.

"If you leave me now, you'll take away the biggest part of me." If You Leave Me Now.

"If you let me, I could be your good friend." Good Friend.

"If you miss the train I'm on, you will know that I am gone." Five Hundred Miles.

"If you need me, call me, no matter where you are." Ain't No Mountain High Enough.

"If you say that all the good times are gone...." That's The Way It's Gonna Be.

"If you search for tenderness, it isn't hard to find." Honesty.

"If you see her, say hello, she might be in Tangier." If You See Her, Say Hello.

"If you see me walkin' down the street and I start to cry...." Walk On By.

"If you see your brother standing by the road." Try A Little Kindness.

"If you smile at me I will understand, 'cause that is something ev'rybody does in the same language." Wooden Ships.

"If you think that we found something good, like I know we had...." Make It Last.

"If you wake up and don't want to smile...." Don't Stop.

"If you wanna be happy for the rest of your life, never make a pretty woman your wife." If You Wanna Be Happy.

"If you want it, better come and get it." Lovey Dovey Kinda' Lovin'.

"If you want it, here it is, come and get it." Come And Get It.

"If you want something to play with, go and find yourself a top." Tell It Like It Is.

"If you wanted that star that shines so brightly...." Sweets For My Sweet.

"If you were a bird and you lived very high, you'd lean on the wind when the breeze came by." Ballad Of You & Me Pooneil.

"If your heart tells you so that you should leave me." Sweetheart.

"If your mem'ry serves you well...." This Wheel's On Fire.

"If you're a long way from home...." Evil (Is Going On).

"If you're down and confused...." Love The One You're With.

"If you're down and out and you feel real hurt...." I'll Play The Blues For You.

"If you're driving into town with a dark cloud above you, dial in the number who's bound to love you." You Turn Me On, I'm A Radio.

"If you're fair game and you look like prey, I'm tellin' you lady better stay away." Animal.

"If you're fond of sand dunes and salty air, quaint little villages here and there...." Old Cape Cod.

"If you're going to San Francisco, be sure to wear some flowers in your hair." San Francisco (Be Sure To Wear Some Flowers In Your Hair).

"If you're in Arizona, I'll follow you." My Heart Cries For You.

"If you're ready (come go with me)." If You're Ready (Come Go With Me).

"If you're thinkin' you're too cool to boogie, boy, oh boy, have I got news for you." Boogie Oogie Oogie.

"If you've been thinkin' you were all that you've got...." Watching The River Run.

"If you've got a problem, I don't care what it is; if you need a hand, I can assure you this, I can help." I Can Help.

"If you've got the time I've got the place (my same old place)." If You've Got The Time.

"I'll always love you the same old way, no matter what may come between." Tell Me You'll Wait For Me.

"I'll always remember the song they were playing the first time we danced." Could I Have This Dance.

"I'll always want you, because my heart is true." ABC's Of Love.

"I'll be alone each and ev'ry night." See You In September.

"I'll be as strong as a mountain or as weak as a willow tree." Any Way You Want Me.

"I'll be here come winter when the cold winds blow." Ashes In The Snow.

"I'll be here when you get home." I'll Be Here.

"I'll be the roundabout." Roundabout.

"I'll be working my way back to you, babe, with a burning love inside." Workin' My Way Back To You.

"I'll be your long haired lover from Liverpool and I'll do anything you say." Long Haired Lover From Liverpool.

"I'll light the fire." Our House.

"I'll never be the one to part." Runaround.

"I'll never let you go, why, because I love you." Why (B. Marcucci & P. De Angelis).

"I'll pack up all my things and walk away." Fairytale.

"I'll play for you." I'll Play For You.

"I'll see you in my dreams." I'll See You In My Dreams.

"I'm a crossroader, speedin' from town to town." Crossroader.

"I'm a gonna raise a fuss, I'm a gonna raise a holler." Summertime Blues.

"I'm a grubworm." Groovy Grubworm.

"I'm a loser, I'm a loser." I'm A Loser.

"I'm a poor Hawaiian beach boy a long way from the beach." Beach Boy Blues.

"I'm a road runner, honey." Road Runner (E. McDaniel).

"I'm a spy in the house of love." Spy.

"I'm a street-walking cheater with a heart full of napalm." Search And Destroy.

"I'm a tangled up puppet spinning round in knots." Tangled Up Puppet.

"I'm a track star, gotta run far." Goin' Home.

"I'm a U.S. male 'cause I was born in a Mississippi town on a Sunday morn." U.S. Male.

"I'm alright; nobody worry 'bout me." I'm Alright.

"I'm as happy as can be." Tweedlee Dee.

"I'm back, I'm back in the saddle again." Back In The Saddle.

"I'm back on dry land once again." Sweet Painted Lady.

"I'm blessed with ev'rything." In The Back Of My Mind.

"I'm comin' home, I've done my time." Tie A Yellow Ribbon Round The Ole Oak Tree.

"I'm coming out." I'm Coming Out.

"I'm dreaming tonight, I'm leaving back home." Last Child.

"I'm ev'ry woman, it's all in me." I'm Every Woman.

"I'm glad you're home." Ring My Bell.

"I'm goin' back to Indiana, back to where I started from." Goin' Back To Indiana.

"I'm goin' to Kansas City; Kansas City, here I come." Kansas City.

"I'm goin' up the country, baby don't you want to go?" Goin' Up The Country.

"I'm going down to Rose Marie's, she never does me wrong." Goin' To Acapulco.

"I'm going to Chicago, that's the last place my baby stayed." Hitch-Hike.

"I'm gonna be a wheel someday." I'm Gonna Be A Wheel Someday.

"I'm gonna do all the things for you a man wants a girl to do." I'm Gonna Make You Love Me.

"I'm gonna go out tonight, gonna feel all right, if it tears me right in two." Dancin' Round And Round.

"I'm gonna raise a fuss, I'm a-gonna raise a holler." Summertime Blues.

"I'm gonna rent myself a house in the shade of the freeway." Pretender.

"I'm gonna tell you how it's gonna be." Not Fade Away.

"I'm gonna wait til the midnight hour." In The Midnight Hour.

"I'm gonna wake you up early 'cause I'm gonna take a ride with you." Little Honda.

"I'm gonna walk away from love." Walk Away From Love.

"I'm gonna write a little letter, gonna mail it to my local D.J." Roll Over, Beethoven.

"I'm, I'm so in love with you." Let's Stay Together.

"I'm in heaven when I see you smile." Diane (E. Rapee & L. Pollack).

"I'm in love with you Honey." Honey (S. Simons, H. Gillespie & R. Whiting).

"I'm in need of someone today." I'm A Cruiser.

"I'm in the mood for love simply because you're near me." I'm In The Mood For Love.

"I'm in the phone booth, it's the one across the hall." Hanging On The Telephone.

"I'm in the 'in' crowd." In Crowd.

"I'm just a lonely boy, lonely and blue." Lonely Boy (P. Anka).

"I'm just a love machine, and I won't work for nobody but you." Love Machine.

"I'm just a roustabout, shiftin' from town to town." Roustabout.

"I'm just a typical American boy from a typical American town." Draft Dodger Rag.

"I'm just a woman, a lonely woman waitin' on the weary shore." Am I Blue.

"I'm just a young girl, dying to learn the ways of love just to please you." Show Me How.

"I'm just like a prairie flow'r, Honey, Honey." Honey Babe.

"I'm just mad about saffron." Mellow Yellow.

"I'm leavin' it all up to you." I'm Leaving It (All) Up To You.

"I'm looking for a place to go so I can be all alone from thoughts and memories." My Melody Of Love.

"I'm Mister Blue, when you say you love me." Mr. Blue.

"I'm not a juvenile delinquent." I'm Not A Juvenile Delinquent.

"I'm not here to forget you." Wurlitzer Prize.

"I'm not Lisa; my name is Julie." I'm Not Lisa.

"I'm on a sailboat ride." Sailboat Song.

"I'm on the outside looking in." I'm On The Outside (Looking In).

"I'm ridin' the rainbow, hittin' the highway to happiness." Ridin' The Rainbow.

"I'm riding in your car." Fire.

"I'm sailing away, set an open course for the virgin sea." Come Sail Away.

"I'm sittin' in the railway station, got a ticket for my destination." Homeward Bound.

"I'm sleepin' and right in the middle of a good dream." I Think I Love You.

"I'm so glad that I met you, baby." Suspicions.

"I'm so happy for you, baby, now that you found somebody new." Happy Anniversary.

"I'm so young and you're so old." Diana.

"I'm the wizard of boogieland." Fess Up To The Boogie.

"I'm tired of slippin and aslidin' with Long Tall Sally." Short Fat Fannie.

"I'm top ground cut of meat, I'm your choice." Elected.

"I'm up on a tight wire, one side's ice and one is fire." Tight Rope.

"I'm walkin', yes indeed, and I'm talkin' 'bout you and me." I'm Walkin'.

"I'm wishin' on a star to follow where you are." Wishin' On A Star.

"I'm writing 'bout the book I read." Book I Read.

"I'm writing this letter to say goodbye." Letter (D. Harris & D. Terry).

"I'm your boogie man, that's what I am." I'm Your Boogie Man.

"I'm your friend, you can talk to me." Better Love Next Time.

"Imaginary lovers never turn you down." Imaginary Lovers.

"Imagine me and you, I do." Happy Together.

"Imagine there's no heaven, it's easy if you try." Imagine.

"In a bar in Toledo, across from the depot, on a barstool she took off her ring. Lucille (R. Bowlins & H. Bynum).

"In a building of gold, with riches untold, lived the families on which the country was founded." Rhythms Of Revolution.

"In a world full of hatred and death and destruction...."
Love Is The Answer (Hugo & Luigi & G. Weiss).

"In America you'll get food to eat, won't have to run
through the jungle and scuff your feet." Sail Away.

"In another time's forgotten space, your eyes looked
from your mother's face." Franklin's Tower.

"In eighteen and fourteen we took a little trip."
Battle Of New Orleans.

"In my heart I have a feeling and I don't know what I'm
gonna do." Young Girl Sunday Blue.

"In my heart I will wait by the stoney gate." Song For
David.

"In my little town, I grew up believing God keeps his eye
on us all." My Little Town.

"In my mind I'm gone to Carolina." Carolina In My Mind.

"In my neighborhood folks don't live so good." I Don't
Want To Hear It Anymore.

"In my sweet little Alice Blue Gown...." Alice Blue
Gown.

"In the attics of my life, full of cloudy dreams unreal...."
Attics Of My Life.

"In the autumn of my madness, when my hair is turning
grey...." In The Autumn Of My Madness.

"In the candle, lights burn away." Wouldn't You Believe
It.

"In the chilly hours and minutes of uncertainty...."
Catch The Wind.

"In the cool of the ev'ning as ev'rything is gettin' kind
of groovy...." Spooky.

"In the corner of an old barroom sat an old cowboy
singing Western tunes." Last Of The Singing Cowboys.

"In the daily rush of things, if we stop to think it seems
we never have time alone." Let's Take The Long Way
Around The World.

"In the darkness of the night, only occasionally relieved
by glimpses of nirvana...." Glimpses Of Nirvana.

"In the day we sweat it out on the streets of a runaway
American dream." Born To Run.

"In the days of my youth I was told what it was to be a
man." Good Times, Bad Times.

"In the early mornin' rain...." Early Mornin' Rain.

"In the event of something happening to me..." N.Y.
Mining Disaster 1941.

"In the fire blue forests faded and forgotten...." When
In Rome.

"In the heart of the night...." Heart Of The Night.

"In the hour of not quite rain when the fog was finger
tip high...." In The Hour Of Not Quite Rain.

"In the jungle, the mighty jungle, the lion sleeps tonight." Lion Sleeps Tonight.

"In the mornin' don't say you love me 'cause I'll only kick
you out of the door." Stay With Me.

"In the mornin' you go gunnin' for the man who stole
your water and you fire 'till he is done in." Do It
Again.

"In the morning when you rise, do you open up your eyes,
see what I see?" Time And A Word.

"In the shadows you got to know your lover mostly by
feel." Love In The Shadows.

"In the sky shines a star." Star.

"In the spring of my life, she came to me." Autumn Of
My Life.

"In the still of the night...." In The Still Of The Night.

"In the summertime when the weather is high...." In The
Summertime.

"In the timbers of Fennario, the wolves are running
around." Dire Wolf.

"In the town where I was born lived a man who sailed to
sea." Yellow Submarine.

"In the tube where I was born, I could have sworn...."
Half A Century High.

"In the wintertime, when all the leaves are brown...."
Winter Time.

"In these days of changing ways...." Killing Of Georgie
(Parts I & II)

"In this cafe the windows are steamin'." Lovin' Stew.

"In this dirty old part of the city...." We Gotta Get Out
Of This Place.

"In this life I've seen ev'rything I can see, woman."
Do Ya.

"In your life I see the hurt he left behind." Got To Believe In Love.

"In your mind you have capacities, you know." Calling
Occupants Of Interplanetary Craft.

"In-a-gadda-da-vida, honey, don't you know that I love
you?' In-A-Gadda-Da-Vida.

"Indiana wants me; Lord, I can't go back there." Indiana
Wants Me.

"Ink is black, the page is white." Black And White.

"Instant karma's gonna get you, gonna knock you right
on the head." Instant Karma.

"Into each heart some tears must fall." Too Many Fish
In The Sea.

"Into my room he creeps without making a sound." Stay
Awhile.

"Irene, good night." Goodnight Irene.

"Is my world not fallen down?" Flying On The Ground
Is Wrong.

"Is there anybody here who'd like to change his clothes
into a uniform?" Is There Anybody Here.

"Is this the little girl I carried?" Sunrise, Sunset.

"Is this the real life?" Bohemian Rhapsody.

"Is this train the Frankfort Special?" Frankfort Special.

"Isn't it a pity; now, isn't it a shame?" Isn't It A Pity.

"Isn't it rich, are we a pair?" Send In The Clowns.

"Isn't she lovely, isn't she wonderful?" Isn't She Lovely.

"It ain't no use to sit and wonder why, babe." Don't
Think Twice, It's All Right.

"It could've been me, but it was you who went and bit off a little bit more than he could chew." <u>Bad Blood</u>.

"It don't matter to me if you really feel that you need some time to be free." <u>It Don't Matter To Me</u>.

"It is the evening of the day." <u>As Tears Go By</u>.

"It is the night." <u>Ride Like The Wind</u>.

"It is the springtime of my loving." <u>Rain Song</u>.

"It makes you want to get away." <u>Dance With The Dragon</u>.

"It must have been the way that you touched me." <u>Need You Bad</u>.

"It seems like yesterday, but it was long ago." <u>Against The Wind</u>.

"It seems so long ago, Nancy was alone." <u>Seems So Long Ago, Nancy</u>.

"It sure was a long, long, long hot summer night." <u>Long Hot Summer Night</u>.

"It takes a fast car, lady, to lead a double life." <u>Double Life</u>.

"It took me a long time to find out my mistakes." <u>Fattening Frogs For Snakes</u>.

"It was a good time." <u>It Was A Good Time</u>.

"It was a hot summer night and the beach was burning." <u>You Took The Words Right Out Of My Mouth</u>.

"It was an early morning yesterday, I was up before the dawn." <u>Goodbye Stranger</u>.

"It was back in nineteen forty two, I was a member of a good platoon." <u>Waist Deep In The Big Muddy</u>.

"It was good for me." <u>Never Be The Same</u>.

"It was late in December, the sky turned to snow." <u>Time Passages</u>.

"It was late last night, I was feelin' something wasn't right." <u>I Saw The Light</u>.

"It was nine twenty-nine, nine twenty-nine, back street, big city." <u>Last Train To London</u>.

"It was the third of June on that younger day." <u>Desiree</u>.

"It was the third of September, that day I'll always remember, yes I will." <u>Papa Was A Rollin' Stone</u>.

"It was thirty days around the horn." <u>Shakedown Cruise</u>.

"It was twenty years ago today that Sergeant Pepper taught the band to play." <u>Sgt. Pepper's Lonely Hearts Club Band</u>.

"It won't be long yeh yeh yeh yeh yeh yeh yeh, it won't be long yeh yeh yeh yeh yeh". <u>It Won't Be Long</u>.

"It'd be a lie to say I'm not gonna miss you." <u>You Don't Love Me Anymore</u>.

"It's a family affair." <u>Family Affair</u>.

"It's a great life; you'll get the things you go after." <u>It's A Great Life</u>.

"It's a heartache, nothin' but a heartache, hits you when it's too late, hits you when you're down." <u>It's A Heartache</u>.

"It's a lesson too late for the learning made of sand, made of sand." <u>Last Thing On My Mind</u>.

"It's a little bit funny this feeling inside." <u>Your Song</u>.

"It's a lonely man who wanders all around." <u>Lonely Man</u>.

"It's a long, long way down to Reno, Nevada; and a long, long way to your home." <u>Reno Nevada</u>.

"It's a mighty hard row that my poor hands have hoed." <u>Pastures Of Plenty</u>.

"It's a sad song I'm singing." <u>Sad Song</u>.

"It's a sayin' that good things always come to those who wait." <u>Drink The Wine</u>.

"It's a shame to complain but we gotta have a lot more love." <u>Got To Have Lovin'</u>.

"It's a still life water color of a now late afternoon." <u>Dangling Conversation</u>.

"It's a time for joy, a time for tears, a time we'll treasure thru the years." <u>Graduation Day</u>.

"It's a way of mine to say just what I'm thinkin'." <u>I Can't Be Myself</u>.

"It's a wild time." <u>Wild Tyme</u>.

"It's all behind me, there's good luck up ahead." <u>Third Time Lucky</u>.

"It's always nice to find a little love along the way." <u>Every Time I Sing A Love Song</u>.

"It's another tequila sunrise." <u>Tequila Sunrise</u>.

"It's been a hard day's night and I've been working like a dog." <u>Hard Day's Night</u>.

"It's been a long, dark night, and I've been awaiting for the morning." <u>Light Of A Clear Blue Morning</u>.

"It's been a long long long time." <u>Long, Long, Long</u>.

"It's been a long time comin', it's goin' to be a long time gone." <u>Long Time Gone</u>.

"It's been a long time since I rock and rolled." <u>Rock And Roll</u>.

"It's been a lover's question ever since time began." <u>Holdin' On For Dear Love</u>.

"It's been such a long time, I think I should be goin'." <u>Long Time</u>.

"It's called the loose caboose." <u>Loose Caboose</u>.

"It's carbon and monoxide, the ole Detroit perfume." <u>Papa Hobo</u>.

"It's gettin' near dawn when lights close a tired eye." <u>Sunshine Of Your Love</u>.

"It's getting late, have you seen my mates?" <u>Saturday Night's Alright</u>.

"It's getting to the point where I'm no fun anymore." <u>Suite: Judy Blue Eyes</u>.

"It's gonna take a lotta love to change the way things are." <u>Lotta Love</u>.

"It's gonna take some time this time to get myself in shape." <u>It's Going To Take Some Time</u>.

"It's impossible, tell the sun to leave the sky." <u>It's Impossible</u>.

"It's in ev'ry one of us to be wise." <u>It's In Every One Of Us</u>.

"It's just your jive talkin', you're tellin' me lies, yeah: jive talkin', you wear a disguise." Jive Talkin'.

"It's knowing that your door is always open and your path is free to walk...." Gentle On My Mind.

"It's late at night and we're all alone with just the music of the radio." Swayin' To The Music.

"It's like looking in the window of a fine boutique, knowing there is nothing I could ever buy." Let Me Love You Once Before You Go.

"It's lonely out tonight and the feelin' just got right for a brand new love song." Another Somebody Done Somebody Wrong Song.

"It's midnight on the bay and lights are shinin'." Midnight On The Bay.

"It's nine o'clock on a Saturday, the regular crowd shuffles in." Piano Man.

"It's not in the way that you hold me...." Hold The Line.

"It's not my way to love you just when no one's looking." I'm Easy.

"It's not that I'm so cheerful, though I'll always raise a smile." All This And More (K. Reid & G. Brooker).

"It's not that lovers are unkind...." Look Through My Window.

"It's not time to make a change." Father And Son.

"It's not unusual to be loved by any one." It's Not Unusual.

"It's now or never, come hold me tight." It's Now Or Never.

"It's one of those nights when you turn out the lights and you sit in the dark." It's One Of Those Nights (Yes Love).

"It's over and done, but the heartache lives on inside." Emotion (B. & R. Gibb).

"It's sad to think we're not gonna make it." Neither One Of Us.

"It's Saturday night and my daddy's up late pickin' with my uncle Bill." Listen To A Country Song.

"It's so easy to be in love with you." It's How I Live.

"It's so easy to fall in love." It's So Easy.

"It's so easy to say, find yourself someone new." It's So Easy To Say.

"It's so hard loving you." Little Darling (I Need You).

"It's so nice to meet an old friend and pass the time of day." Did She Mention My Name.

"It's the best disco in town, funky music by the pound...." Best Disco In Town.

"It's the time of the season when love runs high." Time Of The Season.

"It's tired and I'm getting late, I wanna try to speak but I can't relate." Home To You.

"It's true that all the men you knew were dealers who said they were through with dealing every time you gave them shelter." Stranger Song.

"I've always been the kind of guy who could handle almost anything." Can This Be Real.

"I've been alive forever and I wrote the very first song." I Write The Songs.

"I've been blue since I'm stung by you, don't you just know it?" Don't You Just Know It.

"I've been crying (oo oo) 'cause I'm lonely (for you)." Come See About Me.

"I've been down, but not like this before." All That You Dream.

"I've been drifting on the sea of heartbreak, tryin' to get myself ashore for so long, for so long." Hold On.

"I've been looking for a woman to save my life." I've Been Waiting For You.

"I've been loving you too long to stop now." I've Been Loving You Too Long.

"I've been really tryin', baby, tryin' to hold back this feelin' for so long." Let's Get It On.

"I've been run down, and I've been lied to." Whippin' Post.

"I've been so many places in my life time." Song For You.

"I've been thinkin' 'bout all the times you told me you're so full of doubt you just can't let it be." Keep On Tryin'.

"I've been walkin' these streets so long, singin' the same old song." Rhinestone Cowboy.

"I've been working all week saving my emotions for Saturday night when I use my potion." Boogie Woogie Dancin' Shoes.

"I've been working real hard trying to get my hands clean." Prove It All Night.

"I've been your lover, you've been my friend." Growin'.

"I've cried through many endless nights just holding my pillow tight." Heaven Must Have Sent You.

"I've got a feeling, a feeling deep inside, oh yeah, oh yeah." I've Got A Feeling.

"I've got a never ending love for you." Never Ending Song Of Love.

"I've got a song--I ain't got no melody...." Will It Go 'Round In Circles.

"I've got a story for you; I just don't know what to do." Ups And Downs.

"I've got a whole lotta loving for you." Whole Lotta Loving.

"I've got some money 'cause I just got paid." Another Saturday Night.

"I've got some so-called friends." Paranoia Blues.

"I've got sunshine on a cloudy day." My Girl.

"I've got this feeling all down inside." Who Do Ya Love.

"I've got to tell you I've been racking my brain, hoping to find a way out." Ready For The Times To Get Better.

"I've had bad dreams." Love Has No Pride.

"I've had my fun." Goin' Down Slow.

"I've had my share of life's ups and downs." <u>You're The Best Thing That Ever Happened To Me</u>.

"I've heard it said that the weight of the world's problems is enough to make the ball fall right through space. <u>Here To Love You</u>.

"I've got joy 'round my brain, wait and see." <u>Joy 'Round My Brain</u>.

"I've just closed my eyes again, climbed aboard the dream weaver train." <u>Dream Weaver</u>.

"I've just reached a place where the willow don't bend." <u>Going, Going, Gone</u>.

"I've laid around and played around this old town too long." <u>Gotta Travel On</u>.

"I've neither wealth nor power." <u>I'll Get By</u>.

"I've never worked much, in fact I've been poor all my life." <u>Welfare Cadillac</u>.

"I've paid my dues, time after time." <u>We Are The Champions</u>.

"I've passed a lot of exit signs in my time." <u>Rosecrans Boulevard</u>.

"I've really got to use my imagination to think of good reasons to keep on keepin' on." <u>Imagination</u>.

"I've seen all good people turn their heads each day so satisfied I'm on my way." <u>All Good People</u>.

"I've seen all good people turn their heads each day so satisfied I'm on my way." <u>Your Move</u>.

"I've seen love go by my door." <u>You're Gonna Make Me Lonesome When You Go</u>.

"I've seen the way her head turns when a big, shiny car passes by." <u>Roses And Love Songs</u>.

"I've seen you twice in a short time." <u>Name Of The Game</u>.

"I've seen your picture, your name in lights above it." <u>Peg</u>.

"I've sung this song, but I'll sing it again." <u>So Long, It's Been Good To Know Yuh</u>.

"I've tried to let you down so easy." <u>Don't Take It So Hard</u>.

"I've wondered all my life how I could ever let you go." <u>If Ever I See You Again</u>.

"Jack wanting someone to feel sat upon a hill and waited all day for Jill." <u>Jack And Jill</u>.

"Jackie Blue lives her life from inside a room." <u>Jackie Blue</u>.

"Jackie is a punk, Judy is a runt." <u>Judy Is A Punk</u>.

"Jam up and jelly tight." <u>Jam Up And Jelly Tight</u>.

"Jane, you say it's all over for you and me, girl." <u>Jane</u>.

"Janie, Janie, Janie, Janie, Janie." <u>Down In The Alley</u>.

"Janie was my first love." <u>Me And Baby Jane</u>.

"January to December, we'll have moments to remember." <u>Moments To Remember</u>.

"Jenny, Jenny, Jenny, won't you come along with me?" <u>Jenny, Jenny</u>.

Jeremiah was a bullfrog, was a good friend of mine." <u>Joy To The World</u>.

"Jesse come home, there's a hole in the bed where we slept." <u>Jesse</u> (J. Ian).

"Jesus is just alright with me." <u>Jesus Is Just Alright With Me</u>.

"Jesus loves the little children, all the little children of the world." <u>Everything Is Beautiful</u>.

"Jim Dandy to the rescue." <u>Jim Dandy</u>.

"Jimmy Mack, Jimmy." <u>Jimmy Mack</u>.

"Jimmy Ray was a preachers son." <u>Son Of A Preacher Man</u>.

"Jo Jo was a man who thought he was a loner, but he knew he couldn't last." <u>Get Back</u>.

"Jody girl, Jody girl." <u>Jody Girl</u>.

"Joe Hill came over from Sweden's shore looking for work to do." <u>Joe Hill</u> (P. Ochs).

"Joey was pretty like the flowers he brought me." <u>You Keep Me Dancin'</u>.

"John and Mitchie were gettin' kinda itchie just to leave the folk music behind." <u>Creeque Alley</u>.

"John Wesley Harding was a friend to the poor." <u>John Wesley Harding</u>.

"Johnny Angel, how I love him, he's got something that I can't resist." <u>Johnny Angel</u>.

"Johnny is a joker." <u>Bird Dog</u>.

"Johnny's in the basement mixing up the medicine." <u>Subterranean Homesick Blues</u>.

"Judy in disguise, well, that's what you are." <u>Judy In Disguise (With Glasses)</u>.

"Julie catch a rabbit by his hair." <u>Row Jimmy</u>.

"Julie was an American girl." <u>Girl Of My Dreams</u>.

"Just a dream, just a dream." <u>Just A Dream</u>.

"Just an old fashioned love song playing on the radio." <u>Old Fashioned Love Song</u>.

"Just because you left and said goodbye." <u>Just Because</u>.

"Just because you've become a young woman now." <u>Shop Around</u>.

"Just beyond the mountain lies a city and I hear it calling me." <u>Lonesome Cowboy</u>.

"Just got home from Illinois." <u>Looking Out My Back Door</u>.

"Just, just, just, just let me make love to you baby." <u>Let Me Make Love To You</u>.

"Just let me hear some of that rock and roll music." <u>Rock & Roll Music</u>.

"Just like old saxophone Joe..." <u>Country Pie</u>.

"Just like the driftwood of a dream left on the seashore of sleep...." <u>Driftwood</u>.

"Just look at the mess that I'm in." <u>I Just Can't Say No To You</u>.

"Just one look and I feel so ha-ar-ard." Just One Look.

"Just one voice, singing in the darkness." One Voice.

"Just to admit one mistake; that can be so hard to take." So You Win Again.

"Just to be close to you girl...." Just To be Close To You.

"Just what you need to make you feel better." Doctor Tarr and Professor Fether.

"Just yesterday morning they let me know you were gone." Fire And Rain.

"Just you know why, why you and I will by and by know true love ways." True Love Ways.

"Keep a fire burning in your eye." For A Dancer.

"Keep falling in and out of love." In And Out Of Love.

"Keep it comin', love." Keep It Comin' Love.

"Keep me steady, don't rock me all around." Endless Flight.

"Keep on truckin', baby." Keep On Truckin'.

"Keep the fire bright." Keep The Fire.

"Keep what you got until you get what you need, y'all." Bustin' Loose (Part I).

"Keep your eyes on the road, your hands upon the wheel." Roadhouse Blues.

"Keeping my eyes on the road, I see you." 99 Miles From L.A.

"Kids in Bristol are sharp as a pistol when they do the Bristol Stomp." Bristol Stomp.

"Kind of a drag when your baby don't love you." Kind Of A Drag.

"King Tut." King Tut.

"Kiss me quick while we still have the feeling." Kiss Me Quick.

"Kiss today goodbye, the sweetness and the sorrow." What I Did For Love.

"Know it sounds funny, but I just can't stand the pain." Easy.

"La (37x) much has been written about the world and all its kinds of love." Outside My Window.

"La (36x) when I saw her on the corner...." I've Had It.

"La (24x) you better come home Speedy Gonzales, away from Cannery Row." Speedy Gonzales.

"La (17x) I never fell in love so easily, where the four winds blow I carry on." Spirits (Having Flown).

"La (16x) for you, there might be a brighter star." Another Star.

"La (12x) my cherie amour, lovely as a summer day." My Cherie Amour.

"La la la la la la la la la, ooh ooh, it's gonna take a lotta love to change the way things are." Lotta Love.

"La la la la la la, there ain't nothing in this world I couldn't do." La, La, La.

"La la la la la, the lovely Linda with the lovely flowers in her hair." Lovely Linda.

"L.A. proved too much for the man, so he's leavin' the life he's come to know." Midnight Train To Georgia.

"Lady love, your love is peaceful like the summer's breeze." Lady Love.

"Lady Madonna, children at your feet." Lady Madonna.

"Lady, morning's just a moment away, and I'm without you once again." Still.

"Lady, when you're with me I'm smiling." Lady (D. DeYoung).

"Lady Willpower, it's now or never." Lady Willpower.

"Lamp is burning low upon my table top." Song For A Winter's Night.

"L.A.'s fine, the sun shines most the time and the feelin' is lay back." I Am...I Said.

"Last dance, last chance for love." Last Dance.

"Last December I met a girl; she took a likin' to me." Cinderella.

"Last night as I watched the stars from my window...." Last Night.

"Last night I had the strangest dream I'd ever dreamed before." Last Night I Had The Strangest Dream.

"Last night I made love, I made it with you, at least it was you on my mind." Last Night I Made Love To Somebody Else.

"Last night I said goodbye, now it seems years." Weekend In New England.

"Last night I took a walk after dark, a swingin' place called Palisades Park." Palisades Park.

"Last night I turned out the light, lay down and thought about you." I Woke Up In Love This Morning.

"Last time I saw him, he sweetly kissed my lips." Last Time I Saw Him.

"Last train is nearly due." Poem On The Underground Wall.

"Last week my life had meaning." My Whole World Ended.

"Late afternoon, dreaming hotel...." Redondo Beach.

"Lately I've been thinking how much I miss my lady." Amoreena.

"Laura and Tommy were lovers." Tell Laura I Love Her.

"Lay down, lay down, lay it all down." Lay Down (Candles In The Rain).

"Lay, lady, lay, lay across my big brass bed." Lay, Lady, Lay.

"Lazy stadium night, Catfish on the mound." Catfish.

"Leaning in your corner like a candidate for wax." 11:59.

"Leaves are falling all around." Ramble On.

"Leavin' home, out on the road, I've been down before." Jet Airliner.

"Left a good job in the city." <u>Proud Mary</u>.

"Left her this mornin', I couldn't bear for her to share her love with someone new." <u>Which Way To No-where</u>.

"Legend lives on from the Chippewa on down of the big lake they called 'Gitche Gumee.'" <u>Wreck Of The Edmund Fitzgerald</u>.

"Leroy, boy, is that you?" <u>We Got To Get You A Woman</u>.

"Let me in here." <u>I'd Have You Any Time</u>.

"Let it rain, let it pour." <u>Deep River Blues</u>.

"Let it roll across the floor." <u>Ballad Of Sir Frankie Crisp</u>.

"Let me take you down cause I'm goin' to Strawberry Fields." <u>Strawberry Fields Forever</u>.

"Let me tell ya 'bout the birds and the bees." <u>Birds And The Bees</u>.

"Let me tell you 'bout a boy (girl) I know." <u>Hallelujah I Love Her (Him) So</u>.

"Let the good times roll, let them knock you around." <u>Good Times Roll</u>.

"Let the river rock you like a cradle." <u>Follow</u>.

"Let the spirit flow all through your body." <u>Disco Nights</u>.

"Let the stars fade and fall and I won't care at all as long as I have you." <u>As Long As I Have You</u>.

"Let there be peace on earth and let it begin with me." <u>Let There Be Peace On Earth</u>.

"Let us be lovers, we'll marry our fortunes together." <u>America (P. Simon)</u>.

"Let's all chant." <u>Let's All Chant</u>.

"Let's all get up and dance." <u>Your Mother Should Know</u>.

"Let's build a stairway to the stars." <u>Stairway To The Stars</u>.

"Let's go down by the grapevine, drink my daddy's wine." <u>Sweet Blindness</u>.

"Let's go get stoned." <u>Let's Go Get Stoned</u>.

"Let's go surfin' now." <u>Surfin' Safari</u>.

"Let's take the phone off the hook." <u>Do Not Disturb</u>.

"Let's twist again like we did last summer." <u>Let's Twist Again</u>.

"Levon wears his war wound like a crown." <u>Levon</u>.

"Liberty, laughing and shaking your head." <u>Southbound Train</u>.

"Lido missed the boat that day he left the shack." <u>Lido Shuffle</u>.

"Life ain't so easy in this border town." <u>Border Town</u>.

"Life could be a dream, sh-boom. <u>Sh-Boom</u>.

"Life isn't everything." <u>Song For Guy</u>.

"Life lands a crushing blow." <u>I've Passed This Way Before</u>.

"Life, so they say, is but a game and they let it slip away." <u>We May Never Pass This Way Again</u>.

"Life's dreary for me, days seem to be long as years." <u>Body And Soul</u>.

"Lift me, won't you lift me above the old routine." <u>Jazzman</u>.

"Light up the world with sunshine." <u>Light Up The World With Sunshine</u>.

"Lights out tonight, trouble in the heartland." <u>Badlands</u>.

"Lights shine down the valley." <u>Arms Of Mary</u>.

"Lights turned on and the curtain fell down...." <u>Broken Arrow</u>.

"Like a bird on the wire...." <u>Bird On The Wire</u>.

"Like a fool I went and stayed too long." <u>Signed, Sealed, Delivered I'm Yours</u>.

"Like a long lonely stream I keep runnin' towards a dream, movin' on." <u>Place In The Sun</u>.

"Like a snake crawlin' on a floor, I've got no time to be alone." <u>Stranded</u>.

"Like sailing on a sailing ship to nowhere, love took over my heart like an ocean breeze." <u>All You Get From Love Is A Love Song</u>.

"Like the beat, beat, beat, of the tom-tom...." <u>Night And Day</u>.

"Like the ghost of someone dear she comes to haunt me in my sleep." <u>Pretty Girl Why</u>.

"Like the pine trees lining the winding road, I got a name." <u>I Got A Name</u>.

"Like the tree that grows so tall...." <u>I'm Going Home</u>.

"Lines form on my face and hands." <u>Eighteen</u>.

"Listen baby, ain't no mountain high, ain't no valley low, ain't no river wide enough, baby." <u>Ain't No Mountain High Enough</u>.

"Listen children to a story that was written long ago 'bout a kingdom on a mountain and the valley folk below." <u>One Tin Soldier</u>.

"Listen easy, you can hear God callin'." <u>And The Grass Won't Pay No Mind</u>.

"Listen ev'rybody, 'cause I'm talkin' to you." <u>Wonderful Time Up There</u>.

"Listen to me, and hold me tight." <u>Listen To Me</u>.

"Listen to me baby, I've come to make you see, that I want to be with you, gal, if you want to be with me." <u>If You Gotta Go, Go Now</u>.

"Listen to me, baby, you gotta understand." <u>Lightnin' Strikes</u>.

"Listen to me woman, there's something that is on my mind." <u>Love's Only Love</u>.

"Listen to the emptiness of the raindrops on the ground." <u>Song That Never Comes</u>.

"Listen to the ground." <u>Night Fever</u>.

"Listen to the wind blow; watch the sun rise." <u>Chain</u>.

"Listen while I talk to you." <u>Shake</u>.

"Little bit of soap will wash away your lipstick on my face." <u>Little Bit Of Soap</u>.

"Little bitty pretty one come on and talk to me." <u>Little</u>

Bitty Pretty One.

"Little boy lost in search of little boy found...." Little Boy Lost.

"Little darlin', my little darlin'...." Little Darlin'.

"Little girl, don't you want to stay?" All By Myself (A. Domino & D. Bartholomew).

"Little girl, where did you come from?" She Said "Yeah".

"Little G.T.O., you're really looking fine." G.T.O.

"Little, little little little lit." Little Girl Of Mine.

"Little sleepy boy, do you know what time it is? St. Jude's Comet.

"Little surfer, little one...." Surfer Girl.

"Little things you say and do...." Rave On.

"Little wallflower on the shelf...." Let The Little Girl Dance.

"Little while ago, I went and placed a call." Answering Machine.

"Living in golden temples, my love." Meditation.

"Living is a dream when you make it seem enchanted." Enchanted.

"Local rock group down the street is trying hard to learn their song." Pleasant Valley Sunday.

"Lollipop, lollipop...." Lollipop.

"London Bridge is falling down." Harder They Fall.

"Lonely night, I cry myself to sleep." Lonely Night (Angel Face).

"Lonely teardrops, my pillow's never dry." Lonely Teardrops.

"Lonely women are the desperate kind." Emotion (P. Dahlstrom & V. Sanson).

"Lonesome tears sad and blue...." Lonesome Tears.

"Long ago, a young man sits and plays his waiting game." Long Ago & Far Away.

"Long ago, and, oh, so far away, I fell in love with you before the second show." Superstar (L. Russell & B. Bramlett).

"Long and winding road that leads to your door will never disappear." Long And Winding Road.

"Long as I remember the rain been comin' down." Who'll Stop The Rain.

"Long distance, information, give me Memphis, Tennessee." Memphis, Tennessee.

"Long distance operator, place this call, it's not for fun." Long Distance Operator.

"Long distance run around." Long Distance Run Around.

"Long, long and lonely nights, I cry my eyes out over you." Long Lonely Nights.

"Long, long time ago, I can still remember how that music used to make me smile." American Pie.

"Long, long time ago, on graduation day, you handed me your book, I signed this way." Roses Are Red.

"Long time ago when the earth was green and there were more kinds of animals than you ever seen...." Unicorn.

"Long time forgotten are dreams that just fell by the way." Good Hearted Woman.

"Long time we stayed together, been through the roughest weather, you and I." Take That To The Bank.

"Longer than there've been fishes in the ocean...." Longer.

"Look around you." Lady (G. Goble).

"Look at me, I have fallen so in love with you." Let Me Be Your Angel.

"Look at me, I'm as helpless as a kitten up a tree." Misty.

"Look at us baby, up all night tearin' our love apart." I Can't Tell You Why.

"Look at who the wind's blowing up the road, shining like the northern star." I Know A Heartache When I See One.

"Look at you girl." He Did With Me.

"Look here girls, take this advice." Too Many Fish In The Sea.

"Look! Look! My heart is an open book." My Heart Is An Open Book.

"Look of love is in your eyes." Look Of Love.

"Look out behind you." Jojo.

"Look out now I'm runnin' wild." Never Say Yes.

"Look out of any window, any morning, any evening, any day." Box Of Rain.

"Look outside the window, there's a woman being grabbed." Outside Of A Small Circle Of Friends.

"Look over yonder, what do you see?" Crystal Blue Persuasion.

"Look what man has done." Genius I.

"Look what they done to my song, Ma." What Have They Done To My Song, Ma.

"Lookin' pretty, New York City girl." Native New Yorker.

"Lookin' through the windows, the window to your heart." Lookin' Through The Windows.

"Looking at the world through the sunset of your eyes." Marrakesh Express.

"Looking back on when I was a little nappy headed boy...." I Wish.

"Looking out at the road rushing under my wheels." Running On Empty.

"Looking through some photographs I found inside a drawer...." Fountain Of Sorrow.

"Looking up the sleeve of confidence, I jumped down from the fence." Sweet Green Fields.

"Lookout I'm comin' in with the spirit of the northern wind, yeah." Full Speed Ahead.

"Looks like ev'rybody in this whole round world is down on me." Down On Me.

"Looks like it's over, you knew I couldn't stay." Sad Eyes.

"Loose Lucy is my delight." Loose Lucy.

"Lord, I was born a ramblin' man, try'n to make a livin' and doin' the best I can." Ramblin' Man.

"Lord, it's the same old tune, fiddle and guitar, where do we take it from here?" Are You Sure Hank Done It This Way.

"Lordy, only believe, only believe, all things are possible if you'll only believe." Only Believe.

"Lost and all alone, I always thought that I could make it on my own." Lost Without Your Love.

"Love and happiness, somethin' that can make you do wrong." Love And Happiness.

"Love bug done bit me." Love Is Like An Itching In My Heart.

"Love, exciting and new." Love Boat, Main Title From.

"Love fire, hold me close and breathe my name." Love Fire.

"Love has a strange way of findin' out ev'rything in your heart." Run Home Girl.

"Love has locked us up, peaches." Monkey See--Monkey Do.

"Love is a flower that blooms in the springtime." Everything's Coming Up Love.

"Love is a rose but you better not pick it." Love Is A Rose.

"Love is all we need." Love Is All We Need.

"Love is but a song we sing." Get Together.

"Love is here, and oh my darling, now you're gone." Love Is Here And Now You're Gone.

"Love is higher than a mountain." Thicker Than Water.

"Love is like candy on a shelf." Help Yourself.

"Love is like oxygen." Love Is Like Oxygen.

"Love, look at the two of us, strangers in many ways." For All We Know.

"Love love love, love love love, love love love, there's nothing you can do that can be done." All You Need Is Love.

"Love, love me, darlin', come and go with me." Come Go With Me.

"Love, love me do, you know I love you." Love Me Do.

"Love, love will keep us together." Love Will Keep Us Together.

"Love me good, baby, love me right." My Love Don't Come Easy.

"Love me, love me!" Love Is All We Need.

"Love me or leave me, make your choice." I Do, I Do, I Do, I Do, I Do.

"Love me tender, love me sweet, never let me go." Love Me Tender.

"Love me with all your heart, that's all I want, love." Love Me With All Your Heart.

"Love means you never have to say you're sorry." Love Means.

"Love or let me be lonely, part-time love I can find any day." Love Or Let Me Be Lonely.

"Love, soft as an easy chair." Evergreen.

"Love, you came to my rescue." You're The Love.

"Lovliness of Paris seems somehow sadly gay." I Left My Heart In San Francisco.

"Lovely Linda with the lovely flowers in her hair." Lovely Linda.

"Lovely princess of the islands...." Island Of Love.

"Lover, lover, lover, lover...." Weekend Lover.

"Lover please, please come back." Lover Please.

"Lover you said you're leavin', gotta leave me behind." Silver Lining.

"Lovin' you is easy 'cause you're beautiful; makin' love with you is all I want to do." Lovin' You.

"Loving you isn't the right thing to do." Go Your Own Way.

"Loving you so I was too blind to see you letting me go." It's Gonna Take A Miracle.

"Lucille, won't you do your sister's will?" Lucille (A. Collins & R. Penniman).

"Lucretia MacEvil, little girl what's your game?" Lucretia MacEvil.

"Lullaby of Birdland, that's what I always hear when you sigh." Lullaby Of Birdland.

"Lum dee lum dee lie, lum dee lum dee lie, oh, you know a cat named Mickey came from out of town, yeah." Mickey's Monkey.

"Lyin', cheatin', hurtin', that's all you seem to do." Your Time Is Gonna Come.

"Lyin' in bed with the radio on, moonlight falls like rain." Nights Are Forever Without You.

"Lying by your side I watch you sleeping and in your face the sweetness of a child." I've Lost You.

"Lying on the side of the road, feelin' like he heard a sound...." John Looked Down.

"M, I say M-O, M-O-P, M-O-P-P, Mop! Rag Mop.

"Ma belle amie...." Ma Belle Amie.

"Mabellene, why can't you be true? Mabellene.

"Madman drummers bummers and Indians in the summer with a teenage diplomat." Blinded By The Light.

"Makin' a livin' the old hard way." Draggin' The Line.

"Makin' it, oh, makin' it." Makin' It.

"Mama I'm freezing." Key West.

"Mama, Mama, come here quick." Cocaine Blues.

"Mama pajama rolled out of bed and she ran to the police station." Me And Julio Down By The Schoolyard.

"Mama says yes, Papa says no." Rip This Joint.

"Mama, take this badge off of me." Knockin' On Heaven's Door.

"Mama, where's your pretty little girl tonight?" Tenderness On The Block.

"Mama's got a squeeze box she wears on her chest." Squeeze Box.

"Man in me will do nearly any task." Man In Me.

"Manchester England, England, across the Atlantic sea." Manchester, England.

"Man's got his woman to take his seed." Only Women Bleed.

"Many a tear has to fall, but it's all in the game." It's All In The Game.

"Many roads I've covered...." Time To Kill.

"Many say that I'm too young to let you know just where I'm comin' from." Something He Can Feel.

"Many's the time I've been mistaken and many times confused." American Tune.

"Marching band came down along Main Street; the soldier blues fell in behind." Billy, Don't Be A Hero.

"Martha, she listens for the ticking of my footsteps." Martha.

"Mary Mack dressed in black...." Walking The Dog.

"Mashed potatoes started long time ago." Mashed Potato Time.

"Matchmaker, matchmaker, make me a match." Matchmaker, Matchmaker.

"Matty told Hatty about a thing she saw." Wooly Bully.

"May God bless and keep you always, may your wishes all come true." Forever Young.

"Maybe baby, I'll have you." Maybe Baby.

"Maybe I hang around here a little more than I should." I Honestly Love You.

"Maybe if I pray ev'ry night, you'll come back to me." Maybe.

"Maybe I'll see you again, baby, and maybe I won't." In Thee.

"Maybe the sun gave me the power, but I could swim Loch Lomond and be home in half an hour." Almost Like Being In Love.

"Maybe this time I'll be lucky." Maybe This Time.

"Maybe you think I'm letting you go." Goodbye I Love You.

Maybe you'll wanna give me kisses sweet." I'll Second That Emotion.

"Me and baby brother used to run together." Me And Baby Brother.

"Me and Misses Jones, we've got a good thing going on." Me And Mrs. Jones.

"Me and my arrow, straight up and narrow." Me And My Arrow.

"Measuring a summer's day...." Tangerine.

"Meet me in the middle of the day; let me hear you say ev'rything's okay." Romeo's Tune.

"Meet me in the morning, Fifty Sixth and Wabasha." Meet Me In The Morning.

"Melinda was mine till the time that I found her holding Jim." Solitary Man.

"Melodies bring memories that linger in my heart." Georgia On My Mind.

"Melt my heart, why don't you melt my heart?" Tranquillo (Melt My Heart).

"Mem'ries light the corners of my mind." Way We Were.

"Mended photograph I lent to you." Hot Butterfly.

"Merry Christmas baby, you sure did treat me nice." Merry Christmas Baby.

"Met the girl that I want to get to know a little better." Help Me Make It.

"Michael, row the boat ashore, hallelujah!" Michael, Row The Boat Ashore.

"Michael wakes you up with sweets." Michael From Mountains.

"Michelle ma belle, these are words that go together well, my Michelle." Michelle."

"Mighty Idy, girl, what a shape you're in." Mighty Idy.

"Million to one, that's what our folks think about this love of ours." Million To One.

"Million violins could never sound sweeter than your name." Sunshine Of My World.

"Millionaires and paupers walk the hungry streets." Flower Lady.

"Minute you walked in the joint, I could see you were a man of distinction." Big Spender.

"Minute you're gone I cry." Minute You're Gone.

"Miss Maggie M'Gill she lived on a hill." Maggie M'Gill.

"Mississippi Queen, if you know what I mean." Mississippi Queen.

"Mississippi, you've been on my mind." Mississippi.

"Mister Bass Man, you got that certain something." Mr. Bass Man.

"Mister Big Stuff, who do you think you are." Mr. Big Stuff.

"Mister Moonlight!" Mr. Moonlight.

"Mister Sandman bring me a dream." Mister Sandman.

"Mm ah ah, by the rivers of Babylon there we sat down." Rivers Of Babylon.

"Mm I bet you're wonderin' how I knew 'bout your plans to make me blue." I Heard It Through The Grapevine.

"Mm, it's carbon and monoxide, the ole Detroit perfume." Papa Hobo.

"Mm mm mm mm mm mm mm mm, oh oh oh oh, little bitty pretty one." Little Bitty Pretty One.

"Mm, mm, mm, you want my love and you can't deny." Can't Hide Love.

"Mm, paraphernalia never hides your broken bones." Everything Put Together Falls Apart.

"Mmm, outside my door...." Down To Love Town.

"Mom was cooking bread...." I'm Livin' In Shame.

"Moment I wake up, before I put on my make-up, I say a little prayer for you." I Say A Little Prayer.

"Moment that you smiled is when it all began." In No Time At All.

"Mona, ooh!" Mona.

"Monday, Monday, so good to me." Monday, Monday.

"Monday mornin' feels so bad." Friday On My Mind.

"Money, money, money, money...." For The Love Of Money.

"Money talks, but it don't sing and dance and it don't walk." Forever In Blue Jeans.

"Money, who needs it?" Road Runner (E. Holland, L. Dozier & B. Holland).

"Money, y a get away." Money.

"Moody river, more deadly than the vainest knife." Moody River.

"More than a ripple, less than a splash, the heir to a long line of glory." This Moment In Time.

"Morning comes, she follows the path to the river shore." Weather Report II; Let It Grow.

"Morning has broken like the first morning." Morning Has Broken.

"Mother Earth is waitin' for you, yes she is." Mother Earth.

"Mother, father, sister, brother...." Prayin'.

"Mother, mother, there's too many of you crying." What's Going On.

"Mother told me, yes she told me, I'd meet girls like you." Surrender (R. Nielsen).

"Mountain is high, the valley is low." Free Ride.

"Moving in silent desperation, keeping an eye on the Holy Land." Walking Man.

"Much has been written about the world and all its kinds of love." Outside My Window.

"Muffin warm and basket brown, smiling faces gathered 'round our dinner table close together hand in hand." Cook With Honey.

"Music blastin', there's people laughin'." Dancin' To The Music.

"Music is a high to me." Sky High.

"Music is a world within itself with a language we all understand." Sir Duke.

"Music, music is my thing." Hot Cop.

"Music was my first love." Music.

"Music's sweet, the lights are low." Dum Dum.

"Muskrat candle light, doin' the town and doin' it right in the evenin'." Muskrat Love.

"Mustang Sally, think you better slow your mustang down." Mustang Sally.

"My account is overdrawn; my car slid down the hill." I Need Your Help Barry Manilow.

"My babe, she don't stand no teasin', my babe." My Babe.

"My baby caught the train, left me all alone." Who's Been Talking.

"My baby give me the finance blues." Money Money.

"My baby loves me." My Baby Loves Me.

"My baby makes me proud." Behind Closed Doors.

"My baby moves at midnight, goes right on till the dawn." You Should Be Dancing.

"My boy lollipop, you make my heart go giddy up." My Boy Lollipop.

"My boyfriend's back, and you're gonna be in trouble." My Boyfriend's Back.

"My car broke down in Georgia." Louisville.

"My cherie amour, lovely as a summer day." My Cherie Amour.

"My child arrived just the other day." Cat's In The Cradle.

"My daddy was a family bass man." Baby Driver.

"My eyes adored you 'though I never laid a hand on you." My Eyes Adored You.

"My eyes are dry, my love." Rain In My Heart.

"My father married a pure Cherokee." Half Breed.

"My father sits at night with no lights on." That's The Way I've Always Heard It Should Be.

"My forbidden lover, I don't want no other." My Forbidden Lover.

"My girl baby sits for someone on her block." Babby Sittin' Boogie.

"My grandpa, he's ninety-five, and he keeps on dancin', he's still alive." Dance, Dance, Dance (S. Miller, B. & J. Cooper).

"My heart belongs to only you." My Heart Belongs To Only You.

"My heart breaks open 'cause you're my all." What Gives.

"My lady in the sun with your hair undone...." Thunder Island.

"My life has been a tapestry of rich and royal hue." Tapestry.

"My love, I'll never find the words, my love, to tell you how I feel, my love." You Make Me Feel Brand New.

"My love is warmer than the warmest sunshine, softer than a sigh." My Love (T. Hatch).

"My love must be a kind of blind love." I Only Have Eyes For You.

"My mama done tol' me...." Blues In The Night.

"My mama told me, she said, 'son please beware'." Too Late To Turn Back Now.

"My name should be Trouble, my name should be Woe." Danny.

"My old man, he's a singer in the park." My Old Man.

"My pappy said, 'son you're gonna drive me to drinkin', if you don't stop drivin' that hot rod Lincoln'." Hot Rod Lincoln.

"My sweet Lord, um, my Lord, um, my Lord." My Sweet Lord.

"My tears are fallin' 'cause you're takin' her away." Take Good Care Of My Baby.

"My wish came true when I met you." My Wish Came True.

"My wonderful one...." Wonderful One.

"My world is empty without you, babe." My World Is Empty Without You.

"Name your price, a ticket to paradise." Love Is The Answer (T. Rundgren).

"Nana na nana, nana na nana." Gonna Love You More.

"Need no doctor if 'cause I know what's ailin' me." I Don't Need No Doctor.

"Needless to say I'm sorry, you've made up your mind to go." No Regrets.

"Never been this blue." Stand Tall.

"Never can say goodbye, no, no, no, no, I never can say goodbye." Never Can Say Goodbye.

"Never could believe the things you do for me, never could believe the way you are." Every 1's A Winner.

"Never found a four-leaf clover to bring good luck to me." me." Good Lucky.

"Never mind the reason; you may never know." So Long.

"Never, never, never say never, ne dis ja mais, ja mais." Never Say Never.

"Never saw the mornin' 'til I stayed up all night." San Diego Serenade.

"Never thought about tomorrow." Must Of Got Lost.

"Never thought love had a rainbow on it." Dance Dance Dance (N. Young).

"New Orleans ladies, sassy style that will drive you crazy." New Orleans Ladies.

"Nibblin' on sponge cake, watchin' the sun bake." Margaritaville.

"Nice and easy oh how you please me." Do It Baby.

"Night air is inviting you to walk out on the trail." I've Had Her.

"Night is draggin' her feet." Little More Love.

"Night sets softly with the hush of falling leaves." Patterns .

"Night train that took my baby so far away." Night Train.

"Night was black." Gone At Last.

"Night was clear and the moon was yellow, and the leaves came tumbling down." Stagger Lee.

"Nights in white satin never reaching the end." Nights In White Satin.

"No gal made has got a shade on Sweet Georgia Brown." Sweet Georgia Brown.

"No, I would not give you false hope on this strange and mournful day." Mother And Child Reunion.

"No, I'm not upset, I'm not." Steppin' Out, I'm Gonna Boogie Tonight.

"No matter where you are I will always be with you." No Matter What.

"No more books and studies." School Is Out.

"No more carefree laughter." Knowing Me, Knowing You.

"No more do I see the starlight caress your hair." No More.

"No one can buy tomorrow." Come Live Your Life With Me.

"No one in the world ever had a love as sweet as my love." Hurting Each Other.

"No one's in a hurry." I Think I'm Gonna Like It Here.

"No regrets altho' our love affair has gone astray." No Regrets.

"No regrets, coyote." Coyote.

"No use pretending things can still be right." Never Gonna Fall In Love Again.

"Nobody can do the Shing-a-ling like I do." Nobody But Me.

"Nobody does it better, makes me feel sad for the rest." Nobody Does It Better.

"Nobody feels any pain." Just Like A Woman.

"Nothing but heartaches, oo-oo-oo...." Nothing But Heartaches.

"Nothing so blue as a heart in pain." Baby, Baby, Don't Cry.

"Nothing was delivered." Nothing Was Delivered.

"Nothing you could say could tear me away from my guy." My Guy.

"Nothing's too good for my baby." Nothing's Too Good For My Baby.

"Now a good friend of mine, sat with me and he cried." Don't Be A Drop-Out.

"Now Amos Moses was a Cajun." Amos Moses.

"Now, boys, I'm gonna sing about that Rock Island line." Rock Island Line.

"Now Frankie, she was a fine lookin' woman, had a man named Johnnie and she loved him." New "Frankie And Johnnie" Song.

"Now here we are together." Please Let Me Wonder.

"Now here you go again, you say you want your freedom." Dreams.

"Now if there's a smile upon my face it's only there trying to fool the public." Tears Of A Clown.

"Now if you feel that you can't go on because all of your hope is gone...." Reach Out, I'll Be There.

"Now if you're feelin' kind of low about the dues you've been payin'...." Peace Of Mind.

"Now, I'm craving your body, is this real?" Reasons.

"Now, I'm just a bartender, and I don't like my work." Bartender's Blues.

"Now is the time for your loving, dear, and the time for your company." Children Of Darkness.

"Now it's time for all of us to say goodbye." Because You Are My Friend.

"Now, I've been happy lately." Peace Train.

"Now I've found that the world is round." World.

"Now somewhere in the Black Mountain hills of Dakota there lived a young boy named Rocky Raccoon." Rocky Raccoon.

"Now that I've lost ev'rything to you, you say you wanna start something new." Wild World.

"Now that we've found love, what are we gonna do with it?" Now That We've Found Love.

"Now the curtain is going up." Entertainer (S. Joplin).

"Now the Lord will forgive you if you're cheatin'." It's A Sin When You Love Somebody.

"Now the sun's sittin' high in the sky." Summer Love Sensation.

"Now there is a way to say I love you." Hot Love, Cold World.

"Now, there's a certain thing that I learned from Jim." Open The Door, Homer.

"Now there's a lesson to be learned; you never hurt the one you love." There's A Lesson To Be Learned..

"Now they make new movies in old black and white." Pencil-Thin Mustache.

"Now they up and call me Speedo but my real name is Mister Earl." Speedo.

"Now, this here's a story about the Rock Island Line." Rock Island Line.

"Now, too much of nothing can make a man feel ill at ease." Too Much Of Nothing.

"Now when I get the blues I get me a rockin' chair." Flip, Flop & Fly.

"Now when there's someone else who cares...." Even Now.

"Now when you open your mouth what come out, what's the first word, what's the first line?" Play On Love.

"Now you say ev'ry time you need some affection...." I'm The One You Need.

"Now you're moving on up ah pretty baby, you're leaving me behind." Try It Baby.

"Nowhere to run to, baby, nowhere to hide." Nowhere To Run.

"Now's the time for all good men to get together with a one another." Yes We Can-Can.

"Of war and peace the truth just twists, its curfew gull it glides." Gates Of Eden.

"Oh, a sailor's life is a weary life." Sailor's Life.

"Oh, a sleeping drunkard up in Central Park...." Nice, Nice, Very Nice.

"Oh, a storm is threat'ning my very life today." Gimme Shelter.

"Oh, ain't no problem, carry no heavy load." Road Block.

"Oh, Alabama; the devil fools with the best laid plans." Alabama.

"Oh, baby, ev'rything's gonna be alright, yeah." Every-thing's Gonna Be Alright.

"Oh, baby, I wanna be your lover." Oh, Baby.

"Oh, baby, it's cryin' time." Four Sticks.

"Oh, baby, loving you is all that's on my mind." It Feels So Good To Be Loved So Bad.

"Oh, baby, this time it's goodbye." I Can't Hold On.

"Oh, can't stand it, can't stand your love." I Can't Stand It 76.

"Oh, Carol, don't let him steal your heart away." Carol.

"Oh, C.C. Rider, a-see what you have done." C.C. Rider (H. Ledbetter).

"Oh, come back baby, oh mama, please don't go, yeah." Come Back Baby.

"Oh, darling, doing the best I can." Doing The Best I Can (J. Brown, C. Bobbit & F. Wesley).

"Oh, darling, I'm so lonely without you." Turn Back The Hands Of Time.

"Oh, darling, please believe me, I'll never do you no harm." Oh Darling.

"Oh, dirty Maggie Mae they have taken her away and she'll never walk down Lisle Street any mower." Maggie Mae.

"Oh, don't it get you, get you in your throat." Old Old Woodstock.

"Oh, girl, I've known you very well." More Than A Woman.

"Oh, girls, you know we've got to watch out." Playboy.

"Oh, God said to Abraham kill me a son." Highway 61 Revisited.

"Oh happy day!" Oh Happy Day.

"Oh, hello, Mister Soul, I dropped by to pick up a reason...." Mr. Soul.

"Oh, help me in my weakness, I heard the drifter say." Drifter's Escape.

"Oh, hold me tight, won't you be my woman tonight?" Woman Tonight.

"Oh, how can you tell me how the joy passed from his childhood." Flowers Of Evil.

"Oh, how I remember daddy, he was strong and had a built in tan." Daddy Could Swear, I Declare.

"Oh, how I've loved you, since the day you first told me your name." How You've Changed.

"Oh, how you tried to cut me down to size." Walk Like A Man.

"Oh, hummingbird, mankind was waiting for you to come flying along." Hummingbird.

"Oh, I am just a student sir, and I only want to learn." I'm Gonna Say It Now.

"Oh, I baby, what a fool I am." I Can't Help It.

"Oh, I can't take another heartache though you say you're my friend." Cruel To Be Kind.

"Oh, I could hide neath the wings of the bluebird as she sings." Daydream Believer.

"Oh, I had a one-way love." My Baby's Baby.

161

"Oh, I'm on my way, I know I am somewhere not so far from here." Sitting.

"Oh, I'm really feeling mighty low." Hard Luck.

"Oh, in a little while from now...." Alone Again (Naturally).

"Oh, in the morning feel like the sun." Oh, In The Morning.

"Oh, it's so nice to be with you." Nice To Be With You.

"Oh, jawbone, when did you first go wrong?" Jawbone.

"Oh, kisses sweeter than wine." Kisses Sweeter Than Wine.

"Oh, little girl of mine, gee, you sure look fine." Little Girl Of Mine.

"Oh, little Jeannie, you got so much love, little Jeannie." Little Jeannie.

"Oh, little one, it's so nice to have you near me." Little One.

"Oh, Lord, won't you buy me a Mercedes Benz?" Mercedes Benz.

"Oh, love, so glad I found you." I'm Never Gonna Be Alone Anymore.

"Oh, mama dear, tell me do you hear, they're partying tonight?" Party Lights (C. Clark).

"Oh mamma I'm in fear for my life from the long arm of the law." Renegade.

"Oh, mother, say a prayer for me." Jesse (C. Simon & M. Mainieri).

"Oh, my child, you'll never know just what you mean to me." Jive Talkin'.

"Oh, my love, my darling, I've hungered for your touch a long, lonely time." Unchained Melody.

"Oh, my man, I love him so." My Man.

"Oh, my name it is nothin, my age it means less." With God On Our Side.

"Oh no, I can't write my name, well, don't you know I'm so blasted." I've Never Been In Love.

"Oh, now, I don't hardly know her, but, I think I could love her, crimson and clover." Crimson And Clover.

"Oh, oh! I love you so." I Need Your Love Tonight.

"Oh, oh, oh don't ya know?" Just Go Away.

"Oh, oh, oh, Miss Ann." Miss Ann.

"Oh, oh, oh, oh gee, man oh oh gee, well oh oh gee, do I love that girl." Gee.

"Oh, oh, oh, oh, I got a girl named Rama Lama, Rama Lama Ding Dong." Rama Lama Ding Dong.

"Oh oh oh oh oh Julie, you'll never know how I love you." Oh Julie.

"Oh, oh, oh, oh, oh, oh, I love you, baby, and I want you to be my girl." I Want You To Be My Girl.

"Oh oh oh oh oh oh, you don't have to go." D'yer Mak'er.

"Oh, oh, oh, send her your love with a dozen roses." Send One Your Love.

"Oh, oh! Yea, yea! I love you more than I can say." More Than I Can Say.

"Oh, oh, yeah, oh, listen to me people." Too Busy Thinking About My Baby.

"Oh, once I had a little dog, his color it was brown." Autumn To May.

"Oh people, look around you, the signs are ev'rywhere." Rock Me On The Water.

"Oh, please don't you think, babe, that I am wrong to cry, yeah?" Flower In The Sun.

"Oh Shenandoah I long to hear you." Shenandoah.

"Oh, she's a brick house." Brick House.

"Oh, sister, when I come to lie in your arms, you should not treat me like a stranger." Oh, Sister.

"Oh sit yourself down girl and talk to me." Let's Straighten It Out.

"Oh, Susie-Q, oh, Susie-Q, oh, Susie-Q, how I love you, my Susie-Q." Susie-Q.

"Oh, the benches were stained with tears and perspiration." Day Of The Locusts.

"Oh the cuckoo, she's a pretty bird." Cuckoo.

"Oh, the games people play now, ev'ry night and ev'ry day, now." Games People Play.

"Oh, the path was deep and wide." Son Of Hickory Holler's Tramp.

"Oh, the ragman draws circles up and down the block." Stuck Inside Of Mobile With The Memphis Blues Again.

"Oh the shark has pretty teeth, dear and he shows them pearly white." Mack The Knife.

"Oh, the Sisters of Mercy they are not departed or gone." Sisters Of Mercy.

"Oh, the streets of Rome are filled with rubble, ancient footprints are ev'rywhere." When I Paint My Masterpiece.

"Oh, the summertime is coming and the leaves are sweetly turning." Wild Mountain Thyme.

"Oh the time will come up when the winds will stop and the breeze will cease to be breathin'." When The Ship Comes In.

"Oh very young what will you leave us this time?" Oh Very Young.

"Oh, well I'm sittin' on my la la, waitin' for my ya ya." Ya Ya.

"Oh well, I'm the type of guy that would never settle down." Wanderer (E. Maresca).

"Oh, well, oh well, I feel so good today." Back In The USA.

"Oh well-a put your arms around me now, and try your best to squeeze me." Rock Me My Baby.

"Oh! We're goin' out tonight finger poppin'." Oh, What A Night For Dancing.

"Oh, what a night, late December back in sixty three." December 1963 (Oh, What A Night).

"Oh, what a night to love you dear." Oh, What A Night.

"Oh, what will you give me, say the sad bells of Rhymney." Bells Of Rhymney.

"Oh, what! Wow! He's the greatest dancer." <u>He's The Greatest Dancer</u>.

"Oh, where have you been, my blue-eyed son?" <u>Hard Rain's A Gonna Fall</u>.

"Oh, wild one, I'm a-gonna tame you down." <u>Wild One</u>.

"Oh ye playboys and playgirls ain't gonna run my world." <u>Playboys And Playgirls</u>.

"Oh, yes, I'm the great pretender." <u>Great Pretender</u>.

"Oh yes, it's ladies' night and the feeling's right." <u>Ladies' Night</u>.

"Oh yes, wait a minute Mister Postman." <u>Please Mr. Postman</u>.

"Oh, you can kiss me on a Monday, a Monday, a Monday is very, very good." <u>Never On Sunday</u>.

"Oh you can rock it you can roll it do the slop and even stroll it at the hop." <u>At The Hop</u>.

"Oh-ho, the way that I feel tonight." <u>In Your Arms</u>.

"Ol' black Bascom, don't break no mirrors." <u>Tell Me, Momma</u>.

"Old depression got you guessin'." <u>Everything That 'Cha Do (Will Come Back To You)</u>.

"Old friend told me that you just ran out of chances." <u>No Night So Long</u>.

"Old friends, old friends, sat on their park bench like book ends." <u>Old Friends</u>.

"Old home town looks the same as I step down from the train, and there to meet me is my mama and papa." <u>Green Green Grass Of Home</u>.

"Old man, look at my life, I'm a lot like you were." <u>Old Man</u>.

"Old man lying by the side of the road, with the lorries rolling by...." <u>Don't Let It Bring You Down</u>.

"Old man rhythm is in my shoes." <u>Sea Cruise</u>.

"Old man sailin' in a dinghy boat down there." <u>Apple Sucking Tree</u>.

"On a dark desert highway, cool wind in my hair...." <u>Hotel California</u>.

"On a morning from a Bogart movie...." <u>Year Of The Cat</u>.

"On a night like this...." <u>On A Night Like This</u>.

"On a warm summer's evening on a train bound for nowhere, I met up with a gambler, we were both too tired to sleep." <u>Gambler</u>.

"On Armistice day, the Philharmonic will play, but the songs that we sing will be sad." <u>Armistice Day</u>.

"Oh Saturday night where I was born down on the farm, guitar plinking and we started singing till the break of dawn." <u>Bo Weevil</u>.

"On the day when I was born, daddy sat down and cried." <u>Mississippi Half Step Uptown Toodleoo</u>.

"On the first part of the journey I was looking at all the life." <u>Horse With No Name</u>.

"Once I built a railroad, made it run." <u>Brother, Can You Spare A Dime</u>.

"Once I had a love and it was a gas...." <u>Heart Of Glass</u>.

"Once I had a pretty girl." <u>Hats Off To Larry</u>.

"Once I had a secret love that lived within the heart of me." <u>Secret Love</u>.

"Once I thought I saw you in a crowded, hazy bar." <u>Like A Hurricane</u>.

"Once in ev'ry life, someone comes along, and you came to me." <u>It Was Almost Like A Song</u>.

"Once in morning contemplation...." <u>It's Gonna Come Down</u>.

"Once there were green fields kissed by the sun." <u>Greenfields</u>.

"Once upon a time there was a tavern." <u>Those Were The Days</u>.

"Once upon a time you dressed so fine...." <u>Like A Rolling Stone</u>.

"One and only night you don't need to leave at all, the car rolls up outside on time, a moment from your call." <u>Can't We Just Sit Down And Talk It Over</u>.

"One day a friend took me aside and said 'I have to leave you.'" <u>Prison Song</u>.

"One day I first saw you on passing by." <u>You Beat Me To The Punch</u>.

"One day while I was eating beans at Smokey Joe's Cafe...." <u>Smokey Joe's Cafe</u>.

"One fine day, you'll look at me and you will know our love was meant to be." <u>One Fine Day</u>.

"One is the loneliest number that you'll ever do." <u>One</u>.

"One less bell to answer." <u>One Less Bell To Answer</u>.

"One lonely night at this drivein...." <u>An Empty Cup</u>.

"One more night, the stars are in sight but tonight I'm as lonesome as can be." <u>One More Night</u>.

"One morning I woke up and I knew you were really gone." <u>Carry On</u>.

"One night I was late, came home from a date, slipped out of my shoes at the door." <u>Rock And Roll Waltz</u>.

"One night with you is what I'm now praying for." <u>One Night</u>.

"One of these nights, one of these crazy old nights...." <u>One Of These Nights</u>.

"One pill makes you larger." <u>White Rabbit</u>.

"One summer day, she went away." <u>Sitting On Top Of The World</u>.

"One summer night, we fell in love." <u>One Summer Night</u>.

"One Sunday mornin' we were walkin' down by the old graveyard." <u>Mystic Eyes</u>.

"One too many days I've felt forgotten." <u>Next Time</u>.

"One too many times I fell over you." <u>It's All I Can Do</u>.

"One two, ha cha cha two two, ha cha cha." <u>Ha Cha Cha (Funktion)</u>.

"One, two, three, four, can I have a little more." <u>All Together Now</u>.

"One two three look at Mister Lee." Mister Lee.

"One, two, three o'clock, four o'clock rock." Rock Around The Clock.

"One! Two! Three! One! Two! Three! Oh, uh, alright, uh! You gotta know how to pony like Bony Maronie." Land Of A Thousand Dancers.

"One used to be the shotgun." Funky Street.

"One way or another I'm gonna find ya." One Way Or Another.

"Only on a Friday, never on a Sunday, never on a Monday." Livin' It Up.

"Only two things in life that make it worth livin' is guitars that tune good and firm feelin' women." Luckenbach, Texas.

"Only yesterday, this old man winter came to stay." Only Make Believe.

"Only you can make this world seem right." Only You.

"Oo ah ah ah ah ah, a mended photograph I lent to you." Hot Butterfly.

"Oo, ah, ha, mm, Anthony works in the grocery store, savin' his pennies for some day." Movin' Out (Anthony's Song).

"Oo, and it's all right, and it's comin' 'long." Right Back Where We Started From.

"Oo baby love, my baby love, I need you...." Baby Love.

"Oo bet you're wond'ring how I knew." I Heard It Through The Grapevine.

"Oo, Jackie Blue, lives her life from inside of a room." Jackie Blue.

"Oo, little sleepy boy, do you know what time it is." St. Judy's Comet.

"Oo, oo, ah, oo, oo, oo, oo, oo, oo, oo, ah, there'll never be a better love." There'll Never Be.

"Oo oo any time that you want me...." Anytime.

"Oo, oo, movin', I got my mind made up c'mon you can get it, get it girl anytime." I Got My Mind Made Up.

"Oo, oo, oo, do the hustle." Hustle.

"Oo, sha la la la, oo, sha la la la, sha la la my baby." Hello Stranger.

"Oo weh oo weh oo weh oo weh oo weh oo weh oo weh oo weh woo." Get Off.

"Oo, you're a holiday, such a holiday." Holiday.

"Ooh baby, let's be young tonight." Let's Be Young Together.

"Ooh child, things are gonna get easier." O-o-h Child.

"Ooh I need your love babe, guess you know it's true." Eight Days A Week.

"Ooh, my little pretty one, my pretty one, when you gonna give me some time, Sharona?" My Sharona.

"Ooh oh Lord, yeah, yeah." Coldblooded.

"Ooh, ooh, I met her at the Burger King." Ooh Ooh I Love Her So.

"Ooh, ooh, let me be the clock for the time of your life, oh yeah." Let Me Be The Clock.

"Ooh, ooh, ooh, I'll be working my way back to you babe, with a burning love inside." Workin' My Way Back To You.

"Ooh ooh ooh Mama take this badge off of me." Knockin' On Heaven's Door.

"Ooh, ooh, ooh, ooh, I got a good thing." Stone To The Bone.

"Ooh, ooh, ooh, ooh, wee, ooh, always together, together, forever, always together forever." I Pledge My Love.

"Ooh, ooh, where is love?" Where Is The Love (H.W. Casey, R. Finch, W. Clarke & B. Wright).

"Ooh, there it is." There It Is (Part I).

"Ooh! What a good thing I've got." Thunder And Light'ning.

"Ooh, woman, your show is something else." Release Me (N. Ashford & V. Simpson).

"Ooh, yeah, yeah, yeah, ooh, yeah, you make me laugh." Poetry Man.

"Ooh, you come out of a dream, peaches and cream, lips like strawberry wine." You're Sixteen.

"Ooh, you make me live." You're My Best Friend.

"Ooo, ah, ooo, ah, touch my body, make it funky." Keep On Dancin'.

"Ooo, baby, I hear how you spend night-time wrapped like a candy in a blue, blue neon glow." Fade Away And Radiate.

"Ooo, Friday evenin', what a feelin'." Weekend.

"Ooo, how do you like your love?" More, More, More (Part I).

"Ooo la, la, la, la, I did you wrong." Ooo Baby Baby.

"Ooo ooo you know I've done a lot of livin' in a lifetime." Gimme Something Real.

"Ooo, you have won, take my heart." Please Don't Leave.

"Ooo, you've only got one life to live." One Life To Live.

"Oooh, oooh, this train don't carry no gamblers, this train." This Train.

"Ooo-weh ooo-weh ooo-weh ooo-weh, let's all chant." Let's All Chant.

"Oop oop oop oop oop oop alley oop oop oop oop oop, there's a man in the funny papers we all know, Alley Oop...." Alley Oop.

"Oo-wah, oo-wah, oo-wah, oo-wah, oo-wah, oo-wah, why do fools fall in love?" Why Do Fools Fall In Love.

"Operator, can you help me?" Operator (R. McKernan).

"Operator, could you help me place this call." Operator (That's Not The Way It Feels).

"Operator, give me information." Operator (W. Spivery).

"Other side of Jamie's door is aching loneliness one, two, three, four." Weep For Jamie.

"Our conversation was short and sweet." You're A Big Girl Now.

"Our day will come." Our Day Will Come.

"Our Father who art in heaven, hallowed be Thy name." Lord's Prayer.

"Our love is alive, and so we begin." Stumblin' In.

"Out in the street; it's six a.m." Blue Morning, Blue Day.

"Out of my mind and I just can't take it any more." Out Of My Mind.

"Out of sight, out of mind." Out Of Sight, Out Of Mind.

"Out on the edge of the empty highway, howling at the blood on the moon." Pride Of Cucamonga.

"Out on the road for forty days...." We're An American Band.

"Out on the street I was talkin' to a man." Get It Right Next Time.

"Out where the bright lights are glowing you're drawn like a moth to a flame." Four Walls.

"Outside my door...." Down To Love Town.

"Outside the rain begins and it may never end." We're All Alone.

"Outside the sky is water color grey." Where Are They Now.

"Over and done, but the heartache lives on inside." Emotion (B. & R. Gibb).

"Over and over, I tried to prove my love to you." Personality.

"Over and over, time and again...." Over And Over (N. Ashford & V. Simpson).

"Over by the window there's a pack of cigarettes." Him (R. Holmes).

"Over the mountain, across the sea...." Over The Mountain, Across The Sea.

"Ow! Got to tell you true." Take Care Of Your Homework.

"Ow! Push, push in the bush." In The Bush.

"Oye como va." Oye Como Va.

"Pack up all my care and woe." Bye Bye Blackbird.

"Padre, Padre, in my grief I turn to you." Padre.

"Pain in my heart." Pain In My Heart.

"Pain of losing you, well it made me an angry man." Bluebird Revisited.

"Papa don't take no mess." Papa Don't Take No Mess (Part I).

"Paperback writer, dear sir or madam will you read my book?" Paperback Writer.

"Para bailar la bamba." La Bamba (J. Martinez).

"Paradise waits, on the crest of a wave, her angels in flame." Help On The Way.

"Paraphernalia never hides your broken bones." Everything Put Together Falls Apart.

"Pardon me boy is that the Chattanooga choo choo?" Chattanooga Choo Choo.

"Parrty, parrty." Parrty (Part II).

"Parrty, parrty, parrty," Parrty (Part I).

"Part-time love is bringing me down 'cause I just can't get started with you." Part-Time Love.

"Party's ending." Let's Get A Little Sentimental.

"Pawnbroker roared." She's Your Lover Now.

"Peg o' my heart, I love you." Peg O' My Heart.

"Peggy Day stole my poor heart away." Peggy Day.

"Penny Lane, there is a barber showing photographs of ev'ry head he's had the pleasure to know." Penny Lane.

"People goin', comin', trolley car was hummin' a sweet city song." Sweet City Song.

"People, keep on learnin'." Higher Ground.

"People movin' out, people movin' in, why?" Ball Of Confusion.

"People of the earth can you hear me?" Children Of The Sun.

"People say I'm the life of the party 'cause I tell a joke or two." Tracks Of My Tears.

"People smile and tell me I'm the lucky one." Danny's Song.

"People try to put us down." My Generation.

"Perhaps it's the color of the sun cut flat an' cov'rin the crossroads I'm standin' at." Mama, You Been On My Mind.

"Perhaps the love we feel today tomorrow may be gone." Come Share My Love

"Photographer smiles, take a break for a while, take a rest." Blue Monday.

"Picasso leans out of the window." Floods Of Florence.

"Pick up the pieces." Pick Up the Pieces.

"Picture yourself in a boat on a river with tangerine trees and marmalade skies." Lucy In The Sky With Diamonds.

"Pilot of the airwaves, here is my request." Pilot Of The Airwaves.

"Pilot's playing poker in the cockpit of the plane." White Boots Marchin' In A Yellow Land.

"Pistol shot at five o'clock...." China Doll.

"Pistol shots ring out in the bar room night." Hurricane.

"Play a handful of marked cards, you play life's game." Nevertheless.

"Please don't dominate the rap, Jack, if you got nothing new to say." New Speedway Boogie.

"Please don't let this feeling end." Ice Castles, Theme From.

"Please don't stop loving me." Please Don't Stop Loving Me.

"Please don't talk about love tonight, please don't talk about sweet love." I Love The Nightlife.

"Please, don't wake me up too late." Goodbye.

"Please lock me away and don't allow the day here inside. World Without Love.

"Please love me forever, don't forget me ever." Please Love Me Forever.

"Please, please, please, please, (please, please don't go)." Please, Please, Please.

"Please release me, let me go." Release Me (E. Miller, D. Williams & R. Yount).

"Please stay with me now, don't you let me go." Stay (M. Williams).

"Pop, pop, pop muzik." Pop Muzik.

"Popsicles, icicles, baseball and fancy clothes." Popsicles And Icicles.

"Preacher talked with me and he smiled." I've Got To Get A Message to You.

"Precious and few are the moments we two can share." Precious And Few.

"Precious love I'll give to you blue as the sky and deep in the eyes of a love so true." Count On Me.

"Pretend there is no silence." Forget To Remember.

"Pretty little angel eyes." Pretty Little Angel Eyes.

"Pretty smile, lovely face and a warm breeze, now I you, lady, you're my no tell lover." No Tell Lover.

"Pretty women out walking with gorillas down my street." Is She Really Going Out With Him.

"Price of bread may worry some, but it don't worry me." It Don't Worry Me.

"'Problem is all inside your head,' she said to me." Fifty Ways to Leave Your Lover.

"Problems, problems, problems all day long." Problems.

"Promises, promises, I'm all through with promises, promises, now." Promises, Promises.

"Prudence, won't you come out to play?" Dear Prudence.

"Pucker up buttercup." Pucker Up Buttercup.

"Puff, the magic dragon lived by the sea." Puff (The Magic Dragon).

"Pull the string and I'll wink at you." I'm Your Puppet.

"Pure hell, got to make it hard." Hell.

"Purpose of a man is to love a woman." Game Of Love.

"Pussywillows, cat-tails, soft winds and roses." Pussywillows, Cattails.

"Put a candle in the window, 'cause I've got to move." Long As I Can See The Light.

"Put it on from Jump street, baby." Nanu, Nanu (I Wanna Funcky Wich You).

"Put on your red dress baby." Hi-Heel Sneakers.

"Put your arms around me like a circle 'round the sun." Stealin'.

"Put your hand in the hand of the man who stilled the water." Put Your Hand In The Hand.

"Put your head on my shoulder, hold me in your arms, baby." Put Your Head On My Shoulder.

"Queen of night took her bow and then she turned to go." Battle Of Evermore.

"Rag mama rag, I can't believe it's true." Rag, Mama Rag.

"Rain is falling thru the mist of sorrow that surrounded me." Let It Rain.

"Raindrops keep fallin' on my head." Raindrops Keep Fallin' On My Head.

"Raindrops, so many raindrops." Raindrops.

"Rainy day people always seem to know when it's time to call." Rainy Day People.

"Raise a little hell." Raise A Little Hell.

"Raised to be a lady by the golden rule." All The Girls Love Alice.

"Raven hair and ruby lips, sparks fly from her finger tips." Witchy Woman.

"Reach out and touch somebody's hand, make this world a better place if you can." Reach Out And Touch (Somebody's Hand).

"Reach out, reach out and touch someone." Reach Out.

"Ready, set, go man go." Ready Teddy.

"Red and white, blue suede shoes, I'm Uncle Sam, how do you do?" U.S. Blues.

"Relax, kick your shoes off, baby, relax." Relax.

"Remember the days of the old schoolyard." Old Schoolyard.

"Rescue me, protect me in your arms, rescue me." Rescue Me.

"Rhiannon rings like a bell thru the night, and wouldn't you love to love her." Rhiannon.

"Ribbon of darkness over me since my true love walked out the door." Ribbon Of Darkness.

"Ride, ride my see-saw." Ride My See-Saw.

"Ride-o-rocket." Ride-O-Rocket.

"Ridin' on the City of New Orleans...." City Of New Orleans.

"Riding along in my automobile...." No Particular Place To Go.

"Right before my very eyes, I thought that you were only fakin' it." Baby, What A Big Surprise.

"Right now ha, ha, I am an anti-Christ." Anarchy In The U.K.

"Right outside this lazy summer home you ain't got time to call your soul a critic, no." Eyes Of The World.

"Ring, ring, telephone ring, somebody said baby, what ya doin'?" Rings.

"Risky changes, shot in the dark." Risky Changes.

"Rita May, Rita May, you got your body in the way." Rita May.

"River flows, it flows to the sea." Ballad Of Easy Rider.

"Road is long with many a winding turn." He Ain't Heavy...He's My Brother.

"Rock and roll is here to stay, and it will never die." Rock And Roll Is Here To Stay.

"Rock my soul in the bosom of Abraham." Oh, Rock My Soul.

"Rock, rock, rock, oh baby rock, rock, rock, oh baby." Rock And Roll Is Here To Stay.

"Rockets and moonshots spent it on the have-nots." Inner City Blues.

"Roll up, roll up for the mystery tour." Magical Mystery Tour.

"Rolling, wheeling like I'm feeling." Wheel Of Fortune.

"Round like a circle in a spiral, like a wheel within a wheel...." Windmills Of Your Mind.

"Roxanne, you don't have to put on the red light." Roxanne.

"Rueben James, in my song you'll live again." Rueben James.

"Run Sally run, gotta pull your mind together." Run Sally Run.

"Run through life's meadows, through its green fields." I'll Still Love You.

"Running down the road, make my get away." Running Down The Road.

"Sacred, our love is sacred." Sacred.

"Sadness had been close as my next of kin." Happy (S. Robinson & M. Legrand).

"Safe in my garden an ancient flower grows." Safe In My Garden.

"Said it's party time y'all." Let's Go Down To The Disco.

"Said the fight to make ends meet keeps a man upon his feet." Every Kinda People.

"Sail on down the line 'bout a half a mile or so." Sail On.

"Sail with me into the unknown void that has no end." Highway In The Wind.

"Sailin' away on the crest of a wave, it's like magic." Livin' Thing.

"Sally called when she got the word." Living Next Door To Alice.

"Sam, you've been waiting much too long now, it looks like she's not coming home." Substitute.

"Same dances in the same old shoes." After The Thrill Is Gone.

"Sandy, the fireworks are hailin' over Little Eden tonight." Fourth Of July (Sandy).

"Satin on my shoulder and a smile on my lips, how lucky can you get?" How Lucky Can You Get.

"Satisfaction, that means diff'rent strokes for diff'rent folks, oh yeah." Satisfaction (W. Robinson).

"Saturday in the park, you'd think it was the Fourth of July." Saturday In The Park.

"Saturday night, Saturday night, we all get together on Saturday night." Saturday Night (R. Sparks).

"Save me." Lose Again.

"Say that you love me." Mission Bell.

"Say, where you gonna go, girl, where you gonna hide?" It Keeps You Runnin'.

"Say yea, yea, yeah." Stubborn Kind Of Fellow.

"Say you'll stay until tomorrow." Say You'll Stay Until Tomorrow.

"Scene is set for dreaming." My Foolish Heart.

"Scotch and soda, mud in your eye." Scotch And Soda.

"Sea dogs have all sailed their ships into the docks of dawn." Valhalla.

"Seasons come, seasons go, but people never seem to know how long it will rain, it will shine." Anytime Of The Year.

"See her how she flies, golden sails across the sky." Moon Is A Harsh Mistress.

"See me, feel me, touch me, heal me." See Me, Feel Me.

"See the curtains hangin' in the window in the evening on a Friday night." Summer Breeze.

"See the funny little clown, see him laughin' as you walk by." See The Funny Little Clown.

"See the stop light turnin' red." Too Late.

"See the tree, how big it's grown, but friend it hasn't been too long, it wasn't big." Honey (B. Russell).

"Seems I've got to have a change of scene." Feelin' Alright.

"Seems like only yesterday I left my mind behind down in in the Gypsy Cafe...." Love Is Just A Four Letter Word.

"Sell the house, sell the car, get all the pennies out the cookie jar." Sell The House.

"Send her your love with a dozen roses." Send One Your Love.

"Send me some lovin', send it I pray." Send Me Some Lovin'.

"Set me free why don't cha baby." You Keep Me Hangin' On.

"Seven days, seven days and there's not a word from you." Seven Days.

"Seven little girls sitting in the back seat, huggin' and a kissin' with Fred." Seven Little Girls Sitting In The Back Seat.

"Seven rooms filled with gloom." 7 Rooms Of Gloom.

"Seven thirty seven comin' out of the sky." Travelin Band.

"Seventeen, a beauty queen, she made a ride that caused a scene in the town." Lady Godiva.

"Sha da da da, sha da da da da." Get A Job.

"Sha la la la la la, my lady in the sun with your hair undone." Thunder Island.

"Shadow of your smile when you are gone will color all

my dreams and light the dawn." <u>Shadow Of Your Smile</u>.

"Shadows grow so long before my eyes and they're moving across the page." <u>Baby, I Love Your Way</u>.

"Shake it up, baby, twist and shout." <u>Twist And Shout</u>.

"Shake it up, shake it down." <u>Disco Lady</u>.

"Shake! Shake the little tambourine." <u>Shake That Tambourine</u>.

"Sha-la-boom-boom-yea-ah, sha-la-boom-boom-yea." <u>Heavy Makes You Happy</u>.

"Shattered dreams, worthless years. <u>I Believe (When I Fall In Love It Will Be Forever)</u>.

"She acts sorta teen age." <u>Gidget</u>.

"She came down from Cincinnati." <u>Fins</u>.

"She came in through the bathroom window." <u>She Came In Through The Bathroom Window</u>.

"She came on like the night and she held on tight." <u>Love So Right</u>.

"She came to me, said she knew me, said she'd known me a long time." <u>Carolina In The Pines</u>.

"She can kill with a smile." <u>She's Always A Woman</u>.

"She comes down from Yellow Mountain...." <u>Wildfire</u>.

"She comes on like a rose." <u>Poison Ivy</u>.

"She cried to the southern wind 'bout a love that was sure to end." <u>Showdown</u>.

"She don't care for one-night stands." <u>Good Sculptures</u>.

"She drew out all our money at the Southern Trust." <u>Bye, Bye, Johnny</u>.

"She has seen me changing." <u>See The Changes</u>.

"She keeps Moet and Chandon in her pretty cabinet." <u>Killer Queen</u>.

"She knows me." <u>She Knows Me Too Well</u>.

"She knows when I'm lonesome." <u>How Can I Tell Her</u>.

"She loves you, yeh, yeh yeh...." <u>She Loves You</u>.

"She may be weary, women do get weary wearing the same shabby dress." <u>Try A Little Tenderness</u>.

"She may say she needs fancy bangles and beads." <u>What Every Woman Lives For</u>.

"She moved in down the hall." <u>Down The Hall</u>.

"She packed my bags last night pre-flight, zero hour nine a.m." <u>Rocket Man</u>.

"She packed up her suitcase and walked to the door." <u>She Never Knew Me</u>.

"She said I can't go back to America soon!" <u>Manana</u>.

"She said she don't love me anymore." <u>Stargazer</u>.

"She saw the look in his eyes, and she knew better." <u>Jamie's Cryin'</u>.

"She showed her navel, she wore a label, she wore it thigh high." <u>It's A Plain Shame</u>.

"She sits alone, waiting for suggestions." <u>Da Ya Think I'm Sexy</u>.

"She stood there, bright as the sun, on that California coast." <u>Hollywood Nights</u>.

"She tells him she thinks she wants to be free." <u>Hasten Down The Wind</u>.

"She tells me all the time that she loves me." <u>I'm Her Fool</u>.

"She took my hand." <u>I Looked Away</u>.

"She was a friend to me when I needed one." <u>That Girl Could Sing</u>.

"She was a princess, queen of the highway." <u>Queen Of The Highway</u>.

"She was afraid to come out of the locker." <u>Itsy Bitsy Teenie Weenie Yellow Polkadot Bikini</u>.

"She was all of a lady." <u>Three Times In Love</u>.

"She was black as the night." <u>Brother Louie</u>.

"She was lonely and no one really cared." <u>Midnight Light</u>.

"She was seaside sittin', just asmokin' and adrinkin' on ringside, on top of the world, oh yeah." <u>Beautiful Girls</u>.

"She wore blue velvet." <u>Blue Velvet</u>.

"She would never say where she came from." <u>Ruby Tuesday</u>.

"Sherry don't go." <u>Sherry Don't Go</u>.

"Sherry, Sherry baby, Sherry, Sherry baby." <u>Sherry</u>.

"She's driving away with the dim lights on." <u>Let's Go</u>.

"She's got ev'rything she needs." <u>She Belongs To Me</u>.

"She's got somethin' that moves my soul and she knows I'd love to love her." <u>Temptation Eyes</u>.

"She's got your eyes." <u>Sweet Life</u>.

"She's sitting right over there." <u>Just Tell Her Jim Said Hello</u>.

"She's your adolescent dream, school-boy stuff, a sticky sweet romance." <u>Good Girls Don't</u>.

"Shh, listen my friends while I tell you about a girl that's so divine." <u>Jamie</u>.

"Short people got no reason, short people got no reason, short people got no reason to live." <u>Short People</u>.

"Shotgun, shoot 'em 'fore he run, now." <u>Shotgun</u>.

"Should I reveal exactly how I feel?" <u>Should I</u>.

"Shouldn't I know if you still love me." <u>Shouldn't I Know</u>.

"Show me a river that's so deep." <u>Sweet Love</u>.

"Show me the prison, show me the jail." <u>There But For Fortune</u>.

"Shutters and boards cover the windows of the house where we used to live." <u>Shutters And Boards</u>.

"Sierra mountains rise up as you float down into L.A." <u>California</u> (J. Brooks).

"Sign on the window says 'lonely'." <u>Sign On The Window</u>.

"Silent eyes watching Jerusalem make her bed of stones." <u>Silent Eyes</u>.

"Silent soldiers on a silver screen...." War Is Over.

"Silent weekend, my baby she gave it to me." Silent Weekend.

"Since Eve made you commit the first mistake...." Run To Me (D. Crawford).

"Since I met you baby my whole life has changed." Since I Met You Baby.

"Since my baby left me, found a new place to dwell." Heartbreak Hotel.

"Since she put me down I've been out doin' in my head." Help Me, Rhonda.

"Since you've been gone I've been walking around with my head bowed down to my shoes." Living The Blues.

"Sincerely, oh! yes, sincerely, 'cause I love you so dearly, please say you'll be mine." Sincerely.

"Sing for the day, sing for the moment, sing for the time of your life." Sing For The Day.

"Sing! Sing a song." Sing (J. Raposo).

"Sing, song of songs to me." Sing (L. Gianangelo).

"Singin' in the rain, just singin' in the rain." Singin' In The Rain.

"Singin' to the world, it's time we let the spirit come in." Daybreak.

"Singing in the sunshine...." Ocean.

"Sirens are screaming, and the fires are howling way down in the valley tonight." Bat Out Of Hell.

"Sit by my side, come as close as the air." Changes (P. Ochs).

"Sittin' here eatin' my heart out waitin', waitin' for some lover to call." Hot Stuff.

"Sittin' here thinkin' where does the money go." Money Blues.

"Sittin' in a park in Paris, France." California (J. Mitchell).

"Sittin' in the classroom, thinkin' it's a drag." Smokin' In The Boys Room.

"Sittin' in the morning sun, I'll be sittin' when the evenin' come." Dock Of The Bay.

"Sitting here wond'ring what it's all about." Itchy, Twitchy Feeling.

"Sitting in the stand of the sports arena, waiting for the show to begin." Venus And Mars Rock Show.

"Sixteen candles make a lovely sight." Sixteen Candles.

"Skies are dark and gray." Cowboy.

"Sky is red, I don't understand." Burn.

"Skybird, my bird, we fly so high and then you touch me warm and fly again." Skybird.

"Skylark, have you anything to say to me?" Skylark.

"Sleep all day, out all night." Funk #49.

"Sleepin' single in a double bed, thinkin' over things I wish I'd said." Sleeping Single In A Double Bed.

"Sleepless hours and dreamless nights and faraways...." Wishing You Were Here.

"Slip slidin' away, slip slidin' away...." Slip Slidin' Away.

"Slippin' and a-slidin', peepin' and a-hidin', been told a long time ago." Slippin' And Slidin'.

"Slippin' and slidin' like a weasel on the run...." One More Weekend.

"Slippin' away, sittin' on a pillow...." Celebrate.

"Sloopy lives in a very bad part of town." Hang On Sloopy.

"Slow dancin', it don't turn me on." Slow Dancin' Don't Turn Me On.

"Slow down, you move too fast." 59th Street Bridge Song.

"Slowly but surely, I'm gonna wear you down." Slowly But Surely.

"Slowly I opened my eyes, hazy with mist." Slowly.

"Smile an everlasting smile...." Words.

"Smiling faces sometimes pretend to be your friend." Smiling Faces Sometimes.

"Smoke, smokestack lightning shining like gold." Smokestack Lightning.

"Smoky autumn night, stars up in the sky." Golden Loom.

"Snow cuts loose from the frozen until it joins with the African sea." Eskimo Blue Day.

"So bye bye, Miss American Pie." American Pie.

"So close, yet so far from paradise." So Close, Yet So Far (From Paradise).

"So far away!" So Far Away.

"So full, so warm, like bein' dried out after the storm." So, So Satisfied.

"So I sing you to sleep after the lovin', with a song I just wrote yesterday." After The Lovin.

"So I told him that he'd better shut his mouth and do his job like a man." Great Mandella.

"So I'd like to know where you got the notion." Rock The Boat.

"So in love, sad as could be." Beauty Is Only Skin Deep.

"So long." Reason To Be.

"So long, Frank Lloyd Wright." So Long, Frank Lloyd Wright.

"So long, oh how I hate to see you go." Reconsider Baby.

"So long, sad times!" Happy Days Are Here Again.

"So many nights I'd sit by my window, waiting for someone to sing me his song." You Light Up My Life.

"So many roads, so many trains to ride." So Many Roads.

"So this ain't the end." Barracuda.

"So this is love, real love." So This Is Love.

"So wide can't get around it." One Nation Under A Groove.

"So you think you'll take another piece of me to satisfy your intellectual need." Action.

"So you think you're a Romeo, playing a part in a picture show." Take The Long Way Home.

FIND THAT TUNE

"So you're a little bit older and a lot less bolder than you used to be." Rock And Roll Never Forgets.

"So you're afraid of fallin', for time and time again love's been unkind." Ready Or Not.

"Softly, I will leave you softly for my heart would break if you should wake and see me go." Softly, As I Leave You.

"Some day when I'm aw'fly low, when the world is cold, I will feel a glow just thinking of you." Way You Look Tonight.

"Some folks are born." Fortunate Son.

"Some folks know about it, some don't." Nitty Gritty.

"Some folks like to get away, take a holiday from the neighborhood." New York State Of Mind.

"Some folk's lives roll easy." Some Folk's Lives Roll Easy.

"Some kid's born with a silver spoon." Hard Knocks.

"Some like their women short, some like 'em tall." Smorgasbord.

"Some of my devils upped and left me free to find a quiet space." I'm Comin' Home Again.

"Some of them were dreamers and some of them were fools who were making plans and thinking of the future." Before The Deluge.

"Some other girls are filling your head with jive." One Who Really Loves You.

"Some people are made of plastic." Whatcha See Is Whatcha Get.

"Some people aren't people; some people are rats." Rats.

"Some people call me a teenage idol." Teenage Idol.

"Some people call me the space cowboy." Joker.

"Some people run, some people crawl, some people don't even move at all." Time.

"Some people say a man is made out of mud." Sixteen Tons.

"Some people say I'm a no 'count." Greenback Dollars.

"Some say love it is a river that drowns the tender reed." Rose.

"Some sleepless night, if you should find yourself alone, let me be the one you run to." Let Me Be The One.

"Some things you never get used to." Some Things You Never Get Used To.

"Somebody said tomorrow never brings nothin' new." Who Are You Now.

"Somebody told a lie, said heaven was in the sky." Somebody Told A Lie.

"Somebody told me a long, long time ago, sweet baby, I feel a change in me is comin' on." Just Too Many People.

"Somebody's gonna give you a lesson in leavin'." Lesson In Leavin'.

"Somebody's gonna hurt someone before the night is through." Heartache Tonight.

"Someday has finally come and opened my eyes to you." Nobody But You.

"Someday some old familiar rain will come along and know my name." World I Used To Know.

"Someday someway you'll realize that you've been blind." It's Just A Matter Of Time.

"Someone really loves you, guess who." Guess Who.

"Someone, someone's got you wrong." Love Will Find A Way.

"Someone told me, it's all happening at the zoo." At The Zoo.

"Someone told me long ago...." Have You Ever Seen The Rain.

"Someone's got it in for me." Idiot Wind.

"Somethin' is stirrin', deep down inside." Look What You've Done To My Heart.

"Something in the way she moves attracts me like no other lover." Something.

"Something strange is happening, you don't belong to me any more it seems." It's You That I Need.

"Something sweet as a candy bar." I Can Understand It.

"Something there is about you that strikes a match in me." Something There Is About You.

"Something told me it was over." I'd Rather Go Blind.

"Something you got baby, makes me work all day." Something You Got.

"Something's goin' down like a waterfall, some strong feelings, some old love." Waterfall.

"Something's got a hold on me, something deep inside." Prisoner Of Your Love.

"Something's got a hold on me, yeah, oh, it must be love." Something's Got A Hold On Me.

"Sometimes I feel like a motherless child." Motherless Child.

"Sometimes I feel like I'm getting kinda low." There Goes Another Love Song.

"Sometimes I find I get to thinking of the past." Tonight Will Be Fine.

"Sometimes I listen to the falling rain." Baby, I'm Down.

"Sometimes I tell myself I'm leaving, and I'd like to think I could really go." After You.

"Sometimes I think I love you." Take It Like A Woman.

"Sometimes I will, then again I think I won't." Reelin' And Rockin'.

"Sometimes I wonder where I've been, who I am, do I fit in." Out Here On My Own.

"Sometimes I'm right and I can be wrong." Everyday People.

"Sometimes in our lives, we all have pain, we all have sorrow." Lean On Me.

"Sometimes it's hard to be a woman." Stand By Your Man.

"Sometimes late when things are real and people share the gift of gab between themselves...." Tin Man.

"Sometimes the love rhymes that fill the afternoon lose all their meaning with the rising sun." Do You Wanna Make Love.

"Sometimes we walk hand in hand by the sea and we breathe in the cool salty air." Wonderful! Wonderful!

"Sometimes when I'm down and out and all alone...." All I Ever Need Is You.

"Sometimes when your troubles seem more than you can afford...." I'll Be Your Shelter (In Time Of Storm).

"Sometimes you love me like a good man oughta." See Saw.

"Sometimes you win, sometimes you lose." Sweet Seasons.

"Somewhere back in time you became a friend of mine." Love's Grown Deep.

"Somewhere my love, there will be songs to sing." Somewhere, My Love.

"Somewhere over the rainbow, way up high, there's a land that I heard of once in a lullaby." Over The Rainbow.

"Son of a Tokyo Rose...." Harbor Lights.

"Son of Shaft, gonna be like my dad, son of Shaft." Son Of Shaft.

"Song of love is a sad song, hi-li-li, hi-li-li, hi-lo." Hi-Lili, Hi-Lo.

"Song sung blue, ev'rybody knows one." Song Sung Blue.

"Songbird sings from the heart each word can tear you apart." Songbird (D. Wolpert & S. Nelson).

"Sorry to disturb you, but I was in the neighborhood about a friend." Carrie.

"Sound of your footsteps telling me that you're near." Midnight Confessions.

"Sound that you're listening to is from my guitar that's named Lucille." Lucille (B.B. King).

"Southern man better keep your head." Southern Man.

"Southern nights, have you ever felt a southern night?" Southern Nights.

"Speak softly love and hold me warm against your heart." Speak Softly Love.

"Spendin' all my nights all my money goin' out on the town." Baby Come Back.

"Spending my days thinking about you girl." I'm Still In Love With You (A. Green, W. Mitchell & A. Jackson).

"Spent my days with a woman unkind." Going To California.

"Spirit move me ev'ry time I'm near you, whirling like a cyclone in my mind." Could It Be Magic.

"Splish splash, I was takin' a bath 'long about-a Saturday night." Splish Splash.

"Spring affair...." Spring Affair.

"Spring is here." Spring Is Here.

"Spring was never waiting for us, girl, it ran one step ahead as we followed in the dance." MacArthur Park.

"Springtime mama, be my lady." Springtime Mama.

"Stack your rope, hangman, stack it for a while." Hangman.

"Stand alone waiting on the mornin'...." Just Another Love Song.

"Stand, in the end you'll still be you." Stand.

"Standing at the threshold of a moment in my life." Standing At The Threshold.

"Standing in the shadows of love, I'm getting ready for the heart aches to come." Standing In The Shadows Of Love.

"Standing on a mountain looking down on a city, the way I feel is a doggone pity." Mountain Of Love.

"Standing on my pillow talking to the moon...." Blood Of The Sun.

"Standing on your window, honey, yes, I've been here before." Temporary Like Achilles.

"Star cruisin', lookin' for my star (in the night). Starcruiser.

"Stare at me and ya make me tense." Wimp.

"Starlight falling through your hair, sometimes I wonder if you know I'm there." Don't Cry Baby.

"Starry, starry night, paint your palette blue and grey." Vincent.

"Stars live in the evening, but the very young need the sun." Pretty Baby.

"Stars won't come out if they know that you're about, 'cause they couldn't match the glow of your eyes." Candida.

"Start with a man and you have one." Living Together, Growing Together.

"Starting today I'm teaching my heart not to ache any more." Starting Today.

"Stay away from my window; stay away from my back door too." Tonight's The Night (Gonna Be Alright).

"Stay close to me, give me your heart." Stay Close To Me.

"Stay for just a while." September Morn.

"Stayed in bed all mornin' just to pass the time." It's Too Late.

"Stayin' at home, waitin' for you." I'm Lookin' For Someone To Love.

"Stir it up and serve it." Stir It Up And Serve It.

"Steppin' out, the weekend's open wide." Stomp.

"Stir it up, little darlin', stir it up." Stir It Up.

"Stoned love, oh, yeah." Stoned Love.

"Stop! in the name of love before you break my heart." Stop In The Name Of Love.

"Stop oh yes, wait a minute Mister Postman." Please Mr. Postman.

"Stop playing that crazy thing!" Vo-do-do-de-o Blues.

"Stop, you better save me dear." <u>Love You Save</u>.

"Stories of the street are mine." <u>Stories Of The Street</u>.

"Strange things take place in my moondreams." <u>Moondreams</u>.

"Strolling along country roads with my baby, it starts to rain, it begins to pour." <u>Laughter In The Rain</u>.

"Strollin' in the park...." <u>Feel Like Makin' Love</u>.

"Stuck inside these four walls." <u>Band On The Run</u>.

"Such a feelin's comin' over me." <u>Top Of The World</u>.

"Such are the dreams of the every day housewife you see everywhere, any time of the day." <u>Dreams Of The Everyday Housewife</u>.

"Sugar, ah, honey, honey." <u>Sugar, Sugar</u>.

"Sugar Magnolia, blossoms blooming, heads all empty and I don't care." <u>Sugar Magnolia</u>.

"Sugar pie, honey bunch, you know that I love you." <u>I Can't Help Myself</u>.

"Summer me, winter me, and with your kisses morning me, evening me." <u>Summer Me, Winter Me</u>.

"Summer smiles, the summer knows, and unashamed, she sheds her clothes." <u>Summer Knows</u>.

"Summer time, summertime, sum-sum-sum-mertime." <u>Summertime, Summertime</u>.

"Summertime, time time, oh, an' the livin's easy." <u>Summertime</u>.

"Summer wind came blowing in across the sea." <u>Summer Wind</u>.

"Sun ashining, there's a plenty of life." <u>Since I Lost My Baby</u>.

"Sun goes down on a silky day; quarter moon walkin' thru the Milky Way." <u>Right Time Of The Night</u>.

"Sun is fading away." <u>I'll Be On My Way</u>.

"Sun is out, the sky is blue, there's not a cloud to spoil the view." <u>Raining In My Heart</u>.

"Sun is shining but it's raining in my heart." <u>Sun Is Shining</u>.

"Sunday morning, up with the lark, I think I'll take a walk in the park." <u>Beautiful Sunday</u>.

"Sunflower, good mornin'." <u>Sunflower</u>.

"Sun'll come out tomorrow, bet your bottom dollar that tomorrow there'll be sun." <u>Tomorrow</u>.

"Sunny, yesterday my life was filled with rain." <u>Sunny</u>.

"Sunrise doesn't last all morning, a cloudburst doesn't last all day." <u>All Things Must Pass</u>.

"Sunrise, shine down a little love on the world today." <u>Sunrise</u>.

"Sunshine blue skies please go away." <u>I Wish It Would Rain</u>.

"Sunshine came softly through my window today." <u>Sunshine Superman</u>.

"Sunshine go away today, I don't feel much like dancin'." <u>Sunshine (Go Away Today)</u>.

"Sunshine on my shoulders makes me happy." <u>Sunshine On My Shoulders</u>.

"Surfin' is the only life the only way for me, now, surf." <u>Surfin'</u>.

"Suzanne takes you down to her place near the river." <u>Suzanne</u>.

"Sways with a wiggle with a wiggle when she walks." <u>What Is Love</u>.

"Sweet as a honey bee but like a honey bee stings...." <u>It's The Same Old Song</u>.

"Sweet emotion, sweet emotion...." <u>Sweet Emotion</u>.

"Sweet talkin' guy, talkin' sweet kind of love." <u>Sweet Talkin' Guy</u>.

"Sweet things you do to me...." <u>I Love The Way You Love</u>.

"Sweet, wonderful you...." <u>You Make Loving Fun</u>.

"Swing your daddy, sexy mama." <u>Swing Your Daddy</u>.

"Take a bus, a train or a plane, to Hollywood." <u>In Hollywood (Everybody Is A Star)</u>.

"Take a look around you." <u>Fair Game</u>.

"Take a walk around midnight in the city." <u>Young Blood</u> (R. Jones).

"Take me home, take me home, I wanna feel you close to me." <u>Take Me Home</u>.

"Take me now baby, here as I am." <u>Because The Night</u>.

"Take off your shoes, let down your hair." <u>Slicin' Sand</u>.

"Take one fresh and tender kiss." <u>Memories Are Made Of This</u>.

"Take out the papers and the trash, or you don't get no spending cash." <u>Yakety Yak</u>.

"Take the last train to Clarksville and I'll meet you at the station." <u>Last Train To Clarksville</u>.

"Take the ribbon from your hair, shake it loose and let it fall." <u>Help Me Make It Through The Night</u>.

"Take them for the ride." <u>Rock Me</u>.

"Take to the highway, won't you lend me your name?" <u>Country Road</u>.

"Take your time, I can wait." <u>Take Your Time</u>.

"Takin' in the shade out of the sun." <u>Easy Come, Easy Go</u>.

"Talk to me baby, whisper in my ear." <u>Ko Ko Mo (I Love You So)</u>.

"Talked to my friend again today." <u>Goin' Up In Smoke</u>.

"Talkin' to myself and feelin' old." <u>Rainy Days And Mondays</u>.

"Tell Automatic Slim, tell Ram's Dopey Jim." <u>Wang-Dang-Doodle</u>.

"Tell it all, truth is gonna set yourself free." <u>Tell It All</u>.

"Tell me, how do you feel knowing he's my man?" <u>Leftovers</u>.

"Tell me now to just walk away." <u>Don't Tell My Heart To Stop Loving You.</u>

"Tell me, tell me, tell me, oh, who wrote the book of love." <u>Book Of Love.</u>

"Tell me, what in the world have I done?" <u>Tell Me</u> (C. Burnett).

"Tell me what you're gonna do." <u>Tell Me What You're Gonna Do.</u>

"Tell me where does the lovin' go when it's gone away?" <u>Where Does The Lovin' Go.</u>

"Tell me why nights are lonesome." <u>Tell Me</u> (J.W. Callahan & M. Kortlander).

"Tell me why you are crying son." <u>Day Is Done.</u>

"Tell me why you cried, and why you lied to me." <u>Tell Me Why.</u>

"Ten, nine, eight, seven, six, five, four, three, two, one, ah, ah, ah, ah, you set my lips on fire." <u>Instant Replay.</u>

"Ten percent of something...." <u>Ten Percent.</u>

"Tenement, a dirty street...." <u>Days Of Pearly Spencer.</u>

"Thank you for being a friend." <u>Thank You For Being A Friend.</u>

"Thanks for the times that you've given me, the memries are all in my mind." <u>Three Times A Lady.</u>

"That boy took my love away." <u>Ringo's Theme.</u>

"That day I first saw you on passing by I wanted to know your name but I was much too shy." <u>You Beat Me To The Punch.</u>

"That would be something, it really would be something." <u>That Would Be Something.</u>

"That's all for ev'ryone." <u>That's All For Everyone.</u>

"'That's dang'rous drivin', baby,' the policeman said." <u>Vengeance.</u>

"That's right, that's right I'm sad and blue 'cause I can't do the boo-ga-loo." <u>Gimme Dat Ding.</u>

"That's the way (uh-huh, uh-huh), I like it." <u>That's The Way I Like It.</u>

"That's what, that's what keeps me going." <u>Caretaker.</u>

"That's what you get for lovin' me." <u>For Lovin' Me.</u>

"That's when the music takes me, takes me to a brighter day." <u>That's When The Music Takes Me.</u>

"Then listen to the jingle, the rumble and the roar of the mighty rushing engine as she streams along the shore." <u>Wabash Cannon Ball.</u>

"There ain't no reason why you let me wait." <u>Set Me Free.</u>

"There ain't nothin' like the real thing baby." <u>Ain't Nothing Like The Real Thing.</u>

"There ain't nothing in this world for a boy and a girl but love, love, love." <u>Love, Love, Love.</u>

"There ain't nothing in this world I couldn't do." <u>La, La, La.</u>

"There are diamonds and pearls, em'ralds and rings." <u>Diamonds And Pearls.</u>

"There are places I'll remember all my life though some have changed." <u>In My Life.</u>

"There are times when a woman has to say what's on her mind." <u>Torn Between Two Lovers.</u>

"There been times in my life I've spent wondering why." <u>This Is It.</u>

"There comes Fannie walking down the street." <u>Hey, Miss Fannie.</u>

"There could never be a portrait of my love." <u>Portrait Of My Love.</u>

"There goes another day and I wonder why you and I keep tellin' lies." <u>Child's Claim To Fame.</u>

"There goes my baby movin' on down the line." <u>There Goes My Baby.</u>

"There goes my baby with someone new." <u>Bye, Bye Love.</u>

"There he sits with a pen and a yellow pad." <u>Watchin' Scotty Grow.</u>

"There I was at the immigration scene, shinin' and feelin' clean, could it be a sin?" <u>Immigration Man.</u>

"There I was with the old man, stranded again, so off I'd ran." <u>Dog & Butterfly.</u>

"There is a garden something like the shadow of a butterfly." <u>Magic Garden.</u>

"There is a house in New Orleans they call the Rising Sun." <u>House Of The Rising Sun.</u>

"There is a rose in Spanish Harlem." <u>Spanish Harlem.</u>

"There is a town in North Ontario, with dream-comfort memory to spare." <u>Helpless.</u>

"There is a young cowboy, he lives on the range." <u>Sweet Baby James.</u>

"There is nothing that is wrong in wanting you to stay here with me." <u>Lay Down Sally.</u>

"There is someone walking behind you, turn around, look at me." <u>Turn Around, Look At Me.</u>

"There may be other hands but they're just imitation." <u>Anywhere.</u>

"There must be some misunderstanding." <u>Misunderstanding.</u>

"'There must be some way out of here,' said the joker to the thief." <u>All Along The Watchtower.</u>

"There must be thousands of people out there who search for love and find more than their share." <u>Lucky Me.</u>

"There she stood in the street smiling from her head to her feet." <u>All Right Now.</u>

"There she was just a walkin' down the street." <u>Do Wah Diddy Diddy.</u>

"There there's a place where I can go when I feel low, when I feel blue...." <u>There's A Place.</u>

"There was a girl, there was a boy." <u>Morning Side Of The Mountain.</u>

"There was a lights out television show, there was a Amos and Andy on the radio." <u>Like A Sunday In Salem.</u>

"There was a man." <u>Solitaire</u>.

"There was a tall oak tree that loved the babblin' brook." <u>Tall Oak Tree</u>.

"There was a thrill up on the hill." <u>Do That Stuff</u>.

"There was a time I was so sad." <u>Music In My Life</u>.

"There was a time in this fair land when the railroad did not run." <u>Canadian Railroad Trilogy</u>.

"There was a time not too far gone when I was changed by just a song." <u>Hot Summer Nights</u>.

"There was a time when I was in a hurry as you are." <u>Have You Never Been Mellow</u>.

"There was a wicked messenger from Eli he did come." <u>Wicked Messenger</u>.

"There were two men down, and the score was tied in the bottom of the eighth when the pitcher died." <u>Night Game</u>.

"There you are, looking just the same as you did last time I touched you." <u>Looks Like We Made It</u>.

"There you go and baby, here am I." <u>It Doesn't Matter Anymore</u>.

"There you stood on the edge of your feather, expecting to fly." <u>Expecting To Fly</u>.

"There'll be no strings to bind your hands." <u>Angel Of The Morning</u>.

"There'll come a time when all of us must leave here." <u>Art Of Dying</u>.

"There'll never be a better love." <u>There'll Never Be</u>.

"There's a cold, cold feeling in my heart." <u>Blues Get Off My Shoulder</u>.

"There's a crazy little house beyond the tracks." <u>Sugar Shack</u>.

"There's a girl I know...." <u>One Of Them Is Me</u>.

"There's a kind of hush all over the world tonight." <u>There's A Kind Of Hush</u>.

"There's a lady who's sure all that glitters is gold and she's buying a stairway to heaven." <u>Stairway To Heaven</u>.

"There's a light, a certain kind of light that never shone on me." <u>To Love Somebody</u>.

"There's a little cabin in the sky." <u>Cabin In The Sky</u>.

"There's a lot of things I want." <u>Just Once In My Life</u>.

"There's a lot to learn for wastin' time." <u>Look Out For My Love</u>.

"There's a man at my house, he's so big and strong." <u>Color Him Father</u>.

"There's a man by my side walking." <u>Carry It On</u>.

"There's a man in New Orleans who plays rock and roll." <u>King Creole</u>.

"There's a man in the funny papers we all know Alley Oop...." <u>Alley Oop</u>.

"There's a meetin' here tonight." <u>There's A Meetin' Here Tonight</u>.

"There's a moon out tonight." <u>There's A Moon Out Tonight</u>.

"There's a moon that's big and bright in the Milky Way tonight." <u>Got A Lot O' Livin' To Do</u>.

"There's a new kind of dancing, it's gonna be the rage." <u>Attitude Dancing</u>.

"There's a new sun a-risin'." <u>Biggest Part Of Me</u>.

"There's a new world coming and it's just around the bend." <u>New World Coming</u>.

"There's a new world somewhere they call the promised land." <u>I'll Never Find Another You</u>.

"There's a place I can get to where I'm safe from the city blues." <u>Johnny's Garden</u>.

"There's a place not too far away from here, out with the cows and the Lone Star beer, where the livin' is, lovin' is quite all right with me." <u>Texas</u>.

"There's a reason for the sunshine sky." <u>Let Your Love Flow</u>.

"There's a saying old says that love is blind." <u>Someone To Watch Over Me</u>.

"There's s star up in the sky." <u>Little Star</u>.

"There's a woman that you ought to know." <u>Rock 'N Roll Woman</u>.

"There's a world out there just waiting for you." <u>Take Life A Little Easier</u>.

"There's a wren in a willow wood." <u>Love Song</u>.

"There's a young man that I know, his age is twenty one." <u>Someday Soon</u>.

"There's been some hard feelings here about some words that were said." <u>One Man's Ceiling Is Another Man's Floor</u>.

"There's blood in the streets; it's up to my ankles." <u>Peace Frog</u>.

"There's got to be a morning after, if we can hold on through the night." <u>Morning After</u>.

"There's guns across the river aimin' at ya." <u>Billy</u>.

"There's mosquitoes on the river, fish are rising up like birds." <u>Music Never Stopped</u>.

"There's no cause to think that I won't stay." <u>We're All The Way</u>.

"There's no place in this world where I'll belong when I'm gone." <u>When I'm Gone</u>.

"There's no point in asking, you'll get no reply." <u>Pretty Vacant</u>.

"There's nothin' you can do to turn me away." <u>Right Thing To Do</u>.

"There's nothing left for me, of days that used to be." <u>Among My Souvenirs</u>.

"There's nothing more that I'd like to do than take the floor and dance with you." <u>Shake Your Groove Thing</u>.

"There's nothing 'round here I believe in 'cept you, yeah you." <u>Nobody 'Cept You</u>.

"There's nothing you can do that can't be done." <u>All You Need Is Love</u>.

"There's somebody waiting alone in the street for someone to walk up and greet." Someone To Lay Down Beside Me.

"There's something happening here." For What It's Worth.

"There's talk on the street; it sounds so familiar." New Kid In Town.

"These are the eyes that never know how to smile." Show And Tell.

"These eyes cry ev'ry night for you." These Eyes.

"These here ladies are at our discretion, so we can get off." Get Off.

"They asked me how I knew my true love was true." Smoke Gets In Your Eyes.

"They call her hard hearted Hannah." Hard Hearted Hannah.

"They call it a teen-age crush." Teen Age Crush.

"They call it stormy Monday." Call It Stormy Monday.

"They call me a gypsy man." Gypsy Man.

"They call me poor boy, poor boy, but I ain't lonesome and I ain't blue." Poor Boy.

"They call your daddy 'Big Boots'." Big Boots.

"They get up ev'ry mornin' from the 'larm clock warnin', take the eight fifteen into the city." Takin' Care Of Business.

"They give us a room with a view of the beautiful Rhine." G.I. Blues.

"They paved paradise and put up a parking lot." Big Yellow Taxi.

"They promised us that we would have peace in our time." In Our Time.

"They sat together in the park." Simple Twist Of Fate.

"They say ev'rything can be replaced, yet ev'ry distance is not near." I Shall Be Released.

"They say no fool beneath the sun would die for love." I'm A Fool For You.

"They say that Richard Cory owns one half of this whole town." Richard Cory.

"They say that you're a runaround lover tho you say it isn't so." Night Has A Thousand Eyes.

"They say the neon lights are bright on Broadway." On Broadway.

"They say we're young and we don't know, won't find out till we grow." I Got You Babe.

"They tell us that we lost our tails evolving up from little snails." Jocko Homo.

"They try to tell us we're too young." Too Young.

"They warned me when you kissed me your love would ricochet." Ricochet.

"The're gonna put me in the movies." Act Naturally.

"They're really rockin' in Boston, in Pittsburgh, P.A." Sweet Little Sixteen.

"Think it over, some people say you've been messin' around." Think It Over (C. Houston, A. Fields & M. Zager).

"Think of your fellow man, lend him a helping hand, put a little love in your heart." Put A Little Love In Your Heart.

"Thinkin' 'bout the times you drove in my car." Badge.

"This cat named Mickey came from out of town, yea!" Mickey's Monkey.

"This day and age we're living in gives cause for apprehension." As Time Goes By.

"This girl in her bedroom doin' her homework, she's a-foolin' with her logarithms, she's goin' berserk." Who Listens To The Radio.

"This has got to be the saddest day of my life." Kiss And Say Goodbye.

"This heart of mine carries a heavy load." All I Need.

"This here's a story 'bout Billy Joe and Bobby Sue." Take The Money And Run.

"This I swear is true." This I Swear.

"This is a thing I've never known before--it's called easy living." Easy Living.

"This is for all the lonely people thinking that life has passed them by." Lonely People.

"This is insane; all you did was say hello, speak my name." Deja Vu.

"This is my heaven, being here with you." This Is My Heaven.

"This is my same old coat and my same old shoes." Brand New Me.

"This is not a sad song, a sad song, to sing when you're alone." Song Sung Blue.

"This is the day of the expanding man." Deacon Blues.

"This is the early evening edition of the news." 7 O'Clock News/Silent Night.

"This is the modern world!" Modern World

"This is the story of Sodom and Gomorrah." Sodom And Gomorrah.

"This is the town where we used to live." Sunny And Me.

"This is the way that I feel when I'm with you baby." This Is The Way I Feel.

"This just might be the hardest thing I'll ever have to do." Right Feeling At The Wrong Time.

"This land is your land, this land is my land." This Land Is Your Land.

"This magic moment, so diff'rent and so new was like any other...." This Magic Moment.

"This old heart of mine been broke a thousand times." This Old Heart Of Mine (Is Weak For You).

"This one'll never sell, they'll never understand." This One's For You.

"This poor child was standing on the corner when up walked this woman that looked good all over." Happy Hooker.

"This silver bird takes me 'cross the sky." Home And Dry.

"This song has nothing tricky about it." <u>This Song</u>.

"This song is called Alice's Restaurant." <u>Alice's Restaurant</u>.

"This story has no moral, this story has no end." <u>Frankie And Johnnie</u>.

"This thing called love, I just can't handle it." <u>Crazy Little Thing Called Love</u>.

"This train don't carry no gamblers, this train." <u>This Train</u>.

"Tho we gotta say goodbye for the summer...." <u>Sealed With A Kiss</u>.

"Those school girl days of telling tales and biting nails are gone." <u>To Sir, With Love</u>.

"Thou shall never love another." <u>Ten Commandments Of Love</u>.

"Though we try to be masters of our soul...." <u>It's Not For Me To Say</u>.

"Though we're goin' our sep'rate ways, there can only be brighter days." <u>When I Wanted You</u>.

"Though you sit in another chair, I can feel you here." <u>Let It Down</u>.

"Thought I was in love before, then you moved in next door, pretty blue eyes." <u>Pretty Blue Eyes</u>.

"Thousand stars in the sky, like the stars in your eyes...." <u>Thousand Stars</u>.

"Three angels up above the street." <u>Three Angels</u>.

"Three coins in the fountain...." <u>Three Coins In The Fountain</u>.

"Three nights ago I was at a disco." <u>Ain't Gonna Bump No More</u>.

"Three o'clock in the morning and it looks like it's gonna be another sleepless night." <u>Talkin' In Your Sleep</u>.

"Thrill is gone, the thrill is gone away." <u>Thrill Is Gone</u>.

"Through early morning fog I see visions of the things to be: the pains that are withheld for me." <u>M*A*S*H, Song From</u>.

"Through the corridors of sleep, past the shadows dark and deep, my mind dances and leaps in confusion." <u>Flowers Never Bend With The Rainfall</u>.

"Through the mirror of my mind...." <u>Reflections</u>.

"Throughout history there have been many songs written about the eternal triangle." <u>Tom Dooley</u>.

"Throw my ticket out the window." <u>Tonight I'll Be Staying Here With You</u>.

"Til the morning comes, it'll do you fine." <u>Till The Morning Comes</u>.

"Time is on my side." <u>Time Is On My Side</u>.

"Time is on my side tho' the world keeps gettin' older." <u>Look In My Eyes Pretty Woman</u>.

"Time it was, and what a time it was, it was a time of innocence, a time of confidences." <u>Bookends</u>.

"Time keeps movin' on, friends they turn away." <u>Kozmic Blues</u>.

"Time keeps slippin', slippin', slippin'...." <u>Fly Like An Eagle</u>.

"Time passes slowly up here in the mountains." <u>Time Passes Slowly</u>.

"Time time and again I've seen you staring out at me." <u>Angry Eyes</u>.

"Time, time, time, see what's become of me." <u>Hazy Shade Of Winter</u>.

"Time, you found time enough to love." <u>Somewhere In The Night</u>.

"Tip top tip, doot doot doo doo, time keeps slippin', slippin', slippin...." <u>Fly Like An Eagle</u>.

"To be alone with you...." <u>To Be Alone With You</u>.

"To be with you is nice, though our love seems on ice." <u>One More Try</u>.

"To dream the impossible dream." <u>Impossible Dream</u>.

"To ev'rything (turn, turn, turn), there is a season...." <u>Turn! Turn! Turn</u>.

"To know, know, know, you (him) is to love, love, love you (him)." <u>To Know You (Him) Is To Love You (Him)</u>.

"To lead a better life I need my love to be here." <u>Here, There And Everywhere</u>.

"To make you laugh I'd play the fool for you." <u>Oh Me Oh My I'm A Fool For You Baby</u>.

"To my surprise one hundred stories here...." <u>Disco Inferno</u>.

"To sail on a dream on a crystal clear ocean." <u>Calypso</u>.

"To save my soul I can't get a date." <u>Western Movies</u>.

"Today while the blossoms still cling to the vine, I'll taste your strawberries, I'll drink your sweet wine." <u>Today</u>.

"Today you came by to tell me you are leaving me." <u>Hold On To My Love</u>.

"Today's the day you're telling him that he's got to set you free." <u>Run, Woman, Run</u>.

"Together we will go our way." <u>Go West</u>.

"Told me darlin' that you had to go." <u>Money Won't Change You</u>.

"Tom, get your plane right on time." <u>The Only Living Boy In New York</u>.

"Tonight I wanna give it all to you." <u>I Was Made For Lovin' You</u>.

"Tonight I'm gonna break away." <u>Crazy Love</u>.

"Tonight you're mine completely." <u>Will You Love Me Tomorrow</u>.

"Too many broken hearts have fallen in the river; too many lonely souls have drifted out to sea." <u>Things We Do For Love</u>.

"Too many long conversations, no one is hearing a word." <u>Dancin' Shoes</u>.

"Too many teardrops for one heart to be cryin'." <u>96 Tears</u>.

"Took a walk and passed your house late last night." <u>Silhouettes</u>.

"Took my fam'ly away from my Carolina home." <u>Fire On The Mountain</u>.

"Took the last train to San Tropez." <u>Took The Last Train</u>.

"Toot toot, hey, beep, beep, toot beep, bad girls, talkin' 'bout the sad girls." <u>Bad Girls</u>.

"Touch me in the morning, then just walk away." <u>Touch Me In The Morning</u>.

"Touch me, take me in your arms, shelter me from harm." <u>You Take My Heart Away</u>.

"Touch my body, make it funky." <u>Keep On Dancin'</u>.

"Tough mama meat shakin' on your bones." <u>Tough Mama</u>.

"Tra la la lala la la la la, happy birthday sweet sixteen." <u>Happy Birthday Sweet Sixteen</u>.

"Trailer for sale or rent." <u>King Of The Road</u>.

"Trails of troubles, roads of battles, paths of victory I shall walk." <u>Paths Of Victory</u>.

"Trav'lin', trav'lin', I've been a-trav'elin' on." <u>Lonesome Traveler</u>.

"Trav'ling lady, stay awhile, until the night is over." <u>Winter Lady</u>.

"Treasure of love is easy to find." <u>Treasure Of Love</u>.

"Tried to amend my carnivorous habits." <u>Cheeseburger In Paradise</u>.

"Trina wears her wampum beads." <u>Ladies Of The Canyon</u>.

"Truckin', got my chips cashed in." <u>Truckin'</u>.

"Try just a little bit harder so I can love, love, love you." <u>Try (Just A Little Bit Harder)</u>.

"Try me, try me, darling tell me, I need you." <u>Try Me</u>.

"Try to remember the kind of September when life was slow and oh, so mellow." <u>Try To Remember</u>.

"Try to see it my way." <u>We Can Work It Out</u>.

"Tryin' hard now." <u>Gonna Fly Now</u>.

"Tryin' to find what's heavy, that's been messin' up my mind." <u>Heavy Makes You Happy</u>.

"Tryin' to love two ain't easy to do." <u>Tryin' To Love Two</u>.

"Tuesday afternoon, I'm just beginning to see...." <u>Tuesday Afternoon</u>.

"Turn off the lights and light a candle." <u>Turn Off The Lights</u>.

"Turn on the radio, we'll play it way down low." <u>We'll Never Have To Say Goodbye Again</u>.

"Tutti frutti au rutti." <u>Tutti Frutti</u>.

"Twas in another lifetime, one of toil and blood." <u>Shelter From The Storm</u>.

"Twas in the spring one sunny day my sweetheart left me." <u>Sittin' On Top Of The World</u>.

"'Twas teatime at the circus, Chicky, he was there." <u>'Twas Teatime At The Circus</u>.

"Tweedlee tweedlee tweedlee dee, I'm as happy as can be." <u>Tweedlee Dee</u>.

"Twilight listening...." <u>Miles</u>.

"Twilight on the frozen lake." <u>Never Say Goodbye</u>.

"Two doors down they're laughin' and drinkin' and havin' a party." <u>Two Doors Down</u>.

"Two girls for ev'ry boy." <u>Surf City</u>.

"Two o'clock in the morn, knocking on my door." <u>Sweet Marjorene</u>.

"Ugh! Aw sooky sooky now." <u>Groove Me</u>.

"Um, now is the time for you to be somebody, be anything you want to be, yeah, woh." <u>Here Comes The Sun</u> (A. Middleton, L. Taylor, L. James, L. Barry & A. Austin).

"Um, yea, I swear to you people, it must be my fate." <u>My Roommate</u>.

"Under my thumb's the girl who once had me down." <u>Under My Thumb</u>.

"Understanding is the best thing in the world." <u>Understanding</u>.

"Unless you believe in magic there ain't much left you can be." <u>Buyin' Time</u>.

"Uno mundo, somebody's dreaming." <u>Un-Mundo</u>.

"Up in the mornin' and out to school." <u>School Day (Ring Ring Goes The Bell)</u>.

"Up in the mornin' out on the job, work like the devil for my pay." <u>That Lucky Old Sun</u>.

"Up on the white veranda, she wears a necktie and a Panama hat." <u>Black Diamond Bay</u>.

"Upon the bitter green she walked." <u>Bitter Green</u>.

"Uptown got its hustlers, the Bow'ry got its bums." <u>You Don't Mess Around With Jim</u>.

"Used to think that life was sweet." <u>We Don't Talk Anymore</u>.

"Vernon'll meet me when the BOAC lands." <u>Montego Bay</u>.

"Very old friend came by today." <u>His Latest Flame</u>.

"Very superstitious, writings on the wall." <u>Superstition</u>.

"Village people, now is the time." <u>Village People</u>.

"Virgil Caine is the name, and I served on the Danville train." <u>Night They Drove Old Dixie Down</u>.

"Volare, oh, oh!" <u>Volare</u>.

"Wade into the river." <u>Bracero</u>.

"Wah Wah Wahtusi, c'mon and take a chance and get a with this dance." <u>Wah-Watusi</u>.

"Wait a minute, baby." <u>Sara</u> (S. Nicks).

"Waiting for the break of day." <u>25 Or 6 To 4</u>.

"Wake of the flood, laughing water, forty-nine...." <u>Here Come Sunshine</u>.

"Wake up ev'rybody no more sleepin' in bed." <u>Wake Up Everybody</u>.

"Wake up, little Susie, wake up." <u>Wake Up Little Susie</u>.

"Wake up, Maggie, I think I got something to say to you." <u>Maggie May</u>.

"Wake up, the morning's over." <u>This Girl</u>.

"Walk along the river, sweet lullaby." <u>Blue Sky</u>.

"Walk down to the beach at sunset." <u>Never Ending</u>.

"Walk hand in hand with me through all eternity." <u>Walk Hand In Hand</u>.

"Walk right in, set right down...." <u>Walk Right In</u>.

"Walked all day 'til my feet were tired." <u>Got A Job</u>.

"Walked in the joint; they were lined up back to back." <u>Stuff Like That</u>.

"Walkin' in the park just the other day, baby...." <u>Misty Mountain Hop</u>.

"Walking by myself I hope you understand." <u>Walking By Myself</u>.

"Walking down the street smoggy eyed...." <u>World Is A Ghetto</u>.

"Walking through the park, it wasn't quite dark, there was a man sitting on a bench." <u>Curious Mind</u>.

"Wall is high, the black barn...." <u>Kimberly</u>.

"Wallflow'r, wallflow'r, won't you dance with me?" <u>Wallflower</u>.

"Walls have ears, ears that hear each little sound you make." <u>Walls Have Ears</u>.

"Wanna sing this song for ya'." <u>My Love Ain't Never Been This Strong</u>.

"Wanted man in California...." <u>Wanted Man</u>.

"War! Um, what is it good for?" <u>War</u>.

"Warden threw a party in the county jail." <u>Jailhouse Rock</u>.

"Warm and lovely mystery, fire smiling through." <u>Under The Falling Sky</u>.

"Warm me from the wind and take my hand." <u>Chilling Of The Evening</u>.

"Warmer than sunshine baby, sweeter than tears, that's how my life has been since you first appeared." <u>You Got It</u>.

"Was a hot afternoon the last day of June, and the sun was a demon." <u>Summer</u>.

"Was a sunny day, not a cloud was in the sky." <u>Was A Sunny Day</u>.

"Was ridin' along side the highway." <u>Sweet Hitch-Hiker</u>.

"Wash away my troubles, wash away my pain, with the rain of Shambala." <u>Shambala</u>.

"Wasn't it good the way I touched you late last night?" <u>Wasn't It Good</u>.

"Wasted days and wasted nights I have left for you behind." <u>Wasted Days And Wasted Nights</u>.

"Watch closely now." <u>Watch Closely Now</u>.

"Watch out now, take care, beware of falling swingers, dropping all around you." <u>Beware Of Darkness</u>.

"Watch that band, baby, they've got something." <u>7-6-5-4-3-2-1</u>.

"Watching the sun, watching it come, watching it come up over the rooftops." <u>To The Morning</u>.

"Way back when I saw magic." <u>Way Back When</u>.

"Way down here you need a reason to move." <u>Mexico</u>.

"Way down yonder in the blue bonnet nation, people been a waiting just to hear his sweet name." <u>Blue Bonnet Nation</u>.

"Way downtown foolin' around, took me to the jail." <u>Way Downtown</u>.

"Way I feel is like a robin." <u>Way I Feel</u>.

"'Way I see it,' he said, 'you just can't win it'." <u>Free Man In Paris</u>.

"Way on the other side of the Hudson, deep in the bosom of suburbia...." <u>Ariel</u>.

"Way you make me feel like I belong...." <u>That's Why</u>.

"Way you read the crowd--the way you make them play...." <u>Hollywood</u> (B. Scaggs & M. Omartian).

"We all came out of Montreux on the Lake Geneva shoreline." <u>Smoke On The Water</u>.

"We are amazed but not amused by all the things you say that you'll do." <u>You Haven't Done Nothin'</u>.

"We are family." <u>We Are Family</u>.

"We are not helpless; we are men." <u>We Are Not Helpless</u>.

"We are winners and losers." <u>Shinin' On</u>.

"We been runnin' away from somethin' we both know." <u>One Less Set Of Footsteps</u>.

"We can never know about the days to come but we think about them anyway." <u>Anticipation</u>.

"We carried you in our arms on Independence Day." <u>Tears Of Rage</u>.

"We come from the land of the ice and snow." <u>Immigrant Song</u>.

"We come on the Sloop John B." <u>Sloop John B</u>.

"We don't exist, we are nothing but shadow and mist." <u>Last Tango In Paris</u>.

"We don't need no education." <u>Another Brick In The Wall (Part II)</u>.

"We don't smoke marijuana in Muskogee." <u>Okie From Muskogee</u>.

"We get it on most ev'ry night." <u>Dancin' In The Moonlight</u>.

"We get up early and we work all day." <u>All Night Long</u>.

"We got somethin' we both know it; we don't talk too much about it." <u>Refugee</u>.

"We had been friends for a year and a day, always around for each other." <u>This Is Love</u>.

"We had joy, we had fun, we had seasons in the sun." <u>Seasons In The Sun</u>.

"We hear you're leaving, that's o.k." <u>Rikki, Don't Lose That Number.</u>

"We hold these truths to be self-evident." <u>Declaration.</u>

"We lived in the country when I was a child." <u>Where Did All The Good Times Go.</u>

"We may never love like this again." <u>We May Never Love Like This Again.</u>

"We may still have time." <u>Crazy On You.</u>

"We shall overcome." <u>We Shall Overcome.</u>

"We skipped the light fandango." <u>Whiter Shade Of Pale.</u>

"We starve, look at one another short of breath." <u>Let The Sunshine In.</u>

"We used to laugh, we used to cry." <u>I Need You.</u>

"We walked to the sea, just my father and me, and the dogs played around in the sand." <u>Ships.</u>

"We were born before the wind." <u>Into The Mystic.</u>

"We were born to be alive." <u>Born To Be Alive.</u>

"We were married on a rainy day; the sky was yellow and the grass was grey." <u>I Do It For Your Love.</u>

"We were very happy, well at least I thought we were." <u>Say, Has Anybody Seen My Sweet Gypsy Rose.</u>

"We who are young can know the meaning of love." <u>Why Don't They Understand.</u>

"Wee ooh wimoweh." <u>Lion Sleeps Tonight.</u>

"Welcome back, your dreams were your ticket out." <u>Welcome Back.</u>

"Welcome to my nightmare." <u>Welcome To My Nightmare.</u>

"Well, a hard headed woman, a soft hearted man been the cause of trouble ever since the world began." <u>Hard Headed Woman.</u>

"Well all right so I'm being foolish." <u>Well All Right.</u>

"Well, anytime, anyplace, anywhere, just say the word, you'll be heard." <u>Anytime, Anyplace, Anywhere.</u>

"Well, babe, you could be a-standing in my kitchen or floating on your back in a deep blue sea." <u>Look Away.</u>

"We'll be fighting in the streets with our children at our feet." <u>Won't Get Fooled Again.</u>

"Well come on pretty baby won't you walk with me." <u>Slow Down.</u>

"Well, do you want to dance and hold my hand?" <u>Do You Want To Dance.</u>

"Well, don't leave me baby (no, no, no, no, no)." <u>No, No, No, No.</u>

"Well, don't you know, baby, child...." <u>Don't You Know.</u>

"Well early in the mornin' 'bout the break of day, I asked the Lord help me find the way." <u>Early In The Morning</u> (P. Stookey).

"Well, early in the mornin' til late at night, I got a poison headache but I feel all right." <u>Pledging My Time.</u>

"Well, Frankie Lee and Judas Priest, they were the best of friends." <u>Ballad Of Frankie Lee And Judas Priest.</u>

"Well have you seen that girl in the corner?" <u>Ebony Eyes.</u>

"Well, he went down to dinner in his Sunday best; excitable boy, they all said." <u>Excitable Boy.</u>

"Well, hello there good old friend of mine, you've been reaching for yourself for such a long time." <u>Come In From The Rain.</u>

"Well, honey, I've got what you need when you're layin' down home alone." <u>I Put A Spell On You</u> (L. Russell).

"Well, hop in the hack then turn on the key." <u>Let Me Sing Your Blues Away.</u>

"Well, I been havin' a little trouble, Lord, but I'm keepin' it together, yeah." <u>Gone, Gone, Gone.</u>

"Well, I been lookin' real hard and I'm try'n to find a job, but it just keeps gettin' tougher ev'ry day." <u>Rock 'N Me.</u>

"Well, I built me a raft and she's ready for floatin'." <u>Black Water.</u>

"Well, I can't forget this evening." <u>Without You.</u>

"Well, I could just sit around makin' music all day long." <u>I Believe In Music.</u>

"Well, I dated your big sister, and I took her to a show." <u>Little Sister.</u>

"Well, I don't know where they come from but they sure do come." <u>Cat Scratch Fever.</u>

"Well, I don't know why I came here tonight." <u>Stuck In The Middle With You.</u>

"Well, I dreamed I saw the knights in armor coming, sayin' something about a queen." <u>After The Gold Rush.</u>

"Well, I followed her to the station with a suitcase in my hand." <u>Love In Vain.</u>

"Well, I got my mail late last night." <u>Steel Rail Blues.</u>

"Well, I had just got out from the county prison, doin' ninety days for non support." <u>Workin' At The Car Wash Blues.</u>

"Well, I have known you since you were a small boy." <u>Legend In Your Own Time.</u>

"Well, I heard some people talkin' just the other day." <u>Already Gone.</u>

"Well, I know it's kind of late." <u>I'll Have To Say I Love You In A Song.</u>

"Well, I lay my head on the railroad track, waitin' on the Double E." <u>Poor Poor Pitiful Me.</u>

"Well, I make it all right from Monday morning til Friday night." <u>Lonely Weekends.</u>

"Well, I never been to Spain but I kinda like the music." <u>Never Been To Spain.</u>

"Well, I never kept a dollar past sunset." <u>Happy</u> (M. Jagger & K. Richard).

"Well, I never will forget the first time that we met." <u>Baby Boy (Big Ole Baby Boy).</u>

"Well, I saw my baby walking, with another man today." <u>See You Later, Alligator.</u>

FIND THAT TUNE

"Well, I saw the thing acomin' out of the sky." Purple People Eater.

"Well, I see you got your brand new leopard-skin pill-box hat." Leopard-Skin Pill-Box Hat.

"Well, I see you watching me just like a hawk." I Love The Life I Live.

"Well, I take whatever I want and baby, I want you." Can't Get Enough.

"Well, I think I'm going out of my head." Goin' Out Of My Head.

"Well, I think it's time to get ready to re'lize just what I have found." Love Is Alive.

"Well, I told you once and I told you twice." Last Time.

"Well, I tried to make it Sunday, but I got so damn depressed that I set my sights on Monday and I got myself undressed." Sister Golden Hair.

"Well, I was feelin' oh so bad now." Good Lovin'.

"Well, I was sixteen and sick of school." That's Rock 'N Roll.

"Well, I went to a dance the other night." Over And Over (R. Byrd).

"Well, I woke up Sunday mornin' with no way to hold my head that didn't hurt." Sunday Mornin' Comin' Down.

"Well, I'd rather see you dead little girl than to be with another man." Run For Your Life.

"Well, if you ever go back in the Wooley Swamp, well, you better not go at night." Legend Of The Wooley Swamp.

"Well, if you're trav'lin' in the north country fair...." Girl Of The North Country.

"Well, I'll be back, yeah, I'll be back, like a homesick train on a one way track." I'll Be Back.

"Well, I'll be damned; here comes your ghost again." Diamonds And Rust.

"Well, I'll be doggone if I wouldn't work all day." I'll Be Doggone.

"Well, I'm a voodoo chile, Lord, I'm a voodoo child." Voodoo Chile.

"Well, I'm a-runnin' down the road try'n to loosen my load, I've got seven women on my mind." Take It Easy.

"Well, I'm a-write a little letter, gonna mail it to my local D.J." Roll Over, Beethoven.

"Well, I'm goin' down the road stop in Fanny May's." Don't Start Me Talkin.

"Well, I'm hot blooded, check it and see." Hot Blooded.

"Well, I'm just out of school like a real, real cool." Real Wild Child.

"Well, I'm the same old girl that I used to be, I haven't changed at all." Rhumba Girl.

"Well, in Nineteen Forty One a happy father had a son." 1941.

"Well, it's a marvelous night for a moondance with the stars up above in your eyes." Moondance.

"Well, it's been buildin' up inside of me for oh, I don't know how long." Don't Worry, Baby.

"Well, it's not far down to paradise." Sailing (C. Cross).

"Well, it's one for the money, two for the show, three to get ready, now go, cat, go." Blue Suede Shoes.

"Well, it's Saturday night and I just got paid." Rip It Up.

"Well, it's such a strange world that I'm living in." Roll Away The Stone.

"Well, I've already had two beers, I'm ready for the broom." Please Mrs. Henry.

"Well, I've got to run to keep from hiding." Midnight River.

"Well, I've got two lovers and I ain't ashamed." Two Lovers.

"Well, I've seen you before on that discoteque floor." If You Can't Give Me Love.

"Well, lawdy, lawdy, lawdy Miss Clawdy." Lawdy, Miss Clawdy.

"Well, life on a farm is kinda laid back." Thank God I'm A Country Boy.

"Well, listen, little lady, you're steppin' out of line." Steppin' Out Of Line.

"Well, Lord, I've gotta raise a fuss, Lord, I've gotta raise a holler." Summertime Blues.

"Well, love's got a hold on me, won't let go." Rainbow In Your Eyes.

"Well, my temp'rature's rising and my feet on the floor." Gimme Some Lovin'.

"Well, my time went so quickly, I went lickety-splitly out to my ol' fifty five." Ol' 55.

"Well, no one told me about her, the way she lied." She's Not There.

"Well, not too long ago in nineteen forty-four...." Jump Shout Boogie.

"Well, now Frankie was a woman." Frankie's Blues.

"Well, now, it takes more than a robin to make the winter go." Baby (You've Got What It Takes).

"Well now, listen here people I'm about to sing this song." Wild About My Lovin'.

"Well now, me and Homer Jones and Big John Talley had a big crap game goin' back in the alley." When You're Hot You're Hot.

"Well now they call my baby Patty but her real name, her real name, her real name is Linda Lu." Linda Lu.

"Well, she comes from Tallahassee." Tallahassee Lassie.

"Well, she was just seventeen, and you know what I mean...." I Saw Her Standing There.

"Well, she's all you'd ever want." She's A Lady.

"We'll sing in the sunshine, we'll laugh ev'ry day." We'll Sing In The Sunshine.

"Well smokestack lightnin' shinin' just like gold." Smokestack Lightnin'.

"Well, that big dumb blonde with her wheel in the gorge...." Million Dollar Bash.

"Well, the comic book and me, just us, we caught the bus." Yea! Heavy And A Bottle Of Bread.

"Well, the eagle's been flyin' slow and the flag's been flyin' low." In America.

"Well, the first days are the hardest days...." Uncle John's Band.

"Well, the kids are all hopped up and ready to go." Sheena Is A Punk Rocker.

"Well, the Lone Ranger and Tonto...." Bob Dylan's Blues.

"Well, the rainman comes with his magic wand...." I Wanna Be Your Lover (B. Dylan).

"Well, the southside of Chicago is the baddest part of town." Bad, Bad Leroy Brown.

"Well, the talk on the street says you might go solo." I Need To Know.

"Well, the train they're try'n to switch is runnin' right on time." South's Gonna Do It.

"Well, there's a brand new place I've founda." Going To A Go-Go.

"Well, there's a certain girl I've been in love with a long, long time." Certain Girl.

"Well, there's a dance spreadin' 'round like an awful disease, hully hully gully." Hully Gully.

"Well, there's too many windows in this old hotel and rooms filled with reckless pride." Heart Hotels.

"Well, there's two sides to ev'ry situation." Two Sides.

"Well, they'll stone ya when you're tryin' to be so good." Rainy Day Women #12 & 35.

"Well, we can't take her this week, and her friends don't want another speech." Personality Crisis.

"Well, we got no choice." School's Out.

"Well, well, well I wanna thank you for your love so true." Ffun.

"Well, yes, I've been so lonely." Gonna Try.

"Well, you are such an easy evil, such a sensuous sin." Easy Evil.

"Well, you can tell by the way I use my walk, I'm a woman's man; no time to talk." Stayin' Alive.

"Well, you can tell ev'rybody down in ol' Frisco, tell 'em Tiny Montgom'ry says hello." Tiny Montgomery.

"Well, you give me all your lovin' and your turtle-dovin'." That'll Be The Day.

"Well, your railroad gate, you know I just can't jump it." Absolutely Sweet Marie.

"Well, you're showing me a diff'rent side." Lady Blue.

"Well, you're the cutest thing that I did ever see." Lovey Dovey.

"Well zoom went the strings of my heart." Zoom.

"Wendy, Wendy, what went wrong?" Wendy.

"Went to a party the other night." Disco Duck (Part I).

"Went to my doctor yesterday." Run That Body Down.

"Went to see the captain, strangest I could find." Ship Of Fools (R. Hunter & J. Garcia).

"Went to see the gypsy...." Went To See The Gypsy.

"We're caught in a trap." Suspicious Minds.

"We're doing alright." Driver's Seat.

"We're gonna break out the hats and hooters when Josie comes home." Josie.

"We're gonna start at midnight; party till the morning light." Do Your Dance (Part I).

"We're lost in music; caught in a trap." Lost In Music.

"We're poor little lambs who have lost our way: Baa! Baa! Baa." Whiffenpoof Song.

"We're singin' this song, y'all." Happy Song.

"We're so sorry, Uncle Albert." Uncle Albert/Admiral Halsey.

"We've all got to rise and reach up for the sky." Rise.

"We've been through some things together." Long May You Run.

"We've got trouble, something's just not right." My Angel Baby.

"We've only just begun to live." We've Only Just Begun.

"What a beautiful noise comin' up from the street." Beautiful Noise.

"What a day for a daydream." Daydream.

"What a difference you've made in my life." What A Difference You've Made In My Life.

"What a dream I had!" For Emily, Whenever I May Find Her.

"What a wonderful, wonderful world this could be." Wonderful World.

"What are heavy?" What Are Heavy.

"What are you doing the rest of your life?" What Are You Doing The Rest Of Your Life.

"What can I do?" Tenderness.

"What can I say after I say I'm sorry?" What Can I Say After I Say I'm Sorry.

"What do you get when you fall in love?" I'll Never Fall In Love Again.

"What does it take to win your love for me?" What Does It Take.

"What goes up must come down, spinning wheel got to go 'round." Spinning Wheel.

"What good is sitting alone in your room?" Cabaret.

"What good is the dawn that grows into day?" Warmth Of The Sun.

"What happened to the world we knew." Yester-Me, Yester-You, Yesterday.

"What has happened down here, is the winds have changed." Louisiana 1927.

"What have I ever done to deserve even one of the pleasures I've known?" Why Me.

"What I feel, I can't say." <u>What Is Life</u>.

"What if I fall in love with you, just like normal people do?" <u>Simple Man, Simple Dream</u>.

"What in the world's come over you?" <u>What In The World's Come Over You</u>.

"What it is, I think I've got the feeling comin' on." <u>What It Is</u>.

"What kind of love is this that makes me want to jump and shout." <u>What Kind Of Love Is This</u>.

"What now my love?" <u>What Now My Love</u>.

"What she has is pure pizzzazz, plus a touch of class." <u>Touch Of Class</u>.

"What the world needs now is love, sweet love." <u>What The World Needs Now Is Love</u>.

"What will you do when you get lonely with nobody waiting by your side? <u>Layla</u>.

"What would you do if I sang out of tune, would you stand up and walk out on me?" <u>With A Little Help From My Friends</u>.

"What you think, what you feel, what you know to be real." <u>Got To Be Real</u>.

"What you want baby I got." <u>Respect</u>.

"Whatever gets you thru the night, 'sal-right, 'sal-right, 'sal-right." <u>Whatever Gets You Thru The Night</u>.

"Whatever it is, it'll keep till the morning." <u>Midnight Blue</u>.

"Whatever you got I want, whatever you want, I'll give to you." <u>Whatever You Got, I Want</u>.

"What's goin' on, it's time to get down." <u>TSOP (The Sound Of Philadelphia)</u>.

"What's happened to blue eyes, has anyone seen him?" <u>What Happened To Blue Eyes</u>.

"What's it all about Alfie?" <u>Alfie</u>.

"What's new pussycat whoa." <u>What's New Pussycat</u>.

"What's so good about goodbye." <u>What's So Good About Goodbye</u>.

"What the sense in sharing this one and only life ending up just another lost and lonely wife?" <u>Young Hearts Run Free</u>.

"What's your name?" <u>That's Where I Went Wrong</u>.

"Wheels of life are turning so much faster." <u>Wheels Of Life</u>.

"When a boy like me meets a girl like you...." <u>Boy Like Me, A Girl Like You</u>.

"When a man loves a woman, can't keep his mind on nothin' else." <u>When A Man Loves A Woman</u>.

"When are you gonna come down, when are you going to land?" <u>Goodbye Yellow Brick Road</u>.

"When black Friday comes I'll stand down by the door." <u>Black Friday</u>.

"When he held me in his arms, he said, 'baby, baby, baby, you're the only one for me.'" <u>When A Man Loves A Woman</u>.

"When he opens the door, says, 'I'm home....'" <u>For The Love Of Him</u>.

"When her motor's warm, and she's purrin' sweet...." <u>Spinout</u>.

"When I asked you for my freedom little did I know that I'd long for chains to bind me." <u>Free Me From My Freedom</u>.

"When I became of age my mother called me to her side." <u>Shop Around</u>.

"When I call you up your line's engaged." <u>You Won't See Me</u>.

"When I came to you there, on that cold telephone pole horror of the night." <u>Requiem; 820 Latham</u>.

"When I done quit hollerin' baby I believe...." <u>Hats Off To (Roy) Harper</u>.

"When I find myself in times of trouble Mother Mary comes to me speaking words of wisdom, let it be." <u>Let It Be</u>.

"When I get home babe, gonna light your fire." <u>Kiss You All Over</u>.

"When I get home from work, I wanna wrap myself around you." <u>You And Me</u>.

"When I get off this mountain, ya know where I wanna go." <u>Up On Cripple Creek</u>.

"When I get to the bottom, I go back to the top of the slide." <u>Helter Skelter</u>.

"When I grow too old to dream, I'll have you to remember." <u>When I Grow Too Old To Dream</u>.

"When I grow up to be a man...." <u>When I Grow Up</u>.

"When I had you to myself I didn't want you around." <u>I Want You Back</u>.

"When I lost my baby, I almost lost my mind." <u>I Almost Lost My Mind</u>.

"When I met you in the restaurant, you could tell I was no debutante." <u>Dreaming</u>.

"When I need you, I just close my eyes and I'm with you." <u>When I Need You</u>.

"When I said I needed you, you said you would always stay." <u>You Don't Have To Say You Love Me</u>.

"When I saw her on the corner, then I knew that I was a goner." <u>I've Had It</u>.

"When I see her comin' down the street...." <u>I Go To Pieces</u>.

"When I see my baby, what do I see?" <u>Poetry In Motion</u>.

"When I see your face like the morning sun...." <u>Serpentine Fire</u>.

"When I think about the good love you gave me...." <u>Cry Like A Baby</u>.

"When I think back on all the crap I learned in high school, it's a wonder I can think at all." <u>Kodachrome</u>.

"When I think of those east end lights, muggy nights, the curtains drawn in the little room downstairs...." <u>Someone Saved My Life Tonight</u>.

"When I wake up each morning trying to find myself...." <u>Someone That I Used To Love</u>.

"When I wake up in the morning, love...." <u>Lovely Day</u>.

"When we kiss my heart's on fire." Surrender (D. Pomus, M. Shuman & E. DeCurtis).

"When we used to say good night, I'd always kiss and hold you tight." That's It, I Quit, I'm Movin' On.

"When we're out there dancin' on the floor darlin'...." You Make Me Feel (Mighty Real).

"When when you smile, when you smile at me...." When.

"When you dance, be sure to hold her, hold her tight." When You Dance.

"When you decide it's time for us to part...." Pattern People.

"When you feel down and out, sing a song, it'll make your day." Singa-Song.

"When you get right down to it...." When You Get Right Down To It.

"When you hear the beat you wanna pat your feet and you've got to move 'cause it's really such a groove." California Soul.

"When you just give love, and never get love, you better let love depart." Since I Fell For You.

"When you look into his eyes and he turns away...." Face It, Girl, It's Over.

"When you look over your shoulder and you see the life that you left behind...." You Love The Thunder.

"When you made love to me tonight I felt as if I'd died and gone to heaven." Anyone Who Isn't Me Tonight.

"When you move right up close to me that's when I get the shakes all over me." Shakin' All Over.

"When you remember me, if you remember me, I hope you see it's not the way I want it to be." If You Remember Me.

"When you see some mud upon the ground you lay down so she don't have to walk around...." Carpet Man.

"When you turn misty blue I have eyes on you." All Things Are Possible.

"When you wake up and she's next to you...." I Can't Stand It No More.

"When you walk into a room, your beauty steals my breath away." Should've Never Let You Go.

"When you walked into the room, there was voodoo in the vibes." So Into You.

"When you were young and on your own, how did it feel to be alone?" Only Love Can Break Your Heart.

"When you were young and your heart was an open book, you used to say live and let live." Live And Let Die.

"When you wish upon a star, dreams will take you very far." Shining Star (M. White, P. Bailey & L. Dunn).

"When your baby and you are tight, and e'vything you say or do is mellow...." Ain't That A Groove (Part 1).

"When your eyes met mine, I knew that I had better play it cool." Where Were You When I Was Falling In Love.

"When your heart gets restless, time to move along." Follow That Dream.

"When your heros go up in a puff, and there's not enough to hang on to...." Just You And I.

"When you're down and troubled and you need some love and care...." You've Got A Friend.

"When you're in love with a beautiful woman it's hard, friends." When You're In Love With A Beautiful Woman.

"When you're lost in the rain in Juarez and it's Easter-time too...." Just Like Tom Thumb's Blues.

"When you're out there on your own tryin' to make it all alone...." When You're Loved.

"When you're through with what you think you have to do, I'll pursue." Higher.

"When you're weary, feelin small, when tears are in your eyes, I'll dry them all." Bridge Over Troubled Water.

"When you're young and so in love as we...." Town Without Pity.

"Whenever I am feeling low...." You Are A Song.

"Whenever I call you friend, I begin to think I understand anything we are." Whenever I Call You Friend.

"Whenever I chance to meet some old friends on the street, they wonder how does a man get to be this way!" Kiss An Angel Good Mornin'.

"Whenever I see your smiling face, I have to smile myself." Your Smiling Face.

"Whenever I'm with him, something inside starts burning, and I'm filled with desire." Heat Wave.

"Whenever the day is bringin' you down...." You Gotta Make Your Own Sunshine.

"Where are those happy days, they seem so hard to find?" SOS.

"Where are we going, love?" Questions.

"Where are you going, my little one, little one?" Turn Around.

"Where are you, why do you hide?" Moonraker.

"Where can you find pleasure, search the world for treasure, learn science and technology?" In The Navy.

"Where do I begin to tell the story of how great a love can be." Love Story, Theme From.

"Where do you come from?" Where Do You Come From.

"Where have all the flowers gone?" Where Have All The Flowers Gone.

"Where is the love?" Where Is The Love (R. McDonald & W. Salter).

"Where is the love, where is the love, you promised me?" Where Is The Love (H.W. Casey, R. Finch, W. Clarke & B. Wright).

"Where is the sun that shone on my head?" Spicks And Spacks.

"Where it began, I can't begin to knowin', but then I know it's growin' strong." Sweet Caroline.

"Where the deep blue pearly waters wash upon white silver sands...." White Silver Sands.

"Where the road down by the butternut grove to old Bill Skinner's stream...." Summertime Dream.

"Where's that smile?" So Close.

"Wherever you go, wherever you may wander in your life...." <u>Let Me Be There</u>.

"Whether I'm riding down the highway or walking down the street...." <u>Anyplace Is Paradise</u>.

"While I'm far away from you my baby...." <u>Dedicated To The One I Love</u>.

"While riding in my Cadillac, what to my surprise; a little Nash Rambler was following me, about one-third my size." <u>Beep Beep</u>.

"Whispering while you cuddle near me...." <u>Whispering</u>.

"Whisp'ring bells, whisper low." <u>Whispering Bells</u>.

"White chalk written on red brick...." <u>Jennifer Eccles</u>.

"White light, white light goin' messin' up my mind." <u>White Light, White Heat</u>.

"Who are you?" <u>Who Are You</u>.

"Who can take a sunrise, sprinkle it with dew?" <u>Candy Man</u> (L. Bricusse & A. Newley).

"Who done it?" <u>Who Done It</u>.

"Who draws the crowd and plays so loud, baby it's the guitar man." <u>Guitar Man</u>.

"Who has been the center, world's greatest attraction, since the beginning of time?" <u>Women</u>.

"Who is the hippest happen all over town?" <u>Mohair Sam</u>.

"Who makes my love come tumblin' down?" <u>Yes, It's You</u>.

"Who makes the robins sing?" <u>My Love, My Love</u>.

"Who said it's my year?" <u>Baby (Somethin's Happening)</u>.

"Who will love a little sparrow?" <u>Sparrow</u>.

"Whoa, it's five o'clock in the morning; the party's still goin', still goin' strong." <u>Daylight</u>.

"Whoo yeah, when I'm sittin' home and I'm all alone...." <u>Hot Shot</u>.

"Who's been tellin' you these things?" <u>Trust Me</u>.

"Who's gonna ride that chrome three wheeler?" <u>Fire Lake</u>.

"Who's gonna throw that minstrel boy a coin?" <u>Minstrel Boy</u>.

"Who's peekin' out from under a stairway, calling a name that's lighter than air?" <u>Windy</u>.

"Who's sorry now?" <u>Who's Sorry Now</u>.

"Who's that coming down the road, a sailor from the sea?" <u>Tape From California</u>.

"Who's that coming down the street?" <u>Yes Sir, That's My Baby</u>.

"Who's that knockin' on my door?" <u>Hot Legs</u>.

"Who's the black private dick that's a sex machine to all the chicks?" <u>Shaft, Theme From</u>.

"Who's the livin' dolly with the beautiful eyes?" <u>In The Mood</u>.

"Who's the queen of the locker room, who's the cream of the crop?" <u>Muscle Of Love</u>.

"Whose garden was this?" <u>Whose Garden Was This</u>.

"Why are you still crying?" <u>Behind That Locked Door</u>.

"Why, baby, why don't you treat me like you used to do?" <u>Why Baby Why</u>.

"Why can't you do something right?" <u>Four Wheel Drive</u>.

"Why do birds suddenly appear ev'ry time you draw near?" <u>Close To You</u> (B. Bacharach & H. David).

"Why do fools fall in love?" <u>Why Do Fools Fall In Love</u>.

"Why do I still hear that song?" <u>Music Will Not End</u>.

"Why do we never get an answer when we're knocking at the door?" <u>Question</u>.

"Why do you sit there so strange?" <u>Pause Of Mr. Clause</u>.

"Why don't we stop foolin' ourselves?" <u>Overs</u>.

"Why don't we try a slow dance?" <u>Slow Dance</u>.

"Why don't you ask him if he's gonna stay?" <u>Tusk</u>.

"Why don't you believe me when I say that I love you?" <u>Lovely One</u>.

"Why don't you let me be good to you?" <u>Let Me Be Good To You</u>.

"Why don't you write me?" <u>Why Don't You Write Me</u>.

"Why have you left the one you left me for." <u>Why Have You Left The One (You Left Me For)</u>.

"Why make me plead for what I need?" <u>Say Maybe</u>.

"Why me, Lord?" <u>Why Me?</u> (K. Kristofferson).

"Why must I meet you in a secret rendezvous?" <u>Secretly</u>.

"Why, why can't you love me again?" <u>Why</u> (B. Crompton & T. Sheridan).

"Why'd you tell me this?" <u>You Belong To Me</u>.

"Wide awake in the middle of the night, I wonder how she's feelin'." <u>Trick Of The Light</u>.

"Wild Cat Kelly, looking mighty pale, was standing by the sheriff's side." <u>Don't Fence Me In</u>.

"Wildwood flower grew wild on the farm and we never knowed what it was called." <u>Wildwood Weed</u>.

"Will there come a day where you and I can say we can fin'lly see each other." <u>I'll Meet You Halfway</u>.

"William Zanzinger killed poor Hattie Carroll with a cane...." <u>Lonesome Death Of Hattie Carroll</u>.

"Wind is in from Africa...." <u>Carey</u>.

"Windflowers, my father told me not to go near them." <u>Windflowers</u>.

"Winding paths through tables and glass, first fall was new." <u>Country Girl</u>.

"Winding your way down on Baker street...." <u>Baker Street</u>.

"Winds may blow over the icy sea." <u>Taste Of Honey</u>.

"Winds of chance may blow my way." <u>Winds Of Chance</u>.

"Winter is here again, oh Lord haven't been home in a year or more." <u>Wheel In The Sky</u>.

"Winter is here and it's going on two years." <u>Swallow My Pride</u>.

"Winter rain, now tell me why summers fade and roses die." Weather Report I.

"Winterlude, winterlude, oh darlin', winterlude by the road tonight." Winterlude.

"Winter's day in a deep and dark December." I Am A Rock.

"Wise men say only fools rush in, but I can't help falling in love with you." Can't Help Falling In Love.

"Wish I was a Kellogg's corn flake floatin' in my bowl takin' movies." Punky's Dilemma.

"With a child's heart, go face the worries of the day." With A Child's Heart.

"With a purple umbrella and a fifty cent hat...." Living Loving Maid.

"With pen in hand you sign your name." With Pen In Hand.

"With your mercury mouth in the missionary times...." Sad Eyed Lady Of The Lowlands.

"Woke up, it was Chelsea morning and the first thing that I heard was the song outside my window and the traffic wrote the words." Chelsea Morning.

"Woke up this mornin', dragged myself across the bed." Wanderer (D. Summer & G. Moroder).

"Woke up this morning, feeling low." Poor Me.

"Woman of the country now I've found you." Delta Lady.

"Woman, take me in your arms, rock your baby." Rock Your Baby.

"Wonderful baby, livin' on love, the sandman says maybe he'll take you above." Wonderful Baby.

"Won't you try?" Won't You Try/Saturday Afternoon.

"Won't you wear my ring up around your neck to tell the world I'm yours, by heck." Wear My Ring Around Your Neck.

"Woo ah mercy, mercy me...." Mercy, Mercy Me.

"Words are flying out like endless rain into a paper cup." Across The Universe.

"Words had all been spoken, and somehow the feeling still wasn't right." Late For The Sky.

"Words of love tho' soft and tender won't win a girl's heart anymore." Words Of Love (J. Phillips).

"Working from seven to eleven ev'ry night...." Since I've Been Loving You.

"Working on a barge down in New Orleans...." Muddy Mississippi Line.

"World outside your arms is cold and windy." Green Grass Starts To Grow.

"Worst person I know, Mother-in-law." Mother-In-Law.

"Would you like to learn to sing?" When The Party's Over.

"Would you like to ride in my beautiful balloon?" Up, Up, And Away.

"Ya got to give the people, give the people what they want." Give The People What They Want.

"Ya gotta keep on makin' me high." Dance With Me (P. Brown & R. Rans).

"Ya say that it's over baby, ya say that it's over now." Move Over.

"Y'all come on in now, come right on down front." Do The Funky Chicken.

"Yama, yama, the yama man." Yama-Yama Man.

"Yeah, gonna catch a flight to Nevada, leaving all her friends in L.A." Roller.

"Yeah! Psychedelic shack, that's where it's at." Psychedelic Shack.

"Yeah! Yeah! Oh Yeah! My, my, my." Can't Hold On Much Longer.

"Yeah, yeah, yeah, oh, yeah, when I see your face like the morning sun...." Serpentine Fire.

"Yeah, yeah, yeah, yeah, yeah, yeah, yeah, yeah, I'm talkin', talkin', talkin', talkin', talkin', in my sleep." Sing A Simple Song.

"Yellow bird, up high in banana tree...." Yellow Bird.

"Yellow is the color of my true love's hair." Colours.

"Yes, C.C. Rider, girl see what you have done." C.C. Rider (C. Willis).

"Yes, it means I'm in love again." I'm In Love Again.

"Yesterday a child came out to wonder, caught a dragonfly inside a jar." Circle Game.

"Yesterday a morning came, a smile upon your face." Yours Is No Disgrace.

"Yesterday, all my troubles seemed so far away." Yesterday.

"Yesterday, I would not have believed that tomorrow the sun would shine." Alive Again.

"Yesterday, it was my birthday!" Have A Good Time.

"Y'know girls, it's hard to find a guy that really blows your mind." Maybe.

"Yo, yo, yo, yo, oh yea, I want tell you 'bout ooh poo pah doo." Ooh Poo Pah Doo.

"Yo-de-la-dy, yo-de-la-dy dat I love." Cinderella Rockefella.

"Yonder come Miss-a Rossie." Midnight Special.

"You ain't got no kind of feeling inside." Tell Me Something Good.

"You ain't never been loved like I'm gonna love you." You Ain't Never Been Loved.

"You ain't nothin' but a hound dog, cryin' all the time." Hound Dog.

"You always won, ev'ry time you placed a bet." Still The Same.

"You and I must make a pact; we must bring salvation back." I'll Be There.

"You and I sounds like a whole lot of fun." You And I (J. Bristol).

"You and I travel to the beat of a diff'rent drum." Different Drum.

"You and I, we don't know just where we're goin'." You And I (Michaele & L. & P. Sebastian).

"You and I, we fit together like a glove on hand, that's right." You And I (R. James).

"You and me against the world, sometimes it feels like you and me against the world." You And Me Against The World.

"You angel you, you got me under your wing." You Angel You.

"You are a young man and you're eager to seek." Changes (J. Messina).

"You are all the woman I need, and baby, you know it." Bend Me, Shape Me.

"You are here and warm but I could look away and you'd be gone." Sentimental Lady.

"You are my destiny, you are what you are to me." You Are My Destiny.

"You are my love and my life." Just You 'N' Me.

"You are my pride and joy." Pride And Joy.

"You are my special angel." Special Angel.

"You are on my mind." You Are On My Mind.

"You are so beautiful to me." You Are So Beautiful.

"You are so wonderful ah, being near you is all that I'm living for." You're A Wonderful One.

"You are the one who makes me happy when ev'rything else turns to grey." You (R. Edelman).

"You are the sunshine baby whenever you smile but I call you stormy today." Stormy.

"You are the sunshine of my life." You Are The Sunshine Of My Life.

"You are the woman that I've always dreamed of." You Are The Woman.

"You ask how much I need you, must I explain?" Twelfth Of Never.

"You ask me if there'll come a time when I grow tired of you, never my love." Never My Love.

"You ask me to give up the hand of the girl I love." You Better Move On.

"You asked me to read this letter that you wrote the night before." Go And Say Goodbye.

"You be good to me; you made me glad when I was blue." Thank You Girl.

"You better come home Speedy Gonzales, away from Cannery Row." Speedy Gonzales.

"You broke my heart 'cause I couldn't dance." Do You Love Me.

"You came a long way from St. Louis." You Came A Long Way From St. Louis.

"You came when I was happy." If You Love Me (Let Me Know).

"You can dance ev'ry dance with the guy who gave you the eye; let him hold you tight." Save The Last Dance For Me.

"You can dance, you can jive having the time of your life." Dancing Queen.

"You can find me when you need me." I Still Have Dreams.

"You can have this dance with me." Beechwood 4-5789.

"You can hear it in the street." Relay.

"You can play the game and you can act out the part though you know it wasn't written for you." Shower The People.

"You can run away." If You Should Sail.

"You can take all the tea in China, put it in a big brown bag for me." Tupelo Honey.

"You can take me to paradise and then again you can be cold as ice." Over My Head.

"You can't see the forest if you're lookin' at the trees." Dig A Little Deeper.

"You can't win." You Can't Win.

"You caught me smilin' again." Smilin'.

"You cheated, you lied, you said that you love me." You Cheated.

"You didn't have to love me like you did." I Thank You.

"You didn't know what you were looking for, 'til you heard the voices in your ear." Voices.

"You disbeliever, your eyes are judging me." Tried Tested And Found True.

"You don't bring me flowers; you don't sing me love songs." You Don't Bring Me Flowers.

"You don't drive a big black car." You've Got What It Takes.

"You don't have to be a baby to cry." You Don't Have To Be A Baby To Cry.

"You don't have to go." D'yer Mak'er.

"You don't know how much I love you, but I love you like the sun." Runaway (N. Q. Dewey).

"You don't know me, but I'm your brother." Takin' It To The Streets.

"You don't know that you love me." You Don't Know Where Your Interest Lies.

"You don't like crazy music." Baby I Don't Care.

"You don't love me like I love you." It Do Me So Good.

"You don't need a love in, you don't need a bed pan." Awaiting On You All.

"You don't need anybody to hold you, here I stand with my arms open wide." I'll Keep You Satisfied.

"You don't own me, I'm not just one of your many toys." You Don't Own Me.

"You fill up my senses like a night in a forest." Annie's Song.

"You followed me to Texas." My Elusive Dreams.

"You get a shiver in the dark." Sultans Of Swing.

"You get me runnin', goin' out of my mind." Don't Bring Me Down.

"You get up in the mornin', you hear the ding dong ring." Midnight Special.

"You get your love from dogs and cats you've found in the neighborhood." Lonely One.

"You go where you want, you do what you please." Steppin' Out (N. Sedaka & P. Cody).

"You gonna make me love somebody else if you keep on treatin' me the way you do." You Gonna Make Me Love Somebody Else.

"You got a lotta nerve to say you are my friend." Positively 4th Street.

"You got a real type of thing goin' down." Tear The Roof Off The Sucker.

"You got a smile so bright, you know you could've been a candle." Way You Do The Things You Do.

"You got ants in your pants." I Didn't Have The Nerve To Say No.

"You got me looking at that heaven in your eyes." Shadow Dancing.

"You got me runnin', goin' out of my mind." Don't Bring Me Down.

"You got me runnin', you got me hidin'." Baby, What You Want Me To Do.

"You got the huggin'est arms, the thrillin'est eyes." Shoppin' Around.

"You got to give it to me." Give It To Me.

"You got to know how to pony." Land Of A Thousand Dances.

"You got to learn how to fall before you learn to fly." Learn How To Fall.

"You got to stop and smell the roses." Stop And Smell The Roses.

"You got your Tony Lama's on your jeans pressed tight." Livingston Saturday Night.

"You gotta stop and search your soul." All God's Children Got Soul.

"You had better hold on." Hold What You've Got.

"You, I don't know what to say, you take my breath away." You Take My Breath Away.

"You jump, jump here." Mellow Down Easy.

"You keep comin' back to me again and again." Surrender To Me.

"You keep sayin' you got somethin' for me." These Boots Are Made For Walkin'.

"You knew I could not stay for long when you asked me to come over in the wee hours of the morning." I'm A Drifter.

"You know a cat named Mickey came from out of town, yeah." Mickey's Monkey.

"You know I can be found sitting home all alone." Don't Be Cruel (To A Heart That's True).

"You know, I can't smile without you." Can't Smile Without You.

"You know I feel all right, you know I feel all right children." Shout And Shimmy.

"You know I gassed her up, I'm behind the wheel." Heart Of Saturday Night.

"You know I need your love, you've got that hold over me." Right Down The Line.

"You know, I talked to the Captain this morning." Steamboat.

"You know I've done a lot of livin' in a lifetime." Gimme Something Real.

"You know love makes a fool of you." Love's Made A Fool Of You.

"You know that it would be untrue." Light My Fire.

"You know, there's two ol' maids layin' in the bed." Get Your Rocks Off.

"You know you make me wanna, come on now, come on now, oh let's shout now." Shout.

"You like to keep me a-dangling on a string." Please Don't Drag That String Around.

"You little trustmaker." You Little Trustmaker.

"You live your life in the songs you hear on the rock' and 'roll radio." Angie Baby.

"You look at me that way I know what your eyes say." Baby, I'm Burning.

"You look like an angel." You're The Devil In Disguise.

"You look to me like misty roses." Misty Roses.

"You looked inside my fantasies and made each one come true." I'll Never Love This Way Again.

"You made a fool of me but them broken dreams have got to end." Evil Woman.

"You made me cry when you said goodbye." Ain't That A Shame.

"You make me dizzy, Miss LIzzie, the way you rock and roll." Dizzy Miss Lizzie.

"You make me weep and wanna die." Lovin', Touchin', Squeezin'.

"You may be an ambassador to England or France...." Gotta Serve Somebody.

"You may call me a rollin' stone." Rock Me Baby.

"You might wake up some mornin', to the sound of something moving past your window in the wind." Elusive Butterfly.

"You must be a special lady and a very exciting girl." Special Lady.

"You must leave now, take what you need, you think will last." It's All Over Now, Baby Blue.

"You need a woman, need a woman tonight." You Need A Woman Tonight.

"You need coolin', baby, I'm not foolin'." Whole Lotta Love.

"You never close your eyes anymore when I kiss your lips." You've Lost That Lovin' Feelin'.

"You ought to be the star on a T.V. show." Star On A T.V. Show.

"You ought to know, it's you that he loved, made him feel like a baby boy." Martha (Your Lovers Come And Go).

"You ought to see Mister Jones when he rattles the bones." Alabama Jubilee.

"You packed in the morning, I stared out the window and I struggled for something to say." Just When I Needed You Most.

"You played hookie from school and you can't go out to play." Runaway Child, Running Wild.

"You read about Samson, you read about his birth." If I Had My Way.

"You said you needed time to think it over." Think It Over (B. & B.G. Russell).

"You said you wanted to wait on me." When You're Next To Me.

"You saw me crying in the chapel." Crying In The Chapel.

"You say it's your birthday, it's my birthday too, yeah." Birthday.

"You say that you love me all of the time." Glad All Over.

"You say yes, I say no, you say stop and I say go go go." Hello, Goodbye.

"You say you love me and I hardly know your name." It's Late.

"You say you love me and you're thinkin' of me, but you know you could be wrong." Most Likely You Go Your Way.

"You say you wanna know what you gotta do." Baby I'll Give It To You.

"You say you want a revolution." Revolution.

"You say you want to seek the truth, but it's hard to find." Hurt (C. Stevens).

"You say your heart's been broken and you're left out in the cold." Love To Burn.

"You see that black boy over there runnin' scared?" Bottle.

"You see this guy, this guy's in love with you." This Guy's In Love With You.

"You send cold chills up and down my spine." Mama's Pearl.

"You shake my nerves and you rattle my brain." Great Balls Of Fire.

"You sheltered me from harm, kept me warm, kept me warm." Everything I Own.

"You shook me, baby." You Shook Me.

"You should do it right, each and every night." You Should Do It.

"You should have seen me with the poker man." Junior's Farm.

"You show us ev'rything you've got." Rock And Roll All Nite.

"You stepped into my life and I'm oh, so happy." You Stepped Into My Life.

"You still got that light in your eyes." Days Gone Down (Still Got The Light In Your Eyes).

"You sure have changed, I don't know you any more." Sit Down And Talk To Me.

"You surely must know magic, girl, 'cause you changed my life." You're My Everything.

"You take a bus marked 'Lakewood Drive', and you keep on ridin' 'til you're outa the city." Indian Lake.

"You take a stick of bamboo...." Bamboo.

"You talk too much, you worry me to death." You Talk Too Much.

"You tell me that you're leavin', I can't believe it's true." Breaking Up Is Hard To Do.

"You tell me there's an angel in your tree, did he say he'd come to call on me?" Burn Down The Mission.

"You tell me this town ain't got no heart." Shakedown Street.

"You think I love you for just one thing." Ain't That Loving You (For More Reasons Than One).

"You think that I don't feel love." Love Child.

"You think the love you never had might save you." Prisoner In Disguise.

"You think you had the last laugh now." Race Among The Ruins.

"You think you're gonna take her away with your money and your cocaine." Listen To Her Heart.

"You think you've lost your love." She Loves You.

"You told me, baby once upon a time...." That's All Right.

"You told me goodbye." High Time.

"You took me up to heaven, when you took me in your arms." Fool's Paradise.

"You walked into the party like you were walking onto a yacht." You're So Vain.

"You want my love and you can't deny." Can't Hide Love.

"You want things your way and I want them mine." Everytime Two Fools Collide.

"You want two heads on your body." Two Heads.

"You went away and left me long time ago and now you're knockin' on my door." I Hear You Knocking.

"You went to school to learn girl." ABC.

"You were drowning, my darling, and I saved you." La Bamba.

"You who are on the road must have a code that you can live by." Teach Your Children.

"You wonder why I never ask where you've been." Do What You Wanna Do.

"You wouldn't believe where I been." It's A Miracle.

"You wouldn't read my letters if I wrote them." Wild Side Of Life.

"You, you're the one, you are the only reason." You, You're The One.

"You'll hear my voice." Legend Of Xanadu.

"You'll never find, as long as you live, someone who loves you tender like I do." You'll Never Find Another Love Like Mine.

"You'll never know how I love you." Oh Julie.

"You'll never know how much I really love you." Do You Want To Know A Secret.

"Young America you get food to eat, won't have to run to the jungle and scuff up your feet." Sail Away.

"Young as a circus parade, it's a wonderful world." It's A Wonderful World.

"Young dreams, my heart is filled with young dreams." Young Dreams.

"Young girl, get out of my mind, my love for you is way out of line." Young Girl.

"Young man there's no need to feel down." Y.M.C.A.

"Your breath is sweet; your eyes are like two jewels in the sky." One More Cup Of Coffee.

"Your everlastin' summer, you can see it fadin' fast." Reelin' In The Years.

"Your 'ex' is back in town." Baby Don't Change Your Mind.

"Your kisses take me to Shangri-la." Shangri-la.

"Your lips, your eyes, your soft sweet sighs, I feel that I've known you forever." I Feel That I've Known You Forever.

"Your love is fading." I'm Losing You.

"Your love is liftin' me higher than I've ever been lifted before." Higher And Higher.

"Your love is like a tidal wave spinnin' over my head." Heartbreaker (C. Wade & G. Gill).

"Your mama don't dance and your daddy don't rock & roll." Your Mama Don't Dance.

"Your mama says I'm no good for you." East Is East.

"Your precious love means more to me than any love could ever be." For Your Precious Love.

"Your precious sweetheart, she's so faithful." Shoo-Be-Doo-Be-Doo-Da-Day.

"Your rain falls like crazy fingers, peals of fragile thunder keeping time." Crazy Fingers.

"You're a doll, your eyes see it all...." How Do I Make You.

"You're a runaway love!" Runaway Love.

"You're a stranger to me, then you give me your light." Sugar On The Floor.

"You're a thousand miles away." Thousand Miles Away.

"You're all I need to get by." You're All I Need To Get By.

"You're always dancin' down the street with your suede blue eyes." My Best Friend's Girl.

"You're as cold as ice." Cold As Ice.

"You're fair game and you look like prey." Animal.

"You're far away from me, my love." Someday We'll Be Together.

"You're goin' away on that midnight train." Midnight Train.

"You're gonna say ya miss me!" I'm Gonna Love You Too.

"You're kind, you're so kind." You're Kind.

"You're like quicksand, quicksand." Quicksand.

"You're lookin' kinda lonely girl." Sharing The Night Together.

"You're mine, and we belong together." We Belong Together.

"You're my love, you're my angel, you're the girl of my dreams." Daddy's Home.

"You're my number one dee jay." #1 Dee Jay.

"You're my world, you're ev'ry breath I take." You're My World.

"You're not a dream, you're not an angel, you're a man." Until It's Time For You To Go.

"You're not a ship to carry my life." I Need You To Turn To.

"You're not the only cuddly toy that was ever enjoyed." Cuddly Toy.

"You're sailing softly through the sun." Strange Music.

"You're so fine, you're so fine, you're mine, you're mine." You're So Fine.

"You're so hot teasing me." Does Your Mother Know.

"You're still a young man baby woo." You're Still A Young Man.

"You're sweet as a honey bee." It's The Same Old Song.

"You're takin' all I got and now you're leavin'." Baby Don't Go.

"You've abandoned me." Love Don't Live Here Anymore.

"You've been cheatin' on me and I know, I know it's true." Don't Mess Up A Good Thing.

"You've been treating me bad, misery." Misery.

"You've given me a true love." I Hear A Symphony.

"You've got a cute way of talking." You Make Me Feel Like Dancing.

"You've got me rollin' like a wheel on the road, turnin' 'round and 'round, nowhere to go." I Was Made For Dancin'.

"You've got the cool water when fever runs high." Something So Right.

"You've got to change your evil ways, baby, before I stop lovin' you." Evil Ways.

"You've got to go where you wanna go." Go Where You Wanna Go.

"You've got two lips that look so fine." You've Got Love.

"You've long been on the open road." Thirsty Boots.

4

COMPOSER–LYRICIST INDEX

———

ABERNATHY, Lee Roy
Wonderful Time Up There

ABRAMS, Lester
Minute By Minute (w)

ACQUAVIVA, Nick
My Love, My Love

ADAMS, P.
In The Bush

ADAMS, Ritchie
After The Lovin'
Next Hundred Years
This Moment In Time
Tossin' And Turnin'

ADDRISI, Dick & Don
I Believe You
Never My Love
Slow Dancin' Don't Turn Me On

ADKINS, John
Ways

ADLER, Lou
Poor Side Of Town
Wonderful World

ADLER, Richard
Everybody Loves A Lover

AGER, Milton
Crazy Words-Crazy Tune (m)
Happy Days Are Here Again (m)
Hard Hearted Hannah
Vo-Do-Do-De-O-Blues (m)

AHLERT, Fred E.
I Don't Know Why (I Just Do) (m)
I'll Get By (m)
Love, You Funny Thing (m)

AKST, Harry
Am I Blue (m)
Baby Face (Disco Version)

ALBERT, Morris
Feelings
Gonna Love You More

ALBIN, Peter
Road Block

ALDRIDGE, Tommy
Happy Hooker
Hot Rod

ALEXANDER, Arthur
You Better Move On

ALEXANDER, Dan
Can't Keep A Good Man Down

ALEXANDER, James
Shake Your Rump To The Funk
Too Hot To Stop (Part I)

ALEXANDER, Jules
Lovin' Stew

ALFRED, Roy
Rock And Roll Waltz
That's It, I Quit, I'm Movin' On

ALLEN, Charles
Shake Your Rump To The Funk
Too Hot To Stop (Part I)

ALLEN, Peter
Don't Cry Out Loud
I Go To Rio
I Honestly Love You
I'd Rather Leave While I'm In
Love

ALLEN, Robert
Chances Are (m)
Everybody Loves A Lover
It's Not For Me To Say (m)
Moments To Remember (m)

ALLEN, Shorty
Rock And Roll Waltz

ALLEN, Sylvester
Cisco Kid
Gypsy Man
Me And Baby Brother
Spill The Wine
World Is A Ghetto

ALLER, Michele
Take Me Home
Wasn't It Good

ALLISON, Audrey & Joe
Teen Age Crush

ALLISON, Jerry
Look At Me
More Than I Can Say
Peggy Sue
That'll Be The Day
Well All Right

ALLMAN, Gregg (Gregory L.)
It's Not My Cross to Bear
Melissa
Midnight Rider
Nevertheless
Whippin' Post

ALOMAR, Carlos
Fame

ALPERT, Herb
Wonderful World

ALRIDGE, Ava
Sharing The Night Together

ALTMAN, Mike
M*A*S*H, Song From

AMES, Nancy
Cinderella Rockefella

ANDERSEN, Eric
Thirsty Boots
Weather Report I

ANDERSON, Adrienne
Could It Be Magic
Daybreak (w)
Deja Vu (w)
I Go To Rio
Street Singin'

ANDERSON, Bill
I Can't Wait Any Longer

ANDERSON, Deacon
Rag Mop

ANDERSON, Jon
Long Distance Runaround
Release, Release
Roundabout
Time And A Word
Wonderous Stories
Your Move
Yours Is No Disgrace

193

ANDERSON, Stig
Dancing Queen
Fernando
I Do, I Do, I Do, I Do, I Do
Knowing Me, Knowing You
Name Of The Game
SOS

ANDERSSON, Benny
Dancing Queen
Does Your Mother Know
Fernando
I Do, I Do, I Do, I Do, I Do
Knowing Me, Knowing You
Money, Money, Money
Name Of The Game
SOS
Take A Chance On Me

ANDREW, Sam
Flower In The Sun
I Need A Man To Love

ANDREWS, Lee
Long Lonely Nights

ANGULO, Hector
Guantanamera (m, adapted)

ANKA, Paul
Diana
It Doesn't Matter Anymore
Lonely Boy
Put Your Head On My Shoulder
She's a Lady
You Are My Destiny

ANNARINO, John
Take Life A Little Easier (w)

ANTHONY, Michael
Beautiful Girls
Dance The Night Away
Jamie's Cryin'
Runnin' With The Devil

ANTHONY, Mike
Poetry In Motion

APPEL, Mike
Doesn't Somebody Want To Be
Wanted

APPELL, Dave
Bristol Stomp
Don't Hang Up
Let's Twist Again
Wah-Watusi
Wild One

APPICE, Carmine
Da Ya Think I'm Sexy

ARANDA, JACK
Still Waters Run Deep

ARGENT, Rod
Hold Your Head Up
She's Not There
Time Of The Season

ARKIN, David
Black And White (w)

ARLEN, Harold
Blues In The Night (m)
It's Only A Paper Moon (m)
Over The Rainbow (m)

ARMER, Andy
Rise
Rotation

ARMSTEAD, Josephine (Josie)
I Don't Need No Doctor
Let's Go Get Stoned

ARNOLD, Chris
Can't Smile Without You

ARNOLD, Eddy
That's How Much I Love You

ARSDALE, Douglas Van SEE
Van Arsdale, Douglas

ASCHER, Ken
Watch Closely Now
You And Me Against The World

ASHFORD, Nickolas
Ain't No Mountain High Enough
Ain't Nothing But A Maybe
Ain't Nothing Like The Real
Thing
Anywhere
Believe In Me
Bend Me
Boss
California Soul
Caretaker
Destiny
Drink The Wine
Found A Cure
Genius I
Gimme Something Real
I Don't Need No Doctor
I Wanna Be Selfish
I'm Every Woman
Is It Still Good To Ya
It Came To Me
It'll Come, It'll Come, It'll Come
Let's Go Get Stoned
Over And Over
Reach Out And Touch (Some-
body's Hand)
Release Me
Remember Me
Ride-O-Rocket
Seel The House
Shoe, Shoe Shine
So, So Satisfied

Some Things You Never Get
Used To
Somebody Told A Lie
Stuff Like That
Surrender
Tell It All
Tried, Tested And Found True
Your Precious Love
You're All I Need To Get By

ASKEY, Gilbert A.
Runaway Love

AUSTIN, Art
Here Comes The Sun

AUSTIN, Bobby
Try A Little Kindness

AUSTIN, Tom
Believe Me

AVERRE, Berton
My Sharona

AXTON, Hoyt
Ease Your Pain
Greenback Dollar
Joy To The World
Never Been To Spain

AXTON, Mae Boren
Heartbreak Hotel

AZRAEL, Sam
Shouldn't I Know

BACH, J.S.
Joy (m)

BACHARACH, Burt
Alfie (m)
Always Something There To
Remind Me (m)
Close To You (m)
Do You Know The Way To San
Jose (m)
Don't Make Me Over (m)
Green Grass Starts To Grow (m)
I Say A Little Prayer (m)
I'll Never Fall In Love Again (m)
Living Together, Growing To-
gether (m)
Look Of Love (m)
Make It Easy On Yourself (m)
My Little Red Book (m)
One Less Bell To Answer (m)
Promises, Promises (m)
Raindrops Keep Fallin' On My
Head (m)
This Guy's In Love With You (m)
Walk On By (m)
What The World Needs Now Is
Love (m)
What's New Pussycat (m)

COMPOSER—LYRICIST INDEX

BACHMAN, Randy (Randall)
Four Wheel Drive
Freeways
Let It Ride
My Wheels Won't Turn
Takin' Care Of Business
These Eyes
You Ain't Seen Nothing Yet

BACKER, Bill
I'd Like To Teach The World To
Sing
If You've Got The Time

BADALE, Andy
Face It, Girl, It's Over

BADAZZ, Randy
Rise
Rotation

BAER, Barbara
Sweet Talkin' Guy

BAEZ, Joan
Diamonds And Rust
Song For David

BAHLER, Tom
Julie, Do Ya Love Me

BAILEY, Philip
Evil
Reasons
Shining Star

BAILY, Chris
Stranded

BAKER, Adrian
My Baby's Baby

BAKER, Yvonne
Let Me In

BALIN, Marty
Dance With The Dragon (w)
Miracles
With Your Love
Young Girl Sunday Blue

BALL, Noel
Oh Julie

BALL, Roger
Pick Up The Pieces

BALLARD, Clint, Jr.
Game Of Love
Good Timin'

BALLARD, Hank
Twist

BALLARD, Pat
Mister Sandman

BALLARD, Russ
Liar
So You Win Again

BANKS, Homer
Ain't That Loving You (For
More Reasons Than One)
I Don't Want To Be Right
If You're Ready (Come Go
With Me)
I'll Be Your Shelter (In Time Of
Storm)
Sone Of Shaft
Take Care Of Your Homework
Touch A Hand, Make A Friend
Who's Making Love

BARBATA, Johnny
Sound Asleep

BARBIERI, Gato
Last Tango In Paris (m)

BARE, Bobby
All American Boy

BARER, Marshall
I'm Just A Country Boy

BARGE, Gene
Quarter To Three
School Is Out

BARISH, Jesse
Count On Me
Crazy Feelin'

BARKAN, Mark
How Would You Like To Be

BARLOW, John
Money Money (w)
Music Never Stopped (w)
Weather Report II: Let It
Grow (w)

BARNUM, H.B.
Your Love

BARRERE, Paul
All That You Dream

BARRETT, Richard
ABC's Of Love
Maybe

BARRETT, Vinnie
Just Don't Want To Be Lonely

BARRETTO, Ray
El Watusi (m)

BARRI, Steve
You Baby (Nobody But You)

BARRIE, George
Touch Of Class (m)

BARRIS, Chuck
Palisades Park

BARRY, C.
Boogie Woogie Dancin' Shoes

BARRY, Jeff
Da Doo Ron Ron
Do Wah Diddy Diddy
Heavy Makes You Happy
I Honestly Love You
Montego Bay
Sugar, Sugar
Tell Laura I Love Her

BARRY, John
Born Free (m)
Deep, Theme From (m)
Diamonds Are Forever (m)
Goldfinger (m)
Moonraker (m)

BARRY, Len
Here Comes The Sun
Motown Review

BARTHOLOMEW, Dave
Ain't That A Shame
All By Myself
Blue Monday
Bo Weevil
I Hear You Knocking
I Want You To Know
I'm Gonna Be A Wheel Someday
I'm In Love Again
I'm Walkin'
Let The Four Winds Blow
My Girl Josephine
One Night
Poor Me
Valley Of Tears
Whole Lotta Loving

BASEMORE, Vicki
With A Child's Heart

BASKIN, Don
Little Girl

BASS, Ralph
Dedicated To The One I Love

BATCHELOR, Ruth
Where Do You Come From

BATEMAN, Robert
Playboy
Please Mr. Postman

BATES, Charles
Hard Hearted Hannah

BATORS, Stiv
Sonic Reducer

BATSTONE, Billy
I Still Have Dreams

BATTEAST, Tracy
A' Soalin'

BATTEAU, David
You're The Love

BAUM, Bernie
Do Not Disturb
Everybody Come Aboard
Paradise, Hawaiian Style
Roustabout
Shake That Tambourine
Shout It Out
This Is My Heaven
Today, Tomorrow And Forever
You're The Devil In Disguise

BAXTER, Lou
Merry Christmas Baby

BEACH, Jerry
I'll Play The Blues For You

BEARD, Michael
Shake Your Rump To The Funk
Too Hot To Stop (Part I)

BEATTY, Harold
I'm Gonna Let My Heart Do The
Walking

BEAUMONT, James
Since I Don't Have You (w)
This I Swear (w)

BEAVERS, Jackey
Someday We'll Be Together

BECAUD, Gilbert
It Must Be Him (m)
Let It Be Me (m)
September Morn
What Now My Love (m)

BECKENSTEIN, Jay
Morning Dance

BECKER, Walter
Black Friday
Daddy Don't Live In That New
York City No More
Deacon Blues
Do It Again
FM
Here At The Western World
Josie
My Old School
Peg
Pretzel Logic
Reelin' In The Years
Rikki, Don't Lose That Number

BECKETT, Peter
Baby Come Back
Prisoner Of Your Love
Silver Lining

BECKLEY, Gerry
Daisy Jane
I Need You
Sister Golden Hair

BEDDOE, Albert F.
Copper Kettle (The Pale Moonlight)

BELAFONTE, Harry
Turn Around

BELL, Anthony
I'm Stone In Love With You

BELL, Leroy
Livin' It Up
Mama Can't Buy You Love
Only Make Believe

BELL, Richard
Diane

BELL, Ronald
Jungle Boogie

BELL, Simon Napier SEE Napier-
Bell, Simon

BELL, Theresa
Brand New Me

BELL, Thomas (Thom)
Didn't I (Blow Your Mind This
Time) (m)
I'm Stone In Love With You
Rubberband Man
Wake Up Susan
You Make Me Feel Brand New

BELL, William
All God's Children Got Soul
Born Under A Bad Sign
Tryin' To Love Two

BELLAMY, David
Spiders And Snakes

BELLOTTE, Pete
Heavens Knows
Hot Stuff
Love To Love You, Baby
Spring Affair
Winter Melody

BELOLO, H. (Henri)
Best Disco In Town (w)
Fire Island (w)
Go West
Hot Cop
I Am What I Am (w)
I'm A Cruiser
In Hollywood (Everybody Is A
Star) (w)
In The Navy
Key West (w)
Macho Man

My Roommate
San Francisco (You've Got Me)
(w)
Sodom & Gomorrah (w)
Ups And Downs
Village People (w)
Women
Y.M.C.A.

BELVIN, Jesse
Earth Angel
Guess Who

BENJAMIN, Bennie
Lonely Man

BENNETT, Joe
Black Slacks

BENNETT, Richard
Forever In Blue Jeans

BENNETT, Roy C.
All That I Am
Angel
Beach Boy Blues
Beginner's Luck
Boy Like Me, A Girl Like You
G.I. Blues
Island Of Love
It's A Wonderful World
Lonesome Cowboy
Once Is Enough
Puppet On A String
Relax
Shoppin' Around
Slicin' Sand
Smorgasbord
Walls Have Ears

BENSON, Renauldo
What's Going On

BENTON, Brook
Endlessly
It's Just A Matter Of Time
Lover's Question

BERGMAN, Alan
Hands Of Time (w)
I Was Born In Love With You (w)
Last Time I Felt Like This (w)
Little Boy Lost (w)
Summer Knows (w)
Summer Me, Winter Me (w)
Way We Were (w)
What Are You Doing The Rest
Of Your Life (w)
Windmills Of Your Mind (w)
Yellow Bird (w)
You Don't Bring Me Flowers (w)

BERGMAN, Marilyn
Hands Of Time (w)
I Was Born In Love With You (w)
Last Time I Felt Like This (w)
Little Boy Lost (w)

Summer Knows (w)
Summer Me, Winter Me (w)
Way We Were (w)
What Are You Doing The Rest
    Of Your Life (w)
Windmills Of Your Mind (w)
You Don't Bring Me Flowers (w)

BERNARD, Andrew
    Judy In Disguise (With Glasses)

BERNIE, Ben
    Sweet Georgia Brown

BERNS, BERT
    Piece Of My Heart

BERNSTEIN, Alan
    After The Lovin'
    Next Hundred Years
    This Moment In Time
    Yellow Days (w)

BERNSTEIN, Elmer
    Good Friend (m)

BERRY, Chuck
    Back In The U.S.A.
    Brown Eyed Handsome Man
    Bye, Bye, Johnny
    Carol
    How You've Changed
    Johnny B. Goode
    Little Queenie
    Mabellene
    Memphis, Tennessee
    Nadine (Is It You)
    No Particular Place To Go
    Promised Land
    Reelin' And Rockin'
    Rock & Roll Music
    Roll Over, Beethoven
    School Day
    Surfin' U.S.A.
    Sweet Little Sixteen
    You Can't Catch Me

BERRY, Jan
    Surf City

BETTIS, John
    Only Yesterday
    Top Of The World (w)
    Where Are They Now (m)
    Yesterday Once More

BETTS, Forrest Richard
    Blue Sky
    Jessica (m)
    Just Another Love Song
    Ramblin' Man

BICKERTON, Wayne
    Can't Stop Loving You

BIGELOW, Bob
    Hard Hearted Hannah

BIGGS, Cynthia
    Sweetest Pain

BINDI, Umberto
    You're My World (m)

BINGHAM, J.B.
    Do What You Wanna Do

BIRTLES, Beeb
    Happy Anniversary
    I'll Always Call Your Name

BISHOP, Stephen
    On And On

BJOERKLUND, M.
    Boogie Woogie Dancin' Shoes

BJORN, Frank
    Alley Cat Song (m)

BLACK, Bill
    Smokie (Part I)

BLACK, Charlie
    I Know A Heartache When I
        See One
    Lucky Me

BLACK, Don
    Ben (w)
    Born Free (w)
    Diamonds Are Forever (w)
    Sam
    To Sir, With Love (w)

BLACK, Jet
    Something Better Change

BLACKMAN, Bruce
    Everybody Be Dancin'
    Searching For A Thrill

BLACKMORE, Ritchie
    Burn
    Smoke On The Water

BLACKWELL, DeWayne
    Mr. Blue

BLACKWELL, Otis
    All Shook Up
    Don't Be Cruel (To A Heart
        That's True)
    Easy Question
    Great Balls Of Fire
    Handy Man
    Hey Little Girl
    Please Don't Drag That String
        Around
    We're Coming In Loaded

BLACKWELL, Robert
    All Around The World
    Good Golly Miss Molly
    Long Tall Sally

Reddy Teddy
Rip It Up

BLAIKLEY, Alan
    I've Lost You

BLAIKLEY, Howard
    Legend Of Xanadu

BLAIR, Hal
    I Think I'm Gonna Like It Here
        (w)
    I Was The One
    No More

BLANCHARD, Ollie
    Please Love Me Forever

BLANCHE, Carte
    Don't Go Breaking My Heart

BLAU, Eric
    If We Only Have Love (w)

BLITZ, Johnny
    Sonic Reducer

BLITZSTEIN, Marc
    Mack The Knife (w)

BLOOM, Barry
    Heavy Makes You Happy

BLOOM, Bobby
    Montego
    Mony Mony

BLOOM, Rube
    Fools Rush In

BLOOMFIELD, Michael
    It's Not Killing Me

BLUE, Barry
    Devil's Gun

BOBBIT, Charles
    Doing The Best I Can
    Papa Don't Take No Mess (Part
        I)

BOCAGE, Edwin
    Slippin' And Slidin'

BOCK, Jerry
    Fiddler On The Roof (m)
    If I Were A Rich Man (m)
    Matchmaker, Matchmaker (m)
    Sunrise, Sunset (m)

BOGAN, Lana
    Baby I'll Give It To You (w)

BOHANNON, Hamilton
    Me And The Gang

BOND, Angelo
Free Me From My Freedom

BONHAM, John
Communication Breakdown
Crunge
D'yer Mak'er
Good Times Bad Times
Heartbreaker
How Many More Times
Moby Dick
Ocean
Out On The Tiles
Rock And Roll
When The Levee Breaks
Whole Lotta Love

BONNER, Garry
Celebrate
Happy Together

BONO, Sonny
Bang Bang
Beat Goes On
I Got You Babe
Needles And Pins
She Said Yeah

BONOFF, Karla
Baby Don't Go
I Can't Hold On
Lose Again
Someone To Lay Down Beside
Me

BOONE, Daniel
Beautiful Sunday

BOONE, Steve
Summer In The City

BOOTH, Ann
Run, Woman, Run

BORUSIEWICZ, Kurt
Hot Shot

BOTKIN, Perry, Jr.
Bless The Beasts And Children
Nadia's Theme (m)

BOULANGER, GEORGES
My Prayer (m)

BOURKE, Rory
I Know A Heartache When I
See One
Lucky Me
Most Beautiful Girl

BOUWENS, Hans
Paloma Blanca

BOWEN, James
I'm Stickin' With You
Party Doll

BOWEN, Peter
Home To You

BOWIE, David
Fame
Sound And Vision
Space Oddity

BOWLING, Roger
Lucille

BOWMAN, Don
Wildwood Weed

BOYCE, Tommy
Be My Guest
I Wanna Be Free
Last Train To Clarksville
Monkees, Theme From
Pretty Little Angel Eyes
Where Angels Go, Trouble
Follows

BOYLAN, Terence
Shake It

BRACKEN, James
Dimples
Steppin' Out (m)

BRACKMAN, Jacob
Attitude Dancing
It Was So Easy
That's The Way I've Always
Heard It Should Be

BRADFORD, JANIE
Money (That's What I Want)
Too Busy Thinking About My
Baby

BRAILEY, Jerome
Tear The Roof Off The Sucker

BRAMLETT, Bonnie
Bottle Of Red Wine
Let It Rain
Lovin' You Lovin' Me
Superstar

BRAMLETT, Delaney
Never Ending Song Of Love

BRANDT, Alan
That's All

BRASFIELD, Tom
Angel In Your Arms

BRATTON, John W.
Teddy Bears' Picnic (m)

BREL, Jacques
If We Only Have Love (m)
Seasons In The Sun (m)

BRENT, Earl
Angel Eyes (w)

BREWER, Don
Shining On
We're An American Band

BRICUSSE, Leslie
Can You Read My Mind (w)
Candy Man
Goldfinger (w)
Ride (w)

BRIDGES, Alicia
I Love The Nightlife

BRIGATI, Edward, Jr.
Groovin'
How Can I Be Sure
People Got To Be Free

BRIGGS, David
Happy Anniversary (m)
Lonesome Loser

BRISTOL, Johnny (John)
Daddy Could Swear, I Declare
Hang On In There, Baby
I Don't Want To Do Wrong
If I Could Build My Whole World
Around You
I'll Be Here
My Whole World Ended
Pucker Up Buttercup
Someday We'll Be Together
Twenty Five Miles
What Does It Take
You And I

BRITTAN, Robert
Anytime Of The Year (w)

BRITTEN, Terry
Carrie

BROADWATER, Eleanor
Susie Q

BROCK, Anthony
Silver Dreams

BRODSZSKY, Nicholas
Be My Love (m)
Because You're Mine

BROOD
Saturday Night (w)

BROOKER, Gary
All This And More (m)
Conquistador (m)
Glimpses Of Nirvana
Grand Finale (m)
In The Autumn Of My Madness
Look To Your Soul
Salty Dog (m)
'Twas Teatime At The Circus
Whiter Shade Of Pale

BROOKS, Arthur & Richard
For Your Previous Love

BROOKS, Fred
I'm Just A Country Boy

BROOKS, Joe
California
Come Share My Love
If Ever I See You Again
When It's Over
You Light Up My Life

BROOKS, John Benson
You Came A Long Way From
St. Louis (m)

BROOKS, Mel
Blazing Saddles (w)

BROTHERS, Meredith
Shouldn't I Know

BROUGHTON, Steve
5.7.0.5

BROUSSARD, Joe
Mr. Big Stuff

BROWN, Billie Jean
Here Comes The Judge

BROWN, Charles
Please Come Home For
Christmas
Tell Me You'll Wait For Me

BROWN, Chuck
Bustin' Loose (Part I)

BROWN, Errol
Brother Louie
Every I's A Winner

BROWN, George
Ladies Night
Too Hot

BROWN, Harold R.
Cisco Kid
Gypsy Man
Me And Baby Brother
Spill The Wine
World Is A Ghetto

BROWN, James
Ain't That A Groove (Part I)
Ain't That A Groove (Part 2)
Bring It Up
Can't Stand It 76
Cold Sweat (Parts I & 2)
Coldblooded
Doin' It To Death
Doing The Best I Can
Don't Be A Drop-Out
Fine Old Foxy Self
Gonna Try

Good Good Lovin'
Hell
I Don't Mind
I Got A Bag Of My Own
I Got Ants In My Pants (Part I)
I Got You (I Feel Good)
If You Don't Get It The First
Time Back Up And Try It
Again, Party
I'll Go Crazy
I'll Never, Never Let You Go
Money Won't Change You
My Thang
No, No, No, No
Papa Don't Take No Mess (Part
I)
Papa's Got A Brand New Bag
(Part I)
Papa's Got A Brand New Bag
(Part II)
Parrty (Part I)
Parrty (Part II)
Payback
Please, Please, Please
Shout And Shimmy
Stone To The Bone
Tell Me What You're Gonna Do
There It Is (Part I)
Try Me

BROWN, L. Russell
I Woke Up In Love This Morning
Knock Three Times
Last Night I Made Love To
Somebody Else
Say, Has Anybody Seen My
Sweet Gypsy Rose
Steppin' Out, I'm Gonna Boogie
Tonight
Tie A Yellow Ribbon Round The
Ole Oak Tree

BROWN, Peter (Pete)
Dance With Me
Stargazer
Sunshine Of Your Love
Theme For An Imaginary
Western (w)
You Should Do It

BROWN, Lawrence
One Love In My Lifetime

BROWN, Les
Sentimental Journey

BROWN, Maxine
All In My Mind

BROWN, Nacio Herb
Pagan Love Song
Should I (m)
Singin' In The Rain (m)
Would You (m)

BROWN, Wade, Jr.
Full Speed Ahead
I'll Be Here

BROWN, William
Son Of Shaft

BROWNE, Jackson
Before The Deluge
Boulevard
For A Dancer
For Everyman
Fountain Of Sorrow
Here Come Those Tears Again
Late For The Sky
Pretender
Rock Me On The Water
Running On Empty
Take It Easy
Tenderness On The Block
That Girl Could Sing
Under The Falling Sky
You Love The Thunder

BRUCE, Ed & Patsy
Mammas Don't Let Your Babies
Grow Up To Be Cowboys

BRUCE, Gary D.
Moody River

BRUCE, Jack
Sunshine Of Your Love
Theme For An Imaginary
Western (m)

BRUCE, Michael
Billion Dollar Babies
Eighteen
Elected
Muscle Of Love
No More Mister Nice Guy
School's Out

BRUFORD, Bill
Yours Is No Disgrace

BRYAN, Alfred
Peg O' My Heart (w)

BRYANT, Boudleaux
All I Have To Do Is Dream
Bird Dog
Bye Bye, Love
Devoted To You
Poor Jenny
Problems
Raining In My Heart
Wake Up, Little Susie

BRYANT, Felice
Bye Bye, Love
Poor Jenny
Problems
Raining In My Heart
Wake Up, Little Susie

BRYANT, Don
I Can't Stand The Rain

B.T. EXPRESS
Express

BUCKINGHAM, Lindsey
Chain
Go Your Own Way
That's All For Everyone
Tusk

BUFFETT, Jimmy
Changes In Latitudes, Changes
In Attitudes
Cheeseburger In Paradise
Come Monday
Fins
Livingston Saturday Night
Manana
Margaritaville
Pencil-Thin Mustache
Son Of A Son Of A Sailor
Volcano

BUGATTI, Dominic
Back On My Feet Again
Heaven On The Seventh Floor

BUIE, Buddy
Champagne Jam
Do It Or Die
Don't Miss The Message
I'm Not Gonna Let It Bother Me
Tonight
Imaginary Lover
Sky High
So Into You
Spooky
Stormy
Traces
Ways
Where Did All The Good Times
Go

BULLARD, Jo Ann
Who's Making Love

BULLENS, Cindy
Trust Me

BULLOCK, Robert
Full Speed Ahead

BULLOCK, Vernon
If I Could Build My Whole
World Around You
What Does It Take

BUNNELL, Dewey
Amber Cascades
Green Monkey
Horse With No Name
Sandman
Tin Man
Ventura Highway

BURCH, Don
You Cheated

BURKE, Johnny
Misty (w)

BURKE, Sonny
Serpentine Fire

BURNETT, C.
Back Door Man
Killing Floor
Smokestack Lightning
Who's Been Talking

BURNETT, Chester
Sitting On Top Of The World
Tell Me

BURNETT, Larry
Cinderella

BURNETTE, Billy Joe
Teddy Bear

BURNETTE, Dorsey
Tall Oak Tree

BURNETTE, Rocky
Tired Of Toein' The Line

BURRELL, Boz
Gone, Gone, Gone

BURRIS, Roy Edward
Okie From Muskogee

BURTON, Ray
I Am Woman (m)

BUTANI, Bobby
Rats

BUTLER, Billy
Honky Tonk (Parts 1 & 2)

BUTLER, Jerry
Brand New Me
For Your Precious Love
He Don't Love You (Like I Love
You)
I've Been Loving You Too Long
Only The Strong Survive

BUTLER, Larry
Another Somebody Done Somebody Wrong Song

BUXTON, Glen
Eighteen

BYERS, Joy
C'Mon Everybody
Hard Knocks
I've Got To Find My Baby
Please Don't Stop Loving Me

So Close, Yet So Far (From
Paradise)
Stop, Look, Listen
What's A Matter, Baby

BYNUM, Hal
Lucille

BYRD, Ethel
Hide And Seek

BYRD, Robert
Little Bitty Pretty One
Over And Over

BYRNE, David
Book I Read
Don't Worry About The Govern-
ment
Psycho Killer

BYRON, Al
Roses Are Red

CAHN, Sammy
Be My Love (w)
Because You're Mine
Day By Day
Three Coins In The Fountain (w)
Touch Of Class (w)

CALDERON, Juan Carlos
Eres Tu

CALDWELL, Bobby
What You Won't Do For Love

CALDWELL, Toy
Heard It In A Love Song
Searchin' For A Rainbow

CALE, John J.
After Midnight

CALHOUN, Charles E.
Flip, Flop & Fly
Shake, Rattle And Roll

CALHOUN, Richard
Stay

CALLAHAN, J. Will
Tell Me (w)

CALLANDER, Pete
Billy, Don't Be A Hero
Night Chicago Died (w)

CALLEN, Mickeala
In The Hour Of Not Quite Rain

CALLENDER, Bobby
Little Star

CALLIS, John
Good Sculptures
I Can't Stand My Baby

CALVIN, Billie
Wishin' On A Star

CAMILLO, Tony
Dynomite (Part I)

CAMPBELL, George
Four Walls

CAMPBELL, Jimmy
Good Night Sweetheart
Try A Little Tenderness

CAMPBELL, Michael
Refueee

CAMPBELL, Paul
House Of The Rising Sun
(Adapted)
Kisses Sweeter Than Wine (w)

CANDELARIA, Al
Honest I Do

CANNON, Gus
Stealin'
Walk Right In

CANSLER, Larry
Wildfire (m)

CAPEHART, Jerry
Summertime Blues
Turn Around, Look At Me

CAPITANELLI, Arnold
Sweet Marjorene

CAPIZZI, Leonard
Monster Mash

CAPPS, Al
Half Breed (m)

CARAWAN, Guy
We Shall Overcome (Adapted)

CARILLO, Alvaro
Yellow Days (m)

CARL, Billy
Diane

CARLO, Tyran
Got A Job
Lonely Teardrops
That's Why (I Love You So)
You've Got What It Takes

CARMAN, Brian
Pipeline (m)

CARMEN, Eric
All By Myself
Go All The Way
Hey, Deanie
I Wanna Be With You
Never Gonna Fall In Love Again
She Did It
Sunrise
That's Rock 'N Roll

CARMICHAEL, Hoagy
Baltimore Oriole (m)
Georgia On My Mind (m)
Heart And Soul
Skylark (m)

CARNES, Kim
It Hurts So Bad

CARPENTER, Richard
Only Yesterday
Top Of The World (m)
Yesterday Once More

CARR, Leon
Hey There Lonely Girl

CARR, Robert
We Belong Together

CARRACK, Paul
How Long

CARRADINE, Keith
I'm Easy
It Don't Worry Me

CARRERE, Claude
Don' Tell My Heart To Stop
Loving You

CARROL, Bert
Wear My Ring Around Your
Neck

CARROLL, Gregory
Just One Look

CARROLL, Willis
Seven Days

CARSTARPHEN, V.
Wake Up Everybody

CARTER, A.A.
Wild Side Of Life

CARTER, Blanche
Devil Or Angel

CARTER, Calvin
Goodnight, It's Time To Go
He Don't Love You (Like I
Love You)

CARTER, Carlene
One Step Closer

CARTER, Darryl
Woman's Gotta Have It

CARTER, Valerie
Cook With Honey

CARTER, Lewis
Can't You Hear My Heart Beat

CASEY, H. W. (Harry Wayne)
Boogie Shoes
Dance Across The Floor
Do You Feel All Right
Get Down Tonight
I'm Your Boogie Man
Keep It Comin' Love
Please Don't Go
Rock Your Baby
Shake Your Booty
That's The Way I Like It
Where Is The Love
Who Do Ya Love

CASEY, Kenneth
Sweet Georgia Brown

CASH, John R. (Johnny)
I Walk The Line
Rock Island Line (Adapted)

CASH, Sammy
Midnight Special (Adapted)

CASH, Steve
If You Wanna Get To Heaven
Jackie Blue

CASHMAN, Terry
Friend Is Dying
Song That Never Comes
Sweet City Song

CASON, Buzz
Everlasting Love

CASTENELL, Amadee, Jr.
Action Speaks Louder Than
Words

CASTILLO, E.
You're Still A Young Man

CASTON, Leonard
Boogie Down
Keep On Truckin'

CAVALIERE, Felix
Groovin'
How Can I Be Sure
People Got To Be Free

CAVANAUGH, Jessie
Michael, Row The Boat Ashore
(Adapted)

CERONI, Ray
I've Had It

CERRONE
Got To Have Lovin'

CETERA, Peter
Baby, What A Big Surprise
Feelin' Stronger Every Day
If You Leave Me Now
No Tell Lover
Wishing You Were Here

CHAMBLISS, David G.
Let Me Lay My Funk On You

CHAMPLIN, Bill
After The Love Has Gone

CHANCE, Barry
Fins

CHANNEL, Bruce
Hey Baby

CHAPIN, Harry
Cat's In The Cradle
Circles
I Want To Learn A Love Song
Tangled Up Puppet

CHAPIN, Sandy
Cat's In The Cradle
Tangled Up Puppet

CHAPMAN, Mike
If You Can't Give Me Love
Kiss You All Over
Living Next Door To Alice
Stumblin' In

CHAPMAN, Peter
Every Day (I Have The Blues)

CHAQUICO, Craig
Dance With The Dragon
Jane (m)

CHARLES, Ray
Come Back Baby
Don't You Know
Halleluja I Love Her (Him) So
I Got A Woman
Understanding
What'd I Say

CHARNIN, Martin
Easy Street (w)
Tomorrow (w)

CHASE, Lincoln
Jim Dancy
Name Game
Nitty Gritty

CHATER, Kerry
I Know A Heartache When I
See One

CHATMAN, Peter
Mother Earth

CHEEKS, Judy
Mellow Lovin'

CHIATE, Lloyd
Maybe I'm A Fool

CHILD, Desmond
I Was Made For Lovin' You

CHINN, Nicky
If You Can't Give Me Love
Kiss You All Over
Living Next Door To Alice
Stumblin' In

CHOWNING, Randle
Look Away

CHRISTIAN, Chris
All Things Are Possible
Still The Lovin' Is Fun

CHRISTIAN, Roger
Don't Worry Baby

CHRISTIE, Lou
Lightnin' Strikes

CHRISTOPHER, Gavin
Dance Wit' Me

CHRISTOPHER, Gretchen
Come Softly To Me

CHRISTOPHER, Johnny
If You Talk In Your Sleep
No Love At All

CHROME, Cheetah
Sonic Reducer

CHURCH, Eugene
Pretty Girls Everywhere

CICCHETTI, Carl
Beep Beep

CLANTON, Jimmy
Just A Dream

CLAPS, Donald
Beep Beep

CLAPTON, Eric
Anyday
Badge
Bell Bottom Blues
Bottle Of Red Wine
Hello Old Friend
I Looked Away
Lay Down Sally
Layla
Let It Rain
Lovin' You Lovin' Me
Sunshine Of Your Love

CLARK, Claudine
Party Lights

CLARK, Dave
Any Way You Want It
Catch Us If You Can
Glad All Over

CLARK, Dee
Raindrops

CLARK, Delecta
You Can't Sit Down

CLARK, Rudy
Good Lovin'
It's In His Kiss

CLARKE, Allan
Jennifer Eccles
Tell Me To My Face

CLARKE, Grant
Am I Blue (w)

CLARKE, Mark
Wizard

CLARKE, W.
Where Is The Love

CLAYTON, Paul
Gotta Travel On

CLEVELAND, Alfred
Baby, Baby, Don't Cry
I Second That Emotion
What's Going On

CLIFTON, Dennis
Baby I Want You

CLINGER, Peggy
Rock Me Baby

CLINTON, George
Do That Stuff
One Nation Under A Groove
Tear The Roof Off The Sucker

CLOVERS
Down In The Alley

COBB, ED
Dirty Water

COBB, George L.
Alabama Jubilee (m)
Are You from Dixie (m)

COBB, J. R. (James R.)
Champagne Jam
Do It Or Die
Don't Miss The Message
Searching For A Thrill
Spooky

202

Stormy
Traces
Where Did All The Good Times
  Go?

COBB, Margaret
Hey! Baby

COBURN, Richard
Whispering

COCHRAN, Eddie
Summertime Blues

COCHRAN, Hank
Make The World Go Away

CODY, Phil
Bad Blood
Immigrant
Laughter In The Rain
Love In The Shadows
Should've Never Let You Go
Solitaire
Steppin' Out

COFFEY, Dennis
Scorpio (m)
Taurus

COGGINS, Danny
Pucker, Up Buttercup

COHEN, J.
Ain't No Stoppin' Us Now

COHEN, Leonard
Bird On The Wire
Bunch Of Lonesome Heroes
Butcher
Hey, That's No Way To Say
  Goodbye
Lady Midnight
Master Song
Old Revolution
One Of Us Can Not Be Wrong
Priests
Seems So Long Ago, Nancy
Sisters Of Mercy
So Long, Marianne
Stories Of The Street
Story Of Isaac
Stranger Song
Suzanne
Teachers
Tonight Will Be Fine
Winter Lady
You Know Who I Am

COLACRAI, Cirino
Runaround

COLBY, Robert
I'm A Fool For You

COLEMAN, Cy
Big Spender (m)
What Are Heavy (m)

COLEMAN, Larry
Ricochet

COLEMAN, Ron
Tired Of Toein' The Line

COLEY, John Ford
Gone Too Far

COLLINS, Aaron
Eddie My Love

COLLINS, Albert
Lucille
Slippin' And Slidin'

COLLINS, Bootsie
Tear The Roof Off The Sucker

COLLINS, Gail
Baby I'm Down
Blood Of The Sun
Crossroader

COLLINS, Judy
Maid Of Constant Sorrow
Sailor's Life
Wild Mountain Thyme

COLLINS, Larry
Delta Dawn

COLLINS, Phil
Misunderstanding

COLLINS, Susan
Sweet Life

COLTER, Jessi
I'm Not Lisa
What's Happened To Blue Eyes
You Ain't Never Been Loved

COLTRANE, Chi
Thunder And Light'ning

COLTRANE, John
Welcome (m)

COMANOR, Jeffrey M.
Bobbie's Blues
Lovin' Stew
Sailboat Song
We'll Never Have To Say Good-
  bye Again

CONLEY, Arthur
Funky Street

CONNELL, Melissa A.
I've Never Been In Love

CONNELLY, Reg
Good Night Sweetheart
Try A Little Tenderness

CONNOLLY, Brian
Action
Fox On The Run

CONNORS, Carol
Gonna Fly Now (w)
With You I'm Born Again (w)
You Take My Heart Away (w)

CONTE
Believe Me

CONTI, Bill
Gonna Fly Now (w)
Redemption
Unmarried Woman, Theme From
You Take My Heart Away (m)

CONWAY, Talmadge G.
Ten Percent

COOK, Bill
I'll Come Running Back To You

COOK, Janet J
Let Me Lay My Funk On You

COOK, Paul
Anarchy In the U.K.
God Save The Queen
Pretty Vacant

COOK, R.
I'd Like To Teach The World
  To Sing

COOK, Roger
Doctor's Orders
7-6-5-4-3-2-1 (Blow Your
  Whistle)
Talkin' In Your Sleep
What's Your Name, What's Your
  Number?
You've Got Your Troubles

COOKE, Linda
Woman's Gotta Have It

COOKE, Sam
Another Saturday Night
Bring It On Home To Me
Shake
Wonderful World

COONCE, Rick
Feelings

COOPER, Alice
Billion Dollar Babies
Eighteen
Elected
From The Inside
How You Gonna See Me Now

I Never Cry
Muscle Of Love
No More Mister Nice Guy
Only Women Bleed
School's Out
Welcome To My Nightmare
You And Me

COOPER, Brenda & Jason
Dance, Dance, Dance (w)

COOPER, Mike
Ffun
Shake And Dance With Me

COOPER, S.
In The Bush

COQUATRIX, Bruno
Count Every Star

COR, Peter
Getaway

CORBETTA, Jerry
Green-Eyed Lady

CORCORAN, Tom
Fins

CORDELL, Ritchie
I Think We're Alone Now
Mony Mony

COREA, Chick
Spain (m)

CORNELIUS, Carter
I'm Never Gonna Be Alone Anymore

CORNELIUS, Eddie
Don't Ever Be Lonely
I'm Never Gonna Be Alone Any-
More
Too Late To Turn Back Now
Treat Her Like A Lady

CORNWELL, Hugh
Something Better Change

CORPORATION
ABC
Goin' Back To Indiana
I Want You Back
Love You Save
Mama's Pearl
Maybe Tomorrow
Sugar Daddy

CORRELL, Dennis
Gas Lamps And Clay (w)

CORY, George
I Left My Heart In San Francisco
(m)

COSBY, Henry
Fingertips (Part 2)
I Was Made To Love Her
I'm Livin' In Shame
My Cherie Amour
Nothing's Too Good For My Baby
Shoo-Be-Doo-Be-Doo-Da-Day
Tears Of A Clown
Uptight (Everything's Alright)
With A Child's Heart

COTTON, Gene
Like A Sunday In Salem

COTTON, Paul
Heart Of The Night

COULTER, Phil
Summer Love Sensation

COURAGE, Alexander
Star Trek, Theme From (m)

CONVAY, Don
Letter Full Of Tears
See Saw

COVERDALE, David
Burn

COVINGTON, Joey
With Your Love

COWELL, Johnny
Walk Hand In Hand

COX, Doug
Butterfly For Bucky (m)

COX, Herbert
Little Girl Of Mine

CRAIN, Tom
Devil Went Down To Georgia
In America
Legend Of Wooley Swamp

CRANE, Jimmie
Ev'ry Day Of My Life
Hurt

CRAWFORD, Dave
Run To Me
Young Hearts Run Free

CREATORE, Luigi
Can't Give You Anything (But
My Love)
Can't Help Falling In Love
Disco Baby
Hey Girl, Come And Get It
Lion Sleeps Tonight (Adapted)
Love Is The Answer
Star On A T.V. Show

CREED, Linda
Greatest Love Of All (w)
I'm Stone In Love With You
Rubberband Man
You Make Me Feel Brand New

CRETESCOS, Jim
Doesn't Somebody Want To Be
Wanted

CREWE, Bob
Big Girls Don't Cry
Get Dancin'
Lady Marmalade
My Eyes Adored You
Silhouettes
Tallahassee Lassie
Walk Like A Man

CRIER, Keith
Disco Nights
Standing Ovation

CRISS, Peter
Beth
Love Theme From Kiss

CROCE, Jim
Bad, Bad Leroy Brown
I'll Have To Say I Love You In
A Song
One Less Set Of Footsteps
Operator (That's Not The Way
It Feels)
Time In A Bottle
Workin' At The Car Wash Blues
You Don't Mess Around With Jim

CROFTS, Dash
Blue Bonnet Nation
Diamond Girl (m)
Get Closer
Hummingbird
I'll Play For You (m)
It's Gonna Come Down
Summer Breeze (m)
We May Never Pass This Way
Again (m)

CROMPTON, Bill
Why

CROOK, Max
Runaway

CROPPER, Steve
Dock Of The Bay
Green Onions
Happy Song
In The Midnight Hour
Knock On Wood
See Saw
Soul Clap 69

CROSBY, David
Guinnevere
Long Time Gone

Out Of The Darkness (w)
Wooden Ships

CROSS, Christopher
Never Be The Same
Ride Like The Wind
Sailing

CROSS, Douglas
I Left My Heart In San Francisco (w)

CROWLEY, John C.
Baby Come Back
Prisoner Of Your Love

CRUTCHER, Bettye
Who's Making Love

CUMMINGS, Burton
Stand Tall
These Eyes

CUMMINGS, Steve
Who Listens To The Radio

CUNICO, Gino
When I Wanted You

CUNNINGHAM, James & John
Jo-Ann

CURB, Mike
Burning Bridges (w)
It Was A Good Time (w)

CURTIN, Memphis
Lovey Dovey

CURTIS, Sonny
More Than I Can Say
Walk Right Back

CYMBAL, Johnny
Mr. Bass Man
Rock Me Baby

DABNEY, Herbert A., III
Let Me Lay My Funk On You

D'ABO, Mike
Handbags And Gladrags

DABON, Ernest & Robert
Action Speaks Louder Than Words

DACUS, Donnie
Buyin' Time
Turn Back The Pages

DAHLSTROM, Patti
Emotion (w)

DAILEY, Harry
Volcano

DAL BELLO, Lisa
Pretty Girls

DALE, Jim
Georgy Girl

DANIEL, Eliot
Lavender Blue (m)

DANIELS, Charlie
Devil Went Down To Georgia
In America
Legend Of Wooley Swamp
Mississippi
South's Gonna Do It
Texas

DANIELS, Don
Down To Love Town
Let's Be Young Tonight

DANIELS, Dorothy & Frank
My Heart Belongs To Only You

DANIELS, Jack
Turn Back The Hands Of Time

DANKO, Rick
This Wheel's On Fire (m)

DANOFF, Bill
Afternoon Delight
Take Me Home, Country Roads

DARIN, Bobby
Dream Lover
Simple Song Of Freedom
Splish Splash

DARION, Joe
Impossible Dream (w)
Ricochet

DARLING, Erik
Walk Right In (Adapted)

DASH, Julian
Tuxedo Junction (w)

DAUGHTRY, Dean
I'm Not Gonna Let It Bother Me Tonight
Imaginary Lover
Sky High
So Into You

DAVID, Hal
Alfie (w)
Always Something There To Remind Me (w)
Close To You (w)
Do You Know The Way To San Jose (w)
Don't Make Me Over (w)
Green Grass Starts To Grow (w)
I Never Said I Love You (w)
I Say A Little Prayer (w)

I'll Never Fall In Love Again (w)
It Was Almost Like A Song (w)
Living Together, Growing Together (w)
Look Of Love (w)
Make It Easy On Yourself (w)
Moonraker (w)
My Heart Is An Open Book (w)
My Little Red Book (w)
99 Miles From L.A.
One Less Bell To Answer (w)
Promises, Promises (w)
Raindrops Keep Fallin' On My Head (w)
This Guy's In Love With You (w)
Walk On By (w)
What The World Needs Now Is Love (w)
What's New Pussycat (w)

DAVID, Hod
In Our Time (m)

DAVID, Mack
It Must Be Him (w)
It Was A Good Time (w)
My Own True Love (w)

DAVID, Maxwell
Eddie My Love

DAVID, Sunny
Love Love Love

DAVIDSON, Lenny
Catch Us If You Can

DAVIES, Idris
Bells Of Rhymney (w)

DAVIES, Ray
You Really Got Me

DAVIES, Rick
Give A Little Bit
Goodbye Stranger
Logical Song
Take The Long Way Home

DAVIS, B.
I'd Like To Teach The World To Sing

DAVIS, Benny
Baby Face (Disco Version)
Don't Break The Heart That Loves You

DAVIS, Bernice
Long Lonely Nights

DAVIS, Billy
Country Sunshine

DAVIS, Clifton
Lookin' Through The Windows
Never Can Say Goodbye

DAVIS, Collin
Yama-Yama Man (w)

DAVIS, Don
Disco Lady
Take Care Of Your Homework
Who's Making Love

DAVIS, George
Tell It Like It Is

DAVIS, Hal
Dancing Machine
I'll Be There
Life Of The Party

DAVIS, Mac
Baby Don't Get Hooked On Me
I Believe In Music
Music In My Life
Stop And Smell The Roses
Watchin' Scotty Grow

DAVIS, Patti
I Wish You Peace

DAVIS, Paul
Sweet Life

DAVIS, Rev. Gary
Candy Man
Cocaine Blues
If I Had My Way

DAVIS, Scott
Two Sides

DAVIS, Spencer
Gimme Some Lovin'

DAVIS, Steve
Take Time To Know Her

DAVIS, Tex
Be-Bop-A-Lu-La

DAVIS, Warren
Book Of Love

DAVIS, William E.
Gee

DAWES, Gen. Charles G.
It's All In The Game (m)

DAWSON, John
Friend Of The Devil (m)

DEACON, John
You're My Best Friend

DEAN. J.
You Don't Have To Be A Star

DEAN, James
I've Passed This Way Before
What Becomes Of The Broken
Hearted

DEAN, Mary
Half Breed (w)

DE ANGELIS, Peter
Why

DEBARGE, Bobby
There'll Never Be

DE CURTIS, E.
Surrender

DEE, Joey
Peppermint Twist

DEE, Kiki
Sugar On The Floor

DEE, Sylvia
Too Young

DEES, Rick
Disco Duck (Part I)

DEGREE, Craig
Out Of The Darkness (m)

DEHR, Rich
Greenfields
Memories Are Made Of This

DE KNIGHT, Jimmy
Rock Around The Clock

DE KNIGHT, Rene
Declaration

DEL BARRIO, Eddie
Fantasy
Star

DE LOS RIOS, Orbe-Waldo
Song Of Joy

DEMETRUIS, Claude
Hard Headed Woman
I Was The One
Mean Woman Blues

DEMPSEY, Greg
Roll Away The Stone

DENNIS, Matt
Angel Eyes (m)

DENTON, Johnny
Black Slacks

DENVER, John
Annie's Song
Calypso
Leaving On A Jet Plane
Rocky Mountain High
Sunshine On My Shoulders
Take Me Home, Country Roads

DEODATO, Eumir
Also Sprach Zarathustra (2001)
(m., arranged)
Super Strut

DE PASSE, Suzanne
Here Comes The Judge

DE ROSE, Peter
Deep Purple (m)

DEROSIER, Michael
Barracuda

DERRINGER, Rick
Rock And Roll Hootchie Koo

DE SALVO, John
Nuclear Waste

DE SHANNON, Jackie
Brighton Hill
Dum Dum
Put A Little Love In Your
Heart
River Of Love

DESTRI, James (Jimmy)
11:59
I Didn't Have The Nerve To
Say No
Picture This

DEUTSCH, Helen
Hi-Lili, Hi-Lo (w)

DE VITA, A.
Softly, As I Leave You (m)

DEVO
Jocko Homo

DEVOL, Frank
Happening

DE VORZON, Barry
Bless The Beasts And Children
Nadia's Theme (m)
S.W.A.T., Theme From

DE WALT, Autry
Shotgun

DEWEY, N.Q.
Runaway

DEYOUNG, Dennis
Babe
Come Sail Away
Lady
Lights
Why Me

DIAMOND, Gregg
Dance Little Dreamer
Fess Up To The Boogie
Hot Butterfly

More, More, More (Part I)
Risky Changes
Starcruiser

DIAMOND, Lee
Tell It Like It Is

DIAMOND, Neil
And The Grass Won't Pay No
Mind
Beautiful Noise
Brooklyn Roads
Cherry, Cherry
Cracklin' Rosie
Desiree
Do It
Forever In Blue Jeans
I Am...I Said
If You Know What I Mean
I'm A Believer
Say Maybe
September Morn
Solitary Man
Song Sung Blue
Sunflower
Sweet Caroline
You Don't Bring Me Flowers

DICKERSON, Morris
Cisco Kid
Gypsy Man
Me And Baby Brother
Spill The Wine
World Is A Ghetto

DIDIER, Julie
Anyone Who Isn't Me Tonight

DI FRANCO, Paul
Life Is A Rock

DIGREGORIO, "Taz"
Devil Went Down To Georgia
In America
Legend Of Wooley Swamp

DILENA, Amber
Ready Or Not

DILLON, John
If You Wanna Get To Heaven

DIMIRCO, Vincent
Up The Ladder To The Roof

DINWIDDIE, Gene
Love March

DISCANT, Mack
Summer Place, Theme From (w)

DIXON, Dave
I Dig Rock And Roll Music
Song Is Love

DIXON, Eugene
Duke Of Earl

DIXON, Heather
Mister Lee

DIXON, Julius
Lollipop

DIXON, Luther
Big Boss Man
Hundred Pounds Of Clay
Sixteen Candles
Why Baby Why

DIXON, Mort
Bye Bye Blackbird

DIXON, Willie
Back Door Man
Bring It On Home
Close To You
Evil (Is Going On)
I Can't Quit You Baby
I Love The Life I Live
It Do Me So Good
Mellow Down Easy
My Babe
Seventh Son
Spoonful
Wang-Dang-Doodle
You Shook Me

DOBBINS, Georgia
Please Mr. Postman

DODD, Dorothy
Granada (w)

DODSON, Larry
Shake Your Rump To The Funk
Too Hot To Stop (Part I)

DOGGETT, Bill
Honky Tonk (Parts 1 & 2) (m)

DOHERTY, Dennis
Got A Feeling
I Saw Her Again Last Night

DOLPH, Norman
Life Is A Rock

DOMAN, Harold
Mountain Of Love

DOMINO, Antoine
Ain't That A Shame
All By Myself
Be My Guest
Blue Monday
Do Weevil
I Want To Walk You Home
I Want You To Know
I'm Gonna Be A Wheel Someday
I'm In Love Again
I'm Walkin'
Land Of A Thousand Dances
Let The Four Winds Blow
My Girl Josephine

Poor Me
Valley Of Tears
Whole Lotta Loving

DOMINO, "Fats" SEE Domino,
Antoine

DONAGGIO, P.
You Don't Have To Say You
Love Me

DONALDSON, Walter
What Can I Say After I Say
I'm Sorry
Yes Sir, That's My Baby

DONIDA, C.
Help Yourself (m)
I (Who Have Nothing) (m)

DONOVAN
Catch The Wind
Colours
Mellow Yellow
Sunshine Superman

DOORS
Land Ho! (m)
Light My Fire
Maggie M'Gill (m)
Peace Frog (m)
Roadhouse Blues (m)
Ship Of Fools (m)
Waiting For The Sun (m)

DORE, Charlie
Pilot Of The Airwaves

DORFF, Stephen H.
Fire In The Morning
I Just Fall In Love Again (m)
Let Me Love You Once Before
You Go

DORIS, Jim
Oh Me Oh My (I'm A Fool For
You Baby)

DORSET, Ray
In The Summertime

DOUGLAS, Graeme
Do Anything You Wanna Do

DOUGLAS, Lew
Have You Heard

DOUGLASS, Greg
Jungle Love

DOWDEN, Christopher
Long Haired Lover From Liverpool

DOWE, B.
Rivers Of Babylon

DOWNES, Geoff
  Video Killed The Radio Star

DOZIER, Lamont
  Baby, Don't You Do It
  Baby I Need Your Loving
  Baby Love
  Back In My Arms Again
  Bernadette
  Come See About Me
  Forever Came Today
  Happening
  Heat Wave
  Heaven Must Have Sent You
  How Sweet It Is (To Be Loved
    By You)
  I Can't Help Myself
  I Hear A Symphony
  I'm Ready For Love
  I'm The One You Need
  In And Out Of Love
  It's The Same Old Song
  Jimmy Mack
  Little Darling (I Need You)
  Love Is Here And Now You're
    Gone
  Love Is Like An Itching In My
    Heart
  Mickey's Monkey
  My World Is Empty Without You
  Nothing But Heartaches
  Nowhere To Run
  Quicksand
  Reach Out, I'll Be There
  Reflections
  Road Runner
  7 Rooms Of Gloom
  Shake Me, Wake Me (When It's
    Over)
  Something About You
  Standing In The Shadows Of
    Love
  Stop! In The Name Of Love
  This Old Heart Of Mine (Is
    Weak For You)
  When The Love Light Starts
    Shining Through His Eyes
  Where Did Our Love Go
  You Can't Hurry Love
  You Keep Me Hangin' On
  You're A Wonderful One

DRAKE, Ervin
  Good Morning Heartache
  It Was A Very Good Year

DRAKE, Guy
  Welfare Cadillac

DRAYTON, Clarence
  Life Of The Party

DRIFTWOOD, Jimmy
  Battle Of New Orleans

DRIGGS, C.
  Get Off

DRUMMOND, Burleigh
  Nice, Nice Very Nice (m)

DUBIN, Al
  I Only Have Eyes For You (w)

DUBOFF, Steve
  No Communication

DUDDY, Lyn
  Johnny Angel (w)

DUKE, Vernon
  Cabin In The Sky (m)
  Taking A Chance On Love (m)

DUNAWAY, Dennis
  Eighteen
  Elected

DUNCAN, Jimmy
  My Special Angel

DUNCAN, Wayne M.
  Wasted Days and Wasted Nights

DUNN, Donald
  Soul Clap 69

DUNN, Larry
  Shining Star

DURAND, R.
  Just A Little

DURDEN, Tommy
  Heartbreak Hotel

DURRILL, John
  Dark Lady
  I Saw A Man And He Danced
    With His Wife

DYER, Des
  Love Fire

DYER, Jan
  Everytime Two Fools Collide

DYLAN, Bob
  Abandoned Love
  Absolutely Sweet Marie
  All Along The Watchtower
  All I Really Want To Do
  All The Tired Horses
  Apple Suckling Tree
  As I Went Out One Morning
  Ballad Of Frankie Lee And
    Judas Priest
  Billy
  Black Diamond Bay
  Blowin' In The Wind
  Bob Dylan's Blues
  Buckets Of Rain
  Catfish
  Chimes Of Freedom
  Clothes Line Saga

Country Pie
Crash On The Levee
Day Of The Locusts
Dear Landlord
Dirge
Don't Think Twice, It's All
  Right
Don't Ya Tell Henry
Down Along The Cove
Drifter's Escape
Father Of Night
Forever Young
Fourth Time Around
Gates Of Eden
George Jackson
Get Your Rocks Off
Girl From The North Country
Goin' To Acapulco
Going, Going, Gone
Golden Loom
Gotta Serve Somebody
Hard Rain's A Gonna Fall
Hazel
Highway 61 Revisited
Hurricane
I Am A Lonesome Hobo
I Dreamed I Saw St. Augustine
I Pity The Poor Immigrant
I Shall Be Released
I Threw It All Away
I Wanna Be Your Lover
I Want You
I'd Have You Any Time
Idiot Wind
If Dogs Run Free
If Not For You
If You Gotta Go, Go Now
If You See Her, Say Hello
I'll Be Your Baby Tonight
Isis
It Ain't Me, Babe
It's All Over Now, Baby Blue
It's Alright Ma
John Wesley Harding
Joey
Just Like A Woman
Just Like Tom Thumb's Blues
Knockin' On Heaven's Door
Lay, Lady, Lay
Leopard-Skin Pill-Box Hat
Like A Rolling Stone
Lily, Rosemary And The Jack
  Of Hearts
Living The Blues
Lo And Behold
Lonesome Death Of Hattie
  Carroll
Long Distance Operator
Love Is Just A Four Letter Word
Maggie's Farm
Mama, You Been On My Mind
Man In Me
Masters Of War
Meet Me In The Morning
Million Dollar Bash
Minstrel Boy
Money Blues

FIND THAT TUNE

ENTNER, Warren
  Feelings

ENTWISTLE, John
  Trick Of The Light

ERRY, S.
  Any Way You Want It

ERTEGUN, Ahmet
  Chains Of Love
  Don't Play That Song
  Don't You Know I Love You
  Fool, Fool, Fool
  Hey, Miss Fannie
  Lovey Dovey
  Mess Around
  Yes, It's You

ESCOVEDO, Javier
  Wimp

ESPOSITO, Joe
  Bad Girls
  Make It Last

ESTY, Bob
  Fight
  Take Me Home
  Wasn't It Good

ETRIS, Barry
  Rueben James

EVANS, Paul
  Roses Are Red
  When

EVANS, Tom
  Without You

EVERS, J.
  Boogie Woogie Dancin' Shoes

EVOY, Larry
  Last Song

EYTON, Frank
  Body And Soul (w)

EZRIN, Bob
  Beth

FAGEN, Donald
  Black Friday
  Daddy Don't Live In That New
    York City No More
  Deacon Blues
  Do It Again
  FM
  Here At The Western World
  Josie
  My Old School
  Peg
  Pretzel Logic

Reeling In The Years
Rikki, Don't Lose That Number

FAIN, Sammy
  Secret Love (m)

FAIRFAX, Reuben, Jr.
  Belle

FAITH, Percy
  My Heart Cries For You

FAITH, Russ
  Don't Tell My Heart To Stop
    Loving You

FALTERMEYER, Harold
  Hot Stuff

FARGO, Donna
  Funny Face
  Happiest Girl In The Whole
    U.S.A.

FARIAN, F.
  Rivers Of Babylon

FARINA, Mimi
  Bread And Roses (m)
  Miles

FARINA, Richard
  Children Of Darkness
  Hard Loving Loser
  Joy 'Round My Brain
  Miles
  Reno Nevada

FARINA, Sandy
  Kiss Me In The Rain

FARJEON, Eleanor
  Morning Has Broken (w)

FARNER, Mark
  Closer To Home
  Shinin' On

FARNSWORTH, Nancy
  Here Come Those Tears Again

FARRAR, John
  Have You Never Been Mellow
  Little More Love
  Magic
  Sam
  You're The One That I Want

FARRELL, Wes
  Doesn't Somebody Want To Be
    Wanted
  Hang On Sloopy
  I'll Meet You Halfway
  Sunny And Me

FARROW, Larry
  If It Don't Fit, Don't Force It

FASSERT, Fred
  Barbara Ann

FEASTER, Carl & Claude
  Sh-Boom

FEATHERS, Charlie
  I Forgot To Remember to Forget

FEKARIS, Dino
  I Just Want To Celebrate
  I Pledge My Love
  I Will Survive
  Let Me Know (I Have A Right)
  Makin' It
  Reunited
  Shake Your Groove Thing
  We've Got Love

FELDER, Allan
  Goin' Up In Smoke
  Let Me Make Love To You
  Ten Percent

FELDER, Don
  Hotel California

FELDMAN, Jack
  Copacabana (w)
  Slow Dance (w)

FELDMAN, Richard
  Promises

FELDMAN, Robert
  My Boyfriend's Back

FELICIANO, Jose
  Chico And The Man

FELL, Terry
  You're The Reason

FELLER, Sherm
  Summertime, Summertime

FENDER, Freddy
  Wasted Days And Wasted Nights

FERGUSON, Jay
  Shakedown Cruise
  Thunder Island

FETTER, Ted
  Taking A Chance On Love (w)

FEYNE, Buddy
  Tuxedo Junction (w)

FIEGER, DOUG
  Good Girls Don't
  My Sharona

FIELDS, Alvin
  Let's All Chant
  Think It Over

FIELDS, Dorothy
Big Spender (w)
I'm In The Mood For Love
Way You Look To-Night (w)

FINCH, Richard (R.)
Boogie Shoes
Dance Across The Floor
Do You Feel All Right
Get Down Tonight
I'm Your Boogie Man
Keep It Comin' Love
Please Don't Go
Rock Your Baby
Shake Your Booty
That's The Way I Like It
Where Is The Love
Who Do Ya Love

FINDON, Ben
Light Up The World With Sunshine

FINNERAN, J.L. & V.
Dear One

FINNEY, L.
You're So Fine

FISHER, Andre
Hollywood

FISHER, Bruce
Will It Go 'Round In Circles
You Are So Beautiful

FISHER, Dan
Good Morning Heartache

FISHER, Fred
Peg O' My Heart (m)

FISHER, Matthew
Glimpses Of Nirvana
Grand Finale (m)
In The Autumn Of My Madness
Look To Your Soul
'Twas Teatime at The Circus

FISHER, Roger
Barracuda

FISHERMAN, Jack
Help Yourself (w)
Why Don't They Understand

FLEETWOOD, Mick
Chain

FLEISCHMAN, Robert
Anytime
Wheel In The Sky

FLEMING, Kye
Crackers
Fooled By A Feeling
Sleeping Single In A Double Bed
Years

FLETCHER, Don
Dancing Machine

FLOWERS, Danny
Tulsa Time

FLOYD, Eddie
Knock On Wood

FLOYD, King
Groove Me

FOGELBERG, Daniel
Heart Hotels
Longer
Next Time
Part Of The Plan
To The Morning

FOGERTY, J.C. (John)
Bad Moon Rising
Down On The Corner
Fortunate Son
Have You Ever Seen The Rain
Long As I Can See The Light
Lookin' Out My Back Door
Proud Mary
Someday Never Comes
Sweet Hitch-Hiker
Travelin' Band
Who'll Stop The Rain

FOOTMAN, John
Look What You've Done To My Heart

FORBERT, Steve
Romeo's Tune

FORREST, Jimmy
Night Train

FORSEY, Keith
Boogie Woogie Dancin' Shoes
Hot Stuff

FORSTER, B.Y.
Lullaby Of Birdland (w)

FOSTER, Bruce
Platinum Heroes

FOSTER, David
After The Love Has Gone
Breakdown Dead Ahead
From The Inside
Got To Be Real
Jojo
Look What You've Done To Me (m)
Time And A Word

FOSTER, Fred
Me And Bobby McGee

FOSTER, Patricia
Here I Am Again

FOSTER, Preston
Got My Mo-Jo Working

FOWLER, Wally
That's How Much I Love You

FOX, Charles
I Got A Name (m)
Killing Me Softly With His Song (m)
Love Boat, Main Title From (m)

FOX, Ray
In Our Time (w)

FOXX, Charlie & Inez
Mockingbird

FRAMPTON, Peter
All I Want To Be (Is By Your Side)
Baby, I Love Your Way
Baby Somethin's Happening
I Can't Stand It No More
It's A Plain Shame
Shine On
Show Me The Way

FRANK, Doug
After You

FRANKLIN, Aretha
Since You've Been Gone

FRANKLIN, Carolyn
Angel

FRANKS, Michael
Monkey See-Monkey Do
Popsicle Toes

FRANTZ, Christopher
Psycho Killer

FRASER, Andy
All Right Now
Every Kinda People

FRASER, Ron
Cowboy

FRATTO, Russ
Mabellene

FRAZIER, Dallas
Alley Oop
Mohair Sam
Son Of Hickory Holler's Tramp
Sunshine Of My World

FRED, John
Judy In Disguise (With Glasses)

FREED, Alan
Mabellene
Sincerely

FREED, Arthur
  Pagan Love Song (w)
  Should I (w)
  Singin' In The Rain (w)
  Would You (w)

FREEDMAN, Max C.
  Rock Around The Clock

FREELAND, Roy
  In 25 Words Or Less
  This Night Won't Last Forever

FREEMAN, F.
  Too Hot To Stop (Part I)

FREEMAN, John
  Just Don't Want To Be Lonely

FREEMAN, Robert (Bobby)
  Betty Lou Got A New Pair Of
    Shoes
  Do You Wanna Dance

FREHLEY, Ace
  Love Theme from Kiss

FREIBERG, David
  Jane

FREY, Glenn
  After The Thrill Is Gone
  Best Of My Love
  Desperado
  Heartache Tonight
  Hotel California
  I Can't Tell You Why
  Life In The Fast Lane
  Long Run
  Lyin' Eyes
  New Kid In Town
  One Of These Nights
  Take It Easy
  Take It To The Limit
  Tequila Sunrise

FRICKLER, Sylvia
  You Were On My Mind

FRIED, Gerald
  Roots, Theme From (m)

FRIEDMAN, Dean
  Ariel

FRIEDMAN, Jim
  Hey Nelly Nelly

FRIEDMAN, Ruthann
  Windy

FUKOMOTO, Ken
  Feelings

FULLER, Darrell
  Spinout

FULLER, Dee
  I Got Lucky
  Steppin' Out Of Line

FULLER, Jerry
  Lady Willpower
  Show And Tell
  Young Girl

FULLER, Jesse
  San Francisco Bay Blues

FULSON, Lowell
  Reconsider Baby

FULTON, Kathryn R.
  Fool No. 1

FUNCHES, John
  Oh, What A Night

FUQUA, Harvey
  If I Could Build My Whole World
    Around You
  My Whole World Ended
  Pucker Up Buttercup
  Sincerely
  Someday We'll Be Together
  Twenty Five Miles
  What Does It Take

FURAY, Richie
  Child's Claim To Fame
  In The Hour Of Not Quite Rain
  Kind Woman

GADD, Steve
  Stuff Like That

GALE, Eric
  Stuff Like That

GALLOP, Sammy
  Count Every Star

GALLOWAY, Tob B.
  Whiffenpoof Song

GAMBLE, Kenny (Kenneth)
  Brand New Me
  Don't Leave Me This Way
  Enjoy Yourself
  Expressway To Your Heart
  For The Love Of Money
  Forever Mine
  Give The People What They
    Want
  Hope That We Can Be Together
    Soon
  I Love Music (Part I)
  I'm Gonna Make You Love Me
  Let Me Be Good To You
  Me And Mrs. Jones
  Now That We've Found Love
  One Life To Live

Only The Strong Survive
Sexy (m)
Sit Down And Talk To Me
TSOP (The Sound of Philadel-
  phia)
Turn Off The Lights
When Will I See You Again
You Gonna Make Me Love Some-
  body Else
You'll Never Find Another Love
  Like Mine

GANTRY, Chris
  Dreams Of The Everyday House-
    wife

GARCIA, Jerry (Jerome)
  Attics Of My Life (m)
  Black Peter (m)
  Blues For Allah
  Brokedown Palace (m)
  Candyman (m)
  Casey Jones (m)
  China Doll (m)
  Crazy Fingers
  Cumberland Blues (m)
  Dire Wolf (m)
  Eyes Of The World (m)
  Franklin's Tower
  Friend Of The Devil (m)
  Help On The Way
  Here Comes Sunshine (m)
  High Time (m)
  Loose Lucy (m)
  Mississippi Half Step Uptown
    Toodleoo (m)
  New Speedway Boogie (m)
  Ripple (m)
  Row Jimmy (m)
  Scarlet Begonias (m)
  Shakedown Street (m)
  Ship Of Fools (m)
  Stella Blue (m)
  Till The Morning Comes (m)
  Truckin' (m)
  Uncle John's Band (m)
  U.S. Blues (m)

GARFUNKEL, Arthur (Art)
  Hey Schoolgirl
  Scarborough Fair/Canticle
    (Arrangement & original
    counter melody)
  7 O'Clock News/Silent Night
    (Narration & arrangement)

GARLAND, Joe
  In The Mood

GARNER, Erroll
  Misty (m)

GARNETT, Gale
  We'll Sing In The Sunshine

GARRETT, Lee
  Maybe I'm A Fool

Signed, Sealed, Delivered I'm
Yours

GARRETT, Marilyn
Night Has A Thousand Eyes

GARRETT, William
Please Mr. Postman

GARRICK, Hoyt
New Orleans Ladies

GARSON, Mort
La Bamba (Adapted)
Our Day Will Come (w)

GARTH, Al
Listen To A Country Song

GARVIN, Michael
If The World Ran Out Of Love
Tonight

GARVIN, Rex
Over The Mountain, Across The
Sea

GASPER, Paul
Still Waters Run Deep

GATELY, Jimmy
Minute You're Gone

GATES, David
Baby I'm-A Want You
Everything I Own
Goodbye Girl
Guitar Man
Hooked On You
If
It Don't Matter To Me
Lost Without Your Love
Make It With You
Popsicles And Icicles
Took The Last Train
Where Does The Lovin' Go

GATHERS, Helen
Mister Lee

GAUDIO, Bob
Big Girls Don't Cry
December 1963 (Oh, What A
Night)
Down The Hall
Sherry
Walk Like A Man

GAYDEN, Mac
Everlasting Love

GAYE, Marvin
After The Dance
Beechwood 4-5789
Dancing In The Street
Got To Give It Up (Part 1)
Hitch Hike

Inner City Blues
Let's Get It On
Mercy, Mercy Me
Pride And Joy
Stubborn Kind Of Fellow
What's Going On

GAYLORD, Ronnie
I Will Never Pass This Way
Again

GAYTEN, Paul
But I Do

GELD, Gary
Hurting Each Other (m)
Sealed With A Kiss (m)

GENTILE, Alfonso
There's A Moon Out Tonight

GENTRY, Bo
Mony Mony

GENZALE, John
Personality Crisis (m)

GEORGE, Barbara
I Know

GEORGE, Dona Lyn
Love Song

GERALD, J.
Honey Love

GERSHWIN, George
Rhapsody In Blue (Disco Version)
Someone To Watch Over Me (m)
Summertime (m)

GERSHWIN, Ira
Someone To Watch Over Me (w)

GIANANGELO, Leo
Sing

GIANT, Bill
Do Not Disturb
Everybody Come Aboard
Paradise, Hawaiian Style
Roustabout
Shake That Tambourine
Shout It Out
This Is My Heaven
Today, Tomorrow And Forever
You're The Devil In Disguise

GIBB, Andy
Shadow Dancing
Thicker Than Water

GIBB, Barry
Boogie Child
Come On Over
Desire
Don't Throw It All Away

Emotion
Fanny Be Tender With My Love
Grease
Holiday
How Can You Mend A Broken
Heart
How Deep Is Your Love
I Can't Help It
I Just Want To Be Your Every-
thing
I Started A Joke
If I Can't Have You
I've Got To Get A Message To
You
Jive Talkin'
Lonely Days
Love Me
Love So Right
Massachusetts
More Than A Woman
New York Mining Disaster 1941
Night Fever
Nights On Broadway
Run To Me
Shadow Dancing
Spicks And Specks
Spirits (Having Flown)
Stayin' Alive
Sweetheart
Thicker Than Water
To Love Somebody
Tragedy
Words
World
You Should Be Dancing
You Stepped Into My Life

GIBB, Maurice
Boogie Child
Desire
Fanny Be Tender With My Love
Holiday
How Deep Is Your Love
I Started A Joke
If I Can't Have You
I've Got To Get A Message To
You
Jive Talkin'
Lonely Days
Love So Right
Massachusetts
More Than A Woman
New York Mining Disaster 1941
Night Fever
Nights On Broadway
Run To Me
Shadow Dancing
Spirits (Having Flown)
Stayin' Alive
Sweetheart
To Love Somebody
Tragedy
Words
World
You Should Be Dancing
You Stepped Into My Life

FIND THAT TUNE

GIBB, Robin
 Boogie Child
 Come On Over
 Desire
 Emotion
 Fanny Be Tender With My Love
 Hold On To My Love
 Holiday
 How Can You Mend A Broken
  Heart
 How Deep Is Your Love
 I Started A Joke
 If I Can't Have You
 I've Got To Get A Message To
  You
 Jive Talkin'
 Lonely Days
 Love Me
 Love So Right
 Massachusetts
 More Than A Woman
 New York Mining Disaster 1941
 Night Fever
 Nights On Broadway
 Run To Me
 Shadow Dancing
 Spirits (Having Flown)
 Stayin' Alive
 To Love Somebody
 Tragedy
 Words
 World
 You Should Be Dancing
 You Stepped Into My Life

GIBSON, Bob
 New "Frankie And Johnnie" Song
 That's The Way It's Gonna Be
 There's A Meetin' Here Tonight
  (Adapted)

GIBSON, Steve
 I Just Can't Say No To You (m)

GILBERT, Cary
 Don't Leave Me This Way
 Me And Mrs. Jones

GILBERT, Warwick
 What Gives

GILDER, NICK
 Hot Child In The City
 Rock Me

GILKYSON, Terry
 Greenfields
 Memories Are Made Of This

GILL, Geoff
 Heartbreaker

GILLAN, Ian
 Smoke On The Water

GILLESPIE, Haven
 Honey (w)
 That Lucky Old Sun (w)

GILLESPIE, Jerry
 Gwen

GILLIAM, Michelle SEE Phillips,
 Michelle Gilliam

GILLYARD, Richard E.
 Let Me Lay My Funk On You

GIMBEL, Norman
 Good Friend (w)
 I Got A Name (w)
 Killing Me Softly With His Song
  (w)
 Ricochet

GIOSASI, Harry
 Sorry

GLENN, Artie
 Crying In The Chapel

GLICK, Elmo (Pseud.). See
 LEIBER, Jerry, STOLLER,
 Mike.

GLOVER, Henry
 Let The Little Girl Dance
 Peppermint Twist

GLOVER, J.
 You Don't Have To Be A Star

GLOVER, Roger
 Smoke On The Water

GOBLE, Graham
 Lady
 Reminiscing

GODCHAUX, Keith
 Let Me Sing Your Blues Away
  (m)

GODWIN, Mable
 Ling Ting Tong

GOELL, Kermit
 Slowly

GOFF, Duke
 Run, Woman, Run

GOFFIN, Gerry
 Do You Know Where You're
  Going To (w)
 Go Away Little Girl
 Halfway To Paradise
 Hey Girl
 Hi-De-Ho
 I'll Meet You Halfway
 Imagination
 Just Once In My Life
 Loco-Motion
 One Fine Day
 Pleasant Valley Sunday
 Someone That I Used To Love (w)

Take Good Care Of My Baby
Up On The Roof
Will You Love Me Tomorrow

GOLD, Andrew
 Endless Flight
 Lonely Boy
 Never Let Her Slip Away
 One Of Them Is Me
 Thank You For Being A Friend

GOLD, Jim
 Nice To Be With You

GOLD, Wally
 Good Luck Charm
 In Your Arms
 It's Now Or Never

GOLDBERG, Barry
 Imagination

GOLDBERG, Mark
 How Can This Be Love

GOLDBERG, Neil
 Got To Believe In Love

GOLDE, Frannie
 Gettin' Ready For Love

GOLDNER, George
 ABC's Of Love
 I'm Not A Juvenile Delinquent

GOLDSBORO, Bobby
 Autumn Of My Life
 Butterfly For Bucky
 I'm A Drifter
 Muddy Mississippi Line
 See The Funny Little Clown
 Summer
 With Pen In Hand

GOLDSMITH, Cliff
 Hully Gully
 Western Movies

GOLDSTEIN, Gerald
 My Boyfriend's Back

GOLDSTEIN, Jerry
 It's Nice To Be With You

GOMM, Ian
 Cruel To Be Kind
 Hold On

GONYEA, Dale
 I Need Your Help Barry Manilow

GONZALEZ, Bob
 Little Girl

GOODISON, John
 Lady (Put The Light On Me)

GOODMAN, A.
Special Lady

GOODMAN, Steve
City Of New Orleans

GOODRUM, Randy
Bluer Than Blue
Broken Hearted Me
Lesson In Leavin'
You Needed Me

GOODWYN, Myles
Roller

GORDON, Alan
Celebrate
Happy Together
My Heart Belongs To Me

GORDON, Jim
Layla

GORDON, Mack
At Last (w)
Chattanooga Choo Choo (w)
More I See You (w)

GORDON, Odetta
All My Trials (Adapted)
Fox (Adapted & arranged)
Shenandoah (Adapted & arranged)

GORDY, Berry, Jr.
Do You Love Me
Got A Job
I Love The Way You Love
I'll Be There
I'm Livin' In Shame
Lonely Teardrops
Money (That's What I Want)
Shop Around
That's Why
Try It Baby
You've Got What It Takes
You've Made Me So Very Happy

GORDY, Emory
Traces

GORDY, George
Beechwood 4-5789
Stubborn Kind Of Fellow

GORDY, Gwendolyn (Gwen)
Lonely Teardrops
You've Got What It Takes

GORE, Lesley
Out Here On My Own (w)

GORE, Michael
Fame (m)
Out Here On My Own (m)

GORMAN, Freddie
Please Mr. Postman
Romeo And Juliet

GORNEY, Jay
Brother, Can You Spare A Dime (m)

GORRELL, Stuart
Georgia On My Mind (w)

GOTTEHRER, Richard
My Boyfriend's Back

GOTTLIEB, Alex
Frankie And Johnnie (New words & arranged)

GOULDMAN, Graham
Bus Stop
Things We Do For Love

GOUSSETT, Louis
Handsome Johnny

GRAHAM, Leo
Shining Star

GRAINGER, Gary
Ain't Love A Bitch
I Was Only Joking

GRAMM, Lou
Blue Morning, Blue Day (w)
Cold As Ice (w)
Dirty White Boy
Double Vision (w)
Head Games (w)
Hot Blooded (w)

GRANT, Cornelius
I'm Losing You
You're My Everything

GRAPPELLI, Stephane
Hobo's Blues (m)

GRAVENITES, Nick
Ego Rock
Gypsy Good Times

GRAY, Ed
Crystal Blue Persuasion

GRAY, Von
Lady Love

GRAYDON, Jay
After The Love Has Gone

GREEN, Al
Belle
Call Me (Come Back Home)
I'm Still In Love With You
Let's Stay Together
Love And Happiness
Take Me To the River

GREEN, Bud
Sentimental Journey

GREEN, John
Body And Soul (m)

GREEN, Leroy
Disco Inferno

GREEN, Tony
Come To Me

GREENAN, Johnny
Real Wild Child

GREENAWAY, R.
I'd Like To Teach The World To Sing

GREENAWAY, Robert
Doctor's Orders
It's Like We Never Said Goodbye
Say You'll Stay Until Tomorrow
You've Got Your Troubles

GREENBERG, Elliott
Sweet Talkin' Guy

GREENE, Allen
Turn Around

GREENE, Joe
Outa Space

GREENE, Susaye
Free (Wanna Be Free)

GREENFIELD, Dave
Something Better Change

GREENFIELD, Howard
Amarillo
Breaking Up Is Hard To Do
Calendar Girl
Happy Birthday Sweet Sixteen
Hungry Years
Love Will Keep Us Together
You Gotta Make Your Own Sunshine

GREENWICH, Ellie
Da Doo Ron Ron
Do Wah Diddy Diddy

GREGORY, Miles
Love Don't Live Here Anymore

GREY, Zane
Back In Love Again
Dancin'

GRIFFIN, Billy
Love Machine

GRIFFIN, Paul
Hot Wax Theme

GRIFFIN, Trevor
  Love Is Like Oxygen

GRISBY, John
  That's The Way I Feel About
    Cha

GROFE, Ferde
  Wonderful One (m)

GROSS, Henry
  Shannon
  Springtime Mama

GROSSMAN, Albert
  Great Mandella

GUARD, Dave
  Scotch And Soda

GUEST, William
  I Don't Want To Do Wrong

GUIDA, C.
  If You Wanna Be Happy

GUIDA, Frank J.
  If You Wanna Be Happy
  New Orleans
  Quarter To Three
  School Is Out

GUIDRY, Robert
  But I Do
  See You Later, Alligator

GUNN, Tom
  When You're Next To Me

GUTHRIE, Arlo
  Alice's Restaurant
  Chilling Of The Evening
  Coming In To Los Angeles
  Every Hand In The Land
  Highway In The Wind
  If You Would Just Drop By
  I'm Going Home
  John Looked Down
  Meditation
  Motorcycle Song
  My Front Pages
  Now And Then
  Oh In The Morning
  Pause Of Mister Clause
  Ring Around A Rosy Rag
  Running Down The Road
  Standing At The Threshold
  Stealin' (Adapted)
  Wheel Of Fortune
  Wouldn't You Believe It

GUTHRIE, Woody
  Deportee (w)
  Pastures Of Plenty
  Roll On Columbia (w)
  So Long It's Been Good To Know
    Yuh
  This Land Is Your Land

HADJIDAKIS, Manos
  Never On Sunday (m)

HAGGARD, Merle
  I Can't Be Myself
  Okie From Muskogee

HALL, Bobby Gene, Jr.
  One More Try

HALL, Daryl
  Sara Smile

HALL, J. Graydon
  That's How Much I Love You

HALL, Johanna
  Half Moon
  Let There Be Music

HALL, John
  Half Moon

HALL, Reginald
  You Talk Too Much

HALL, Rich
  Sweet And Innocent

HAM, Peter
  Day After Day
  No Matter What
  Without You

HAMILTON, Bob
  Romeo And Juliet

HAMILTON, Frank
  We Shall Overcome (Adapted)

HAMILTON, Tom
  Sweet Emotion

HAMLISCH, Marvin
  Ice Castles, Theme From (m)
  If You Remember Me (m)
  Last Time I Felt Like This (m)
  Nobody Does It Better (m)
  Way We Were (m)
  What I Did For Love (m)

HAMMER, Jack
  Great Balls Of Fire

HAMMERSTEIN, OSCAR, II
  I've Told Ev'ry Little Star (w)
  When I Grow Too Old To Dream
    (w)

HAMMOND, Albert
  Air That I Breathe
  Gimme Dat Ding
  It Never Rains In Southern
    California
  99 Miles From L.A.
  When I Need You (w)

HAMMOND, Ronnie
  Do It Or Die
  Sky High

HAMPTON, Carl
  I Don't Want To Be Right
  If You're Ready (Come Go With
    Me)
  I'll Be Your Shelter (In Time Of
    Storm)
  Touch A Hand, Make A Friend

HANDMAN, Lou
  Are You Lonesome Tonight

HANDY, John
  Hard Work

HANKS, Len Ron
  Back In Love AGain
  Dancin'

HARBACH, Otto
  Smoke Gets In Your Eyes (w)

HARBURG, E.Y.
  Brother, Can You Spare A Dime
    (w)
  It's Only A Paper Moon (w)
  Over The Rainbow (w)

HARDAWAY, Lula Mae
  I Was Made To Love Her
  Signed, Sealed, Delivered I'm
    Yours

HARDIN, Charles
  Every Day
  Listen To Me
  Maybe Baby
  Not Fade Away

HARDIN, Louis
  All Is Loneliness

HARDIN, Tim
  If I Were A Carpenter
  Misty Roses
  Reason To Believe
  Soft Summer Breeze

HARDY, Hagood
  Homecoming (m)

HARJU, Gary
  Fire In The Morning

HARLAN, Jack
  Alley Cat Song (w)

HARNICK, Sheldon
  Fiddler On The Roof (w)
  If I Were A Rich Man (w)
  Matchmaker, Matchmaker (w)
  Sunrise, Sunset (w)

HARRIS, Bobby
Catchin' Up On Love

HARRIS, Don
I'm Leaving It All Up To You
Justine
Letter

HARRIS, Jimmy. See HOLVAY, James.

HARRIS, Lloyd, Jr.
Action Speaks Louder Than Words

HARRIS, Norman
Goin' Up In Smoke

HARRISON, George
All Things Must Pass
Apple Scruffs
Art Of Dying
Awaiting On You All
Badge
Ballad Of Sir Frankie Crisp
Behind That Locked Door
Beware Of Darkness
Crackerbox Palace
For You, Blue
Give Me Love
Hear Me Lord
Here Comes The Sun
I Dig Love
I'd Have You Any Time
Isn't It A Pity
Let It Down
Long, Long, Long
Love You To
Maggie Mae (Arranged)
My Sweet Lord
Old Brown Shoe
Photograph
Piggies
Run Of The Mill
Savoy Truffle
Something
This Song
What Is Life
While My Guitar Gently Weeps
You

HARRISON, Larry
Why Baby Why

HARRISON, Nigel
One Way Or Another

HARRISON, Paul
Love To Burn

HARRY, Deborah
Call Me
Dreaming
Heart Of Glass
I Didn't Have The Nerve To Say No
In The Flesh

Just Go Away
One Way Or Another
Picture This
Pretty Baby
Rip Her To Shreds
X Offender

HART, Bobby
Hurt So Bad
I Wanna Be Free
Keep On Singing
Last Train To Clarksville
Monkees, Theme From
Where Angels Go, Trouble Follows

HART, Bruce
Who Are You Now (w)
You Take My Breath Away (w)

HART, Freddie
Easy Loving

HART, Gladys
White Silver Sands

HART, Lorenz
Blue Moon (w)
I Married An Angel (w)
Spring Is Here (w)

HART, William
Didn't I (Blow Your Mind This Time) (w)

HARTFORD, John
Gentle On My Mind

HARTMAN, Dan
Free Ride
Hangin' Round
Instant Replay

HARVEY, Alex
Delta Dawn
Rings
Rueben James

HATCH, Tony
My Love

HAVENS, Richie (Richard)
Handsome Johnny
Midnight Train

HAWES, Bruce
They Just Can't Stop It

HAWKER, Mike
I Only Want To Be With You

HAWKINS, Dale
Susie-Q

HAWKINS, Edwin R.
Oh Happy Day

HAWKINS, Erskine
Tuxedo Junction (m)

HAWKINS, Jay
I Put A Spell On You

HAWKINS, M.
Can This Be Real

HAWKINS, Roy
Thrill Is Gone

HAYES, Isaac
Deja Vu (m)
Do Your Thing
Hold On I'm Coming
I Thank You
Shaft, Theme From
Show Me How
Soul Man
You Got Me Hummin'

HAYES, Roy
I'm Gonna Be A Wheel Someday

HAYES, Woody
Scarborough Fair (Adapted)

HAYMES, Bob
My Love, My Love
That's All

HAYS, Lee
If I Had A Hammer
Lonesome Traveler
Sloop John B (Adapted)

HAYWARD, Charlie
Devil Went Down To Georgia
In America
Legend Of Wooley Swamp

HAYWARD, Justin
Driftwood
Nights In White Satin
Question
Tuesday Afternoon

HAZELWOOD, Lee
These Boots Are Made For Walkin'

HAZELWOOD, Mike
Air That I Breathe
Gimme Dat Ding
It Never Rains In Southern California

HAZZARD, Tony
Me, The Peaceful Heart

HEAD, Roy
Treat Her Right

HEATHER, Susan
Rock Me My Baby

HEBB, Bobby
Sunny

HELL, Richard
Blank Generation
Love Comes In Spurts

HENDERSON, Douglas
Long Lonely Nights

HENDERSON, Harvey
Shake Your Rump To The Funk
Too Hot To Stop (Part I)

HENDERSON, Joe
Why Don't They Understand

HENDERSON, Michael
In The Night Time
Take Me I'm Yours

HENDERSON, Patrick
Real Love

HENDERSON, Ray
Bye Bye Blackbird (m)

HENDLER, Joel
Hangman (Adapted)

HENDRICKS, Belford
It's Just A Matter Of Time

HENDRICKS, James
Long Lonesome Highway
Look To Your Soul

HENDRIX, Jimi
Have You Ever Been (To Electric
Ladyland)
Long Hot Summer Night
Voodoo Chile

HENLEY, Don
After The Thrill Is Gone
Best Of My Love
Desperado
Heartache Tonight
Hotel California
I Can't Tell You Why
Life In The Fast Lane
Long Run
Lyin' Eyes
New Kid In Town
One Of These Nights
Take It To The Limit
Tequila Sunrise
Witchy Woman

HENLEY, Fred
You're The Reason

HENLEY, Larry
Holdin' On For Dear Love

HENNING, John
Hot Love, Cold World

HENRY, Clarence
Ain't Got No Home

HENRY, Sonny
Evil Ways

HENSLEY, Ken
Easy Living
Wizard

HERBERT, Twyla
Lightnin' Strikes
Two Faces Have I

HERBSTRITT, Larry
Fire In The Morning
I Just Fall In Love Again (m)

HERNANDEZ, Patrick
Born To Be Alive

HESS, David
Come Along

HESTER, Tony
Whatcha See Is Whatcha Get

HEYMAN, Edward
Body And Soul (w)

HEYWARD, DuBose
Summertime (w)

HEYWARD, Sammy
Day Light Break (New words &
new music adaptation)

HICKERSON, Joe
Where Have All The Flowers
Gone (Additional verses)

HICKEY, Ersel
Bluebirds Over The Mountain

HICKS, Joe
That's The Way I Feel About
Cha

HICKS, Tony
Tell Me To My Face

HIGGENBOTHAM, Robert
Hi-Heel Sneakers

HIGGINBOTHAM, Irene
Good Morning Heartache

HILDERBRAND, Diane
Easy Come, Easy Go

HILDERBRAND, Ray
Hey Paula

HILL, David
Speedy Gonzales

HILL, Dedette Lee
Old Folks (w)

HILL, Jessie
Ooh Poo Pah Doo

HILL, Tommy
Teddy Bear

HILLIARD, Bob
Seven Little Girls Sitting In The
Back Seat
Our Day Will Come (m)

HIRSCH, Nurit
Anytime Of The Year (m)

HIRSCH, Ricky
Everything That' Cha Do (Will
Come Back To You)

HIRSCHHORN, Joel
Morning After
We May Never Love Like This
Again

HODGE, Gaynell
Earth Angel

HODGES, Mabon
Love And Happiness
Take Me To The River

HODGSON, Roger
Give A Little Bit
Goodbye Stranger
Logical Song
Take The Long Way Home

HOFFMAN, Al
Secretly

HOFFMAN, Dan
Run, Woman, Run

HOFFMAN, Martin
Deportee (m)

HOKENSON, Eddie
Bad Girls (m)

HOLIDAY, Jimmy
All I Ever Need Is You
Brighton Hill
Don't Change On Me
Put A Little Love In Your Heart
River Of Love
Understanding

HOLLAND, Brian
Baby, Don't You Do It
Baby, I Need Your Loving
Baby Love
Back In My Arms Again
Bernadette
Come See About Me
Forever Came Today
Happening
Heat Wave
Heaven Must Have Sent You

How Sweet It Is (To Be Loved
By You)
I Can't Help Myself
I Hear A Symphony
I'm Gonna Let My Heart Do The
Walking
I'm Ready For Love
I'm The One You Need
In And Out Of Love
It's The Same Old Song
Jimmy Mack
Little Darling (I Need You)
Love Is Here And Now You're
Gone
Love Is Like An Itching In My
Heart
Mickey's Monkey
My World Is Empty Without You
Nothing But Heartaches
Nowhere To Run
Please Mr. Postman
Quicksand
Reach Out, I'll Be There
Reflections
Road Runner
7 Rooms Of Gloom
Shake Me, Wake Me (When It's
Over)
Something About You
Standing In The Shadows Of
Love
Stop! In The Name Of Love
This Old Heart Of Mine (Is Weak
For You)
When The Love Light Starts
Shining Through His Eyes
Where Did Our Love Go
You Can't Hurry Love
You Keep Me Hangin' On
You're A Wonderful One

HOLLAND, Eddie
Ain't Too Proud To Beg
All I Need
Baby, I Need Your Loving
Baby Love
Back In My Arms Again
Beauty Is Only Skin Deep
Bernadette
Come See About Me
Forever Came Today
Happening
Heat Wave
Heaven Must Have Sent You
How Sweet It Is (To Be Loved By
You)
I Can't Help Myself
I Hear A Symphony
I'm Gonna Let My Heart Do The
Walking
I'm Losing You
I'm Ready For Love
I'm The One You Need
In And Out Of Love
It's The Same Old Song
Jimmy Mack
Little Darling (I Need You)

Love Is Here And Now You're
Gone
Love Is Like An Itching In My
Heart
Mickey's Monkey
My World Is Empty Without You
Nothing But Heartaches
Nowhere To Run
Quicksand
Reach Out, I'll Be There
Reflections
Road Runner
7 Rooms Of Gloom
Shake Me, Wake Me (When It's
Over)
Something About You
Standing In The Shadows Of Love
Stop! In The Name Of Love
This Old Heart Of Mine (Is Weak
For You)
Too Many Fish In The Sea
When The Love Light Starts
Shining Through His Eyes
Where Did Our Love Go
You Can't Hurry Love
You Keep Me Hangin' On
You're A Wonderful One

HOLLER, Dick
Abraham, Martin And John

HOLLIS, Ed
Do Anything You Wanna Do

HOLLOWAY, Brenda & Patrice
You've Made Me So Very Happy

HOLLY, Buddy
I'm Lookin' For Someone To Love
It's So Easy
Lonesome Tears
Look At Me
Love's Made A Fool Of You
Peggy Sue
Stay Close To Me
Take Your Time
That'll Be The Day
True Love Ways
Well All Right
Words Of Love

HOLMES, Jake
So Close

HOLMES, Robert
Answering Machine
Escape
Him

HOLMES, Wally
Rock The Boat

HOLT, Will
Lemon Tree

HOLVAY, James
Kind Of A Drag

HOLYFIELD, Wayland
Could I Have This Dance
She Never Knew Me

HOMER, Ben
Sentimental Journey

HOOKER, John Lee
Boom Boom
Dimples
I'm Mad Again

HOOVEN, Joseph
Gimme Little Sign
Lovey Dovey Kinda Lovin'

HOPPEN, Larry
Let There Be Music (w)

HORN, Trevor
Video Killed The Radio Star

HORTON, Zilphia
We Shall Overcome (Adapted)

HOSCHNA, Karl
Yama-Yama Man (m)

HOSONO, Haruomi
Computer Game

HOTLEN, Allen
Don't Tell My Heart To Stop
Loving You

HOUSE, Bob
Could I Have This Dance

HOUSTON, Cissy
Think It Over

HOWARD, Gus
Ma Belle Amie (Arranged)

HOWARD, Harlan
Heartaches By The Number

HOWARD, Ken
I've Lost You

HOWE, Steve
Roundabout
Yours Is No Disgrace

HUBBARD, Jerry
Amos Moses
When You're Hot You're Hot

HUDDLESTON, Floyd
I'm A Fool For You

HUDSON, James
Goodnight, It's Time To Go

HUFF, Leon
Do It Anyway You Wanna
Don't Leave Me This Way

Enjoy Yourself
Expressway To Your Heart
For The Love Of Money
Forever Mine
Give The People What They Want
Hope That We Can Be Together
   Soon
I Love Music (Part I)
Let Me Be Good To You
Me And Mrs. Jones
Now That We've Found Love
One Life To Live
Only The Strong Survive
Sexy
Sit Down And Talk To Me
TSOP (The Sound Of Philadelphia)
Turn Off The Lights
When Will I See You Again
You Gonna Make Me Love Some-
   body Else
You'll Never Find Another Love
   Like Mine

HUGO & LUIGI. See CREATORE,
  Luigi & PERETTI, Hugo.

HULL, Bunny
  Let Me Be Your Angel

HUNTER, Ian
  Ships

HUNTER, Ivory Joe
  I Almost Lost My Mind
  I Need You So
  My Wish Came true
  Out Of Sight, Out Of Mind
  Since I Met You Baby

HUNTER, Ivy
  Dancing In The Street
  My Baby Loves Me

HUNTER, Robert
  Attics Of My Life (w)
  Black Peter (w)
  Blues For Allah
  Box Of Rain (w)
  Brokedown Palace (w)
  Candyman (w)
  Casey Jones (w)
  China Doll (w)
  Crazy Fingers (w)
  Cumberland Blues (w)
  Dire Wolf (w)
  Easy Wind
  Eyes Of The World (w)
  Franklin's Tower
  Friend Of The Devil (w)
  Help On The Way
  Here Comes Sunshine (w)
  High Time (w)
  Let Me Sing Your Blues Away (w)
  High Time (w)
  Loose Lucy (w)
  Mississippi Half Step Uptown
    Toodleoo (w)

New Speedway Boogie (w)
Rippel (w)
Row Jimmy (w)
Scarlet Begonias (w)
Shakedown Street (w)
Ship Of Fools (w)
Stella Blue (w)
Sugar Magnolia (w)
Till The Morning Comes (w)
Truckin' (w)
Uncle John's Band (w)
U.S. Blues (w)

HUPFELD, Herman
  As Time Goes By

HUPP, Debbie
  You Decorated My Life

HURLEY, John
  Son Of A Preacher Man

HURTT, P. (Phil)
  Best Disco In Town (w)
  Fire Island (w)
  In Hollywood (Everybody Is A
    Star) (w)
  San Francisco (You've Got Me)
    (w)
  Village People (w)

HUTCH, Willie
  I'll Be There

HUTCHESON, Susan
  I Love The Nightlife

HUTCHINSON, Willie
  California My Way
  Learn How To Fly

IAN, Janis
  At Seventeen
  Jesse
  Lonely One
  When The Party's Over

IMES, Mildred
  You're The Reason

INFANTE, Frank
  I Know But I Don't Know

INGLE, Doug
  In-A-Gadda-Da-Vida

INGRAHAM, Roy
  No Regrets (m)

INGRAM, Arnold
  Float On

INGRAM, Butch
  Motown Review

INGRAM, John
  Baby I Want You

INGRAM, Luther
  Respect Yourself

IRWIN, Randy
  Oh, Baby

ISBELL, Alvertis
  I'll Take You There

ISLEY, O'Kelly, Ronald & Rudolph
  Nobody But Me
  Shout

IVEY, Clayton
  Angel In Your Arms

JABARA, Paul
  Last Dance
  Main Event/Fight

JACKS, Terry
  That's Where I Went Wrong

JACKSON, Al
  Call Me (Come Back Home)
  Green Onions
  I'm Still In Love With You
  Let's Stay Together
  Soul Clap 69

JACKSON, Anthony
  For The Love Of Money

JACKSON, Brian
  Bottle (m)

JACKSON, Christopher Mark
  You Little Trustmaker

JACKSON, Gary
  Higher And Higher

JACKSON, George
  This Is The Way I Feel

JACKSON, Jill
  Let There Be Peace On Earth

JACKSON, Joe
  Is She Really Going Out With
    Him

JACKSON, Michael
  Lovely One

JACKSON, MICK
  Weekend

JACKSON, Mike
  My Love Don't Come Easy

COMPOSER—LYRICIST INDEX

JACKSON, Randy
Lovely One

JACKSON, Raymond
I Don't Want To Be Right
If You're Ready (Come Go With Me)
I'll Be Your Shelter (In Time Of Storm)
Take Care Of Your Homework
Touch A Hand, Make A Friend
Who's Making Love

JACKSON, Roddy
She Said Yeah

JACKSON, Rudolph
Hearts Of Stone (m)

JACOBS, Al
Ev'ry Day Of My Life
Hurt

JACOBS, W.
Can't Hold On Much Longer

JACOBS, Walter
Everything's Gonna Be Alright

JACOBSEN, Erik
Cuckoo

JACOBSON, Kenny
Swingin' Shepherd Blues (w)

JACQUES-BURNEL, Jean
Something Better Change

JAGGER, Mick
Angie
As Tears Go By
Brown Sugar
Gimme Shelter
Happy
Honky Tonk Women
It's Only Rock 'N' Roll
Jumpin' Jack Flash
Last Time
Let's Spend The Night Together
Love In Vain
Midnight Rambler
Rip This Joint
Ruby Tuesday
Satisfaction
Street Fighting Man
Under My Thumb
You Can't Always Get What You Want

JAMES, Arthur
For All We Know (w)

JAMES, Brian
New Rose

JAMES, Casey
Livin' It Up

Mama Can't Buy You Love
Only Make Believe

JAMES, Doug
After You

JAMES, Elmore
Sun Is Shining

JAMES, Etta
Dance With Me Henry
Something's Got A Hold On Me

JAMES, Jesse
Boogaloo Down Broadway

JAMES, Larry
Here Comes The Sun

JAMES, Mark
Everybody Loves A Rain Song
Hooked On A Feeling
Roller Coaster
Suspicious Minds

JAMES, Paul
Freight Train

JAMES, Rick
Come Into My Life
Mary Jane
You And I

JAMES, Tommy
Crimson And Clover
Crystal Blue Persuasion
Draggin' The Line
Gotta Get Back To You
Mony Mony
Three Times In Love

JAMESON, Tom
Summertime, Summertime

JANIS, Lu
Nanu, Nanu (I Wanna Funcky Wich You)

JANSSEN, Danny
Keep On Singing
La, La, La
Little Woman
Sherry Don't Go

JANSSEN, Myrna
Sherry Don't Go

JARRE, Maurice
It Was A Good Time (m)
Somewhere, My Love (m)

JARRELL, Phillip
Torn Between Two Lovers

JARRETT, Tommy
How Time Flies

JAY, Fred
I Cried A Tear

JEFFERSON, Joseph B.
They Just Can't Stop It

JEFFREY, Allan
I Feel That I've Known You Forever
Old Cape Cod

JENKINS, David
Love Will Find A Way

JENKINS, Gordon
This Is All I Ask

JENNINGS, Waylon
Are You Sure Hank Done It This Way
Good Hearted Woman

JENNINGS, Will
I'll Never Love This Way Again (w)
Looks Like We Made It (w)
No Night So Long
Somewhere In The Night (w)
Street Life (w)

JOBE, Steve
Where Were You When I Was Falling In Love

JOEL, Billy
Entertainer
Honesty
Just The Way You Are
Movin' Out (Anthony's Song)
New York State Of Mind
Piano Man
Say Goodbye To Hollywood
She's Always A Woman
You May Be Right

JOHANSEN, David
Personality Crisis (w)

JOHN, Elton
All The Girls Love Alice
Amoreena
Bennie And The Jets
Bitch Is Back
Border Song
Burn Down The Mission
Candle In The Wind
Crocodile Rock
Daniel
Don't Let The Sun Go Down On Me
Goodbye Yellow Brick Road
I Need You To Turn To
Island Girl
Let Me Be Your Car
Levon
Little Jeannie
Michelle's Song

221

Part-Time Love
Philadelphia Freedom
Rocket Man
Saturday Night's Alright
Someone Saved My Life Tonight
Song For Guy
Sweet Painted Lady
Take Me To The Pilot
Tiny Dancer
Valhalla
Your Song

JOHN, Robert
Sad Eyes

JOHNS, Carolyn
If It Don't Fit, Don't Force It
(w)

JOHNSEN, Julius
Declaration (m)

JOHNSON, Buddy
Since I Fell For You

JOHNSON, Emanuel
Gloria

JOHNSON, Enotris
Jenny, Jenny
Long Tall Sally
Miss Ann

JOHNSON, Fred
All In My Mind

JOHNSON, George
Stomp

JOHNSON, Howard
When The Moon Comes Over The
Mountain

JOHNSON, J.J.
Across 110th Street

JOHNSON, Janice Marie
Boogie Oogie Oogie

JOHNSON, Louis
Stomp

JOHNSON, Peyton F.
Let Me Lay My Funk On You

JOHNSON, Roy Lee
Mr. Moonlight

JOHNSON, Terry
Baby, Baby, Don't Cry

JOHNSON, Valerie
Stomp

JOHNSON, Walter
Your Love

JOHNSON, William
Tuxedo Junction (m)

JOHNSTON, Bruce
I Write The Songs

JOHNSTON, Tom
Captain And Me
China Grove
Eyes Of Silver
Listen To The Music
Long Train Runnin'

JON, Mikol
I Love The Way You Love

JONES, Allen
Ain't That Loving You (For More
Reasons Than One)
Son Of Shaft

JONES, Andrew
When You Dance

JONES, Bessie
Come By Here (New words & new
music adaptation)

JONES, Booker T.
All God's Children Got Soul
Born Under A Bad Sign
Green Onions
Soul Clap 69

JONES, David H., Jr.
Full Speed Ahead
I'll Be Here

JONES, George, Jr.
Rama Lama Ding Dong

JONES, Gloria
Haven't Stopped Dancing Yet
If I Were Your Woman
There's A Lesson To Be Learned

JONES, Isham
I'll See You In My Dreams (m)

JONES, Jimmy
Handy Man

JONES, Joe
You Talk Too Much

JONES, John Paul
Black Dog
Bron-Y-Sur Stomp
Celebration Day
Communication Breakdown
Crunge
D'yer Mak'er
Good Times Bad Times
Heartbreaker
How Many More Times
Misty Mountain Hop

Moby Dick
No Quarter
Ocean
Rock And Roll
Since I've Been Loving You
When The Levee Breaks
Whole Lotta Love
Your Time Is Gonna Come

JONES, Mick
Blinded By Science
Blue Morning, Blue Day
Cold As Ice
Dirty White Boy
Double Vision
Feels Like The First Time
Head Games
Hot Blooded

JONES, Nat
Ain't That A Groove (Part I)
Ain't That A Groove (Part II)
Don't Be A Drop-Out
Money Won't Change You

JONES, Quincy
Anderson Tapes, Theme From (m)
Stuff Like That

JONES, Rickie Lee
Chuck E.'s In Love
Young Blood

JONES, Steven
Anarchy In The U.K.
God Save The Queen
Pretty Vacant

JONES, Tom
Try To Remember (w)

JOPLIN, Janis
Down On Me
Ego Rock
I Need A Man To Love
Kozmic Blues
Mercedes Benz
Move Over
Road Block

JOPLIN, Scott
Entertainer (m)
Maple Leaf Rag (m)

JORDAN, Archie
I Never Said I Love You (m)
In No Time At All
It Was Almost Like A Song
Let's Take The Long Way
Around The World
What A Difference You've Made
In My Life

JORDAN, Cyril
Shake Some Action
Yes It's True
You Tore Me Down

JORDAN, Dazz
  Down By The Riverside

JORDAN, E.
  I'd Rather Go Blind

JORDAN, Leroy "Lonnie"
  Cisco Kid
  Gypsy Man
  Me And Baby Brother
  Spill The Wine
  World Is A Ghetto

JORDAN, Fred
  Belle

JOSEA, Joe
  Cherry Pie

JOSIE, Lou
  Midnight Confessions

JOYCE, Roger
  It Feels So Good To Be Loved
    So Bad

JOYNER, Anthony W.
  Let Me Lay My Funk On You

JULIA, Al
  I Cried A Tear

JUNIOR, Marvin
  Oh, What A Night

JUSTMAN, Seth
  Give It To Me
  Must Of Got Lost

KAEMPFERT, Bert
  Spanish Eyes (m)
  Wooden Heart

KAHN, Andy
  Hot Shot

KAHN, Gus
  I'll See You In My Dreams (w)
  Yes Sir, That's My Baby

KALMANOFF, Martin
  Young Dreams

KALMAR, Bert
  Who's Sorry Now

KANDER, John
  Cabaret (m)
  How Lucky Can You Get
  Maybe This Time (m)

KANTER, Paul
  Ballad Of You And Me Pooneil
  Dance With The Dragon (w)
  Eskimo Blue Day (w)

Jane (m)
Martha
Watch Her Ride
Wild Tyme
Won't You Try/Saturday After-
  noon
Young Girl Sunday Blue

KAPER, Bronislau
  Hi-Lili, Hi-Lo (m)

KARGER, Fred
  Frankie And Johnnie (New
    words & Arranged)
  Gidget

KARLIN, Fred
  Come Saturday Morning (m)
  For All We Know (m)

KASENETZ, Jerry
  Free As The Wind

KASHA, Al
  Morning After
  We May Never Love Like This
    Again

KATZ, Jeff
  Free As The Wind

KAUFMAN, Paul
  Poetry In Motion

KAUKONEN, Jorma
  Last Wall Of The Castle

KAYE, Buddy
  Never Ending
  Speedy Gonzales

KAYE, Florence
  Do Not Distrub
  Everybody Come Aboard
  Paradise, Hawaiian Style
  Roustabout
  Shake That Tambourine
  Shout It Out
  This Is My Heaven
  Today, Tomorrow And Forever
  You're The Devil In Disguise

KAYE, Lenny
  Redondo Beach

KAYE, Tony
  Yours Is No Disgrace

KAYLAN, Howard
  Sound Asleep

KAZ, Eric
  Deep Inside My Heart
  Love Has No Pride

KEITH, Barbara
  Free The People

KEITH, Larry
  Better Love Next Time
  This Time I'm In It For Love

KEITH, Marilyn
  Yellow Bird (w)

KEITH, Vivian
  Before The Next Teardrop
    Falls

KELLEM, Milton
  Gonna Get Along Without Ya
    Now

KELLER, Jack
  Easy Come, Easy Go
  It's So Easy To Say
  Ready Or Not

KELLY, Casey
  Anyone Who Isn't Me Tonight
  Love To Burn

KELLY, Chet
  Time Won't Let Me (w)

KELLY, Sherman
  Dancin' In The Moonlight

KELLY, Tom
  Take Care Of Your Homework

KENNEDY, Jimmy
  My Prayer (w, musical adaptation)
  Teddy Bear's Picnic (w)

KENNEDY, Mike
  Heartbeat, It's A Lovebeat

KENNER, Chris
  I Like It Like That
  Land Of A Thousand Dances
  Something You Got

KENT, James
  Funk #49

KERN, Jerome
  I've Told Ev'ry Little Star (m)
  Smoke Gets In Your Eyes (m)
  Way You Look To-Night (m)

KERR, Richard
  I'll Never Love This Way Again
    (m)
  Looks Like We Made It (m)
  Mandy
  No Night So Long
  Somewhere In The Night (m)
  Where Are They Now (w)

KERSEY, Ron
  Disco Inferno

KESKE, Wally
  Sherry Don't Go

KESLER, Stanley A.
I Forgot To Remember To
Forget

KETTNER, Alfons
What You Won't Do For Love

KEYES, James
Sh-Boom

KHAN, Chaka
Stay

KHENT, Allyson R.
Sixteen Candles

KIBBLE, Perry
Boogie Oogie Oogie (m)

KIDD, Johnny
Shakin' All Over

KILLEN, Buddy
Ain't Gonna Bump No More
I Can't Wait Any Longer

KIM, Andy
Sugar, Sugar

KINDT, William
Wabash Cannon Ball

KING, B.B.
Lucille

KING, Ben E.
Stand By Me

KING, Bob
Draggin' The Line
Gotta Get Back To You

KING, Carole
Corazon
Go Away Little Girl
Halfway To Paradise
Hard Rock Cafe
Hey Girl
Hi-De-Ho
I Feel The Earth Move
It's Going To Take Some Time
Its Too Late (m)
Jazzman
Just Once In My Life
Loco-Motion
One Fine Day
Pleasant Valley Sunday
So Far Away
Sweet Seasons
Take Good Care Of My Baby
Tapestry
Up On The Roof
Will You Love Me Tomorrow
You've Got A Friend

KING, Pearl
I Hear You Knocking
One Night

KING, Tom
Time Won't Let Me (m)

KING, William
Brick House

KING, Windsor
Dance, Dance, Dance

KIPNER, Nat
Too Much, Too Little, Too Late

KIPPS, Charles H., Jr.
Walk Away From Love

KIRKE, Mikael
Who's Been Sleepin' Here

KIRKLAND, Leroy
All In My Mind
Something's Got A Hold On Me

KIRKMAN, Terry
Cherish

KIRWAN, Danny
Bare Trees

KLAATU
Calling Occupants Of Interplanetary Craft

KLEBAN, Edward
What I Did For Love (w)

KNECHTEL, Larry
Took The Last Train (m)

KNIGHT, Baker
Wonder Of You

KNIGHT, Frederick
Ring My Bell

KNIGHT, Gladys
Daddy Could Swear, I Declare
I Don't Want To Do Wrong

KNIGHT, Jimmy De. See
DEKNIGHT, Jimmy.

KNIGHT, Merald
Daddy Could Swear, I Declare
I Don't Want To Do Wrong

KNISS, Richard L. (Dick)
Song Is Love
Sunshine On My Shoulders (m)

KNOPFLER, Mark
Dire Straits
Sultans Of Swing

KNOX, Buddy
I'm Stickin' With You
Party Doll

KNUDSEN, Keith
One Step Closer

KODA, Cub
Smokin' In The Boys' Room

KOFFMAN, Moe
Swingin' Shepherd Blues (m)

KOLBER, Larry
I Love How You Love Me

KONTE, Skip
Gas Lamps And Clay

KOOL & THE GANG
Hollywood Swinging
Jungle Boogie
Ladies Night
Too Hot

KORDULETSCH, J. S.
Boogie Woogie Dancin' Shoes

KORTLANDER, Max
Tell Me (m)

KOSLOFF, Ira
I Want You, I Need You, I Love
You (m)

KRAEMER, P.
Hello Hello

KRAL, Ivan
Ask The Angels
Kimberly

KREIDER, Mark
Such A Woman

KRENSKI, John & Mike
Cheater

KREUTZMANN, William
Franklin's Tower

KRIEGER, Robbie
Indian Summer
Queen Of The Highway

KRISTOFFERSON, Kris
For The Good Times
Help Me Make It Through The
Night
Loving Her Was Easier
Me And Bobby McGee
Sunday Mornin' Comin' Down
Why Me

KRUEGER, Jim
We Just Disagree

KUEPPER, Ed
Stranded

KUPKA, S.
You're Still A Young Man

KUSIK, Larry
Come Live Your Life With Me (w)
Speak Softly Love (w)

LA BOSTRIE, Dorothy
Tutti Frutti

LABOUNTY, Bill
In 25 Words Or Less
This Night Won't Last Forever

LADEMACHER
Saturday Night (m)

LAI, Francis
Love Story, Theme From
Ride (m)

LAING, Corky
Mississippi Queen

LAMB, Kevin
Right Feeling At The Wrong
Time

LAMBERT, Dennis
Ain't No Woman
Don't Pull Your Love
It Only Takes A Minute
Look In My Eyes Pretty Woman
One Tin Soldier

LAMM, Robert
Beginnings
Does Anybody Really Know What
Time It Is
Saturday In The Park
25 Or 6 To 4

LAND, Harry
Mashed Potato Time

LANDAU, Bill
Sacred

LANE, Herb
Disco Nights
Standing Ovation

LANE, J. A.
Walking By Myself

LANE, Jeff
What It Is

LANE, John
Beethoven's Fifth (Disco Version)
(Adapted & arranged)

LANGE, Lee
Cara Mia

LANIER, Allen
In Thee
Kimberly

LANIER, Verdell
It's You That I need

LAPREAD, Ronald
Brick House
Fancy Dancer

LARA, Agustin
Granada

LARSON, Mel
Whatever You Got, I Want

LASLEY, David
Jojo
Lead Me On
Love Me Again

LATIMORE, Benny
Dig A Little Deeper
Let's Straighten It Out

LATOUCHE, John
Cabin In The Sky (w)
Taking A Chance On Love (w)

LAUBER, Terry
Martha (Your Lovers Come
And Go)

LAURIE, Linda
Leave Me Alone
You Got It

LAVERE, Frank
Have You Heard

LAVOIE, Kent
Me And You And A Dog
Named Boo

LAWRENCE, Bert
Let The Little Girl Dance

LAWRENCE, Stephen
Who Are You Now (m)
You Take My Breath Away (m)

LAWSON, Herbert Happy
Any Time

LEADON, Bernie
I Wish You Peace
Witchy Woman

LEANDER, Mike
Early In The Morning
Lady Godiva
Let's Get A Little Sentimental

LEBISH, Louis
Dance With Me

LE BLANC, Emmanuel Rahiem
Disco Nights
Standing Ovation

LE BLANC, Lenny
Falling
Midnight Light

LEDBETTER, Huddie
C. C. Rider
Cotton Fields
Goodnight Irene
Midnight Special (Adapted)
Rock Island Line (Adapted)
Roll On Columbia (m)

LEDESMA, L.
Get Off

LEE, Curtis
Pretty Little Angel Eyes

LEE, Dor
It's How I Live (w)

LEE, Ethel
Speedy Gonzales

LEE, Jack
Hanging On The Telephone
Will Anything Happen

LEE, Larry
Jackie Blue

LEE, Leonard
Let The Good Times Roll

LEE, Nancy
Stroll

LE GLAIRE, Sonny
Fool's Paradise

LEGRAND, Michel
Hands Off Time (m)
Happy (m)
I Was Born In Love With You (m)
Little Boy Lost (m)
Summer Knows (m)
Summer Me, Winter Me (m)
Summer Of 42 (Disco Version)
(m)
What Are You Doing The Rest
Of Your Life (m)
Windmills Of Your Mind (m)

LEHMAN, Kenny
Dance, Dance, Dance (Yowsah,
Yowsah, Yowsah)

LEIBER, Jerry
Baby, I Don't Care
Bossa Nova, Baby
Charlie Brown

Don't
Fools Fall In Love
Hound Dog
I (Who Have Nothing)
Jailhouse Rock
Just Tell Her Jim Said Hello
Kansas City
King Creole
Love Potion Number Nine
Loving You
On Broadway
Poison Ivy
Ruby Baby
Searchin'
Smokey Joe's Cafe
Spanish Harlem
Stand By Me
Treat Me Nice
Yakety Yak
Yound Blood

LEIGH, Mitch
Impossible Dream (m)

LEIGH, Richard
Don't It Make My Brown Eyes
Blue
In No Time At All

LEIKIN, Molly Ann
Let Me Love You Once Before
You Go

LEITCH, Donovan. See DONOVAN.

LENNON, John
Across The Universe
All My Loving
All Together Now
All You Need Is Love
And I Love Her
Baby, You're A Rich Man
Back In The U.S.S.R.
Bad To Me
Birthday
Can't Buy Me Love
Carry That Weight
Come Together
Day In The Life
Day Tripper
Dear Prudence
Do You Want To Know A Secret
Drive My Car
Eight Days A Week
Eleanor Rigby
Fame
Fool On The Hill
From Me To You
Get Back
Give Peace A Chance
Good Day Sunshine
Goodbye
Got To Get You Into My Life
Hard Day's Night
Hello, Goodbye
Help
Helter Skelter
Here, There And Everywhere
Hey Jude

I Saw Her Standing There
I Should Have Known Better
I Wanna Be Your Man
If I Fell
I'll Be On My Way
I'll Keep You Satisfied
I'm A Loser
I'm Happy Just To Dance With
You
Imagine
In My Life
Instant Karma
It Won't Be Long
I've Got A Feeling
Lady Madonna
Let It Be
Long And Winding Road
Love Me Do
Lucy In The Sky With Diamonds
Maggie Mae (Arranged)
Magical Mystery Tour
Michelle
Misery
Norwegian Wood
Nowhere Man
Ob La Di, Ob La Da
Oh Darling
Paperback Writer
Penny Lane
P. S. I Love You
Revolution
Rocky Racoon
Run For Your Life
Sgt. Pepper's Lonely Hearts
Club Band
She Came In Through The
Bathroom Window
She Loves You
Strawberry Fields Forever
Tell Me Why
Thank You Girl
There's A Place
Ticket To Ride
We Can Work It Out
Whatever Gets You Thru The
Night
With A Little Help From My
Friends
World Without Love
Yellow Submarine
Yesterday
You Won't See Me
Your Mother Should Know
You've Got To Hide Your Love
Away

LENORE, J. B.
You Shook Me

LERIOS, Cory
Love Will Find A Way

LERNER, Alan Jay
Almost Like Being In Love (w)
They Call The Wind Maria (w)

LESH, Philip
Box of Rain (m)

Cumberland Blues (m)
Pride Of Cucamonga (m)
Truckin' (m)
Unbroken Chain (m)

LESLIE, Edgar
Among My Souvenirs

LESTER, Walter
Since I Don't Have You (w)
This I Swear (w)

LEVAY, Sylvester
Fly, Robin, Fly

LEVEL, Don
Good Morning, Little School Girl

LEVERT, Eddie
My Love Don't Come Easy

LEVINE, Irwin
Candida
I Woke Up In Love This Morning
Knock Three Times
Last Night I Made Love To
Somebody Else
Say, Has Anybody Seen My
Sweet Gypsy Rose
Steppin' Out, I'm Gonna Boogie
Tonight
Tie A Yellow Ribbon Round The
Ole Oak Tree

LEVINE, Joe
Life Is A Rock

LEVY, Adam R.
Walkin' Miracle

LEVY, Eunice
Ko Ko Mo (I Love You So)

LEVY, Jacques
Black Diamond Bay (w)
Catfish (w)
Hurricane (w)
Isis (w)
Joey (w)
Money BLues (w)
Mozambique (w)
Oh, Sister (w)
Rita May (w)
Romance In Durango (w)

LEVY, Marcy
Lay Down Sally

LEVY, Morris
Dance, Dance, Dance
Gee
I Want You To Be My Girl
Little Girl Of Mine
LIttle Star
My Boy Lollipop
Why Do Fools Fall In Love
Ya Ya

COMPOSER—LYRICIST INDEX

LEWIS, Al
Blueberry Hill

LEWIS, Barbara
Hello Stranger

LEWIS, Calvin
When A Man Loves A Woman

LEWIS, Clarence L.
Ya Ya

LEWIS, Edna
Judy's Turn To Cry

LEWIS, Jack
Teenage Idol

LEWIS, Stanley J.
Susie-Q

LIGHTFOOT, Gordon
Beautiful
Bitter Green
Canadian Railroad Trilogy
Did She Mention My Name
Early Mornin' Rain
For Lovin' Me
Got My Way
I Can't Make It Anymore
If You Could Read My Mind
Pussywillows, Cattails
Race Among The Ruins
Rainy Day People
Ribbons Of Darkness
Rich Man Spiritual
Song For A Winter's Night
Street Rail Blues
Summer Side Of Life
Summertime Dream
Sundown
That Same Old Obsession
Way I Feel
Wreck Of The Edmund
Fitzgerald

LIND, Bob
Elusive Butterfly

LIND, Jon
Boogie Wonderland

LINDE, Dennis
I'm Her Fool

LINDEMAN, Edith
Little Things Mean A Lot

LINDSAY, Mark
Don't Take It So Hard

LING, Sam
Eddie My Love

LINN, Roger
Promises

LINSLEY, Horace
Fool's Paradise

LINZER, Sandy
Can I Carry Your Balloon
Native New Yorker
Weekend Lover
Workin' My Way Back To You
You Keep Me Dancin'

LIPPMAN, Sid
Too Young

LIPSIUS, Fred
Go Down Gamblin' (m)

LIPTON, Leonard
Puff, (The Magic Dragon)

LIPUMA, Tommy
La Bamba (Adapted)

LIVGREN, Kerry
Carry On Wayward Son
Dust In the Wind
Reason To Be

LIVINGSTON, Jerry
Twelfth Of Never

LLOYD, Harry
He Did With Me
I Just Fall In Love Again (w)

LLOYD, Michael
I Was Made For Dancin'
Kiss In The Dark

LOBO
How Can I Tell Her (About You)
There Ain't No Way

LODGE, John
Ride My See-Saw

LOESSER, Frank
HEart And Soul

LOEWE, Frederick
Almost Like Being In Love (m)
They Call The Wind Maria (m)

LOGAN, Harold
I'm Gonna Get Married
Personality
Stagger Lee

LOGGINS, Eva Ein
Keep The Fire

LOGGINS, Kenny
Angry Eyes
Danny's Song
Growin'
House At Pooh Corner
I'm Alright
Keep The Fire

Love Song
My Music
This Is It
Watching The River Run
What A Fool Believes
Whenever I Call You "Friend"
Your Mama Don't Dance

LOMAX, Alan
Amazing Grace (Collected,
adapted & arranged)
Come By Here (Additional
lyrics)
Tom Dooley (Collected, adapted
& arranged)

LOMAX, John A.
Amazing Grace (Collected,
adapted & arranged)
Goodnight Irene
Roll On Columbia (m)
Tom Dooley (Collected,
adapted & arranged)

LONDON, Marc
To Sir With Love (m)

LONG, Frederick
Devil With The Blue Dress On
Here Comes The Judge

LONG, Shorty
Rock Me My Baby

LOPEZ, Gilbert
Happy, Happy Birthday, Baby

LORBER, Sam
Where Were You When I Was
Falling In Love

LORD, Jon
Burn
Smoke On The Water

LORDAN, Jerry
Apache

LOUDERMILK, John D.
Tobacco Road

LOUGHNANE, Lee
Call On Me
No Tell Lover

LOVE, Bob
Good Morning, Little School
Girl

LOVE, Mike
Please Let Me Wonder
Surfin'
Surfin' Safari
Warmth Of The Sun

LOVETT, Winfred
  Kiss And Say Goodbye

LOWE, Bernie
  Wild One

LOWE, Nick
  Cruel To Be Kind

LOWRY, F.
  Whispering Bells

LUBOFF, Norman
  Yellow Bird (m)

LUCAS, Buddy
  Steamboat

LUCAS, David
  Reach Out (m)

LUCCISANO, Joseph
  There's A Moon Out Tonight

LUCIA, Peter
  Crimson And Clover

LUKE, Robin
  Susie Darlin'

LUTZ, Michael
  Smokin' In The Boys Room

LYMAN, Abe
  What Can I Say After I Say I'm
    Sorry

LYMON, Frankie
  Why Do Fools Fall In Love

LYNN, Cheryl
  Got To Be Real

LYNNE, Jeff
  Do Ya
  Don't Bring Me Down
  Evil Woman
  Last Train To London
  Livin' Thing
  Shine A Little Love
  Showdown
  Strange Magic
  Sweet Talkin' Woman
  Telephone Line
  Turn To Stone

LYNOTT, Phil
  Boys Are Back In Town

MACALUSO, Leonard
  Dancin' To The Music

MACAULAY, Tony
  Can't We Just Sit Down And
    Talk It Over

McBROOM, Amanda
  Rose

McCANN, Peter
  Do You Wanna Make Love
  Right Time Of The Night

McCARTHY, Joseph
  Alice Blue Gown (w)

McCARTNEY, Linda
  Another Day
  Band On The Run
  Junior's Farm
  Live And Let Die
  My Love
  Uncle Albert/Admiral Halsey

McCARTNEY, Paul
  Across The Universe
  All My Loving
  All Together Now
  All You Need Is Love
  And I Love Her
  Another Day
  Baby, You're A Rich Man
  Back In The U.S.S.R.
  Bad To Me
  Band On The Run
  Birthday
  Can't Buy Me Love
  Carry That Weight
  Come And Get It
  Come Together
  Day In The Life
  Day Tripper
  Dear Prudence
  Do You Want To Know A
    Secret
  Drive My Car
  Eight Days A Week
  Eleanor Rigby
  Every Night
  Fool On The Hill
  From Me To You
  Get Back
  Give Peace A Chance
  Good Day Sunshine
  Goodbye
  Got To Get You Into My Life
  Hard Day's Night
  Hello, Goodbye
  Help
  Helter Skelter
  Here, There And Everywhere
  Hey Jude
  I Am The Walrus
  I Feel Fine
  I Saw Her Standing There
  I Should Have Known Better
  I Wanna Be Your Man
  If I Fell
  I'll Be On My Way
  I'll Keep You Satisfied
  I'm A Loser
  I'm Happy Just To Dance With
    You

In My Life
It Won't Be Long
I've Got A Feeling
Junior's Farm
Lady Madonna
Let It Be
Listen To What The Man Said
Live And Let Die
Long And Winding Road
Love Me Do
Lovely Linda
Lucy In The Sky With Diamonds
Maggie Mae (Arranged)
Magical Mystery Tour
Maybe I'm Amazed
Michelle
Misery
My Love
Norwegian Wood
Nowhere Man
Ob La Di, Ob La Da
Oh Darling
Paperback Writer
Penny Lane
P. S. I Love You
Revolution
Ringo's Theme
Rocky Racoon
Run For Your Life
Sgt. Pepper's Lonely Hearts
  Club Band
She Came In Through The
  Bathroom Window
She Loves You
Strawberry Fields Forever
Tell Me Why
Thank You Girl
That Would Be Something
There's A Place
Ticket To Ride
Uncle Albert/Admiral Halsey
Venus And Mars Rock Show
We Can Work It Out
With A Little Help From My
  Friends
World Without Love
Yellow Submarine
Yesterday
You Won't See Me
Your Mother Should Know
You've Got To Hide Your Love
  Away

McCLARY, Thomas
  Brick House
  Flying High

McCLURE, Michael
  Mercedes Benz

McCOLL, Deborah
  Fins

MacCOLL, Ewan
  First Time Ever I Saw Your
    Face

COMPOSER—LYRICIST INDEX

McCORKLE, George
Fire On The Mountain
Last Of The Singing Cowboys

McCORMACK, Keith
Sugar Shack

McCORMICK, Randy
Suspicions

McCOY, Van
Baby Don't Change Your Mind
Baby, I'm Yours
Change With The Times
Everything's Coming Up Love
Hustle
Party

McCRAE, Teddy
Love Love Love

McCULLOCH, James
Hot Child In The City
Rock Me

McCURDY, Ed
Last Night I Had The Strangest
Dream

McDANIEL, Ellas
Bo Diddley
Call Me
Here Tis
I Can Tell
Mona
Road Runner
Who Do You Love

McDANIELS, Eugene
Feel Like Makin' Love

MacDERMOT, Galt
Aquarius (m)
Aquarius/Let The Sunshine In
(m)
Easy to Be Hard (m)
Good Morning Starshine (m)
Let The Sunshine In (m)
Manchester England (m)

McDILL, Bob
She Never Knew Me

McDONALD, Joe
I Feel Like I'm Fixin' To Die
Rag

McDONALD, Michael
Dependin' On You
Here To Love You
It Keeps You Runnin'
Minute By Minute
Real Love
Takin' It To The Streets
This Is It
What A Fool Believes
You Belong To Me (m)

McDONALD, Ralph
Stuff Like That
Where Is The Love

McDOWELL, Ronnie
Animal

McFADDEN, Gene
Ain't No Stoppin' Us Now
Prayin'
Wake Up Everybody

McFADDIN, Terri
Look What You've Done To My
Heart
One Love In My Lifetime

McFEE, John
One Step Closer

McGEE, Parker
I Just Can't Say No To You
I'd Really Love To See You
Tonight
Nights Are Forever Without You

McGINTY, Bennie Lee
Ain't Gonna Bump No More

MacGREGOR, Mary
This Girl

McGUINN, Roger
Ballad Of Easy Rider

McGUIRE, Barry
Green Green

McGUIRE, Raymond
Raise A Little Hell

McHUGH, Jimmy
I'm In The Mood For Love

McKAY, Al
Best Of My Love
September
Singasong

McKENNA, Danny
My Angel Baby

McKENZIE, M.
Little Town Flirt

McKENZIE, Scott
What About Me

McKERNAN, Ron
Operator

McKUEN, Rod
Love's Been Good To Me
Pastures Green
Seasons In The Sun (w)
World I Used To Know

McLAUGHLIN, John
Birds Of Fire (m)

McLEAN, Don
American Pie
And I Love You So
Vincent
Wonderful Baby

MacLELLAN, Gene
Put Your Hand In The Hand
Snowbird

McLEOD, Marilyn
Love Hangover

McMURRAY, Clay
Here I Am Again
If I Were Your Woman

McNAUGHTON, F.
Rivers Of Babylon

MacNEIL, T.
Hello Hello

McPHATTER, Clyde
Honey Love

McPHERSON, Jim
Jane

McQUEEN, Rod
Beautiful Sunday

McRAE, Floyd F.
Sh-Boom

McREYNOLDS, Denny
It's A Great Life

McVIE, Christine
Chain
Don't Stop
Over & Over
Over My Head
Say You Love Me
Songbird
Think About Me
You Make Loving Fun

McVIE, John
Chain

McWILLIAMS, David
Days Of Pearly Spencer

MADARA, John
You Don't Own Me

MAGNUM, Jeff
Sonic Reducer

MAHER, Brent
Lesson In Leavin'

MAINEGRA, Richard
Home Made Love

MAINIERI, Mike
Jesse (w)

MALLOY, David
Suspicions

MALNECK, Matt
Shangri-la (m)
Stairway To The Stars (m)

MALONE, Deadric
Blind Man

MALONE, George
Book Of Love

MALONE, Johnny
Please Love Me Forever

MANCHESTER, Melissa
Come In From The Rain
Just Too Many People
Just You And I
Midnight Blue
Whenever I Call You "Friend"
(w)

MANDEL, Johnny
M*A*S*H, Song From (m)
Shadow OF Your Smile (m)

MANILOW, Barry
Beautiful Music
Copacabana (m)
Could It Be Magic
Daybreak (m)
Even Now (m)
It's A Miracle
It's Just Another New Year's
Eve (m)
Jump Shout Boogie
One Voice
Slow Dance (m)
Street Singin'
This One's For You (m)

MANN, Barry
Here You Come Again (m)
How Much Love
I Just Can't Help Believin'
I Love How You Love Me
I'm Gonna Be Strong
New World Coming
On Broadway
We Gotta Get Out Of This
Place
When You Get Right Down To
It
You've Lost That Lovin' Feeling

MANN, Curtis
Let It Be Me (w)

MANN, Kal
Bristol Stomp
Don't Hang Up
Let's Twist Again
Wah-Wahtusi
Wild One
You Can't Sit Down

MANN, Mono
Don't Jump Me Mother
Mighty Idy

MANNING, Dick
Morning Side Of The Mountain
Secretly

MANUEL, Richard
Jawbone

MANZANERO, A.
It's Impossible (m)

MARASCALCO, John
Be My Guest
Good Golly Miss Molly
Ready Teddy
Rip It Up
Send Me Some Lovin'

MARCELLINO, Gene & Jerry
Whatever You Got, I Want

MARCUCCI, Bob
Why

MARCUS, Sol
Lonely Man

MARDIN, Arif
Tranquillo (Melt My Heart)

MARENO, Ricci
Gwen

MARESCA, Ernie
Wanderer

MARINELL, LeRoy P.
Excitable Boy
Werewolves Of London

MARKWELL, Mark
Secretly

MARLEY, Bob
I Shot The Sheriff
Stir It Up

MARLOW, Ric
Taste Of Honey (w)

MARSHALL, Edward H.
Venus

MARSHALL, James W. (Jim)
Devil Went Down To Georgia

In America
Legend Of Wooley Swamp

MARSHALL, Sherman
Then Came You
Wake Up Susan

MARTI, Jose
Guantanamera (w)

MARTIN, Bill
Summer Love Sensation

MARTIN, Bobbi
For The Love Of Him

MARTIN, David
Can't Smile Without You

MARTIN, Lennie
Since I Don't Have You (m)
This I Swear (m)

MARTIN, Moon
Bad Case Of Loving You
Cadillac Walk
Rolene

MARTIN, Naomi
Let's Take The Long Way Around
The World

MARTIN, Steve
King Tut

MARTINE, Layng, Jr.
Way Down

MARTINEZ, Jose
La Bamba (Adapted)

MARTINEZ, Rudy
96 Tears

MARTINOLI, Carlos Alberto
Love Me With All Your Heart
(m)

MARVIN, Hank
Sam

MASON, Barbara
Yes I'm Ready

MASON, Barry
Delilah
I Believe In Miracles
Love Me Tonight
Say You'll Stay Until Tomorrow

MASON, Dave
Feelin' Alright?
Let It Go, Let It Flow

MASON, James
I Dig Rock And Roll Music

MASON, Lol
5.7.0.5.

MASSER, Michael
Do You Know Where You're
Going To? (m)
Greatest Love Of All (m)
I Thought It Took A Little Time
It's My Turn
Last Time I Saw Him (m)
Someone That I Used To Love
(m)
Touch Me In The Morning (m)

MATASSA, C.
Just A Dream

MATHER, Bob
Sexy Eyes

MATLOCK, Glen
Anarchy In The U.K.
God Save The Queen
Pretty Vacant

MATSON, Vera
Love Me Tender
Poor Boy

MATTHEW, Eric
Keep On Dancin'

MATTHEWS, Charles G. (Red)
White Silver Sands

MAULDIN, Joe
I'm Gonna Love You Too
Last Night
Well All Right

MAXWELL, Robert
Ebb Tide (m)
Shangri-la (m)

MAY, Brian
Fat Bottomed Girls
It's Late
We Will Rock You

MAYER, Henry
My Melody Of Love (m)
Summer Wind (m)

MAYER, Tommy
Weekend

MAYFIELD, Curtis
Curious Mind
Get Down
Gypsy Woman
He Don't Love You (Like I Love
You)
Let's Do It Again
Something He Can Feel
Superfly

MAYFIELD, Percy
Hit The Road Jack
Please Send Me Someone To
Love

MEDICA, Leon
New Orleans Ladies

MEDLEY, Phil
Million To One
Twist And Shout

MEDLOCKE, Rick
Highway Song

MEDORA, J.
At The Hop

MEISNER, Randy
Deep Inside My Heart
Take It To The Limit

MEKLER, Gabriel
Kozmic Blues

MEMPHIS MINNIE
When The Levee Breaks

MERCHANT, Michael
Time

MERCURY, Eric
You Are My Heaven

MERCURY, Freddie
Bicycle Race
Bohemian Rhapsody
Crazy Little Thing Called Love
Killer Queen
Lazing On A Sunday Afternoon
Somebody To Love
We Are The Champions

MERINO, Dana
You Need A Woman Tonight

MERRICK, Jerry
Follow

MERRILL, Bob
You Don't Have To Be A Baby To
Cry

MERSHON, Norman
Such A Woman

MESHEL, Billy
Come Love Your Life With Me
(w)

MESSINA, Jim (James)
Angry Eyes
Changes
Listen To A Country Song
My Music
Nobody But You

Watching The River Run
Your Mama Don't Dance

MEVIS, Blake
If The World Ran Out Of Love
Tonight

MEZZETTI, Elena
A' Soalin'

MICHAEL, William
Mission Bell

MICHAELE
You And I (w)

MIDDLEBROOKS, Harry
Spooky

MIDDLETON, Anthony
Here Comes The Sun

MILCHBERG, JORGE
El Condor Pasa (m)

MILES, John
Music

MILLER, BERNARD
I Can't Stand The Rain

MILLER, Charles W.
Cisco Kid
Gypsy Man
Me And Baby Brother
Spill The Wine
World Is A Ghetto

MILLER, Eddie
Release Me

MILLER, Frank
Greenfields
Memories Are Made Of This

MILLER, Glenn
Moonlight Serenade (m)

MILLER, Kim
I Got My Mind Made Up

MILLER, Roger
King Of The Road

MILLER, Ronald
For Once In My Life (w)
Heaven Help Us All
Place In The Sun (w)
Touch Me In The Morning (w)
Yester-Me, Yester-You, Yester-
day (w)

MILLER, Scott
I Got My Mind Made Up

MILLER, Steve
Dance, Dance, Dance
Fly Like An Eagle
Joker
Rock 'N Me
Take The Money And Run
Winter Time

MILLER, Sy
Let There Be Peace On Earth

MILLER, William
Daddy's Home
Thousand Miles Away

MILLET, M.
All Around The World

MILLS, Chas.
Lady Godiva

MILLS, Gordon
It's Not Unusual

MINER, Raynard
Higher And Higher
Rescue Me

MINNIGERODE, Meade
Whiffenpoof Song

MITCHELL, Adam
Dancin' Round And Round

MITCHELL, James
Float On

MITCHELL, Johnny
We Belong Together

MITCHELL, Joni
All I Want
Amelia
Big Yellow Taxi
Blue
Both Sides Now
California
Carey
Chelsea Morning
Circle Game
Coyote
Fiddle And The Drum
For The Roses
Free Man In Paris
Help Me
In France They Kiss On Main
Street
Ladies Of The Canyon
Michael From Mountains
My Old Man
Raised On Robbery
Song To A Seagull
Woodstock
You Turn Me On, I'm A Radio

MITCHELL, Paul F.
Tryin' To Love Two

MITCHELL, Phillip
Leftovers

MITCHELL, Willie
Call Me (Come Back Home)
Echoes Of Love (w)
I'm Still In Love With You
Let's Stay Together
Twenty Seventy Five

MODUGNO. Domenico
Volare (m)

MOFFITT, Kenneth R.
Oh Julie

MOLINARY, Phyllis
Every Time I Sing A Love Song

MOMAN, Chips
Another Somebody Done Some-
body Wrong Song
Everybody Loves A Rain Song
Luckenbach, Texas
Wurlitzer Prize

MONEY, Eddie
Can't Keep A Good Man Down
Maybe I'm A Fool
Two Tickets To Paradise

MONN, T.
Mellow Lovin'

MONROE, Bill
Blue Moon Of Kentucky

MONTANA, Vincent, Jr.
#1 Dee Jay

MONTGOMERY, Bob
Heartbeat
Love's Made A Fool Of You

MOODY, Russell
Wear My Ring Around Your
Neck

MOORE, Daniel
Shambala

MOORE, James
Baby Scratch My Back

MOORE, Johnny
Merry Christmas Baby

MOORE, Marvin
Four Walls

MOORE, Oscar
Tell Me You'll Wait For Me

MOORE, Pete
Love Machine

MOORE, Warren
Ain't That Peculiar
Going To A Go-Go
I'll Be Doggone
Ooo Baby Baby
Since I Lost My Baby
Tracks Of My Tears

MORALI, J. (Jacques)
Best Disco In Town (m)
Fire Island (m)
Go West
Hot Cop
I Am What I Am
I'm A Cruiser
In Hollywood (Everybody Is A
Star) (m)
In The Navy
Key West (m)
Macho Man
My Roommate
San Francisco (You've Got Me)
(m)
Sodom And Gomorrah (m)
Ups And Downs
Village People (m)
Woman
Y.M.C.A.

MOREY, Larry
Lavender Blue (w)

MORGAN, Dennis W.
Crackers
Fooled By A Feeling
Sleeping Single In A Double Bed
Years

MORODER, Giorgio
Call Me
Chase (m)
Heaven Knows
Love To Love You, Baby
Spring Affair
Wanderer (m)
Winter Melody

MORRIS, Charles
Let Me Lay My Funk On You

MORRIS, Doug
Sweet Talkin' Guy

MORRIS, Joe
Anytime, Anyplace, Anywhere

MORRIS, John
Blazing Saddles

MORRIS, Lee
Blue Velvet

MORRISON, Bob
You Decorated My Life

MORRISON, Jim
Blue Sunday
Indian Summer
Land Ho (w)
Maggie M'Gill (w)
Peace Frog (w)
Queen Of The Highway
Roadhouse Blues (w)
Ship Of Fools (w)
Spy
Waiting For The Sun (w)
You Make Me Real

MORRISON, Van
Blue Money
Brown Eyed Girl
Domino
I Shall Sing
Into The Mystic
Moondance
Mystic Eyes
Old Old Woodstock
Tupelo Honey
Wild Night

MORRISON, Vonie
Act Naturally

MORRISON, W.
One Nation Under A Groove

MORROW, Geoff
Can't Smile Without You

MORTIMER, Al
For The Love Of Him

MORTON, Gladys
Playboy

MOSS, Leonard
Also Sprach Zarathustra (m, arranged)

MOURET, J.J.
Masterpiece (m)

MOY, Sylvia
I Was Made To Love Her
My Baby Loves Me
My Cherie Amour
Nothing's Too Good For My Baby
Shoo-Be-Doo-Be-Doo-Da-Day
Uptight (Everything's Alright)
With A Child's Heart

MULDAUR, Geoffrey
Wild About My Lovin'

MULDROW, Cornell
You Can't Sit Down

MULLER, Randy
Ha Cha Cha (Funktion)
What It Is

MURDEN, Orlando
For Once In My Life (m)

MURPHEY, Michael
Carolina In The Pines
Wildfire (w)

MURPHY, Audie
Shutters And Boards

MURPHY, Ralph
Half The Way

MURPHY, Walter
Fifth Of Beethoven (m)
Music Will Not End (m)

MURRAY, Jean
Splish Splash

MURRAY, Mitch
Billy, Don't Be A Hero
Night Chicago Died (m)

MURRY, Ted
Don't Break The Heart That Loves You

MUSIC, Henrietta & Lorenzo
Home To Emily (m)

MUSKER, Frank
Back On My Feet Again
Heaven On The Seventh Floor

MYERS, Randy
Brighton Hill
Put A Little Love In Your Heart
River Of Love

MYSELS, Maurice
I Want You, I Need You, I Love You (w)

NAHAN, Irv
Dance With Me

NAPIER-BELL, Simon
You Don't Have To Say You Love Me (w)

NASH, Graham
Immigration Man
Jennifer Eccles
Marrakesh Express
Our House
Out Of The Darkness
Prison Song
Southbound Train
Teach Your Children
Tell Me To My Face

NASH, Johnny
Hold Me Tight
I Can See Clearly Now
What Kind Of Love Is This

NAVARRO, Esther
Speedo
Zoom

NEHLS, H., III
Too Hot To Stop (Part I)

NEIL, Fred
Everybody's Talkin'
Just A Little Bit Of Rain

NEILEN, Marshall
Wonderful One (Adapted from his theme)

NELSON, Benjamin
There Goes My Baby

NELSON, Betty
Don't Play That Song

NELSON, Rick
Garden Party

NELSON, Steve
Songbird

NELSON, Willie
Good Hearted Woman

NESMITH, Michael
Different Drum

NEVILLE, Naomi
Certain Girl
Pain In My Heart

NEVINS, Al & Morty
Twilight Time (m)

NEWBORN, Ira
Hot Wax Theme

NEWLEY, Anthony
Candy Man
Goldfinger (w)

NEWMAN, Alfred
Winds Of Chance (m)

NEWMAN, Herb
Birds And The Bees
So This Is Love

NEWMAN, Joel
Kisses Sweeter Than Wine (m)

NEWMAN, Randy
I Don't Want To Hear It Any More
Louisiana 1927
Sail Away
Short People

NICHOL, Al
Sound Asleep

NICHOLLS, Horatio
Among My Souvenirs

NICHOLS, Billy
Do It ('Til You're Satisfied)

NICHOLS, Dan
You, You're The One (w)

NICHOLS, Roger
I Won't Last A Day Without You
(m)
Let Me Be The One (m)
Rainy Days And Mondays (m)
We've Only Just Begun (m)

NICKS, Stevie
Chain
Dreams
Rhiannon
Sara

NIELSEN, Reed
If You Should Sail

NIELSEN, Rick
Dream Police
I Want You To Want Me
Surrender
Voices

NILSSON, Harry
Cuddly Toy
Me And My Arrow
1941
One
Without Her

NIMS, Walter D.
Precious And Few

NITZSCHE, Jack
Needles And Pins

NIVERT, Taffy
Take Me Home, Country Roads

NIX, Robert
Champagne Jam
Don't Miss The Message
I'm Not Gonna Let It Bother Me
Tonight
Imaginary Lover
Sky High
So Into You

NOBLE, Harry
Hold Me, Thrill Me, Kiss Me

NOBLE, Ray
Good Night Sweetheart

NOE, Dale
After The Storm

NOLAN, Kenny
Get Dancin'
I Like Dreamin'
Lady Marmalade
Love's Grown Deep
My Eyes Adored You
Swing Your Daddy
Us And Love

NORTH
Nice, Nice, Very Nice

NORTH, Alex
Unchained Melody

NUGENT, Ted
Cat Scratch Fever
Need You Bad
Yank Me, Crank Me

NUGETRE SEE Ertegun, Ahmet

NYRO, Laura
And When I Die
Eli's Coming
I Never Meant To Hurt You
Save The Country
Stoned Soul Picnic
Stoney End
Sweet Blindness
Wedding Bell Blues

NYX, James, Jr.
Inner City Blues

OATES, John
Sara Smile (w)

OBSCURE, Charles
Hats Off To (Roy) Harper
(Arranged)

OCASEK, Ric
Candy-O
Double Life
Good Times Roll
It's All I Can Do
Just What I Needed
Let's Go
My Best Friend's Girl

OCHS, Phil
Bracero
Cannons Of Christianity
Changes
Cops Of The World
Cross My Heart
Crucifixion
Draft Dodger Rag
Floods Of Florence
Flower Lady
Half A Century High
Harder They Fall
I'm Gonna Say It Now
Is There Anybody Here

I've Had Her
Joe Hill
Love Me, I'm A Liberal
Miranda
Outside Of A Small Circle Of
Friends
Party
Pleasures Of The Harbor
Rhythms Of Revolution
Santo Domingo
Tape From California
That's The Way It's Gonna Be
There But For Fortune
War Is Over
When I'm Gone
When In Rome
White Boots Marchin' In A
Yellow Land

O'CONNOR, Robert
Sweet Marjorene

O'DAY, Alan
Angie Baby
Easy Evil
Started Out Dancing, Ended Up
Making Love
Undercover Angel

O'DELL, Kenny
Behind Closed Doors

ODEN, J.
Goin' Down Slow

O'HARA, Karen
It's A Great Life

O'KEEFE, Danny
Good Time Charlie's Got The
Blues

O'KEEFE, Johnny
Real Wild Child

OKUN, Milton
All My Trials (Adapted)
Come And Go With Me (Adapted
& arranged)
Cuckoo
Hangman (Adapted)
Monday Morning (Adapted & ar-
ranged)
Motherless Child
Tell It On The Mountain
(Adapted)

OLDFIELD, Mike
Tubular Bells (m)

OLDHAM, Andrew Loog
As Tears Go By

OLDHAM, Linden
I'm Your Puppet

OLDHAM, Spooner
Cry Like A Baby
Denver
Sweet Inspiration

OLIVER, Jimmy
Itchy, Twitchy Feeling

OMARTIAN, Michael
Get Used To It
Hollywood (m)

OPPENHEIM, James
Bread And Roses (w)

ORANGE, Walter
Brick House

ORBISON, Roy
Empty Cup
You've Got Love

ORNADEL, Cyril
Portrait Of My Love (m)

ORSBORN, Victor
Dance (Disco Heat)

ORSON, Ann
Don't Go Breaking My Heart

OSBORN, Rev. Earl
Michael (Adapted)

OSBORNE, Gary
Little Jeannie
Part-Time Love

OSKAR, Lee
Cisco Kid
Gypsy Man
Me And Baby Brother
Spill The Wine
World Is A Ghetto

OSMOND, Alan, Merrill & Wayne
Goin' Home

OSTERBERG, James
Search And Destroy

O'SULLIVAN, Raymond
Alone Again (Naturally)

OTIS, Clyde
Baby (You've Got What It Takes)
Endlessly
It's Just A Matter Of Time
Out Of Sight, Out Of Mind
Stroll
What's A Matter, Baby

OTIS, P.
Dance With Me Henry

OWENS, Cliff
Any Way You Want Me

OWENS, Dave
Real Wild Child

OWENS, Shirley
Oh, Baby

PACK, David
Biggest Part Of Me
Nice, Nice, Very Nice (m)

PAGE, Billy
In Crowd

PAGE, Jimmy
Babe, I'm Gonna Leave You
Battle Of Evermore
Black Dog
Black Mountain Side
Bron-Y-Aur Stomp
Celebration Day
Communication Breakdown
Crunge
Dancing Days
Dazed And Confused
Four Sticks
Friends
Gallows Pole
Going To California
Good Times Bad Times
Heartbreaker
How Many More Times
Immigrant Song
Living Loving Maid
Measuring A Summer's Day
Misty Mountain Hop
Moby Dick
No Quarter
Ocean
Out On The Tiles
Over The Hills And Far Away
Rain Song
Ramble On
Rock And Roll
Since I've Been Loving You
Song Remains The Same
Stairway To Heaven
Thank You
That's The Way
What Is And What Should Never
Be
When The Levee Breaks
Whole Lotta Love
Your Time Is Gonna Come

PAICE, Ian
Burn
Smoke On The Water

PAICH, David
Got To Be Real
Hold The Line
It's Over
Lido Shuffle
Lowdown

PALMER, David
Jazzman

PANKOW, James
Alive Again
Colour My World
Feelin' Stronger Every Day
Just You 'N' Me
Make Me Smile
Searchin' So Long
You Are On My Mind

PANZER, Marty
Beautiful Music
Even Now (w)
It's A Miracle (w)
It's Just Another New Year's
Eve (w)
This One's For You (w)

PANZERI, M.
Love Me Tonight (m)

PAPPALARDI, Felix
Baby I'm Down
Blood Of The Sun
Crossroader
Flowers Of Evil
Mississippi Queen

PARISH, Mitchell
Deep Purple (w)
Moonlight Serenade (w)
Stairway To The Stars (w)
Volare (w)

PARKER, Bobby
Blues Get Off My Shoulder

PARKER, Johnny
Baby Sittin' Boogie

PARKER, Judy
December 1963 (Oh, What A
Night) (w)
Down The Hall

PARKER, Ray, Jr.
Honey I'm Rich
Jack And Jill
Two Places At The Same Time
You Can't Change That

PARKER, Robert
Barefootin'

PARKER, Ross
Song Of Joy (w)

PARKER, Tom
Joy (m, adapted & arranged)

PARKS, Weldon Dean
Dancing Machine

PARNES, Paul
Masterpiece (m)

PARRIS, Fred
  In The Still Of The Night

PARSONS, Alan
  Doctor Tarr And Professor
    Fether

PARTON, Dolly
  Baby, I'm Burning
  Light Of A Clear Blue Morning
  Two Doors Down

PATRICK, Charles
  Book Of Love

PATTERSON, Lover
  There Goes My Baby

PATTERSON, Massie
  Day Light Break (New works &
    new music adaptation)

PAUL, Clarence
  Fingertips (Part 2)
  Hitch Hike

PAUL, M.
  Ten Commandments Of Love

PAUL, Marshall
  So Many Roads

PAULING, Lowman
  Dedicated To The One I Love

PAXTON, Tom
  Bottle Of Wine
  Last Thing On My Mind
  Whose Garden Was This

PAYNE, Bill
  All That You Dream (m)

PAYNE, Doris
  Just One Look

PAYNE, Harold
  Daylight

PAYNE, K.
  Midnight Rider

PEABODY, John
  Little Star

PEARSON, Gene
  Thousand Stars

PEARSON, Mark
  If You Should Sail

PEDRICK, Robert John & Tom
  Give A Little More

PEEBLES, Ann
  I Can't Stand The Rain

PEEK, Catherine L.
  Lonely People

PEEK, Dan
  All Things Are Possible
  California Revisited
  Don't Cry Baby
  Lonely People
  Today's The Day
  Woman Tonight

PENA, Paul
  Jet Airliner

PENDLEBURY, Andrew
  Who Listens To The Radio

PENN, Dan
  Cry Like A Baby
  Denver
  I'm Your Puppet
  Sweet Inspiration

PENNIMAN, Richard
  Bama Lama Bama Loo
  Boo, Hoo, Hoo, Hoo (I'll Never
    Let You Go)
  Hey, Hey, Hey, Hey (Goin' Back
    To Birmingham)
  Jenny, Jenny
  Long Tall Sally
  Lucille
  Miss Ann
  Slippin' And Slidin'
  Tutti Frutti

PENRIDGE, Stan
  Beth

PENZABENE, Roger
  End Of Our Road
  I Could Never Love Another
  I Wish It Would Rain
  You're My Everything

PEPPERS, Bill
  I Was The One

PERETTI, Hugo
  Can't Give You Anything (But
    My Love)
  Can't Help Falling In Love
  Disco Baby
  Hey Girl, Come And Get It
  Lion Sleeps Tonight (Adapted)
  Love Is The Answer
  Star On A T.V. Show

PERKINS, Carl Lee
  Blue Suede Shoes

PERPER, Bob
  Still Waters Run Deep

PERREN, Freddie
  Boogie Fever
  Do It Baby

Hallelujah Day (m)
I Pledge My Love (m)
I Will Survive
It's So Hard To Say Goodbye To
  Yesterday
Let Me Know (I Have A Right)
Makin' It
Reunited
Shake Your Groove Thing
We've Got Love
Who Done It

PERRY, Joe
  Back In The Saddle
  Draw The Line
  Walk This Way

PERRY, Leonard
  One Love In My Lifetime

PERRY, Steve
  Lights
  Lovin', Touchin', Squeezin'
  Too Late

PETERS, Ben
  Before The Next Teardrop Falls
  Daytime Friends
  Kiss An Angel Good Mornin'

PETERS, Dale Thomas
  Funk #49

PETERS, Jerry
  Love Or Let Me Be Lonely

PETERSON, Robert
  Pride Of Cucamonga (w)
  Unbroken Chain (w)

PETTY, Norman
  Empty Cup
  Every Day
  Fool's Paradise
  Heartbeat
  I'm Gonna Love You Too
  I'm Lookin' For Someone To Love
  It's So Easy
  Last Night
  Listen To Me
  Look At Me
  Maybe Baby
  Moondreams
  Not Fade Away
  Oh Boy
  Peggy Sue
  Rave On
  Take Your Time
  That'll Be The Day
  True Love Ways
  Well All Right
  You've Got Love

PETTY, Tom
  Don't Do Me Like That
  I Need To Know
  Listen To Her Heart
  Refugee

PEVERETT, Dave
Third Time Lucky

PHILLIPS, J.C.
Green Eyed Lady

PHILLIPS, John
California Dreamin'
Creeque Alley
Go Where You Wanna Go
Hey Girl
I Got A Feeling
I Saw Her Again Last Night
Look Through My Window
Monday, Monday
Safe In My Garden
San Francisco (Be Sure To Wear
Some Flowers In Your Hair)
Somebody Groovy
Straight Shooter
Words Of Love

PHILLIPS, Marvin
Cherry Pie

PHILLIPS, Michelle Gilliam
California Dreamin'
Creeque Alley
Hey Girl

PICCIRILLO, Mike
Give A Little More

PICKETT, Bobby
Monster Mash

PICKETT, Wilson
In The Midnight Hour

PICKNEY, St. Clair
There It Is (Part I)

PIKE, Victoria
Forget To Remember
It Feels So Good To Be Loved So
Bad
Rain In My Heart

PILAT, L.
Love Me Tonight (m)

PINKARD, Marco
Sweet Georgia Brown

PIPPIN, Steve
Better Love Next Time
Holdin' On For Dear Love
This Time I'm In It For Love

PISCARIELLO, Frederick A.
Tallahassee Lassie

PISTILLI, Gene
Music Will Not End (w)
Song That Never Comes

PITCHFORD, Dean
Fame (w)

PLACE, Mary Kay
Baby Boy (Big Ole Baby Boy)

PLANT, Robert
Battle Of Evermore
Black Dog
Bron-Y-Aur Stomp
Celebration Day
Crunge
Dancing Days
D'yer Mak'er
Four Sticks
Friends
Gallows Pole
Going To California
Heartbreaker
Immigrant Song
Living Loving Maid
Misty Mountain Hop
No Quarter
Ocean
Out On The Tiles
Over The Hills And Far Away
Rain Song
Ramble On
Rock And Roll
Since I've Been Loving You
Song Remains The Same
Stairway To Heaven
Thank You
That's The Way
What Is And What Should Never
Be
When The Levee Breaks
Whole Lotta Love

PLANTE, Jacques
Don't Tell My Heart To Stop
Loving You

PLEHN, David
Easy Driver

POCKRISS, Lee
Itsy Bitsy Teenie Weenie Yellow
Polkadot Bikini
Johnny Angel (m)
My Heart Is An Open Book (m)
Playground In My Mind
Run Sally Run
Seven Little Girls Sitting In The
Back Seat
What Is Love

POINTER, Anita & Bonnie
Fairytale

POLLACK, Lew
Charmaine
Diane

POLLOCK, Channing
My Man (w)

POMERANZ, David
It's In Every One Of Us
Tryin' To Get The Feeling Again

POMEROY, George S.
Whiffenpoof Song

POMUS, Doc
Doin' The Best I Can
Gonna Get Back Home Somehow
His Latest Flame
Hushabye
I Count The Tears
I Feel That I've Known You For-
ever
Kiss Me Quick
Little Sister
Mess Of Blues
Never Say Yes
Save The Last Dance For Me
Surrender (w)
Suspicion
Sweets For My Sweet
This Magic Moment
True Love, True Love
What Every Woman Lives For
Young Blood

PONCIA, Vincent (Vini)
I Was Made For Lovin' You
Just Too Many People
You Make Me Feel Like Dancing

PONS, Jim
Sound Asleep

POREE, Anita
Boogie Down
Keep On Truckin'
Love Or Let Me Be Lonely

PORTER, Cole
Begin The Beguine
Don't Fence Me In
Night And Day

PORTER, David
Hold On I'm Coming
I Thank You
Show Me How
Soul Man
You Got Me Hummin'

PORTER, Jake
Ko Ko Mo (I Love You So)

POST, Jim
Reach Out In The Darkness

POTTER, Brian
Ain't No Woman
Don't Pull Your Love
It Only Takes A Minute
Look In My Eyes Pretty Woman
One Tin Soldier

POUGHT, Emma Ruth & Jannie
Mister Lee

POWELL, Roger
Set Me Free

POWERS, Chet
Get Together

PRAGER, Stephen
Fly, Robin, Fly

PRESLEY, Elvis
All Shook Up
Don't Be Cruel (To A Heart
That's True)
Heartbreak Hotel
Love Me Tender
Only Believe
Poor Boy

PRESTON, Billy
Outa Space
Will It Go 'Round In Circles
You Are So Beautiful

PREVIN, Andre
Valley Of The Dolls, Theme
From (m)
You're Gonna Hear From Me (m)

PREVIN, Dory
Come Saturday Morning (w)
Last Tango In Paris (w)
Valley Of The Dolls, Theme
From (w)
You're Gonna Hear From Me (w)

PRICE, Alan
House Of The Rising Sun
(Adapted)

PRICE, Harvey
Temptation Eyes

PRICE, Leo
Send Me Some Lovin'

PRICE, Lloyd
I'm Gonna Get Married
Just Because
Lawdy, Miss Clawdy
Personality
Stager Lee

PRIEST, Steve
Action
Fox On The Run

PRINCE
I Wanna Be Your Lover

PRINE, John
Paradise

PROFFER, Spencer
Children Of The Sun

PROVISOR, Dennis
Walking Through The Country

PUENTE, Tito
Oye Como Va

PUERTA, Joe
Nice, Nice, Very Nice

PUGH, Phil
Then Came You

PUTMAN, Curly
Green Green Grass Of Home
My Elusive Dreams

QUICK, C.E.
Come Go With Me
Whispering Bells

QUITTENTON, Martin
Maggie May

RABBITT, Eddie
Suspicions

RABIN, Buzz
Beaucoups Of Blues

RADER, Paul
Only Believe

RADO, James
Aquarius (w)
Aquarius/Let The Sunshine In (w)
Easy To Be Hard (w)
Good Morning Starshine (w)
Let The Sunshine In (w)
Manchester England (w)

RAFFERTY, Gerry
Baker Street
Days Gone Down (Still Got The
Light In Your Eyes)
Get It Right Next Time
Home And Dry
Right Down The Line
Stuck In The Middle With You

RAGNI, Gerome
Aquarius (w)
Aquarius/Let The Sunshine In (w)
Easy To Be Hard (w)
Good Morning Starshine (w)
Let The Sunshine In (w)
Manchester England (w)

RAGOVOY, Jerry
Piece Of My Heart
Time Is On My Side
Try (Just A Little Bit Harder)
You Got It

RAKSIN, David
Laura
Slowly

RALEIGH, Ben
How Would You Like To Be
Love Is All We Need
Tell Laura I Love Her
Wonderful! Wonderful

RALPHS, M.
Can't Get Enough

RAM, Buck
Enchanted
Great Pretender
Only You
Twilight Time

RAMONE, Joey, Dee Dee, Tommy,
& Johnny
Blitzkrieg Bop
I Wanna Be Your Boyfriend
Judy Is A Punk
Oh Oh I Love Her So
Ramona
Rockaway Beach
Sheena Is A Punk Rocker
Swallow My Pride

RAMSEY, Ken
Greenback Dollar

RAMSEY, Willis Alan
Muskrat Love

RAND, Ande
Only You

RANDAZZO, Teddy
Forget To Remember
Goin' Out Of My Head
Hurt So Bad
I'm On The Outside (Looking In)
It Feels So Good To Be Loved So
Bad
It's Gonna Take A Miracle
Pretty Blue Eyes
Rain In My Heart

RANDELL, Denny
Can I Carry Your Balloon
Native New Yorker
Weekend Lover
Workin' My Way Back To You
You Keep Me Dancin'

RANDLE, Earl
Echoes Of Love (w)

RANS, Robert
Dance With Me
You Should Do It (w)

RAPEE, Erno
Charmaine
Diane

RAPOSO, Joe
Sing

RASCEL, R.
Arrivederci, Roma (m)

RASKIN, Gene
Those Were The Days

RATNER, Lisa
Kiss Me In The Rain

RAY, Alan
You Don't Love Me Anymore

RAY, Don
Got To Have Lovin'

RAY, Eddy
Hearts Of Stone (w)

RAY, H.
Special Lady

RAYMOND, Jeff
You Don't Love Me Anymore

RAYMONDE, Ivor
I Only Want To Be With You

RAZAF, Andy
Honeysuckle Rose (w)

REA, David
Flowers Of Evil
Mississippi Queen

REARDON, Jack
When

REBENNACK, Mac
Right Place Wrong Time

REDD, Gene
Please Come Home For Christmas

REDD, Hank
Free (Wanna Be Free)

REDDING, Otis
Dock Of The Bay
Happy Song
I've Been Loving You Too Long
Respect
Security

REDDY, Helen
I Am Woman (w)

REDINGTON, Ginny
You, You're The One (m)

REED, Jerry
U.S. Male

REED, Jimmy
Baby, What You Want Me To Do
Bright Lights, Big City
Honest I Do

REED, Les
Delilah
I Believe In Miracles
It's Not Unusual
There's A Kind Of Hush

REED, Lou
White Light, White Heat

REEVES, Eddie
All I Ever Need Is You
Don't Change On Me
Rings

REGGIE, R.
Billion Dollar Babies

REGNEY, Noel
Dominique (w)

REICHNER, Bix
I Need Your Love Tonight

REID, Keith
All This And More (w)
Conquistador (w)
Glimpses Of Nirvana
Grand Finale (m)
In The Autumn Of My Madness
Look To Your Soul
Salty Dog (w)
'Twas Teatime At The Circus
Whiter Shade Of Pale

REINHARD, Keith
You, You're The One (w)

RENE, Malou
Tossin' And Turnin'

RENWICK, Tim
Keep On Running Away

RESNICK, Art
Good Lovin'
Under The Boardwalk

REYAM, G.
Rivers Of Babylon

REYNOLDS, Allen
Ready For The Times To Get Better

REYNOLDS, Art
Jesus Is Just Alright

REYNOLDS, Dick
Silver Threads And Golden Needles

REYNOLDS, Malvina
Turn Around

RHODES, Jack
Silver Threads And Golden Needles

RICE, Bonny
Mustang Sally

RICE, Mack
Respect Yourself

RICE, Tim
I Don't Know How To Love Him (w)
Superstar (w)

RICH, Charlie
Every Time You Touch Me
Lonely Weekends
Who Will The Next Fool Be

RICHARD, Frank
Action Speaks Louder Than Words

RICHARD, Keith
Angie
As Tears Go By
Brown Sugar
Gimme Shelter
Happy
Honky Tonk Women
It's Only Rock 'N' Roll
Jumpin' Jack Flash
Last Time
Let's Spend The Night Together
Love In Vain
Midnight Rambler
Rip This Joint
Ruby Tuesday
Satisfaction
Street Fighting Man
Under My Thumb
You Can't Always Get What You Want

RICHARD, Renald
Greenbacks

RICHARDS, Deke
Love Child

RICHARDS, Dwight
Action Speaks Louder Than Words

RICHARDSON, J.P.
Chantilly Lace

RICHIE, Lionel
Brick House
Easy
Fancy Dancer
Flying High
Just To Be Close To You

239

Sail On
Still
Sweet Love
Three Times A Lady

RICHMOND, Paul
Shining Star

RIDGELEY, Tommy
Jam Up Twist (m)

RIGUAL, Carlos
Love Me With All Your Heart
(m)

RIOFELLE, Jerry
Easy Driver

RIORDAN, David
Green Eyed Lady

RIPERTON, Minnie
Lovin' You

RISER, Paul
What Becomes Of The Broken
Hearted

RITCHIE, Jean
Black Waters

RIVERS, Johnny
Poor Side Of Town

RIVERS, Sylvester
In The Night Time

ROACH, Jimmy
My Whole World Ended

ROBBINS, Ayn
Gonna Fly Now (w)
You Take My Heart Away (w)

ROBERTS, Bob
Where Do You Come From

ROBERTS, Bruce
I'm Comin' Home Again
Main Event/Fight
Skybird

ROBERTS, Johnny
My Boy Lollipop

ROBERTS, Paul
Driver's Seat

ROBERTS, Rhoda
Swingin' Shepherd Blues (w)

ROBERTS, Rick
Colorado
Goodbye I Love You
Just Remember I Love You
Livin' Ain't Livin'

So Long
Strange Way
You Are The Woman

ROBERTS, Solomon, Jr.
Give It What You Got

ROBERTS, William M.
Hey Joe

ROBERTSON, Brian
Carrie

ROBERTSON, Don
I Don't Hurt Anymore (m)
I Think I'm Gonna Like It Here
No More
Starting Today

ROBERTSON, J. Robbie
Get Up, Jake
Jawbone
Night They Drove Old Dixie
Down
Rag Mama Rag
Time To Kill
Up On Cripple Creek

ROBINSON, Bill SEE Robinson,
William "Smokey"

ROBINSON, Earl
Black And White (m)
Joe Hill

ROBINSON, Eric
Dance (Disco Heat)

ROBINSON, Frank F.
I've Found Someone Of My Own

ROBINSON, Gerald
No Communication

ROBINSON, Jessie Mae
Party

ROBINSON, William "Smokey"
Ain't That Peculiar
Baby, Baby, Don't Cry
Cruisin'
Don't Mess With Bill
Get Ready
Going To A Go-Go
Got A Job
Happy (w)
I Like It Like That
I Second That Emotion
I'll Be Doggone
Let Me Be The Clock
My Baby Must Be A Magician
My Girl
My Guy
One Who Really Loves You
Ooo Baby Baby
Satisfaction

Shop Around
Since I Lost My Baby
Tears Of A Clown
Tracks Of My Tears
Two Lovers
Way You Do The Things You Do
What's So Good About Goodbye
You Beat Me To The Punch
You've Really Got A Hold On Me

ROBISON, Willard
Old Folks (m)

ROBLES, Daniel
El Condor Pasa (m)

ROCCO, Len
#1 Dee Jay

ROCK, Joseph
Since I Don't Have You (m)
This I Swear (m)

RODDE, Roy
Have You Heard

RODDENBERRY, Gene
Star Trek, Theme From (w)

RODGERS, Nile
Dance, Dance, Dance (Yowsah,
Yowsah, Yowsah)
Everybody Dance
Good Times
He's The Greatest Dancer
I Want Your Love
I'm Coming Out
Le Freak
Lost In Music
My Feet Keep Dancing
My Forbidden Lover
Upside Down
We Are Family

RODGERS, Paul
All Right Now
Rock 'N' Roll Fantasy

RODGERS, Richard
Blue Moon (m)
I Married An Angel (m)
Spring Is Here (m)

ROE, Tommy
Dizzy
Jam Up And Jelly Tight
Stir It Up And Serve It

ROESER, D.
Reaper

ROGERS, Charles
Louisville

ROGERS, Jimmy
That's All Right

ROGERS, Kay
Hundred Pounds Of Clay

ROGERS, Robert
Ain't That Peculiar
Going To A Go-Go
Way You Do The Things You Do

ROKER, Ron
Devil's Gun

ROLIE, Gregg
Anytime

ROLLINS, Jack
I Don't Hurt Anymore (w)

ROMANS, Alain
Padre (m)

ROMBERG, SIGMUND
When I Get Too Old To Dream
(m)

ROME, Richard
Best Disco In Town (m)

ROMEO, Tony
I Think I Love You
Indian Lake
It's One Of Those Nights (Yes
Love)
Sunny And Me

ROPER, Ray
Love Struck

ROSE, Billy
It's Only A Paper Moon (w)

ROSE, Peter De. See
DE ROSE, Peter.

ROSE, Vincent
Blueberry Hill
Whispering

ROSS, Adam
Sacred

ROSS, Beverly
Judy's Turn To Cry
Lollipop

ROSS, Bud
#1 Dee Jay

ROSS, Jerry
I'm Gonna Make You Love Me

ROSTILL, John
If You Love Me (Let Me Know)
Let Me Be There

ROTA, Nino
Come Live Your Life With Me
(m)
Speak Softly Love (m)

ROTH, David Lee
Beautiful Girls
Dance The Night Away
Jamie's Cryin'
Runnin' With The Devil

ROTHROCK, Claire
Old Cape Cod

ROTTEN, Johnny
Anarchy In The U.K.
God Save The Queen
Pretty Vacant

ROWAN, Peter
Home To You

ROYAL, Dale
Teddy Bear

ROYSTER, Joseph
If You Wanna Be Happy
New Orleans
Quarter To Three

RUBY, Harry
Who's Sorry Now

RUDOLPH, Richard
Lovin' You

RUNDGREN, Todd
Hello It's Me
I Saw The Light
Love Is The Answer
Real Man
Set Me Free
We Got To Get You A Woman

RUSH, Otis
All Your Love

RUSSELL, Bert
Hang On Sloopy
Little Bit Of Soap
Twist And Shout

RUSSELL, Bob
He Ain't Heavy...He's My
Brother (w)
I Didn't Know About You (w)
You Came A Long Way From St.
Louis (w)

RUSSELL, Bobby
Honey
Little Green Apples

RUSSELL, Brenda Gordon
Think It Over
Way Back When

RUSSELL, Brian
Think It Over

RUSSELL, Graham
Lost In Love

RUSSELL, Johnny
Act Naturally

RUSSELL, Leon
Delta Lady
I Put A Spell On You
Lady Blue
Me And Baby Jane
Rainbow In Your Eyes
Roll Away The Stone
Song For You
Superstar
Sure Gonna Miss Her
This Masquerade
Tight Rope

RUTHERFORD, Michael
Your Own Special Way

RYAN, Charles
Hot Rod Lincoln

RYAN, Paul
Love's Only Love

SACCO, Lou
Two Faces Have I

SAFAN, Mark
How Can This Be Love
I'm On My Way

SAFKA, Melanie
Beautiful People
Brand New Key
Lay Down (Candles In The Rain)
Sad Song
What Have They Done To My
Song, Ma

SAGER, Carole Bayer
Come In From The Rain
Don't Cry Out Loud
Ice Castles, Theme From (w)
I'd Rather Leave While I'm In
Love
If You Remember Me (w)
I'm Comin' Home Again
It's My Turn (w)
Just You And I
Midnight Blue
Nobody Does It Better (w)
Skybird
When I Need You (m)

SAIN, Oliver
Don't Mess Up A Good Thing

SAINTE-MARIE, Buffy
Until It's Time For You To Go

SAKAMOTO, Ryuichi
Computer Game

SALEN, Jeff
  Nuclear Waste
  Rats
  Who's Been Sleepin' Here

SALLITT, Norman
  Take It Like A Woman

SALTER, William
  Where Is The Love

SAMOHT, Yennik
  Stoned Love

SAMPLE, Joe
  Street Life (m)

SAMUDIO, Domingo
  Wooly Bully

SANDERS, William
  Angel

SANDS, Lee
  Lord's Prayer (m, arranged)

SANSON, Veronique
  Emotion (m)

SAPAUGH, Carl
  Try A Little Kindness

SAWYER, Pam
  I Thought It Took A Little Time
  If I Were Your Woman
  I'm Livin' In Shame
  Last Time I Saw Him (w)
  Love Child
  Love Hangover
  My Whole World Ended
  There's A Lesson To Be Learned

SAYER, Leo
  How Much Love
  You Make Me Feel Like Dancing

SCAGGS, Boz
  Breakdown Dead Ahead
  Harbor Lights
  Hard Times
  Hollywood
  It's Over
  Jojo
  Lido Shuffle
  Look What You've Done To Me
  Lowdown
  We're All Alone

SCALES, Harvey
  Disco Lady

SCARBOROUGH, Skip
  Can't Hide Love
  Love Ballad
  Love Music
  Lovely Day (m)

SCHAFFNER, Catherine
  I Don't Want To Do Wrong

SCHARF, Stuart
  Like To Get To Know You

SCHARF, Walter
  Ben (m)

SCHIFRIN, Lalo
  Burning Bridges (m)
  Mission Impossible Theme (m)
  Where Angels Go, Trouble
    Follows

SCHLITZ, Don
  Gambler

SCHMIDT, Harvey
  Try To Remember (m)

SCHMIDT, Timothy B.
  I Can't Tell You Why
  Keep On Tryin'

SCHOCK, Harriet
  Ain't No Way To Treat A Lady

SCHOFIELD, W.
  You're So Fine

SCHOLZ, Donald T.
  Hitch A Ride
  Long Time
  More Than A Feeling
  Peace Of Mind

SCHON, Neal
  Any Way You Want It
  Anytime
  Lights
  Too Late
  Wheel In The Sky

SCHONBERGER, John
  Whispering

SCHROEDER, Aaron
  Any Way You Want Me
  Big Hunk O' Love
  Don't Leave Me Now
  Good Luck Charm
  Got A Lot O' Livin' To Do
  I Was The One
  In Your Arms
  It's Now Or Never
  Shoppin' Around
  Young Dreams

SCHWARTZ, Marvin
  Baby Talk

SCHWARTZ, Stephen
  Corner Of The Sky
  Day By Day

SCOTT, Andy (Andrew)
  Action
  Fox On The Run
  Love Is Like Oxygen

SCOTT, Bobby
  He Ain't Heavy...He's My Brother
  Taste Of Honey (m)

SCOTT, Clifford
  Honky Tonk (Parts 1 & 2)

SCOTT, Clive
  Love Fire

SCOTT, Howard
  Cisco Kid
  Gypsy Man
  Me And Baby Brother
  Spill The Wine
  World Is A Ghetto

SCOTT, Jack
  My True Love
  What In The World's Come Over
    You

SCOTT, Joseph W.
  Blind Man

SCOTT, ROBIN
  Pop Muzik

SCOTT, Ronnie
  If I Sing You A Love Song
  It's A Heartache

SCOTT, Thomas W.
  Starsky & Hutch Theme

SCOTT, Tom
  Tom Cat (m)

SCOTT, Winfield
  Easy Question
  Please Don't Drag That String
    Around
  Tweedlee Dee
  We're Coming In Loaded

SCOTT-HERON, Gil
  Bottle (w)

SEAGO, Eddie
  Early In The Morning
  Let's Get A Little Sentimental
  My Baby's Baby

SEALS, Danny
  Windflowers

SEALS, James
  Ashes In The Snow
  Baby I'll Give It To You (m)
  Blue Bonnet Nation
  Diamond Girl
  Get Closer

Hummingbird
I'll Play For You
It's Gonna Come Down On You
King Of Nothing
Summer Breeze
Sweet Green Fields
We May Never Pass This Way
    Again
Windflowers

SEARS, Pete
Dance With The Dragon (m)
Play On Love (m)

SEBASTIAN, John B.
Daydream
Didn't Want To Have To Do It
Do You Believe In Magic
On The Road Again
Summer In The City
Welcome Back
Wild About My Lovin'

SEBASTIAN, L. & P.
You And I (m)

SEBASTIAN, Mark
Summer In The City

SEDAKA, Neil
Amarillo
Bad Blood
Breaking Up Is Hard To Do
Calendar Girl
Happy Birthday Sweet Sixteen
Hungry Years
Immigrant
Laughter In The Rain
Lonely Night (Angel Face)
Love In The Shadows
Love Will Keep Us Together
Should've Never Let You Go
Solitaire
Steppin' Out
That's When The Music Takes Me
You Gotta Make Your Own
    Sunshine

SEEGER, Pete
Bells Of Rhymney (m)
Guantanamera (m, adapted)
If I Had A Hammer
Turn! Turn! Turn! (Adapted)
Waist Deep In The Big Muddy
We Shall Overcome (Adapted)
Where Have All The Flowers
    Gone

SEGER, Bob
Against The Wind
Beautiful Loser
Fire Lake
Heartache Tonight
Hollywood Nights
Jody Girl
Katmandu
Mainstreet

Night Moves
Ramblin' Gamblin' Man
Rock And Roll Never Forgets
Still The Same
We've Got Tonite
You'll Accomp'ny Me

SERAPHINE, Danny
Little One
No Tell Lover

SERNO, Del
That's It, I Quit, I'm Movin' On

SEROTA, Ronald
Three Times In Love

SERVICE, Paul
Disco Nights
Standing Ovation

SEVERINSEN, Doc
Stop And Smell The Roses

SHAND, Terry
You Don't Have To Be A Baby
    To Cry

SHANKLIN, Wayne
Chanson D'Amour

SHANNON, Del
Hats Off To Larry
I Go To Pieces
Little Town Flirt
Runaway

SHANNON, Harry
Cowboy

SHANNON, Jackie De. See
    DE SHANNON, Jackie.

SHAPER, Hal
Softly, As I Leave You (w)

SHAPIRO, Hal
Treasure Of Love

SHAPIRO, Mike
Spooky

SHARPE, Ray
Linda Lu

SHAW, Tommy
Lights
Never Say Never
Renegade
Sing For The Day

SHEARING, George
Lullaby Of Birdland

SHEELEY, Sharon
Dum Dum

SHELDON, Jon
Mashed Potato Time

SHELTON, Louis
You're The Love (m)

SHEPHERD, Shep
Honky Tonk (Parts 1 & 2)

SHAPPARD, James
Daddy's Home
Thousand Miles Away

SHERIDAN, Tony
Why

SHERMAN, Robert B. (Bob) &
    Richard M (Dick)
When You're Loved
You're Sixteen

SHERMAN, Joe
Graduation Day (m)

SHERMAN, Noel
Graduation Day (w)
It's So Easy To Say

SHERRILL, Billy
Every Time You Touch Me
Most Beautiful Girl
My Elusive Dreams
Stand By Your Man
Sweet And Innocent
Too Far Gone
Very Special Love Song

SHIDER, Gary
Do That Stuff
One Nation Under A Groove

SHIRE, David
With You I'm Born Again (m)

SHORROCK, Glenn
Cool Change

SHUBERT, Albert
Good Good Lovin'

SHUMAN, Carl
Hey There Lonely Girl

SHUMAN, Mort
Doin' The Best I Can
Gonna Get Back Home Somehow
His Latest Flame
Hushabye
I Count The Tears
If We Only Have Love (w)
Kiss Me Quick
Little Sister
Mess Of Blues
Never Say Yes
Save The Last Dance For Me
Surrender (w)
Suspicion

Sweets For My Sweet
This Magic Moment
True Love, True Love
What Every Woman Lives For

SHURY, Gerry
Devil's Gun

SIGLER, Bunny
Let Me Make Love To You
South Shore Commission

SIGMAN, Carl
Arrivederci, Roma (w)
Ebb Tide (w)
It's All In The Game (w)
My Heart Cries For You
Shangri-la (w)
Love Story, Theme From (w)
You're My World (w)

SIGNORELLI, Frank
Stairway To The Stars (m)

SILBAR, Jeff
Where Were You When I Was
Falling In Love

SILHOUETTES
Get A Job

SILVA, Balde
My Angel Baby

SILVER, Roger
Anytime

SILVERSTEIN, Shel
Hey Nelly Nelly
New "Frankie And Johnnie" Song
Unicorn

SIMMONS, Charles
Oh, Baby
They Just Can't Stop It

SIMMONS, Gene
Love Theme From Kiss
Rock And Roll All Nite

SIMMONS, Patrick
Black Water
Dependin' On You
Echoes Of Love (m)

SIMMS, Earl
Funky Street

SIMON, Carly
Anticipation
Attitude Dancing
It Was So Easy
Jesse
Legend In Your Own Time
Right Thing To Do
That's The Way I've Always
Heard It Should Be

Tranquillo (Melt My Heart)
Vengence
Waterfall
You Belong To Me (w)
You're So Vain

SIMON, Paul
America
American Tune
April Come She Will
Armistice Day
At The Zoo
Baby Driver
Big Bright Green Pleasure Ma-
chine
Blessed
Bookends
Boxer
Bridge Over Troubled Waters
Cecilia
Church Is Burning
Cloudy
Congratulations
Dangling Conservation
Duncan
El Condor Pasa
Everything Put Together Falls
Apart
Fakin' It
59th Street Bridge Song
Fifty Ways To Leave Your Lover
Flowers Never Bend With The
Rainfall
For Emily, Whenever I May Find
Her
Gone At Last
Have A Good Time
Hazy Shade Of Winter
Hey Schoolgirl
Hobo's Blues
Homeward Bound
I Am A Rock
I Do It For Your Love
Kathy's Song
Keep The Customer Satisfied
Kodachrome
Late In The Evening
Learn How To Fall
Leaves That Are Green
Loves Me Like A Rock
Me And Julio Down By The
Schoolyard
Most Peculiar Man
Mother And Child Reunion
Mrs. Robinson
My Little Town
Night Game
Old Friends
One Man's Ceiling Is Another
Man's Floor
One Trick Pony
Only Living Boy In New York
Overs
Papa Hobo
Paranoia Blues
Patterns
Peace Like A River

Poem On The Underground Wall
Punky's Dilemma
Red Rubber Ball
Richard Cory
Run That Body Down
Save The Life Of My Child
Scarborough Fair/Canticle
(Arrangement & original
counter melody)
7 O'Clock News/Silent Night
(Narration & arrangement)
Silent Eyes
Simple Desultory Philippic
Slip Slidin' Away
So Long, Frank Lloyd Wright
Some Folk's Lives Roll Easy
Something So Right
Somewhere They Can't Find Me
Song For The Asking
Sound Of Silence
Sparrow
St. Judy's Comet
Still Crazy After All These Years
Stranded In A Limousine
Take Me To The Mardi Gras
Tenderness
Was A Sunny Day
Wednesday Morning, 3 a.m.
We've Got A Groovy Thing Goin'
Why Don't You Write Me
You Don't Know Where Your
Interest Lies
You're Kind

SIMONS, Seymour
Honey

SIMPKINS, Lewis C.
Mother Earth
Night Train

SIMPSON, Richard
One More Try

SIMPSON, Valerie
Ain't No Mountain High Enough
Ain't Nothing But A Maybe
Ain't Nothing Like The Real Thing
Anywhere
Believe In Me
Bend Me
Boss
California Soul
Caretaker
Destiny
Drink The Wine
Found A Cure
Genius I
Gimme Something Real
I Don't Need No Doctor
I Wanna Be Selfish
I'm Every Woman
Is It Still Good To Ya
It Came To Me
It'll Come, It'll Come, It'll Come
Let's Go Get Stoned
Over And Over

Reach Out and Touch (Some-
  body's Hand)
Release Me
Remember Me
Ride-O-Rocket
Sell The House
Shoe, Shoe Shine
So, So Satisfied
Some Things You Never Get Used
  To
Somebody Told A Lie
Stuff Like That
Surrender
Tell It All
Tried Tested And Found True
Your Precious Love
You're All I Need To Get By

SINGER, A.
At The Hop

SINGLETON, Charles
Spanish Eyes (w)

SKLEROV, Gloria
Every Time I Sing A Love Song
He Did With Me
I Just Fall In Love Again (w)

SKYLAR, Sunny
Love Me With All Your Heart (w)

SLARBROUGH, C. "Skip"
Love Or Let Me Be Lonely

SLATE, Johnny
Better Love Next Time
Holdin' On For Dear Love

SLAY, Frank C., Jr.
Silhouettes
Tallahassee Lassie

SLICK, Darby
Somebody To Love

SLICK, Grace
Dance With The Dragon (w)
Eskimo Blue Day
Play On Love (w)
Rejoyce
Two Heads
White Rabbit

SLOAN, P.F.
You Baby (Nobody But You)

SMALLS, Charlie
Ease On Down The Road
You Can't Win

SMITH, Al
Big Boss Man

SMITH, Alfred
Gimme Little Sign
Lovey Dovey Kinda Lovin'

SMITH, Arthur
Duelling Banjos (m)

SMITH, Beasley
That Lucky Old Sun (m)

SMITH, Billy Dawn
To The Aisle

SMITH, Brian
Raise A Little Hell

SMITH, Carl
Higher And Higher
Rescue Me

SMITH, Fred
Hully Gully
Western Movies

SMITH, Huey "Piano"
Don't You Just Know It
Rockin' Pneumonia And The
  Boogie Woogie Flu
Sea Cruise

SMITH, James
Slippin' And Slidin'

SMITH, Johnny
Walk, Don't Run (m)

SMITH, Joseph, III
Action Speaks Louder Than
  Words

SMITH, Kate
When The Moon Comes Over The
  Mountain

SMITH, Lloyd
Shake Your Rump To The Funk
Too Hot To Stop (Part I)

SMITH, Marshall F.
Let Me Lay My Funk On You

SMITH, Michael L.
Let's Be Young Tonight

SMITH, Mike
Glad All Over

SMITH, Neal
Eighteen
Elected

SMITH, Patti
Ask The Angels
Because The Night
Frederick
Kimberly
Redondo Beach

SMITH, Russell
Amazing Grace (Used To Be Her
  Favorite Song)

SMITH, Samuel
I Can Tell

SMITH, Tamy
Life Of The Party

SMITH, Victor
With Your Love

SNOW, Phoebe
Poetry Man

SNOW, Tom
Gettin' Ready For Love
You

SNYDER, Eddie
Spanish Eyes (w)

SNYDER, Richie
Superman

SNYDER, Ted
Who's Sorry Now

SOHL, Richard
Redondo Beach

SOLBERG, Chris
Can't Keep A Good Man Down

SOMMERS, John Martin
Thank God I'm A Country Boy

SONDHEIM, Stephen
Send In The Clowns

SOUR, Robert
Body And Soul (w)

SOURIRE, Soeur, O.P.
Dominique

SOUTH, Joe
Don't It Make You Wanta Go
  Home
Down In The Boondocks
Games People Play
I Knew You When
Rose Garden
Walk A Mile In My Shoes
Yo Yo

SOUTHER, John David (J.D.)
Best Of My Love
Border Town
Faithless Love
Heartache Tonight
New Kid In Town
Prisoner In Disguise
Simple Man, Simple Dream
You're Only Lonely

SOVINE, Red
Teddy Bear

SPARKS, Randy
Green Green
Saturday Night
Today

SPECTOR, Phil
Da Doo Ron Ron
Just Once In My life
Spanish Harlem
To Know You (Him) Is To Love
You (Him)
You've Lost That Lovin' Feelin'

SPENCER, Carl
Let The Little Girl Dance

SPENCER, Kevin
Take That To The Bank

SPENCER, Richard
Color Him Father

SPENCER, Tim
Room Full Of Roses

SPICKARD, BOB
Pipeline (m)

SPIELMAN, Fred
Paper Roses (m)

SPINAZOLA, Joe
Anything You Want
I Wrote This Song For You

SPIRES, Jackson
Highway Song

SPIVERY, William
Operator

SPRINGER, Philip
Never Ending

SPRINGFIELD, Tom
Georgy Girl
I'll Never Find Another You
World Of Our Own

SPRINGSTEEN, Bruce
Badlands
Because The Night
Blinded By The Night
Born To Run
Fire
Fourth Of July (Sandy)
Prove It All Night

SQUIRE, Chris
All Good People
Release, Release
Yours Is No Disgrace

ST. JOHN, R.P., Jr.
Bye, Bye Baby

ST. LEWIS, Keni
Boogie Fever
Who Done It

STAFFORD, Jim
Spiders And Snakes
Wildwood Weed

STALLMAN, Lou
It's Gonna Take A Miracle
Treasure Of Love

STANKEY, Damon
Honest I Do

STANLEY, Paul
I Was Made For Lovin' You
Love Theme From Kiss
Rock And Roll All Nite

STANTON, Albert
Lion Sleeps Tonight (Adapted)
Michael, Row The Boat Ashore
(Adapted)

STANTON, Frank H.
Face It, Girl, It's Over

STARKEY, Richard
Back Off Boogaloo
Maggie Mae (Arranged)
Photograph

STARKS, John
Papa Don't Take No Mess
(Part I)
Payback

STARR, Edwin
H.A.P.P.Y. Radio
Twenty Five Miles

STARR, Ringo. See STARKEY,
Richard.

STEGALL, Keith
Sexy Eyes

Stein, Chris
Dreaming
Fade Away And Radiate
Heart Of Glass
In The Flesh
Picture This
Pretty Baby
Rip Her To Shreds
Sunday Girl

STEIN, Murray
Baby (You've Got What It Takes)

STEINBERG, Billy
How Do I Make You

STEINBERG, Lewis
Green Onions

STEINER, Max
Honey Babe (m)
My Own True Love (m)
Summer Place, Theme From (m)
Summer Place '76 (m)

STEINHARDT, Robby
Point Of No Return

STEINMAN, Jim
All Revved Up With No Place
To Go
Bat Out Of Hell
For Crying Out Loud
Heaven Can Wait
Paradise By The Dashboard Light
Two Out Of Three Ain't Bad
You Took The Words Right Out
Of My Life

STEPHENS, Geoff
Doctor's Orders
It's Like We Never Said Goodbye
There's A Kind Of Hush

STEPHENS, Tennyson
Party Lights

STEPNEY, Charles
Reasons
That's The Way Of The World

STERN, Toni
It's Going To Take Some Time
It's Too Late (w)
Sweet Seasons

STEVENS, Cat
Bonfire
Father And Son
Hurt
Morning Has Broken (m)
Oh Very Young
Old Schoolyard
Peace Train
Sitting
To Be A Star
Wild World

STEVENS, Even
Suspicions
When You're In Love With A
Beautiful Woman

STEVENS, Mort
Hawaii Five-O (m)

STEVENS, Ray
Everything Is Beautiful

STEVENS, T.M.
I Shoulda Loved Ya

STEVENSON, Bobby
Hey Little Girl

STEVENSON, Rudy
Don't Cha Hear Me Callin' To Ya

STEVENSON, W.S.
Hot Rod Lincoln
Release Me

STEVENSON, William
Beechwood 4-5789
Dancing In The Street
Devil With The Blue Dress On
Hitch Hike
Jamie
My Baby Loves Me
Nothing's Too Good For My Baby
Playboy
Pride And Joy
Stubborn Kind Of Fellow

STEWART, Al
On The Border
Song On The Radio
Time Passages
Year Of The Cat

STEWART, Eric
Things We Do For Love

STEWART, John
Daydream Believer

STEWART, Rod
Ain't Love A Bitch
Da Ya Think I'm Sexy
Hot Legs
I Was Only Joking
Killing Of Georgie (Part I & II)
Maggie May
Stay With Me
Tonight's The Night (Gonna Be
   Alright)
You're In My Heart

STEWART, Sylvester
Dance To The Music
Everyday People
Family Affair
Higher
Hot Fun In The Summertime
I Want To Take You Higher
Sex Machine (m)
Sing A Simple Song
Smilin'
Stand

STEWART, Winston
Shake Your Rump To The Funk
Too Hot To Stop (Part I)

STILLMAN, Al
Chances Are (w)
It's Not For Me To Say (w)
Moments To Remember (w)

STILLS, Stephen
Bluebird Revisited
Buyin' Time

Carry On
Change Partners
Dark Star
Fair Game
For What It's Worth
4 + 20
Go And Say Goodbye
Helplessly Hoping
Johnny's Garden
Love The One You're With
Pretty Girl Why
Questions
Rock 'N' Roll Woman
See The Changes
Suite: Judy Blue Eyes
Turn Back The Pages
Un Mundo
We Are Not Helpless
Wooden Ships

STING
Roxanne

STOCK, Larry
Blueberry Hill
Morningside Of The Mountain

STOKES, Michael (Mike)
Gloria
It's You That I Need

STOLLER, Mike
Baby, I Don't Care
Bossa Nova, Baby
Charlie Brown
Don't
Fools Fall In Love
Hound Dog
I (Who Have Nothing)
Jailhouse Rock
Just Tell Her Jim Said Hello
Kansas City
King Creole
Love Potion Number Nine
Loving You
On Broadway
Poison Ivy
Ruby Baby
Searchin'
Smokey Joe's Cafe
Stand By Me
Treat Me Nice
Yakety Yak
Young Blood

STONE, Bob
Gypsys, Tramps And Thieves

STONE, Jesse
Don't Let Go
Down In The Alley

STOOKEY, Paul
All My Trials (Adapted)
A' Soalin'
Autumn To May
Come And Go With Me (Adapted
   & arranged)

Cruel War
Cuckoo
Early In The Morning
Hangman (Adapted & arranged)
I Dig Rock And Roll Music
Man Of Constant Sorrow
Monday Morning (Adapted)
Single Girl
Song Is Love
Tell It On The Mountain (Adapted)
This Train

STORDAHL, Axel
Day By Day

STORIE, Carl
Dancin' Shoes

STORY, Dwain
Cuckoo

STRALS, Arnold (M)
Lord's Prayer

STRANDLUND, Robb
Already Gone

STRAUSS, Richard
Also Sprach Zarathustra (2001)
   (m)

STREISAND, Barbra
Evergreen (m)

STRIANO, Alfred
There's A Moon Out Tonight

STRONG, Barrett
Ball Of Confusion
Cloud Nine
End Of Our Road
I Can't Get Next To You
I Could Never Love Another
I Heard It Through The Grapevine
I Wish It Would Rain
Jamie
Just My Imagination
Papa Was A Rollin' Stone
Psychedelic Shack
Runaway Child, Running Wild
Smiling Faces Sometimes
That's The Way Love Is
Too Busy Thinking About My Baby
War

STROUSE, Charles
Easy Street (m)
Tomorrow (m)

STRUNK, Jed
Daisy A Day

STRUZICK, Eddie
Falling
Midnight Light
Sharing The Night Together

STRZELECKI, Harry
Long Tall Texan

STUART, Hamish
Pick Up The Pieces

STUTZ, Carl
Little Things Mean A Lot

STYNE, Jule
Three Coins In The Fountain (m)

SUBWAY,
Chinese Kung Fu (m)

SUDANO, Bruce
Bad Girls (m)
Make It Last (m)

SULLIVAN, Niki
I'm Gonna Love You Too

SULTON, Kasim
Set Me Free

SUMMER, Donna
Bad Girls (w)
Dim All The Lights
Heaven Knows
Love To Love You, Baby
Spring Affair
Wanderer (w)
Winter Melody

SUMMIT, Art
House Of The Rising Sun
(Adapted)

SUNSHINE, Madeline
This Is Love (w)

SURFARIS
Wipe Out

SUSSMAN, Bruce
Copacabana (w)
Jump Shout Boogie (w)
Slow Dance (w)

SUTHERLAND, Gavin
Sailing

SUTHERLAND, Ian (Iain)
Arms Of Mary
Moonlight Lady

SUTTON, Michael B.
Down To Love Town

SVANOE, Willard
Walk Right In (Arranged)

SWAN, Billy
I Can Help
I'm Her Fool
Lover Please

SWEET, Sam
Sun's Gonna Shine Again

SYKES, Keith
Volcano

SYLVERS, Leon F., III
New Horizons
Take That To The Bank

SYLVERS, Ricky
New Horizons

SYLVESTER
You Make Me Feel (Mighty Real)
(w)

SYLVIA, Margo
Happy, Happy Birthday Baby

SZABO, Gabor
Gypsy Queen (m)

TABLEPORTER, Frank
Come What May

TAKAHASHI, Yukihiro
Computer Game (m)

TARNEY, Alan
We Don't Talk Anymore

TARPLIN, Marv (Marvin)
Ain't That Peculiar
Cruisin'
Going To A Go-Go
I Like It Like That
I'll Be Doggone
Tracks Of My Tears

TATE, Laurie
Anytime, Anyplace, Anywhere

TAUPIN, Bernie
All The Girls Love Alice
Amoreena
Bennie And The Jets
Bitch Is Back
Border Song
Burn Down The Mission
Candle In The Wind
Crocodile Rock
Daniel
Don't Let The Sun Go Down On
Me
From The Inside
Goodbye Yellow Brick Road
How You Gonna See Me Now
I Need You To Turn To
Island Girl
Let Me Be Your Car
Levon
Michelle's Song
Philadelphia Freedom
Rocket Man

Saturday Night's Alright
Someone Saved My Life Tonight
Sweet Painted Lady
Take Me To Your Pilot
Tiny Dancer
Valhalla
Your Song

TAYLOR, Beloyd
Getaway

TAYLOR, Carmen
Seven Days

TAYLOR, Chip
Angel Of The Morning
Try (Just A Little Bit Harder)

TAYLOR, James
Bartender's Blues
Carolina In My Mind
Country Road
Don't Let Me Be Lonely Tonight
Fire And Rain
Hey Mister, That's Me Up On
The Jukebox
Long Ago & Far Away
Mexico
Mockingbird
Shower The People
Sweet Baby James
Tranquillo (Melt My Heart)
Walking Man
Your Smiling Face

TAYLOR, John
Since I Don't Have You (w)
This I Swear (w)

TAYLOR, Larry
Here Comes The Sun

TAYLOR, Mike
Rocky Mountain High
Sunshine On My Shoulders (m)

TAYLOR, R. Dean
All I Need
I'm Livin' In Shame
Indiana Wants Me
Love Child

TAYLOR, Robert
Maybe I'm A Fool

TEE, Richard
Stuff Like That

TEK, Deniz
What Gives

TEMPCHIN, Jack
Already Gone
Peaceful Easy Feeling
Slow Dancing
Swayin' To The Music

TEMPERTON, Rod
Always And Forever
Boogie Nights
Off The Wall
Rock With You
Stomp

TENNILLE, Toni
Do That To Me One More Time

TEPPER, Robert
This Is Love (m)

TEPPER, Sid
All That I Am
Angel
Beach Boys Blues
Beginner's Luck
Boy Like Me, A Girl Like You
G.I. Blues
Island Of Love
It's A Wonderful World
Lonesome Cowboy
Once Is Enough
Puppet On A String
Relax
Shoppin' Around
Slicin' Sand
Smorgasbord
Walls Have Ears

TERRISS, Dorothy
Wonderful One (w)

TERRY, Dewey, Jr.
I'm Leaving It (All) Up To You
Justine
Letter

TERRY, George
Lay Down Sally
Stayin' Alive

TERRY, Johnny
Please, Please, Please

TETTEROO, Peter
Ma Belle Amie

TEX, Joe
Hold What You've Got
Loose Caboose

THEODORAKIS, Mikis
Zorba The Greek, Theme From
(m)

THOMAS, Carla
Gee Whiz

THOMAS, David
Sonic Reducer

THOMAS, David Clayton
Go Down Gamblin' (w)
Lucretia MacEvil
Spinning Wheel

THOMAS, Ian
Painted Ladies

THOMAS, J.
Rockin' Robin

THOMAS, Joe
Anyplace Is Paradise

THOMAS, Ronald
Girl Of My Dreams

THOMAS, Rufus
Do The Funky Chicken
Walking The Dog

THOMAS, Truman
Free Me From My Freedom

THOMASSON, Hugh Edward, Jr.
There Goes Another Love Song

THOMPSON, Bonnie
Turn Back The Hands Of Time

THOMPSON, Frank
Shake Your Rump To The Funk
Too Hot To Stop (Part I)

THOMPSON, Gloria
Loose Caboose

THOMPSON, James
Get Down

THOMPSON, Wayne Carson
Letter
No Love At All

THORNTON, Blair
Four Wheel Drive

THORPE, Billy
Children Of The Sun

THROCKMORTON, Sonny
I Wish I Was Eighteen Again

TIERNEY, Harry
Alice Blue Gown (m)

TILGHMAN, Bill
Oh Boy
Rave On

TILLOTSON, Johnny
It Keeps Right On A-Hurtin'

TIO, Mario G.
Action Speaks Louder Than
Words

TIOMKIN, Dimitri
High And The Mighty (m)
Town Without Pity (m)

TITUS, Libby
Love Has No Pride (Additional
Lyrics)

TOBIAS, Fred
Good Timin'

TOBIAS, Harry
No Regrets (w)

TOBIAS, Ken
Stay Awhile

TOOMBS, Rudolph
Daddy, Daddy
5-10-15 Hours
One Mint Julep

TORRE, Janice
Paper Roses (w)

TORRY, Clare
Love For Living

TOUSSAINT, Allen
Happiness
I Like It Like That
Mother-In-Law
Southern Nights
Yes We Can Can

TOWNE, Billy
Never On Sunday (w)

TOWNSEND, Ed
For Your Love
Let's Get It On

TOWNSHEND, Peter (Pete)
I Can See For Miles
Magic Bus
My Generation
Pinball Wizard
Relay
See Me, Feel Me
Squeeze Box
Who Are You
Won't Get Fooled Again

TRAPANI, Tulio
Cara Mia

TRAVERS, Mary
Come And Go With Me (Adapted
& arranged)
Cuckoo
Great Mandella
Hangman (Adapted & arranged)
Monday Morning (Adapted)
Motherless Child
Single Girl
Song Is Love
Tell It On The Mountain (Adapted)

TRAVIS, Merle
Sixteen Tons

TREADWELL, George
Dance With Me
There Goes My Baby

TRIMACHI, Sal
Free As The Wind

TROXEL, Gary
Come Softly To Me

TRUE, Mark
Why Have You Left The One
(You Left Me For)

TUBBS, Pierre
Gotta Be The One
Right Back Where We Started
From

TUCKER, Alonzo
Baby Workout

TUCKER, Mick
Action
Fox On The Run

TURK, Roy
Are You Lonesome Tonight
I Don't Know Why (I Just Do) (w)
I'll Get By (w)
Love, You Funny Thing (w)

TURNER, C.F.
Let It Ride

TURNER, D.
Do Your Dance (Part I)

TURNER, Gil
Carry It On

TURNER, Lonnie
Jungle Love

TURNER, Lou Willie
Flip, Flop & Fly
Honey Hush

TURNER, Scott
Shutters And Boards

TURNER, Tina
Nutbush City Limits

TURNER, Titus
Hey, Doll Baby

TURNIER, Gary
Keep On Dancin'

TWEEL, Jeff
Every Time Two Fools Collide

TWOMEY, Kay
Wooden Heart

TYLER, Steven
Back In The Saddle
Draw The Line
Dream On
Last Child
Sweet Emotion
Walk This Way

TYLER, West
Diamonds And Pearls

TYSON, Ian
Four Strong Winds
Red Velvet
Someday Soon

TYSON, Ronnie
Free Man

UDELL, Pete
Hurting Each Other (w)
Sealed With A Kiss (w)

ULVAEUS, Bjorn
Dancing Queen
Does Your Mother Know
Fernando
I Do, I Do, I Do, I Do, I Do
Knowing Me, Knowing You
Money, Money, Money
Name Of The Game
SOS
Take A Chance On Me

UNIMAN, Mimi
Long Lonely Nights

UPTON, Pat
More Today Than Yesterday

VALE, Mike
Crystal Blue Persuasion

VALENS, Ritchie
Donna

VALENTI, John
Anything You Want
I Wrote This Song For You

VALENTINE, Gary
X-Offender

VALLEE, Rudy
Whiffenpoof Song (Revision)

VALLINS, John
Too Much, Too Little, Too Late

VALORY, Diane
Wheel In The Sky

VALORY, Ross
Anytime

VAN ARSDALE, Douglas
Tumbleweed

VANCE, Al
Disco Lady

VANCE, Kenny
Hot Wax Theme

VANCE, Paul
Itsy Bitsy Teenie Weenie Yellow
Polkadot Bikini
Playground In My Mind
Run Sally Sun
What Is Love

VANDA, Harry
Friday On My Mind

VAN EIJCK, Hans
Ma Belle Amie

VAN HALEN, Alex & Edward
Beautiful Girls
Dance The Night Away
Jamie's Cryin'
Runnin' With The Devil

VANHOY, Rafe
Sail Away

VAN LEEUWEN, Bobby
Mighty Joe

VANNELLI, Gino
Wheels Of Life

VANNELLI, Ross
I Just Wanna Stop

VAN RONK, Dave
Bamboo
Frankie's Blues

VANWARMER, Randy
Just When I Needed You Most

VAUGHN, Sharon
My Heroes Have Always Been
Cowboys

VERSCHAREN, Joseph
Since I Don't Have You (w)
This I Swear (w)

VILLA, Joe
Believe Me

VINCENT, Gene
Be-Bop-A-Lula

VINCENT, John
Don't You Just Know It

Rockin' Pneumonia And The
Boogie Woogie Flu
Sea Cruise

VINCENT, Stan
O-o-h Child

VINTON, Bobby
My Melody Of Love (w)

VITO, Rick
Surrender To Me

VOGEL, Janet
Since I Don't Have You (w)
This I Swear (w)

VOLMAN, Mark
Sound Asleep

VONNEGUT, Kurt, Jr.
Nice, Nice, Very Nice (w)

VOSS, Faye
Sugar Shack

VOUDOURIS, Roger
Get Used To It

WACHTEL, Robert & Waddy
Werewolves Of London

WADDINGTON, Tony
Can't Stop Loving You

WADE, Cliff
Heartbreaker

WAGNER, Dick
From The Inside
How You Gonna See Me Now
I Never Cry
Only Women Bleed
Welcome To My Nightmare
You And Me

WAINMAN, Phil
Lady (Put The Light On Me)

WAITE, John
Back On My Feet Again
Silver Dreams

WAITS, Tom
Heart Of Saturday Night
Ol' 55
San Diego Serenade

WAKEFIELD, Kathy
Down To Love Town

WALDEN, Narada Michael
I Shoulda Loved Ya
Let Me Be Your Angel

WALKER, Aron T.
Call It Stormy Monday

WALKER, Jerry Jeff
Mr. Bojangles

WALKER, T-Bone
I'm Still In Love With You

WALLER, Thomas
Honeysuckle Rose (m)

WALSH, Dan
Temptation Eyes

WALSH, Joe (Joseph Fidler)
All Night Long
Funk #49
Life In The Fast Lane
Life's Been Good

WALSH, Steve
Point Of No Return

WALTER, L.
Special Lady

WANSEL, Dexter
Sweetest Pain

WARE, La Verne
If I Were Your Woman

WARE, Leon
After The Dance

WARNER, Frank
Tom Dooley (Collected, adapted
& arranged)

WARREN, B.
Groovy Grubworm

WARREN, Harry
At Last (m)
Chattanooga Choo Choo (m)
I Only Have Eyes For You (m)
More I See You (m)

WARREN, W.
Wild Side Of Life

WASHINGTON, Carrol
Mr. Big Stuff

WASHINGTON, Ned
High And The Mighty (w)
My Foolish Heart (w)
Town Without Pity (w)

WASHINGTON, Oscar
Night Train

WASHINGTON, Patti
Gidget

WATERS, Chris
Sexy Eyes

WATERS, Roger
Another Brick In The Wall (Part
II)
Money

WATKINS, Dave
It's How I Live

WATSON, Doc
Deep River Blues
Sittin' On Top Of The World
Way Downtown (Adapted &
arranged)

WATSON, Melvin L.
Let Me Lay My Funk On You

WATTS, Nathan
Free (Wanna Be Free)

WAYNE, Bernie
Blue Velvet

WAYNE, Dottie
Night Has A Thousand Eyes

WAYNE, Sid
Big Boots (w)
Didja Ever (w)
Frankfort Special (w)
Hard Luck
I Need Your Love Tonight
I'll Be Back (w)
It's Impossible (w)
See You In September (w)
Slowly But Surely (w)
Spinout

WEATHERLY, Jim
I'll Still Love You
Love Finds Its Own Way
Midnight Train To Georgia
Neither One Of Us
Once In A Lifetime Thing
Roses And Love Songs
Where Peaceful Waters Flow
You Are A Song
You're The Best Thing That Ever
Happened To Me

WEATHERSPOON, William
I've Passed This Way Before
What Becomes Of The Broken
Hearted

WEAVER, Blue
Don't Throw It All Away
Hold On To My Love

WEAVER, Jerry
My Love Ain't Never Been This
Strong

WEBB, Danny
One Summer Night

WEBB, Jim (Jimmy)
All I Know
By The Time I Get To Phoenix
Carpet Man
Everybody Gets To Go To The
  Moon
Girls Song
It's A Sin When You Love Some-
  body
MacArthur Park
Magic Garden
Moon Is A Harsh Mistress
Never Gonna Be The Same
Paper Cup
Pattern People
Requiem; 820 Latham
Rosecrans Boulevard
Up, Up And Away
Which Way To Nowhere
Wichita Lineman
Worst That Could Happen

WEBB, Laura
Mister Lee

WEBBER, Andrew Lloyd
I Don't Know How To Love Him
  (m)
Superstar (m)

WEBSTER, Paul Francis
Baltimore Oriole (w)
Honey Babe (w)
Padre (w)
Secret Love (w)
Shadow Of Your Smile (w)
Somewhere, My Love (w)
Twelfth Of Never (w)
Winds Of Chance (w)

WEIL, Cynthia
Here You Come Again (w)
I Just Can't Help Believin' (w)
I'm Gonna Be Strong
New World Coming
On Broadway
We Gotta Get Out Of This
  Place
You've Lost That Lovin' Feelin'

WEILL, Kurt
Mack The Knife (m)

WEINSTEIN, Bobby
Goin' Out Of My Head
I'm On The Outside (Looking In)
It's Gonna Take A Miracle
Pretty Blue Eyes

WEIR, Bob
Money Money (m)
Music Never Stopped (m)
Sugar Magnolia
Truckin' (m)

Weather Report I
Weather Report II; Let It Grow
  (m)

WEISMAN, Ben
As Long As I Have You (m)
Danny (m)
Don't Leave Me Now
Fame And Fortune (m)
Follow That Dream (m)
Frankie And Johnnie (New words
  & arranged)
Got A Lot O' Livin' To Do
Hard Luck
I Got Lucky
I Slipped, I Stumbled, I Fell
  (m)
I'll Be Back (m)
Night Has A Thousand Eyes
Ridin' The Rainbow (m)
Slowly But Surely (m)
Spinout
Steppin' Out Of Line
Wooden Heart

WEISS, George David
Can't Give You Anything (But
  My Love)
Can't Help Falling In Love
Disco Baby
Hey Girl, Come And Get It
Lion Sleeps Tonight (Adapted)
Love Is The Answer
Star On A T.V. Show
Walkin' Miracle

WEISS, Larry
Rhinestone Cowboy

WEISS, Laurence
Bend Me, Shape Me

WEISS, Sam
We Belong Together

WELCH, Bob
Ebony Eyes
Hot Love, Cold World
Sentimental Lady

WELLER, F.
Dizzy
Jam Up And Jelly Tight
Stir It Up And Serve It

WELLER, Paul
Modern World

WELLS, Bryan
Place In The Sun (m)
Yester-Me, Yester-You, Yester-
  day (m)

WESLEY, Fred
Doing The Best I Can
Papa Don't Take No Mess
  (Part I)
Payback

WESSEN, Margaret
Security

WEST, Bob
I'll Be There

WEST, Bobby "Red"
If You Talk In Your Sleep

WEST, David
Portrait Of My Love (w)

WEST, Dottie
Country Sunshine

WEST, Hedy
Five Hundred Miles

WEST, Jim
Honest I Do

WEST, Leslie
Because You Are My Friend
Blood Of The Sun
Flowers Of Evil
Mississippi Queen

WEST, Norman
Hearsay

WEST, R.
You're So Fine

WEST, Ricky
Hollywood Swinging

WEST, Sonny
Oh Boy
Rave On

WEST, T.P.
Friend Is Dying
Song That Never Comes
Sweet City Song

WESTON, Paul
Day By Day

WEYMOUTH, Martina
Psycho Killer

WHITE, Alan
Release, Release

WHITE, Barry
Oh, What A Night For Dancing

WHITE, Chris
Hold Your Head Up
I Love You
Keep On Running Away

WHITE, David (Dave)
At The Hop
Rock And Roll Is Here To Stay
You Don't Own Me

WHITE, Edgar
Hangin' Round

WHITE, Maurice
Best Of My Love
Evil
Fantasy
Reasons
September
Serpentine Fire
Shining Star
Singasong
Star
That's The Way Of The World

WHITE, Peter
Time Passages

WHITE, Ronald
My Girl
You Beat Me To The Punch

WHITE, Ted
Since You've Been Gone

WHITE, Tony Joe
I've Got A Thing About You Baby
Rainy Night In Georgia

WHITE, Verdine
Fantasy
Serpentine Fire
That's The Way Of The World

WHITEHEAD, John (J.)
Ain't No Stoppin' Us Now
Prayin'
Wake Up Everybody

WHITEHEAD, P.
Fire Island (w)
I Am What I Am (w)
Key West (w)
Macho Man
San Francisco (You've Got Me)
(w)
Sodom And Gomorrah (w)
Village People (w)

WHITELAW, Reid
Diane

WHITEMAN, Paul
Wonderful One (m)

WHITFIELD, Norman
Ain't Too Proud To Beg
Ball Of Confusion
Beauty Is Only Skin Deep
Cloud Nine
Do Your Dance (Part I)
End Of Our Road
I Can't Get Next To You
I Could Never Love Another
I Heard It Through The Grapevine
I Wish It Would Rain

I'm Losing You
Just My Imagination
Let's Go Down To The Disco
Papa Was A Rollin' Stone
Pride And Joy
Psychedelic Shack
Runaway Child, Running Wild
Smiling Faces Sometimes
That's The Way Love Is
Too Busy Thinking About My
Baby
Too Many Fish In The Sea
War
You + Me = Love
You're My Everything

WHITFORD, Brad
Last Child

WHITING, Richard A.
Honey

WHITLOCK, Bobby
Anyday
I Looked Away

WHITTEN, Danny
I Don't Want To Talk About It

WICKHAM, Vicki
You Don't Have To Say You Love
Me (w)

WIENER, Sturt
To The Aisle

WILCOX, Harlo
Groovy Grubworm

WILCOX, John
Set Me Free

WILDER, Warner
Love Means

WILDING, Bobby
Hurt So Bad

WILKIN, John
G.T.O.

WILKINS, Geoff
Light Up The World With Sunshine

WILKINS, Ronnie
Growin'
Son Of A Preacher Man

WILLENSKY, Elliot
Got To Be There

WILLIAMS, Bernice
Duke Of Earl

WILLIAMS, Dennis
My Love Don't Come Easy

WILLIAMS, Don
We're All The Way

WILLIAMS, Dootsi
Earth Angel

WILLIAMS, Fred
Freight Train

WILLIAMS, Greg
Heartbeat, It's A Lovebeat

WILLIAMS, J. Deniece
Free (Wanna Be Free)

WILLIAMS, Jerry
I'm Gonna Make You Love Me

WILLIAMS, Jimmy
Lover's Question

WILLIAMS, John
Can You Read My Mind (m)
Close Encounters Of The Third
Kind, Theme From (m)
Star Wars (m)

WILLIAMS, Kenneth
Action Speaks Louder Than
Words

WILLIAMS, Larry (E.)
Bad Boy
Bony Moronie
Carol
Dizzy Miss Lizzie
Let Your Love Flow
Short Fat Fannie
Slow Down

WILLIAMS, Lawton
Fraulein

WILLIAMS, Mason
Cinderella Rockefella
Classical Gas (m)

WILLIAMS, Maurice
Little Darlin'
Stay

WILLIAMS, Mentor
Drift Away

WILLIAMS, Milan
Brick House
Machine Gun (m)
Wonderland

WILLIAMS, Paul
Evergreen (w)
I Won't Last A Day Without You
(w)
Let Me Be The One (w)
Love Boat, Main Title From (w)
Old Fashioned Love Song
Rainy Days And Mondays (w)

We've Only Just Begun (w)
You And Me Against The World

WILLIAMS, R.
Mellow Lovin'

WILLIAMS, Ralph
Mr. Big Stuff

WILLIAMS, Thomas
Pretty Girls Everywhere

WILLIAMSON, James
Search And Destroy

WILLIAMSON, "Sonny Boy"
Checkin' Up On My Baby
Don't Start Me Talkin'
Fattening Frogs For Snakes
Good Morning, Little School Girl

WILLIS, Allee
Boogie Wonderland
I Shoulda Loved Ya
Lead Me On
September
Star

WILLIS, Chuck
C.C. Rider

WILLIS, Marvin
Float On

WILLIS, V.
Go West
Hot Cop
I Am What I Am
I'm A Cruiser
In The Navy
Key West (w)
Macho Man
My Roommate
Sodom And Gomorrah (w)
Ups And Downs
Women
Y.M.C.A.

WILLS, Dave
Love Struck

WILLS, Johnnie Lee
Rag Mop

WILSON, Alan
Goin' Up The Country

WILSON, Ann & Nancy
Barracuda
Crazy On You
Dog & Butterfly
Dreamboat Annie
Even It Up
Heartless
Magic Man

WILSON, Brian
Dance, Dance, Dance
Don't Worry, Baby
Good Timin'
Help Me Rhonda
I Get Around
In The Back Of My Mind
Little Honda
Man With All The Toys
Please Let Me Wonder
She Knows Me Too Well
Sloop John B (Adapted)
Surf City
Surfer Girl
Surfin'
Surfin' Safari
Surfin' U.S.A. (w)
Warmth Of The Sun
Wendy
When I Grow Up

WILSON, Carl
Dance, Dance, Dance
Good Timin' (w)

WILSON, Chris
Shake Some Action
Yes It's True
You Tore Me Down

WILSON, Forest
Ko Ko Mo (I Love You So)

WILSON, Frank
All I Need
Boogie Down
I'm Livin' In Shame
Keep On Truckin'
Look What You've Done To My
    Heart
Love Child
Stoned Love
You've Made Me So Very Happy

WILSON, Ian
Run Home Girl

WILSON, Jackie
Baby Workout

WILSON, Jimmy
You've Got love

WILSON, Kelly & Steve
If The World Ran Out Of Love
    Tonight

WILSON, Meri
Telephone Man

WILSON, Norris
Most Beautiful Girl
Very Special Love Song

WILSON, Philip
Love March

WILSON, Robb
For All We Know (w)

WILSON, T.
Brother Louie

WILSON, Vance
Oh, What A Night For Dancing

WILSON, Willie Harry
Substitute

WINCHESTER, Jesse
Rhumba Girl
Yankee Lady

WINE, Toni
Candida

WINGFIELD, Pete
Making A Good Thing Better

WINLEY, Paul
Hide And Seek

WINN, Jerry
Gimme Little Sign
Lovey Dovey Kinda Lovin'

WINTER, Edgar
Frankenstein

WINWOOD, Muff & Steve
Gimme Some Lovin'

WIRRICK, James "Tip"
You Make Me Feel (Mighty Real)
    (m)

WISE, Fred
As Long As I Have You (w)
Danny (w)
Fame And Fortune (w)
Follow That Dream (w)
I Got Lucky
I Slipped, I Stumbled, I Fell (w)
Ridin' The Rainbow (w)
Steppin' Out Of Line
Wooden Heart

WITHERS, Bill
Ain't No Sunshine
Lean On Me
Lovely Day (w)

WITHERSPOON, William
What Becomes Of The Broken-
    hearted

WOLF, Don
Love Is All We Need

WOLF, Peter
Give It To Me
Must Of Got Lost

COMPOSER—LYRICIST INDEX

WOLFE, Steve
If I Sing You A Love Song
It's A Heartache

WOLINSKI, David "Hawk"
Do You Love What You Feel
Hollywood
Little One

WOLOSHIN, Sid
Take Life A Little Easier (m)

WOLPERT, David
Songbird

WOMACK, Bobby
Across 110th Street
Breezin' (m)
Daylight
I Can Understand It
That's The Way I Feel About Cha
Woman's Gotta Have It

WONDER, Stevie
All In Love Is Fair
Another Star
Boogie On Reggae Woman
Don't You Worry 'Bout A Thing
Happier Than The Morning Sun
Higher Ground
I Believe (When I Fall In Love It
Will Be Forever)
I Was Made To Love Her
I Wish
Isn't She Lovely
Living For The City
My Cherie Amour
Outside My Window
Send One Your Love
Shoo-Be-Doo-Be-Doo-Da-Day
Signed, Sealed, Delivered I'm
Yours
Sir Duke
Superstition
Tears Of A Clown
Tell Me Something Good
Uptight (Everything's Alright)
You Are My Heaven
You Are The Sunshine Of My
Life
You Haven't Done Nothin'

WOOD, Bobby
Half The Way

WOOD, Don
Reach Out (w)

WOOD, Lauren
Please Don't Leave

WOOD, Peter
Time Passages
Year Of The Cat

WOOD, Ronald David
Stay With Me

WOODFORD, Terry
Angel In Your Arms

WOODLEY, Bruce
Red Rubber Ball

WOODS, Bobby
Talkin' In Your Sleep
What's Your Name, What's Your
Number

WOODS, H.
Walk Right In

WOODS, Harry
Try A Little Tenderness
When The Moon Comes Over The
Mountain

WOODS, Pearl
Something's Got A Hold On Me

WOOLEY, Bruce
Video Killed The Radio Star

WOOLEY, Sheb
Purple People Eater

WOLFSON, Eric
Doctor Tarr And Professor
Fether

WORRELL, Bernie
Do That Stuff

WRIGHT, Andrew
When A Man Loves A Woman

WRIGHT, B.
Where Is The Love

WRIGHT, Gary
Dream Weaver
Love Is Alive
Water Sign

WRIGHT, Syreeta
Signed, Sealed, Delivered I'm
Yours

WRIGHT, Yvonne
I Believe (When I Fall In Love It
Will Be Forever)

WYCHE, Sid
Big Hunk O' Love
Love Love Love
Woman, A Lover, A Friend

WYNETTE, Tammy
Stand By Your Man

WYRICK, Barbara
Right Feeling At The Wrong Time

YARROW, Peter
All My Trials (Adapted)
Autumn To May
Come And Go With Me (Adapted
& arranged)
Cruel War
Cuckoo
Day Is Done
Gilgarra Mountain (Adapted &
arranged)
Great Mandella
Hangman (Adapted & arranged)
Man Of Constant Sorrow
Monday Morning (Adapted)
Oh, Rock My Soul (Adapted &
arranged)
Puff (The Magic Dragon)
Song Is Love
Tell It On The Mountain
(Adapted)
This Girl
This Train
Torn Between Two Lovers
Weep For Jamie

YELLEN, Jack
Alabama Jubilee (w)
Are You From Dixie (w)
Crazy Words-Crazy Tune (w)
Happy Days Are Here Again (w)
Hard Hearted Hannah
Vo-Do-Do-De-O Blues (w)

YOHO, Byron Lamont
There Goes Another Love Song

YOUNG, Dennis De. See
DEYOUNG, Dennis.

YOUNG, George
Friday On My Mind

YOUNG, Joe
I'm Alone Because I Love You

YOUNG, Kenny
Don't Go Out Into The Rain
Under The Boardwalk

YOUNG, Neil
After The Gold Rush
Alabama
Broken Arrow
Cinnamon Girl
Country Girl
Cowgirl In The Sand
Dance Dance Dance
Do I Have To Come Right Out
And Say It
Don't Let It Bring You Down
Expecting To Fly
Flying On The Ground Is Wrong
Harvest
Heart Of Gold
Helpless
Hey Babe
Hey Hey, My My

I Am A Child
If I Could Have Her Tonight
I've Been Waiting For You
Like A Hurricane
Long May You Run
Look Out For My Love
Lotta Love
Love Is A Rose
Midnight On The Bay
Mr. Soul
Needle And The Damage Done
Nowadays Clancy Can't Even Sing
Old Man
On The Way Home
Only Love Can Break Your Heart
Out Of My Mind
Southern Man
Walk On

YOUNG, Paul
  Run Home Girl

YOUNG, Rusty
  Crazy Love

YOUNG, Victor
  My Foolish Heart

YOUNT, Robert
  Release Me

YVAIN, Maurice
  My Man

ZAGER, Michael
  Let's All Chant
  Think It Over

ZARET, Hy
  Unchained Melody (w)

ZERO, Jimmy
  All This And More
  I Won't Look Back
  Sonic Reducer

ZESSES, Nick
  I Just Want To Celebrate

ZEVON, Warren
  Carmelita
  Excitable Boy
  Hasten Down The Wind
  Johnny Strikes Up The Band
  Lawyers, Guns And Money
  Poor Poor Pitiful Me
  Tenderness On The Block
  Werewolves Of London

ZWIRN, Artie
  Sorry

ZWOL, Wally. See
  ZWOLINSKI, Walter.

ZWOLINSKI, Walter
  New York City I Love You

5

PERFORMER INDEX

———

ABBA
Dancing Queen
Does Your Mother Know
Fernando
I Do, I Do, I Do, I Do, I Do
Knowing Me, Knowing You
Money, Money, Money
Name Of The Game
SOS
Take A Chance On Me

ACE
How Long
I Can't Help Myself

ADDERLEY, Nat
I Married An Angel

ADDRISI BROTHERS
Slow Dancin' Don't Turn Me On

AEROSMITH
Back In The Saddle
Come Together
Draw The Line
Dream On
Last Child
Sweet Emotion
Walk This Way

AIR SUPPLY
Lost In Love

AKINS, Jewel
Birds And The Bees

ALAIMO, Steve
Denver

ALAN PARSONS PROJECT
Doctor Tarr And Professor
Fether

ALBERT, Morris
Feelings

ALDRICH, Ronnie
Diamonds Are Forever

ALEXANDER, Arthur
You Better Move On

ALICE COOPER. See COOPER,
Alice.

ALLEN, Peter
Don't Cry Out Loud

I Go To Rio
I Honestly Love You
I'd Rather Leave While I'm In
Love
More I See You

ALLISON, Mose
Cabin In The Sky
I Love The Life I Live
Seventh Son
That's All Right

ALLMAN, Greg. See also
ALLMAN BROTHERS BAND.
Don't Mess Up A Good Thing

ALLMAN BROTHERS BAND
It's Not My Cross To Bear
Jessica
Just Another Love Song
Melissa
Mignight Rider
Nevertheless
Ramblin' Man
Whippin Post

ALMANAC SINGERS
Alabama Jubilee

ALPERT, Herb. See also HERB
ALPERT & THE TIJUANA
BRASS.
Rise
Rotation
Street Life
This Guy's In Love With You

AMAZING RHYTHM ACES
Amazing Grace (Used To Be Her
Favorite Song)

AMBROSIA
Biggest Part Of Me
Nice, Nice, Very Nice

AMERICA
Amber Cascades
California Revisited
Daisy Jane
Green Monkey
Horse With No Name
I Need You
Lonely People
Muskrat Love
Sandman
Sister Golden Hair
Tin Man

Today's The Day
Ventura Highway
Woman Tonight

AMERICAN BREED
Bend Me, Shape Me

AMMONS, Gene
Pagan Love Song

ANDERSEN, Eric
Honey (S. Simmons, H. Gillespie
& R. Whiting)
Ol' 55
Thirsty Boots

ANDERSON, Bill
I Can't Wait Any Longer

ANDERSON, Lynn
Angel In Your Arms
I Love How You Love Me
Right Time Of The Night
Rose Garden

ANDREA TRUE CONNECTION
More, More, More (Part I)
What's Your Name, What's Your
Number

ANDY GIBB & OLIVIA NEWTON-
JOHN. See also GIBB, Andy;
NEWTON-JOHN, Olivia.
I Can't Help It

ANGELS
My Boyfriend's Back

ANIMALS
Boom Boom
Bright Lights, Big City
Bring It On Home To Me
House Of The Rising Sun
How You've Changed
We Gotta Get Out Of This Place

ANKA, Paul
Diana
Lonely Boy
Put Your Head On My Shoulder
This Is Love
You Are My Destiny

ANNIE, Cast Of
Easy Street

APOLLO 100
Joy

APRIL WINE
Roller

ARBOR
Graduation Day

ARCHIES
Sugar, Sugar

ARDEN, Tony
Padre

ARGENT
Hold Your Head Up
Liar

ARMSTRONG, Louis
Sunrise, Sunset
That Lucky Old Sun
Whiffenpoof Song

ARNOLD, Eddie
Cowboy
Make The World Go Away
With Pen In Hand

ART & DOTTY TODD
Chanson D'Amour

ARTISTICS
That Lucky Old Sun
What The World Needs Now Is
Love

ASHFORD & SIMPSON. See also
SIMPSON, Valerie.
Ain't Nothing But A Maybe
Anywhere
Believe In Me
Bend Me
Caretaker
Destiny
Found A Cure
Gimme Something Real
I Wanna Be Selfish
Is It Still Good To Ya
It Came To Me
It'll Come, It'll Come, It'll Come
One More Try
Over And Over
Sell The House
So, So Satisfied
Somebody Told A Lie
Tell It All
Tried Tested And Found True

ASSOCIATION
Cherish
Never My Love
Windy

ATKINS, Chet
I'll See You In My Dreams
Masterpiece
Susie-Q

ATLANTA RHYTHM SECTION
Champagne Jam
Do It Or Die
Don't Miss The Message
I'm Not Gonna Let It Bother Me
Tonight
Imaginary Lover
Sky High
So Into You
Spooky

AUSTIN, Sil
Let The Sunshine In

AVALON, Frankie
Come Softly To Me
Splish Splash
Venus
Why (B. Marcucci &
P. DeAngelis)

AVERAGE WHITE BAND
Pick Up The Pieces
Walk On By

AVIATOR
Get Your Rocks Off

AXTON, Hoyt
Ease Your Pain

BABYS
Back On My Feet Again
Silver Dreams

BACHARACH, Burt
Living Together, Growing
Together
Promises, Promises

BACHELORS
Diane (E. Rapee & L. Pollack)

BACHMAN-TURNER OVERDRIVE
Four Wheel Drive
Freeways
Let It Ride
My Wheels Won't Turn
Takin' Care Of Business
You Ain't Seen Nothing Yet

BACK PORCH MAJORITY
That's The Way It's Gonna Be

BAD COMPANY
Can't Get Enough
Feel Like Makin' Love
Gone, Gone, Gone
Rock 'N' Roll Fantasy
Young Blood (J. Leiber, M.
Stoller & D. Pomus)

BADFINGER
Come And Get It
Day After Day
No Matter What

BAEZ, Joan. See also BOB DYLAN
& JOAN BAEZ.
All My Trials (O. Gordon)
Blue Sky
Children Of Darkness
Daddy, You Been On My Mind
Dear Landlord
Deportee
Diamonds And Rust
Don't Think Twice, It's All Right
Fountain Of Sorrow
Green Green Grass Of Home
Guantanamera
Hard Rain's A Gonna Fall
House Of The Rising Sun
I Dreamed I Saw St. Augustine
I Shall Be Released
It Ain't Me, Babe
It's All Over Now, Baby Blue
Jesse (J. Ian)
Joe Hill (E. Robinson)
Just Like A Woman
Last Thing On My Mind
Let Your Love Flow
Love Is Just A Four Letter Word
Night They Drove Old Dixie
Down
Sad Eyed Lady Of The Lowlands
Song For David
Tears Of Rage
There But For Fortune
Tumbleweed
We Shall Overcome
Where Have All The Flowers
Gone
With God On Our Side
You Ain't Goin' Nowhere

BAJA MARIMBA
Yes Sir, That's My Baby

BAKER, La Vern
I Cried A Tear
Tweedlee Dee

BAND. See also BOB DYLAN &
THE BAND.
Baby, Don't You Do It
Georgia On My Mind
Get Up, Jake
I Shall Be Released
Jawbone
Night They Drove Old Dixie
Down
Rag Mama Rag
Tears Of Rage
This Wheel's On Fire
Time To Kill
Up On Cripple Creek
When I Paint My Masterpiece

BANZAII
Chinese Kung Fu

BARBIERI, Gato
Last Tango In Paris

BARBRA STREISAND & KRIS
KRISTOFFERSON. See also
STREISAND, Barbra;
KRISTOFFERSON, Kris.
Watch Closely Now

BARBRA STREISAND & NEIL
DIAMOND. See DIAMOND,
Neil & STREISAND, Barbra.

BARE, Bobby
All American Boy
Four Strong Winds
Green Green Grass Of Home

BAR-KAYS
Shake Your Rump To The Funk
Son Of Shaft
Too Hot To Stop (Part I)

BARRETTO, Ray
El Watusi

BARRY, Claudia
Boogie Woogie Dancin' Shoes

BARRY DE VORZON & PERRY
BOTKIN, JR.
Nadia's Theme

BASIE, Count
Let The Good Times Roll

BASSEY, Shirley
All In Love Is Fair
Alone Again (Naturally)
Angel Eyes
Come In From The Rain
Day By Day (S. Schwartz)
Diamonds Are Forever
First Time Ever I Saw Your Face
Goldfinger
I Don't Know How To Love Him
I Only Have Eyes For You
I (Who Have Nothing)
I Won't Last A Day Without You
If (D. Gates)
If We Only Have Love
I'll Never Fall In Love Again
I'm In The Mood For Love
The Look Of Love
Moonraker
Over The Rainbow
Spring Is Here
Taking A Chance On Love
Way We Were
What Are You Doing The Rest
Of Your Life
What I Did For Love
You Take My Heart Away
You're Gonna Hear From Me

BATDORF & RODNEY
You Are A Song

BAZUKA
Dynomite (Part I)

BEACH BOYS
Barbara Ann
Come Go With Me
Dance, Dance, Dance (B. Wilson
& C. Wilson)
Do You Wanna Dance
Don't Worry Baby
Good Timin' (B. Wilson & C.
Wilson)
Graduation Day
Help Me Rhonda
Hushabye
I Get Around
In The Back Of My Mind
Just Once In My Life
Little Honda
Man With All The Toys
Please Let Me Wonder
Rock And Roll Music
She Knows Me Too Well
Sloop John B
Surfer Girl
Surfin'
Surfin' Safari
Surfin' U.S.A.
Warmth Of The Sun
Wendy
When I Grow Up
Why Do Fools Fall In Love

BEATLES
Across The Universe
Act Naturally
All My Loving
All Together Now
All You Need Is Love
And I Love Her
Baby, You're A Rich Man
Back In The U.S.S.R.
Bad Boy
Bad To Me
Birthday
Can't Buy Me Love
Carry That Weight
Come Together
Day In The Life
Day Tripper
Dear Prudence
Dizzy Miss Lizzie
Do You Want To Know A Secret
Drive My Car
Eight Days A Week
Eleanor Rigby
Fool On The Hill
For You, Blue
From Me To You
Get Back
Good Day Sunshine
Good Golly Miss Molly
Got To Get You Into My Life
Hard Day's Night
Hello, Goodbye
Help
Helter Skelter
Here Comes The Sun
Here, There And Everywhere
Hey Jude

I Am The Walrus
I Feel Fine
I Saw Her Standing There
I Should Have Known Better
I Wanna Be Your Man
If I Fell
I'll Be On My Way
I'm A Loser
I'm Happy Just To Dance With
You
In My Life
It Won't Be Long
I've Got A Feeling
Kansas City
Lady Madonna
Let It Be
Long And Winding Road
Long, Long, Long
Long Tall Sally
Love Me Do
Lucy In The Sky With Diamonds
Maggie Mae
Magical Mystery Tour
Michelle
Misery
Money (That's What I Want)
Mr. Moonlight
Norwegian Wood
Nowhere Man
Ob La Di, Ob La Da
Oh Darling
Old Brown Shoe
Paperback Writer
Penny Lane
Piggies
Please Mr. Postman
P.S. I Love You
Revolution
Ringo's Theme
Rock & Roll Music
Rocky Raccoon
Roll Over, Beethoven
Run For Your Life
Savoy Truffle
Sentimental Journey
Sgt. Pepper's Lonely Hearts
Club Band
She Came In Through The
Bathroom Window
She Loves You
Slow Down
Something
Strawberry Fields Forever
Taste Of Honey
Tell Me Why
Thank You Girl
There's A Place
Ticket To Ride
Twist And Shout
We Can Work It Out
While My Guitar Gentle Weeps
Why (B. Crompton & T. Sheridan)
With A Little Help From My
Friends
Yellow Submarine
Yesterday
You Won't See Me

FIND THAT TUNE

Your Mother Should Know
You've Got To Hide Your Love
Away

BEAU BRUMMELS
Just A Little
Laugh, Laugh

BEE GEES
Boogie Child
Fanny Be Tender With My Love
Holiday
How Can You Mend A Broken
Heart
How Deep Is Your Love
I Started A Joke
If I Can't Have You
I've Got To Get A Message To
You
Jive Talkin'
Love So Right
Massachusetts
More Than A Woman
Night Fever
Nights On Broadway
New York Mining Disaster 1941
Run To Me (B., R., & M. Gibb)
Sgt. Pepper's Lonely Hearts Club
Band
Spicks And Specks
Spirits (Having Flown)
Stayin' Alive
To Love Somebody
Tragedy
Words
World
You Should Be Dancing

BELAFONTE, Harry
Day Light Break
Try To Remember
Turn Around

BELL, Madeline
I'm Gonna Make You Love Me

BELL, Vincent
Winds Of Chance

BELL, William
All God's Children Got Soul
Tryin' To Love Two

BELL & JAMES
Livin' It Up
Only Make Believe

BELL NOTES
I've Had It

BELLAMY BROTHERS
Let Your Love Flow

BELVIN, Jesse
Guess Who

BENATAR, Pat
Heartbreaker (C. Wade & G.
Gill)

BENNETT, Tony
Blue Moon
I Don't Know Why (I Just Do)
I Left My Heart In San Francisco
Shadow Of Your Smile
Something
Spring Is Here
This Is All I Ask

BENSON, George
Breezin'
Chattanooga Choo Choo
Gonna Love You More
Greatest Love Of All
Hey, Girl (G. Goffin & C. King)
It's All In The Game
Love Ballad
My Cherie Amour
On Broadway
That Lucky Old Sun
This Masquerade
Unchained Melody

BENT FABRIC. See FABRIC,
Bent.

BENTON, Brook. See also BROOK
BENTON & DINAH WASHING-
TON.
Endlessly
It's Just A Matter Of Time
Rainy Night In Georgia
Still Waters Run Deep

BERRY, Chuck
Back In The U.S.A.
Bye, Bye, Johnny
Carol
Johnny B. Goode
Mabelline
Memphis, Tennessee
Nadine (Is It You)
No Particular Place To Go
Reelin' And Rockin'
Rock And Roll Music
Roll Over, Beethoven
Runaround
School Day (Ring Ring Goes The
Bell)
Sweet Little Sixteen
Tutti Frutti
You Came A Long Way From
St. Louis
You Can't Catch Me

BIDDU ORCHESTRA
Summer Of 42 (Disco Version)

BIG BOPPER
Chantilly Lace

BILL BLACK COMBO
Smokie (Part I)
White Silver Sands

BILL HALEY & THE COMETS
Bony Moronie
Hide And Seek
I'm Walkin'
Lawdy, Miss Clawdy
Rip It Up
Rock Around The Clock
See You Later, Alligator
Shake, Rattle And Roll
Who'll Stop The Rain

BILLY DAVIS JR. & MARILYN
MC COO. See MARILYN
MC COO & BILLY DAVIS JR.

BILLY J. KRAMER & THE
DAKOTAS
Bad To Me

BILLY PRESTON & SYREETA.
See also PRESTON, Billy.
With You I'm Born Again

BIONIC BOOGIE
Dance Little Dreamer
Hot Butterfly

BISHOP, Stephen
On And On

BLACK, Bill. See BILL BLACK
COMBO.

BLACK OAK ARKANSAS
Happy Hooker
Hot Rod
Jim Dandy

BLACKFOOT
Highway Song

BLACKWELL, Otis
All Shook Up
Handy Man
Hey Little Girl

BLAKE, Eubie
Maple Leaf Rag

BLAND, Billy
Let The Little Girl Dance

BLAND, Bobby
Ain't That Loving You (For More
Reasons Than One)
Blind Man
Georgia On My Mind
Goin' Down Slow
Since I Fell For You
Today

BLISS, Don
Peg O' My Heart

BLONDIE
Call Me (D. Harry & G. Moroder)
Dreaming

11:59
Fade Away And Radiate
Hanging On The Telephone
Heart Of Glass
I Didn't Have The Nerve To Say
No
I Know But I Don't Know
I'm Gonna Love You Too
In The Flesh
Just Go Away
One Way Or Another
Picture This
Pretty Baby
Rip Her To Shreds
Sunday Girl
Will Anything Happen
X-Offender

BLOOD, SWEAT & TEARS
And When I Die
Go Down Gamblin'
Hi-De-Ho
Lucretia MacEvil
Roller Coaster
Spinning Wheel
You've Made Me So Very Happy

BLOOMFIELD, Michael
It's Not Killing Me

BLUE CHEER
Summertime Blues

BLUE OYSTER CULT
In Thee
Reaper

BLUE RIDGE RANGERS
Hearts Of Stone

BLUE SWEDE
Never My Love

BLUES BROTHERS
Gimme Some Lovin'
Soul Man

BLUES IMAGE
Gas Lamps And Clay

BO DONALDSON & THE
HEYWOODS
Billy, Don't Be A Hero

BOB & MARCIA
But I Do

BOB DYLAN & JOAN BAEZ. See
also BAEZ, Joan; DYLAN, Bob.
With God On Our Side

BOB DYLAN & THE BAND. See
also BAND; DYLAN, Bob.
Apple Suckling Tree
Clothes Line Saga
Crash On The Levee
Don't Ya Tell Henry

Goin' To Acapulco
Going, Going, Gone
Hazel
Lo And Behold
Long Distance Operator
Million Dollar Bash
Nothing Was Delivered
Odds And Ends
Open The Door, Homer
Please Mrs. Henry
Quinn The Eskimo
Tears Of Rage
This Wheel's On Fire
Tiny Montgomery
Too Much Of Nothing
Yea! Heavy And A Bottle Of
Bread
You Ain't Goin' Nowhere

BOB KUBAN & THE IN-MEN
Cheater

BOB SEGER & THE SILVER
BULLET BAND. See also
SEGER, Bob.
Against The Wind
Fire Lake
Hollywood Nights
Still The Same
We've Got Tonight
You'll Accomp'ny Me

BOBBETTES
Mister Lee

BOBBIE GENTRY & GLEN
CAMPBELL. See GLEN
CAMPBELL & BOBBIE GENTRY.

BOBBY HART & TOMMY
BOYCE. See TOMMY BOYCE
AND BOBBY HART.

BOHANNON, Hamilton
Me And The Gang

BONDS, Gary "U.S."
New Orleans
Quarter To Three
School Is Out

BONEY M
Rivers Of Babylon

BONO, Sonny. See SONNY &
CHER.

BONOFF, Karla
Baby Don't Go
I Can't Hold On
Lose Again
Someone To Lay Down Beside
Me

BOOKER T. AND THE M.G.'S
Green Onions
Soul Clap '69

BOONE, Daniel
Beautiful Sunday

BOONE, Debby
Baby I'm Yours
California (J. Brooks)
Come Share My Love
If Ever I See You Again
When It's Over
When You're Loved
You Light Up My Life

BOONE, Pat
Moody River
Speedy Gonzales
That's How Much I Love You
Why Baby Why
Wonderful Time Up There

BOSTON
Hitch A Ride
Long Time
More Than A Feeling
Peace Of Mind

BOSTON POPS
Blue Moon
Chattanooga Choo Choo
Laura
Moonlight Serenade
Stairway To The Stars
Wonderful One

BOTKIN, Perry, Jr. See Barry
DeVorzon & Perry Botkin Jr.

BOWEN, Jimmy
I'm Stickin' With You

BOWIE, David
Fame (D. Bowie, J. Lennon &
C. Alomar)
Friday On My Mind
Sound And Vision
Space Oddity

BOX TOPS
Cry Like A Baby
I Shall Be Released
Letter (W. Thompson)

BOYCE, Tommy. See TOMMY
BOYCE & BOBBY HART.

BRAMLETT, Bonnie. See
DELANEY & BONNIE.

BRASS CONSTRUCTION
Ha Cha Cha (Funktion)

BREAD
Baby I'm-A Want You
Everything I Own
Guitar Man
Hooked On You
If
It Don't Matter To Me

FIND THAT TUNE

Lost Without Your Love
Make It With You

BREWER, Teresa
Ricochet

BRIDGES, Alicia
I Love The Nightlife

BRISTOL, Johnny
Hang On In There, Baby
You And I (J. Bristol)

BROMBERG, David
Mr. Blue
To Know You (Him) Is To Love
You (Him)

BROOD, Herman
Saturday Night

BROOK BENTON & DINAH
WASHINGTON. See also
BENTON, Brook.
Baby, (You've Got What It Takes)

BROOKLYN BRIDGE
Free As The Wind
Worst That Could Happen

BROOKLYN DREAMS
Make It Last

BROOKS, Donnie
Mission Bell

BROOKS, Joe
California (J. Brooks)

BROTHERS FOUR
Greenfields
Have You Never Been Mellow
Killing Me Softly With His Song
Mandy
Most Beautiful Girl In The World
Seasons In The Sun
Sundown
Sunshine On My Shoulder
Tomorrow Is A Long Time
Try To Remember
Yesterday Once More

BROTHERS JOHNSON. See
JOHNSON BROTHERS.

BROWN, Charles
Tell Me You'll Wait For Me

BROWN, Chuck. See CHUCK
BROWN & THE SOUL
SEARCHERS.

BROWN, James
Ain't That A Groove (Part I)
Ain't That A Grove (Part II)
Bring It Up
Cold Sweat (Parts I & II)

Coldblooded
Doin' It To Death
Doing The Best I Can (J. Brown,
C. Bobbit & F. Wesley)
Don't Be A Drop-Out
Fine Old Foxy Self
Gonna Try
Good Good Lovin
Hello
I Can't Stand It 76
I Don't Mind
I Got A Bag Of My Own
I Got Ants In My Pants (Part I)
I Got You (I Feel Good)
If You Don't Get It The First
Time, Back Up And Try It
Again, Party
I'll Go Crazy
I'll Never Let You Go
Money Won't Change You
My Thang
No, No, No, No
Papa Don't Take No Mess (Part
I)
Papa's Got A Brand New Bag
(Part I)
Papa's Got A Brand New Bag
(Part II)
Parrty (Part I)
Parrty (Part II)
Payback
Please, Please, Please
Shout And Shimmy
Stone To The Bone
Tell Me What You're Gonna Do
There It Is (Part I)
Try Me

BROWN, Maxine. See also CHUCK
JACKSON & MAXINE BROWN.
All In My Mind

BROWN, Peter
Dance With Me
Stargazer
You Should Do It

BROWN, Ruth
Daddy, Daddy
5-10-15 Hours

BROWNE, Jackson
Before The Deluge
Boulevard
For A Dancer
For Everyman
Fountain Of Sorrow
Here Come Those Tears Again
Late For The Sky
Pretender
Rock Me On The Water
Running On Empty
Take It Easy
That Girl Could Sing
Under The Falling Sky
You Love The Thunder

BROWNSVILLE STATION
Lady (Put The Light On Me)
Smokin' In The Boys Room

BRUBECK, Dave
Laura

B.T. EXPRESS
Do It ('Til You're Satisfied)
Express
Give It What You Got

BTO. See BACHMAN-TURNER
OVERDRIVE.

BUCKINGHAMS
Kind Of A Drag
Lawdy Miss Clawdy

BUDDY HOLLY & THE CRICKETS.
See also HOLLY, Buddy.
It's So Easy
Maybe Baby
Oh Boy
That'll Be The Day
Words Of Love (B. Holly)

BUFFALO SPRINGFIELD
Bluebird Revisited
Broken Arrow
Child's Claim To Fame
Do I Have To Come Right Out
And Say It
Expecting To Fly
Flying On The Ground Is Wrong
For What It's Worth
Go And Say Goodbye
I Am A Child
In The Hour Of Not Quite Rain
Kind Woman
Mr. Soul
Nowadays Clancy Can't Even
Sing
On The Way Home
Out Of My Mind
Pretty Girl Why
Questions
Rock 'N' Roll Woman
Un Mundo

BUFFETT, Jimmy
Changes In Latitudes, Changes
In Attitudes
Cheeseburger In Paradise
Come Monday
Fins
Livingston Saturday Night
Manana
Margaritaville
Pencil-Thin Mustache
Volcano

BUGGLES
Video Killed The Radio Star

BULLENS, Cindy
Trust Me

264

BURDON, Eric. See also ERIC
BURDON & WAR.
Boom Boom
Mother Earth

BURNETTE, Dorsey
Tall Oak Tree

BURNETTE, Johnny
You're Sixteen

BURNETTE, Rocky
Tired Of Toein' The Line

BURNS, George
I Wish I Was Eighteen Again

BUTLER, Jerry
He Don't Love You (Like I Love
You)
Make It Easy On Yourself
Only The Strong Survive

BUTTERFIELD, Paul
Mellow Down Easy
Please Send Me Someone To
Love

BUTTERFIELD BLUES BAND
Everything's Gonna Be Alright
Love March

BYRDS
All I Really Want To Do
Ballad Of Easy Rider
Chimes Of Freedom
It's All Over Now, Baby Blue
Mr. Tambourine Man
My Back Pages
Positively 4th Street
Times They Are A-Changin'
Turn, Turn, Turn

CADILLACS
Speedo
Zoom

CALDWELL, Bobby
What You Won't Do For Love

CAMERON, G.C.
It's So Hard To Say Goodbye To
Yesterday

CAMPBELL, Glen. See also
GLEN CAMPBELL & BOBBIE
GENTRY.
By The Time I Get To Phoenix
Dreams Of The Everyday
Housewife
Gentle On My Mind
I Will Never Pass This Way
Again
It Ain't Me, Babe
It's A Sin When You Love
Somebody

Oh Happy Day
Rhinestone Cowboy
Southern Nights
Sunflower
Time
Try A Little Kindness
Wichita Lineman

CANDYMEN
Ways

CANNED HEAT
Can't Hold On Much Longer
Evil (Is Going On)
Goin' Down Slow
Goin' Up The Country
Walking By Myself

CANNIBAL & THE HEAD
HUNTERS
Land Of A Thousand Dances

CANNON, Ace
It Was Almost Like A Song
With Pen In Hand

CANNON, Freddie
Palisades Park
Tallahassee Lassie

CAPRIS
There's A Moon Out Tonight

CAPTAIN & TENNILLE
Come In From The Rain
Do That To Me One More Time
Happier Than The Morning Sun
Happy Together
I'm On My Way
Lonely Night (Angel Face)
Love Will Keep Us Together
Muskrat Love
Shop Around
Since I Fell For You
You Need A Woman Tonight

CARA, Irene
Fame (D. Pitchford & M. Gore)
Out Here On My Own

CARAVELLES
You Don't Have To Be A Baby
To Cry

CARDINALS
Shouldn't I Know

CARLTON, Carl
Everlasting Love

CARLY SIMON & JAMES
TAYLOR. See also SIMON,
Carly; TAYLOR, James.
Devoted To You
Mockingbird

CARMEN, Eric
All By Myself (E. Carmen)
Never Gonna Fall In Love Again
She Did It
Sunrise
That's Rock 'N Roll

CARN, Jean
My Love Don't Come Easy

CARNES, Kim
It Hurts So Bad

CARPENTERS
All You Get From Love Is A
Love Song
Bless The Beasts And Children
Breaking Up Is Hard To Do
Calling Occupants Of Inter-
planetary Craft
Close To You (B. Bacharach &
H. David)
Da Doo Ron Ron
For All We Know
Hurting Each Other
I Believe In You
I Just Fall In Love Again
I Won't Last A Day Without You
I'll Never Fall In Love Again
It's Going To Take Some Time
Johnny Angel
Let Me Be The One
Only Yesterday
Piano Picker
Please Mr. Postman
Rainy Days And Mondays
Sing (J. Raposo)
Solitaire
Song For You
Superstar (L. Russell & B.
Bramlett)
This Masquerade
Top Of The World
Two Sides
We've Only Just Begun
Yesterday Once More
You (R. Edelman)

CARR, Vikki
It Must Be Him
Lean On Me
Over The Rainbow
With Pen In Hand

CARRADINE, Keith
I'm Easy
Mr. Blue

CARROLL, Diahann
Alfie

CARS
Candy-O
Double Life
Good Times Roll
It's All I Can Do
Just What I Needed

Let's Go
My Best Friend's Girl

CARTER, Mel
Hold Me, Thrill Me, Kiss Me

CARTER, Valerie
O-o-h Child

CASH, Johnny
I Walk The Line
Red Velvet
Rock Island Line

CASHMAN & WEST. See also
PISTILLI, CASHMAN & WEST.
Friend Is Dying
Sweet City Song

CASSIDY, David
Cherish
How Can I Be Sure
Rock Me Baby

CASSIDY, Shaun
Bad Boy
Da Doo Ron Ron
Do You Believe In Magic
Hey, Deanie
Rip It Up
That's Rock 'N Roll

CASTELLS
Sacred
So This Is Love

CASTLE, Joann
Pagan Love Song

CATHY JEAN & THE ROOM-
MATES
Please Love Me Forever

CHAD & JEREMY
Early Mornin' Rain

CHALLENGERS
Sunshine Of Your Love

CHAMBERLAIN, Richard
Hi-Lili, Hi-Lo

CHAMBERS BROTHERS
Blues Get Off My Shoulder
Johnny B. Goode

CHANDLER, Gene
Duke Of Earl
Get Down (J. Thompson)

CHANNEL, Bruce
Hey Baby

CHANTAYS
Pipeline

CHANTELS
Maybe

CHAPIN, Harry
Cat's In The Cradle
Circles
I Want To Learn A Love Song
Tangled Up Puppet

CHARLES, Jimmy
Million To One

CHARLES, Ray
Blues In The Night
Come Back Baby
Don't You Know
Greenbacks
Hallelujah I Love Her (Him) So
Hit The Road Jack
I Got A Woman
Let The Good Times Roll
Mess Around
One Mint Julep
Sun's Gonna Shine Again
That Lucky Old Sun
Understanding
What'd I Say

CHARLIE DANIELS BAND
Devil Went Down To Georgia
In America
Legend Of Wooley Swamp
Mississippi
South's Gonna Do It
Texas

CHARMS
Hearts Of Stone
Ling Ting Tong

CHEAP TRICK
Ain't That A Shame
Dream Police
I Want You To Want Me
Surrender (R. Nielson)
Voices

CHECKER, Chubby
Let's Twist Again
Ooh Poo Pah Doo
Twist

CHEEKS, Judy
Mellow Lovin'

CHER. See also SONNY & CHER.
Alfie
Am I Blue
Dark Lady
Fire And Rain
Gypsys, Tramps And Thieves
Half Breed
I Saw A Man And He Danced
  With His Wife
Knock On Wood
Rescue Me
Take Me Home
Wasn't It Good

CHIC
Dance, Dance, Dance (Yowsah,
  Yowsah, Yowsah)
Everybody Dance
Good Times
I Want Your Love
Le Freak
My Feet Keep Dancing
My Forbidden Lover

CHICAGO
Alive Again
Baby, What A Big Surprise
Beginnings
Call On Me
Colour My World
Does Anybody Really Know What
  Time It Is
Feelin' Stronger Every Day
If You Leave Me Now
Just You 'N' Me
Little One
Make Me Smile
No Tell Lover
Saturday In The Park
Searchin' So Long
25 Or 6 To 4
Wishing You Were Here
You Are On My Mind

CHICK COREA AND RETURN TO
FOREVER
Spain

CHIFFONS
Da Doo Ron Ron
One Fine Day
Sweet Talkin' Guy

CHI-LITES
Twelfth Of Never
Yes I'm Ready

CHILLY
Friday On My Mind

CHOCOLATE MILK
Action Speaks Louder Than
  Words

CHORDETTES
Lollipop
Mister Sandman
Never On Sunday

CHORDS
Sh-Boom

CHRISTIE, Lou
Lightnin' Strikes
Two Faces Have I

CHUCK BROWN & THE SOUL
SEARCHERS
Bustin' Loose (Part I)

CHUCK JACKSON & MAXINE
BROWN. See also BROWN,
Maxine.
Something You Got

CHURCH, Eugene
Pretty Girls Everywhere

CITY BOY
5. 7. 0. 5

C.J. & CO.
Devil's Gun

CLANTON, Jimmy
Just A Dream

CLAPTON, Eric
After Midnight
Badge
Bell Bottom Blues
Bottle Of Red Wine
Hello Old Friend
I Shot The Sheriff
Lay Down Sally
Layla
Let It Rain
Lovin' You Lovin' Me
Promises
Spoonful
Sunshine Of Your Love
We're All The Way

CLARK, Claudine
Party Lights (C. Clark)

CLARK, Dave. See DAVE CLARK
FIVE.

CLARK, Dee
Raindrops

CLARK, Petula
My Love (T. Hatch)
Wedding Song (There Is Love)

CLARKE, Kenny
I Married An Angel

CLASSICS IV. See DENNIS YOST
& THE CLASSICS IV.

CLEFTONES
Little Girl Of Mine

CLIFFORD, Buzz
Baby Sittin' Boogie

CLIFFORD, Linda
Runaway Love

CLIMAX
Precious And Few

CLIMAX BLUES BAND
Seventh Son

CLOUT
Substitute

CLOVERS
Devil Or Angel
Don't You Know I Love You
Down In The Alley
Fool, Fool, Fool
Hey, Doll Baby
Hey, Miss Fannie
Love Love Love
Love Potion Number Nine
Lovey Dovey
One Mint Julep
Yes, It's You

COASTERS
Charlie Brown
Poison Ivy
Searchin'
Smokey Joe's Cafe
Yakety Yak
Young Blood (J. Leiber, M.
Stoller & D. Pomus)

COCKER, Joe
Catfish
Delta Lady
Lawdy, Miss Clawdy
Let's Go Get Stoned
Letter (W. Thompson)
Moon Is A Harsh Mistress
She Came In Through The
Bathroom Window
Superstar (L. Russell & B.
Bramlett)
With A Little Help From My
Friends
You Are So Beautiful

COFFEY, Dennis
Scorpio
Taurus

COHEN, Leonard
Bird On A Wire
Bunch Of Lonesome Heroes
Butcher
Hey, That's No Way To Say
Goodbye
Lady Midnight
Master Song
Old Revolution
One Of Us Can Not Be Wrong
Priests
Seems So Long Ago, Nancy
Sisters Of Mercy
So Long, Marianne
Stories Of The Street
Story Of Isaac
Stranger Song
Suzanne
Teachers
Tonight Will Be Fine
Winter Lady
You Know Who I Am

COLD BLOOD
You Got Me Hummin'

COLE, Nat King
Because You're Mine
Honeysuckle Rose

COLE, Natalie
Party Lights (T. Stephens)
Someone That I Used To Love
Stairway To The Stars

COLLINS, Judy
Amazing Grace
Both Sides Now
Bottle Of Wine
Bread And Roses
Brother Can You Spare A Dime
Carry It On
Chelsea Morning
Cook With Honey
Deportee
Early Mornin' Rain
Hard Loving Loser
I Didn't Know About You
Ice Castles, Theme From
In My Life
Just Like Tom Thumb's Blues
Last Thing On My Mind
Lonesome Death Of Hattie
Carroll
Maid Of Constant Sorrow
Mama, You Been On My Mind
Masters Of War
Moon Is A Harsh Mistress
Mr. Tambourine Man
Sailor's Life
Send In The Clowns
Someday Soon
Suzanne
Thirsty Boots
Tomorrow Is A Long Time
Wild Mountain Thyme

COLTER, Jessi. See also
WAYLON JENNINGS & JESSI
COLTER.
I'm Not Lisa
What's Happened To Blue Eyes
You Ain't Never Been Loved

COLTRANE, Chi
Thunder And Light'ning

COLTRANE, John
Spring Is Here
Stairway To The Stars

COMMANDER CODY & THE
LOST PLANET AIRMEN
Don't Let Go
Hot Rod Lincoln
Rip It Up

COMMODORES
Brick House
Easy

Fancy Dancer
Flying High
Just To Be Close To You
Machine Gun
Sail On
Still
Sweet Love
Three Times A Lady
Wonderland

COMO, Perry
And I Love You So
It's Impossible
Ko Ko Mo (I Love You So)

CON FUNK SHUN
Ffun
Shake And Dance With Me

CONIFF, Ray. See RAY
CONIFF SINGERS.

CONLEY, Arthur
Funky Street
Shake, Rattle And Roll

CONSUMER RAPPORT
Ease On Down The Road

CONTI, Bill
Gonna Fly Now
Redemption
Unmarried Woman, Theme From

CONTOURS
Do You Love Me

COOKE, Sam
Another Saturday Night
Bring It On Home To Me
I'll Come Running Back To You
Send Me Some Lovin'
Shake
That's It, I Quit, I'm Movin' On

COOLIDGE, Rita. See also KRIS
KRISTOFFERSON & RITA
COOLIDGE.
Higher And Higher
Hungry Years
I'd Rather Leave While I'm In
Love
Love Me Again
Way You Do The Things You Do
We're All Alone
When You're Loved
You (T. Snow)

COOPER, Alice
Billion Dollar Babies
Eighteen
Elected
From The Inside
How You Gonna See Me Now
I Never Cry
Muscle Of Love
No More Mister Nice Guy

Only Women Bleed
School's Out
Welcome To My Nightmare
You And Me

COREA, Chick. See CHICK
COREA & RETURN TO
FOREVER.

CORNELIUS BROTHERS &
SISTER ROSE
Don't Ever Be Lonely
I'm Never Gonna Be Alone
Anymore
Too Late To Turn Back Now
Treat Her Like A Lady

COSTA, Don
Never On Sunday

COTTON, Gene
Like A Sunday In Salem

COUNTRY JOE & THE FISH
I Feel Like I'm Fixin' To Die
Rag

COVEN
One Tin Soldier

CRADDOCK, Billy "Crash"
Knock Three Times

CRAMER, Floyd
It Was Almost Like A Song
It's A Heartache
Nadia's Theme

CRAWFORD, Randy
At Last

CREAM
Badge
Sitting On Top Of The World
Spoonful
Sunshine Of Your Love

CREEDENCE CLEARWATER
REVIVAL
Bad Moon Rising
Down On The Corner
Fortunate Son
Have You Ever Seen The Rain
I Heard It Through The Grape-
vine
I Put A Spell On You (J.
Hawkins)
Long As I Can See The Light
Lookin' Out My Back Door
Proud Mary
Someday Never Comes
Susie-Q
Sweet Hitch-Hiker
Travelin' Band
Who'll Stop The Rain

CRESCENDOS
Oh Julie

CRESTS
Sixteen Candles

CREW CUTS
Ko Ko Mo (I Love You So)
Sh-Boom

CROCE, Jim
Bad, Bad Leroy Brown
I Got A Name
I'll Have To Say I Love You In
A Song
One Less Set Of Footsteps
Operator (That's Not The Way
It Feels)
Time In A Bottle
Workin' At The Car Wash Blues
You Don't Mess Around With
Jim

CROSBY, David. See DAVID
CROSBY & GRAHAM NASH;
CROSBY, STILLS & NASH.

CROSBY, STILLS & NASH
Dark Star
Fair Game
Long Time Gone
See The Changes
Suite: Judy Blue Eyes
Wooden Ships

CROSBY, STILLS, NASH &
YOUNG
Carry On
Country Girl
Cowgirl In The Sand
4 + 20
Guinnevere
Helpless
Helplessly Hoping
Long Time Gone
Love The One You're With
Marrakesh Express
Suite: Judy Blue Eyes
Teach Your Children
Wooden Ships
Woodstock

CROSS, Christopher
Never Be The Same
Ride Like The Wind
Sailing (C. Cross)

CROWS
Gee

CRUISE, Pablo. See PABLO
CRUISE.

CRUSADERS
Street Life

CUFF LINKS
Run Sally Run

CUMMINGS, Burton
Stand Tall
You Ain't Seen Nothing Yet

CY COLEMAN CO-OP
What Are Heavy

CYMBAL, Johnny. See also
DEREK.
Mr. Bass Man

CYRKLES
Red Rubber Ball

D. GOOD AND G. PLENTY
Sunny And Me

DALE & GRACE
I'm Leaving It (All) Up to You

DAMNED
New Rose

DAN FOGELBERG & TIM
WEISBERG. See Also
FOGELBERG, Dan.
Tell Me To My Face

DANIELS, Charlie. See CHARLIE
DANIELS BAND.

DANLEERS
One Summer Night

DANNY & THE JUNIORS
At The Hop
Rock And Roll Is Here To Stay

DANTE'S INFERNO
Brand New Key

DARIN, Bobby
Blue Monday
Dream Lover
Happy (S. Robinson &
M. Legrand)
If I Were A Carpenter
Mack The Knife
Simple Song Of Freedom
Splish Splash

DARRELL, Johnny
With Pen In Hand

DARREN, James
Gidget

DAVE & SUGAR
It's A Heartache

DAVE CLARK FIVE
Any Way You Want It (D. Clark)

Catch Us If You Can
Glad All Over
I Like It Like That (C. Kenner &
A. Toussaint)
Over And Over (R. Byrd)
Reelin' And Rockin'

DAVE, DEE, DOZY, BEAKY,
MICK & TICH
Legend Of Xanadu

DAVE VAN RONK & THE HUDSON
DUSTERS. See VAN RONK,
Dave.

DAVID BROMBERG BAND. See
BROMBERG, David.

DAVID CROSBY & GRAHAM
NASH. See also CROSBY,
STILLS & NASH; NASH,
Graham.
Immigration Man
Out Of The Darkness
Southbound Train

DAVIDSON, John
Every Time I Sing A Love Song

DAVIS, Billy, Jr. See MARILYN
MC COO & BILLY DAVIS JR.

DAVIS, Mac
Baby Don't Get Hooked On Me
I Believe In Music
Music In My Life
Stop And Smell The Roses
Superstar (L. Russell & B.
Bramlett)
Watchin' Scotty Grow

DAVIS, Miles
Diane (E. Rapee & L. Pollack)
Whispering

DAVIS, Paul
Sweet Life

DAVIS, Rev. Gary
Candy Man (G. Davis)
If I Had My Way

DAVIS, Sammy, Jr.
Candy Man (L. Bricusse & A.
Newley)
Mr. Bojangles
Night And Day

DAVIS, Spencer. See SPENCER
DAVIS GROUP.

DAVIS, Tyrone
Turn Back The Hands Of Time
DAWN. See also TONY
ORLANDO & DAWN.
Candida
Knock Three Times

DAY, Bobby
Rockin' Robin

DEAD BOYS
All This & More (J. Zero)
I Won't Look Back
Little Girl
Sonic Reducer

DEE, Kiki. See ELTON JOHN &
KIKI DEE.

DEEP PURPLE
Burn
Smoke On The Water

DEES, Michael
What Are You Doing The Rest
Of Your Life

DEES, Rick. See RICK DEES &
HIS CAST OF FRIENDS.

DE FRANCO, Tony
Heartbeat, It's A Love Beat

DE FRANCO FAMILY
Save The Last Dance For Me

DEL VIKINGS
Come Go With Me
Whispering Bells

DELANEY & BONNIE
Long Tall Sally
Never Ending Song Of Love
What The World Needs Now Is
Love

DELFONICS
Didn't I (Blow Your Mind This
Time)
When You Get Right Down To It

DELIGHTS
Maybe

DELIVERANCE. See ERIC
WEISSBERG & DELIVERANCE.

DELLS
Oh, What A Night

DENIECE WILLIAMS & JOHNNY
MATHIS. See JOHNNY MATHIS
& DENIECE WILLIAMS.

DENNIS YOST & THE CLASSICS
IV
Spooky
Stormy
Traces
Where Did All The Good Times
Go

DENVER, John. See also JOHN
DENVER & THE MUPPETS.
Annie's Song
Calypso
Rocky Mountain High
Sunshine On My Shoulder
Take Me Home, Country Roads
Thank God I'm A Country Boy
Today
Whose Garden Was This

DEODATO
Also Sprach Zarathustra (2001)
Rhapsody In Blue
Star Trek, Theme From
Super Strut

DEREK. See also CYMBAL,
Johnny.
Back Door Man

DEREK & THE DOMINOES
Anyday
I Looked Away
Layla

DE SARIO, Teri. See TERI DE
SARIO & K.C.

DE SHANNON, Jackie
Brighton Hill
Needles And Pins
Put A Little Love In Your Heart
What The World Needs Now Is
Love

DETROIT EMERALDS
Treat Her Like A Lady

DE VILLE, Mink
Cadillac Walk

DEVO
Jocko Homo

DE VORZON, Barry. See
BARRY DE VORZON & PERRY
BOTKIN JR.

DIAMOND, Gregg
Dance Little Dreamer
Fess Up To The Boogie
Risky Changes
Starcruiser

DIAMOND, Neil. See also
BARBRA STREISAND & NEIL
DIAMOND.
And The Grass Won't Pay No
Mind
Beautiful Noise
Brooklyn Roads
Cherry, Cherry
Cracklin' Rosie
Desiree
Do It
Forever In Blue Jeans

He Ain't Heavy...He's My
Brother
I Am...I Said
Last Thing On My Mind
Say Maybe
September Morn
Solitary Man
Song Sung Blue
Stagger Lee
Sweet Caroline
Until It's Time For You To Go

DIAMONDS
Little Darlin'
Stroll

DIANA ROSS & MICHAEL JACK-
SON. See also JACKSON,
Michael; ROSS, Diana.
Ease On Down The Road

DIANA ROSS & THE SUPREMES.
See also ROSS, Diana;
SUPREMES.
I'm Gonna Make You Love Me
Love Is Here And Now You're
Gone
Some Things You Never Get
Used To

DIDDLEY, Bo
Bo Diddley
Call Me (E. McDaniel)
Road Runner (E. McDaniel)

DINAH WASHINGTON & BROOK
BENTON. See BROOK BENTON
& DIANE WASHINGTON.

DION
Abraham, Martin And John
Ruby Baby
Stagger Lee
Wanderer (E. Maresca)

DIONNE WARWICK & ISAAC
HAYES. See ISAAC HAYES &
DIONNE WARWICK.

DIRE STRAITS
Sultans Of Swing

DISCO TEX & HIS SEX-O-LETTER
Get Dancin'

DMZ
Don't Jump Me Mother
Mighty Idy

DOBKINS, Carl
My Heart Is An Open Book

DOE, Ernie K.
Mother-In-law

DOGGETT, Bill
Honky Tonk (Parts I & II)

DOMAN, Harold
Mountain Of love

DOMINO, Fats
Ain't That A Shame
All By Myself (A. Domino & D.
Bartholomew)
Be My Guest
Blue Monday
Blueberry Hill
Bo Weevil
I Hear You Knocking
I Want To Walk You Home
I Want You To Know
I'm A Fool For You
I'm Gonna Be A Wheel Someday
I'm In Love Again
I'm In The Mood For Love
I'm Walkin'
Let The Four Winds Blow
My Girl Josephine
Poor Me
Valley Of Tears
Whole Lotta Loving

DON ELLIS & SURVIVAL
Star Wars

DONALDSON, Bo. See BO DON-
ALDSON & THE HEYWOODS.

DONNY & MARIE OSMOND. See
also OSMOND, Donnie;
OSMOND, Marie; OSMONDS.
Ain't Nothing Like The Real
Thing
Deep Purple
I'm Leaving It (All) Up To You
Make The World Go Away
Morningside Of The Mountain

DONNY HATHAWAY & ROBERTA
FLACK. See ROBERTA FLACK
& DONNY HATHAWAY.

DONOVAN
Catch The Wind
Colours
Mellow Yellow
Sunshine Superman

DOOBIE BROTHERS
Black Water
Captain And Me
China Grove
Dependin' On You
Echoes Of Love
Eyes Of Silver
Here To Love You
It Keeps You Runnin'
Jesus Is Just Alright
Listen To The Music
Little Darling (I Need You)
Long Train Runnin'
Minute By Minute
One Step Closer
Real Love

Takin' It To The Streets
What A Fool Believes

DOORS
Back Door Man
Blue Sunday
Close To You (W. Dixon)
Indian Summer
Land Ho
Light My Fire
Maggie M' Gill
Peace Frog
Queen Of The Highway
Roadhouse Blues
Ship Of Fools (J. Morrison & The Doors)
Spy
Waiting For The Sun
Who Do You Love
You Make Me Real

DORE, Charlie
Pilot Of The Airwaves

DORSEY, Lee
Ya Ya

DOTTIE WEST & KENNY ROGERS. See KENNY ROGERS & DOTTIE WEST.

DOUBLE EXPOSURE
Ten Percent

DOUGLAS, Carol
Doctor's Orders

DOVELLS
Bristol Stomp
You Can't Sit Down

DOZIER, Lamont
It's The Same Old Song

DR. FEELGOOD
I Can Tell

DR. HOOK
Better Love Next Time
Ooh Poo Pah Doo
Sexy Eyes
Sharing The Night Together
When You're In Love With A BeautifulWoman

DR. JOHN
Right Place Wrong Time

DRAKE, Guy
Welfare Cadillac

DRAMATICS
Whatcha See Is Whatcha Get

DRIFTERS
Dance With Me (L. Lebish, G. Treadwell, I. Nahan & E. Glick)
Fools Fall In Love
Honey Love
I Count The Tears
On Broadway
Ruby Baby
Save The Last Dance For Me
Steamboat
Sweets For My Sweet
There Goes My Baby
This Magic Moment
True Love, True Love
Under The Boardwalk
Up On The Roof

DUPREES
Have You Heard

DYLAN, Bob. See also BOB DYLAN & JOAN BAEZ; BOB DYLAN & THE BAND.
Absolutely Sweet Marie
All Along The Watchtower
All I Really Want To Do
All The Tired Horses
As I Went Out One Morning
Ballad Of Frankie Lee And Judas Priest
Billy
Black Diamond Bay
Blowin' In The Wind
Blue Moon
Bob Dylan's Blues
Buckets Of Rain
Chimes Of Freedom
Copper Kettle (The Pale Moonlight)
Country Pie
Day Of The Locusts
Dear Landlord
Dirge
Don't Think Twice, It's All Right
Down Along The Cove
Drifter's Escape
Early Mornin' Rain
Father Of Night
Forever Young
Fourth Time Around
Gates Of Eden
George Jackson
Girl From North Country
Going, Going, Gone
Gotta Serve Somebody
Gotta Travel On
Hard Rain's A Gonna Fall
Highway 61 Revisited
Hurricane
I Am A Lonesome Hobo
I Dreamed I Saw St. Augustine
I Pity The Poor Immigrant
I Shall Be Released
I Threw It All Away
I Want You
Idiot Wind
If Dogs Run Free
If Not For You
If You See Her Say Hello
I'll Be Your Baby Tonight

Isis
It Ain't Me, Babe
It's All Over Now, Baby Blue
It's Alright Ma
Joey
John Wesley Harding
Just Like A Woman
Just Like Tom Thumb's Blues
Knockin' On Heaven's Door
Lay, Lady, Lay
Leopard-Skin Pill-Box Hat
Like A Rolling Stone
Lily, Rosemary And The Jack Of Hearts
Living The Blues
Lonesome Death Of Hattie Carroll
Maggie's Farm
Mama, You Been On My mind
Man In Me
Masters Of War
Meet Me In The Morning
Minstrel Boy
Most Likely You Go Your Way
Mozambique
Mr. Tambourine Man
My Back Pages
Nashville Skyline Rag
Never Say Goodbye
New Morning
Nobody 'Cept You
Obviously Five Believers
Oh, Sister
On A Night Like This
One More Cup Of Coffee
One More Night
One More Weekend
One Of Us Must Know
Only A Pawn In Their Game
Peggy Day
Playboys And Playgirls
Pledging My Time
Positively 4th Street
Rainy Day Women #12 & 35
Romance In Durango
Sad Eyed Lady Of The Lowlands
Sara (B. Dylan)
She Belongs To Me
Shelter From The Storm
Sign On The Window
Simple Twist Of Fate
Something There Is About You
Stuck Inside Of Mobile With The Memphis Blues Again
Subterranean Homesick Blues
Talking Folklore Center
Tangled Up In Blue
Tears Of rage
Tell Me That It Isn't true
Temporary Like Achilles
Three Angels
Time Passes Slowly
Times They Are A-Changin'
To Be Alone With You
Tomorrow Is A Long Time
Tonight I'll Be Staying Here With You

Tough Mama
Visions Of Johanna
Wanted Man
Watching The River Flow
Wedding Song
Went To See The Gypsy
When I Paint My Masterpiece
When The Ship Comes In
Wicked Messenger
Wigwam
Winterlude
With God On Our Side
Woogie-Boogie
You Angel You
You're A Big Girl Now
You're Gonna Make Me Lonesome
    When You Go

DYNAMIC SUPERIORS
    Release Me (N. Ashford & V.
        Simpson)
    Shoe, Shoe Shine

EAGLES
    After The Thrill Is Gone
    Already Gone
    Best Of My Love (D. Henley, G.
        Frey & J.D. Souther)
    Desperado
    Heartache Tonight
    Hotel California
    I Can't Tell You Why
    I Wish You Peace
    Life In The Fast Lane
    Long Run
    Lyin' Eyes
    New Kid In Town
    Ol' 55
    One Of These Nights
    Peaceful Easy Feeling
    Please Come Home For
        Christmas
    Take It Easy
    Take It To The Limit
    Tequila Sunrise
    Witchy Woman

EARTH, WIND & FIRE
    After The Love Has Gone
    Best Of My love (M. White & A
        McKay)
    Boogie Wonderland
    Can't Hide Love
    Evil
    Fantasy
    Getaway
    Got To Get You Into My Life
    Love Music
    Reasons
    September
    Serpentine Fire
    Shining Star (M. White, P. Bailey
        & L. Dunn)
    Singasong
    Star
    That's The Way Of The World

EASYBEATS
    Friday On My Mind

EDDIE & THE HOTRODS
    Do Anything, You Wanna Do

EDGAR WINTER GROUP
    Frankenstein
    Free Ride
    Hangin' Round
    Rock And Roll Hootchie Koo
    Tobacco Road

EDMUNDS, Dave
    I Hear You Knocking

EDSELS
    Rama Lama Ding Dong

EDWARD BEAR
    Last Song

EDWARDS, Jonathan
    Beautiful Sunday
    Sunshine (Go Away Today)

EDWARDS, Tommy
    Love Is All We Need

EDWIN HAWKINS SINGERS
    Oh Happy Day

EGAN, Walter
    Hot Summer Nights

ELECTRIC LIGHT ORCHESTRA
    Do Ya
    Don't Bring Me Down
    Evil Woman
    Last Train To London
    Livin' Thing
    Roll Over Beethoven
    Shine A Little Love
    Showdown
    Strange Music
    Sweet Talkin' Woman
    Telephone Line
    Turn To Stone

ELEGANTS
    Little Star

ELGINS
    Heaven Must Have Sent You

ELLIMAN, Yvonne
    Hello Stranger
    Love Me

ELLINGTON, Duke
    Honeysuckle Rose
    Misty

ELLIS, Don. See DON ELLIS &
SURVIVAL.

ELLIS, Shirley
    Name Game

ELO. See ELECTRIC LIGHT
ORCHESTRA.

ELTON JOHN & KIKI DEE. See
also JOHN, Elton.
    Don't Go Breaking My Heart

EMERALDS
    Paloma Blanca
    Yellow Bird

EMERSON, LAKE & PALMER
    Maple Leaf Rag

EMOTIONS
    Ain't No Sunshine
    Best Of My Love (M. White & A.
        McKay)
    Show Me How

ENCHANTMENT
    Gloria
    It's You That I Need

ENGLAND DAN & JOHN FORD
COLEY
    Gone Too Far
    I'd Really Love To See You To-
        night
    If The World Ran Out Of Love
    Love Is The Answer (T. Rundgren)
    Nights Are Forever Without You
    We'll Never Have To Say Good-
        bye Again

ERIC BURDON & WAR. See also
BURDON, Eric.
    Spill The Wine

ERIC WEISSBERG & DELIVER-
ANCE
    Duelling Banjos

ERUPTION
    I Can't Stand The Rain
    Way We Were

ESSEX
    Walkin' Miracle

ESTHER & ABI OFARIM
    Cinderella Rockefella

EVANS, Paul
    Seven Little Girls Sitting In The
        Back Seat

EVERLY BROTHERS
    All I Have To Do Is Dream
    Bird Dog
    Bye Bye, Love
    Devoted To You
    Poor Jenny
    Problems
    Wake Up Little Susie

EXILE
  Kiss You All Over

FABARES, Shelly
  Johnny Angel

FABRIC, Bent
  Alley Cat Song

FAITH, Percy
  M*A*S*H*, Song From
  Summer Place 76

FAITHFUL, Marianne
  As Tears Go By

FALCONS
  You're So Fine

FANTASTIC JOHNNY C
  Boogaloo Down Broadway
  Some Kind Of Wonderful

FARGO, Donna
  Funny Face
  Gone At Last
  Happiest Girl In The Whole USA

FARINA, Mimi. See MIMI &
  RICHARD FARINA.

FARINA, Richard. See also
  MIMI & RICHARD FARINA.
  Joy 'Round My Brain
  Reno Nevada

FARINA, Sandy
  Strawberry Fields Forever

FARROW, Tal
  Cabin In The Sky

FAT LARRY'S BAND
  Here Comes The Sun (A. Middle-
    ton, L. Taylor, L. James, L.
    Barry & A. Austin)

F.C.C.
  Baby I Want You

FELICIANO, Jose
  Bye Bye Blackbird
  Chico And The Man
  Light My Fire
  Susie-Q

FENDER, Freddy
  Before The Next Teardrop Falls
  I'm Leaving It (All) Up To You
  Secret Love
  Wasted Days And Wasted Nights

FERGUSON, Jay
  Shakedown Cruise
  Thunder Island

FERGUSON, Maynard
  Gonna Fly Now
  Star Trek, Theme From

FERRANTE & TEICHER
  Be My Love
  I'm In The Mood For Love
  Laura
  Stairway To The Stars

FIDDLER ON THE ROOF, Cast
  Of
  Fiddler On The Roof
  Matchmaker, Matchmaker
  Sunrise, Sunset

FIFTH DIMENSION
  Aquarius/Let The Sunshine In
  Bobbie's Blues
  California My Way
  California Soul
  Carpet Man
  Declaration
  Don't Cha Hear Me Callin' To
    Ya
  Girls Song
  Learn How To Fly
  Lovin' Stew
  Magic Garden
  Misty Roses
  Never Gonna Be The Same
  Never My Love
  One Less Bell To Answer
  Paper Cup
  Pattern People
  People Got To Be free
  Poor Side Of Town
  Requiem; 820 Latham
  Rosecrans Boulevard
  Sailboat Song
  Save The Country
  Stoned Soul Picnic
  Sweet Blindness
  Up, Up And Away
  Wedding Bell Blues
  Which Way To Nowhere
  Worst That Could Happen

FINNEGAN, Larry
  Dear One

FIREBALLS
  Bottle Of Wine

FIREFALL
  Cinderella
  Goodbye I Love You
  Just Remember I Love You
  Livin' Ain't Livin'
  So Long
  Strange Way
  You Are The Woman

FIREHOUSE 5 PLUS 2
  Pagan Love Song

FITZGERALD, Ella
  Honeysuckle Rose
  I'm Walkin'
  Lullaby Of Birdland
  Misty

FIVE AMERICANS
  No Communication

FIVE FLIGHTS UP
  Do What You Wanna Do

FIVE KEYS
  Ling Ting Tong
  Out Of Sight, Out Of Mind

FIVE MAN ELECTRICAL BAND
  Signs

FIVE SATINS
  In The Still Of The Night
  To The Aisle

FIVE STAIRSTEPS
  Dear Prudence

FLACK, Roberta. See also
  ROBERTA FLACK & DONNY
  HATHAWAY.
  Feel Like Makin' Love
  First Time Ever I Saw Your Face
  For All We Know
  If Ever I See You Again
  Jesse (J. Ian)
  Killing Me Softly With His Song
  When It's Over
  Will You Love Me Tomorrow
  You Are My Heaven

FLAMIN' GROOVIES
  Shake Some Action
  Werewolves Of London
  Yes, It's True
  You Tore Me Down

FLAMINGOS
  I Only Have Eyes For You

FLEETWOOD MAC
  Bare Trees
  Chain
  Don't Stop
  Dreams
  Go Your Own Way
  Over & Over (C. McVie)
  Over My Head
  Rhiannon
  Sara (S. Nicks)
  Say You Love Me
  Sentimental Lady
  Songbird (C. McVie)
  That's All For Everyone
  Think About Me
  Tusk
  You Make Loving Fun

FLEETWOODS
Come Softly To Me
Mr. Blue

FLOATERS
Float On

FLOYD, Eddie
Knock On Wood

FLOYD, King
Groove Me

FLYING BURRITO BROS.
Bony Moronie

FOGELBERG, Dan. See also DAN
FOGELBERG & TIM WEISBERG.
Heart Hotels
Longer
Next Time
Part Of The Plan
To The Morning

FOGHAT
Third Time Lucky

FONTAINE SISTERS
I'm In Love Again

FONTANA, Wayne. See WAYNE
FONTANA & THE MINDBEND-
ERS.

FORBERT, Steve
Romeo's Tune

FORD, Frankie
Sea Cruise

FORD, Tennessee Ernie
Sixteen Tons

FOREIGNER
Blinded By Science
Blue Morning, Blue Day
Cold As Ice
Dirty White Boy
Double Vision
Feels Like The First Time
Head Games
Hot Blooded

FORTUNES
You've Got Your Troubles

FOSTER, Bruce
Platinum Heroes

FOUR ACES
Peg O' My Heart
Three Coins In The Fountain

FOUR FRESHMEN
Graduation Day

FOUR LADS
Moments To Remember

FOUR LEAVES
I Just Want To Be Your Everything

FOUR SEASONS
Big Girls Don't Cry
December 1963 (Oh, What A
Night)
Down The Hall
Sherry
Walk Like A Man
Will You Love Me Tomorrow
Workin' My Way Back To You

FOUR TOPS
Ain't No Woman
Baby I Need Your Loving
Bernadette
For Once In My Life
I Can't Help Myself
It's The Same Old Song
Reach Out I'll Be There
7 Rooms Of Gloom
Shake Me, Wake Me (When It's
Over)
Something About You
Standing In The Shadows Of Love

FOXY
Get Off

FRAMPTON, Peter
All I Want To Be (Is By Your
Side)
Baby, I Love Your Way
Baby (Somethin's Happening)
I Can't Stand It No More
It's A Plain Shame
Jumpin' Jack Flash
Road Runner (E. Holland, L.
Dozier & B. Holland)
Shine On
Show Me The Way
Signed, Sealed, Delivered (I'm
Yours)

FRANCIS, Connie
Among My Souvenirs
Don't Break The Heart That
Loves You
Who's Sorry Now

FRANKIE LYMON & THE TEEN-
AGERS
ABC's Of Love
I Want You To Be My Girl
I'm Not A Juvenile Delinquent
Why Do Fools Fall In Love

FRANKLIN, Aretha
Angel (W. Saunders & C. Frank-
lin)
Border Song
Didn't I Blow Your Mind This Time
Don't Play That Song
I Say A Little Prayer
Love The One You're With
Reach Out And Touch
Respect
See Saw
Since You've Been Gone
Something He Can Feel
Son Of A Preacher Man
Spanish Eyes
Spanish Harlem
You're All I Need To Get By

FRANKS, Michael
Popsicle Toes

FRAZIER, Dallas
Sunshine Of The World

FRED, John. See JOHN FRED &
HIS PLAYBOY BAND.

FREE
All Right Now

FREE MOVEMENT
I've Found Someone Of My Own

FREEMAN, Bobby
Betty Lou Got A New Pair Of
Shoes
Do You Want To Dance

FRIEDMAN, Dean
Ariel

FRIEND & LOVER
Reach Out In The Darkness

FRIENDS OF DISTINCTION
Love Or Let Me Be Lonely

FRIJID PINK
House Of The Rising Sun

FULLER, Jesse
San Francisco Bay Blues

FULSOM, Lowell
Let's Go Get Stoned

FUNKADELIC
One Nation Under A Groove

FUNKY KINGS
Slow Dancing

FURAY, Richie. See also
SOUTHER-HILLMAN-FURAY.
I Still Have Dreams

GABRIEL
Martha (Your Lovers Come And
Go)

GALLERY
Nice To Be With You

GARFUNKEL, Art. See also
SIMON & GARFUNKEL.
All I Know
I Believe (When I Fall In Love
It Will Be Forever)
I Only Have Eyes For You
I Shall Sing
99 Miles From L.A.
Since I Don't Have You
Wonderful World

GARLAND, Charles
Aquarius

GARLAND, Judy
Singin' In The Rain

GARNETT, Gale
We'll Sing In The Sunshine

GARRETT, Leif
Bad To Me
I Was Made For Dancin'

GARTER, Clarence
I'd Rather Go Blind

GARY, John
Eres Tu
Yellow Bird

GARY LEWIS & THE PLAYBOYS.
See also LEWIS, Gary.
Sure Gonna Miss Her

GARY PUCKETT & THE UNION
GAP
Lady Willpower
Young Girl

GARY, TOMS' EMPIRE
7-6-5-4-3-2-1

GATES, David
Goodbye Girl
Took The Last Train
Where Does The Lovin' Go

GATLIN, Larry
After The Storm

GAYE, Marvin. See also
MARVIN GAYE & TAMMI
TERRELL.
After The Dance
Ain't That Peculiar
Baby Don't You Do It
Got To Give It Up (Part I)
Hitch Hike
How Sweet It Is (To Be Loved
By You)
I Heard It Through The Grape-
vine
I'll Be Doggone

Inner City Blues
Let's Get It On
Little Darlin' (I Need You)
Mercy, Mercy Me
Pride And Joy
Stubborn Kind Of Fellow
That's The Way Love Is
Too Busy Thinking About My
Baby
Try It Baby
What's Going On
You're A Wonderful One

GAYLE, Crystal
Don't It Make My Brown Eyes
Blue
Half The Way
It's Like We Never Said Goodbye
Ready For The Times To Get
Better
Someday Soon
Talkin' In Your Sleep
Why Have You Left The One
(You Left Me For)

GAYNOR, Gloria
I Will Survive
Let Me Know (I Have A Right)
Never Can Say Goodbye

GENESIS
Misunderstanding
Your Own Special Way

GENTRY, Bobbie. See GLEN
CAMPBELL & BOBBIE GENTRY.

GEORGE, Barbara
I Know

McCRAE, George & Gwen
Change With The Times

GEORGIA SEA ISLAND SINGERS
Come By Here

GERRY & THE PACEMAKERS
Reelin' And Rockin'
Rip It Up

GIBB, Andy. See also ANDY
GIBB & OLIVIA NEWTON-JOHN.
Desire
Don't Throw It All Away
I Just Want To Be Your Every-
thing
Shadow Dancing
Thicker Than Water

GIBB, Robin
Oh Darling

GIBBS, Georgia
Arrivederci, Roma
Tweedlee Dee

GILDER, Nick
Hot Child In The City
Rock Me

GILLEY, Mickey
Room Full Of Roses

GILMER, Jimmy. See JIMMY
GILMER & THE FIREBALLS.

GILSTRAP, Jim
Swing Your Daddy

GLADYS KNIGHT & THE PIPS.
See also KNIGHT, Gladys.
Baby Don't Change Your Mind
Daddy Could Swear, I Declare
End Of Our Road
For Once In My Life
Here I Am Again
I Can See Clearly Now
I Don't Want To Do Wrong
I Heard It Through The Grape-
vine
I Wish It Would Rain
If I Were Your Woman
I'll Be There
Imagination
Letter Full Of Tears
Love Finds Its Own Way
Midnight Train To Georgia
Neither One Of Us
Nitty Gritty
Once In A Lifetime Thing
There's A Lesson To Be Learned
Way We Were
Where Peaceful Waters Flow
You're The Best Thing That
Ever Happened To Me

GLASS BOTTLE
Love For Living

GLEN CAMPBELL & BOBBIE
GENTRY. See also CAMPBELL,
Glen; GENTRY, Bobbie.
All I Have To Do Is Dream
Let It Be Me

GODSPELL, Cast Of
Day By Day (S. Schwartz)

GOLD, Andrew
Do Wah Diddy Diddy
How Can This Be Love
Lonely Boy (A. Gold)
Never Let Her Slip Away
One Of Them Is Me
Thank You For Being A Friend

GOLDEN GATE
Diane (B. Carl, R. Whitelaw &
R. Bell)

GOLDSBORO, Bobby
Autumn Of My Life
Butterfly For Bucky

Honey (B. Russell)
I'm A Drifter
Muddy Mississippi Line
See The Funny Little Clown
Summer
Watchin' Scotty Grow
With Pen In Hand

GOMM, Ian
Hold On

GONZALEZ
Ain't No Way To Treat A Lady
Haven't Stopped Dancing Yet

GOODMAN, Steve
City Of New Orleans

GOODY GOODY
#1 Dee Jay

GOOFUS FIVE
Vo-Do-Do-De-O Blues

GORE, Lesley
Judy's Turn To Cry
You Don't Own Me

GORME, Eydie
Softly, As I Leave You

GOULET, Robert
Old Cape Cod

G.Q.
Boogie Oogie Oogie
Disco Nights
Standing Ovation

GRAHAM CENTRAL STATION
I Can't Stand The Rain

GRAND FUNK
Closer To Home
Loco-Motion
Shinin' On
Some Kind Of Wonderful
We're An American Band

GRASS ROOTS
Feelings (R. Coonce, W. Entner
& K. Fukomoto)
Midnight Confessions
Temptation Eyes
Walking Through The Country

GRATEFUL DEAD
Attics Of My Life
Black Peter
Blues For Allah
Box Of Rain
Brokedown Palace
Candyman (J. Garcia & R.
Hunter)
Casey Jones
China Doll
Crazy Fingers

Cumberland Blues
Dire Wolf
Easy Wind
Eyes Of The World
Franklin's Tower
Friend Of The Devil
Good Lovin'
Help On The Way
Here Comes Sunshine
High Time
Johnny B. Goode
Let Me Sing Your Blues Away
Loose Lucy
Mississippi Half Step Uptown
Toodleoo
Money Money
Music Never Stopped
New Speedway Boogie
Operator (R. McKernan)
Pride Of Cucamonga
Ripple
Row Jimmy
Scarlet Begonias
Shakedown Street
Ship Of Fools (R. Hunter & J.
Garcia)
Stagger Lee
Stella Blue
Sugar Magnolia
Till The Morning Comes
Truckin'
Unbroken Chain
Uncle John's Band
U.S. Blues
Weather Report I
Weather Report II; Let It Grow

GRAVENITIES, Nick
Gypsy Good Time

GRAY, Dobie
Drift Away

GREAN, Charles Randolph
Masterpiece

GREEN, Al
Belle
Call Me (Come Back Home)
I'm Still In Love With You (A.
Green, W. Mitchell & A. Jack-
son)
Let's Stay Together
Love And Happiness
To Sir, With Love

GREY & HANKS
Dancin'

GROSS, Henry
Shannon
Springtime Mama

GUESS WHO
Shakin' All Over
These Eyes

GUTHRIE, Arlo
Alice's Restaurant
Any Time
Chilling Of The Evening
City Of New Orleans
Coming In To Los Angeles
Deportee
Every Hand In The Land
Highway In The Wind
If You Would Just Drop By
I'm Going Home
John Looked Down
Kisses Sweeter Than Wine
Last Night I Had The Strangest
Dream
Meditation
Midnight Special
Motorcycle Song
My Front Pages
Now And Then
Oh, In The Morning
Pause Of Mr. Clause
Ring Around A Rosy Rag
Rock Island Line
Running Down The Road
Standing At The Threshold
Stealin'
Wheel Of Fortune
When The Ship Comes In
Wouldn't You Believe It

GUTHRIE, Woody
Pastures Of Plenty
Roll On Columbia
So Long It's Been Good To Know
Yuh

GWEN & GEORGE MCCRAE. See
GEORGE & GWEN MCCRAE.

HAGGARD, Merle
I Can't Be Myself
Okie From Muskogee

HAGGERS, Loretta. See
PLACE, Mary Kay.

HAIR, Cast Of
Aquarius
Good Morning Sunshine
Manchester England

HALEY, Bill. See BILL HALEY &
THE COMETS.

HALL & OATES
Sara Smile

HAMILTON, George, IV
Why Don't They Understand

HAMILTON, JOE FRANK &
DENNISON
Light Up The World With Sun-
shine

HAMILTON, JOE FRANK &
REYNOLDS
Don't Pull Your Love

HAMLISCH, Marvin
Entertainer (S. Joplin)
What I Did For Love

HAMMOND, Albert
It Never Rains In Southern California
99 Miles From L.A.

HAMMOND, John
Don't Start Me Talkin'
I Can Tell
Seventh Son

HANDY, John
Hard Work

HAPPENINGS
Go Away Little Girl
See You In September

HARDIN, Tim
If I Were A Carpenter
Misty Roses
Reason To Believe
Soft Summer Breeze

HARDY, Hagood
Homecoming

HARLO WILCOX & THE OAKIES
Groovy Grubworm

HARMONICATS
Charmaine
Peg O' My Heart

HAROLD MELVIN & THE BLUE-
NOTES
Hope That We can Be Together
Soon
Prayin'
Wake Up Everybody

HARPO, Slim
Baby (Scratch My Back)

HARPTONES
I Almost Lost My Mind

HARRIS, Emmylou
Here, There And Everywhere
Too Far Gone

HARRIS, Richard
MacArthur Park

HARRIS, Thurston
Little Bitty Pretty One

HARRISON, George
All Things Must Pass
Apple Scruffs

Art Of Dying
Awaiting On You All
Ballad Of Sir Frankie Crisp
Behind That Locked Door
Beware Of Darkness
Crackerbox Palace
Give Me Love
Hear Me Lord
Here Comes The Sun (G. Harrison)
I Dig Love
I'd Have You Any Time
Isn't It A Pity
Let It Down
Love You Too
My Sweet Lord
Run Of The Mill
Something
This Song
What Is Life
While My Guitar Gently Weeps
You

HARRISON, Wilbert
Kansas City

HART, Bobby. See TOMMY
BOYCE & BOBBY HART.

HART, Freddie
Easy Loving

HARTMAN, Dan
Instant Replay

HATHAWAY, Donny. See
ROBERTA FLACK & DONNY
HATHAWAY.

HAVENS, Ritchie
Follow
Handsome Johnny
I Can't Make It Anymore
Just Like A Woman
Midnight Train
San Francisco Bay Blues

HAWKINS, Dale
Susie-Q

HAWKINS, "Screamin'" Jay
I Put A Spell On You (J. Hawkins)

HAYES, Isaac. See also ISAAC
HAYES & DIONNE WARWICK.
Do Your Thing
Don't Let Go
Don't Let Me Be Lonely Tonight
Never Can Say Goodbye
Shaft, Theme From

HEAD, Roy
Treat Her Right

HEART
Barracuda
Crazy On You

Dog & Butterfly
Dreamboat Annie
Even It Up
Heartless
Magic Man
Tell It Like It Is

HEARTBEATS
Thousand Miles Away

HEATWAVE
Always And Forever
Boogie Nights

HEBB, Bobby
Sunny (B. Hebb)

HELL, Richard
Blank Generation
Love Comes In Spurts

HELMS, Bobby
Fraulein
My Special Angel

HENDERSON, Michael
In The Night-Time
Take Me I'm Yours

HENDRICKS, Bobby
Itchy, Twitchy Feeling

HENDRIX, Jimi
Have You Ever Been (To Electric
Ladyland)
Hey Joe
Johnny B. Goode
Like A Rolling Stone
Long Hot Summer Night
Voodoo Chile

HENRY, Clarence "Frogman"
Ain't Got No Home
But I Do

HERB ALPERT & THE TIJUANA
BRASS. See also ALPERT,
Herb.
Last Tango In Paris
Taste Of Honey
What Now My love

HERMAN'S HERMITS
Can't You Hear My Heart Beat
Don't Go Out Into The Rain
Mother-In-Law
Silhouettes

HERNANDEZ, Patrick
Born To Be Alive

HESITATIONS
Impossible Dream

HICKEY, Ersel
Bluebirds Over The Mountain

FIND THAT TUNE

HIGHWAYMEN
Cotton Fields
Michael, Row The Boat Ashore

HILL, Jesse
Ooh Poo Pah Doo

HILLSIDE SINGERS
I'd Like To Teach The World To
Sing

HINES, Earl "Fatha"
Yellow Days

HIRT, Al
Down By The Riverside
Granada
Lullaby Of Birdland

HOLIDAY, Billie
My Man

HOLLAND, Eddie
Jamie

HOLLIES
Air That I Breathe
Bus Stop
Fourth Of July
He Ain't Heavy...He's My
Brother
Jennifer Eccles

HOLLY, Buddy. See also BUDDY
HOLLY & THE CRICKETS.
Empty Cup
Every Day
Fool's Paradise
Heartbeat
I'm Gonna Love You Too
I'm Lookin' For Someone To Love
It Doesn't Matter Anymore
Last Night
Listen To Me
Lonesome Tears
Look At Me
Love's Made A Fool Of You
Maybe Baby
Moondreams
Not Fade Away
Peggy Sue
Raining In My Heart
Rave On
Real Wild Child
Rock Me My Baby
Slippin' And Slidin'
Stay Close To Me
Take Your Time
True Love Ways
Well All Right
You've Got Love

HOLLYWOOD ARGYLES
Alley Oop

HOLMAN, Eddie
Hey There Lonely Girl

HOLMES, Clint
Playground In My Mind

HOLMES, Jake
So Close

HOLMES, Rupert
Answering Machine
Escape
Him (R. Holmes)

HOOKER, John Lee
Dimples
I'm Mad Again

HOPKIN, Mary
Goodbye
Those Were The Days

HOPKINS, Lightnin'
Honey Babe

HORNE, Jimmy "Bo"
Dance Across The Floor

HORTON, Johnny
Battle Of New Orleans

HOT
Angel In Your Arms
Right Feeling At The Wrong Time

HOT CHOCOLATE
Every 1's A Winner
So You Win Again

HOUSTON, Cisco
Deportee

HOUSTON, Cissy
Think It Over (C. Houston, A.
Fields & M. Zager)

HOUSTON, Thelma
Don't Leave Me This Way
Everybody Gets To Go To The
Moon
Suspicious Minds

HOWLING WOLF
Tell Me (C. Burnett)
Wang-Dang-Doodle

HUDSON, Jay
Goodnight, It's Time To Go

HUES CORPORATION
Rock The Boat

HUMBLE PIE
Baby Don't You Do It
Drift Away
I Can't Stand The Rain
I Don't Need No Doctor

HUMPERDNICK, Englebert
After The Lovin

I Believe In Miracles
Just The Way You Are
Love's Only Love
Release Me (E. Miller, D. Wil-
liams & R. Yount)
Sweet Marjorene
Sweetheart
This Moment In Time
What I Did For Love
When I Wanted You

HUNTER, Ian
Ships

HUNTER, Ivory Joe
I Almost Lost My Mind
I Need You So
Since I Met You Baby

HYLAND, Brian
Gypsy Woman
Itsy Bitsy Teenie Weenie Yellow
Polkadot Bikini
Sealed With A Kiss

IAN, Janis
At Seventeen
Go Away Little Girl
Jesse (J. Ian)
Lonely One
When The Party's Over

IAN & SYLVIA
For Lovin' Me
Four Strong Winds
Tomorrow Is A Long Time
You Were On My mind

IGGY POP AND THE STOOGES
Search And Destroy

IKE & TINA TURNER. See also
TURNER, Ike.
My Man
Nutbush City Limits
Ooh Poo Pah Doo
Reconsider Baby
Your Precious Love

IMPALAS
Sorry

IMPRESSIONS
Gypsy Woman

INGRAM, Luther
I Don't Want To Be Right
I'll Be Your Shelter (In Time Of
Storm)

INNOCENTS. See also KATHY
YOUNG & THE INNOCENTS.
Honest I Do (D. Stankey, J.
West & A. Candelaria)

INSTANT FUNK
  I Got My Mind Made Up

IRISH ROVERS
  Unicorn

IRON BUTTERFLY
  In-A-Gadda-Da-Vida

ISAAC HAYES & DIONNE WAR-
  WICK. See also HAYES, Isaac;
  WARWICK, Dionne.
  Have You Never Been Mellow

ISLEY BROTHERS
  Don't Let Me Be Lonely Tonight
  Fire And Rain
  It's Too Late
  Love The One You're With
  Nobody But Me
  Put A Little Love In Your Heart
  Shout
  Summer Breeze
  This Old Heart Of Mine (Is Weak
    For You)
  Twist And Shout

IVES, Burl
  Tell Me (J.W. Callahan & M.
    Kontalander)

J. GEILS BAND
  Give It To Me
  Must Of Got Lost

JABARA, Paul
  Last Dance

JACKIE & ROY
  Day By Day (S. Schwartz)

JACKSON, Chuck. See CHUCK
  JACKSON & MAXINE BROWN.

JACKSON, Jermaine. See also
  JACKSON 5; JACKSONS.
  Isn't She Lovely
  Let's Be Young Tonight

JACKSON, Joe
  Is She Really Going Out With
    Him

JACKSON, Michael. See also
  DIANA ROSS & MICHAEL
  JACKSON; JACKSON 5;
  JACKSONS.
  Ben
  Got To Be There
  Off The Wall
  Rock With You
  Rockin' Robin
  With A Child's Heart
  You Can't Win

JACKSON, Mick
  Weekend

JACKSON, Millie
  Angel In Your Arms
  Didn't I (Blow Your Mind This
    Time)
  I Don't Want To Be Right
  Leftovers
  Summer

JACKSON 5. See also JACKSON,
  Jermaine; JACKSON, Michael;
  JACKSONS.
  ABC
  Corner Of The Sky
  Dancing Machine
  Goin' Back To Indiana
  Got To Be There
  Hallelujah Day
  I Want You Back
  I'll Be There
  Life Of The Party
  Little Bitty Pretty One
  Lookin' Through The Windows
  Love You Save
  Mama's Pearl
  Maybe Tomorrow
  Never Can Say Goodbye
  Sugar Daddy
  Whatever You Got, I Want

JACKSONS
  Enjoy Yourself
  Lovely One

JAM
  Modern World

JAMES, Elmore
  Sun Is Shining

JAMES, Etta
  Dance With Me Henry
  Security
  Something's Got A Hold On Me

JAMES, Joni
  My Love, My Love

JAMES, Rick. See also RICK
  JAMES & THE STONE CITY
  BAND.
  Come Into My Life
  Mary Jane

JAMES, Sonny
  My Love (T. Hatch)

JAMES, Tommy. See also TOM-
  MY JAMES & THE SHONDELLS.
  Draggin' The Line
  Three Times In Love

JAMES & BOBBY PURIFY
  I'm Your Puppet

JAMES GANG
  Funk #49

JAMES TAYLOR & CARLY
  SIMON. See CARLY SIMON &
  JAMES TAYLOR.

JAMIES
  Summertime

JAN & DEAN
  Baby Talk
  Heart And Soul
  Surf City

JANE, Billy
  Last Night I Made Love To Some-
    body Else

JANE OLIVER & JOHNNY MATHIS.
  See JOHNNY MATHIS & JANE
  OLIVER.

JARMELS
  Little Bit Of Soap

JAY AND THE AMERICANS
  Cara Mia

JAYE, Jerry
  My Girl Josephine

JEFFERSON AIRPLANE
  Ballad Of You & Me Pooneil
  Eskimo Blue Day
  Last Wall Of The Castle
  Martha
  Rejoyce
  Somebody To Love (D. Slick)
  Two Heads
  Watch Her Ride
  White Rabbit
  Wild Tyme
  Won't You Try Saturday After-
    noon
  Young Girl Sunday Blue

JEFFERSON STARSHIP
  Count On Me
  Crazy Feelin'
  Dance With The Dragon
  Jane
  Miracles
  Play On Love
  Runaway (N. Dewey)
  With Your Love

JENNINGS, Waylon. See also
  WAYLON & WILLIE; WAYLON
  JENNINGS & JESSI COLTER.
  Are You Sure Hank Done It This
    Way
  Brown Eyed Handsome Man
  Good Hearted Woman
  Luckenbach, Texas

JESUS CHRIST SUPERSTAR,
Cast Of
Superstar (T. Rice & A. Webber)

JIGSAW
Love Fire

JIM KWESKIN & THE JUG BAND
Crazy Words-Crazy Tune

JIMMY & JESSE
Sweet Little Sixteen

JIMMY CASTOR BUNCH
I Just Wanna Stop

JIMMY GILMER & THE FIRE
BALLS. See also FIREBALLS.
Sugar Shack

JIVE BOMBER
Bad Boy

JOAN BAEZ & BOB DYLAN. See
BOB DYLAN & JOAN BAEZ.

JOE & EDDIE
They Call The Wind Maria

JOE COCKER & THE GREASE
BAND. See also COCKER,
Joe.
Feelin' Alright

JOEL, Billy
Entertainer (B. Joel)
Honesty
Just The Way You Are
Movin' Out (Anthony's Song)
New York State Of Mind
Piano Man
Say Goodbye To Hollywood
She's Always A Woman
You May Be Right

JOHN, Elton. See also ELTON
JOHN & KIKI DEE.
All The Girls Love Alice
Amoreena
Bennie And The Jets
Bitch Is Back
Border Song
Burn Down The Mission
Candle In The Wind
Crocodile Rock
Daniel
Don't Let The Sun Go Down On
Me
Goodbye Yellow Brick Road
I Need You To Turn To
Island Girl
Levon
Little Jeannie
Lucy In The Sky With Diamonds
Mama Can't Buy You Love
Michelle's Song
Part-Time Love

Philadelphia Freedom
Pinball Wizard
Rocket Man
Saturday Night's Alright
Someone Saved My Life Tonight
Song For Guy
Sugar On The Floor
Sweet Painted Lady
Take Me To The Pilot
Tiny Dancer
Valhalla
Your Song

JOHN, Olivia Newton. See
NEWTON-JOHN, Olivia.

JOHN, Robert
Give A Little More
Sad Eyes

JOHN DENVER & THE MUPPETS.
See also DENVER, John.
It's In Every One Of Us

JOHN FRED & HIS PLAYBOY
BAND
Judy In Disguise (With Glasses)

JOHN McLAUGHLIN/
MAHAVISHNU ORCHESTRA
Birds Of Fire

JOHN TRAVOLTA & OLIVIA
NEWTON-JOHN. See also
NEWTON-JOHN, Olivia;
TRAVOLTA, John.
You're The One That I Want

JOHNNIE & JOE
Over The Mountain, Across The
Sea

JOHNNY & JACK
Goodnight, It's Time To Go

JOHNNY MATHIS & DENIECE
WILLIAMS. See also MATHIS,
Johnny; WILLIAMS, Deniece.
Too Much Too Little, Too Late
You're All I Need To Get By

JOHNNY MATHIS & JANE
OLIVER. See also MATHIS,
Johnny.
Last Time I Felt Like This

JOHNNY MOORE'S THREE
BLAZERS
Merry Christmas Baby

JOHNSON, Marv
Baby (You've Got What It Takes)
I Love The Way You Love
You've Got What It Takes

JOHNSON, Michael
Bluer Than Blue
This Night Won't Last Forever

JOHNSON BROTHERS
Ride-O-Rocket
Stomp

JOLI, France
Come To Me

JONES, Etta
This Guy's In Love With You
Yes Sir, That's My Baby

JONES, Grandpa
Are You From Dixie

JONES, Jack
Impossible Dream
Love Boat, Main Title From
Somewhere My Love

JONES, Jimmy
Good Timin' (C. Ballard & F.
Tobias)
Handy Man

JONES, Jo
Should I

JONES, Joe
You Talk Too Much

JONES, Quincy
Anderson Tapes, Theme From
Roots, Theme From
Stuff Like That

JONES, Rickie Lee
Chuck E.'s In Love
Young Blood (R. Jones)

JONES, Tom
Can't Stop Loving You
Delilah
Green Green Grass Of Home
Help Yourself
It's Not Unusual
Love Me Tonight
Say You'll Stay Until Tomorrow
She's A Lady
What's New Pussycat

JONES GIRLS
You Gonna Make Me Love Somebody Else

JOPLIN, Janis
All Is Loneliness
Bye, Bye, Bye
Down On Me
Ego Rock
Flower In The Sun
Half Moon
I Need A Man To Love
Kozmic Blues
Me And Bobby McGee
Mercedes Benz
Move Over
Piece Of My Heart

Road Block
Summertime
Try (Just A Little Bit Harder)

JOURNEY
Any Way You Want It (S. Perry &
  N. Schon)
Anytime
Lights (S. Perry & N. Schon)
Lovin', Touchin', Squeezin'
Too Late
Wheel In The Sky

JR. WALKER & THE ALL STARS
How Sweet It Is (To Be Loved
  By You)
Money (That's What I Want)
Pucker Up Buttercup
Road Runner (E. Holland, L.
  Dozier & B. Holland)
Shotgun
What Does It Take

KALIN TWINS
When

KANE, Madleen
You And I (L. & P. Sebastian &
  Michaele)

KANSAS
Carry On Wayward Son
Dust In The Wind
Point Of Know Return
Reason To Be

KATHY YOUNG & THE
  INNOCENTS. See also
  INNOCENTS.
Thousand Stars

KAZ, Eric
Love Has No Pride

KC & THE SUNSHINE BAND
Boogie Shoes
Do You Feel All Right
Get Down Tonight
I'm Your Boogie Man
It's The Same Old Song
Keep It Comin' Love
Please Don't Go
Shake Your Booty
That's The Way I Like It
Who Do Ya Love

KEANE BROTHERS
Dancin' In The Moonlight

KEEFER, James Barry. See
  KEITH.

KEITH
Tell Me To My Face

KELLUM, Murry
Long Tall Texan

KENDRICKS, Eddie
Boogie Down
Goin' Up In Smoke
Keep On Truckin'

KENNER, Chris
I Like It Like That (C. Kenner &
  A. Toussaint)

KENNY ROGERS & DOTTY WEST.
  See also ROGERS, Kenny; WEST,
  Dotty.
All I Ever Need Is You
Another Somebody Done Some-
  body Wrong Song
Anyone Who Isn't Me Tonight
Every Time Two Fools Collide
Just The Way You Are
Let's Take The Long Way Around
  The World

KHAN, Chaka. See also RUFUS
  FEATURING CHAKA KHAN.
I'm Every Woman

KIKI DEE & ELTON JOHN. See
  ELTON JOHN & KIKI DEE.

KING, Albert
Born Under A Bad Sign
I'll Play The Blues For You
Killing Floor

KING, B.B.
Come By Here
Every Day (I Have The Blues)
Lucille (B.B. King)
Please Send Me Someone To Love
Thrill Is Gone (R. Hawkins)
Whole Lotta Loving

KING, Ben E.
Don't Play That Song
I (Who Have Nothing)
Spanish Harlem
Stand By Me

KING, Carole
Corazon
Hard Rock Cafe
I Feel The Earth Move
It's Too Late
Jazzman
One Fine Day
So Far Away
Sweet Seasons
Will You Love Me Tomorrow
You've Got A Friend

KING HARVEST
Dancin' In The Moonlight

KING PLEASURE
What Can I Say After I Say I'm
  Sorry   281

KINGSMAN DAZZ
Catchin' Up On Love

KINGSTON TRIO
Greenback Dollar
If I Had My Way
Scotch And Soda
Sloop John B
Tom Dooley
Tomorrow Is A Long Time
Where Have All The Flowers
  Gone

KING
You Really Got Me

KISS
Beth
I Was Made For Lovin' You
Love Theme From Kiss
Rock And Roll All Nite

KNACK
Good Girls Don't
My Sharona

KNIGHT, Frederick
Let The Sunshine In

KNIGHT, Gladys. See also GLADYS
  KNIGHT & THE PIPS.
I (Who Have Nothing)
I'm Comin' Home Again

KNIGHT, Jean
Mr. Big Stuff

KNOX, Buddy
Party Doll

KOOL & THE GANG
Hollywood Swinging
Jungle Boogie
Ladies Night
Too Hot

KRAMER, Billy J. See also BILLY
  J. KRAMER & THE DAKOTAS.
I'll Keep You Satisfied

KRIS KRISTOFFERSON & BARBRA
  STREISAND. See BARBRA
  STREISAND & KRIS
  KRISTOFFERSON.

KRIS KRISTOFFERSON & RITA
  COOLIDGE. See also COOLIDGE,
  Rita; KRISTOFFERSON, Kris.
Lover Please

KRISTOFFERSON, Kris
For The Good Times
Help Me Make It Through The
  Night
Loving Her Was Easier
Me And Bobby McGee
Sunday Mornin' Comin' Down
Why Me (K. Kristofferson)

KUBAN, Bob. See BOB KUBAN &
THE IN-MEN.

KWESKIN, Jim. See JIM KWESKIN
& THE JUG BAND.

LA BELLE, Patty
Don't Let Go

LABELLE
Lady Marmalade

LA BOUNTY, Bill
In 25 Words Or Less

LADD, Cheryl
Think It Over (B. & B.G. Russell)

LADY FLASH
Street Singin'

LAINE, Frankie
Blazing Saddles

LARSON, Nicolette
Lotta Love
Rhumba Girl

LATIMORE
Dig A Little Deeper
Let's Straighten It Out

LATTISAW, Stacy
Let Me Be Your Angel

LAWRENCE, Steve
Go Away Little Girl
Pretty Blue Eyes
You Take My Heart Away

LAWRENCE, Vicki
He Did With Me

LAZY RACER
Keep On Running Away

LEADBELLY
C.C. Rider (H. Ledbetter)
I'm Alone Because I Love You

LEAVES
Hey Joe

LE BLANC & CARR
Falling
Midnight Light

LED ZEPPELIN
Babe, I'm Gonna Leave You
Battle Of Evermore
Black Dog
Black Mountain Side
Bring It On Home
Bron-Y-Aur Stomp
Celebration Day

Communication Breakdown
Crunge
Dancing Days
Dazed And Confused
D'yer Mak'er
Four Sticks
Friends
Gallows Pole
Going To California
Good Times Bad Times
Hats Off To (Roy) Harper
Heartbreaker (J. Page, R. Plant,
    J.P. Jones & J. Bonham)
How Many More Times
Immigrant Song
Living Loving Maid
Misty Mountain Hop
Moby Dick
No Quarter
Ocean
Out On The Tiles
Over The Hills And Far Away
Rain Song
Ramble On
Rock And Roll
Since I've Been Loving You
Song Remains The Same
Stairway To Heaven
Tangerine
Thank You
That's The Way
What Is And What Should Never
    Be
When The Levee Breaks
Whole Lotta Love
You Shook Me
Your Time Is Gonna Come

LEDBETTER, Huddy. See LEAD-
BELLY.

LEE, Brenda
Dum Dum
Fool No. 1

LEE, Curtis
Pretty Little Angel Eyes

LEE, Peggy
Big Spender
I'll Get By

LEE ANDREWS & THE HEARTS
Long Lonely Nights

LEGRAND, Michel. See also
SARAH VAUGHAN & MICHEL
LEGRAND.
Hands Of Time
Windmills Of Your Mind

LENNON, John
Ain't That A Shame
Bony Moronie
Give Peace A Chance
Imagine
Instant Karma

Send Me Some Lovin'
Slippin' And Slidin'
Sweet Little Sixteen
Whatever Gets You Thru The
    Night

LEON & MARY RUSSELL. See
also RUSSELL, Leon.
Daylight
Rainbow In Your Eyes

LETTERMEN
Eres Tu
It Never Rains In Southern
    California
Love Me With All Your Heart
Love Means
Portrait Of My Love
Put A Little Love In Your Heart
Shangri-La
Sherry Don't Go
Somewhere My Love
Summer Place, Theme From
Turn Around, Look At Me
Walk Hand In Hand
Way You Look Tonight
You Were On My Mind
You've Got A Friend

LEWIS, Barbara
Baby, I'm Yours

LEWIS, Bobby
Tossin' And Turnin'

LEWIS, Gary. See also GARY
LEWIS & THE PLAYBOYS.
Sealed With A Kiss

LEWIS, Jerry Lee
Chantilly Lace
Don't Let Go
Good Time Charlie's Got The
    Blues
Great Balls Of Fire
Johnny B. Goode
Let The Good Times Roll
Lucille (A. Collins & R. Penni-
    man)
Mabellene
Money (That's What I Want)
Over The Rainbow
Rita May
Sweet Little Sixteen

LEWIS, Smiley
I Hear You Knocking

LIGHTFOOT, Gordon
Beautiful
Bitter Green
Cabaret
Canadian Railroad Trilogy
Did She Mention My Name
Early Mornin' Rain
First Time Ever I Saw Your Face
For Lovin' Me

Go My Way
If You Could Read My Mind
Just Like Tom Thumb's Blues
Pussywillows, Cattails
Race Among The Ruins
Rainy Day People
Ribbon Of Darkness
Rich Man Spiritual
Song For A Winter's Night
Steel Rail Blues
Summer Side Of Life
Summertime Dream
Sundown
That Same Old Obsession
Way I Feel
Wreck Of The Edmund Fitz-
   gerald

LIMELITERS
Gotta Travel On
There's A Meetin' Here Tonight
This Train
Those Were The Days

LIND, Bob
Elusive Butterfly

LIQUID GOLD
My Baby's Baby

LITTLE ANTHONY & THE
   IMPERIALS
Goin' Out Of My Head
Hurt So Bad
I'm On The Outside (Looking In)
Out Of Sight, Out Of Mind
Over The Rainbow
Ten Commandments Of Love

LITTLE BEAVER
Never Can Say Goodbye

LITTLE EVA
Loco-Motion

LITTLE MISS CORNSHOCK
It Do Me So Good

LITTLE RICHARD
All Around The World
Bama Lama Bama Loo
Boo, Hoo, Hoo, Hoo (I'll Never
   Let You Go)
Good Golly Miss Molly
Hey, Hey, Hey, Hey (Goin' Back
   To Birmingham)
Jenny, Jenny
Long Tall Sally
Lucille (A. Collins & R. Penni-
   man)
Miss Ann
Ready Teddy
Rip It Up
Send Me Some Lovin'
Slippin' And Slidin'
Tutti Frutti

LITTLE RIVER BAND
Cool Change
Happy Anniversary
I'll Always Call Your Name
Lady (G. Goble)
Lonesome Loser
Reminiscing

LIVERPOOL FIVE
If You Gotta Go, Go Now

LIVING VOICES
You'll Never Find Another Love
   Like Mine

LOBO
Holdin' On For Dear Love
How Can I Tell Her (About You)
Me And You And A Dog Named
   Boo
Rings
There Ain't No Way
Where Were You When I Was
   Falling In Love

LOCKLIN, Hank
Minute You're Gone

LOGGINS, Kenny. See also
LOGGINS & MESSINA.
Easy Driver
I'm Alright
Keep The Fire
This Is It
Whenever I Call You "Friend"

LOGGINS & MESSINA
Angry Eyes
Changes (J. Messina)
Danny's Song
House At Pooh Corner
Listen To A Country Song
Love Song
My Music
Nobody But You
Splish Splash
Watching The River Run
Your Mama Don't Dance

LOMBARDO, Guy
Love, You Funny Thing

LONDON SYMPHONY
ORCHESTRA
Close Encounters Of The Third
   Kind, Theme From
Star Wars

LONG, Shorty
Devil With The Blue Dress On
Here Comes The Judge

LOPEZ, Trini
If I Had A Hammer
It's A Great Life

LOUISIANA'S LE ROUX
New Orleans Ladies

LOVE
My Little Red Book

LOVEMAKERS
When You're Next To Me

LOVIN' SPOONFUL
Daydream
Do You Believe In Magic
Wild About My Lovin'

LOWE, Nick
Cruel To Be Kind

LTD
Back In Love Again

LUKE, Robin
Susie Darlin'

LULU
Me, The Peaceful Heart
Oh Me Oh My (I'm A Fool For
   You Baby)
To Sir With Love

LUNCEFORD, Jimmie
I'll See You In My Dreams

LYMON, Frankie. See FRANKIE
LYMON & THE TEENAGERS.

LYNN, Cheryl
Got To Be Real

LYNN, Loretta
Another Somebody Done Somebody Wrong Song

M
Pop Muzik

McCANN, Peter
Do You Wanna Make Love
Right Time Of The Night

McCARTNEY, Paul. See also
PAUL & LINDA McCARTNEY;
PAUL McCARTNEY & WINGS.
Every Night
Lovely Linda
Maybe I'm Amazed
That Would Be Something

McCOO, MARILYN. See
MARILYN McCOO & BILLY
DAVIS, JR.

McCOY, Charlie
Silver Threads And Golden
   Needles

McCOY, Van. See also VAN
McCOY & THE SOUL CITY
SYMPHONY.
Change With The Times
Party (V. McCoy)

McCOYS
Call It Stormy Monday
Hang On Sloopy

McCRAE, George. See also
GEORGE & GWEN McCRAE.
Rock Your Baby

McCRAE, Gwen
For Your Love

McDANIELS, Gene
Hundred Pounds Of Clay

McDOWELL, Ronnie
Animal

McFADDEN & WHITEHEAD
Ain't No Stoppin' Us Now

MC 5
Back In The USA

McGEE, Parker
I Just Can't Say No To You

McGHEE, Brownie
Down By The Riverside

McGOVERN, Maureen
Can You Read My Mind
I Won't Last A Day Without You
Morning After
We May Never Love Like This
Again
Yes I'm Ready

MacGREGOR, Mary
Good Friend
This Girl
Torn Between Two Lovers

McGUINN, Roger
Up To Me

McGUINN, CLARK & HILLMAN
Surrender To Me

McGUIRE SISTERS
Little Things Mean A Lot
Sincerely

McKENZIE, Scott
San Francisco (Be Sure To Wear
Some Flowers In Your Hair)

McKUEN, Rod
Love's Been Good To Me
Pastures Green
Seasons In The Sun

McLAURIN, Betty
My Heart Belongs To Only You

McLEAN, Don
American Pie
And I Love You So
Crying In The Chapel
Vincent
Wonderful Baby

McNAMARA, Robin
Got To Believe In Love

McPHATTER, Clyde
Long Lonely Nights
Lover Please
Lover's Question
Lovey Dovey
Seven Days
Treasure Of Love

McRAE, Carmen
Song For You

McWILLIAMS, David
Days Of Pearly Spencer

MAGNUM FORCE
Almost Like Being In Love

MAHAL, Taj
Checkin' Up On My Baby

MAIN INGREDIENT
Just Don't Want To Be Lonely

MAMA CASS
New World Coming

MAMAS & THE PAPAS
California Dreamin'
Creeque Alley
Dedicated To The One I Love
Do You Want To Dance
Go Where You Wanna Go
Got A Feeling
Hey Girl (J. Phillips & M.
Gilliam Phillips)
I Saw Her Again Last Night
In Crowd
Look Through My Window
Monday, Monday
Safe In My Garden
Somebody Groovy
Straight Shooter
Words Of Love (J. Phillips)
You Baby

MANCHESTER, Melissa
Come In From The Rain
Don't Cry Out Loud
Fire In The Morning
I Don't Want To Hear It Anymore
Ice Castles, Theme From
Just Too Many People
Just You And I
Midnight Blue
Monkey See-Monkey Do

Pretty Girls
Rescue Me

MANCINI, Henry
If You've Got The Time (I've Got
The Place)

MANDRELL, Barbara
After The Lovin'
Crackers
Fooled By A Feeling
I Don't Want To Be Right
I Never Said I Love You
Sleeping Single In A Double Bed
Very Special Love Song
Years

MANFRED MANN'S EARTH BAND.
See also MANN, Manfred.
Blinded By The Light

MANHATTAN TRANSFER
Body And Soul
Don't Let Go
Operator (W. Spivery)
Tuxedo Junction

MANHATTANS
After You
It Feels So Good To Be Loved By
You
Kiss And Say Goodbye
Shining Star (L. Graham & P.
Richmond)
Tomorrow

MANILOW, Barry
Beautiful Music
Can't Smile Without You
Copacabana
Could It Be Magic
Daybreak
Even Now
I Write The Songs
It's A Miracle
It's Just Another New Year's Eve
Jump Shout Boogie
Looks Like We Made It
Mandy
M*A*S*H, Song From
My Baby Loves Me
One Voice
Ships
Slow Dance
Somewhere In The Night
This One's For You
Tryin' To Get The Feeling Again
Weekend In New England
When I Wanted You
Where Are They Now

MANN, Manfred. See also
MANFRED MANN'S EARTH
BAND.
Get Your Rocks Off
If You Gotta Go, Go Now
Quinn The Eskimo

MANNE, Shelly
I Married An Angel

MANTOVANI
Alice Blue Gown
Almost Like Being In Love
Charmaine
Diane (E. Rapee & L. Pollack)
Good Night Sweetheart
It Was A Good Time
Laura
My Own True Love
Three Coins In The Fountain
Whiffenpoof Song
Whispering
Zorba The Greek, Theme From

MARCELS
Blue Moon

MARCOVICCI, Andrea
In Our Time

MARIE, Buffy Sainte. See
SAINTE-MARIE, Buffy.

MARILYN MCCOO & BILLY DAVIS
JR.
Look What You've Done To My
Heart
You Don't Have To Be A Star
Your Love

MARSHALL TUCKER BAND
Fire On The Mountain
Heard It In A Love Song
Last Of The Singing Cowboys
Searchin' For A Rainbow

MARTHA & THE VANDELLAS.
See also REEVES, Martha.
Dancing In The Street
I'm Ready For Love
Jimmy Mack
Heat Wave
My Baby Loves Me
Nowhere To Run
Quicksand

MARTIN, Bobbi
For The Love Of Him

MARTIN, Dean
Memories Are Made Of This

MARTIN, Moon
Rolene

MARTIN, Steve
King Tut

MARTINO, Al
Make The World Go Away
My Foolish Heart
Next Hundred Years
Spanish Eyes
Volare

MARVELETTES
Beechwood 4-5789
Don't Mess With Bill
My Baby Must Be A Magician
Playboy
Please Mr. Postman
Too Many Fish In The Sea

MARVIN GAYE & TAMMI TER-
RELL. See also GAYE, Marvin.
Ain't No Mountain High Enough
Ain't Nothing Like The Real
Thing
If I Could Build My Whole World
Around You
Your Precious Love
You're All I Need To Get By

MASON, Barbara
Yes I'm Ready

MASON, Dave
Bring It On Home To Me
Let It Go, Let It Flow
We Just Disagree
Will You Love Me Tomorrow

MATHIS, Johnny. See also
JOHNNY MATHIS & DENIECE
WILLIAMS; JOHNNY MATHIS &
JANE OLIVER.
As Time Goes By
Begin The Beguine
Chances Are
Deep Purple
Every Time You Touch Me
Hands Of Time
If We Only Have Love
I'm Stone In Love With You
It Was Almost Like A Song
It's Not For Me To Say
Little Boy Lost
Misty
99 Miles From L.A.
Ready Or Not
Since I Fell For You
Speak Softly Love
When Will I See You Again
Wonderful! Wonderful

MATTHEWS, Ian
Shake It

MATTHEWS SOUTHERN COMFORT
Da Doo Ron Ron

MAURIAT, Paul
Burning Bridges

MAXINE BROWN & CHUCK
JACKSON. See CHUCK
JACKSON & MAXINE BROWN.

MAXWELL, Robert
Shangri-La

MAYALL, John
All Your Love
I Can't Quit You Baby
So Many Roads
Steppin' Out (J. Bracken)

MAYFIELD, Curtis
Get Down (C. Mayfield)
Superfly

MAYFIELD, Percy
Please Send Me Someone To
Love

MEAD, Sister Janet
Lord's Prayer

MEATLOAF
All Revved Up With No Place To
Go
Bat Out Of Hell
For Crying Out Loud
Heaven Can Wait
Paradise By The Dashboard Light
Two Out Of Three Ain't Bad
You Took The Words Right Out
Of My Mouth

MECO
Star Wars

MEDALLIONS
Letter (D. Harris & D. Terry)

MEISNER, Randy
Deep Inside My Heart

MELANIE
Beautiful People
Brand New Key
I'd Rather Leave While I'm In
Love
Knock On Wood
Lay Down (Candles In The Rain)
Ruby Tuesday
Sad Song
What Have They Done To My
Song, Ma

MELVIN, Harold. See HAROLD
MELVIN & THE BLUENOTES.

MFSB
Philadelphia Freedom
Sexy
Touch Me In The Morning
TSOP (The Sound of Philadelphia)

MICHAEL JACKSON & DIANA
ROSS. See DIANA ROSS &
MICHAEL JACKSON.

MICHAEL ZAGER BAND
Let's All Chant

MICHEL LEGRAND & SARAH
VAUGHAN. See SARAH
VAUGHAN & MICHEL
LEGRAND.

MIDLER, Bette
Delta Dawn
Do You Want To Dance
In The Mood
Rose
Say Goodbye To Hollywood
Skylark
Superstar (L. Russell & B.
Bramlett)
When A Man Loves A Woman

MIKE CURB CONGREGATION
Burning Bridges

MILES, John
Music

MILLER, Glenn
Alice Blue Gown
Chattanooga Choo Choo
Moonlight Serenade
Pagan Love Song
Tuxedo Junction
Wonderful One

MILLER, Roger
King Of The Road

MILSAP, Ronnie
Four Walls
In No Time At All
It Was Almost Like A Song
Let's Take The Long Way Around
The World
What A Difference You've Made
In My Life

MIMI & RICHARD FARINA. See
also FARINA, Richard.
Children Of Darkness
Hard Loving Loser
Miles

MIMMS, Garnet
What It Is

MINELLI, Liza
Cabaret
Good Morning Starshine
It Was A Good Time
Look Of Love
Maybe This Time

MIRACLES. See also SMOKEY
ROBINSON & THE MIRACLES.
Dancing Machine
Do It Baby
Going To A Go-Go
I'm The One You Need
Love Machine
Money (That's What I Want)
Shop Around

MIRAN, Wayne. See WAYNE
MIRAN & RUSH RELEASE.

MIRETTES
In The Midnight Hour

MITCHELL, Guy
My Heart Cries For You

MITCHELL, Joni
All I Want
Amelia
Big Yellow Taxi
Blue
Both Sides Now
California (J. Mitchell)
Carey
Chelsea Morning
Circle Game
Coyote
Fiddle And The Drum
For The Roses
Free Man In Paris
Help Me
In France They Kiss On Main
Street
Ladies Of The Canyon
Michael From Mountains
My Old Man
Raised On Robbery
Song To A Seagull
Why Do Fools Fall In Love
Woodstock
You Turn Me On, I'm A Radio

MITCHELL, Willie
Twenty Seventy Five

MODUGNO, Domenico
Volare

MOE KOFFMAN & HIS
ORCHESTRA
Swingin' Shepherd Blues

MONEY, Eddie
Can't Keep A Good Man Down
Maybe I'm A Fool
Two Tickets To Paradise

MONKEES
Cuddly Toy
Daydream Believer
I Wanna Be Free
I'm A Believer
It's Nice To Be With You
Last Train To Clarksville
Pleasant Valley Sunday
Monkees, Theme From

MONOTONES
Book Of Love

MONROE, Vaughn
Good Night Sweetheart

MONTANA
Let's Get A Little Sentimental

MONTGOMERY, Wes
Scarborough Fair

MOODY BLUES
Driftwood
Nights In White Satin
Question
Ride My See-Saw
Tuesday Afternoon

MOONGLOWS
Sincerely

MOORE, Johnny. See JOHNNY
MOORE'S THREE BLAZERS.

MOORE, Melba
Easy To Be Hard
You Stepped Into My Life

MORRIS, Joe
Anytime, Anyplace, Anywhere

MORRISON, Van. See also VAN
MORRISON & THEM.
Blue Money
Brown Eyed Girl
Domino
Into The Mystic
Midnight Special
Moondance
Old Old Woodstock
Tupelo Honey
Wild Night

MOSTEL, Zero
If I Were A Rich Man

MOUNTAIN
Blood Of The Sun
Crossroader
Flowers Of Evil
Mississippi Queen
Theme For An Imaginary
Western

MUNGO JERRY
In The Summertime

MURMAIDS
Popsicles And Icicles

MURPHEY, Michael
Carolina In The Pines
Wildfire

MURPHY, Walter. See WALTER
MURPHY BAND.

MURRAY, Anne
Broken Hearted Me
Could I Have This Dance
Danny's Song
Daydream Believer

Dream Lover
Ease Your Pain
Fire And Rain
I Just Fall In Love Again
Let Me Be The One
Love Song
Lucky Me
Put Your Hand In The Hand
Snowbird
Walk Right Back
What About Me
You Needed Me
You've Got A Friend

MUSIQUE
In The Bush

MYSTICS
Hushabye

NASH, Graham. See also
CROSBY, STILLS & NASH;
DAVID CROSBY & GRAHAM
NASH.
Prison Song

NASH, Johnny
Hold Me Tight
I Can See Clearly Now
It's So Easy To Say
Stir It Up

NASHVILLE BRASS
Moonlight Serenade
Wabash Cannon Ball

NASHVILLE TEENS
Tobacco Road

NATALIE COLE & PEABO
BRYSON. See also COLE,
Natalie.
What You Won't Do For Love

NATURAL FOUR
Can This Be Real

NAUGHTON, David
Makin' It

NEIL DIAMOND & BARBRA
STREISAND. See also DIAMOND,
Neil; STREISAND, Barbra.
You Don't Bring Me Flowers

NEIL YOUNG & CRAZY HORSE.
See also CROSBY, STILLS,
NASH & YOUNG; YOUNG, Neil.
Hey Hey, My My

NELSON, Rick
Fools Rush In
Garden Party
I'm In Love Again
I'm Walkin'

She Belongs To Me
Teenage Idol
That's All

NELSON, Willie. See also
WAYLON & WILLIE; WILLIE
NELSON & LEON RUSSELL.
Fire And Rain
My Heroes Have Always Been
Cowboys
Someone To Watch Over Me
That Lucky Old Sun

NERO, Peter
Summer Knows

NEVILLE, Aaron
Tell It Like It Is

NEW BIRTH
I Can Understand It
It's Impossible

NEW CHRISTY MINSTRELS
Green Green
Saturday Night (R. Sparks)
This Land Is Your Land
Today

NEW RIDERS OF THE PURPLE
SAGE
I Don't Need No Doctor

NEW SEEKERS
I'd Like To Teach The World To
Sing
What Have They Done To My
Song, Ma

NEW YORK DOLLS
Personality Crisis

NEWMAN, Randy
Louisiana 1927
Sail Away (R. Newman)
Short People

NEWTON, Wayne
Years

NEWTON-JOHN, Olivia. See also
ANDY GIBB & OLIVIA NEWTON-
JOHN: JOHN TRAVOLTA &
OLIVIA NEWTON-JOHN.
Air That I Breathe
Angel Of The Morning
Come On Over
Dancin' Round And Round
Free The People
Have You Never Been Mellow
I Honestly Love You
If You Could Read My Mind
If You Love Me (Let Me Know)
Let Me Be There
Little More Love
Magic
Making A Good Thing Better

Sam
Who Are You Now

NICHOLAS, Paul
Heaven On The Seventh Floor

NIELSEN & PEARSON
If You Should Sail

NIGHT
Hot Summer Nights

NIGHTINGALE, Maxine
Gotta Be The One
Lead Me On
Right Back Where We Started
From

NILSSON
As Time Goes By
Everybody's Talkin'
Lean On Me
Me And My Arrow
Without Her
Without You

NINO & APRIL
Deep Purple
Whispering

NITTY GRITTY DIRT BAND
All I Have To Do Is Dream
Crazy Words--Crazy Tune
Gotta Travel On
Hard Hearted Hannah
Mr. Bojangles
Teddy Bears' Picnic

NOLAN, Kenny
I Like Dreamin'
Love's Grown Deep
Us And Love

NORMAN, Chris. See SUZI
QUATRO & CHRIS NORMAN.

NORTHCOTT, Tom
1941

NUGENT, Ted
Cat Scratch Fever
Need You Bad
Yank Me, Crank Me

NYRO, Laura
I Never Meant To Hurt You
Save The Country
Stoney End
Up On The Roof
Wedding Bell Blues

OCEAN
Put Your Hand In The Hand

OAK RIDGE BOYS
 Sail Away (R. Vanhoy)

OCHS, Phil
 Bracero
 Cannons Of Christianity
 Changes (P. Ochs)
 Cops Of The World
 Cross My Heart
 Crucifixion
 Draft Dodger Rag
 Floods Of Florence
 Flower Lady
 Half A Century High
 Harder They Fall
 I'm Gonna Say It Now
 Is There Anybody Here
 I've Had Her
 Joe Hill (P. Ochs)
 Love Me, I'm A Liberal
 Miranda
 Outside A Small Circle of
  Friends
 Party (P. Ochs)
 Pleasures Of The Harbor
 Rhythms Of Revolution
 Santo Domingo
 Tape From California
 War Is Over
 When I'm Gone
 When In Rome
 White Boots Marching In A
  Yellow Land

O'DAY, Alan
 Started Out Dancing, Ended Up
  Making Love
 Undercover Angel

ODETTA
 All My Trials (O. Gordon)
 Fox
 Pastures Of Plenty
 Rock Island Line
 Shenandoah

ODYSSEY
 Native New Yorker
 Weekend Lover

OFARIM, Esther & Abi. See
 ESTHER & ABI OFARIM.

O'HARA, Mary
 Tapestry

O'JAYS
 Feelings
 For The Love Of Money
 Forever Mine
 Give The People What They Want
 I Love Music (Part I)
 Let Me Make Love To You
 Now That We've Found Love

O'KEEFE, Danny
 Good Time Charlie's Got The
  Blues

OLDFIELD, Mike
 Tubular Bells

OLIVER
 Good Morning Starshine

OLIVER, Jane. See JOHNNY
 MATHIS & JANE OLIVER.

OLIVIA NEWTON-JOHN & ANDY
 GIBB. See ANDY GIBB &
 OLIVIA NEWTON-JOHN.

OLIVIA NEWTON-JOHN & JOHN
 TRAVOLTA. See JOHN
 TRAVOLTA & OLIVIA NEWTON-
 JOHN.

OLSEN, Nigel
 Dancing Shoes

OLYMPICS
 Hully Gully
 Western Movies

ORBISON, Roy
 Mean Woman Blues

ORIGINAL CASTE
 One Tin Soldier

ORIGINALS
 Down To Love Town

ORIOLES
 Crying In The Chapel

ORION
 I Hear You Knocking

ORLANDO, Tony. See also
 DAWN; TONY ORLANDO &
 DAWN.
 Sweets For My Sweet

ORLEANS
 Let There Be Music

ORLONS
 Don't Hang Up
 Wah-Watusi

OSMOND, Donny. See also
 DONNY & MARIE OSMOND;
 OSMONDS.
 Go Away Little Girl
 Hey, Girl (G. Goffin & C. King)
 I Knew You When
 Long Haired Lover From Liver-
  pool
 Sweet And Innocent
 Too Young
 Twelfth Of Never

OSMOND, Marie
 Paper Roses
 This Is The Way I Feel

OSMONDS
 Goin' Home
 He Ain't Heavy...He's My
  Brother
 Hey There Lonely Girl
 Yo Yo
 You Are So Beautiful

OUTLAWS
 There Goes Another Love Song

OUTSIDERS
 Time Won't Let Me

OVERSTREET, Tommy
 Gwen

OWENS, Buck
 Memphis Tennessee

OZARK MOUNTAIN DAREDEVILS
 If You Wanna Get To Heaven
 Jackie Blue
 Look Away

PABLO CRUISE
 I Go To Rio
 Love Will Find A Way

PAIGE, Sharon
 Hope That We Can Be Together
  Soon

PALMER, Robert
 Bad Case Of Loving You
 Every Kinda People

PAPER LACE
 Night Chicago Died

PAPPALARDI, Felix
 Baby, I'm Down

PARADONS
 Diamonds And Pearls

PARIS SISTERS
 I Love How You Love Me

PARKER, Robert
 Barefootin'

PARKS, Michael
 Long Lonesome Highway

PARLIAMENT See also
 FUNKADELIC
 Do That Stuff
 Tear The Roof Off The Sucker

PARTON, Dolly
 Baby, I'm Burning
 Here You Come Again
 Light Of A Clear Blue Morning
 Two Doors Down

PARTRIDGE FAMILY
Breaking Up Is Hard To Do
Doesn't Somebody Want To Be
Wanted
I Think I Love You
I Woke Up In Love This Morning
I'll Meet You Halfway
It's One Of Those Nights (Yes
Love)

PATIENCE & PRUDENCE
Gonna Get Along Without You
Now

PATTERSON, Kellee
If It Don't Fit, Don't Force It

PATTI SMITH GROUP
Ask The Angels
Because The Night
Frederick
Kimberly
Redondo Beach

PAUL, Billy
Me And Mrs. Jones

PAUL & LINDA MCCARTNEY.
See also MCCARTNEY, Paul.
Uncle Albert/Admiral Halsey

PAUL & PAULA
Hey Paula

PAUL MCCARTNEY & WINGS
Another Day
Band On The Run
Juniors Farm
Listen To What The Man Said
Live And Let Die
My Love (P. & L. McCartney)
Venus And Mars Rock Show

PAUL REVERE & THE RAIDERS
Don't Take It So Hard

PAXTON, Casey
East Is East

PAXTON, Tom
Last Thing On My Mind
Pastures Of Plenty
Whose Garden Was This

PEABO BRYSON & NATALIE
COLE. See NATALIE COLE
& PEABO BRYSON.

PEACHES & HERB
For Your Love
I Pledge My Love
Reunited
Shake Your Groove Thing
We've Got Love

PEEK, Dan
All Things Are Possible

PENDERGRASS, Teddy
Turn Off The Lights

PENGUINS
Earth Angel

PEOPLE
I Love You

PEOPLES CHOICE
Do It Anyway You Wanna

PERKINS, Carl
Baby, What You Want Me To Do
Blue Suede Shoes
Rock Around The Clock

PETER & GORDON
I Go To Pieces
Lady Godiva
World Without Love

PETER, PAUL & MARY
All My Trials
A'soalin
Autumn To May
Bamboo
Blowin' In The Wind
Come And Go With Me
Cruel War
Cuckoo
Day Is Done
Don't Think Twice, It's All Right
Early In the Morning (P. Stookey)
Early Mornin' Rain
First Time Ever I Saw Your Face
Five Hundred Miles
For Lovin' Me
Freight Train
Gilgarra Mountain
Great Mandella
Hangman
I Dig Rock 'N' Roll Music
If I Had A Hammer
If I Had My Way
Last Thing On My Mind
Leaving On A Jet Plane
Lemon Tree
Man Of Constant Sorrow
Monday Morning
Motherless Child
Oh Rock My Soul
Puff (The Magic Dragon)
Single Girl
Song Is Love
Tell It On The Mountain
This Train
Too Much Of Nothing
Weep For Jamie
When The Ship Comes In

PETERSON, Ray
Tell Laura I Love Her

PETTY, Tom. See TOM PETTY &
THE HEARTBREAKERS.

PHILLY CREAM
Motown Review
Soul Man

PICKETT, Bobby "Boris"
Monster Mash

PICKETT, Wilson
Hey Joe
In The Midnight Hour
Land Of A Thousand Dances
Mustang Sally
Stagger Lee

PINK FLOYD
Another Brick In The Wall (Part
II)
Burning Bridges
Money

PINK LADY
Kiss In The Dark

PIPKINS
Gimme Dat Ding

PISTILLI, CASHMAN & WEST.
See also CASHMAN & WEST.
Song That Never Comes

PITNEY, Gene
I'm Gonna Be Strong
Town Without Pity

PLACE, Mary Kay
Baby Boy (Big Ole Baby Boy)

PLATTERS
Enchanted
Great Pretender
My Prayer
Only You
Smoke Gets In Your Eyes
Twilight Time

PLAYER
Baby Come Back
Prisoner Of Your Love
Silver Lining
This Time I'm In It For Love

PLAYER'S ASSOCIATION
I Wish

PLAYMATES
Beep Beep
Jo-Ann
What Is Love

POCO
Crazy Love
Heart Of The Night
Keep On Tryin'

POINTER, Bonnie. See also
POINTER SISTERS.
Free Me From My Freedom

Heaven Must Have Sent You
I Can't Help Myself

POINTER SISTERS
Fairytale
Fire
Happiness
Wang-Dang-Doodle
Yes We Can Can

POISON
Let Me Lay My Funk On You

POLICE
Roxanne

POPPY FAMILY
That's Where I Went Wrong

PRELUDE
After The Gold Rush

PRESLEY, Elvis
All Shook Up
All That I Am
Angel (S. Tepper & R. Bennett)
Any Way You Want Me
Anyplace Is Paradise
Are You Lonesome Tonight
As Long As I Have You
Baby, I Don't Care
Beach Boy Blues
Beginner's Luck
Big Boots
Big Boss Man
Big Hunk O'Love
Blue Moon
Blue Moon Of Kentucky
Blue Suede Shoes
Bossa Nova, Baby
Boy Like Me, A Girl Like You
Can't Help Falling In Love
C'mon Everybody
Come Along
Come What May
Crying In The Chapel
Danny
Didja Ever
Do Not Disturb
Doin' The Best I Can (D. Pomus
& M. Shuman)
Don't
Don't Be Cruel (To A Heart
That's True)
Don't Leave Me Now
Easy Question
Everybody Come Aboard
Fame And Fortune
Follow That Dream
Fools Fall In Love
Frankie And Johnnie
Frankfort Special
G.I. Blues
Gonna Get Back Home Somehow
Good Luck Charm
Good Time Charlie's Got The
Blues

Got A Lot O' Livin' To Do
Green Green Grass Of Home
Hard Headed Woman
Hard Knocks
Hard Luck
Heartbreak Hotel
His Latest Flame
Hound Dog
How Would You Like To Be
Hurt (J. Crane & A. Jacobs)
I Feel That I've Known You
Forever
I Forgot To Remember To
Forget
I Got A Woman
I Got Lucky
I Just Can't Help Believin'
I Need Your Love Tonight
I Slipped, I Stumbled, I Fell
I Think I'm Gonna Like It Here
I Want You, I Need You, I Love
You
I Was The One
If You Talk In Your Sleep
I'll Be Back
In Your Arms
Island Of Love
It's A Wonderful World
It's Now Or Never
I've Got A Thing About You Baby
I've Got To Find My Baby
I've Lost You
Jailhouse Rock
Johnny B. Goode
Just Tell Her Jim Said Hello
King Creole
Kiss Me Quick
Lawdy, Miss Clawdy
Little Sister
Lonely Man
Lonesome Cowboy
Long Tall Sally
Love Me Tender
Loving You
Make The World Go Away
Mean Woman Blues
Memphis, Tennessee
Mess Of Blues
My Babe
My Wish Came True
Never Ending
Never Say Yes
No More
Once Is Enough
One Night
Only Believe
Paradise, Hawaiian Style
Party (J. Robinson)
Please Don't Drag That String
Around
Please Don't Stop Loving Me
Poor Boy
Promised Land
Puppet On A String
Relax
Ridin' The Rainbow
Rip It Up

Roustabout
Shake Rattle & Roll
Shake That Tambourine
Shoppin' Around
Shout It Out
Slicin' Sand
Slowly But Surely
Smorgasbord
So Close, Yet So Far From
Paradise
Softly, As I Leave You
Spanish Eyes
Spinout
Starting Today
Steppin' Out Of Line
Stop, Look, Listen
Surrender (D. Pomus, M. Shuman
& E. DeCurtis)
Suspicion
Suspicious Minds
This Is My Heaven
Today, Tomorrow And Forever
Treat Me Nice
Tutti Frutti
Unchained Melody
U.S. Male
Walls Have Ears
Way Down
Wear My Ring Around Your
Neck
We're Coming In Loaded
What Every Woman Lives For
Where Do You Come From
Wonder Of You
Wooden Heart
You Don't Have To Say You
Love Me
Young Dreams
You're The Devil In Disguise
You've Lost That Lovin' Feelin'

**PRESTON, Billy. See also BILLY
PRESTON & SYREETA.**
Get Back
My Sweet Lord
Outa Space
Slippin' And Slidin'
Will It Go 'Round In Circles
You've Lost That Lovin' Feelin'

PRICE, Alan
House Of The Rising Sun

PRICE, Lloyd
I'm Gonna Get Married
Just Because
Lawdy, Miss Clawdy
Personality
Stagger Lee

PRICE, Ray
For The Good Times
Roses And Love Songs

PRIDE, Charley
Kiss An Angel Good Mornin'

PRINCE
I Wanna Be Your Lover

PRINE, John
Paradise

PROCOL HARUM
All This And More (K. Reid & G. Brooker)
Conquistador
Glimpses Of Nirvana
Grand Finale
In The Autumn Of My Madness
Look To Your Soul (G. Brooker, M. Fisher & K. Reid)
Salty Dog
'Twas Teatime At The Circus
Whiter Shade Of Pale

PROPHETS OF SOUL
Ain't No Sunshine

PUCKETT, Gary. See GARY PUCKETT & THE UNION GAP.

QUATRO, Suzi. See also SUZI QUATRO & CHRIS NORMAN.
If You Can't Give Me Love
I've Never Been In Love

QUEEN
Bicycle Race
Bohemian Rhapsody
Crazy Little Thing Called Love
Fat Bottomed Girls
It's Late
Killer Queen
Lazing On A Sunday Afternoon
Somebody To Love (F. Mercury)
We Are The Champions
We Will Rock You
You're My Best Friend

? AND THE MYSTERIANS
96 Tears

QUICKSILVER MESSENGER SERVICE
Mona

RABBITT, Eddie
Suspicions
You Don't Love Me Anymore

RADIO BIRDMAN
What Gives

RAFFERTY, Gerry
Baker Street
Days Gone Down (Still Got The Light In Your Eyes)
Get It Right Next Time

Home And Dry
Right Down The Line

RAGTIMERS
Next Hundred Years
What Have They Done To My Song, Ma

RALSTON, Bob
I Was Born In Love With You

RAMONES
Blitzkrieg Bop
Do You Wanna Dance
I Wanna Be Your Boyfriend
Judy Is A Punk
Needles And Pins
Ooh Ooh I Love Her So
Ramona
Rockaway Beach
Sheena Is A Punk Rocker
Swallow My Pride

RANDOLPH, Boots
Deep Purple
I'm In The Mood For Love
Laura
Shangri-La
Wabash Cannon Ball

RANKIN, Kenny
On And On

RARE EARTH
Get Ready
I Just Want To Celebrate
I'm Losing You

RASCALS
Groovin'
How Can I Be Sure
In The Midnight Hour
People Got To Be Free

RASBERRIES
Go All The Way
I Wanna Be With You

RAWLS, Lou
Lady Love
Let Me Be Good To You
One Life To Live
Send In The Clowns
Sir Duke
Sit Down And Talk To Me
Tomorrow
You'll Never Find Another love Like Mine

RAY, Don
Got To Have Lovin'

RAY CONIFF SINGERS
My Little Town
Somewhere My Love

RAY, GOODMAN & BROWN
Special Lady

RAY PARKER JR. & RAYDIO.
See also RAYDIO.
Two Places At The Same Time

RAYDIO
Honey I'm Rich
Jack And Jill
You Can't Change That

RAYS
Silhouettes

REDDING, Otis
Dock Of The Bay
Happy Song
I've Been Loving You Too Long
Pain In My Heart

REDDY, Helen
Ain't No Way To Treat A Lady
Angie Baby
Delta Dawn
Emotion (P. Dahlstrom & V. Sanson)
I Am Woman
I Don't Know How To Love Him
Keep On Singing
Leave Me Alone
Ready Or Not
Somewhere In The Night
This Masquerade
You And Me Against The World
You're My World

REED, Jerry
All I Ever Need Is You
Amos Moses
Are You From Dixie
When You're Hot You're Hot

REED, Jimmy
Honest I Do (J. Reed)

REEVES, Jim
Four Walls

REEVES, Martha. See also MARTHA AND THE VANDELLAS.
You've Lost That Lovin' Feelin'

REFLECTIONS
Romeo & Juliet

REGENTS
Barbara Ann

RENAISSANCE
Do You Know The Way To San Jose
Look Of Love
Walk On By

REUNION
Life Is A Rock

FIND THAT TUNE

REYNOLDS, Debbie
  Singin' In The Rain
  Would You

REZILLOS
  Good Sculptures
  I Can't Stand My Baby

RHYTHM HERITAGE
  Gonna Fly Now
  S.W.A.T., Theme From

RICH, Charlie
  Behind Closed Doors
  Every Time You Touch Me
  Lonely Weekends
  Mohair Sam
  Most Beautiful Girl
  Very Special Love Song
  Who Will The Next Fool Be

RICHARD, Cliff
  Carrie
  We Don't Talk Anymore

RICHARD & MIMI FARINA. See
MIMI & RICHARD FARINA.

RICK DEES & HIS CAST OF IDIOTS
  Disco Duck (Part I)

RICK JAMES & THE STONE CITY
  BAND. See also JAMES, Rick.
  You And I (R. James)

RIDGELEY, Tommy
  Jam Up Twist

RIGHTEOUS BROTHERS
  Ebb Tide
  Justine
  Unchained Melody
  You've Lost That Loving Feeling

RIOS, Miguel
  Song Of Joy

RIPERTON, Minnie
  Lovin' You

RIPPY, Rodney Allen
  Take Life A Little Easier

RITA COOLIDGE & KRIS
  KRISTOFFERSON. See KRIS
  KRISTOFFERSON & RITA
  COOLIDGE.

RITCHIE, Jean
  Black Waters

RITCHIE FAMILY
  Best Disco In Town

RIVERS, Johnny
  Baby I Need Your Loving
  Curious Mind

  Look To Your Soul (J. Hendricks)
  Memphis Tennessee
  Midnight Special
  Mountain Of Love
  Poor Side Of Town
  Rocking Pneumonia And The
    Boogie Woogie Flu
  Seventh Son
  Swayin' To The Music
  Tracks Of My Tears

ROBBINS, MARTY
  Ribbon Of Darkness

ROBERT & JOHNNY
  We Belong Together

ROBERTA FLACK & DONNY
  HATHAWAY. See also FLACK,
  ROBERTA.
  Where Is The Love (R. MacDonald
    & W. Salter)
  You've Got A Friend
  You've Lost That Lovin' Feelin'

ROBINS
  Smokey Joe's Cafe

ROBINSON, Vicki Sue
  Daylight

ROBINSON, William "Smokey."
See also "SMOKEY" ROBINSON
& THE MIRACLES.
  Cruisin'
  Let Me Be The Clock

ROCKIN' HORSE
  Dancin' To The Music

ROD STEWART & FACES. See
Also STEWART, Rod.
  Stay With Me

RODERICK, Judy
  Baltimore Oriole

RODGERS, Jimmie
  Kisses Sweeter Than Wine
  Secretly
  Today
  World I Used To Know

ROE, Tommy
  Carol
  Dizzy
  Jam Up And Jelly Tight
  Stir It Up And Serve It

ROGERS, Kenny. See also
KENNY ROGERS & DOTTIE
WEST.
  Daytime Friends
  Gambler
  Home Made Love
  Lucille (R. Bowling & H. Bynum)
  Old Folks

  Rueben James
  You Decorated My Life

ROLLING STONES
  Ain't Too Proud To Beg
  Angie
  As Tears Go By
  Brown Sugar
  Carol
  Gimme Shelter
  Happy (M. Jagger & K. Richard)
  Honky Tonk Women
  It's Only Rock N Roll
  Johnny B. Goode
  Jumpin' Jack Flash
  Last Time
  Let's Spend The Night Together
  Little Queenie
  Love In Vain
  Midnight Rambler
  Mona
  Money (That's What I Want)
  Rip This Joint
  Ruby Tuesday
  Satisfaction
  She Said "Yeah"
  Street Fighting Man
  Susie-Q
  Time Is On My Side
  Under My Thumb
  You Can't Always Get What You
    Want

RONNY & THE DAYTONAS
  G.T.O.

RONSTADT, Linda
  All That You Dream
  Back In The U.S.A.
  Carmelita
  Colorado
  Desperado
  Different Drum
  Faithless Love
  Hasten Down The Wind
  Heat Wave
  Hey Mister, That's Me Up On The
    Jukebox
  How Do I Make You
  Hurt So Bad
  I'm Leaving It (All) Up To You
  Just A Little Bit Of Rain
  Lawyers, Guns And Money
  Look Out For My Love
  Lose Again
  Love Is A Rose
  Ooo Baby Baby
  Poor Poor Pitiful Me
  Prisoner In Disguise
  Rivers Of Babylon
  Rock Me On The Water
  Sail Away (R. Newman)
  Silver Threads And Golden
    Needles
  Simple Man, Simple Dream
  Someone To Lay Down Beside Me
  Tracks Of My Tears
  When I Grow Too Old To Dream

ROOFTOP SINGERS
Walk Right In

ROSE ROYCE
Do Your Dance (Part I)
Love Don't Live Here Anymore
Wishin' On A Star

ROSS, Diane. See also DIANA
ROSS & THE SUPREMES; DIANA
ROSS & MICHAEL JACKSON.
Ain't No Mountain High Enough
Ain't Nothing But A Maybe
Boss
Come In from The Rain
Do You Know Where You're
Going To
Gettin' Ready For Love
Good Morning Heartache
I Thought It Took A Little Time
I'm Coming Out
It's My Turn
Last Time I Saw Him
Love Hangover
My Man
Money (That's What I Want)
One Love In My Lifetime
Reach Out And Touch (Some-
body's Hand)
Remember Me
Surrender (N. Ashford & V.
Simpson)
Touch Me In The Morning
Upside Down
You Got It

ROYAL, Billy Joe
Down In The Boondocks

ROYAL TEENS
Believe Me

ROYALETTES
It's Gonna take A Miracle

RUBINOOS
I Think We're Alone Now

RUBY & THE ROMANTICS
Our Day Will Come

RUDY WEST & THE FIVE KEYS
Out Of Sight, Out Of Mind

RUFFIN, David
Everything's Coming Up Love
My Whole World Ended
Walk Away From Love

RUFFIN, Jimmy
Hold On To My Love
I've Passed This Way Before
What Becomes Of The Broken-
hearted

RUFUS
Ain't Nothing But A Maybe
Tell Me Something Good

RUFUS, FEATURING CHAKA
KHAN
Dance Wit Me
Do You Love What You Feel
Hollywood (D. Wolinski & A.
Fisher)
Jive Talkin'
Stay (C. Khan & R. Calhoun)

RUNDGREN, Todd. See also
TODD RUNDGREN & UTOPIA.
Dust In The Wind
Hello It's Me
I Saw The Light
Real Man
We Got To Get You A Woman

RUSH, Merrilee
Angel Of The Morning

RUSSELL, Bobby
Little Green Apples

RUSSELL, Brenda
Think It Over (B. & B.G. Russell)
Way Back When

RUSSELL, Leon. See also LEON
& MARY RUSSELL; WILLIE
NELSON & LEON RUSSELL.
Delta Lady ·
I Put A Spell On You (L. Russell)
Lady Blue
Me And Baby Jane
Roll Away The Stone
Song for You
Superstar (L. Russell & B. Bram-
lett)
This Masquerade
Tight Rope

RYDELL, Bobby
Volare
Wild One

RYDER, Mitch
Devil With The Blue Dress On

SAD CAFE
Run Home Girl

SAHM, Doug
Wallflower

SAINTE-MARIE, Buffy
Circle Game
Until It's Time For You To Go
Wedding Song

SAINTS
Stranded

SAM & DAVE
Hold On I'm Coming
Soul Man

SAM THE SHAM & THE
PHARAOHS
Wooly Bully

SANDPIPERS
Come Saturday Morning
Guantanemera
Old Fashioned Love Song
Spanish Eyes

SANDS, Tommy
Teen Age Crush

SANG, Samantha
Emotion (B. & R. Gibb)
You Keep Me Dancin'

SANTA ESMERALDA
House Of The Rising Sun

SANTANA
Evil Ways
Gypsy Queen
Oye Como Va
She's Not There
Stormy
Welcome

SARAH VAUGHN & MICHEL
LEGRAND. See LEGRAND,
Michel; VAUGHAN, Sarah.
Hands Of Time

SAUSAGE, Doc
Rag Mop

SAYER, Leo
Endless Night
How Much Love
More Than I Can Say
Raining In My Heart
When I Need You
You Make Me Feel Like Dancing

SCAGGS, Boz
Breakdown Dead Ahead
Harbor Lights
Hard Times
Hollywood (B. Scaggs & M. Omar-
tian)
It's Over
Jojo
Lido Shuffle
Look What You've Done To Me
Lowdown

SCHORY, Dick
Mission Impossible Theme

SCOTT, Jack
My True Love
What In The World's Come Over
You

SCOTT, Linda
  Count Every Star
  I've Told Ev'ry Little Star

SCOTT, Tom
  Starsky & Hutch Theme

SCOTT-HERON, Gil
  Bottle

SCREAMING MOTHERS
  Spoonful

SEALS & CROFTS
  Arkansas Traveler
  Ashes In The Snow
  Baby I'll Give It To You
  Blue Bonnet Nation
  Diamond Girl
  Hummingbird
  I'll Play For You
  It's Gonna Come Down
  King Of Nothing
  Summer Breeze
  Sweet Green Fields
  We May Never Pass This Way
    Again
  Windflowers
  You're The Love

SEALS & CROFTS, FEATURING
  CAROLYN WILLIS
  Get Closer

SEARCHERS
  Love Potion Number 9
  Needles And Pins

SEATRAIN
  Home To You

SEBASTIAN, John
  Didn't Want To Have To Do It
  On The Road Again
  Summer In The City
  Welcome Back

SEDAKA, Neil
  Amarillo
  Bad Blood
  Breaking Up Is Hard To Do
  Calendar Girl
  Happy Birthday Sweet Sixteen
  Immigrant
  Laughter In The Rain
  Love In The Shadows
  Should've Never Let You Go
  Steppin' Out (N. Sedaka & P.
    Cody)
  That's When The Music Takes Me
  You Gotta Make Your Own Sun-
    shine

SEEGER, Pete
  Bells Of Rhymney
  Goodnight Irene
  Guantanamera

If I Had A Hammer
Paths Of Victory
Playboys And Playgirls
Turn! Turn! Turn
Waist Deep In The Big Muddy
We Shall Overcome
Where Have All The Flowers Gone

SEEKERS
  Georgy Girl
  I'll Never Find Another You
  This Land Is Your Land
  World Of Our Own

SEGAL, George
  Yama-Yama Man

SEGER, Bob. See also BOB SEGER
& THE SILVER BULLET BAND.
  Beautiful Loser
  Jody Girl
  Katmandu
  Love The One You're With
  Mainstreet
  Night Moves
  Nutbush City Limits
  Ramblin' Gamblin' Man
  Rock And Roll Never Forgets

SENSATIONS
  Let Me In

SERGIO MENDES & BRASIL 66
  Scarborough Fair

7TH WONDER
  My Love Ain't Never Been This
    Strong

SEX PISTOLS
  Anarchy In The U.K.
  God Save The Queen
  Pretty Vacant

SHA NA NA
  Rock And Roll Is Here To Stay

SHADOWS
  Apache

SHALAMAR
  Take That To The Bank

SHANNON, Del
  Handy Man
  Hats Off To Larry
  Little Town Flirt
  Runaway (D. Shannon & M.
    Crook)

SHANNON, Jackie De. See DE
SHANNON, JACKIE.

SHANNON, Pat
  It's How I Live

SHARP, Dee Dee
  Mashed Potato Time

SHARPE, Ray
  Linda Lu

SHEILA & B.
  Singin' In The Rain

SHEP AND THE LIMELIGHTS
  Daddy's Home

SHERMAN, Bobby
  Easy Come, Easy Go
  Julie, Do Ya Love Me
  La, La, La
  Little Woman

SHIELDS
  You Cheated

SHIRELLES
  Dedicated To The One I Love
  Everybody Loves A Lover
  It's Gonna Take A Miracle
  Will You Love Me Tomorrow

SHOCKING BLUE
  Mighty Joe

SHORT, Bobby
  At Last

SILHOUETTES
  Get A Job

SILKIE
  You've Got To Hide Your Love
    Away

SILVER CONVENTION
  Fly, Robin Fly

SILVERSTEIN, Shel
  Hey Nelly Nelly

SIMON, Carly. See also CARLY
SIMON & JAMES TAYLOR.
  Anticipation (C. Simon)
  Attitude Dancing
  It Was So Easy
  Jesse (C. Simon & M. Mainieri)
  Legend In Your Own Time
  Nobody Does It Better
  Right Thing To Do
  That's The Way I've Always
    Heard It Should Be
  Tranquillo (Melt My Heart)
  Vengeance
  Waterfall
  You Belong To Me
  You're So Vain

SIMON, Paul. See also SIMON &
GARFUNKEL.
  American Tune
  Armistice Day

What's So Good About Goodbye
You've Really Got A Hold On Me

SMOKIE
Living Next Door To Alice

SNIFF 'N' THE TEARS
Driver's Seat

SNOW, Phoebe
No Regrets
Poetry Man
San Francisco Bay Blues

SONNY & CHER. See also CHER.
All I Ever Need Is You
Bang Bang
Beat Goes On
I Got You Babe
Unchained Melody

SOPWITH CAMEL
Hello Hello

SOUL, Jimmy
If You Wanna Be Happy

SOUL CHILDREN
Hearsay

SOUL SURVIVORS
Expressway To Your Heart

SOUND OF SUNSHINE
Love Means

SOUTH, Joe
Don't It Make You Wanta Go
Home
Games People Play
Walk A Mile In My Shoes

SOUTH SHORE COMMISSION
Free Man

SOUTHER, J.D.
Faithless Love
You're Only Lonely

SOUTHER-HILLMAN-FURAY
BAND
Border Town

SOVINE, Red
Teddy Bear

SPANIELS
Goodnight, It's Time To Go

SPANKY & OUR GANG
Brother, Can You Spare A Dime
Like To Get To Know You

SPARKLETONES
Black Slacks

SPEARS, BILLIE JO
I Will Survive

SPENCER DAVIS GROUP
Gimme Some Lovin'

SPINNERS
Rubberband Man
Then Came You
They Just Can't Stop It
Wake Up Susan
Workin' My Way Back To You

SPIRAL STAIRCASE
More Today Than Yesterday

SPITBALLS
Knock On Wood

SPORTS
Who Listens To The Radio

SPRINGFIELD, Dusty
Brand New Me
I Just Fall In Love Again
I Only Want To Be With You
Let Me Love You Once Before
You Go
Stay Awhile
Windmills Of Your Mind
You Don't Have To Say You Love
Me

SPRINGFIELDS
Silver Threads And Golden
Needles

SPRINGSTEEN, Bruce
Badlands
Blinded By The Light
Born To Run
Fourth Of July
Prove It All Night

SPYRO GYRA
Morning Dance

STAFFORD, Jim
Spider And Snakes
Wildwood Weed

STAFFORD, TERRY
Suspicion

STAMPEDERS
Hit The Road Jack

STANDELLS
Dirty Water

STAPLE SINGERS
Heavy Makes You Happy
If You're Ready (Come Go With
Me)
I'll Take You There
Let's Do It Again
Respect Yourself
Touch A Hand, Make A Friend

STAPLES
I Honestly Love You

STARBUCK
Everybody Be Dancin'
Searching For A Thrill

STARLAND VOCAL BAND
Afternoon Delight
American Tune

STARR, Edwin
H.A.P.P.Y. Radio
Twenty Five Miles
War

STARR, Kay
Rock And Roll Waltz

STARR, Ringo
Back Off Boogaloo
Beaucoups Of Blues
Hey Baby
Photograph
You're Sixteen

STATON, Candi
Nights On Broadway
Run To Me (D. Crawford)
Young Hearts Run Free

STEALERS WHEEL
Stuck In The Middle With You

STEELY DAN
Black Friday
Daddy Don't Live In That New
York City No More
Deacon Blues
Do It Again
FM
Here At The Western World
Josie
My Old School
Peg
Pretzel Logic
Reelin' In The Years
Rikki, Don't Lose That Number

STEVE MILLER BAND
Dance, Dance Dance (S. Miller,
B. Cooper & J. Cooper)
Fly Like An Eagle
Jet Airliner
Joker
Jungle Love
Rock 'N Me
Take The Money And Run
Winter Time

STEVENS, Cat
Another Saturday Night
Bonfire
Father And Son
Hurt (C. Stevens)
Morning Has Broken
Oh Very Young

Old Schoolyard
Peace Train
Sitting
To Be A Star
Wild World

STEVENS, Ray
Everything Is Beautiful
I Need Your Help Barry Manilow
Misty
You Are So Beautiful

STEVENSON, B.W.
River Of Love

STEWART, Al
On The Border
Song On The Radio
Time Passages
Year Of The Cat

STEWART, Rod. See also ROD
STEWART & FACES.
Ain't Love A Bitch
Da Ya Think I'm Sexy
Drift Away
Good Morning, Little School
Girl (D. Level & B. Love)
Handbags And Gladrags
Hot Legs
I Don't Want To Be Right
I Don't Want To Talk About It
I Was Only Joking
I'd Rather Go Blind
Killing Of Georgie (Part I & II)
Let Me Be Your Car
Maggie May
Mama, You Been On My Mind
Memphis, Tennessee
Only A Hobo
Sailing (G. Sutherland)
Tonight's The Night (Gonna Be
Alright)
Wild Side Of Life
You're In My Heart

STILLS, Stephen. See also
CROSBY, STILLS & NASH;
STILLS-YOUNG BAND.
Buyin' Time
Change Partners
Johnny's Garden
Love The One You're With
Turn Back The Pages
We Are Not Helpless

STILLS-YOUNG BAND
Long May You Run
Midnight On The Bay

STONEBOLT
Love Struck

STOOKEY, Paul. See also PETER,
PAUL & MARY.
Wedding Song (There Is Love)

STORIES
Brother Louie

STORM, Gale
I Hear You Knocking

STRANGE, Billy
Chattanooga Choo Choo

STRANGLERS
Something Better Change

STREISAND, Barbra. See also
BARBRA STREISAND & KRIS
KRISTOFFERSON; NEIL DIA-
MOND & BARBRA STREISAND.
All In Love Is Fair
Evergreen
Growin'
Happy Days Are Here Again
How Lucky Can You Get
I Won't Last A Day Without You
Kiss Me In The Rain
Let The Good Times Roll
Main Event/Fight
My Heart Belongs To Me
My Man
New York State Of Mind
Songbird (D. Wolpert & S. Nelson)
Splish Splash
Stoney End
Superman
Taking A Chance On Love
Tomorrow
Way We Were
What Are You Doing The Rest
Of Your Life
You And I (Michaele, L. Sebastian
& P. Sebastian)

STRONG, Barrett
Money (That's What I Want)

STRUNK, Jud
Daisy A Day

STUCKEY, NAT
Roll Over, Beethoven

STUFF
Up On The Roof

STYLISTICS
Baby Don't Change Your Mind
Can't Give You Anything (But
My Love)
Hey Girl, Come And Get It
I'm Stone In Love With You
Love Is The Answer (Hugo &
Luigi & G. Weiss)
Star On A T.V. Show
Unchained Melody
You Make Me Feel Brand New

STYX
Babe
Come Sail Away

Lady (D. DeYoung)
Lights (T. Shaw & D. DeYoung)
Never Say Never
Renegade
Sing For The Day
Why Me (D. DeYoung)

SUGAR CANE
Montego Bay

SUGARLOAF
Green-Eyed Lady

SUMMER, Donna
Bad Girls
Can't We Just Sit Down And
Talk It Over
Could It Be Magic
Deep, Theme From
Dim All The Lights
Heaven Knows
Hot Stuff
Last Dance
Love To Love You, Baby
MacArthur Park
Spring Affair
Wanderer (D. Summer & G.
Moroder)
Winter Melody

SUPERTRAMP
Give A Little Bit
Goodbye Stranger
Logical Song
Take The Long Way Home

SUPREMES. See also DIANA
ROSS & THE SUPREMES.
Baby Love
Back In My Arms Again
Come See About Me
Forever Came Today
Happening
I Hear A Symphony
I'm Gonna Let My Heart Do The
Walking
I'm Livin' In Shame
In And Out Of Love
Love Child
Love Is Like An Itching In My
Heart
My World Is Empty Without You
Nothing But Heartaches
Reflections
Someday We'll Be Together
Stoned Love
Stop In The Name Of Love
Up The Ladder To The Roof
When The Love Light Starts
Shining Through His Eyes
Where Did Our Love Go
You Can't Hurry Love
You Keep Me Hangin' On

SURFARIS
Wipe Out

SUTHERLAND BROS. & QUIVER
Arms Of Mary

SUZI QUATRO & CHRIS NORMAN.
See also QUATRO, Suzi.
Stumblin' In

SWAMPSEEDS
Can I Carry Your Balloon

SWAN, Billy
I Can Help
I'm Her Fool

SWEET
Action
Fox On The Run
Love Is Like Oxygen

SWEET INSPIRATIONS
Sweet Inspirations

SWITCH
There'll Never Be

SILVERS
Boogie Fever
New Horizons

SYLVESTER
Dance (Disco Heat)
I (Who Have Nothing)
Over And Over (N. Ashford & V.
Simpson)
You Make Me Feel (Mighty Real)

SYNDICATE OF SOUND
Little Girl

SYREETA. See BILLY PRESTON
& SYREETA.

TALKING HEADS
Book I Read
Don't Worry About The Govern-
ment
Psycho Killer
Take Me To The River

TAMMI TERRELL & MARVIN
GAYE. See MARVIN GAYE &
TAMMI TERRELL.

TANER, Gary
Over The Rainbow

TASTE OF HONEY
Boogie Oogie Oogie
Your Love

TATA VEGA
Full Speed Ahead

TATUM, Art
I'll See You In My Dreams

TAVARES
It Only Takes A Minute
Who Done It

TAYLOR, James. See also CARLY
SIMON & JAMES TAYLOR.
Bartender's Blues
Carolina In My Mind
Country Road
Don't Let Me Be Lonely Tonight
Fire And Rain
Handy Man
How Sweet It Is (To Be Loved By
You)
Long Ago & Far Away
Mexico
Shower The People
Sweet Baby James
Up On The Roof
Walking Man
Woman's Gotta Have It
Your Smiling Face
You've Got A Friend

TAYLOR, Johnnie
Disco Lady
Take Care Of Your Homework
Who's Making Love

TAYLOR, Kate
It's In His Kiss

TAYLOR, Livingston
Over The Rainbow

TAYLOR, R. Dean
Indiana Wants Me

TCHAIKOWSKY, Bram
Girl Of My Dreams

TEDDYBEARS
To Know You (Him) Is To Love
You (Him)

TEE SET
Ma Belle Amie

TEEMATES
Matchmaker, Matchmaker

TEEN QUEENS
Eddie My Love

TEMPTATIONS
Ain't Too Proud To Beg
All I Need
Ball Of Confusion
Beauty Is Only Skin Deep
Cloud Nine
I Can't Get Next To You
I Could Never Love Another
I Wish It Would Rain
I'm Losing You
Just My Imagination
My Girl
Papa Was A Rollin' Stone

Psychedelic Shack
Runaway Child, Running Wild
Since I Lost My Baby
Song For You
Way You Do The Things You Do
You're My Everything

10 CC
Things We Do For Love

TEN YEARS AFTER
Good Mornin' Little School Girl

TERI DE SARIO & K.C.
Yes I'm Ready

TERRELL, Tammi. See MARVIN
GAYE & TAMMI TERRELL.

TEX, Joe
Ain't Gonna Bump No More
Baby (You've Got What It Takes)
Hold What You've Got
Loose Caboose

THIN LIZZY
Boys Are Back In Town

THIRD WORLD
Now That We've Found Love

THOMAS, B.J.
Another Somebody Done Some-
body Wrong Song
Everybody Loves A Rain Song
Help Me Make It
Here You Come Again
Hooked On A Feeling
No Love At All
Raindrops Keep Fallin' On My
Head
Still The Lovin' Is Fun

THOMAS, Carla
Gee Whiz

THOMAS, Ian
Painted Ladies

THOMAS, Rufus
Do The Funky Chicken
Walking The Dog

THOMPSON, Chris
If You Remember Me

THORNTON, Big Mama
Hound Dog

THORPE, Billy
Children Of The Sun

THREE BLAZERS. See JOHNNY
MOORE'S THREE BLAZERS.

THREE DEGREES
Maybe
When Will I See You Again

THREE DOG NIGHT
Black And White
Celebrate
Easy To Be Hard
Eli's Comin'
Joy To The World
Liar
Never Been To Spain
Old Fashioned Love Song
One
Shambala
Try A Little Tenderness

TIJUANA BRASS. See also HERB
ALPERT & THE TIJUANA
BRASS.
If I Were A Rich Man
Never On A Sunday
Zorba The Greek, Theme From

TILLOTSON, Johnny
Heartaches By The Number
It Keeps Right On A-Hurtin'
Poetry In Motion
You're The Reason

TIOMKIN, Dimitri
High And The Mighty

TOBY BEAU
My Angel Baby

TODD, ART & DOTTY. See ART
& DOTTY TODD.

TODD RUNDGREN & UTOPIA.
See also RUNDGREN, Todd
Love Is The Answer

TOKENS
Lion Sleeps Tonight
Portrait Of My Love

TOM & JERRY. See also SIMON
& GARFUNKEL.
Hey, Schoolgirl

TOM PETTY & THE HEART-
BREAKERS
Don't Do Me Like That
I Need To Know
Listen To Her Heart
Refugee

TOM SCOTT & THE L.A. EXPRESS
Tom Cat

TOMMY BOYCE & BOBBY HART
Where Angels Go, Trouble
Follows

TOMMY JAMES & THE SHON-
DELLS. See also JAMES,
Tommy.
Crimson And Clover
Crystal Blue Persuasion
Gotta Get Back To You

I Think We're Alone Now
Mony, Mony

TONEY, Oscar Jr.
For Your Precious Love

TONY ORLANDO & DAWN. See
also DAWN, ORLANDO, Tony.
He Don't Love You (Like I Love
You)
Look In My Eyes Pretty Woman
Say, Has Anybody Seen My Sweet
Gypsy Rose
Sing (L. Gianangelo)
Skybird
Steppin' Out, I'm Gonna Boogie
Tonight
Tie A Yellow Ribbon Round The
Old Oak Tree
You're All I Need To Get By

TOOTS & THE MAYTALS
I Shall Sing

TOTO
Hold The Line

TOWER OF POWER
You're Still a Young Man

TRAMMPS
Disco Inferno

TRAVERS, Mary. See also
PETER, PAUL & MARY.
Air That I Breathe

TRAVOLTA, John. See also
JOHN TRAVOLTA & OLIVIA
NEWTON-JOHN.
Right Time Of The Night

TROOPER
Raise A Little Hell

TROY, Doris
Just One Look

TUCKER, Tommy
Hi-Heel Sneakers

TUFF DARTS
Nuclear Waste
Rats
Who's Been Sleepin' Here

TUNE WEAVERS
Happy, Happy Birthday, Baby

TURBANS
When You Dance

TURNER, Gil
Carry It On

TURNER, Ike. See also IKE &
TINA TURNER.
Lean On Me

TURNER, Joe
Chains Of Love
Flip Flop And Fly
Honey Hush
Shake, Rattle And Roll

TURNER, Sammy
Lavender Blue

TURNER, Spyder
I Can't Make It Anymore

TURNER, Tina. See IKE & TINA
TURNER.

TURRENTINE, Stanley
Cabin In The Sky
Take Me Home

TURTLES
Happy Together
It Ain't Me, Babe
Sound Asleep
You Baby (Nobody But You)

TUXEDO JUNCTION
Chattanooga Choo Choo
Moonlight Serenade

TYCOON
Such A Woman

TYLER, Bonnie
If I Sing You A Love Song
It's A Heartache

TYMES
Twelfth Of Never
You Little Trustmaker

UNDISPUTED TRUTH
Let's Go Down To The Disco
Smiling Faces Sometimes
You + Me = Love

UNION GAP. See GARY PUCKETT
& THE UNION GAP.

UNIQUES
House Of The Rising Sun

URIAH HEEP
Easy Living
Wizard

UTOPIA
Set Me Free

VALE, Jerry
  Don't Tell My Heart To Stop
    Loving You

VALENS, Ritchie
  Donna
  La Bamba

VALENTI, John
  Anything You Want
  I Wrote This Song For You

VALLI, Frankie
  Grease
  My Eyes Adored You
  We're All Alone

VAN DYKE, Leroy
  Louisville

VAN McCOY & THE SOUL CITY
SYMPHONY. See also McCOY,
Van.
  Disco Baby
  Hustle

VAN HALEN
  Beautiful Girls
  Dance The Night Away
  Jamie's Cryin'
  Runnin' With The Devil
  You Really Got Me

VAN MORRISON & THEM. See
also MORRISON, Van.
  Mystic Eyes

VAN RONK, Dave
  Bamboo
  Chelsea Morning
  Cocaine Blues
  Frankie's Blues

VANILLA FUDGE
  She's Not There

VANITY FAIR
  Early In The Morning (M.
    Leander & E. Seago)

VANNELLI, Gino
  I Just Wanna Stop
  Wheels Of Life

VANWARMER, Randy
  Just When I Needed You Most

VAUGHAN, Sarah. See also
SARAH VAUGHAN & MICHEL
LEGRAND.
  Alone Again (Naturally)
  Love Story, Theme From
  Slowly
  Summer Me, Winter Me

VEE, Bobby
  Night Has A Thousand Eyes
  Take Good Care Of My Baby

VELVET UNDERGROUND
  White Light, White Heat

VENTURES
  Hawaii Five-O
  Nadia's Theme
  Night Train
  Raindrops Keep Fallin' On My
    Head
  Walk, Don't Run
  Who'll Stop The Rain

VERA, Billy
  With Pen In Hand

VILLAGE PEOPLE
  Fire Island
  Go West
  Hot Cop
  I Am What I Am
  I'm A Cruiser
  In Hollywood (Everybody Is A
    Star)
  In The Navy
  Key West
  Macho Man
  My Roommate
  San Francisco (You've Got Me)
  Sodom And Gomorrah
  Ups And Downs
  Village Peope
  Women
  Y.M.C.A.

VINCENT, Gene
  Be-Bop-A-Lula

VINTON, Bobby
  Blue Velvet
  Ev'ry Day Of My Life
  Halfway To Paradise
  Hurt (J. Crane & A. Jacobs)
  Love Me With All Your Heart
  Moonlight Serenade
  My Elusive Dreams
  My Heart Belongs To You
  My Melody Of Love
  Please Love Me Forever
  Roses Are Red
  Sealed With A Kiss
  Seasons In The Sun
  Summer Love Sensation
  Wooden Heart

VOGUES
  My Special Angel
  Turn Around, Look At Me

VOUDORIS, Roger
  Get Used To It

WAITS, Tom
  Heart Of Saturday Night
  San Diego Serenade

WALDEN, Naranda Michael
  I Shoulda Loved Ya

WALKER, Jerry Jeff
  Mr. Bojangles

WALKER, T-Bone
  I'm Still In Love With You (T.
    Walker)

WALL, Eugene
  Rock Me On The Water

WALLACE, Jerry
  How Time Flies
  Shutters And Boards

WALLINGTON, George
  I Married An Angel

WALSH, Joe
  All Night Long
  Life's Been Good

WALTER MURPHY BAND
  A Fifth Of Beethoven
  Music Will Not End
  Rhapsody In Blue (Disco Version)

WAMMACK, Travis
  Easy Evil

WANSEL, Dexter
  Sweetest Pain

WAR. See also ERIC BURDON &
WAR.
  Cisco Kid
  Gypsy Man
  Me And Baby Brothers
  World Is A Ghetto

WARD, Anita
  Ring My Bell

WARNES, Jennifer
  Don't Make Me Over
  I Know A Heartache When I See
    One
  Right Time Of The Night

WARWICK, Dionne. See also
ISAAC HAYES & DIONNE
WARWICK.
  After You
  Alfie
  Always Something There To Re-
    mind Me
  Close To You (B. Bacharach &
    H. David)
  Deja Vu
  Do You Know The Way To San
    Jose

Don't Make Me Over
Green Grass Starts To Grow
I Say A Little Prayer
I'll Never Fall In Love Again
I'll Never Love This Way Again
Make It Easy On Yourself
No Night So Long
One Less Bell To Answer
This Guy's In Love With You
Valley Of The Dolls, Theme From
Walk On By

WASHINGTON, Deborah
Standing In The Shadows Of Love

WASHINGTON, Dinah. See also
BROOK BENTON & DINAH
WASHINGTON.
I Don't Hurt Anymore
Since I Fell For You

WATSON, Doc
Deep River Blues
Sittin' On Top Of The World
Sweet Georgia Brown
Wabash Cannon Ball
Way Downtown

WAYLON & WILLIE. See also
JENNINGS, Waylon; NELSON,
Willie.
Mammas Don't Let Your Babies
Grow Up To Be Cowboys
Wurlitzer Prize

WAYLON JENNINGS & JESSI
COLTER. See also COLTER,
Jessi; JENNINGS, Waylon.
Suspicious Minds

WAYNE FONTANA & THE MIND-
BENDERS
Game Of Love

WAYNE MIRAN & RUSH RELEASE
Oh, Baby

WE FIVE
You Were On My Mind

WEATHERLY, Jim
I'll Still Love You

WEAVERS
Goodnight, Irene
If I Had A Hammer
Kisses Sweeter Than Wine
Last Night I Had The Strangest
Dream
Lion Sleeps Tonight
Lonesome Traveler
Michael Row The Boat Ashore
Rock Island Line
Sloop John B
This Land Is Your Land

WEBB, Jimmy
Alice Blue Gown

WEBS
We Belong Together

WEBSTER, Ben
Should I

WEISSBERG, Eric. See also
ERIC WEISSBERG & DELIV-
ERANCE.

WEISSMAN, Dick
Hard Rain's A Gonna Fall

WELCH, Bob
Ebony Eyes
Hot Love, Cold World
I Saw Her Standing There
Sentimental Lady

WELCH, Lenny
Since I Fell For You

WELCH, Mary
Take It Like A Woman

WELLER, Freddy
Indian Lake

WELLS, Mary
My Guy
One Who Really Loves You
Two Lovers
You Beat Me To The Punch

WEST, Dottie. See also KENNY
ROGERS & DOTTIE WEST.
Country Sunshine
Lesson In Leavin'

WEST, Leslie
Because You Are My Friend

WEST, Rudy. See RUDY WEST &
THE FIVE KEYS.

WET WILLIE
Everything That 'Cha Do (Will
Come Back To You)
Weekend

WHITE, Barry
Oh, What A Night For Dancing

WHITEHEAD, J. See McFADDEN
& WHITEHEAD.

WHITLOCK, Bobby
Ease Your Pain

WHITMAN, Slim
It's All In The Game

WHO
I Can See For Miles
Magic Bus
My Generation
Pinball Wizard
Relay
See Me Feel Me
Summertime Blues
Squeeze Box
Trick Of The Light
Who Are You
Won't Get Fooled Again

WILDARE EXPRESS
Walk On By

WILLIAMS, Andy
Born Free
Love Story, Theme From
Summer Knows

WILLIAMS, Deniece. See also
JOHNNY MATHIS & DENIECE
WILLIAMS.
Free (Wanna Be Free)

WILLIAMS, Don
I'm Just A Country Boy
She Never Knew Me
Tulsa Time

WILLIAMS, John
Star Wars

WILLIAMS, Larry
Bony Moronie
Dizzy Miss Lizzie
Good Golly Miss Molly
Short Fat Fanny
Slow Down

WILLIAMS, Mason
Classical Gas

WILLIAMS, Maurice
Stay (M. Williams)

WILLIAMS, Paul
Old Fashioned Love Song
Rainy Days And Mondays
You And Me Against The World

WILLIAMS, Robin
Nanu, Nanu

WILLIAMS, Roger
Impossible Dream
M*A*S*H, Song From

WILLIAMSON, "Sonny Boy"
Fattening Frogs For Snakes

WILLIE NELSON & LEON RUS-
SELL. See also NELSON, Willie;
RUSSELL, Leon.
Am I Blue
Don't Fence Me In

WILLIS, Carolyn. See SEALS
& CROFTS FEATURING
CAROLYN WILLIS.

WILLIS, Chuck
C.C. Rider (C. Willis)

WILSON, Al
I Won't Last A Day Without You
Show And Tell

WILSON, Jackie
Baby Workout
For Once In My Life
For Your Precious Love
Lonely Teardrops
Over The Rainbow
That Lucky Old Sun
That's Why
Woman, A Lover, A Friend

WILSON, Meri
Telephone Man

WILSON, Nancy
Face It, Girl, It's Over

WINCHESTER, Jesse
Yankee Lady

WING & A PRAYER FIFE & DRUM
CORPS
Baby Face (Disco Version)
Those Were The Days

WINGS. See also PAUL McCART-
NEY & WINGS.
Long And Winding Road
Live And Let Die
Maybe I'm Amazed
Yesterday

WINSTONS
Color Him Father

WINTER, Johnny
Bony Moronie
Good Morning, Little School
Girl (D. Level & B. Love)
Highway 61 Revisited
Johnny B. Goode
Slippin' And Slidin'

WINTERHALTER, Hugo
Count Every Star

WITHERS, Bill
Ain't No Sunshine
Lean On Me
Lovely Day

WOMACK, Bobby
Across 110th Street
Woman's Gotta Have It

WONDER, Stevie
All In Love Is Fair
Another Star
Boogie On Reggae Woman
Don't You Worry 'Bout A Thing
Fingertips (Part II)
For Once In My Life
Heaven Help Us All
Higher Ground
I Was Made To Love Her
I Wish
Isn't She Lovely
Living For The City
My Cherie Amour
Nothing's Too Good For My Baby
Outside My Window
Place In The Sun
Send One Your Love
Shoo-Be-Doo-Be-Doo-Da-Day
Signed, Sealed, Delivered I'm
Yours
Sir Duke
Superstition
Tell Me Something Good
Uptight (Everything's Alright)
Yester-Me, Yester-You, Yester-
day
You Are The Sunshine Of My
Life
You Haven't Done Nothin'

WOOD, Brenton
Gimme Little Sign
Lovey Dovey Kinda' Lovin'

WOOD, Lauren
Please Don't Leave

WOOLEY, Sheb
Purple People Eater

WRIGHT, Betty
Where Is The Love (H.W. Casey,
R. Finch, W. Clarke & B.
Wright)

WRIGHT, Gary
Dream Weaver
Love Is Alive
Water Sign

WRIGHT, O.V.
That's The Way I Feel About Cha

WYNETTE, Tammy
Run, Woman, Run
Stand By Your Man

YARBOROUGH, Glen
New "Frankie And Johnnie" Song
That's The Way It's Gonna Be

YARDBIRDS
Good Morning, Little School
Girl (S. Williamson)

Here Tis'
Smokestack Lightnin'

YELLOW MAGIC ORCHESTRA
Computer Game

YES
All Good People
Long Distance Runaround
Release, Release
Roundabout
Time And A Word
Wonderous Stories
Your Move
Yours Is No Disgrace

YOST, Dennis. See DENNIS
YOST & THE CLASSICS IV.

YOUNG, Karen
Hot Shot

YOUNG, Kathy. See KATHY
YOUNG & THE INNOCENTS.

YOUNG, Neil. See also CROSBY,
STILLS, NASH & YOUNG;
NEIL YOUNG & CRAZY HORSE;
STILLS-YOUNG BAND.
After The Gold Rush
Alabama
Cinnamon Girl
Cowgirl In The Sand
Dance Dance Dance (N. Young)
Don't Let It Bring You Down
Four Strong Winds
Harvest
Heart Of Gold
Helpless
Hey Babe
If I Could Have Her Tonight
I've Been Waiting For You
Like A Hurricane
Lotta Love
Love Is A Rose
Needle And The Damage Done
Old Man
Only Love Can Break Your Heart
Song For You
Southern Man
Walk On

YOUNGBLOODS
Get Together

YURO, TIMI
What's A Matter, Baby

ZAGER, Michael. See MICHAEL
ZAGER BAND.

ZEROS
Wimp

ZEVON, Warren
  Certain Girl
  Excitable Boy
  Johnny Strikes Up The Band
  Tenderness On The Block
  Werewolves Of London

ZOMBIES
  She's Not There
  Time Of The Season

ZWOL
  New York City I Love You

Z.Z. TOP
  I Thank You